TO

SIR DIETRICH BRANDIS, K.C.I.E., PH.D., F.R.S.

(LATE INSPECTOR-GENERAL OF FORESTS TO THE GOVERNMENT OF INDIA)

I DEDICATE THESE VOLUMES

AS A TRIBUTE OF PERSONAL FRIENDSHIP

AND OF ADMIRATION FOR AN OFFICIAL CAREER

WHICH, MARKED THROUGHOUT BY DEVOTION TO THE PUBLIC GOOD

HAS BORNE FRUIT IN LASTING BENEFITS

TO THE INDIAN EMPIRE

NOTICE

In 1882, the Government of India printed at Calcutta a *Manual of the Land-Tenures and Land-Revenue Systems of British India*, which was written by me under the orders of Government. The edition was exhausted in two or three years; but as about that time great changes in the law were under consideration, it was thought desirable to await the passing of the Bengal Tenancy Act (1885), the Oudh Rent Act (1886), and the Panjáb Land-Revenue and Tenancy Acts (1887)—to say nothing of minor enactments—before preparing a new edition.

When (in 1888–9) things seemed ripe for a new issue corrected and brought up to date, I found that so much had to be altered and added, and that such improvements might be made, especially in the chapters on Land-Tenures, that it would be better to write a new book. The present work is therefore independent of the original volume, except as regards a very few pages. It has also been illustrated by maps. In this form it is much larger, and may be less adapted for the purposes of some officials who have to pass an examination in Land-Revenue subjects: on the other hand, it will have become, I hope, much better suited to the needs of others; and it is certainly more complete as a general handbook of the Land-Systems of British India.

As regards Forest-Officers and others for whom the present work is too detailed, or contains too much on branches of Revenue work—such as Assessment—with which they are not practically concerned, it will be easy to meet their requirements by the subsequent issue of a 'Primer' or Shorter Manual especially written for them.

B. H. B. P.

OXFORD:
March, 1892.

TABLE OF CONTENTS

L.R. = Land-Revenue. S. = Settlement.

VOL. I.—GENERAL, BENGAL.

BOOK I.—GENERAL.

VOL. II.

BOOK III.—THE SYSTEM OF VILLAGE OR MAHÁL SETTLEMENTS.

PART I.—THE NORTH-WESTERN PROVINCES AND OUDH.

PART II.—ÁJMER-MERWÁRA.

PART III.—THE CENTRAL PROVINCES.

PART IV.—THE PANJÁB.

VOL. III.

BOOK IV.—THE RAIYATWÁRÍ AND ALLIED SYSTEMS.

Part I.—MADRAS.

CHAP. PART II.—BOMBAY (AND SINDH). PAGE

PART III.—BERÁR.

PART IV.—ASSAM.

PART V.—COORG.

PART VI.—BURMA.

LIST OF MAPS, ETC.

VOL. I.

VOL. II.

VOL. III.

ERRATA

VOL. I

P. 15, l. 26. Panjáb also, *dele* also

P. 19, l. 6. The closing bracket should be at the end of the sentence, just before the full stop.

P. 103, l. 6 from the bottom, *for* for *read* from

P. 104, l. 1, *for* has *read* have

P. 110, l. 9, *for* is *read* are

P. 118, l. 3, *for* for instance *read* possible

P. 172, l. 3, *for* and *read* or

P. 183, *note* (last line but one), *for* were *read* was

P. 197, l. 20, *for* for *read* from

P. 232, l. 11, *after* Malleson says *insert* ([2]) *note reference.*

P. 301, l. 11, *for* Sec. VII. *read* Sec. VI.

P. 323 (heading of section), *for* Sec. IX. *read* Sec. VIII. *and so on, to the end.*

P. 407, § 8, *should be headed* SECTION II. THE PROCEDURE OF THE SETTLEMENT.

P. 412, l. 29, *for* were *read* had been

P. 466, l. 1, *for* from *read* for

P. 552, l. 18, *for* it at all *read* it all

LIST OF ABBREVIATIONS

EMPLOYED TO INDICATE CERTAIN WORKS FREQUENTLY REFERRED TO.

Full Title.	Referred to as
Fifth Report of the Select Committee of the House of Commons on the Affairs of the East India Company (1812). This was reprinted at Madras in 1866 and 1883 (2 vols.)	'Fifth Report.'
Harington's Analysis of the Bengal Regulations, 1821 (3 vols.). (I have used also a Reprint of the portion relating to the Revenue System, published at Calcutta, Government Press, 1866) . . .	'Harington.'
A Memoir of Central India, including Malwa and adjoining Provinces, &c., by Major-General Sir John Malcolm, 1824. (Reprint from the 3rd Edition. 2 vols. Calcutta, Thacker & Spink, 1880)	'Malcolm.'
Annals and Antiquities of Rajast'han, or the Central and Western Rajpoot States of India, by Lieutenant-Colonel James Tod, 1829. (Third Reprint. 2 vols. Madras, Higginbotham, 1880)	'Tod.'
The Present Land-Tax in India, &c. (Lt.-Col.) John Briggs. (1 vol. London, Longmans, 1830)	'Briggs.'

Full Title.	Referred to as
The Administration of the East India Company. John William Kaye. (London, R. Bentley, 1853)	'Kaye.'
The Land Tax of India, by Neil B. E. Baillie. (London, Smith & Elder, 1873)	'Baillie.'
Lectures on Indian Law, by W. Markby, M.A., one of the Judges of the High Court. (Calcutta, 1873)	'Markby.'
The Law relating to the Land-Tenures of Lower Bengal. Tagore Law Lectures, 1874–75, by Arthur Phillips. (Calcutta, 1876)	'Phillips.'
Report on the Land-Revenue System, Bengal, Behar, and Orissa, 1882–83, submitted by the Board to Government of Bengal, October 31st, 1883. (Calcutta, Secretariat Press)	'Report, 1883.'
Landholding and the Relation of Landlord and Tenant in Various Countries, by C. D. Field, LL.D. 2nd edition. (Calcutta, Thacker and Spink, 1885)	'Field.'
The Bengal Tenancy Act, VIII of 1885 (as amended by Act VIII of 1886), with notes and rulings, &c., by R. F. Rampini and M. Finucane. 2nd edition. (Calcutta, Thacker, Spink & Co., 1889)	'R. and F. Tenancy Act.'
'Settlement Report' (of various districts) . .	'S. R.'

BOOK I.

GENERAL.

CHAPTER I.

INTRODUCTORY.

The student who approaches the subject of Indian Land-tenures, and of the systems under which the State levies a revenue from the land, has probably a vague idea that he is about to enter on a *terra incognita* or to plunge into some mysterious and unintelligible darkness. A few words of encouragement at the outset seem therefore desirable. I do not wish to pretend that the subject of land-tenure is free from difficulty, still less that it is impossible to be in doubt regarding many questions which have to be decided on a comparison of more or less fragmentary evidence, some of which is traditional and much of it matter of direct or indirect inference. Holt Mackenzie, an eminent authority on Revenue matters—he was Secretary to the first Revenue Commission which originated the Board of Revenue for the North-West Provinces—said that he had been all his life studying land-tenures without understanding them; and the older text-books abound with remarks to the same general effect. But it should be remembered that Holt Mackenzie lived and studied in the early years of the present century, when village-tenures were only just discovered, and when everybody's mind was filled with the one idea, that the only possible form of land-holding was by a landlord who let his lands to tenants at a stated rent. The early forms of property had not been considered. No Haxthausen, Von Maurer, De Laveleye, H. S. Maine, or Seebohm, had yet arisen to set men thinking and comparing and making use of the materials that were to be found in different countries. Sanskrit and Arabic literature and law were only beginning to be explored, and no one had found out anything about the history of the Aryan conquerors and colonizers of India[1], still less about the so-called Dravidian races which before the Aryan inroad had formed organized States in Central and Southern India, or about the Kolarian tribes whose remnants are still found in that part of Western Bengal called Chota (properly Chutiyá) Nágpur, in the 'Santál Parganas,' and in the Vindhyan Mountains which divide Upper and Central India.

Our sources of information have immensely multiplied since those days. Not only have we works whose chief value is that they suggest the right use of materials—tell us how to extract the pure metal from the crude ore of tradition and semi-mythical literature, and to read the meaning of ancient forms and customs, but we have for nearly every district in India valuable materials in the form of 'Manuals' (for the Madras districts) and the volumes known as 'Settlement Reports' in other Provinces. I may explain that when the Land Revenue Settlement operations of a district (or part of a district) are concluded, when rights have been recorded, and the interests of all classes in the land set down in due form, and when the assessment of the revenue on the field, the 'village' or the estate (as the case may be), has been determined,—the Settlement officer gathers up the results of his work in a printed volume (in English) which contains the history of the district and all peculiarities of its *locale*, its people and their land-tenures. In preparing this Manual I have studied some dozens of such reports. They are not indeed always easily obtained, nor are they light reading—especially to

[1] I doubt whether Holt Mackenzie had known Col. Tod's Study of the Aryan (Rájput) tribes whose last permanent home was in the States of modern Rájputána, or whether he knew of Col. Wilk's Study of the Hindu State organization as exemplified in Mysore.

those who have not official knowledge and experience[1]—but many of them are storehouses of valuable information. At the beginning of the century no such aids were available, for one of the many misfortunes attaching to our first Settlements in Bengal and Madras (Permanent Settlements as they are called) was that no information about tenures and agricultural customs was recorded. The early writers could find in the celebrated 'Fifth Report on the affairs of the East Indies,' presented to the House of Commons (1812, and since reprinted in Madras), a multitude of unarranged and rather confused details about the landholders in Bengal and North Madras called 'Zamíndárs,' but that is all. And without enlarging on a subject which must be unintelligible till we come to our chapter on land-tenures, I will only say that the tenure of the 'Zamíndár' of Bengal represents a late—if not the latest—development in land-interest, and was the localized outcome of a dying and corrupt system of State management. The study of it threw no light on the real customary tenures of the country.

It is true that I have found a single report of 1796 describing the real natural tenures of the Benares districts: but I have rarely seen it quoted; and all our early authorities, who are responsible for the dissemination of the idea that Indian land-tenures are unintelligible, appear only just to have heard of 'village' tenures, and to have started with the idea, derived from Bengal, that all land must have *some landlord*, with tenants under him.

In studying, then, the land-tenures of India, we must be prepared for difficulties, and expect to find *lacunæ* which we cannot fill up or only supply conjecturally and provisionally; but it would be exaggeration to go on saying that a fair amount of clear knowledge on the subject is

[1] There are also volumes of reprints of special reports and papers known as 'Selections from the Records' of the several Governments. Among the notable Settlement Reports I may instance as samples (but there are many others almost equally valuable) Elliott's Report on Hoshangábád (Central Provinces), Benett's on Gondá (Oudh), Ibbetson on Karnál (Panjáb), Roe on Multan (Panjáb), Logan on Malabar (Madras), and Pedder's Bombay Reports.

unattainable[1] with moderate study and a fair memory for facts.

And as to the systems under which the Land-Revenue is assessed and afterwards collected, there is no excuse for regarding their study as of excessive difficulty, when there is scarcely a province that has not its Land-Revenue and Tenancy Acts and Regulations besides many hand-books and volumes of circular orders, and special Reports. In the aggregate, no doubt, these documents form an extensive and even a forbidding literature; and they are often written so as to be puzzling to a beginner, or a non-official reader. A guide to them is necessary, and it is the express object of my present work to supply the need: whether the object has been in any degree satisfactorily attained, it will be for the reader to judge; but I may explain, that I have endeavoured to give only the essential features of the Acts and orders, confining myself to what is really important and practical, while I have indicated in footnotes the sources whence a more detailed knowledge may be obtained.

May I be permitted also to add a word of general explanation as to my method. It may be said that subjects are treated in too positive or even dogmatic a manner. But in the first place, space is limited, and room could not be afforded for many qualifying and apologetic paragraphs and for repeated drawbacks on the statements made. Moreover, a continued hesitancy, a suggestion of conflicting possibilities and an atmosphere of scepticism and uncertainty, is apt to be puzzling to a beginner; and it is beginners and 'outsiders' to the Revenue official circle that have been kept in mind. I have endeavoured to give my authorities, and to state as fact only what is fairly receivable as such: if any one thinks the facts lead to other

[1] If by 'understanding' land-tenures we mean possessing a complete theory of origin and growth, perhaps land-tenures will long remain 'not understood.' But if we mean that we cannot accomplish the more modest task of getting an adequate knowledge of the *facts* as they are, or as they have become, then I see no reason for supposing that we are or need be in any such position of difficulty.

conclusions than those I have drawn, he will have no great difficulty in working out another view. Possessed in the first instance of a definite outline of the subject, even if it is too strongly drawn in parts, the student who afterwards goes into detail in Indian official life, will fast enough discover where he would prefer to draw the lines a little more faintly or uncertainly, or where he would desire to give a different colour to the phenomena of landholding customs. The text will always afford a sufficient indication where there is room for an interpretation other than that which it adopts.

With these few prefatory explanations I may at once proceed to the direct subject of the chapter. I have to discuss certain general topics which it will be useful to explain by way of preparation for the study which we are to enter on.

§ 1. *The term 'India.'*

Sir John Strachey, in his admirable Lectures on India[1]—a work which I advise every student to read—has already spoken of the dangers attaching to the use of a general term like 'India.' It is geographical only. In no other sense is there any one country which can properly be called 'India.' Within the confines of the area so marked on the map, we have a series of provinces inhabited by different races, and often speaking different languages. The inhabitants of the Panjáb for example—even in the same province—are so different, that a Pesháwar tribesman in the north could hardly make himself understood at Delhi or Hisár in the south-east. Religious and other differences divide the populations, and racial antipathies are not unknown: Sikhs have no love for Hindustánis, and a Bengálí Bábú[2] at Lahore is regarded as a foreigner almost

[1] 'India,' by Sir John Strachey. London: Kegan Paul, Trench & Co. (1888). 1 vol.

[2] The term properly means a cadet or younger son of a noble family, then a native gentleman in general. It is now commonly employed to designate a pleader, attorney, or office-clerk.

as much as the Englishman is. The mere fact that one portion of the general population is Hindu and the other Muhammadan is in itself a permanent source of difference. And there is little internal uniformity among those who are called Hindus, and little more than a semblance of it among the Muhammadan races, despite the fact of a common creed and a common form of worship.

Those who have read Sir A. Lyall's *Asiatic Studies* know how protean in form Hinduism is; local deities and deified personages are readily adopted, thus giving a different complexion to the worship of each locality: in fact there is nothing common to Hindus as a body, except certain social ideals and rules. Otherwise the Hindu castes in the several provinces, have very little connection. The Sikh religion, again, is far removed from the Hindu ideal; and the great bulk of the peasant population of the Panjáb that is returned as 'Hindu,' is so only in the sense that the people are not Sikhs and are not Muhammadan. They have learned a certain respect for Hindu festivals and for Brahmans, because those ubiquitous caste-men travel everywhere and skilfully introduce at least a portion of their ideas; but the Hindu law of the books and commentaries is unknown to the Jat and Gújar and Rájput landholding peasantry.

Even among Muhammadans, to say nothing of hostile sects of Shíá and Sunní, great numbers are perfectly ignorant converts, knowing nothing beyond the simple *formula* of the faith. In the Panjáb, for instance, these people follow their local customs of inheritance; and it is perhaps chiefly the action of the law-courts that enforces a certain respect for the regular law in matters of marriage, divorce, minority and bastardy, otherwise it is not known or respected in practice. In a word, the various castes and races in the different provinces diverge from one another as much (or more) as the people of Scotland do from those of Naples, or the peasantry of Normandy from the mountaineers of the Tyrol.

Common *influences* there are, which have extended far and wide. The Muhammadan conquest, for example, introduced the use of Persian or Arabic terms regarding land all over India, and with the terms, many practices and principles of Revenue management. And certain land-customs and family customs derivable from early Dravidian and Aryan traditions among Hindus, as well as official titles derived from the Rájput State System, may be traced in provinces widely separated. But while we shall take note of such wide-spread influences, and make the best use of the facts they disclose, we shall not be misled into supposing that all Indian peoples are more or less identical, or their ideas the same. Of the mistaken supposition of unity throughout 'India' we shall soon meet with practical examples. I shall shortly have to explain how the same conditions of life have brought about everywhere the aggregation of the cultivating classes into groups, which we call 'villages,' but they are not all in one form. Yet we find the standard histories of India giving general accounts of the 'Indian Village' as if the form described was prevalent everywhere and one general description sufficed for all. Another instance of confusion is perhaps more due to the use of a common name than to any assumption of unity among the provinces. I allude to the term 'Zamíndár.' We first came in contact with a certain class of landholder in Bengal known by this name, and from the language of some of the earlier Regulations and minutes, it would seem as if the same form of landholding must exist everywhere. This of course is not the case. But unfortunately the vernacular term (in itself) means 'holder' of 'land,' and so it easily got used to designate entirely different things. It is applied to particular forms of landed interest, entirely special or local, it is also used in the widest sense to signify the landholding class generally. If you meet a peasant in Northern India, for example, and ask him who he is, he will probably reply, 'I am a poor man—a zamíndár.' He does not mean that he is a great estate holder.

§ 2. *Some common geographical terms used in India.*

While we are on the subject of India, it may be well to explain some common terms used to denote different parts of the country which have often distinctive features, though they do not coincide with provinces or express divisions recognized for Government purposes. In reading these remarks, the student should have a map of India before him.

Northern India.

'Northern India' is applied to the part of the country which is north of the Vindhyan Mountains, and north-west of Benares or thereabout. 'Southern India' applies to the province or Presidency of Madras, including part of the State of Hyderabad. 'Central India' will not be confused with the 'Central Provinces'; the former is an area really central, and consists mostly of Native States; the latter is a British province, having its capital in Nágpur, and lies between the Tapti and Narbada rivers on the north-west, and the Wardha and Godávari on the south-east.

Southern India. Central India. Central Provinces.

The Dakhan.

The 'Dakhan,' commonly written Dekkan or Deccan, is a convenient term which is employed to signify the part of India south of the Narbada river and inland of the Ghâts or range of hills that run down the western as well as the eastern side of the Peninsula; but it is not employed to include the whole of the Peninsula, and may be said to terminate southwards about the line of the Mysore State, and to include Hyderabad. Its southern limit is however rather indefinite. The eastern and western coasts of the Peninsula are less commonly spoken of as the Coromandel and Malabar coasts respectively. Along each, at a greater or less distance from the sea-shore, runs a line of hills much more continuous on the west side than it is on the east. On the west side also the country between the crest of the hills (or 'Ghát' as they are called) and the sea-shore is more distinct in character than it is on the east. The sea-board, for instance, below Bombay to the Kistná river, is called the Konkán (Concan), and southward of that come the interesting and specialized districts of Kánnaḍa (Canara or Kanara) and Malabar.

The east and west coasts and their hill ranges.

I may mention that 'Ghát,' besides meaning the hillrange itself, is the common Indian term for any pass, gorge or passage leading into the hills, especially in Central, Eastern, and Southern India. Thus the visitor who has taken the beautiful drive up to Ootacamund—the favourite summer resort of the Southern presidency—will remember that he heard the people talk of 'going up the Ghát[1]': so in all these countries the districts on the uplands are said to be 'above Ghát' or 'bálághát,' while those at the foot are said to be 'below Ghát' or 'payín-ghát.' Ghát.

We shall hear much in the sequel of native chiefs whose freehold land is spoken of as held on the 'Ghátwálí' tenure, because they held the land free of revenue or on privileged terms, on condition of maintaining a force to keep the passes into the hills clear of robbers and prevent raids on to the low-lying lands.

'Hindustán' is a term which is properly applied to that northern-central region that lies above the Vindhyan Mountains and about the great plain or valley of the Ganges river as far west as the Jamná. 'Hindustán.'

The 'Panjáb'—the land of the five (panj, P.) rivers or waters (áb, P.) properly means the area bounded on the north-west by the Sindh Ságar or Indus river[2] and contained between the Rivers Jihlam, Chináb, Rávi, Biás and Sutlej (Satlaj). 'Panjáb.'

The tracts of land between these rivers are called 'Doábs' (between 'two-' 'waters'), each distinguished by a special addition: but '*the* Doáb' *par excellence* is the great tract in the North-Western Provinces between the Ganges and the Jamná rivers. 'Doáb.'

[1] The word means 'Gate' or 'pass.' In the case of Ootacamund there is a long natural cleft or gully in the hills along the side of which the carriage road zigzags upwards first on to one plateau and then on to the higher one.

[2] The word Ságar is shown in the dictionaries as meaning 'ocean,' but in the Panjáb and its hills, and doubtless elsewhere inland where the people have never seen the sea, it means the big river of the locality. Thus in the Simla hills the people will tell you that such and such a stream (nadí or nála) runs into the 'Ságar,' or great River—Sutlej in those parts—at such and such a point.

§ 3. *Remarks about the Provinces.*

In Chapter II a list is given of all the provinces or administrative divisions of British India. A few remarks may be here made as to the meaning of the names and what territories they include.

The Panjáb.

Commencing with the north, I have already explained the term 'Panjáb'—but have to add that the Panjáb *as a province* extends beyond the Indus to the north-west, and includes also the country beyond the Sutlej up to the Jamná, where the 'North-Western Provinces' begin. Bilúchistán, coloured as British territory on modern maps, is a separate political Chief Commissionership, and is not part either of Sindh or of the Panjáb.

North-Western Provinces.

The 'North-Western Provinces' consist (1) of the tract known as 'Rohilkhand,' because it was the site where the Rohillas or Rohelas, a tribe of adventurers from Afghánistán, established a cruel and oppressive rule till they were dislodged at the end of last century. (2) 'The Doáb' (as already stated) comprises all the districts between the Ganges and the Jamná; (3) and the districts of Bándá, Hamírpur, Jhánsi, Lalitpur and Jaláun are in Bundélkhand—the country which was formerly the site of the conquest of an Aryan tribe called Bundélá[1]. (4) There remain the districts east of Oudh; and the group of permanently settled districts adjoining the Bengal frontier which, speaking generally, form the old 'Benares Province,' acquired in 1775. The provinces as a whole are called 'North-Western,' because at first they formed part of the Bengal Presidency, and were 'north-west' of Bengal and Bihár.

Bengal.

The term 'Bengal' is now generally used to mean the entire territory under the Lieutenant-Governor of Bengal. It includes (1) 'Bihár,' i.e. the districts north of the hills about Hazáribágh (the Rájmahál hills), as far east as the Mahánadi River. (2) Chota (or Chutiyá) Nágpur, between Bihár and Orissa, occupying the western part of the province. (3) Orissa along the south-east coast, from near the

[1] Its name is still found in books as 'Bundlecund,' apparently to be pronounced like the English word bundle!

Subarnarekha River to the frontier of Madras[1]. (4) The 'Santál parganas' district (often written Sonthal, and also called in some books 'Santália') is a hilly tract of frontier country lying to the south-west of the Ganges and extending from the river to the Chutiyá Nágpur boundary. (5) 'Bengal Proper' is the rest of the Province. But it is usual further to divide it into Bengal (or Central Bengal), and Eastern Bengal; for the latter country is in many ways distinct: it includes the districts of Chittagong, Tipperah (Tiprá), Noacolly (Nawákhálí), and as far north as Maimansingh and Rangpur, while along the mouths of the Húghlí the country is known as the 'Sundarband,' and consists of an extent of swampy 'Delta' country, intersected by tidal creeks, and covered with dense jungle and forest, except on the higher lands where cultivation is possible.

'Assam' has been separated from Bengal since 1874, and though 'Assam Proper' or the 'Valley districts' refers to the districts (beginning with Goálpára) which lie along the valley of the Tísta river, the province as a whole includes the group of hills to the south of the river, viz. the Garos, Khásia, Jaintiyá, &c., and the districts of Sylhet and Cachar. 'Assam.'

The 'Central Provinces' include the old 'Ságar and Narbada (Saugor and Nerbudda) territories in the north and north-west as well as the Nimár district, the Nágpur districts (escheated, on the death without heirs of the Bhônslá king), the 'Chhatísgarh plain,' and Sambalpur. These various parts will at once be understood by a glance at the map, and further details about their history will be found in Chapter II and in the chapters of the sequel specially relating to the Central Provinces. 'Central Provinces.'

None of the other presidencies or provinces call for any general explanation. Purely local details will be mentioned in introducing the special chapters relating to the various provinces.

[1] That is the present extent of Orissa. The 'Orissa' of 1765—when the E. I. Company received the grant of 'Bengal, Bihár and Orissa'—referred only to the small portion of the coast between the Subarnarekha river and the Húghlí (now nearly conterminous with the Midnapore district.

§ 4. *Certain features connected with land.—Seasons and harvests.*

The seasons.

It may be convenient to remark that everywhere they recognize three main divisions of the seasons—the cold season, the hot season, and the 'rains.'

But of course there are great local differences. In some parts, as in the south, the cold season is only marked by a slight diminution of temperature, and that for a short time. In the Panjáb, on the other hand, the climate is temperate from November to March, and quite cold in December and January, often with sharp frosts; while an intense heat reigns from May to September or October.

On the southern part of the east coast, the N.E. monsoon brings rain in November or later, but in other parts of India there is no rain at this time; what rain falls in the cool season falls in December or January and is due to other causes.

The general rainy season is due to the S.W. monsoon, which brings rain from the end of May to September, varying of course in the direction of beginning earlier or later, lasting a longer or shorter time, in different parts. In some parts the rainy season is a matter of occasional downpours between June and September; in others there is a steady wet season from the end of May often to half through October. Again, there are almost rainless regions, where the 'rainy season' does not mean much, and where cultivation is only possible by the aid of river-overflow, or canals taken shorter or longer distances inland and wells sunk where the subsoil is still moist by percolation from the river.

Two principal harvests.

The general division of the year into a dry season (part of it colder than the rest) and a rainy season, has commonly resulted in the people of a large part of India recognizing two main harvests, one called 'rabí'' (A.): or by Hindi names as Hári, &c., and the other 'Kharíf' (Sáwani, &c.).

These terms will be remembered because they constantly occur, and regulate many matters connected with land-administration.

The 'rabí'[1] (or spring) harvest, in Northern and Northern-Central India, consists mainly of wheat, barley, and a pulse called by the English 'Gram' (*Cicer arietinum*). It is often the principal harvest, sown about October[2] and reaped in April to May. The Kharíf (or autumn) harvest (sown as soon as the rains set in) ripens in October and November or earlier, according to the staple grown. Sugar-cane, which is an important item of this harvest, does not ripen till later, and is frequently cut gradually, and is not off the ground all the winter.

'The Kharíf' is the time when the millets and maize grow, and also fodder for the cattle. In Bengal the great rice harvest is the Kharíf[3].

All these dates and details vary from place to place, but as a general indication they will be useful.

§ 5. *The Agricultural and the 'Faslí' Year.*

When Akbar began his reign, he desired to adopt an universal official year, which should correspond to the harvest seasons better than the Hijrí year (with its changing lunar months) or the Hindu Samvat era. He began with the 10th Sept. 1555 (A.D.), and arbitrarily called it 'Faslí 963,' being the Hijrí year of his ascending the throne. This era (which can be found by deducting 592, or 593 according to the month, from the year A.D.) was used for all Revenue accounts. The 'Fasli' in use in the

[1] Having once indicated the correct spelling of 'rabí,' we will hereafter use 'rabi' (without accents) for simplicity of printing.

[2] The land having been ploughed and prepared towards the close of the rains.

[3] People have an idea that the Indian populations live on rice. The general cultivation of rice is by no means widely extended, and is confined to Eastern and Central Bengal, to Lower Burma, and to the moister parts of Madras and Bombay. Rice is locally cultivated elsewhere, of course, but is regarded as a luxury rather than as a staple food.

Dakhan was begun by Sháh Jahán in A.D. 1636, and is somewhat different.

The 'agricultural year,' which is defined in Tenant and Land-Revenue Acts, is fixed for the convenience of date in enhancing rents and putting an end to tenancies. The year begins on some day between the 15th April and 1st July, as the provincial climate may render convenient. It is not used as a date or era.

§ 6. *Irrigation.*

Irrigation.

The details of irrigation also affect many questions regarding land-revenue management, and, as we shall see, originate some customs of land-tenure.

Canals.

'Inundation' canals.

Canal irrigation is of two kinds; regular canals which flow perennially, and those called 'inundation' canals, which only flow when the rivers are in full flood, being swelled by the rains of the 'Monsoon' season, or by the melting of snows in the Himáláyá, or both, as the case may be.

Private canals.

Some canals are small cuts made by private enterprise and managed according to local custom, as regards the distribution of water and the supply of labour, or the cost of labour for keeping the channels clear of silt. These are mostly inundation canals, and have no regularly constructed masonry head-works at the source.

Hill torrents.

In some places on the north-west frontier, and I daresay the same is true elsewhere, there are curious customs depending on the use of water in streams descending from the barren hills which only fill when a rainfall occurs. The successive rights to take the water, and the time during which it is to run on to each lot, as well as the dams to be maintained and the height above which they must not be piled up, are all regulated by custom.

Wells.

Irrigation from wells is a feature of Northern and Northern-Central India.

In the Panjáb, water is raised by the Persian wheel[1] all over the plain country as far to the south-east as the Sutlej, where (for what reason I cannot say) it gives way to other methods of which two are found more or less all over India. One consists in raising water in a large leather bag which is pulled over a wheel by means of a long rope drawn by bullocks: in the other the water is lifted in an earthen pot or a leather bucket fixed at one end of a long lever-pole, the other being weighted so as to let the empty vessel descend readily.

Modifications of the 'well' are to be found in various parts, as where a small reservoir is constructed by the side of a river or channel, and some form of wheel or lift is employed to raise the water ('Dheṅkudi' of Bombay, and the small wheel on canals, 'Jhalár' and 'ráotí' of the Panjáb and Sindh).

Customs connected with 'wells.'

In the Panjáb we shall find that the area watered (or protected, for the whole is not watered at once) by a well, and the number of wells in a village, is often a matter intimately connected with land customs and sharing among co-proprietors. A person has a fraction of a well—a sixteenth or half perhaps—or his *land* is otherwise estimated, and he has a share in the *water*, represented by so many 'turns' (varhí) at working the well in the course of a week or other stated time.

In the Panjáb also, and perhaps in other dry districts also, the term 'kuh' or well is constantly used, not merely of the actual water-shaft, but to mean the entire *area of land* cultivated under or in connection with, the well.

Tank.

Tank irrigation[2] is a great feature in Ajmer, in parts of

[1] This is a skeleton wheel fixed over the mouth of the well and carrying a long belt or ladder of rope to which a series of earthen pots are attached. As they successively dip into the water they fill and remain full till they come to the top, when the movement of the belt inverts them and turns the contents into a wooden trough. The wheel is fitted with stout pegs or teeth which work into one upright wheel or drum moved round by oxen.

[2] The Ajmer chapter contains some rather curious details.

Bombay, and in Madras. A 'tank' does not mean a rectangular masonry-lined reservoir:—that sort of tank is no doubt common, but mostly for bathing or in connection with a sacred place or temple. The irrigation tank is in fact a suitable soil-depression, storing up the rain and drainage water, and varying in size from a pond filling the upper part of a small valley, to a vast lake covering hundreds of acres. The tank is closed in by an embankment of earth and masonry, or both. In some cases this is an enormous work, and the bursting of it is the cause of great destruction to agriculture. The 'tank' is always so situated that the rain water reaches it by flowing down all the water-courses, hill-sides, &c. of the neighbouring hills—it is in fact the catchment area of the high land. An escape is afforded in case the water threatens to overtop the embankment. In some cases the tank represents a lake which is never dry: in others, the whole of the water is run off or dries up early in the season, and the bed, enriched with slime, and moistened by the previous soaking of the water, is ploughed up and cultivated.

§ 7. *Orthography of Vernacular Names.*

The mention of Indian provinces and some of their general features has already led me to introduce local terms, and this again suggests the question of the method of writing the native names of places, and the words indicating tenures, offices, and persons, and how far the use of such terms untranslated is permissible. Two methods of writing are possible—one is to endeavour to represent the word *as pronounced*, by writing it phonetically or with such English letters and syllables as the writer thinks will convey the desired sound. The other is to transliterate the real word into Roman letters. Unfortunately for the first method, English vowels (at any rate) have no uniform value or sound maintained under all circumstances: hence it is impossible to be sure what sound is meant to be represented. Especially in the case of 'out-of-the-way' words. It is only a limited number of words that can be phonetically written with fair certainty. The method therefore neither gives the true *word*, nor does it give the real *pronunciation*, because hardly two people would read the combination of letters in the same way. I have adopted then, perforce, the other plan, wherever possible. I give the vernacular word transliterated into the Roman character[1]. At any rate this represents the true *word*, though it does not indicate the pronunciation.

But this latter is of little consequence, because the value of the vernacular vowels being *fixed and uniform*, the student has only to master a very few rules or principles in order to pronounce quite accurately enough to be intelligible. And I wish at once to give the necessary instructions applicable to the reading of the vernacular terms throughout the book. Speaking generally, the words are read as if they were Italian—or with the 'continental' sound to the vowels. The short vowels are printed plain, the long (or broad sound) vowels have an accent. Thus :—

		Uniformly sounded as
a — á	=	must — mast
i — í	=	pit — peat
u — ú	=	pull — pool

Of the other vowels 'e' is always like the French e in 'tête,' so that the Hindí word 'pet' (=stomach) is pronounced like the English word 'pate,' and not like the word 'pet,' and an accent is not ordinarily required. In a few instances, I have put an accent on the (é) so as to *remind* the reader. And in *Southern* Indian names I have always added the accent, because there they use a short ĕ sound as well as the long é.

'O' also needs no accent; it is always long as in 'depôt,' not as in 'pot.' Thus we speak of Gônd tribes—Goand, not short as in 'pond.'

[1] In order to indicate the origin of the terms, a *capital* letter is often added: thus P. means the word is Persian; Pj. means Panjábí; A Arabic, S. Sanskrit, and H. a Hindí dialect.

Of the *diphthongs*, 'ai' is always pronounced like the English 'eye' (not like 'jay'). 'Au' is as in 'bough' (not as in 'awe').

As regards the accented and plain vowels, short 'a' has the sound of '*a*' in 'organ,' *never* of '*a*' in 'pan.' As this vowel naturally inheres in every Sanskrit or Hindí consonant, it is constantly occurring, and attention to this one rule will almost secure a tolerable enunciation of words. 'Parasú-Rámá,' e.g., must be read like the English syllables purr-us-soo-Râmâ, and not as if it were the English 'parasol' or 'rammer.'

The accented 'á' is always broad. 'Alláhábád' has all the 'a's,' except the first, as in the French 'gâteau' or Italian 'lago.'

The 'i' is as in the English 'pit,' and the accented 'í' as our 'ee,' or 'ea' in 'cheat'; thus, Pitiká (Pity-kah), Pílíbhít (Pee-lee-bheet).

The 'u' is *always* as in 'push' or 'put,' *never* as in 'jug,' 'pug' (which latter sounds would be supplied by short 'a,' without any accent, as above described).

The accented 'ú' is *always* as our 'oo' and *never* the 'you' sound peculiar to English. Thus read 'Telugu' as Teloogoo, not as 'Tell-you-gou,' and 'púram' as in 'poor,' not 'pure.'

Of *consonants* little need be said. The ordinary reader need not attempt the niceties of sound; but I may mention a general distinction in t's and d's (which are very common letters), viz. that some are *dental* (pronounced with a touch of the tongue against the teeth), and others *palatal* (touch against the palate). The latter are distinguished by a *dot* under the letter.

These dots will however not concern the ordinary student, and are retained for the use of those who are going to learn the vernacular dialects regularly.

'Th' is not sounded in any Indian dialect as a sibilant (i.e. like 'thin' or 'that'). It is simply a hard 't' with a slight aspirate after it.

The gutturals 'kh' and 'gh' of Arabic and Persian words

are indicated by drawing a line under the two letters, thus—'kh' and 'gh' (pronounced like 'loch' in Scotch).

The Arabic consonant *'ain* is a sound the student need not trouble himself to try and pronounce; it is hardly noticed except in writing, and is represented by the *apostrophe* (or by *a'*) at the end of a word. Thus 'jama'' =a total sum; ra'íyat=a subject, a cultivating tenant, 'mu'áf'=pardoned.

As there are two letters 'k' in the Perso-Arabic alphabet, one distinguished by the long 'tail' and the other by two diacritical points, in the native character,—I use 'k' for the former, and 'q' (without any conventional 'u' added) for the latter.

The letter 'y' is *always* a consonant, and is never used as a vowel in transliterating.

When an 'n' is intended to be merely a nasal intonation, not a distinct letter, it is written with a dot 'ṇ' and then it is hardly sounded: e.g. gáṇw=a village, which is pronounced like 'gow' with a nasal intonation.

'G' is *always* hard, never as in 'gin,' which would be the 'j' sound. I have only to add that these instructions suffice for all words in Sanskrit, Arabic, Persian, Hindí, Hindustání, Bengálí, Maráthí, &c., i.e. for Northern, Eastern, Western and Central India, and to a great extent in Madras also. But in this latter Presidency there are several separate languages—Tamil, Telugu, Canarese and Malayálam; there are also many names which are virtually Anglicized, and I have not knowledge enough—if any change were desirable—to restore a strict transliteration. In Burma also the language is wholly different, with a variety of additional vowel-sounds, and a transliteration system has not yet been fixed. In writing about that province I could, therefore, only adopt the common spelling; but the native words I have used are very few, and by giving accented vowels the value above assigned, no great error will be perceptible.

§ 8. *Retention of Anglicized Names.*

Where a name of a river or place has become thoroughly English, I have retained the familiar form, indicating (if it is known) the real vernacular word in brackets. It would be affectation to ignore the common 'Calcutta' (Kalkaṭṭa or Kálíghát ?), 'Cawnpore' (Káhanpur [1]), Oudh (Awadh [2]), Lucknow (Lakhnau), Sutlej River (Satlaj), Sylhet (Srihaṭṭa or Silhaṭṭ), Chittagong (Cháṭṭágráoṇ) Lahore (Láhaur), &c. The names of Burmese towns—Rangoon, Prome, Moulmein, Mandalay, again, are virtually English words ;—they have hardly any recognizable connection with the local vernacular names, and I have retained them as they are.

In conclusion, I may say that if the student will only remember to give the 'continental' sound to his vowels, giving the *accented* vowels their broad or full sound, he will be able before he has finished a chapter, to read all the Indian names without hesitation, and quite correctly enough to be intelligible. Indian students will, on the other hand, have the *real words*, so that they can look them up in dictionaries and glossaries [3].

§ 9. *Employment of Vernacular terms.*

A few remarks have also to be made about the use of vernacular terms—other than the names of places. A great number of vernacular revenue terms have not only come into use in the common speech of the people, but have been adopted into official language—many of them

[1] The name is derived from Káhn or Káhan, one of the names of the god Krishna (city of Káhn), and not the Persian Khán, as sometimes said.

[2] But the word should be pronounced 'Owd,' not 'Ood,' as I have heard done (i.e. as in *proud*—not *prude*).

[3] I can assure the reader that not the least part of the very great labour of getting up these volumes has been the endeavour to trace the *real* form of vernacular words fancifully spelt (and rendered absolutely unintelligible) by the writers of Reports and text-books, especially the earlier ones. I have had to conjecture of half-a-dozen possible sounds which was right, and search and search again in dictionaries till I found it. Even so, I fear there may be several mistakes.

being Persian terms, survivals from the Revenue System of the Muhammadan Empire. How far may we use the original words in a book of this kind, and how far should we use translations? No doubt the plain rule is, when writing English, to use English words. But in matters of land-revenue and land-tenure there are necessarily many of the local and general terms which have no exact English equivalent; they represent institutions, offices, customs and forms of proceeding which do not belong to anything English or in England. Sooner or later the reader will find it necessary to know familiarly a few of the common land-terms, and when he has mastered the not very onerous task, he will find the vernacular words both shorter and more expressive than any attempted English substitutes. I cannot pretend to any system in determining when to use an English and when an Indian term; I can only trust to the method adopted proving practically convenient.

I have everywhere used the English word 'village' as the commonly accepted equivalent for the group of lands which is called in Revenue or official language 'Mauza' or 'Dih' (P.), or in Hindí dialects gáṇw, gráma, gaum, &c. But the reader will at once understand that by 'village' we do not mean a small collection of houses with a green, a few shops, and a church-spire rising above the 'immemorial elms'; we mean always *a group of landholdings aggregated in one place*; there is generally one, or more than one, group of dwellings situated somewhere in the area, and the 'village' has a common tank, graveyard and cattle-stand, and probably an area of scrub jungle and grazing ground attached to it. Village.

Again, I may well use the English term *Headman* to indicate the person who in some forms of village tenure is an essential part of the community,—an hereditary officer of some consideration. Even where such a person is not essential to the social constitution of the village, the Government has generally appointed or recognized a headman in some form or other, because it is more convenient to deal with one man and make him the medium 'Headman.'

of communication and the representative. At the same time, while the English does well enough to replace the great variety of local names that exist[1], it does not distinguish between one form and another, as the vernacular does. The term 'lambardár,' for example, for the headman, in the North Indian and Central Provinces villages, at once indicates that we are speaking of a village of the joint type of which we shall afterwards hear, while 'Mandal' or 'Pátel' at once suggests the other type of village prevailing in Bengal and in Southern India.

'Lambardár.' 'Pátel.'

'Patwárí.' Another very common Indian revenue term is *Patwárí*, meaning the person who keeps the village accounts, and, above all, looks after the maps and records of rights, and registers changes in land proprietorship and in tenancies. Some books call him 'village accountant,' others 'village registrar,' but neither term is satisfactory. Synonymous with *Patwárí* (in Northern India and the Central Provinces) is the name 'Karnam' in the South, and 'Kulkarní' in the West.

'Karnam.' 'Kulkarní.'

I am tempted to illustrate my point by one or two more examples, because they will serve at the outset to explain the most frequently used terms, which will occur at every page almost of our reading.

'Raiyat.' The word 'ryot,' as it is incorrectly written, is familiar as a word to English readers, and they mostly suppose it to mean 'tenant.' So it does to a certain extent; but it marks also that it is 'tenant' of a sort which does not necessarily arise out of any *contract* between a landlord and a cultivator.

I write it 'raiyat' to save trouble, though in strict accuracy it is 'ra'íyat' (A.), meaning 'subject, protected,' &c.

In Bengal it has always been the custom to call the village cultivators under the persons constituted landlords

[1] The village headman was 'Pátel' all over Central and Western India, 'Mandal' in Bengal, and in the North 'Muqaddam'; but there are many other local names. In the joint-villages of Northern India the headman is not a natural part of the system. He is only one among the heads of families selected to represent them with the Government, and primarily to pay in the revenue due by the body.

in 1793, as 'raiyats'; and we shall see the term continued in the latest Tenancy law of Bengal. Some of these are modern contract-tenants, but a great many are really the descendants of the original clearers and settlers, who would have been regarded as owners of their holdings, but for subsequent historical circumstances and changes.

But perhaps the commonest use of the term is to signify the landholder who does not claim—or at any rate has long lost any tangible right to—the ownership of anything beyond his own field or fields. Such landowners exist all over Bombay, Madras, and indeed in other parts, whereever what we shall presently describe as the 'landlord village' has not come into sight, owing to the growth of a landlord class. Technically, the position of such a landholder may be differently defined in different parts. The Bombay Revenue Code calls him 'occupant,' and defines his rights. There is no Code in Madras and no definition, but judicial decisions have recognized the occupant who pays revenue as *de facto* proprietor of his holding. Hence it is very convenient to have a term like 'raiyat' to indicate the members of village communities of a certain type; and especially because in its compound form we can talk of a *Raiyat*-wárí village, and of the Settlement being *Raiyat*-wár—meaning that each occupant is separately assessed for his own field without responsibility for anything else, as opposed to the Bengal 'Zamíndárí' system, where one landlord engages for the revenue of a considerable—sometimes a very large—area, including many villages; or to the 'village' system where a smaller estate—very often a single village—is settled for, and assessed at a lump sum, the body of co-sharers of the village or estate being in theory jointly and severally liable for the whole, and arranging among themselves, according to their own custom and constitution, how much of the total each has to contribute. 'Raiyat wári.' 'Raiyat-wár.'

Another convenient term is 'jama',' and its derivative 'jamabandi.' 'Jama.'

'Jama' is Arabic for 'total,' and means the entire revenue-assessment (exclusive of certain road, education and other

cesses separately levied under special laws). To say that the 'jama' of village A. is Rs. 300' means that the Government Land Revenue demand on the village as a whole, is Rs. 300 each year. Or in a '*raiyatwárí*' settlement it would be—the '*jama*' of the single field or survey number, 'No. 703 is 16 Rs. 8 as.'

'Jamabandi.' 'Jamabandi' is the account 'fixing' or definitely recording (*bandi*) the Revenue demand (*Jama'*). In *raiyatwárí* provinces it has this meaning quite intact. Every year an account is made out showing what fields each *raiyat* has held, and what revenue (jama') he has accordingly become liable for. Under other systems the term has naturally become modified in meaning. In the North-West and Central Provinces, for example, it has come to mean the list of the *tenants* and their *rents*. In the Panjáb it has come to mean a complete record of right, a list showing concisely every holder of land, whether co-sharing proprietor or tenant cultivating (under a co-sharer or under the whole body jointly), and the payment, whether revenue or rent, due from each.

I do not think that terms like these gain anything by attempted translations or equivalents, and I have described the meaning at some length, with the double object of justifying my retaining the original words, and also, at the same time, familiarizing the reader with the words. If he will make himself at home with the terms (headman) 'lambardár' and 'pátel'; with 'raiyat,' 'jama'' and 'jamabandi,' he will have taken a useful step forward.

10. *Connection of the Land-Revenue Administration with other branches.*

One other topic demands perhaps a few words of explanation: why is it that the systems of Land-Revenue Administration are of so much importance in India, that everybody who aims at understanding the Administration generally, must understand this first?

The present book had its origin in a desire to bring a class of public officers—those who have the care of the State Forests in India—into closer contact with the civil administration; and it was felt that to let them understand the land system was the best way to begin.

But for every other class of public officer, and for the economist who interests himself in the welfare of India, the comprehension of the broad features of land-revenue administration is hardly less necessary, if the reasons are less direct or less easily stated [1].

The State derives its principal revenue from the land: it has done so at all times, and the people are accustomed to pay it: it is with them the very nature of things. The collection, when once the assessment is arranged for a term of years, is effected without inquisitorial proceedings and without trouble or extortion. The population is so largely agricultural, and the different classes so wedded to custom, that the speculative administrator who should conceive the idea of getting rid of the land-revenue would soon find himself in a position of difficulty which language could hardly do justice to. The 'land-tax' in England is only one item, and not a very large one, among a host of other taxes; it falls on a small class. In India the land-revenue is a totally different thing. With the necessity for fairly adjusting the amount of revenue which each class of land has to pay, comes the necessity of thoroughly understanding the agricultural conditions of the country, the caste of the people as it affects their cultivating capacity, the modes of holding land, the interests each class has in the land, and

[1] There are, indeed, in the case of forest officers, special reasons for requiring the study. Besides regarding a 'forest' as an organic whole—an arrangement of nature destined to fulfil certain objects—a forest may be looked on as a piece of property of a particular kind; and when it is so regarded we find it subject to peculiar requirements for its protection. Rights of various kinds are claimed and exercised in a manner which does not happen in other properties, and hence the delimitation of forest boundaries and the definition of vague rights and interests are matters of peculiar importance. In attempting either, the forest officer is sure to be brought into contact with Land Revenue maps, records and officials of the neighbouring lands, and he must understand them all—at least in a general way—to deal with them efficiently.

on what classes, and to what extent on each respectively, the revenue burden is to fall. Considering what a large portion of the total population gets its living wholly or in part from the land, it is obvious that the determination of landed rights and the record of everything which concerns the agricultural and social habits of the people is an immense business; consequently a knowledge of the land administration and of the records it requires and the procedure it employs, is, in fact, a knowledge of the largest class of the population and of the conditions under which it lives.

And as the collection of the land-revenue, and the management of all the affairs that are connected with the maintenance of the land-holders in prosperity, demand a subdivision of the entire country into districts and minor official charges, this subdivision and the hierarchy of officers which it entails, naturally becomes the basis of the entire administrative system. Considerations connected with it find their way into every department, the Post-office, the Irrigation department, the Public Works and many others. Nor is the territory organized and officers appointed to the charge of each local area, merely with a view to collecting fixed sums of revenue at fixed dates. The administration has to take a sort of paternal or 'lord of the manor' interest in the whole range of agricultural conditions. It is on this account that the Government is sometimes represented as the 'universal landlord.' The term, it is true, is used with some reference to the fact that the Government has the right over all waste and unoccupied land (as will be explained in the sequel), and that to secure its revenue it holds in a sort of hypothecation the ultimate right over every acre. But there is more than that. In order that the revenue may not be reduced below what a prosperous country should yield, the State officers—among whom the District officer or Collector vested with magisterial powers, is the most prominent—have continually to watch the state of the country. They have to take note of the approach of famine, and by suspending or even remitting the revenue in due time, prevent any undue strain being laid on the people; they have to watch the state of the crops, the failure of rain, the occurrence of floods, locusts and blight, the spread of cattle-disease, all of which may affect the revenue-paying capacity of the land. They have to repress crime and other sources of social disturbance, which demoralize and tend to pauperize the people; to consider how estates may be improved and protected against famine, by studying the requirements of the district in respect of communications which improve the market, of canals which render the waste cultivable, of drainage and embankment works and other improvements. Local Acts empower the Collector to distribute advances from the Treasury to enable the agriculturist to buy stock and to sink wells and undertake individual and local improvements; and this duty requires intimate knowledge of the land.

Even education is not unconnected with the land system. Village schools and the dissemination of agricultural knowledge are matters which indirectly—or perhaps I should say directly—affect the welfare of the villages, and thus affect their power to bear up against calamity and pay with ease instead of with pressure the demands of the State.

Every officer of every department will in some way or at some time be brought into communication with the Collector, his records and his subordinate officials.

The Police-officer has to deal with the village headmen and rural notables, who, as land-holders, have by law certain duties laid on them in connection with the repression and discovery of crime. The details of offences, and especially cattle thefts, demand a knowledge of local land customs and agricultural habits to make them intelligible. The Canal Officer can neither assess water-rates nor distribute the water without some acquaintance with the land system. Even the Commandant of a regiment is thrown into contact with the local Revenue officer, the rural deputy of the Collector, for the supplies and the carts and camels he needs on the march. In fact, I cannot think of any public servant who will not be the better for a general idea of the Land System, while for many such knowledge is absolutely indispensable.

And it also follows, almost without saying, that any one who aims at understanding India, its people and its requirements, and who would gauge at their real value the outcry of half-educated newspaper writers and students of our colleges at the great capitals, and who would understand where there is really a reform to be wisely introduced, and where there is mere clamour and the expression of a natural discontent and aspiration that does not know really what it wants, or what is best for it,—it follows that for him, at least a general idea of the land-system and of the land-tenures cannot fail to be of primary value and importance.

I think I have now discussed all the purely preliminary questions that arise; so, after devoting a chapter to a brief history of the Provinces into which British India is divided —describing how they came to be, and on what legal basis they are constituted—we may proceed to a general account of the land-tenures and landholding customs of the several provinces, especially noting the *factors* which went to their making and shaping: after this will follow an equally general account of the different systems under which the Land-Revenue is assessed and collected, and the administration carried on.

These chapters are especially designed for the home reader and the non-official student, while I hope they will serve as a useful and introductory study to all classes.

I only add that, as in the course of our study we repeatedly mention 'Acts' of the Legislature of India and of the Local Government's 'Regulations,' and Acts of Parliament relating to India, I have thought that it would tend to completeness to interpolate a short chapter on the Indian Legislatures and their powers. Thus the first or 'General' volume, looks at the subject as a whole, and is intended to prepare the way for the volumes which follow and which deal in more detail with the separate provinces *seriatim*. It will be observed that each provincial account is divided into chapters, the first being introductory and calling attention to any special historical or local features that affect the administration; the next describes the process of 'Settlement,' i.e. assessing the Land Revenue; the next deals with land-tenures and customs; and the last with the classes of revenue-officers and the powers they exercise, and with the principal heads of business which they daily transact in camp or in the Collector's office[1] connected with the collection of the revenue, the realization of arrears, the hearing of petitions and cases relating to revenue business, and to the affairs of the estates generally as far as those are of public concern.

[1] In India a public office in the provinces is always called 'Kutcherry,' an Anglicized form of the Hindí 'Kachhahrí.'

CHAPTER II.

OF THE PROVINCES UNDER THE GOVERNMENT OF INDIA, AND HOW THEY WERE CREATED.

§ 1. *Introductory.*

BRITISH INDIA is divided into Provinces, each under a separate local government, and each having its own special laws relating to Land-Revenue. It will be well, therefore, to understand how these provinces came into separate existence for the purposes of administrative government. The limits of my work, however, preclude me from entering on anything like a historical sketch of the progress of those great and unforeseen events which led to so vast a territory being brought under British rule: for such information the standard Histories of India must be consulted. I must plunge at once *in medias res*, only pausing briefly to remind the reader that the history of the British rule in India is the history of a trading Company, which in the course of events was entrusted with the government of the country until 1858, when its delegated powers being resumed, the Crown undertook the direct administration by its own officers.

§ 2. *The Presidencies.*

So long as the East India Company[1] was, as a body, chiefly concerned with trade, the charters granted to it

[1] The title 'East India Company' originated with the Act of Parliament 3 and 4 Wm. IV, cap. 85 (A. D. 1833). Section 111 says that the Company may be described as the 'East India Company.' At first

by the Crown (from the first memorable grant of December 31st, A.D. 1600, onwards) related, as might be expected, chiefly to trading interests.

The first settlements—at Surát (A.D. 1613), on the Coromandel Coast, at Fort St. George (A.D. 1640), and at Fort William in Bengal (A.D. 1698)—were mere 'factories' for trading purposes [1]. These factories then became 'settlements,' which were governed internally each by a 'President and Board.' In the course of time, out-stations or dependent factories grew up under the shelter of the parent, and then the original factory was spoken of as the 'Presidency town,' or centre of the territory where the President resided. In this way, what we now call 'the three Presidencies [2],' Bengal, Madras, and Bombay, came into existence.

In 1773 the government of the Presidency of Fort William was entrusted to a Governor and Council of four members. The style of the 'Governor' was changed to 'Governor-General,' and as such he had a certain control over the other two Presidencies, particularly as regards the declaration of war and concluding peace. This was provided by the Act (13 Geo. III, cap. 63) known as the 'Regulating Act.' It was not till twenty years after (33 Geo. III, cap. 52) that the government of Bombay and Madras, respectively, was formally vested in a Governor with three Councillors [3].

the Company was called 'the Governor and Company of Merchants trading to the East Indies.' Then a rival Company was formed, called 'the English Company trading to the East Indies.' These two Companies were afterwards united, and, by the Act of Queen Anne (6 Anne, cap. 17, Sec. 13), the style became 'the United Company of Merchants of England trading to the East Indies.' Last of all, the Act of William IV, first quoted, legalized the formal use of the designation ever since in use. It is, however, frequently used in the titles of Statutes prior to this, e.g. 9 Anne, cap. 7; 10 Geo. III, cap. 47; 13 Geo. III, cap. 63.

[1] And, indeed, they were not 'possessions,' but the traders were the tenants of the Mughal Emperor. The first actual possession was the Island of Bombay, ceded by Portugal, in 1661, to Charles II, as part of the marriage dowry of the Infanta. This island was granted to the Company in 1669.

[2] The use of this term has never, even in Acts of Parliament, been precise: sometimes it is meant to signify the *form* of government, sometimes the *place* which was the seat of that government; at other times it meant the *territories* under such government.

[3] The term '*Governor* or President,' however, begins to appear before

These territorial divisions of India, called Presidencies, could not be authoritatively defined from the first; they gradually grew up under the effect of circumstances.

Territories that were conquered or ceded to the Company were, naturally enough, in the first instance attached to the Presidency whose forces had subdued them, or whose Government had negotiated their cession. Thus, for instance, Bengal, Bihár, and (old) Orissa, granted in 1765, went to Fort William; the territory acquired from the Nawáb of the Carnatic (1801), the Ceded districts (1800) and the acquisitions from Mysore (Maisúr) 1792–99, went to Fort St. George; and the Bombay territories, taken in 1803–1818 from the Maráthá King or Peshwá, to Bombay; and so on.

No one could foresee what course events would take; and when it is recollected under what very different circumstances, at what different dates, and under what unexpected conditions, province after province was added to the government of the Company, it is not surprising that the Legislature should not, *ab initio*, have hit upon a convenient and uniform procedure, which would enable all acquisitions of territory to be added on to one or other of the existing centres of Government in a systematic

that; e.g. in Section 39 of the Regulating Act itself; and in 26 Geo. III, cap. 57.

It would be beyond the scope of this work to go into any detail about the powers of the E. I. C.: it may be useful to state so much, that the Act of 1773 was the first in which the new position of the Company as territorial potentate seems to have been fully realized. After this, further statutes were usually passed about every twenty years, when the charters came up for reconsideration, with the general result, as Mr. J. S. Cotton puts it, 'of tightening the authority of Parliament and of transforming the Company itself from a trading corporation into an administrative machine' (Statement of *Moral and Material Progress*, Parl. Blue-Book, 1882–3, p. 3). The Company was never sovereign, its power was always derivative. In 1813 (50 Geo. III, c. 155) an express reservation is made of the 'undoubted sovereignty of the Crown over the territorial acquisitions of the Company'; and the Statutes from 1833 onwards speak of the Company as trustee for the Crown as regards its possessions, its rights and its powers. See also *Field*, § 348, p. 632, where the learned author discusses the question at what time the Company can be held to have begun to act as a Government (by delegation for the Crown). For a long time the Company, even after it had acquired territory, neither desired nor exercised sovereign rights. But the treaties of 1801, 1803, and 1805 clearly show that by that time such rights were exercised.

manner. The student will not therefore be surprised to find that the legislative provisions for the formation and government of the provinces of India are not contained in one law, but were developed gradually by successive Acts, each of which corrected the errors, or enlarged the provisions, of the former ones.

§ 3. *Method of dealing with new Territories.*

Until quite a late date (as will be seen hereafter) no Statute gave any power to provide for any new territory, otherwise than by attaching it to one or other of the three historical Presidencies. But as a matter of fact, large areas of country, when conquered or ceded to the British by treaty, were not definitely attached to any Presidency; at any rate, it was doubtful whether they were intended to be so or not. This was especially the case with the Bengal Presidency; it became in fact difficult to say with precision what were the exact limits of that Presidency, or whether such and such a district was in it or not; and this afterwards gave rise to questions as to whether particular laws were in force or not.

The Act 39 and 40 Geo. III, cap. 79 (A.D. 1800), was the first distinctly to empower[1] the Court of Directors in England, to determine what places should be subject to either Presidency, and set the example by declaring the districts forming the province of Benares (ceded in 1775) to be formally 'annexed' to the Bengal Presidency.

§ 4. *List of Provinces.*

At this point, and before describing the further legislative enactments relating to the constitution of provinces, it will be well to give a list of the existing provinces in British India, and to describe how they were constituted; then we shall be in a better position to understand the legal enactments which settle their territorial constitution and government.

[1] There are Acts of 1773 and 1793 which make allusion to the subject, but the Act of 1800 is the first which directly deals with it.

The student will clearly understand—

I. That originally there were certain centres of trade managed by a President and Council, and that in the first instance such territories as were acquired, were attached to one or other of these three centres called 'Presidencies.' And it appears to have been supposed that they would embrace all the British territories in India. But this afterwards proved impossible.

II. That the Presidencies of Bengal, of Madras and Bombay, do not cover the whole of British India, and that the following list summarizes the whole. The capitals or head-quarters are noted in the margin.

Calcutta (Fort William).

(1) Presidency of Bengal. (Lieutenant-Governor and Council.) This at first included 'Benares province' (1775–1800) and the 'North-Western Provinces' (1801–3).

Madras (Fort St. George).

(2) Presidency of Madras. (Governor and Council.)

Bombay (Bombay Castle).

(3) Presidency of Bombay. (Governor and Council.) (Aden belongs to this Presidency.)

N.W. Provinces. Allahábád.

(4) The North-Western Provinces and Oudh. The former was separated from Bengal in 1834. Oudh was annexed in 1856, and placed under a Chief Commissioner. In 1877 the Provinces were amalgamated, so that the official title of the head of the administration is 'Lieutenant-Governor and Chief Commissioner.' A Legislative Council was formed in 1886.

Lahore. (5) The Panjáb. (Lieutenant-Governor, no Council.)

Nágpur. (6) The Central Provinces. (Chief Commissioner.)

Ajmer. (7) Ajmer and Merwára. (Chief Commissioner.)

Shillong. (8) Assam. (Chief Commissioner; separated from Bengal in 1874.)

Bangalore (local capital Mérkára).

(9) Coorg. (Chief Commissioner.)

Rangoon.

(10) Burma. (Chief Commissioner. Lower Burma acquired 1824–1852, Upper Burma, 1885.)

Port Blair. (11) The Andaman Islands. (Chief Commissioner.)

The Residency, Hyderábád.

(12) The Hyderabad (Haidarábád) assigned districts or Berár, governed by the Viceroy (through the Resident of Hyderabad). This constitutes a special territory as will be explained.

§ 5. *Notice of their Acquisition.*

Taking these provinces in the order stated, we will now give the essential particulars regarding each, *seriatim.*

And this seems the place to introduce and explain a general map of India, which shows at a glance when the various territories were acquired. The States which are still more or less independent—that is, managing their own affairs under a native administration, but acknowledging the suzerainty of the British Crown—are left uncoloured in the map.

I will only explain that the number of colours being limited, I could only adopt one for each period of years, not one for every separate war or treaty by which territory was acquired. Thus in Madras in 1800–1 territory was acquired by assignments which had nothing whatever to do with the acquisition of the 'Ceded Districts' of the North-West Provinces (1801), though the colour is the same. On the other hand, in 1803, the Maráthá treaty gave us territory in various parts of India—viz. near Delhi, in Bombay, and in Orissa[1].

§ 6. *Bengal and the North-West Provinces.*

The Presidency of Bengal was the one which first necessitated legal steps with a view to providing for the distribution of territory. Madras never received any territory that was not naturally and conveniently attached to it. Bombay was also compact, and though Sindh (annexed by war in 1843) was added to it as an outlying province, it was a natural addition, as in 1843 the Panjáb was foreign terri-

[1] It is curious to observe from this map, first, that territory was not eagerly—but most reluctantly—acquired. Certain powers that continued to resist, e. g. Mysore, were not deprived of their provinces at once—but at first of only such districts as were absolutely needed for security. It will also be seen that the annexations were not haphazard, but arranged with forethought to secure the sea-board and to prevent the hostile action of certain States. I do not mean to defend every acquisition of territory in detail, but a study of such a map will certainly exculpate the rulers of past days from many vague charges of wantonness. A large area, it will be observed, has come to us by escheat on failure of heirs.

tory and Sindh was nearer to Bombay than to any other centre[1].

It was otherwise with Bengal. The addition of Benares in 1775 by itself would not have been a difficulty, and even the annexation of the modern Orissa (Cuttack (Katák) Bálásúr and Púrí) in 1803 was not inconvenient from an administrative point of view. But the first Burmese war, in 1824, gave Assam, Arrakan, and Tennasserim; and the additions in 1801–3 to the North-West[2], would have extended the Presidency beyond all reasonable limits.

3 and 4 Will. IV, cap. 85, sec. 38.

The subject of territorial division was accordingly again dealt with in the year 1833 (3 and 4 Will. IV, cap. 85). This Act proposed to divide the Presidency into two parts, to be called 'the Presidency of Fort William in Bengal,' and the 'Presidency of Agra[3].'

It was to be determined locally what territories should be allotted to each.

§ 7. *The first Lieutenant-Governorship (North-West Provinces).*

Though a 'Governor of Agra' was actually appointed[4], the scheme was early abandoned, and instead of forming a new Presidency, the 'North-West Provinces' were separated from the rest of Bengal and placed under a Lieutenant-Governor. This was ordered in 1836, and was legalized by the 5 and 6 Will. IV, cap. 52 (1835), which suspended the

[1] Aden, the military station at the entrance to the Red Sea, was placed under the Governor of Bombay for the same reason.

[2] These large additions in the north-west (besides the Benares territory above alluded to) consisted of the districts ceded in 1801 by the Nawáb of Oudh, and comprised the country now known as the districts of Allábábád, Fatihpur, Cawnpore (Káhnpur), part of 'Ázimgarh, Gorakhpur, Bareli, Murádábád, Bijnaur, Badáon, and Sháhjahánpur. Soon after, a subordinate of the Nawáb's ceded Farukhábád; and not long after followed the districts conquered in the Maráthá War (which began in 1803): these were Etáwa, Mainpúri, Aligarh, Bulandshahr, Meerut (Mírath), Muzaffarnagar, Sahádranpur, Agra, Muttra (Mathurá), and Delhi (the latter including the districts on the right bank of the Jamná, now in the Panjáb); also Bánda and parts of Bundélkhand.

[3] This attempt to attach the historic reminiscences involved in the term 'Presidency' to Agra, which had never known the system of 'President and Board,' is curious.

[4] See Notification (in the Political Department) of the 14th November, 1834.

previous enactment ordering the creation of two presidencies, and rendered valid the appointment of the Lieutenant-Governor. Bengal was thus partly relieved and reduced to more reasonable dimensions.

§ 8. *The Government of Bengal.*

But still there was another difficulty. There was no separate Governor or Lieutenant-Governor for Bengal. The Governor-General of India was *ex-officio* Governor of Bengal; that is to say, he had to do the work of a local Governor in addition to his functions as Governor-General with supreme control over all Governments. It is true that the Governor-General was empowered to appoint a Deputy-Governor of Bengal, but that did not relieve him of the direct responsibility. Accordingly, the Statute 16 and 17 Vict., cap. 95 (1853), authorized the appointment of a separate Governor of Bengal, or (until such an officer should be appointed) a Lieutenant-Governor. This Act also looks back on the arrangements made for the North-West Provinces (just described), and again confirms them, going on to say that the Lieutenant-Governorship of Bengal was to consist of such part of the territories of the Presidency as for the time being was not under the new Lieutenant-Governorship of the North-West Provinces.

A Lieutenant-Governor of Bengal was accordingly appointed under this Act[1].

§ 9. *Unattached Provinces.*

With this relief, the management of Assam, though the province was early exempted from the Regulation Law of Bengal, presented no difficulty; and even the Burma districts did not call for any special measures till several years later.

[1] See Resolution, Home Department, No. 415, dated 28th April, 1854. And by order of the Government of India, 26th January, 1855, 'the authority of the Lieutenant-Governor of Bengal extends to all matters relating to civil administration heretofore under the authority of the Governor of Bengal.'

So far then as the territory actually attached to the Bengal Presidency is concerned, the matter was settled. But before long other territories also were acquired, and they were so large and important, that some further provision for their government was needed; for on annexation they were not formally attached to either of the existing Presidencies. Such were the 'Saugor and Nerbudda' (Ságar and Narbada) territories (ceded after the Maráthá War of 1817–18), Coorg (Kodagu) 1834, Nágpur (1854), the Panjáb (1849), and Pegu (1852). How were these to be provided for[1]?

It is probable that at first the case was not thoroughly understood; at all events, the only additional provision made by the law of 1853, was a general power to create one other Presidency besides those existing, and if it was not desired to make a '*Presidency*' then to appoint a Lieutenant-Governor of the territories to be provided for.

But a glance at the list of provinces or districts just given as 'unattached,' and a thought as to their geographical position, will show that this provision was not sufficient; the 'unattached' provinces were too far apart to make it possible to provide for them by uniting them under one new 'Presidency.'

What are now called 'The Central Provinces' were mainly formed by the cession of the 'Saugor and Nerbudda' (Ságar and Narbada) territories in 1817–18 and by the escheat of the territory of the Bhônslá family (one of the members of the Maráthá Confederacy) in 1854; and they were far removed from the older territories. The second Burmese war added the rest of Lower Burma, across the Bay of Bengal. The important acquisition of the Panjáb was in the extreme north-west of India.

None of these provinces—either from their geographical position or owing to the requirements of their administration, or both—could be attached to either of the Presidencies; nor would the Lieutenant-Governorship of the North-

[1] Sindh, annexed in 1843, had been attached to Bombay. Oudh was not annexed till afterwards (1856).

West Provinces bear extension so as to include any of them.

The Act of 1853, above alluded to, by which the Lieutenant-Governorship of Bengal was constituted, had empowered the Government to create *one* other 'Presidency' besides those existing, or, if that was not desired, then to appoint a Lieutenant-Governor for the territories in question. This provision was held to authorize the appointment of a Lieutenant-Governor for the Panjáb, but it was insufficient to meet the other cases.

In the year 1854 the deficiency was supplied. By the 17 and 18 Vict., cap. 77, provision was made for the government of such territories or parts of territories as 'it might not be advisable to include in any Presidency or Lieutenant-Governorship.' Section 3 empowers the Governor-General by proclamation (under Home sanction) to take such territories under his 'immediate authority and management,' or otherwise to provide for the administration of them. Under this Act the 'Local Administrations' under Chief Commissioners, as they now exist, were constituted. As they are under the 'direct orders' of the Governor-General, the Government of India is itself the Local Government[1], and the Chief Commissioner constitutes a 'Local Administration' as administering the orders of the Local Government.

It would of course be inconvenient if the Governor-General had to exercise directly, in every one of these provinces, all the powers of a Local Government; and therefore, in 1867, an Indian Act (XXXII) was passed to enable him to relieve himself of such detailed work, by delegating certain of his powers as the 'Local Government' to the Chief Commissioners then existing, which were those of Oudh, the Central Provinces, and British Burma. Since then, this process has been further simplified by inserting in Section 2, clause 10 of Act I of 1868 ('The General

[1] The provinces under Lieutenant-Governors are called 'Local Governments,' because such provinces, though subordinate to the Government of India, are not *immediately* under the orders of the Governor-General.

Clauses Act'), a definition of the term 'Local Government.' In all Acts passed after 1868, when anything is provided to be done by a Local Government, that *includes* the Chief Commissioner of any province; in fact, the delegation of the Governor-General's power as a Local Government is in all such cases implied by, or contained in, the legal meaning of the term Local Government[1]. Of course the term has this wider meaning only when the context, or some express provision, does not control or limit it.

The powers of the Governor-General were further enlarged by the 46th section of the 24 and 25 Vict., cap. 67 ('The Indian Councils Act, 1861') which gives him power to constitute new provinces and to appoint Lieutenant-Governors for them. The Act also makes provision for fixing the limits of every 'Presidency division, province or territory in India' for the purposes of the Act; and for altering those limits.

In 1865 the 28th Vict., cap. 17, provided the power to apportion or re-apportion the different territories among the existing Governorships and Lieutenant-Governorships.

There are also provisions of the Indian Legislature regarding minor divisions of territory, i.e. creating new districts and altering the existing boundaries of districts, of which it is not here necessary to speak.

§ 10. *Notes on the Provinces—Bengal—Madras.*

I may now add a few particulars regarding the different provinces as constituted under the laws above enumerated. The growth of Bengal has been already indicated. Madras calls for no explanation; the table at the end of the chapter gives the facts.

[1] The 'General Clauses Act' of 1868 defines the term 'Local Government' to mean, 'the person authorized by law to administer executive government in the part of British India in which the Act containing such expression shall operate, and shall include a Chief Commissioner.' In Assam, where it was not convenient that this should take effect, Acts VIII and XII of 1874 were specially enacted to regulate the powers of the Chief Commissioner.

§ 11. *Bombay.*

The earliest acquisitions, leaving aside Bombay itself, were Surát, Bharôch, and Kairá, which were acquired partly from the Nawáb of Surát in 1800, partly from the Gaikwár of Baroda (one of the Maráthá confederacy) between 1802–1805. Ahmadábád was also acquired from the Gaikwár between 1802 and 1817.

The Maráthá war of 1803 was the cause of some of these cessions. The rest of the districts were variously acquired, but the bulk of them were annexed after the last war in 1818. In 1822 a treaty with the Nizám of Haidarábád resulted in several exchanges and cessions with a view to simplifying boundaries and jurisdictions. The Bombay presidency still remains much interspersed with native states, and, as might be expected, occasional lapses for want of heirs, and some confiscations, have occurred. Thus the Satárá district was acquired on the deposition of the Rájá in 1837; and the part of Belgám that was not ceded in 1818 was acquired from the Rájá of Kolapur in 1827.

A treaty with Sindhia of December 12th, 1860 (also for the purpose of adjusting boundaries), resulted in several exchanges of small tracts in Poona and elsewhere.

In 1862, the North Kánara district, which was previously under Madras, was transferred to Bombay.

§ 12. *The North-West Provinces and Oudh.*

I have already been obliged to include much of what has to be said of this province in my account of Bengal. It will only be necessary here to repeat that the province consists of the Benares districts which came under the Permanent Settlement—viz. Benares (Banáras), Ballia, Jaunpur, Ghzipur, and part of Mirzapur; the 'Ceded districts' of 1801, already enumerated in a footnote; and certain districts called the 'Conquered territories,' acquired by treaty from the Maráthás in 1803. These were Agra, Muttra (Mathurá), Aligarh, Bulandshahr, Meerut (Mírath), Muzaffarnagar, and Sahāranpur, as well as the Bundélkhand districts of Bándá and Hamírpur. The remaining districts of this last local group, viz. Jhánsí, Jaláun, and Lalitpur, were acquired by lapse, forfeiture, and treaty after 1840.

The Maráthá treaty of 1803 also ceded certain territory on the right bank of the Jamná river known as 'the Delhi territory.' In 1858 it was transferred to the Panjáb, because at the time the mutiny at Delhi made it impossible to communicate with it from the North-West Provinces. Further particulars will be given in the next paragraph.

The only other addition to the North-West Provinces was the hill and sub-montane tract taken after the Nepál war of 1815 (Dehra-dún, Jáunsar-Báwar, Kumáon and British Garhwál.)

The North-West Provinces, as already explained, are under a Lieutenant-Governor, whose capital was moved to Allahábád shortly after 1860. The Province is under a High Court and a Board of Revenue.

OUDH was annexed in 1856, and placed under a Chief Commissioner. In 1877 it was amalgamated with the North-West Provinces, so far, that the Lieutenant-Governor became also the Chief Commissioner, and is the chief controlling Revenue authority[1]. The Board of Revenue does not control Oudh, nor has the High Court jurisdiction: the Judicial Commissioner is still the highest local Court.

§ 13. *The Panjáb.*

The first acquisition of territory, which now forms part of the Panjáb, resulted from Lord Lake's Maráthá campaign and the treaty of Sarjí-Anjangám (Dec. 30, 1803). This was the country on the right bank of the Jamná, and is comprised in the present districts of Delhi (Dihlí), Gurgáoṇ, Rohtak, Karnál, Hisár, and the Sirsá tahsil of Firozpur.

[1] The official particulars are to be found in the Resolution, Home Department (Government of India) No. 45, Jan. 17, 1877. In order to facilitate the action of Government, Act XIV of 1878 was passed to assimilate the powers of the Chief Commissioner of Oudh to those which the Lieutenant-Governor would exercise as such. The assimilation is chiefly effected by repealing some of the provisions (in various Acts) which require the Governor-General's sanction to the Chief Commissioner's proceedings.

The country was at first under the general political control of the North-West Provinces. It was then our policy to make the Jamná the frontier, and to provide for the districts beyond by granting them to great chiefs who were to receive the revenue, and be responsible for the administration. The plan failed; and after some years under the North-West Provinces government, the events of the Mutiny (as already stated) compelled the transfer of the districts (1858) to the Panjáb[1].

The next important occurrence was the Protection treaty of 1809 with the chiefs on this side (i. e. the side nearest the British capital) of the Sutlej. The chiefs became alarmed by the incursions of Ranjít Singh, who indeed in 1806 advanced as far as the British cantonment at Karnál.

The greater chiefs have since been confirmed as feudatory princes (Farídkot, Patiála, Jínd, Nábhá, and the minor states of Malér-Kotlá and Kalsiá), the others became

[1] One of the above-named districts—Karnál—as it now is, does not wholly consist of territory taken in 1803; other neighbouring lands lapsed to the Government, and there were several changes. First, there were two districts, Karnál and Thanesar, and then, on the abolition of the latter, there was a remodelling of the district of Karnál.

The districts named in the text are commonly called the 'Delhi territory,' and were equally commonly, but erroneously, supposed to be the territory spoken of in the Regulations of 1803–5 which provided for the administration of the 'Conquered districts.' The territory therein declared exempt from the Regulations was only the country round the city of Delhi, including the 'ṭaiyúl' villages—lands the income of which went to the privy purse of the titular king of Delhi, and certain other tracts, *the revenues of which were assigned for the expenses of the Court.* Certainly Karnál as it then was, and Hisár, Rohtak, &c., though called the Delhi territory, were never assigned for the support of the king of Delhi. The fact is that the Regulations ignored the country on the right bank of the Jamná. Reg. VIII of 1805 professes to provide for the whole of the conquered territories: but by the direction to form them into districts, and then specifying the law applicable *to those districts*, the country we are speaking of is virtually excluded, because geographically it never was or could be included in any of the five districts prescribed by the Regulation. Legally then the Regulation law generally applied, but practically there was no one to administer it, as most of the territory had been granted to native chiefs under political control only. Karnál was (for example) granted to the Mandal family, who still hold the pargana of Karnál. As a whole, the plan failed, and some of the chiefs resigned their grants. Gradually these districts came under British Government, and the grantees (such of them as remained) became great private estate holders under the Government. In 1832, Reg. V was passed to declare the laws in force, and British officers made the Revenue Settlements. This Regulation was repealed in 1858 (Act XXXVIII), and since then the districts have been under the Panjáb, and of course subject to the ordinary Panjáb law.

'jágírdárs' or smaller chiefs to whom the revenue of the territory was granted. Some of the states have since lapsed from failure of heirs, e.g. part of Jínd in 1834, Kaithal (now part of Karnál district) in 1843, and Thanesar in 1850[1]. In 1845 the Ladwá state was forfeited for rebellion, and now forms part of Karnál district.

In this part of the country there have naturally been minor exchanges of villages and adjustments of boundary which it is not necessary to detail.

Things so remained till Ranjít Singh's death, and some years afterwards, when the Darbár (or Sikh Court) was foolishly moved to interfere on the other side of the Sutlej; this led to the first Sikh war, and the annexation of the cis-Sutlej districts, Firozpur, Lúdíána, Ambála[2], as well as (for security) the districts of Jálandhar, Húshyárpur, and Kangra, which were trans-Sutlej, or between the Sutlej and the Bíás Rivers. A British Resident was appointed to aid the Darbár in administering the Panjáb to the north-west of the Bíás River; but a second Sikh war broke out, and, in 1849, Lord Dalhousie (very reluctantly) annexed the whole.

The province was not attached to any presidency, but simply annexed to the British dominion; hence

[1] Thanesar was at first formed into a separate district, but was afterwards divided between Ambála and Karnál districts.

The history of the Sikhs is a very interesting one, but I cannot, of course, go into it. By the Treaty of 1809, the states cis-Sutlej were protected from being swallowed up by the power of Ranjít Singh. At first, the reader will remember, a number of Sikh chiefs, with their followers, each conquering and holding what territory he could (as his taluqa or state), formed a number of groups called 'misl,' confederated together, till Rája Mahan Singh of the Sukrchakyá misl began to take the lead and reduce the others to subjection. The plan was consummated by the force and genius of his son Ranjít Singh, who became the 'Mahárájá' or great over-lord of the whole.

[2] Ambála was only partly annexed: most of it is made up of territory which lapsed to Government by failure of heirs. A certain number of the cis-Sutlej chiefs intrigued with the Sikhs before the war. Ladwá was confiscated on this account, and on the conclusion of the war, safety was secured by acknowledging sovereign powers only to the greater (and thoroughly loyal) chiefs, Patiálá, Jínd, and Nábhá, of the Phúlkián misl, while sovereign powers were withdrawn from the petty territories. It was obviously impossible long to tolerate, among the British districts, a series of semi-independent kingdoms, each the size of half a county, and at bitter enmity one with the other.

the Regulations did not apply. A despatch (dated 31st March, 1849) from the Governor-General, gave directions as to the form and method of administration, and appointed a 'Board of Administration' consisting of three members. By the Government of India, Notif. No. 660, dated 4th February, 1853, a single Chief Commissioner was substituted. (Differences of opinion arose in the Board, and, as might be expected, it was found that the responsible executive functions in a province must be in a single hand.) The Chief Commissioner was assisted by a Financial Commissioner and a Judicial Commissioner as the chief Revenue and Judicial authorities under Government. Lastly, by Notification No. 1, dated 1st January, 1859 (under the 16 and 17 Vict., cap. 95) the Governor-General 'proclaimed that a separate Lieutenant-Governorship for the territories on the extreme northern frontier of Her Majesty's Indian Empire shall be established, and that the Panjáb and the tracts commonly called the trans-Sutlej States, the cis-Sutlej States, and the Delhi territory, shall be the jurisdiction of the Lieutenant-Governor.' These limits are maintained to the present day. As they include more than the Panjáb proper, the official style is 'Lieutenant-Governor of the Panjáb and its dependencies.' The Chief Court (virtually a High Court, but not by Royal Charter) has become the chief judicial controlling authority (Act IV of 1866), and there are now two Financial Commissioners for Revenue control.

§ 14. *The Central Provinces.*

It will be observed that there are certain groups which will facilitate the remembrance of the main parts—(1) Nimár; (2) the districts adjoining the Taptí and Narbada rivers in the North; (3) the Central districts; (4) Sambalpur; and (5) the small tract in the south on the Godávarí river.

(1) The first portions of Nimár were acquired after the Maráthá war from Sindhia in 1818. But the rest of the district was made over to our management, the northern

part in 1820–25, the southern (adjoining the Taptí) in 1844. The sovereignty of both was ceded in 1860.

(2) Of the Northern districts, Baitul, Seoni, Jabalpur[1], and Mandla were ceded after the war, in 1818, so was most of Narsinghpur, and Hoshangabad. A few parganas of Narsinghpur north of the Taptí were first made over to British management (1820–5) and ceded in 1860, and the southern part of Hoshangabad (Hardá-Hándia) was made over in 1844, and ceded in 1860. The two northern districts, Ságar and Dámoh, were acquired piecemeal; portions of both were acquired in 1818 from the Bhônslá Maráthás of Nágpur, and from the Peshwá; and the rest, having been made over for management in 1820–5, was ceded in 1860[2]. One pargana (Sháhgarh) in Ságar was forfeited for rebellion in 1857.

(3) The central districts, escheated for want of heirs in 1854. The same was the case with Sambalpur (4) in 1849.

Lastly, the tract now called the Sironchá tahsil of the Chándá district, along the Godávarí, was ceded by the Nizám (in exchange for other lands) in 1860.

By Resolution (Foreign Department, No. 9 of 2nd November, 1861) the Chief Commissionership of the Central Provinces was constituted. The notification contains a long history of the administration of these provinces. It recites that Nágpur had been under a Commissioner as Agent for the Governor-General. The Ságar and Narbada districts had at various times been transferred from one Government to another. They were originally under the Supreme Government; subsequently they were placed under the Lieutenant-Governor of the North-West Provinces. Again, in 1842, the general control of them was vested in a Commissioner and Governor-General's Agent, in direct communication with the Supreme Government, while the supervision of fiscal and judicial affairs re-

[1] The north-east pargana of Jabalpur formed a separate state (Bijragogarh), which was forfeited for mutiny in 1857.

[2] Both Ságar and Damoh districts were further altered by some transfers from British territory in Bundélkhand, but that was an administrative transfer not a territorial acquisition.

mained with the Sudder Board and Sudder Court of the North-West Provinces respectively. After this, the general jurisdiction was again transferred to the Lieutenant-Governor of the North-West Provinces, and so remained till the notification issued in 1861. Nimár had been managed chiefly as an 'assigned district' till its cession as a whole in 1860. Sambalpur was added to the Central Provinces in 1862, Nimár in 1864, and a small estate called Bijragogarh in 1865. The fact that some tracts in Nágpur were ceded in 1817 does not place Nágpur first in the list of acquisitions. The province as a whole had been managed since the defeat of Appa Sáhib in 1817, on behalf of the minor Bhônslá Rájá (Raghújí III). He succeeded to the estates in 1830, but died without heirs in 1853, and the province lapsed to the British Government.

§ 15. *Ajmer and Merwára.*

Ajmer was ceded by treaty in 1818 and Merwára also, but the latter district was in so disturbed a state that it had to be restored to order by military occupation. Such details as are necessary will best find a place in the chapter specially devoted to an account of this province. The whole was constituted a Chief Commissionership under the authority of the 17 and 18 Vict., cap. 77, sec. 3[1]. The Governor-General's Agent for the Rájputána States is *ex officio* Chief Commissioner.

Previously the province had been under the North-West Provinces Government, and it was owing to that fact that the first regular settlement was made on the system of village settlements prevalent in those provinces.

§ 16. *Assam.*

This province was separated from Bengal and placed under a Chief Commissioner under the provisions of the Act of 1854 (17 and 18 Vict., cap. 77). As it was not desirable to give the Chief Commissioner, as such, all the

[1] Notification (Foreign Department), No. 1007, dated 26th May, 1871.

powers which had been exercised by the Government of Bengal, special acts were passed dealing with the subject of powers. The detail of this will be more appropriately given in the chapter devoted to Assam.

Assam includes the Assam valley districts, acquired in 1824, the Hill districts (Garo Hills, Khásí and Jaintya Hills, &c.), and the older districts of Goálpárá, Sylhet (properly Silhaṭṭ or Srihaṭṭa), and Kachár [1].

§ 17. *Coorg.*

The little province of *Coorg* (Koḍagu) was annexed in 1834 owing to the continued misgovernment of its Rájá [2]. It is a hill country along the top of the Western Ghât range; only a tract to the north and a strip to the east is 'below Ghât.' Its people and its tenures were peculiar, so that its administration was provided for separately. The Resident of Mysore is the Chief Commissioner.

It is a scheduled district under Act XIV of 1874, and is governed by such of the General Acts as have been declared in force, and by Regulations under the 33 Vict., cap. 3.

§ 18. *Burma.*

British Burma was constituted a Chief Commissionership on its present footing in 1862 [3]. As in the case of the Central Provinces, the Resolution gives a history of the previous administration. It recites that there had been three separate Commissioners of Arracan, Pegu, and Tenasserim respectively: the first had been under the Government of Bengal (annexation after the war of 1824); Pegu (second Burmese war, 1852) had been directly under the Government of India.

After the third Burmese war (1885–6) the provinces of Upper Burma and the Shán States were annexed, and formed into seventeen districts, the States being under political con-

[1] Notification, No. 379, dated 7th February, 1874 (*Gazette of India*, Part II, p. 53).

[2] Proclamation issued May, 1834.

[3] Resolution, Foreign Department (General), No. 212, dated 31st January, 1862.

trol only[1]. The Chief Commissioner has jurisdiction over the whole, but the Upper Burma territories are governed by several separate Regulations under the 33 Vict., cap. 3.

§ 19. *The Andaman Islands.*

The small settlement at Port Blair has importance chiefly as a penal settlement for convicts; the government is by a Chief Commissioner at Port Blair.

§ 20. *Berár.*

Berár (the Hyderabad Assigned Districts) is governed by British officers in virtue of the treaties of 1853 and 1860[2]. By the first treaty Berár and some other territories were assigned for the payment of interest on the debt due to the East India Company for the support of the Hyderabad Contingent force, and for some other purposes. The assignment was subject to an annual account of receipts and expenses. By the treaty of 1860 the debt was declared cancelled; certain of the territories assigned under the first treaty were restored, and Berár alone retained (within the general limits it now occupies, but including certain taluqas inside the boundaries which were before exempt from management). No account is now rendered to the Nizám, but the British Government pays to him any surplus it may have in hand after meeting the cost of administration, the cost of the troops of the Contingent, and certain allowances and pensions specified in the treaty.

No laws are in force as such; but the Governor-General makes rules on certain subjects and also directs such Acts as are suitable, to be followed. They are then 'in force,'

[1] Proclamation, 3rd March, 1886 (*British Burma Gazette*, 6th March, 1886, Part I, p. 89).

[2] Article 6 of the treaty of 1853 and article 6 of the treaty of 26th December, 1860 (Aitchison's *Treaties*, vol. v. pp. 214-224). By the treaty of 1853 the districts are assigned 'to the exclusive management of the British Resident for the time being at Hyderabad and to such officers acting under his orders, as may from time to time be appointed by the Government of India to the charge of those districts.'

not as Acts of the Legislature, but as expressions of the will of the Governor-General[1].

§ 21. *The term 'Non-Regulation' Province.*

There remains one more topic of the administrative system to be noticed. We still hear of 'Regulation' Provinces and 'Non-Regulation' Provinces; and these terms should be explained, if it is only for the sake of history, as it must be admitted that the terms, having lost their former force, are going out of use.

Starting with the idea of the 'Presidencies' as the centres of government, we have already seen that each Presidency under its Governor and Council was empowered to enact a code of 'Regulations' for its government, in the days before 1834, when a General Legislative Council was formed. When therefore any territory was added by conquest or treaty to a presidency—as it was first supposed would be the ordinary course—such territory or province came under the existing 'Regulations'; and further, the course of its *official appointments* was governed by an Act of Parliament. But when, as we have seen, provinces were acquired which were not, and could not be, annexed to any of the three Presidencies, their official staff could be provided as the Governor-General pleased, and was not governed by any Statute; and what was perhaps of greater importance still, the existing Regulations of the Bengal, Madras, or Bombay Codes did not apply *proprio vigore*. Such provinces were then called 'Non-Regulation Provinces.' Besides the whole provinces never 'regulationized,' there

[1] There have been proposals from time to time to restore the territory to the rule of the Nizám. But it is believed that these have now received their final *quietus*. It would certainly be extremely hard on the population, which has grown well to do if not rich and contented, under British rule, for nearly half a century, if a change was now made. Treaty obligations to respect the moderation of our Revenue Settlement might be made on paper, but they could not be enforced, especially when the term of settlement expired. It should also be fairly borne in mind that the Nizám is not the indigenous or natural ruler any more than the British crown. The country was conquered by the Mughal emperors, and the Nizám, who was originally their local deputy, established his independence in the last days of the collapse of the empire, and owes his continuance in his existing territory entirely to the moderation of the British rulers of the time.

were also parts of the older presidencies which it was desirable to exempt from the ordinary law. The 'Non-Regulation Provinces,' in fact, soon came to comprise the larger portion of the total number of districts in British India [1].

Of the two features which distinguished the Non-Regulation districts, one relating to the difference of the laws in force cannot be fully explained till we have further studied the legislative powers of the Indian Government in the next chapter. I must therefore defer my remarks for the present, only saying that the difference in law has now almost disappeared as regards the bulk of the districts; but as regards a few which are really backward, or exceptional tracts of country requiring a simpler and more 'paternal' form of government, the old distinction has given way to a new and real one.

The second feature of the original distinction survives still, but only in the titles and salaries of certain officials, and also in the fact that in Regulation Provinces certain posts are, by law, reserved to be held by members of the Covenanted Civil Services [2]. Under the Act of 33 Geo. III. (1793), it was provided that offices under Government should be filled by Covenanted Civil Servants of the Presidency to which the vacant office belonged. Consequently districts *not attached to any Presidency* were not bound by this rule, and the Governor-General could provide for their administration as he pleased.

[1] Colonel Chesney (*Indian Polity*, 2nd edition, p. 193) gives a list showing that there are 111 Non-Regulation to 97 Regulation districts. Readers must beware of certain inaccuracies in this otherwise excellent book, as regards the legal position of the Non-Regulation Provinces. The author is mistaken in supposing that the Non-Regulation Provinces were excluded from the operation of *Legislative enactments* till 1861. They were exempt from the *Regulations*, but all *Acts* applying generally to British India, passed by the Legislative Council (which began in 1834), applied equally to these territories, provided the province formed part of British India when the Act was passed. Thus, any general Act passed after 1849 would apply to the Panjáb, and one passed after 1856 to Oudh.

[2] The question what appointments in India, generally, must be held by Covenanted Civil Servants and what must be so held in the Judicial and Revenue Branches in *Regulation Provinces*, is now determined by the Act of Parliament, 24 and 25 Vict., cap. 54.

It was both natural and advisable in such cases that military and political officers (who had been, in many cases, engaged in the affairs of a province before its annexation) should be appointed to the task of first organizing and conducting the new administration. Besides this, as time went on, an increasing staff of native and European and Eurasian 'uncovenanted' officers came into existence. It consisted of qualified persons appointed in India or otherwise, but who had not signed a covenant under the old forms with the Court of Directors, or passed through Haileybury College, or been selected by competitive examination under the later rules (since 1856).

Such officers could of course be also employed. At the same time there was nothing to prevent civilians of the Covenanted Services being also appointed as their services became available: consequently the Commission in those provinces is always a mixed one[1].

In the 'Non-Regulation' districts also the district officer (called 'Deputy Commissioner'[2]) originally had civil as well as criminal and revenue powers, and this is still maintained in a few cases, though the later tendency has been to confine the district officer to his revenue and executive duty; he however has in all provinces criminal powers as magistrate, because that is necessary, though of course he does not take any large share in the disposal of ordinary Criminal Court cases. As magistrate he hears appeals and superintends the administration, and in some provinces is invested with special powers enabling him to deal directly with heavy cases (all offences not punishable with death) without committing them for trial to the Sessions Court.

[1] And local rules exist as to what appointments should ordinarily be open to or be held by each class, —Military in Civil employ, Civilian and Uncovenanted—with a view to giving a fair proportion to each.

[2] This special title of the district officer is about the most tangible 'outward and visible sign' that a district is 'Non-Regulation' that I am aware of.

§ 22. *List of Districts in India.*

The following provincial lists will prove useful to the student, who will in the course of this book find continual reference to the 'Districts' and 'Divisions' (aggregates of three or more districts under a Commissioner).

The table shows the form of government, whether a 'local government' (i.e. under a Governor or Lieutenant-Governor), or a 'local administration' (under a Chief Commissioner)[1], and also the groups of districts under 'Divisions'—a plan which, as we shall see, interposes a certain intermediate superintendence and control over the districts before coming to the chief revenue and executive control vested in the Financial Commissioners or Boards of Revenue, and in the head of the Government. I have also given the chief facts regarding the acquisition of the districts, and the date of their passing under British rule[2]. Tho date of the Land-Revenue Settlements is also given as far as possible.

[1] See pp. 39-40.

[2] This is stated generally: in some cases the district was acquired piecemeal, and small portions acquired by treaty, exchango and other arrangement for simplifying boundaries, which it is impossible to include in a general table.

LIST OF DISTRICTS IN INDIA.—BENGAL.

Name of Province, with form of Government and chief Revenue Control.	Date of Acquisition, and former territorial designation.	Name of Revenue and Administrative Division.	Name of present District.	Taluk, Pergana, or other sub-division of District.	Date of Land Revenue Settlement.	Date of Revision Settlement.	REMARKS.
BENGAL. (Presidency of Fort William in Bengal.)		Bardwán Division.	Bardwán.	....	Permanently settled 1793.		
			Bankúrá.	....	"		
			Bírbhúm.	....	"		
			Midnapore (Mednipur).	....	"	......	All except the Pátáspur pargana.
—	'Bengal, Bihár, and Orissa,' granted in 1765, (Orissa as far as the Subarnrekhá River, i.e. part of the Midnapore District).		Húghli & Howrah.	....	"		
		Presidency Division.	24-Pergunnahs.	....	"		
			Calcutta.	....	"		
Lieutenant-Governor (1854). Legislative Council (1862).			Nadiya.	....	"		
			Jessore (Jasúr).	....	"	......	Jessore was divided into two districts. Jessore (N.) and Khulná (S.).
			Khulná.	....	"		
			Múrshidábád.	....	"		
		Rájsháhí Division.	Dinájpur.	....	"		
			Rájsháhí.	....	"		
			Rangpur.	....	"		
—			Bogra (Bagurá).	....	"		
			Patná.	....	"		
Board of Revenue.			Darjiling.	....	Temporarily settled.	......	Scheduled district Act XIV. of 1874.
—	Ceded in 1838, 1850, and after Bhután-war, 1865.		Jalpaigúrí.	....	....	......	Part is permanently settled (being part of the old Rangpur district) the 'Dwárs,' are treated as a temporarily settled 'Raiyatwári tract.'

Bengal, Bihár and Orissa, 1765.	Dacca Division.	Dacca (Dákhá).	....	Permanently settled.		
" " "		Farídpur.	....	"		
		Bákirganj.	....	"		
		Maimansingh.	....	"		
" " "	Chittagong Division.	Chittagong.	....	Permanent and temporary settlement.	......	The 'Noábád' estates are temporarily settled: settlement expires in 1892.
		Noacolly (Nawákhálí).	....	Permanent settlement.		
		Tipperah (Típrá).	....	"		
(Bihár) A.D. 1765.	Patná Division.	Patná.	....	"		
		Gáyá.	....	"		
		Shahábád.	....	"		
		Muzaffarpur.	....	"	......	These two districts together formed the old Tirhút district.
		Darbhanga.	....	"	......	
		Sáran.	....	"		
		Champáran.	....	"		
" "	Bhágulpur Division.	Monghyr (Mungér).	....	"		
		Bhágulpur.	....	"		The Dáman-i-Koh exempt from the Regulations (and Permanent Settlement) since 1780 and forms a Government estate settled under Act XXXVII of 1855, and now under Reg. III of 1872.
		Purneah (Parniyá).	....	"		
		Maldá.	....	"		
		Sántál Parganas.	....	Part permanently settled.	....	

Name of Province, with form of Government and chief Revenue Control.	Date of Acquisition, and former territorial designation.	Name of Revenue and Administrative Division.	Name of present District.	Taluk, Pergana, or other sub-division of District.	Date of Land Revenue Settlement.	Date of Revision Settlement.	REMARKS.
BENGAL (*concluded*).		Orissa Division.	Katák.	....	Temporary settlement (under Reg. VII of 1822, continued under (Ben) Act X of 1867. Expires in 1897).	......	This is the modern Orissa, after the cession from the Maráthás. Some estates are permanently settled.
			Púrí.	....			
			Bálásúr.	....			
	Chutiya Nágpur (or Chota Nagpore). After Kol rebellion of 1831–2 placed under 'S. W. Frontier Agency' by Reg. XIII of 1833. Became the Chota Nagpore Division by Act XX of 1854.	Chota Nagpore Division.	Hazáribágh.	....	In large part permanently settled; with several large Government estates.	......	'Scheduled districts' (Act XIV of 1874).
			Lohárdaggá.	....		......	
			Mánbhúm.	....		......	
			Singhbhúm.	....		......	

MADRAS.

The 'Presidency of Fort St. George' or MADRAS. — Governor in Council (A. D. 1793), by 33 George III, cap. 52. — Board of Revenue. —	The Northern Sirkárs (Circars of old reports) ceded by Mughal power in 1765 and confirmed by the Nizám of the Dakhan shortly after.	Ganjam.	Chicacole. Berhampore. Gúmsoor.	1878-9 1879-80 1883-4	....	These were the five 'Sirkárs' or districts. Gantúr did not immediately pass with the others but fell in in 1788. The others were all managed politically under tribute till 1823. In these districts the Permanent Settlement chiefly took effect. The 'Settlement' dates of course refer to the tracts under Raiyatwári Settlement. In Godávarí are now included two talúks, Rékapalle and Bhadráchalam, which were formerly part of the Central Provinces, viz. that part of Chánda (Upper Godávarí) ceded in 1860 by the Nizám. Transferred in 1874. The two districts, now called by the names of the great rivers which constitute their main features, were for administrative reasons made out of the three older districts of 'Rajamundry,' 'Masulipatam,' and 'Guntoor.' The change was made in 1860.
		Vizagapatam.	....	Settlement in progress.	...	
		Godávarí.	Tanuku. Bhimávaram. Narsápuram (part only).	1862-3	......	
			The rest of the district.	1866-7	......	
		Kistná.	Gudiváda. Bandar. Nandigáma. Bezwáda.	1866-7	......	
			The rest of the District.	1873-4	......	

Name of Province, with form of Government and chief Revenue Control.	Date of Acquisition, and former territorial designation.	Name of Revenue and Administrative Division.	Name of present District.	Taluk, Pergana, or other sub-division of District.	Date of Land Revenue Settlement.	Date of Revision Settlement.	REMARKS.
MADRAS (*continued*).	The 'Ceded' districts (by the Nizám in 1800).	......	Cuddapah.	Cuddapah. Proddutur. Jamalamadugu.	1874–5	......	These districts (with the exception mentioned below) are the 'Ceded districts,' settled under the old system by MUNRO. Anantapur was formed in 1882 in order to reduce the excessive size of the Bellary collectorate.
				Sidhout.	1877–8	......	
				Badvél.	1878 9	......	
				Pulivendla. Pulampet.	1879–80	......	
				Váyalpád. Ráyachoti.	1881–2	.... .	
				Kadirí. Madanapalle.	1882–3	......	
			Anantapur. Bellary (Balárí).	....	In progress.		
	Kurnool (the old district) was also formally included in the Ceded districts; but was left under the rule of a local Nawáb till 1839. Four talúks, Pattikonda, Koilkuntla, Kambam and Márkápur, which were also ceded in 1800, were transferred to the Kurnool district in 1858-9.	......	Kurnool (Karnúl).	Rámalakota.	1864–9		
				Nandíkotkúr.	1864 6		
				Nandyál.	1864–8		
				Sirvel.	1866–7		
				Pattikonda.	1872–3		
				Koilkuntla.	1874–5		
				Kumbum. Márkápur.	1877–8		

	The 'Jágír'—1750–63—(ceded by the Nawáb of the Carnatic in parts, in 1750 and 1760, confirmed by Emperor's *Sanad* of 1763).		Madras.	....	....	......	The Presidency town and adjacent country separated into a district for administrative convenience.
			Chingleput.	Part of Saidápet.	1875-6		
				Part of Saidápet and other talúks.	1877–8		
	The 'Carnatic districts,' ceded by the Nawáb in 1801.	......	Nellore.	All talúks.	1873-5		
	Part of North Arcot,—(the Kángundi zamíndári) was obtained in 1792, and the Palmanér talúk and the Panganúr zamíndári in 1799.		North Arcot.	Wálajápet.	1881-2		
				Arcot.	1882–3		
				Vellore. Gudiyátam. Chandragiri. Chitúr.	1883–4		
				Polúr. Palmanér.	1884–5		
				Wandiwash.	1885–6		
			South Arcot.	Chidambaram.	1861–2		
				Other talúks.	In progress.		
			Tanjore.	....	Not settled.		
			Trichinopoly.	All talúks.	1864–5		
	The Dindigal part of this district (Palni, Dindigal and Periyakulam talúks) was acquired 1792.		Madura.	Palni.	1885–6		
				Periyakulam.	1886-7		
				Other talúks.	In progress.		
			Tinnevelly.	Tinnevelly. Tenkási.	1873–4		
				Tenkarai.	1874-5		
				Ambásamudram.	1874 6		
				Nángunéri.	1876-7		
				The remaining talúks.	1877–8		

Name of Province, with form of Government and chief Revenue Control.	Date of Acquisition, and former territorial designation.	Name of Revenue and Administrative Division.	Name of present District.	Taluk, Pergana, or other sub-division of District.	Date of Land Revenue Settlement.	Date of Revision Settlement.	REMARKS.
MADRAS (*concluded*).	Partition of Mysore, 1799.	......	Coimbatore.	Bhárání.	1878-9		
				Palladam.			
				Eroda.			
				Karúr.			
				Dhárápuram.	1879-80		
				Satyamangalam.			
				Coimbatore.			
				Udamalpet.	1880-1		
				Polláchi.	1881-2		
				Kollegál.			
	,, ,, ,,	......	Nílgiris.	....	1881-7		
	The 'Bára-mahál' (with Dindigal and Palni) acquired by treaty 1792. The Hosúr talúk acquired in 1799.	......	Salem (Sélam).	Atúr.	1870-1		
				Salem.			
				Námakal.	1871-2		
				Tiruchengod.			
				Uttankarai.			
				Dharmapúri.	1872-3		
				Krishnagiri.			
				Hosúr.	1873 4		
				Tripatúr.			☞ All the years of the date of settlement are calculated as from the 1st of July—which is the Madras 'fasli' (or Revenue year) reckoning.
			South Kánara.	....	Not settled.		
			Malabar.	....	Not settled.		

BOMBAY.

The Presidency of BOMBAY.	From the Nawáb of Surát and the Gaikwár, 1800-3.	...... (Northern Division.)	Surát.	....	1865-72	......	Surát and Bharoch were made into separate districts in 1865.
	1803.	......	Broach (Bharoch).	....	1870-6		
—	1802-5.	......	Kairá.	....	1856-67		
Governor in Council, A. D. 1793 (33 Geo. III, Cap. 52).	Ceded by Sindhia in 1861.	......	Pánchmaháls.	....	1870-80	1885	Revision effected in three talukas: is a 'scheduled district.'
	From the Gaikwár, 1802-17.	......	Ahmadábád.	....	1856-64		
—	From the Peshwá in 1818.	......	Thána.	....	1854-67		
Under Commissioners of Divisions in direct correspondence with Government.	From the Peshwá, 1818.	...... (Central Division.)	Khándésh.	....	1854-71	1886	Revision settlement in progress.
	1818.	......	Násik.	....	1842-69	1871	,, ,, ,,
	From the Peshwá and the Nizám, 1818 and 1822.	......	Ahmadnagar.	....	1841-56	1875	,, ,, ,,
—	From the Peshwá, 1818.	......	Pooná (Púná).	....	1836-54	1867	,, ,, ,,
	From the Peshwá and the Rájá of Satárá, 1818-37 and 1848.	......	Satárá.	....	1852-64		
	From the Peshwá and the Nizám, 1818 and 1822.	......	Sholápur.	....	1839-58	1870	,, ,, ,,

Name of Province, with form of Government and chief Revenue Control.	Date of Acquisition, and former territorial designation.	Name of Revenue and Administrative Division.	Name of present District.	Taluk, Pergana, or other sub-division of District.	Date of Land Revenue Settlement.	Date of Revision Settlement.	REMARKS.
BOMBAY (*concluded*).	From the Peshwá, 1818.	......	Kolábá.				
	" " "	......	Ratnágirí.	....	1865	......	Original settlement only now finished.
	" ,, 1817–18.	...... Southern Division.	Dhárwár.	....	1843-60 1849-61	1874–81 1880–8	
	From the Peshwá and the Rájá of Kolapur, 1818 and 1827.		Belgáum.	....			Revision settlement in progress. This district was formed from the old Kaládgi district in 1884–5. (See Administration Report, 84-5.)
	From the Peshwá and the Nizám, 1818 and 1822.		Bíjapur.	....	1843-60	1874	
	(1799) Transferred to Bombay Presidency from Madras in 1862.	......	Kánara (North).	....	1863	......	Original settlement finished. (All the Revisions are expected to be finished in 1893.)
The Province of Sindh.	Annexed after the War, 5th of March, 1843.	Under the Commissioner of Sindh.	Karáchi.	....	With the exception of one taluka of the Frontier District and one of Karáchi all talukas settled between 1862–4 and 1888–9.	......	Sindh is a Scheduled district under Act XIV of 1874.
			Shikárpur.	....			
			Upper Sindh Frontier.	....			
			Thar and Párkar.	....	....	......	All talukas unsettled.

NORTH-WESTERN PROVINCES.

						Date of Second Regular Land Revenue Settlement.		
Presidency of Agra' (1834) altered to—Lieutenant-Governorship of the NORTH-WESTERN PROVINCES (1836). United with the Chief Commissionership in Oudh (1877). Has a Legislative Council (1886).	Benares province. Ceded A.D. 1775 by Asaf-ud-daula, Nawáb of Oudh. Brought under Regulations 1795.		Benares Division.	Benares.	....	Permanently settled.		*Ballia* district formed in 1879 to include the Bhadáon and Sikandurpur pargans—being the 'part of Azamgarh' permanently settled, together with some tracts formerly in Bihár.
				Gházipur.	....			
				Ballia.	....			
				Jaunpur.	....			
				Mirzapur (part).	....			
				Rest of Mirzapur.	Certain tappas, the tract south of the Khaimúr hill range.	Temporary settlement.	......	Scheduled district.
	The 'Ceded districts,' by treaty with the Nawáb of Oudh, 1801.			Azamgarh.	....	1866–77		
				Gorakhpur.	....	1859–71	In progress.	Older settlement about to expire.
				Basti.	....	"		
		The 'Doáb' from between Jamná and Ganges.	Alláhábád Division.	Alláhábád.	....	1867–78		
				Fatihpur.	....	1870–7		
—				Cawnpore (Káhnpur).	....	1868–78		
			Ágra Division.	Etáwa.	....	1868–74		
Board of Revenue (for the N.W. Provinces only).				Farukhábád.	....	1863–75		
				Etáh.	....	1863–73		
				Mainpuri.	....	1866–74		
			Rohilkhand Division.	Sháhjahánpur.	....	1867–74		
				Budáon (Badáyún).	....	1864–72		
				Bareli.	....	1865–72		
				Pilíbhít.	....	1865–72		
—				Murádábád.	....	1872–80		
				Bijnaur.	....	1864–74		

Name of Province, with form of Government and chief Revenue Control.	Date of Acquisition, and former territorial designation.	Name of Revenue and Administrative Division.	Name of present District.	Taluk, Pergana, or other sub-division of District.	Date of Second Regular Land Revenue Settlement.	Date of Revision Settlement.	REMARKS.
NORTH-WESTERN PROVINCES (*continued*).		Kumaon Division.	The Tarái parganas.	....	....	(New Settlement completed.)	Scheduled district. Reg. IV of 1876.
	The 'Conquered Districts' (Treaty of Sirjí-Anjangám, 1803. Dec. 30 after Marátha war by Lord Lake).	Ágra Division.	Ágra.	....	1872–80		
			Muttra (Mathurá).	....	1872 9		
			'Alígarh.	....	1866–74		
		Meerut Division.	Bulandshahr.	....	1858 65	New Settlement in progress.	Settlement about to expire.
			Meerut (Mírath).	....	1865–70		
			Muzaffarnagar.	....	1860–75	,, ,,	,, ,, ,,
			Saháranpur.	....	1854–70	,, ,,	,, ,, ,,
	Sovereignty acquired in 1803 and brought under administration in 1817, and part in 1840. These were the 'Bundélkhand district' of the Regulation of 1805.	Alláhábád Division.	Bándá.	....	1873-82		
			Hamirpur.	....	1872–80		

Acquired by lapse, forfeiture, or treaty since 1840. (Bundélkhand country.)	Jhánsi Division.	Jaláun.	....	1853-74	New Settlement of part just made.	Various portions separately settled. Settlement of part has expired.
		Jhánsi.	....	1854-67	....	Settlement expired; new Settlement postponed till 1891.
		Lalitpur.	....	1853-69	....	Expired in 1888; new Settlement postponed till 1898.
						This Division is a 'Scheduled district' under Act XIV of 1874. But ordinary Revenue and Rent law is applicable.
After Nepál war, 1815.	In Division. Meerut.	Dehra-Dún.	....	1860-7	New Settlement complete.	Since 1871 (July) has been under ordinary law, except pargana Jáunsar-Báwar.
			Jáunsar-Báwar.	1874	....	Settlement expired, but has been extended for twenty years, i. e. till 1904.
	Division. Kumáon	Kumáon.	....	1863-73	....	Scheduled districts. Under special law. Ordinary Revenue law only partly in force.
		British Garhwál	....	1856-64		

OUDH.

Name of Province, with form of Government and chief Revenue Control.	Date of Acquisition, and former territorial designation.	Name of Revenue and Administrative Division.	Name of present District.	Taluk, Pergana, or other sub-division of District.	Date of Land Revenue Settlement	Date of Revision Settlement	REMARKS.
OUDH. Annexed in Feb. 1856. Under Chief Commissioner till March 1877. The office united with the Lieutenant-Governorship N.W. Provinces (1877). — The Chief Commissioner is the Chief Controlling Revenue authority. —		Sítapur Division.	Kheri.	....	1868-76	....	Regular Settlement for thirty years.
			Sítapur.	....	1866-71		
			Hardoi.	....	1866-8		
		Lucknow Division.	Lucknow (Lakhnau).	....	1866-8		
			Unáo.	....	1862-7		
			Bará Bánki.	....	1865-8	....	In pargana Bhitauli the 'summary' Settlement of 1858-59 was fixed in perpetuity.
		Rái-Bareli Division.	Rái-Bareli.	....	1865-9		
			Partábgarh.	....	1863-6		
			Sultánpur.	....	1865-70		
		Faizábád Division.	Faizábád.	....	1866-74		
			Gondá.	....	1875-6		
			Bahraich.	....	1867-71		

AJMER-MÉRWÁRA.

AJMER-MERWÁRA. Chief Commissioner, 1871, (who is the Governor-General's Agent for Rájputána.) A Commissioner has the immediate management; with two Assistants who live at Ájmér and Beáwar.	Ceded in 1818, after the Pindárí war. Merwára was reduced in 1819–22.	......	Ajmer. Merwára.	....	First settled in 1849–50, revised in 1874.	1887	The Settlement of 1874 was for ten years, the present Settlement is for twenty years, on the North-west system: but for sixty-one villages the assessment is on a fluctuating scale.

CENTRAL PROVINCES.

Name of Province, with form of Government and Chief Revenue Control.	Date of Acquisition, and former territorial designation.	Name of Revenue and Administrative Division.	Name of present District.	Taluk, Pergana, or other sub-division of District.	Date of Land Revenue Settlement.	Date of Revision Settlement.	REMARKS.
THE CENTRAL PROVINCES. Constituted in 1862, under a Chief Commissioner (in place of the former various administrations of the 'Ságar and Narbada territories,' the Nágpur Province, Nimár, &c.) — The Chief Commissioner is the Chief Controlling Revenue authority.	The districts marked * constitute the old 'Ságar and Narbada' territories. The bulk of them were ceded by the Peshwa or the Bhônslá Rájá after the Marátha war in 1818. The Ságar district was altered by additions made under treaty with Sindhia, 1820-5-60: by confiscation during the Mutiny, and by territorial transfer from Bundélkhand. Two parganas (Máriadoh and Fatihpur) were also transferred from Bundélkhand.	Japalpur Division.	*Saugor (Ságar).	…………	Various parts from 1863-67.		
			*Dámoh.	…………	1863-4		
			*Jabalpur.	Bijragogarh.	1863 1867	…………	The Bijragogarh pergana was added by confiscation after the Mutiny and settled for twenty years.
			*Mandlá.	…………	1868-9	In progress.	Settlement was for twenty years, and expired 1888-9.
			*Seoni.	…………	1864-7	…………	Thirty years Settlement.
			*Narsinghpur.	…………	1863-6	…………	The greater part of the Settlement expires in 1894-5.

pargana was ceded by Sindhia, 1844–60. Ceded by Sindhia in 1818, and added to by treaty 1820-5-60.	Narbada Division.	*Hushangábád.	....	1864–5	....	For thirty years.
		Nimár.	....	1866	....	" "
		*Betúl.	....	1864–7	....	" "
Escheated from the Bhônslá family in 1854. Formed the old 'Nágpur province.'	Nágpur Division.	Chhindwára.	....	1865–7	....	" "
		Wardhá.	....	1863–5	....	" "
		Nágpur.	....	1862–5	....	" "
		Chándá.	....	1865–8	Revision of part completed.	Pargana Sironcha was acquired by territorial transfer from the Nizám in 1860. Part settled for thirty years and part for twenty years (expired).
		Bhandára.	....	1864	....	For thirty years.
		Bálághát.	....	1864–7	....	Part of the present district transferred from Mandlá and Seoní. Settled for thirty years.
Ceded 1818 by the Bhônslá Rájá: placed under a Chief in 1826: escheated in 1849.	Chhatísgarh Division.	Raipur.	....	1865–8	In progress.	Settlement for twenty years expired.
		Biláspur.	....	1868	In progress.	Part transferred from Sambalpur. Settlement for twenty years expired.
		Sambalpur.	....	1876	In progress.	Settlement, which is practically raiyatwárí, was for twelve years. Resettlement in progress.

PANJÁB.

Name of Province, with form of Government and chief Revenue Control.	Date of Acquisition, and former territorial designation.	Name of Revenue and Administrative Division.	Name of present District.	Taluk, Pargana, or other sub-division of District.	Date of Regular Land Revenue Settlement (in force).	Date of Revision Settlement.	Remarks.
'The PANJÁB and its Dependencies.' Under a 'Board of Administration,' 1849–1853. Under a 'Chief Commissioner,' 1853–1858. Under 'Lieutenant-Governor,' Jan. 1, 1859. — Two Financial Commissioners (First and Second).	Annexed by proclamation of 31st March, 1849, after second Sikh war.	Peshâwar Division.	Peshâwar.	....	1873		There were formerly ten divisions: under reorganization of 1884 made into six. The first six districts on the list are scheduled under Act XIV of 1874: a Special Criminal Regulation is in force. Ordinary Revenue and Tenancy law, except as to Hazára which has some special features.
			Kohát.	....	1881		
			Hazára.	....	1872		
		Deráját Division.	Bannu.	....	1877		
			Dera Ismaíl Khán.	....	1878		
			Dera Ghází Khán.	....	1874		
			Muzaffargarh.	....	1879		
		Lahore Division.	Multán.	....	1872–80		
			Jhang.	....	1879		
			Montgomery.	....	1873	....	Formerly called 'Gugaira.'
			Lahore.	....	1868	In progress.	Expired in 1888.
			Amritsar.	....	1864	" "	Expired in 1885.
			Gurdáspur.	....	1849	" "	(Settlement expired.)
			Gujránwála.	....	1868	" "	Settlement expired in 1888.
		Rávalpindi Division.	Gujrát.	....	1868		
			Sialkot.	....	1864	" "	(Settlement expired.)
			Sháhpur.	....	1854	" "	" "
			Jihlam.	....	1879	....	Sanction of Government of India not received.
			Ráwalpíndi.	....	....		

Ceded by treaty (March 1846), after first Sikh war.	Jálandhar Division.	Firozpur.	Half the district.	Expired 1881–5.	Revision in progress.	The Wattú pargana near Fázilka was taken in exchange from Baháwalpur in 1844: the Buhak pargana was taken from the Nawáb of Mamdot 1858.
			Fázilka Tetsíl.	Expired 1875–87.	Revision complete.	
			Mukatsar T. Mamdot Iláqa.	1873		
Ceded by treaty (March 1846) after first Sikh war.		Jálandhar.	....	1879–85		
		Húshyárpur.	....	1879 84		
		Kángra.	....	1849	Expired in 1879.	Revision in progress.
After Nepál war, 1815.	......	Simla.	....	1882	....	Consists only of twenty square miles for the Station of Simla.
Cis-Sutlej States, 1845–6.*	Delhi Division.	Ambála.	....	1849–54	Expired 1879 87.	Revision completed.
		Lúdiána.	....	1878–83		
Part of Karnál came with the 'Conquered districts in 1803.'		Karnál.	....	1879	....	
The 'districts on the right bank of the River Jamná' (Reg. VIII of 1805).		Delhi (Dihlí).	....	1880		
		Rohtak.	....	1879		The old Sirsa district has been divided, part to Firozpur, part to Hisár.
		Gúrgaon.	....	1882		
Transferred to the Panjáb in Feb. 1858 by Act of Legislature.		Hisár.	....	1860–64	Expired. Revision in progress.	(Sirsa and) Hisár border towards Bikanír was defined in 1828, and the Patiálá border in 1835.

* The term 'Cis-Sutlej States, 1845-6,' is used shortly to denote (*a*) the possessions of the Mahárájá east of Sutlej which came into British territory by treaty; (*b*) territories which lapsed on failure of heirs in the Protected States, 1806–9, or were confiscated for misconduct of the chiefs during the second Sikh war.

ASSAM.

Name of Province, with form of Government and Chief Revenue Control.	Date of Acquisition, and former territorial designation.	Name of Revenue and Administrative Division.	Date of present District.	Taluk, Pargana, or other sub-division of District.	Date of Land Revenue Settlement.	REMARKS.
ASSAM. Chief Commissioner (Acts VIII and XII of 1874).	First Burmese war, 1824-6.	Commissioner of Assam. Assam Proper.	Kámrup. Darrang. Naugong. Sibságar. Lakhimpur.	....	....	Under Annual Settlement or periodic leases, expiring 1892-3. Half-revenue paying land-leases expire between 1887-8 and 1892 3.
	Originally part of Rangpur and acquired with Bengal in 1765.		Goálpára.	....	1793 (Permanent Settlement).	
	Annexed after Bhutan war in 1866.		Eastern Dwárs.	....	....	Annual Settlements under Assam Rules.
	Partly acquired with Goalpára in 1765, and occupied from time to time up to 1872.	(Political Control.) Assam Hill Range.	Garo Hills.	....	....	Portion towards plains under Annual Settlement. No Settlement in Hills. House-tax levied.
	Jaintya hills in 1835: the rest is foreign territory except Shillong and a few villages (1829-35).		Khási and Jaintya.	....	....	House-tax and Annual Settlement.
			Nágá Hills.	....	....	Only house-tax levied.
	Lapsed in 1830.	....	Cachár Hills, &c.	....	....	In the hill portions only house-tax.
		Directly ruled by the Chief Commissioner.	Cachár.	(Plains.)	1882-4	Settlement expires 31st of March, 1898.
	With Bengal in 1765.		Sylhet.	....	1793 (Permanent Settlement).	Ilám and other non-permanently settled estates, under temporary Settlements which expire from 1892-3 to 1906-7.
	Annexed in 1835.		Jaintya parganas.	.. ..	1878-80	ettlements expire 1893-4.

BURMA.

BURMA.						
Chief Commissioner (1862).	Arakan—first Burmese war, 1824.	Arakan Division.	Hill tracts.	....	None.	Under the Arakan Hill Districts Regulation of 1874.
			Kyaukpyú. Sandoway.	....	....	Annual Settlements (Act II of 1876).
——			Akyab.	....	1885-8	Regular Settlement with Survey.
Financial Commissioner (1888).	Pegu—second Burmese war, 1852.	Pegu Division.	Rangoon Town.			
			Hanthawady.	....	1880-84	16 circles regularly settled.
			Pegu.	....	1879 84	41 " " "
			Tharawady.	....	1880-4	39 " " "
			Prome.	....	1883-5	86 " " "
			Thongwá.	....	....	Annual Settlements (part about to be regularly settled).
	" " "	Irrawaddy Division.	Bassein.	....	1879-85	56 circles regularly settled.
			Henzada.	....	1883 6	41 " " "
			Thayetmyo.	....	None.	Annual Settlements.
	Tennasserim — first Burmese war, 1824.	Tennasserim Division.	Karennee. Toungoo. Shwégyin. Salween. Amherst. Tavoy. Merguí.	....	....	Under Annual Settlements: Act II of 1876 in force (except in Karennee).
	Upper Burma—third Burmese war, 1886.	Four Divisions, Northern, Southern, Eastern, Central.	Seventeen districts.	....	None.	Not yet settled. Under Upper Burma Regulation VII of 1887 and Land Revenue Regulation III of 1889.

COORG.

Name of Province, with form of Government and chief Revenue Control.	Date of Acquisition, and former territorial designation.	Name of Revenue and Administrative Division.	Name of present District.	Taluk, Pergana, or other sub-division of District.	Date of Land Revenue Settlement.	REMARKS.
COORG (Kodagu). Under Chief Commissioner, who is the Resident of Mysore (at Bangalore).	Annexed in May, 1834.	....	One district (headquarters at Merkára).	Six taluks. Yelusávirashime.	Old Settlement of the Coorg Rajas still in force. Survey is in contemplation.	Two taluks have been separated and added to the South Kánara district (Madras Presidency).

BERAR.

'BERÁR,' formerly called 'the Berárs' because it formed two portions, East and West Berár, under two Commissioners. Now supervised by one 'Commissioner' under the Resident of Hyderabad.	'Assigned' to the Government of the British power by treaties, 1853–1860, with the Nizám of Hyderabad (Haidarábád).		Baldána.	....	1862–3	Revenue-Survey under the Bombay system (Raiyatwárí).
			Akola.	....	1864-5	
			Amráotí.	....	1868-9	
			Ellichpur (Alichpur).	....	1868-9	Settlement does not extend to the Melghát hill taluk, which is a great forest. Forest Survey is being carried out demarcating cultivated villages inside.
			Básim.	....	1872–3	
			Wún.	....	1873–4	In Básím and Wún a large number of villages were under lease before the Revenue-Survey, and as these are now expiring a new Settlement is in progress.

CHAPTER III.

OF THE INDIAN LEGISLATURES, AND THE LAWS BY WHICH INDIA IS GOVERNED.

---

§ 1. *Reason for describing them.*

As I have already alluded to 'Acts' and 'Regulations' of the Indian Legislature, and shall have occasion continually to refer to such Acts and Regulations in the sequel, it will be desirable to give a brief account of the legislative powers under which laws have been, and are, enacted for the Indian Empire.

Just as in the last chapter we learned that the organization of the several provinces for administrative purposes was only accomplished gradually and by a series of Acts of Parliament, so the Indian Legislature has gradually grown into its present form after several statutes for organizing it have been made, amended, and repealed. The tentative and changeful nature of the arrangements provided are due to the same causes in both instances.

At first it was only necessary to provide for the internal affairs of the Company's factories, to determine what laws the settlers were to be deemed to carry with them, and were to be bound by, in their new home, and what courts were to administer justice among them. Soon, however, the sphere widened; whole provinces were acquired and added on to the original settlements; and then came the necessity of controlling, not only the European settlers, but of providing for the government of the country at large.

Trading charters had then to be supplemented by Acts of Parliament, providing for the direction and control of the East India Company (now that it was a governing body), regulating the appointment of high functionaries and subordinate agents in India, determining the constitution of Courts of Justice, and giving powers of local legislation.

The first Act, as already intimated, passed for this purpose was the 'Regulating' Act of 1772–3 (13 Geo. III, cap 63). This had to be amended on the subject of framing 'Regulations' in 1780–1, and further in 1784 and 1786 (26 Geo. III, cap. 16). The subsequent Acts were passed at intervals of twenty years (when the charters were renewed), thus:—

1792–3 (33 Geo. III, cap. 52).
1812–3 (53 Geo. III, cap. 155).
1833 (3 and 4 Will. IV, cap. 85).
1853 (16 and 17 Vict., cap. 95).

§ 2. *Home Government of the present day.*

It would serve no useful purpose, even if I had space available, to describe the early history of the Government which, in former days, as at present, was, from the necessity of the case, carried on partly in England and partly in India.

The 'Court of Directors' of the Company, afterwards supervised by the 'Board of Control' (which acted as a check on the part of the Crown)[1], passed away in 1858. The Home Government is now provided for by the Act 21 and 22 Vict., cap. 106 (A.D. 1858), known as the 'Act for the better government of India,' amended in 1869 (32 and 33 Vict., cap. 97). This Statute received the Royal assent on the 2nd August, 1858, and came into force thirty days later. In the proclamation that was issued throughout India, the Governor-General is for the first time styled 'Viceroy.' This Act transferred the government of the Company's possessions to the Crown, and provides that all the rights of the Company are to be exercised by the Crown, and all

[1] This was constituted by 'Pitt's Act' of 1784 (24 Geo. III, cap. 25).

revenues to be received for and in the name of the Queen, and to be applied for the purposes of the government of India alone, subject to the provisions of the Act[1].

One of Her Majesty's Principal Secretaries of State is to exercise all the control that the Court of Directors of the old Company did, whether alone or under the Board of Control.

A Council of fifteen members, styled the 'Council of India[2],' is also established. The number has been since reduced to ten (1889), by enabling the Secretary of State not to fill up five vacancies out of the fifteen. The Act fixes the salary of the members (payable out of the Indian revenue) and prohibits them from sitting or voting in Parliament. The Council is under the direction of the Secretary of State, and its duty under the Act, is to 'conduct the business transacted in the United Kingdom in relation to the government of India and the correspondence with India.'

It may be, and is, divided into Committees for different departments of business. If the Council differs from the Secretary of State, the opinion of the Secretary is final, except in some matters, for the decision of which the law declares a majority of votes necessary[3].

§ 3. *Legislative power in England.*

The Parliament has full power to legislate for India whenever it thinks fit. Not only has Parliament this general power, but the local Indian Legislature is expressly barred from dealing with certain subjects which it was thought wiser to reserve for the Imperial Parliament.

I may here mention that it is a settled rule of interpretation that Acts of Parliament applicable to 'British

[1] In 1876 (39 Vict., cap. 10) the authority of the Queen was further recognized and Her Majesty was authorized to adopt the style and title of Empress of India which she did by Proclamation, 28th April, 1876. The assumption of the title 'Empress of India' (Kaisar-i-Hind) was celebrated with great pomp before an immense assemblage of native princes and chiefs at Delhi on 1st January, 1877.

[2] See the Act, sects. 7 and 19.

[3] The most important of such cases is provided by section 41 of the Act itself. No grant or appropriation of Indian revenue or public property can be made without such majority.

India' give the law to the whole of those territories, not only as they happen to be at the time, but however they may be constituted thereafter. No matter how many provinces may be added to British India in future, Acts of Parliament now in force and applying to 'British India' would equally apply to the new provinces added[1]. The meaning of the terms 'British India' and 'India' (including territories which are under native princes, but under 'the suzerainty of Her Majesty') is more formally defined in the 'Interpretation Act,' 52 and 53 Vict., cap. 63 (1889), but sect. 18 makes this apply only to Acts passed after the Interpretation Act.

I shall not here notice the Acts of Parliament applicable to India, as that would be beyond the direct scope of my work[2].

Such being the powers of the Secretary of State for India and his Council, and of the Imperial Parliament, we may now consider the powers and constitution of the Government of India.

§ 4. *The Government of India.*

There is a Viceroy[3] and Governor-General with the supreme power of control and supervision over all the Governors and Lieutenant-Governors (who are the 'Local Governments'). The Governors of Madras and Bombay retain some special powers (such as that of direct correspondence with the Home Government) not enjoyed by other Local Governments, and which in some respects affect their relation to the Government of India; but this it is not necessary to enter upon.

[1] See Sir H. (then Mr.) Maine's remarks in the Abstract of the Proceedings of the Legislative Council of 22nd March, 1867 (*Calcutta Gazette*, 30th March, 1867). Not so with Indian Acts:—if applicable to the 'whole of the territories of the East India Company,' that means the territories as they existed at the time. For example, an Act passed in 1848 would not (unless afterwards extended) apply to the Panjáb, because it was not till 1849 that the Panjáb formed part of the territories of the East India Company.

[2] An excellent collection of 'Statutes relating to India' (up to 1881, and Supplement) is published at the Government Central Printing Office, Calcutta, by the Legislative Department.

[3] So first styled in the Queen's Proclamation of 1858.

The Governor-General may also himself become the Local Government of certain provinces by taking them under his direct management (under the Act 17 and 18 Vict., cap. 77) in the manner described in the last chapter [1]. The Central Provinces, Oudh, Assam, and Burma, are examples of this. In such cases there is a Chief Commissioner who constitutes the 'Local Administration.'

The Governor-General is now assisted by a Council of five Ordinary Members [2]. This is the Executive Council.

§ 5. *The first form of Indian Legislature.*

The first Act which directly provided for the form of government in India is the 13 Geo. III, cap. 63 (passed in 1773), known as 'The Regulating Act.' It provided that the Government of Bengal should consist of a Governor-General and Council (four Councillors), and this was to be the Supreme Government, subject, however, to control of the Home authorities [3].

Legislative powers were given under this Statute to the Governor-General for the 'Settlement of Fort William' and other factories and places subordinate thereto.

Madras and Bombay had not yet any power of making Regulations. To the former of these Presidencies powers were given by an Act of Parliament in 1800 (which extended powers similar to those which an Act of 1781, presently to be mentioned, had given to Bengal).

In 1807 Bombay was provided for, and the powers of Madras were at the same time improved and placed on the same footing.

The chief feature of the Regulating Act as it affected legislation, was, that all laws required to be registered in the Supreme Court of Judicature at Calcutta, in order to give them validity. This plan did not answer; and it was amended by an Act of 1781 [4].

[1] See Chapter II, p. 8.

[2] 24 and 25 Vict., cap. 67 (Indian Councils Act), sect. 3.

[3] *Vide* the Act, secs. 7, 8, and 9, and *Tagore Lectures for* 1872, p. 44.

[4] The causes of the change were the antagonism which sprang up between the Supreme Court and the Council. All such matters must necessarily be here omitted.

§ 6. *The Regulations.*

Under this amending Act of 1781, a large body of Regulations was passed[1]. The Marquis of Cornwallis revised and codified the Regulations in 1793, and on the 1st of May, 1793, forty-eight Regulations, so revised, were passed, of which the forty-first declares the purpose of forming into a regular Code, all Regulations that might be enacted for the internal government of the British territories in Bengal.

That these Regulations did not exactly comply with the terms of the Act of 1773, while they exceeded the limits of the powers given by the Act of 1781, there can be no doubt. However, Parliament in 1797 (37 Geo. III, cap. 142) recognized them as in fact valid, approved of the formation of a Code of such Regulations, and only added that they should be registered in the 'Judicial Department,' and that the reasons for each Regulation should be prefixed to it[2]. The Code thus issued in 1793 and added to down to 1833, forms what is called the 'Code of Bengal Regulations[3].' There are local Codes of Regulations also for Madras and Bombay.

§ 7. *No provision for Provinces not annexed formally to the Bengal Presidency.*

It was noted in the last chapter that the force of the Regulations was in 1800 (39 and 40 Geo. III, cap. 79) extended to the province of Benares and 'all other factories, districts, and places which now are, or hereafter shall be, subordinate, and to all such provinces and districts *as may at any time hereafter be annexed to the Presidency* of Fort William in Bengal.'

The student who desires to pursue the subject, may refer to the *Tagore Lectures*, 1872 (Lecture III), and the standard Histories.

[1] *Tagore Law Lectures*, 1872, p. 80.

[2] This is the reason why long, and sometimes very instructive, preambles are to be found prefixed to some of the earlier Regulations, these preambles being, in fact, 'explanatory memoranda' of the object and purpose of the law.

[3] Part of this is still in force. The various repealing Acts have done away with all obsolete Regulations; others, of course, have been specially repealed in the course of legislation.

In the course of the preceding chapter I have noticed the importance of this provision, and also the fact that various new acquisitions of territory, though annexed in general terms to the British dominions, were *not specifically made subordinate*, or annexed to, the Presidency of Bengal. Consequently, no Regulations applied to such provinces, nor was there any direct power of making laws for them till 1834; nor was all difficulty connected with the subject completely removed till 1861.

§ 8. *The second Indian Legislature.*

The 28th August, 1833—on which day the 3 and 4 Will. IV, cap. 85, was passed—brought to a close the era of the Regulations. By the 43rd section, the 'Governor-General in Council' was to make *Laws* and Regulations for all persons, for all courts of justice, and for all places and things within British territory and regarding servants of the Company in allied Native States.

The Act provided also certain limits to the power of the Indian Legislature with regard to certain subjects of legislation.

In the former period, the legislative power had been to make 'Rules, Regulations, and Ordinances;' the term 'Regulation' was consequently adopted as most properly describing the enactments issued. Under the 3 and 4 Will. IV, cap. 85, the power was given to make *laws* as well as Regulations; and it thenceforward became the custom to call the enactments of the Governor-General in Council 'Acts.'

There is but little specific difference in the nature of a Regulation and an Act, except that the former were less concisely and technically drafted, and were usually preceded by the detailed expositions of the motives and purpose of the enactments previously alluded to. This, in 'Acts,' has been replaced by the brief 'preamble[1].'

[1] There are also some differences in the manner of interpretation; but it is not here necessary to enter on such details. The introduction to 'Field's *Chronological Index* explains the subject clearly. The

From 1793 to 1833, therefore, we have 'Regulations,' and from 1834 down to the present day we have 'Acts.'

These Acts are numbered consecutively through the year, and follow the calendar, not the official, year. This plan has ever since been adhered to, notwithstanding the modifications which have affected the constitution of the Legislature down to the present time.

By the Act of 1833, the Governments of Madras and Bombay were deprived of the power of legislation, and did not regain this power till 1861.

The Act gave the Governor-General a Council of four members, of whom one was to be conversant with legal subjects. He was not a member of the Executive Council, and only sat when legislation was in question. Even then he was not necessarily present; nor need he concur when an Act was passed [1]. Under this Act, however, Commissioners were appointed *in India* to consider and propose drafts of laws [2].

§ 9. *The Indian Legislature in its third stage.*

Our present system is nothing more than a development of the Legislature of the 3 and 4 Will. IV, cap. 85. The first important change was made by the Act of 1853 (16 and 17 Vict., cap. 15). It will be interesting to follow, in a very general manner, the changes made [3].

'Statement of Objects and Reasons,' which is always published with the proposed law while it is yet in the stage of a 'Bill,' does away with the necessity for any lengthy preamble to the Act itself when passed. It is, however, itself probably a relic of the old exposition prefixed to the Regulations.

[1] For an excellent comparison of the various Legislatures in more detail, see *Tagore Law Lectures*, 1872, page 105 *et seq.*

[2] It was under these provisions that Lord Macaulay came out, the result of the Commissioners' labours being the Indian Penal Code, now so famous. By the Act of 1853 a Law Commissioner in England was appointed to advise the Crown, on the recommendations of the Law Commissioners in India.

[3] Acts passed under the constitution of 1834 are technically styled *Acts of the Governor-General of India in Council*; those under the system of 1853 are *Acts of the Legislative Council of India*; those made since the Indian Councils' Act of 1861 are *Acts of the Council of the Governor-General of India assembled for the purpose of making Laws and Regulations.* At the present day the drafts of proposed Acts are published in the *Gazette of India*, for the purpose of giving notice of the proposed law and of invoking criticism, and in that stage the draft is spoken of as

By this Act some purely *legislative* members were added to the Council. These were appointed, one by each Governor of a presidency or Lieutenant-Governor of a province. The Chief Justice of Bengal and one of the Judges, were also made members.

While, however, the Council was thus improved in two important features—(*a*) local representation of provinces, and (*b*) special adaptation for legislative functions—it did not satisfy the ideas of many who could make their opinions heard. In those days the plan of a local legislature for each province was strongly advocated, and in 1859 Lord Canning sent home a despatch, in which not only this subject was dealt with, but the practice of the existing Council was criticised. Lord Canning advocated a separate legislature for Bombay, Madras, Bengal, the North-West Provinces, and the Panjáb. He also desired that natives of the country should be consulted, and that they should be able to give their opinions in their own language.

a 'Bill.' When the Acts are passed by the Council and have received the assent of the Governor-General, they are also published in the *Gazette*.

The Superintendent of Government Printing (at his office, No. 8, Hastings Street, Calcutta) publishes authorized copies of all Acts, which can be bought by the public at a small price, varying according to the length of the Act. The Legislative Department is also issuing a collected series of the Acts, grouped in volumes of 'General Acts,' and in 'Codes,' i. e. the Acts referring specially or solely to each province. In these editions, which are of great value, tables are published showing how all the Acts and Regulations are disposed of—by repeal, &c. Only unrepealed enactments are printed, with the alterations introduced by later Acts (if passed in time for the printing). The provincial volumes, or 'Codes,' of Bengal, Madras, and Bombay, give all the Regulations and Acts of the Local Legislatures, as well as the Acts of the Supreme Legislature; and all the provincial volumes contain the 'Regulations' issued for certain districts under the Act 33 Vict., cap. 3. They do not, however, give the 'rules made pursuant to various Acts,' which are now so conspicuous a feature in recent Acts. These must be looked for in local Gazettes or reprints. Such 'rules' are, however, of great convenience, enabling a multitude of details to be locally provided for which could not be entered in the Act itself without swelling its bulk enormously, since the 'rules' are as various as are the conditions of the provinces. The Forest Officer will remember how important a place 'rules' have in the Forest Acts of 1878 and 1881.

§ 10. *The Indian Legislature as it is at present (under the Indian Councils Act).*

In 1861 was passed the 24 and 25 Vict., cap. 67, the 'Indian Councils' Act,' which (as amended in some particulars by later Statutes) is the law under which our present legislature subsists[1].

The nucleus of the Council is the Executive Council of the Governor-General. This now consists of five Ordinary Members (with the Commander-in-Chief as an Extraordinary Member, if so appointed by the Secretary of State). The Governor of Madras or Bombay becomes also another Extraordinary Member when the Council sits in his Presidency.

Of the five Ordinary Members, three are officials, Civil or Military (of ten years' standing at least), and of the remaining two, one must be a Barrister (or Scotch Advocate) of not less than five years' standing. The Barrister Member is generally spoken of as the 'Legal Member' and the other as the 'Financial Member.' When the Council sits for legislative purposes, it has to be supplemented by a number of 'Additional' Members[2], for the purpose of making Laws and Regulations only. These Additional Members have no power of voting except at legislative meetings. In number they must be not less than six nor more than twelve; one-half the number so nominated must (by section 10) be non-official persons.

Provision is made for the Council meeting in the absence of the Governor-General; and for the Governor-General, when visiting any part of India, exercising his power without his Council.

[1] All the recent Acts of Parliament, viz. from 1855, can be found in the Collection of Statutes issued by Mr. Whitley Stokes in continuation of the 'Law relating to India and the East India Company'; the former can easily be obtained, the latter is now out of print and scarce. But an edition of all the Statutes is being printed in the Legislative Department.

[2] When the Council sits in any province, the Lieutenant-Governor (and by the 33 Vict., cap. 3, sect. 3, a Chief Commissioner also) becomes *ex-officio* a Member *for legislative purposes* only. The *ex-officio* Members may be in excess of the maximum of twelve Additional Members.

But this power does not extend to legislation. The Governor-General can never legislate apart from his Council; but the Council may sit notwithstanding the absence of the Governor-General. In such cases a 'President in Council' is appointed according to the Act.

The Governor-General (alone) has, however, a special[1] power to issue ordinances for the peace and good government of the country in cases of emergency.

Power is reserved to the Crown (through the Secretary of State in Council) to disallow any law or Regulation passed in India; and the powers of the Council are restricted by section 22 in respect of certain subjects of legislation.

The Indian Councils Act was amended by the 32–33 Vict., cap. 98 (1869), and by 37–38 Vict., cap. 91 (1874), and by the 39 Vict., cap. 7 (1876).

§ 11. *Powers of Local Legislatures.*

The Act gives legislative powers to the Madras and Bombay Governments; consequently, the Local Codes which show a blank after 1833, begin to have Local Acts from 1862 onwards. For the other provinces the matter is differently stated. The provisions of the Act *are* to be extended to the Lieutenant-Governorship of Bengal, and *may* be extended to the North-West Provinces[2] and the Panjáb as soon as the Governor-General deems it expedient.

[1] See section 23. This remains in force for a limited period only, and is subject to a 'veto' from the Home Government (Secretary of State).

[2] Under these provisions the Bengal Council was constituted by proclamation on the 17th January, 1862. A Local Council of nine Members for the North-West Provinces and Oudh was created by Notification, No. 1704, dated Calcutta, 26th November, 1886, with effect from the 1st December, 1886. No local legislature for the Panjáb has yet been constituted.

The following passage from the *Tagore Lectures for* 1872 may be here quoted as well describing the functions of the Councils when sitting as *legislative bodies* (pages 122–23):—

'The character of these Legislative Councils is simply this, that they are Committees for the purpose of making laws, Committees by means of which the Executive Government obtains advice and assistance in their legislation, and the public derive the benefit of full publicity being ensured at every stage of the law-making process. Although the Government enacts the laws through its Council, private legislation being unknown, yet the public has a right to make itself heard, and the Executive is bound to defend its legislation.

'And when the laws are once

The local Governor is bound to transmit an authenticated copy of any Law or Regulation to which he has assented, to the Governor-General [1]. No such local law has any validity till the Governor-General has assented thereto, and such assent shall have been signified by him to and published by the Governor. If the assent is withheld, the Governor-General must signify his reasons in writing for so doing.

made, the Executive is as much bound by them as the public, and the duty of enforcing them belongs to the Courts of Justice. Such laws are in reality the orders of Government, but they are made in a manner which ensures publicity and discussion, are enforced by the Courts and not by the Executive, cannot be changed but by the same deliberate and public process as that by which they were made, and can be enforced against the Executive or in favour of individuals whenever occasion requires. The Councils are not deliberative bodies with respect to any subject but that of the immediate legislation before them. They cannot enquire into grievances, call for information, or examine the conduct of the Executive. The acts of administration cannot be impugned, nor can they be properly defended in such assemblies, except with reference to the particular measure under discussion.'

[1] And if the Bill contains penal clauses, it is ordered (as a matter of administrative regulation) by a despatch of the Secretary of State of 1st December, 1862, that it should be submitted to the Governor-General *before* it is locally passed into an Act.

Diagram or Table giving a 'Conspectus of the Legislatures.'

Legislature of **1834** (3 & 4 William IV, Cap. 85).	Legislature of **1853** (16 & 17 Vict., Cap. 95).	Legislature of **1861** (24 & 25 Vict., Cap. 67).
Governor-General and Council of three, with a fourth member (a lawyer) for Legislative duty only.	Governor-General and Council of four (all four being on the Executive Council); *also* The Chief Justice of Bengal, One Judge, *and* One 'Legislative Member' appointed by each Governor and Lieutenant-Governor.	(A) Governor-General and Council of five 'Ordinary' Members. (Three of them officials and two non-officials, usually one 'Legal Member' and one 'Financial Member'); *and as* 'Extraordinary' Members— (1) Commander-in-Chief (if appointed), (2) Governor of Madras or Bombay, *ex-officio* when Council sits in his territories; [Supreme Council.] *to which is added* (B) For legislative purposes only (no vote on other matters), 'Additional Members' (not more than twelve nor less than six, one-half to be non-official), *and* (1) Lieutenant-Governor, (2) Chief Commissioner, *ex-officio* (and without reference to maximum of 12) when the Council sits for making Laws in their territories. [Council of Governor-General assembled for purpose of making Laws and Regulations.]
No Local Legislative Councils at Madras, Bombay, or Fort William.		Legislative Council, Bengal. — Act *directs* Governor-General to appoint. (Done Jan. 17th, 1862.) / Legislative Council, Bombay. Legislative Council, Madras. — Constituted by the Act itself. / Legislative Councils for other Provinces. — Act *allows* Governor-General to appoint. (Not yet done, except for N.W. Prov.) / Their 'Acts' require the assent of the Governor-General.

§ 12. *Law of 'Non-Regulation' Provinces.*

One section (25) of the Indian Councils Act I have reserved for notice till the conclusion of this chapter.

I have already spoken of 'Non-Regulation Provinces,' and so far explained how they came into existence. We have seen that, unless expressly made subordinate to the presidency, a province did not come within the operation of the Regulations. Consequently, up to 1833, no provision existed by which anything in the nature of a legislative power existed for such places.

The Act 3 and 4 Will. IV, cap. 85, afforded only a partial remedy. It gave, it is true, power to legislate for all British territory, so that provinces which were already British territory at the time were provided for; but nothing was said about the application of such Acts, if general in their character, to provinces not at the time British provinces, but added afterwards [1]. It soon became doubtful how far such Acts were practically in force. But the chief difficulty was, that in the newer provinces a number of matters had been provided for by local rules, circular orders, and official instructions, which emanated from the executive, but not from any legislative, authority. Business could not have been carried on without such rules, yet there was no legal basis for them, only the sanction of practice.

The Indian Councils Act of 1861 removed the difficulty, and by section 25 provides that 'no rule, law, or regulation which, prior to the passing of this Act, shall have been made by'

the Governor-General,
the Governor-General in Council,
the Governor,
the Governor in Council,
the Lieutenant-Governor,

[1] *Vide* note, p. 79; the remarks there quoted were made in the Council with reference to the Act XI of 1835, which, though applicable to all British territory, was not legally in force, e. g. in the Panjáb, because in 1835 the Panjáb was not British territory.

for and in respect of any such non-regulation province (i.e. territory known from time to time as a non-regulation province) shall be deemed invalid, 'only by reason of the same not having been made in conformity' with the provisions of Acts regarding the powers and constitution of Councils and other authorities [1].

§ 13. *Local Laws Acts.*

In order to remove any possible doubt on the subject, the Indian Legislature has since expressly enacted 'Local Laws Acts,' which state what Rules and Acts and Regulations are to be deemed to be in force in the chief non-regulation provinces. In the Panjáb we have Act IV of 1872 (amended by XII of 1878); for Oudh, Act XVIII of 1876; for the Central Provinces, Act XX of 1875.

In 1874, also, an Act was passed (No. XV of 1874) which is called the 'Laws Local Extent Act,' and this, in a series of schedules, gives a list of previous Acts and Regulations which extend to the whole of India, or to the particular province (as the case may be), and the applicability of which was, or might be, previously doubtful.

§ 14. *Scheduled Districts.*

As regards the extent and nature of the law in force, the old distinction of 'Regulation' and 'Non-Regulation' has entirely lost its meaning. Many of the old Regulations have been repealed or superseded, and some of those that remain have been expressly declared to apply to the Non-Regulation Provinces. Not only so, but all the more important branches of legislation—Civil and Criminal Procedure, Land Revenue, Stamps, Excise, Irrigation, the

[1] When rules and orders were made by 'Boards of Administration' or 'Chief Commissioners,' they would not have validity under the Indian Councils Act, unless they had been confirmed by the Governor-General, in which case they virtually became rules made by the Governor-General. In this way the Panjáb Forest Rules of 1855 had validity, owing to their confirmation by the Governor-General in Council. This validity has since been affirmed by the insertion of the rules in the schedule of the Panjáb Laws Act.

Law of Contract, the Criminal Law—have been provided for either by general Acts which apply to all the provinces at large, or by special Acts containing local details, but resembling each other in principle. But there is still a practical distinction of another kind to be mentioned, which is of importance and likely long to be maintained.

There are portions of the older Regulation Provinces, and also portions of the newer Non-Regulation Provinces themselves, which are 'Extra Regulation' in a perfectly valid and current sense. These are now spoken of as the 'Scheduled districts,' under the Act (XIV of 1874) passed to place them on an intelligible basis as regards the laws in force in them [1].

The districts are called 'Scheduled' because they are noted in the 'Schedules' of Act XIV of 1874.

None of the Acts of a general character passed before 1874, the local application of which is settled by Act XV of

[1] The list may be summarised as follows:—

Scheduled Districts, Bengal

I.—The Jalpaigúri and Darjiling Divisions.
II.—The Hill Tracts of Chittagong.
III.—The Santál Parganas.
IV.—The Chutiyá Nágpur Division.

North-Western Provinces.

I.—The Jhánsi Division, comprising the districts of Jhánsi, Jaláun, and Lalitpur.
II.—The Province of Kumáon and Garhwál.
III.—The Tarái Parganas, comprising Bázpur, Káshípur, Jáspur, Rudarpur, Gadarpur, Kilpúri, Nának-Matthá, and Bilherí.
IV.—In the Mirzapur District—
(1) The tappas of Agori Khás and South Kon in the pargana of Agori.
(2) The tappa of British Singraulí in the pargana of Singrauli.
(3) The tappas of Phulwá, Dudhi, and Barhá in the pargana of Bichipár.
(4) The portion lying to the south of the Kaimúr range.
V.—The Family Domains of the Mahárájá of Benares.
VI.—The tract of country known as Jaunsár-Báwar in the Dehra-Dún district.

Panjáb.

The districts of Hazára, Pesháwar, Kohát, Bannú, Dera Ismáil Khán, Dera Gházi Khán, Lahaul, and Spiti.

Central Provinces.

No part of the Central Provinces is now 'scheduled.'

The Chief Commissionership of Ajmer and Merwára.

The Chief Commissionership of Assam.

British Burmá.

The Hill Tracts of Arracan.

Madras.

Certain estates in Ganjam, Vizagapatam, and Godávari districts (besides the Laccadive Islands).

Bombay.

Sindh, the Panch Maháls (attached to the Kairá Collectorate), Aden, and certain villages of Mehwásí Chiefs.

Coorg.

The whole province (Chief Commissionership).

this same year, apply directly to the *Scheduled* districts; it is left to the Local Government to define by notification in each case,—

(*a*) what laws are *not* in force (so as to remove doubts in case it might be supposed that some law was in force);

(*b*) what laws *are* in force;

(*c*) and to extend Acts or parts of Acts to the district in question.

Of course all Acts *passed since* 1874 themselves define to what territories they extend, so that there can be no further doubt on the matter.

§ 15. *Regulations under* 33 *Vict., cap.* 3.

In order to provide a still more elastic and adaptable method of making rules which have legal validity, for provinces in an elementary stage of progress, the Act 33 Vict., cap. 3 (1870), provides that certain territories may at any time be declared by the Secretary of State to be territories for which it is desirable that special Regulations (other than the Acts of the Legislature) should be made. The districts so declared (if not already under Act XIV) *become* 'Scheduled' whenever such declaration is made, so that there is in fact a power of creating new scheduled districts in addition to those in that Act. The Regulations regarding Hazára in the Panjáb, the Santál Parganas in Bengal, regarding Assam, Ajmer, and the Hill Tracts of Arracan, &c., are all under this law. They are at once known from the old 'Regulations' (of 1793–1833) by their bearing date since 1870.

§ 16. *Résumé.*

In order to aid the student in remembering the *principal stages* in the growth of the Legislature, I present the following skeleton or abstract:—

(1) Originally each presidency had its own President and Council: no formal legislature being needed for settlers who bring their own law with them to the 'factory' in which they settle.

(2) Territories acquired and formal government begins; Courts have to deal with natives of the country; Legislative power necessary; given by the 'Regulating Act' of 1773, subject to supervision of Supreme Court. This does not work, and is amended in 1781, but incompletely.

A. D. 1773. 1781. 1797.

(3) A number of 'Regulations' made; codified in 1793; recognised as valid by Act of Parliament, 1797. This, with subsequent additions up to 1833, forms the Code of 'Bengal Regulations.'

Applies to Bengal. Similar powers given to Madras in 1800; and both Madras and Bombay were still further empowered in 1807.

(4) Legislature of 1834 (3 and 4 Will. IV, cap. 85) for British India.

A. D. 1833.

The 'Acts' begin 1834 and onwards.

(5) Improved in 1853 by adding local members from provinces and some judicial authorities.

A. D. 1853.

Legislative powers *taken away* from Madras and Bombay, and do not yet exist in other provinces.

(6) Finally improved by Indian Councils' Act, 1861.

A. D. 1861.

Legislative Councils (Acts subject to assent of Governor-General) for Bombay and Madras. One *to be* provided for Bengal (this done in 1862); *may* be provided for other provinces (North-West Provinces and Oudh in 1886).

(7) Special power given to Secretary of State to declare certain territories amenable to the 33 Vict., cap. 3. Thereon the head of the Local Government or Administration may propose to the Governor-General in Council a Regulation, which, on being approved by him, becomes law.

A. D. 1870.

CHAPTER IV.

A GENERAL VIEW OF THE LAND-TENURES OF BRITISH INDIA.

SECTION I—THE LINES OF STUDY.

§ 1. *Object of the Chapter.*

THE heading of this chapter is perhaps a somewhat startling one. I may therefore express a hope that it will not be misunderstood or taken as indicating an attempt to propound a general theory of origin for all the varieties of land-tenure that are to be found in India. It may well be doubted whether any such theory is, at present at any rate, possible; certainly I have no pretensions to be competent to suggest one. And, even if such a theory were possible, it might be further questionable whether it would be of use to the student of practical land-administration.

At the same time there may be great advantage to be derived from bringing together in one chapter various leading facts about Indian land-tenures. It would be strange if the comparative method, which has been found fruitful in other branches of study bearing on the language and progress of mankind, should be infructuous here. I am not aware of any treatise in which facts regarding various provincial and local forms of land-holding in India have been brought together for the purpose of comparative treatment. The attempt made in this chapter will not then be going over old ground.

§ 2. *Value of the Comparative Method.*

A comparative study of land-tenures will bring out one thing: there are certain common factors which have, at least within wide geographical or ethnical limits, always been at work in the production of the tenures we actually see around us in the several provinces. Had these been always observed, we should have been spared some strange mistakes. I may instance the case of that curious district on the west coast of India known as Malabár. From the tenure point of view Malabár presents in its limited area quite a number of instructive and, in one sense, unique facts. It is like one of those little glens sometimes found by botanists, in which a group of plant-treasures—not to be found over many square miles outside—all at once reward his search. Malabár was long a source of puzzled remarks from reporters on land affairs. It was supposed, for instance, that here 'private property' in land had existed, while it could not be found anywhere else. It was also asserted that here, exceptionally, no land-revenue had been levied on the 'proprietor' before the Mysore conquest. Both remarks, though often repeated, are quite without foundation. A study of the early Dravidian-Hindu organization, and a comparison of the history of the military chiefs of the country with that observable in Oudh and other parts, would have enabled a more correct interpretation to be put on the facts. The strong proprietary holdings of Malabár in all probability grew up in exactly the same way as similar rights did in Northern India. And as to land-revenue, wherever chiefs of a conquering or military caste are known to have held estates on a sort of feudal system, they will be found never to have paid land-revenue to the Rájá or over-lord. But when in the ups and downs of fortune the rule was lost, and the chiefs' estates became dismembered, and the descendants (as often happens in such cases) managed to regain the land in a new capacity, it was not to be supposed that they could escape the natural responsibilities of the changed position;

in other words, it was not in the nature of things to be supposed—in Malabár any more than elsewhere—that the next ruling power should abstain from levying a land-revenue on such lands. However, this is all by way of anticipation: I must not go into details; what has been said is only with a view to illustrate the uses of comparison in the study of land-tenures. It cannot be a matter of chance, nor a case in which we must abstain from drawing inferences, that a claim to strong 'birth-right' tenures is, all over India, found to arise among the descendants of military chieftains who had been colonizers or conquerors and who have undergone the usual changes. And if so, the origin of Malabár claims, and their relative value, is explained.

Whatever may be thought, however, of the benefits to be derived from a comparison of local tenures, it can hardly be doubted that by a preliminary study of this kind, we can gain a certain familiarity with common forms and with terms of constant occurrence in revenue literature, which will greatly simplify our after study, and will enable the separate provincial chapters in the sequel to be written without the necessity for explaining over and over again terms and facts which must recur in each.

And, fortunately, there are certain features in the circumstances of our Indian provinces which indicate the lines on which a general study may be pursued.

§ 3. *Land grouped in 'Villages.'*

We can hardly help beginning with the general fact that all the races of India whose history we are to any extent acquainted with, have, when they passed the nomadic or pastoral stage, and took to settled agriculture, formed certain groups of land-holdings, more or less connected together, and which we call 'VILLAGES.' At least that is true for all the districts in the plain country where there are no exceptional features.

I have already explained, in an introductory chapter, that

the term 'village,' as we use it, means a group of land-holdings, with (usually) a central aggregate of residences, the inhabitants of which have certain relations, and some kind of union or bond of common government[1]. In the course of time modifications arise in the ownership and constitution of village societies; but once given a local name, the 'village' remains a feature on the district map in spite of all. Family partitions, for instance, and transfers, may cause one village to be divided between several estates, or may unite twenty villages under one owner, but as a local feature the 'village' always remains.

The village, its various forms and the modifications it undergoes, will then form a natural starting-point for our study of tenures.

§ 4. *Effects of Land-Revenue Administration and Revenue-farming.*

Then again, the greater Oriental governments which preceded ours, have always, in one form or another, derived the bulk of their State-revenues and Royal property from the land. In one system known to us, 'Royal lands' were allotted in the principal villages, and this fact may have suggested to the Mughals their plan of allotting special farms and villages to furnish the privy purse, and has had other survivals. But, speaking generally, the universal plan of taking revenue was by taking a share of the actual grain heap on the threshing-floor from each holding. Afterwards this was commuted for a money payment levied on each estate or each field as the case

[1] In revenue language, I may repeat, the village is the 'mauza' or 'dih' (P.). In the Hindi dialects it is variously gáñw, grámam, gráoñ, gaum, or some similar form. In Elphinstone's *History of India* and many other works, the 'village' is called a 'township.' I am not aware of any advantage possessed by this term, except that it is equivalent to the Saxon 'vill' which had features in common with some forms of Indian village. The 'village' group varies in size. In the Panjáb it *averages* 900 acres, in the Central Provinces 1300 acres, in the North-West Provinces, where population is denser, and land highly cultivated and much subdivided, it is 600 acres (Stack's *Memorandum on Temporary Settlements*, 1880, p. 8).

might be. The nature and consequence of this system as it affects our modern land-revenue, will be dealt with in detail in the next chapter. Here I only state the fact. To collect this revenue, the ruler appointed or recognized not only a headman and accountant in each village, but also a hierarchy of graded officials in districts and minor divisions of territory formed for administrative purposes. These officers were often remunerated by holdings of land, and a class of land-tenures will be found in some parts of India owing its origin to these hereditary official holdings. Not only so, but during the decline which Oriental governments have usually undergone, the Revenue officials have been commonly found to merge in, or be superseded by, revenue-farmers—persons who contracted for a certain sum of revenue to be paid into the Treasury from a given area, as representing the State dues exigible from the land-holdings within that area. Such revenue-farmers, or officials, whatever their origin, have always tended to absorb the interests of the land-holders [1] and to become in time the virtual landlords *over them.*

Nor is it only that landlord tenures arise in this way. No sooner does the superior right take shape than we find many curious new tenures created by the landlord or arising out of his attempts to conciliate or provide for certain eminent claims in the grade below him.

§ 5. *Effects of Assignment or Remission of Land-Revenue.*

Yet another class of tenures arises in connection with the State Revenue-administration; and that is when the ruler either excuses an existing land-holder from paying his revenue, either wholly or in part; or 'alienates' or assigns the revenue of a certain estate or tract of country in favour of some chief, or other person of importance, or to provide funds for some special objects, or to serve as a recompense for services to be rendered.

[1] See Maine, *Early History of Institutions*, p. 150.

At first such grants are carefully regulated, are for life only, and strictly kept to their purpose, and to the amount fixed. But as matters go on, and the ruler is a bad or unscrupulous one, his treasury is empty, and he makes such grants to avoid the difficulty of finding a cash salary. The grants become permanent and hereditary; they are also issued by officials who have no right to make them; and not only do they then result in landlord tenures and other curious rights, but are a burden to after times, and have furnished a most troublesome legacy to our own Government when it found the revenues eaten up by grantees whose titles were invalid, and whose pretensions, though grown old in times of disorder, were inadmissible.

Such grants may have begun with no title to the land but only a right to the revenue, but want of supervision and control has resulted in the grantee seizing the landed right also. Here we have another 'common factor' which has everywhere been at work—the influence of State organization and revenue systems on landholding.

§ 6. *Superimposition of Landed Rights.*

The mention of tenures arising out of official relations with the land and revenue-farming, reminds us that these tenures do not always, or even generally, arise over unoccupied lands, or where there are no pre-existing interests. They strike, in fact, the key-note of 'superimposition' and 'modification'; one set of tenures supervening on another and producing changes.

This will not be understood as leading the reader to suppose that the great historic conquests with their new systems of government produced any radical or wholesale disruption of the previous state of things, as the Roman conquest did in Europe. The changes were gradual and often insensible; the modified tenures were not the result of any defined purpose to change, or any distinct principle which was enforced. They represented an indefinite sort of compromise between old facts and new conditions: still there was modification. For example; a man represents the family of the leader of a party of colonizers who founded a Bengal village generations ago. As such he is the virtual, though not legally defined, proprietor of the best lands in the village formed by the groups of colonists. But time goes on, and a State 'Zamíndár' arises to contract for the revenues, and gradually destroys the rights under him; but the man we have spoken of is strong enough or respected enough to influence even the 'Zamíndár,' who thereon gives him a writing acknowledging or granting to him a perpetual tenure at a fixed and unalterable rent. Practically the man is as well off as he was before—perhaps better; but it is impossible to deny that the colour of his tenure is changed.

Or again, let us go back to an early cultivating settlement, perhaps in the days of the Gond or other ancient kingdoms. Even this represents a somewhat advanced stage, for before the ideas of the people had got to appreciate a definite right to clear and cultivate permanently a given area, there must have been a previous stage of nomadic and shifting cultivation in the forest. But let that pass. The village may remain for centuries in this stage. The different members all claim their own cleared holdings, and perhaps one or two leading men hold a hereditary headship with certain customary powers and privileges. The time however comes when it is conquered by a marauding Rájput clan, or interfered with by some of the indigenous princes converted to Hinduism and adopting Aryan ideas of government; or the Rájá or chief makes a grant of the village to some member of his family. In short, a landlord is found for the village. The lord dies and is succeeded by sons and grandsons. A change in the village constitution thus occurs. The family form a 'community' jointly claiming to own the whole. They have themselves cleared and cultivated the surrounding waste; they have bought up some of the older cultivated lands, and got rid of the holders of others, and the relics of the original village body that remain are now the 'tenants' of the superior family. This landlord family, or 'proprietary body,' is at first closely united; all have equal rights, and they do not divide. But in time quarrels arise, and a desire for separate enjoyment grows. The 'community' then divide the land into major and minor shares or lots, but still hold together and have certain common rights and the waste in common. This state of things is, however, in its turn affected by the Muhammadan conquest and by the organized system which the Mughal Empire introduced. Not so much at first: they are ruthlessly assessed to a full revenue, and this a little damps their pretensions; they are more and more evidently graded as peasant-proprietors, that is all. But in time the proprietary body find their rights ignored; a revenue-farmer first *acts* as their landlord, and ends by *calling himself* so, till his descendants are found, after a generation or two, talking about their 'ancient rights' under the 'law and constitution of the country!' The old village rights have disappeared altogether.

Then come Maráthá plunderers, Rohilla adventurers, or an advance of Sikh clans. All fasten on the land, and all devise some scheme of making a profit out of it, which in the end affects the land-tenures.

§ 7. *Effect of Modern Laws.*

Lastly, the British rule comes upon the confusion and ruin caused by centuries of such changes. Able administrators, often actuated by the highest motives, but necessarily guided by the ideas which are natural to their age and antecedents, endeavour to settle landed rights and the revenues of the State on some equitable system. They perceive that the result of all that has gone before has been not merely to efface old tenures, and substitute new interests in their places, but rather to leave traces of several different rights, and to impose, as it were, layer upon layer of interests, each revealing itself in varying degrees of strength or preservation.

In dealing with such a state of things many mistakes are

made. Tenures are not understood, or are misunderstood; faulty systems of revenue-assessment and collection are adopted, and great distress and much injustice result. In the end matters slowly right themselves; and then it is desired to fix by law, in a definite manner, the principles on which rights are to be enjoyed and the form in which they are to be secured and recorded. The task is one of great difficulty: as its accomplishment progresses, divergence of authorities occurs, evidence is found conflicting, and public opinion changes. With the best intention of avoiding special theories, Western terms and the principles of Western jurisprudence make their influence felt, and the last stage in modification of the old order is only reached when the British legislation, earnestly desiring to do practical justice to all classes of rights, establishes, confers and consolidates rights, defining and classifying them as best it may, calling this man a landlord and that a tenant, and shading off the intermediate claims into defined grades of 'inferior-proprietor,' 'tenure-holder,' 'occupancy-tenant,' and what not; trying always to provide equitably, but not always succeeding in doing so, in order that no really surviving rights may be ignored.

§ 8. *Effects of Economic Conditions.*

Nor must we attribute all modification to historical events and legislative efforts. All the time economic conditions are silently bearing their part in modifying ideas and customs of land-holding. Originally the foundation of every one's interest in land, whether it is the king's, or the landlord-family's, or the cultivator's, is the grain heap, the natural produce, divided by some process or another, in kind.

But as cultivation occupies more and more of the area, and waste for new tillage diminishes, population increases, and farms become more and more subdivided. No doubt subdivision means increased care and effort bestowed on the land, the increase of works of irrigation and the use of manure, and thus the produce is largely increased; but this cannot go on for ever, and the time comes when the shares of the produce for the different parties cannot all be taken. For the share which meets the expense of cultivation and feeds and clothes the ploughman, remains a constant, at any rate a not diminishing quantity, and the surplus from each diminished holding becomes less. Meanwhile coined money comes into common use, and the king or the chief, instead of facing the inevitable and reducing his grain share to a lower fraction, seizes on the fact that he can take coin instead of grain. Grain shares are given up, and money payments adjusted in the rough, and without attempting a valuation of the actual produce, still less of appraising the acres according to their different productive capacities. This changes the relations of cultivator and over-lord, and modifies the whole basis of agricultural society. 'Rent,' 'enhancement,' 'competition,' or their equivalent phrases begin to be talked of. When population increases also, land ceases to be over-abundant, the race to secure land for cultivation begins, and not as before to coax cultivators to the land. Waste is increasingly broken up and new forms of tenure depending on arrangements for utilizing the waste land multiply. Here again is a new field for settled law and orderly administration to define, to regulate, and to protect.

§ 9. *Résumé.*

Let us now gather up these various heads of study, and we may arrange our subjects for a 'general view' in the following order:—

(1) The village and its modifications.

(2) Tenures arising from official position, State grants, and assignment or remission of State revenue, as well as for the conversion of revenue-farmers or collecting agencies into proprietors and proprietary bodies.

(3) The grades of land-right resulting from the superposition, by conquest or otherwise, of new layers of interest in the soil.

(4) The growth and present position of what has become 'cultivating tenancies' under the newly recognized landlords.

(5) To these I shall add a section containing some general ideas regarding 'property' in land as it is understood in India. This is a sort of episode or collateral subject, the consideration of which is rendered necessary by every remark we make on land-tenures.

SECTION II.—THE VILLAGE.

§ 1. *Existing accounts of the Village.*

Considering the very great interest which attaches to the VILLAGE, as it is found under its varied conditions and with its different origins, in different parts of India, it is surprising to find that it is practically impossible to put one's hand on a single book that has collected and reduced to shape the information which exists in Settlement Reports and local and special papers and minutes, official and other [1].

The only detailed attempt to account for the village constitution I have met, is in Mr. Phillips' *Tagore Lectures* for 1874–5. The author has set about, with his usual skill and industry, to collect facts from different sources; but unfortunately he has been dominated with the idea that villages are always 'Hindu,' and that there is one kind of

[1] In Dr. Field's valuable work on *Landholding* in various countries, very little is said about the villages;—the perfect communities of the Panjáb are hardly alluded to, and those of the North-West Provinces described only in extracts from some official *Minutes*, which, whatever may have been the ability of their authors, still were written when the settlement enquiries under the new system of 1822 had hardly commenced, and when knowledge on the subject was most elementary.

The Cobden Club Essays contain a valuable paper by Sir G. Campbell, but it is too brief and generalized to be altogether satisfactory. There are, of course, the valuable conclusions as to early forms of property, which Sir H. Maine has made us familiar with in his *Village Communities* and other works; but these do not, and do not profess to, specially analyze the Indian village or give any details as to the actual facts of origin, constitution, and history, of the different types of village in the various countries of India.

village only; the consequence is that he tries to explain everything by the ideas of the much later Hindu law-books; he pieces together various items of information gathered from totally different provinces; and thereout evolves a picture of a single form of village constitution, which thus represents nothing that really exists, or ever did exist, as far as *evidence* goes. 'The village referred to in *Manu*[1]' (he writes) 'was, we can hardly doubt, the well-known village community, the constitution and position of which are so important in the Hindu land system; the village is, in fact, the key to that system.' 'From the slight reference to it in *Manu*,' he continues, 'we have to pass by a long stride of centuries, to what has been observed in such recent times as the period since British rule. It is from such observations, with the aid of analogies from similar institutions existing in modern times in other countries, that we have to *construct the idea of the village community of Hindu times*.'

§ 2. *Remarks on the Quotation.—Origin of Villages.*

But in order to get a notion how the village system arose and grew in early times, and how it has since been modified, it is necessary to throw away all theories and to observe and collate the facts as far as they can be established by evidence, carefully distinguishing different localities, and only generalizing when we have a safe basis.

The first point to be noted is that there is no such thing as *one* form of the 'well-known village community'; and that the village-system should not be referred to *Hindu law* influences without a great deal of consideration—at any rate, if by 'Hindu law' we mean the later embodiment of modified custom in the now well-known commentaries and text-books.

In the first place, as I have already remarked, there can

[1] Mánava-dharma-sástra, or the Institutes of Manu, with the gloss of Kullukă Bhattă. I always refer to the best and most recent English version, that by Bühler, forming vol. xxv. of Trübner's series of *Sacred Books of the East*. See Phillips, Lect. I, p. 6.

hardly be any doubt that the formation of village groups—that is the aggregation of land-holdings in one place, and with a certain degree of union among the cultivators—is not peculiar to Hindu races, either original or converted. It is found in India, among the great races which were certainly antecedent to the Hindus, and which still survive (with their institutions) in widely distant parts of the country. The village—apart from questions of particular forms—is not so much the result of any system as it is of a natural instinct. We find it everywhere, especially in the plain country, where circumstances invited it; at the same time, we do not find it in other places—on the Himalayan hill-sides, on the west coast (Kánara and Malabár) and in the dry regions of the Southern Panjáb. In these latter situations we find individuals, or a few connected families with individual holdings; the residences are separately located within the holdings, or perhaps (as on the west coast) a few family houses are arranged in a group; and we find that on the west coast there is no word for 'village,' but the term for a family group of houses with its dependencies is some word such as 'tara,' meaning a 'street.' It is true that for Government purposes these holdings are artificially grouped into circles of some kind, and that some sort of headman, or chief over the circle, is recognized, partly as a matter of social convenience, partly as a matter of State management with a view to the collection of revenue or taxes.

But over the greater part of India aggregates of cultivators forming regular villages are the rule, the other cases are the exception.

§ 3. *Two types of Village distinguished.*

And then, there is not one type of village community, but two very distinct types, one of which, again, has marked and curious forms or varieties. And, without anticipating details, which must come later, I may say at once that these two types are distinct in origin.

In the one type the aggregates of cultivators have no claim as a joint-body to the whole estate, dividing it among themselves on their own principles; nor will they acknowledge themselves in any degree jointly liable for burdens imposed by the State. Each man owns his own holding, which he has inherited, or bought, or cleared from the original jungle. The waste surrounding the village is *used* for grazing and wood-cutting, but no one in the village claims it as his, to appropriate and cultivate without leave; still less do the whole group claim it jointly, to partition when they please.

In the other type—owing to causes which we shall presently investigate—a strong joint-body, probably descended (in many cases) from a single head, or single family, has pretensions to be of higher caste and superior title to the 'tenants' who live on the estate. The site on which the village habitations, the tank, the graveyard, and the cattle-stand are, is claimed by them; and the others live in and use it only by permission—perhaps on payment of small dues to the proprietary body. The same body claim jointly (whether or not they have separate enjoyment of portions) the entire area of the village[1], both the cultivated land and the waste. If this waste is kept as such, they alone will receive and distribute any profits from grazing, sale of grass or jungle fruits or fisheries; if it is rented to tenants, they will divide the rents; if it is partitioned and broken up for tillage, each sharer will get his due portion. There are other differences, but these suffice for our immediate purpose.

As a matter of fact, the first type of village is the one most closely connected with Hindu government and Hindu ideas. And the second type is found strongly developed among the Panjáb frontier tribes who were converted to Muhammadanism: it is also universal among Jat, Gujar, and other tribes in the Central Panjáb, as well

[1] There may be two or more such bodies, each claiming a certain known section of a village; but I take the case of a simple village as better expressing my point.

as among conquering Aryan tribes and descendants of chiefs and nobles in other parts.

So much then for there being one general type of village to be described, and for that type being due to Hindu influences. In making the latter remark, I wish, however, to qualify it by adding that it is perfectly true that the second type of village *does* arise largely from those deep-seated archaic notions of *family* property and of the joint and equal inheritance of the members which have formed the basis of the later Hindu *law*, as much as they do that of the *custom* which governs the Panjáb tribes.

§ 4. *Sources of information regarding Villages.*

Let us now proceed to examine our sources of information as to the two types of village I have indicated, and see how such villages grew up and how they have been modified.

§ 5. *Causes of Village grouping.*

It has been said that the idea of aggregating men in *village* groups for the purposes of agriculture is a matter of natural instinct; so it is to a great extent[1]. Not only is it true that 'union is strength,' but the situation of villages in most parts of India was such as specially to call for some kind of union. In the first place, the early villages would be situated in the midst of often dense jungle; and the depredations of deer and pig on the crops, and of the danger to human life from the larger beasts of the forest, are such as an English farmer could hardly realize. Then, too, there were adventurous armies on the move, hill-tribesmen and local robbers to be dreaded, to say nothing of the need of presenting an united front against forces employed by iniquitous revenue-farmers in the later days of misrule.

[1] And we shall hereafter find evidence from several provinces that many villages owe their existence to more or less ancient or recent associations of enterprising settlers—perfectly voluntary and quite unconnected with any tribal notions or dynastic changes.

Nor were neighbouring villages always friendly to one another. It would often happen that a group of settlements on one side of a boundary would be at feud with those on the other, and union for defence became a normal condition on either side.

It is not wonderful, therefore, that 'village grouping' should have been adopted, where local circumstances suited it, by all races in India.

And then there was another influence which tended to fix the institution, as well as to determine the size and composition of the groups. Some land-owning castes in parts of India still retain a distinct *tribal* organization. What happened in this respect with the earlier races we only know partially. But we have the example of tribes who settled in parts of the Panjáb at a comparatively late date —long after the Aryans—and we find them not only forming villages, the holders of which have a strong joint-claim to the whole, but forming them on the plainly evident basis of tribal divisions and sub-divisions. First, we find an allotment of certain larger areas to whole tribes or clans, and then sub-divisions forming villages, the elders carrying out the scheme down to making a specific allotment for their several family holdings. *Some* villages are then clearly due to *tribal* instincts. And even among the Aryan tribes who had Rájás and chiefs over them, and among whom we cannot trace a detailed tribal allotment, we shall occasionally find certain clans or branches among whom no family was sufficiently predominant to furnish a Rájá; and among these we shall find villages divided up and allotted from the first on a tribal and family basis.

In fact, we can follow out three conditions of the existence of villages. The *first* is where, as with Dravidian and Aryan tribes, there is a central government and a series of territorial officers, but where the villages are aggregates of cultivators, and no principle of allotting the original village areas—if there ever was any—is now traceable, and where the village grouping appears to depend partly on the natural necessities of the population, partly on the

State jurisdiction of headmen. The *second* is where we can trace the village back to the settlement of a clan or tribe, and have evidence of the formation of village groups and the allotment of lands on tribal principles from the first. The *third* is where a landlord-body, having acquired predominance in an existing village, or having founded a new one themselves, and being now represented by a more numerous body of descendants, the existing grouping and distribution of holdings is the result of joint-inheritance and partition.

§ 6. *Villages how far 'joint.'—The stages of property.*

It may not unnaturally be asked why are the two distinct types of village spoken of not always recognized and kept apart by Revenue writers? I think it is due to the fact that they have been too often regarded as if one was only some kind of modification of the other. Even if it were so, it would not justify us in overlooking the distinction that certainly now exists; but the existence of such an opinion gives me an opportunity of introducing some remarks that ought to be made at an early stage, regarding ideas of 'joint property' and 'communities,' as these terms are applied to villages.

It is commonly said that property in land passes through three stages. First, it is held by the tribe or clan, and is regarded as the common property of the whole body. Holdings indeed are allotted or recognized, because without that agricultural labour could not be performed; but periodically the holdings are exchanged or redistributed, showing (it is said) that no one regards any particular field as his private property. The next stage is reached when redistribution is abandoned, because each several holding—that of the man with his sons, has become improved, and each family desires to retain permanently its own. But still the *paterfamilias* is not the individual owner: he cannot sell or will away the holding. He must share it equally with his sons if he makes a partition, and on his death it will go to all sons equally, or to all other heirs if there are no surviving sons.

That is said to be the stage when property vests in the *family*. This stage evidently subsists to a great extent in most parts of India. The Hindu law and local custom (as I have mentioned) recognize a joint succession, and provide some other rules which I need not here allude to, for keeping the property in one family.

But gradually the desire to profit by one's own skill and labour *individualizes* property. A number of things conduce to this end. Family quarrels are an unfortunate but very common factor. Differences of taste and agricultural capability also have their sphere. Coined money comes into use, and men begin to buy and sell land. Finally, families break up, and *individual ownership*, such as we see it in Europe, with or without the last restraints and survivals of the preceding stage, is the third or final condition.

These stages must certainly be borne in mind in any attempt to account for Indian villages. At the same time it must be clearly stated that we have no actual evidence of the first stage—evidence, I mean, showing that *universally* at one time, there was no such thing as individual or even a family right, but that the whole *tribe* or *clan* regarded the land as really 'common' in a communistic or socialist sense.

It is true that we have ample evidence of a primal custom of re-distributing the holdings in particular tribes; but it always followed a distinct allotment of lands, and an allotment which showed that there was a desire to equalize the holdings, and not give all the best to some and the inferior to others. It is, therefore, open to us to interpret the distribution, not so much as indicating a communistic idea of property as indicating a desire to equalize. For after all devices (and very inconvenient devices we shall find them to have been) adopted by the tribesmen for classifying lands, and giving families a bit of this and a bit of that, instead of one compact lot in one place, still inequality was not completely remedied, and therefore a periodic interchange may have been intended rather to give each his turn at the best and inferior holdings [1].

If we look to the earliest villages found under the Aryans, or before that, we have no evidence (other than that of the re-distribution, which I do not regard as conclusive) of a tribal stage; and even among the later Panjáb tribes, where tribal occupation and allotment are clearly discernible, any previous stage of the *joint* holding by the tribe collectively, hardly seems deducible from the known facts.

But we certainly must recognize that, as regards most villages, property is still in the 'family' stage. The principle of joint succession when the head of the family deceases, is clearly an indication of 'family' property, and so are the devices of excluding females (who marry, and so would take the land into another family), the restrictions on alienation by sonless male proprietors, and the right of pre-emption by which strangers can be kept out.

And it may be argued that this idea of the family owning is necessarily the sequel of an earlier idea of a common holding by the tribe or clan. Those who think so point to certain large areas in the Panjáb, now forming separate villages, which were once believed to have formed units of tribal holdings divided into shares [2]. I do not then wish to deny the *possibility* of some early stage of joint tribal holding, but to point out that it is a theory, and not a matter that can be asserted with any approach to certainty.

[1] We have no *evidence* of any such stage as mentioned by M. de Laveleye, pp. 4, 5. 17): 'Peu a peu une partie de la terre est momentanément mise en culture, et la régime agricole s'établit : mais la territoire que le clan ou la tribu occupe demeure sa propriété indivise. La terre arable, le pâturage et le forêt sont exploités en commun. Plus tard, la terre cultivée est divisée en lots, répartis entre les familles par voie du sort : l'usage temporaire est seul attribué ainsi à l'individu. Le fonds continue a rester la propriété collective du clan à qu'il fait retour de temps en temps, afin qu'on puisse procéder à un nouveau partage,' &c. Still less have we any trace of Virgil's 'Golden Age' (Georg. i. 125):

'Ante Jovem nulli subigebant arva coloni ;
Nec signare quidem aut partiri limite campum
Fas erat: in medio quaerebant ; ipsaque tellus
Omnia liberius, nullo poscente, ferebat.'

[2] See some curious instances given in Tupper's *Customary Law* (Panjáb Government, 5 vols.) regarding the Jihlam district.

§ 7. *Meaning of the term 'Community.'*

And this leads me to remark that though we talk about 'village communities,' we ought not to give that term any meaning of such a kind as to indicate anything like a communistic or socialistic right or interest. As regards a large proportion of villages there is no evidence whatever of their being held actually in common in that sense. Villages held for a time in common are always so held by the joint descendants of a conqueror or chief who in some way acquired the estate. The descendants are jealously disposed to insist on equal privileges and position, and so remain joint as long as circumstances render it possible. I have come across a few instances where a tribe (in the Panjáb) has from the first held a part of the land in common, but there it is due to local circumstances, and the produce is always divided out according to certain shares. The term 'community' might, if not explained, be apt to mislead. It can be correctly used only with reference to the fact that in many villages families live together under a system which makes them joint owners; while in others the people merely live under similar conditions and under a sense of tribal or caste connection, and with a common system of local government. It cannot be used as suggesting any idea of having the land or anything else 'in common.'

§ 8. *Kinds of right actually found to be asserted.*

But whatever the truth may be in this matter, we are introduced at a very early stage to the existence of an idea of an individual (or rather family) right to the land *in favour of the person who cleared and reclaimed it from the jungle.* In such a situation as the forest-clad, or again the very dry, portions of India, it is hardly surprising that this feeling should have arisen at a very early stage and rapidly gained ground. There are of course places where the soil is soft and the labour of preparing it for its first ploughing is comparatively light. But in large areas the most severe and protracted labour has to be undergone in getting the dense forest and jungle cleared, and in digging out masses of stumps and roots, with no aid beyond manual labour, and very rude if not inefficient tools. And this labour has to be unremittingly continued or the jungle again encroaches. In other parts, agriculture is impossible without embanking and terracing fields on the hill side, and making water courses to divert the streams of hill torrents. In all these cases the man (or family) whose hands and funds have effected the change, is sure, at an early stage, to regard himself, and be regarded by others, as peculiarly entitled. In the concluding section on property we shall find that at least 500 years B.C. the *Institutes of Manu* had acknowledged this principle, and it is highly improbable that it was then a new idea inscribed in the text for the first time.

I have said that right resides in the *family*,—though the sentiment is slowly disappearing. The principle just spoken of does not militate against this. For it is the man and his relations together, who 'cleared' the fields; and to this day in the most purely *raiyatwárí* villages,—where nothing but the most ancient several holding is traceable, the sons or other heirs succeed jointly to the holding. And as for the cases where (as in the Panjáb) we see the tribes allotting land to families who hold separately, but in village groups; or where (as in villages acquired in landlord right by families) there is at first a joint holding by all the members collectively, we are obviously in the 'family' stage.

But while we see especially the influence of the 'right of the first clearer' in one type of village where the individual or family holdings are all separate, and never were (as far as we know) anything else; we also see an idea of right by *conquest* which is not so called, but is distinguished as the 'birthright' or claim by inheritance. It prevails in villages of the second type where, between the ruling power and the cultivating families, there is a *landlord*, or a family claiming superior rights as owners. How these landlords came to have such rights we shall presently see.

Here the object of these remarks is to disabuse the reader's mind of the idea that in some way a 'joint' village is necessarily the earliest or original type, and that it is a process of decay and flux of time, whereby joint rights are forgotten, and the other type (which I have suggested to be really the oldest) arises. That cases of decay, by which one form passes into the other, have occurred, I do not doubt; but it is not the general rule. We shall also see the joint villages partitioned, splitting up, and becoming individual properties, but that again is quite a different and easily recognizable condition.

§ 9. *Successive immigrations into India.*

It is well known that India has been the scene of a series of tribal immigrations—a phenomenon which stretches back into the remote past. Antiquarians will long continue to explore such authorities as the *Bráhmanas* for evidence as to the successive races,—some coming from the north, others by sea from the west. But in a work of this kind, I must avoid the path of antiquarian speculation, however tempting, and leave the real detail to others. For our present purpose we shall find it sufficient to take note of three great races,—those whose effect on the land-tenures is evident. One of the early races, which still survives, is the Kolarian (or, as some write it, Kolharian). Tribes belonging to this race are still to be found in South-western Bengal, and in Central India along the Vindhyan mountains. Their origin I cannot discuss, but they were followed by Dravidian tribes, whose rule they often accepted. The Kol races are still represented by the Ho and Munda tribes in the Chutiyá Nágpur division of Bengal, by some primitive tribes called Korwá in the same country, and by the Hors of Singhbhúm. The Bhúmij and the Santál people, who settled in what are known as the 'Santál Parganas' of Bengal, belong to the same race. Along the Vindhyan hills these races are traced in the Kols of Gujarát, the Bhíls of Málwa, the Kuárs of Ellichpur (in Berár), and the Kúrkú tribe of Hushangábád in the Northern-Central Provinces. To the present day they represent various stages of tribal progress.

The Kolarian races hardly interest us from the tenure-point of view so much as the Dravidians—except in this respect that, while some of these tribes mixed with the Dravidians and submitted to their government, others remained distinct, and still remain, to show us all gradations of tribal progress. Some are still nomadic, living only in the forest by hunting and collecting forest produce, and if they practise cultivation, it is by that method of *shifting* or temporary cultivation which is common in many parts of India.

§ 10. *Shifting Cultivation in the Hill Forests.*

As this shifting cultivation marks the first stage in progress from the pastoral and hunting stage, I may briefly describe the method adopted. The tribes who practise it, commence by selecting a suitable site on not too steep a slope, and cutting down all the smaller tree and shrub vegetation, which is heaped on the ground to dry during the hot season. The larger trees are killed by ringing; the rest is burned. As soon as the rains fall, the ashes mixed with seed—usually hill-rice, pulses, and (in places) cotton—are dibbled into the ground. One crop is taken, perhaps followed by a second, on the same place, and then the tribe moves to a new locality. They return to the first only after a period sufficient for the vegetation to grow up again. If space is ample and the tribes not numerous, it may be twenty, thirty, or forty years before the same place is cut again. But where the population is denser, and space limited, the rotation is reduced to ten or even seven years, and less.

In Burma we shall see an instance of this form of cultivation becoming organized, and evidently on the way to change into settled land-holding[1].

[1] Shifting cultivation is practised largely in Assam and Eastern Bengal under the name of 'júm' (and many other tribal names). It is

§ 11. *The Kol Institutions.*

The Kol tribes do not appear to have had any central government. Their village settlements—when they were of a permanent character—were united in tribal areas, as were those of the Dravidians, and known as 'parhá' in that part of India where they still survive. A chief or 'mánkí' presided over the parhá. In each village, a hereditary headman called 'mundá' was acknowledged. The final reference was to the *mánkí*, or to the mánkís in council united with the *mundás* and chief land-holders. This resembles the Dravidian form, so clearly traceable in South India, where the village or other family groups were aggregated into unions called 'nád' or 'nádu,' with some kind of chief, acting alone as regards the nád, or in council with the other chiefs in affairs affecting the whole country. Nothing under this system indicates that the village land-holder claimed any other right than to hold his own clearing. The mundá, Mr. Hewitt informs us, disposed of lapsed or abandoned holdings; and probably no theory as to general right in unoccupied land existed, except possibly that it belonged to the 'parhá'—representing the original territory allotted to a tribal section. In time each village expanded by new cultivation; hamlets, offshoots of existing villages, spreading into the waste.

No regular system of revenue can be traced, but the mundá and the mánkí held lands in their respective villages, and gifts of grain—the early forerunner of the regular grain share—were received.

§ 12. *The Dravidian Races.*

These tribes are said to have come from the west, and undoubtedly spread over a great part of India. They

a great feature in the forests of Burma where forest officers have carefully to deal with the custom, and arrange grounds for its practice. In Burma it is called 'toungyâ' (and the tangled jungle that springs up where a cutting has taken place is 'punzô'). In South India it is Kumri or Kumerí (Canarese) or pôdû in Telugu. In the Central Provinces it is 'dahyá' or 'bewar.' It was formerly known in the Simla hills.

established great kingdoms in South and Central India, and it is difficult to say how far their influence extended. It appears, for instance, that the Tákshakas, a race which occupied the northern-central regions of the Panjáb, and were snake worshippers, were Dravidians. The Central Provinces and Berár were peopled by Gonds or Khonds, who were Dravidians—and the Central Provinces 'Zamíndárí estates' are the surviving traces of the chiefships held by Gond nobles. These people left more than others a strong mark, because they had a central government—a king whose territories were in the centre, and chiefs holding the outer circle of estates—like the Aryans. It is fairly certain that the Dravidians were partly conquered and partly peaceably mingled with the Aryan races who came afterwards. They had the habit of educating their children; hence Brahmans of the literary Aryan stock were welcomed, and thus it was that while the Sanskrit language adopted those peculiar letters, which are found in none of the Europaeo-Aryan tongues, in time the Dravidian princes took Brahman counsellors, adopted Hinduism, and often took Hindu names and called themselves Rájputs, with fanciful genealogies derived from the heroes of the *Mahábhárata* [1]. Dravidian tenures and institutions still survive in Chutiyá Nágpur side by side with the Kolarian. The Uráoṇs, who conquered and gave their name to Orissa, were also Dravidians.

Some interesting details will be found in the chapters in the Bengal section devoted to Orissa and Chutiyá Nágpur [2].

As already stated, the Dravidians had a central government of a king or Rájá—the original title has perished—and chiefs. They occupied (as far as the Kol countries are concerned) lands already cultivated. What is interesting

[1] The Dravidians are also represented by the Bhárs who had important kingdoms in Oudh, and represent the 'Bhárata' tribes of the *Bráhmanas*. It is curious also to note the Burman institutions which show a Dravidian origin. Dravidian institutions have also been observed in Sumatra.

[2] The vernacular terms given in the text in connection with these institutions are those which now obtain in the South-west of Bengal, where the institutions are still most clearly in evidence. Similar institutions survive elsewhere, and of course the names are different.

about them, besides the system of Rájás and chiefs, which is thus a pre-Aryan organization, is, that at first the chiefs raised their principal revenue by holding *special lands* in each village throughout the country; the whole produce being taken by the ruler. The villages were divided into lots called 'Khúnt.' One of these was the 'majhas' land or royal farm spoken of; another went to the headman, and another to the 'páhan' or priest; this being subdivided into shares for the worship of the great goddess, the *district* god, and the *village* deity respectively. After a time the kings, not feeling satisfied with the 'majhas' produce, *took a grain-share also*, from all lands except the priest's, and the headman's; and then it was that some further changes took place. The king first introduced a State headman or accountant called 'Mahto,' who speedily reduced to a shadow the position of the old 'Mundá' or natural headman. Of course the 'Mahto' got his allotment of land: and the lands held by the 'bhúíṇhár' families —those of the original settlers who furnished the headman and other chief men including the *Mahto*, were exempt from revenue. In this stage, the king also, to provide for the cultivation of the royal farm or 'majhhas' land, made an allotment (beṭkhéta) to certain cultivators, which was exempt from revenue, on condition that they should work the 'majhhas' lands. Then it was that, excepting the lands of the bhúíṇhár officials and the 'beṭkhéta,' all other land paid a share to the king or chief, and so was called 'Rájhas' land.

§ 13. *How far the Aryans copied the Dravidian System.*

It is certainly a remarkable fact, that while we know the Aryan races to have been originally a pastoral race, but including a strong military caste, the institution of the Rájá and his chiefs forming a sort of feudal government, as well as taking a grain-share by way of revenue, were apparently in existence before the Aryans came.

This fact has led Mr. J. F. Hewitt to study the whole question. This author has had exceptional facilities for examining the evidence on the spot, having long resided in the Central Provinces, and also been Commissioner of the Chutiyá Nágpur division of Bengal [1].

Seeing the undoubted influence that the Dravidian and Aryan races had on one another, and that *something* must have brought about the change in the Aryans from a conquering and pastoral people to a settled ruling race, with an orderly government and village cultivation and a regular hierarchy of officials over the land; it is at least a probable explanation to suggest that they simply copied the Dravidian institutions which they found ready to hand. On the other side, it may be urged that the plan of forming villages is a natural one, and that taking a grain-share is also natural. We see it among the Arabians. (The early Muhammadan plan was that of the tithe, or *'ashr*, paid by the faithful, and the 'khiráj,' or tribute taken from the conquered, and both probably in kind.) [2] But I must leave the question an open one. At any rate, we have a very perfect coincidence, amply justifying a prominent notice in this place. We must admit that, whether or no the Aryans could have had the 'grain-share' idea of revenue by nature, they certainly found it practised when they came.

I must also add that the Dravidian institution of the 'Majhhas' lands explains the prevalence of 'Royal' lands or farms in Burma, and in many parts of India, where, for instance in Coorg, we also find it, the land being worked by slaves. It seems to have been at one time adopted in Malabár, and perhaps affords one (alternative) explanation

[1] See on the subject of the tribes, Cunningham, *Ancient Geography* (Trübner, 1871) pp. 505-7. and Mr. Hewitt's paper in the *Journal of the Society of Arts for May* 6, 1887 (vol. xxxv. p. 613) and subsequent papers in the *Journal of the Royal Asiatic Society*, April 1890.

[2] And so in the remote times of the Old Testament. The instance of the one-fifth produce taken by the Pharaohs is familiar. Having acquired the land in exchange for food during the protracted famine, the ruler could not of course dispense with the original cultivators; so he left them in possession, stipulating for an annual fifth of the produce (Gen. xlvii. 20-24).

of the fact that the king did not take a general land-revenue. There is also no doubt, to my mind, that the 'waṭan,' or land held *ex officio* by village headmen—of which we shall presently hear—is a distinct Dravidian survival.

In short, when our books speak of the pre-Muhammadan government and land organization as 'ancient Hindu,' it is really a fusion of Aryan and Dravidian ideas which they refer to; a system the original elements of which can hardly be separated.

§ 14. *The Aryan Immigration.*

Notwithstanding the question of origin alluded to, I shall speak of the Aryan or Hindu system when referring to the revenue-system which preceded the Muhammadan conquest, chiefly because the Aryan and Dravidian races merged into one another, and also because the system is more perfectly preserved to us *through Aryan writings*, and is most clearly exhibited to us in the Aryan (Rájput) states, where it has found an enthusiastic historian in Colonel Tod, whose well-known *Rajásthán*—fortunately reprinted—is a mine of information on the subject.

So that the Aryan immigration is really, for our special purpose, the most important. To this we will now turn.

At some remote period one of the great waves of immigration brought a race from the North-west, which was originally pastoral; it is believed that their taking to settled agriculture was a later development, and may perhaps be traced to the time when they began to leave the hill kingdoms which they first occupied—where cultivation was limited to narrow valleys or terraced fields on the mountain-side—and descend to the wider spaces of the alluvial plains of Upper India. It is certain that such a change did take place. There can be no reasonable doubt that the Aryan tribesmen at first established themselves, with their chiefs, along the Himáláyan slopes—in Kashmír, in the hills now forming the Chamba State, and in the hills near Simla. In the Kángra district (Panjáb Himáláya) we find a distinct tradition that the present Rájput chiefs and landholders were only the successors of a much earlier race of Hindu settlers and conquerors, they themselves having occupied land in those hills at a period no earlier than the beginning of the Muhammadan conquest, when they fled from oppression. In Chamba and in Kashmír there are stone temples marking colonies of great antiquity. In the latter valley many ruins—like those celebrated ones of Mártand—are Buddhist; but in Chamba the old conical stone temples, with their finials resembling a grooved or fluted and flattened sphere (called by Fergusson the 'Amlika'), may go back to a really ancient establishment of the princes and people who afterwards conquered India, and fought in the battles which have been half mythically, half historically, described in the epic of the Mahábhárata. It is common to find in books, statements to the effect that after a long sojourn—perhaps of centuries—in the hills, they descended on to the 'plains of the Panjáb.' But the Aryans at first did not descend far, if at all, into the Panjáb plains[1] properly so called. The Rájput bodies now found there are all, by tradition, later settlements; princes, with their followers, or individual adventurers (whose descendants have since multiplied into clans) returned from kingdoms established further on into

[1] We have no old Hindu remains in the Panjáb plains; but the Greek writers tell us of a number of (Aryan) kingdoms to the north (near the hills), and beside them we have traces of tribes of non-Aryan origin, viz. the Malli, Cathœi and other tribes (of the Greek authors) to the south and east, and the Tákshakas or Takkás who had their capital at Takáshilá (Taxiles of the Greeks) not far from Ráwalpindi. Presumably Porus (Purushá) was an Aryan prince, but his conflict with Alexander was on the Jihlam river, and that is not far from the hills which the Rájputs certainly occupied. In time, too, Aryan families allied themselves with the Panjáb tribes and formed mixed races, but that was later. I do not venture here to discuss what was the origin or date of the Jat tribes and many others who form so large a portion of the Panjáb village population, but they certainly were much later than the Aryan immigration, and they were not Aryans in that sense. Dr. Muir (*Sanskrit Texts*, ii. 482, &c.) cites passages from the Mahábhárata which confirm this. The people 'who dwell between the five rivers which are associated with the Sindhu (Indus) as a sixth' are 'those impure *Bahikas* who are outcast from righteousness.' 'Let no Aryan dwell there even for two days. There dwell degraded Brahmans. . . . They have no Veda nor Vedic ceremony nor any sacrifice.'

Hindustán. But the site of the first Aryan settlement in the plains of India was to the north-west of Delhi, in the vicinity of the Jamná river, where they established kingdoms—of which Hastinapúra is a historic example—and thence they spread over the North-West Provinces and Oudh (properly Awadh—the ancient Ayodhyá). The advance could not stop here. Although the old writers attempted to describe 'the country where the antelope was found' as the proper abode of the Aryans—and this phrase points to the open plains about the Jamná and Ganges—the tribes or clans gradually advanced over Bengal and Bihár [1], and conquering portions of them, at any rate obtained a kingdom in Orissa [2]; others went to Central, and perhaps to Southern India; others conquered Guzarát in Northern Bombay, where their remains are found to the present day. The group of states now known as Rájputána and Káthiáwár, represent the last refuge of these clans at a time when the Muhammadan conquest began to disturb them. It is impossible to state in what order these conquests and settlements occurred, except that they were after the primal settlement in the region of the Jamná.

Pure Aryan settlements were, however, not the only feature of the immigration; it is certain that many alliances—both political and social—early took place [3]. Dravidian and Aryan rapidly mingled, both as to race, language, and forms of government; and the influence of their religious, social, and political system spread in other ways. Brahmans travelled to the remotest parts, and soon, as I have said, converted the Dravidian chiefs to Hindu ideas and made them 'Rájputs.' In reading accounts of the southern kingdoms—the Chéra, Chola, and Pándyan dynasties, in the Madras territories, or the states on the west coast, now

[1] A distinct legend describes how the ancestor of the Videhas of Bihár set out bearing the sacred fire with him towards Bihár.

[2] As set forth by Stirling in the *Asiatic Researches*, an authority rendered more accessible to us in the graphic pages of Hunter's *Orissa*, 2 vols.

[3] Mr. Hewitt has endeavoured to trace many of these movements and alliances in his interesting papers on the *Early History of Northern India*, Journal R. A. S., vol. xx. July 1888, and vol. xxi. April 1889.

called Kánara and Malabár—it is impossible to feel certain whether we are to read through the records of Brahmanical authors, that the princes and chiefs were actually Rájput immigrants, or were (as is more probable) local Dravidian princes who had adopted the Hindu system. It is quite certain that the Gond kingdoms of Central India, and the Assam dynasty in the north-east, were 'Hinduized' in this way, and we shall see the same thing in south-west Bengal.

Then, again, in spite of caste prohibitions and a great strictness in marriage rules observed by the purest families, it is quite certain that the Aryans mixed freely with other tribes, their predecessors, and that tribes of half-blood multiplied rapidly; some of them, at least, would be Hindu and claim to be Rájput. Among the Jats of the Panjáb, for example, while some of the clans assert a separate tribal immigration from beyond what is now Afghánistán, others declare they are Rájputs who lost caste by adopting irregular marriage customs. There are castes in the North-west Himáláya who are known to be of this mixed origin, and very sturdy races they are. The Bihár people are probably a mixture of the antecedent 'Magadhás' and Aryans; and the important agricultural caste of Kurmís, or Kunbis, are said to be a mixed race from the Kaurava or Kuru clan. Tribes of this kind, and Rájputs of purer origin also, spread (as I have already remarked) over the Panjáb and other places, by what I may call a reflex movement—settling as individuals or groups, who returned upon their steps, after the original tribes had advanced to the country of the Jamná and beyond it. The once extensive settlement of 'Chíb' Rájputs in the Gujrat district of the Panjáb, may with tolerable certainty be ascribed to this origin[1].

[1] Many settlements now forming groups of Rájput villages, in the Panjáb were due to single adventurers, cadets and members of families who, dissatisfied with their position and prospects in Bikanír or Mewár, or wherever else they had settled in Hindustán returned, founded villages, and gradually multiplied into clans. The Rájput race is everywhere noted as extremely prolific.

§ 15. *Importance of the Hindu system.*

The land-system of the Aryans—whether really Dravidian or not—is the one that has come down to us in the greatest perfection. It survives to this day in Rájputána and in the Hindu states of the Himáláyan mountains. We can see its identity, at least in all main features, with the system of the Aryan tribes as it was in Manu's time. We have also evidence of what it was in the small Hindu states that once spread over Oudh; we trace it in Orissa; we can follow the same organization as it was adopted by the Maráthás and by the Sikhs. We can gather similar information also about the Hindu states in South India. Everywhere we have the same broad outlines of State and social organization in their relation to land-holding.

The Rájás of one place may regard those of other parts as having lost caste, and they may refuse intermarriage; they may regard themselves as the representatives of the pure stock, and other princes as nobodies; but all that has nothing to do with the fact that they all adopt, and have adopted from time immemorial, a system of organization and land-administration which is the same in all essentials.

What is more strange, the Muhammadan conquest did little directly to modify the old system of Hindu land-holding; though indirectly, as we shall see, it caused a new race of landlords to arise, who ignored and gradually caused the decay of, the special features of village organization. But it is not to the Muhammadan conquest, speaking of the country as a whole, that we owe any irrecoverable loss of evidence as to what the old forms of land-holding were.

§ 16. *The Hindu Land-system.*

Although in the chapter (which follows this) on the Land-Revenue Systems, I have fully described the method of State organization which marks the Hindu Ráj or kingdom, and all others which assimilated to it, I had better give a similar outline here, and the repetition will be forgiven. No doubt the different clans or sections of the Aryan tribe occupied defined territories which they conquered. There is everywhere evidence that the tendency was to form a number of comparatively small States or territories, and the Rájás, or head chiefs, and minor chiefs, called Thákur, Ráná, Bábú, &c., of each, divided the land amongst themselves. Sometimes particular clans had no Rájás, and they then made an equal division into villages and family estates. There was also a marked tendency for a number of these States to be united in a sort of confederacy under some greater emperor. Such was the case in the days of the great kings of Kanauj, and with the empire of Chandragupta and Asoka [1]. The Chinese pilgrim in the seventh century A.D., notes that he saw the State barge of the Mahárájá, or great king of Kanauj, being drawn along on some ceremonial occasion, by eighteen minor Rájás.

We are, however, only concerned with the individual States. The Rájá, as the chief power of the clan, received the largest and best group of lands [2] (usually in the centre of the country) as his royal demesne, and this was in after times called his 'Khálsa,' the Persian term of course indicating its later introduction. Smaller estates were assigned to the other tribal or clan chieftains (Thákur, Ráná, &c.), and they governed these estates without interference from the Rájá. They were only bound to feudal service, to appear at the Rájá's court from time to time, to receive investiture, and to pay a succession fee on the occasion of a succession by inheritance.

§ 17. *Manu's idea of land-holding.*

Unfortunately we have no information as to how individual families and members of the clans received holdings of

[1] Just as there was an overlord, a *Rex gentis Anglorum*, in the days of the heptarchy in England.

[2] Stirling, in his remarks on Orissa, (*Asiatic Researches*, vol. xv. p. 220) says: 'The domains reserved for the crown constituted, if not the largest, at least the most valuable and productive share of the whole territory.'

land. By the time which Manu's Institutes represent, the tribes had settled down, and agriculture was well established. Manu has nothing to tell us of how individual (family) holdings were apportioned. In the times represented by his Code, there were already separate villages, a headman over each village, and other officials over groups of villages, and over larger areas (deṣ), which probably still survive under the more familiar revenue name of 'pargana,' a term introduced at a later period by the Mughals. who simply followed the old Hindu organization of territory under new names.

It is not easy to explain why Manu tells us nothing of the original possession of cultivating holdings. He is, however, chiefly concerned with the Rájá of high or military caste and his learned Bráhman counsellors, and how these allotted the country for rule and overlordship. It is probable that the cultivators, who were called Vaisyas and Sudras by caste, were some of them, dependents or followers of particular chiefs, who settled on the territories of their respective heads; but they must also have represented the mixed race formed by the union of Hindus and Dravidians. They cultivated each man (or family) according to his ability. The higher military caste, when not of rank to hold estates as chiefs, or become headmen and district officers, either lived apart as soldiers, or fell into the humbler position of cultivators. In a great many instances the land occupied must have been waste and covered with jungle, and its reclamation may have been without any formal division other than the allotment (of ultimate holdings) under the direction of headmen, such as we see in so many parts in later times [1]. However this may be, all that Manu notices is the *right possessed by the 'first clearer' of the jungle.* He has the right, just as the hunter who first wounded the deer in the chase.

In the concluding section on property we shall give

[1] I refer to the process of village founding in the Central Provinces, described more fully in the chapter devoted to the tenures of those provinces.

some further details about Manu, and the state of things in his time. Here I am only concerned to note that it is doubtful if there is any suggestion of a landlord between the cultivators and the Rájá, and certainly nothing like a tribal or a joint ownership on the part of the body of cultivators or holders of land in the 'Grámam' or village[1]. Indeed, if there had *originally* been a joint ownership, I do not see how any such ownership could have grown up afterwards, not universally, but in particular cases, as it certainly did. The process of such growth is clearly traceable in the Hindu states of Oudh, and is well described in Mr. Bennett's excellent *Settlement Report on the Gonda District* (1878). It is also clearly traceable in Guzarát (Bombay Presidency), not to mention numerous other instances.

§ 18. *The Right to the Waste.*

The conclusion that the earliest villages consisted of aggregates of individual holders, with only the Rájá or chief over them as ruler not landlord, depends to some extent on what was held regarding the ownership of the *un*cultivated and unoccupied lands. Where there is a true joint village, as we shall presently see, we find some person (or body) claiming the entire area in a ring fence, uncultivated as well as cultivated. But in the ordinary village of Manu, the individual cultivators, each strongly attached to his own holding, make use of the adjacent waste for grazing and wood-cutting, but do not claim it as theirs. Certainly the Rájá or the chief exercised the right of making grants and locating settlers on this waste, and the village headman was applied to to authorize the breaking up of fresh waste. In some parts of Oudh, where there was valuable timber on

[1] It is quite certain that no phrase in Manu gives the slightest hint of any joint-body owning in common a certain group of territory in a ring-fence. Mr. Phillips in his first lecture, and M. de Laveleye, if I rightly understand his use of the term 'communauté' (*Propriété Primitive*, p. 66), would seem to imply the contrary. I have carefully re-examined Bühler's translation, and find nothing approaching an indication of anything beyond a group of cultivators (under a common headman) whose *individual* right depends on the *first clearing* of the jungle.

the land, we find the Rájá levying (as one of his State rights) an 'axe-tax' on the felling of timber, from all outsiders. This is, again, quite inconsistent with the idea of a communal group or body owning the waste. As a matter of practice, the rulers and the headmen of the villages (on their behalf) would allow any one to extend his tillage to the neighbouring waste, because the king's share of the produce at once became due, and so the total was augmented. Naturally, as long as waste was abundant and land had no great value, the authorities were only too glad to see cultivation extended and a title acquired by first clearing the land, and did not think of asking questions, or raising objection to its occupation.

§ 19. *Conclusion as to the oldest known form of Village.*

Thus we must conclude that the first (and, as far as we know, the oldest) form of village is where the cultivators —practically owners of their several family holdings— live under a common headman, with certain common officers and artisans who serve them, of which presently; and there is no landlord (class or individual) over the whole. The Rájás *now* (where they survive, as in the Himáláyan States) claim to be themselves landlords or owners of all the soil, and only recognize landholders as tenants, hereditary indeed, after holding for some generations; but then they are conquerors, or rather descended from conquerors or adventurers who gained the superior position, in one way or another, only a few centuries ago. No such claim on the part of a Rájá (as we shall presently see) is traceable in Manu. The Rájá had his own private lands; but as ruler of the whole country, his right is represented, not by a claim to general soil-ownership, but by the ruler's right to the revenue, taxes, cesses, and the power of making grants of the waste. For this reason I have called the first of the two types of village above spoken of the RAIYATWÁRÍ or NON-LANDLORD VILLAGE.

§ 20. *Modes in which the second type arises.*

Let us now enquire how the second class of village which I have stated to exist, comes to light or has grown up. It is distinguished by the fact, which the reader will have already surmised, that there is a landlord, or a body of landlords, claiming right over an entire village, intermediate between the Rájá or chief, and the humbler body of resident cultivators and dependants. It will be found to be (*a*) a growth among and over the villages of the first type; and (*b*) to be the form resulting from the original conquest and occupation of land—as far as we know—previously unoccupied, by certain tribes and leaders of colonists who settled in the Panjáb and elsewhere. I shall first enumerate the different origins of which we have distinct evidence, and then I shall offer explanatory remarks on each head *seriatim*.

Every one of these heads is derived from an observation of the recorded facts in Oudh, the North-West Provinces, Madras, Bombay, and the Panjáb.

The village of the second type arises:—

(*a*) Landlord rights have grown up *over* the village of the first type.

(1) Out of the dismemberment of the old Rájá's or chief's estate, and the division or partition of larger estates.

(2) Out of grants made by the Rájá to courtiers, favourites, minor members of the Royal family, &c.

(3) By the later growth and usurpation of Government Revenue officials.

(4) In quite recent times by the growth of Revenue farmers and purchasers, when the village has been sold under the first laws for the recovery of arrears of revenue.

(*b*) Landlord rights were (as far as we know) claimed from the first allotment or foundation.

(5) From the original establishment of special clans and families by conquest or occupation, and by the settlement of associated bands of village families and colonists in comparatively late times. (This applies specially to the Panjáb.)

§ 21. (1.) *The dismemberment of the Ráj.*

The Rájá's position was distinctly that of an overlord; the title and its appanages descended by primogeniture to one son only, so that as long as affairs went prosperously, there was no tendency to any alteration. But cases occurred, where, from family dissensions, or misfortune of war, or both, the Rájá's principality broke up; and then individual members of the family seized upon, or managed to retain in their hands, certain portions, and of that they became in process of time the practical owners—landlords in something of the modern sense.

Still more easily would this follow with the smaller chief's estates that were not, like the 'Ráj,' indivisible. Primogeniture is there the exception, not the rule; and I cannot state any definite rule as to the particular grade of rank at which there ceases to be a 'coronet' or a 'throne' right which only goes to the eldest. Among the chiefs who held estates in the ancient Oudh kingdoms, some families divided the estates, and some did not. When such an estate divided, it was almost certain to be the case that one member got one village, another two or three, and so on, till it came to pass that each family endeavoured to reproduce in the small area of one or two villages, the rights of the chief to the grain-share and other dues; and of course seized on the waste as an important means of increasing its wealth. In time these claims have *always developed into a landlord right* over the village. And when the original acquirer of such rights dies, and a body of joint heirs succeeds, *we soon find a number of co-sharers*, all equally entitled, claiming the whole estate, and (whether remaining joint or partitioning the fields) forming what is called a 'joint village-community.'

§ 22. (2.) *The Rájá's Grants.*

In Oudh we have instances where the Rájá has made *grants* to younger members of his family, or to courtiers, or where some family in the village of higher caste or more energy than the rest, has asked for and obtained the king's favour. The grant is called 'birt,' or, in the Sanskrit form, 'vṛittí.'

As long as the old Hindu kingdoms remained in their pristine state, such grants were only made for life to members of the king's family for their subsistence (jewan birt), or were grants of the waste—in revenue language jangal-taráshí—to clear the forest and found new villages. But when the Rájás came into conflict with the Muhammadan power, and were dispossessed or reduced to subordinate positions, we find cases where they raised money by selling 'birts.' This can be clearly traced in Oudh, where we have a full account of the ancient States within what is now the Gondá district[1]. The Utraulá State is one that exhibits examples of the sale of *birts*. In all these cases we find that the management of a village, the whole or a part of the Rájá's grain-share, and the manorial rights (tolls, ferries, local taxes) were made over to the grantee, the aggregate of such rights being called the 'zamíndárí,' and the *birt* being called a 'zamíndárí birt[2].'

Exactly the same thing happened when powerful families settled in the villages, raised their position, either with the Rájá's tacit consent, or merely by usurpation.

In Ajmer, among the Rájputs, we shall find certain holdings called 'bhúmiyá,' which were in fact landlord holdings, created apparently for smaller chiefs and others who had fallen out of the ruling rank; and thus holding the land more directly than the chief in his greater estate, they became in every sense the *landlord* over the cultivators.

In all these cases it might be asked what became of the

[1] Benett's *Settlement Report of Gondá*, 1878. Mr. Benett remarks that such grants were made chiefly when the Rájá was in a precarious position or out of possession altogether. The taking money was *sub rosá*, as beneath the dignity of the prince.

[2] The grant disposed of the Rájá's right over the waste, to tolls, fishing rights, &c., with the formula 'sa-jal' (water), 'sakát' (forest rights), 'sa-path' (right over roads, ferries, &c.) In Utraulá, besides the Rájá's grants, the Muhammadan power settled its own soldiers in some villages, granting them the Revenue as petty 'jágírdárs.' In time their families became landlords of the granted villages.

rights of the original villagers whose title by clearing the waste had already been acknowledged? But in Oriental affairs we must not look for definiteness and for consistency: doubtless in practice the old holders went on exactly as before, and had an hereditary right, which, though undefined, was practically respected by all decent grantees and landlords.

§ 23. *Illustration of the effect of dismemberment of a 'Ráj' or Chief's Estate.*

It is exceedingly important to remember how easily in the course of a few generations a single family multiplies—and the Rájput race is extraordinarily prolific—so that when we now see a whole group of villages in one locality having the same origin, we might almost suspect the settlement of a whole tribe; whereas really it is a case of multiplication of descendants and the separation of interests, consequent on the dismemberment of one single family estate. I cannot help alluding to the remarkable illustration of this afforded by the clan of Tilôk Chand Báis in the Rái Barelí district of Oudh[1]. This locality once formed the centre of an extensive kingdom or overlordship, established by Rájá Tilôk Chand. After his death—spite of the usual rule of primogeniture which applies to the *ruling* family as regards the chiefship, though not otherwise—the family broke up into a number of petty estates; i.e. the heads claimed the landlordship over numerous villages and founded other new ones. After some time *the family agreed to divide no further*. The result has been a large number of small (village) estates, and a certain number of larger estates of many villages—537 of the former and 60 of the latter—all, of course, of the landlord or joint type. Out of 1735 villages in the district, no less than 1719 are owned by descendants of this one Rájá's family—in fact, the 'Tilôk Chand Báis' have become a

[1] See *Gazetteer of Oudh*, s. v. Rái Barelí, vol. iii., and Mr. Benett's *Clans of Rái Barelí*.

numerous clan, forming a section of some great branch of the Rájput race.

Many other instances, perhaps not on quite such a large scale, could be quoted from Oudh, the North-West Provinces, and from the Panjáb.

§ 24. *Special features noticed in connection with these first heads.*

The discussion of the two first named among the modes of origin assignable to the present joint villages, leads me to invite attention to the fact that the claim to be landlord is due to the same feeling of superior caste, with its sentiment of graded rank and obedience to the ruler, as produced the organization of Rájá and subordinate chiefs[1]. It is also worth noticing that it is this kind of claim to the soil which is the subject of discussion when we find 'property in land' brought into question in books and reports. The humbler but strongly-felt right of cultivators not claiming 'birthright,' under the name of 'janmí' or 'mirási' right, or other similar title—in other words, the right of the 'first clearer' of the soil, is not so much asserted and talked about. But what I desire especially to press on the attention of the reader is how, as long as the superior caste is represented by a Rájá, or a chief holding a great estate *as ruler*, the original title of the soil-occupants is not, either in theory or practice, interfered with. The chief remains apart, receiving revenue, levying tolls and taxes, administering justice, with perhaps some vague claim as conqueror to be lord of all, but not claiming any actual concern with the occupied land in the villages. But no sooner is this domain

[1] As a matter of fact, in a majority of cases, landlord villages which derive their origin from some distant but still remembered ancestor who was of the Rájá's family, or was a royal grantee, or simply a man of superior energy and talent who pushed his way, will be found to be held, or once to have been held, on *ancestral shares* in preference to any other principle. They are usually high caste, or military caste. Of course some are due to strong and able families not originally of high caste, and these will derive their origin from Revenue farming arrangements, not being under the head we are at present confining our attention to.

dismembered owing to war or family feuds, and the members of the family retain or seize upon separate villages; no sooner is there a succession and a partition of the family estate, than the sense of lordship, focussed as it were on the more limited area, becomes fixed on the land itself, and developes into a claim to be owner of the actual acres of the village area.

But there is the same feeling of superiority that the Rájá or the chief had in his domain when it was in its original state and dignity, the same sense that the family, even though it now is a peasant family engaged in agriculture[1], is far above the plough-drivers and humbler occupants of the fields. In the case of the great estate, the feeling is expressed by holding the ruler's seat and taking the revenue; in the petty estate, it is expressed by the claim to be owner of everything within the boundaries of the village—which is now called the 'birthright' of the family or joint body.

This claim invariably results in the ultimate overshadowing of all preceding rights. In time these would have become ignored altogether, were it not for the existence of provinces in which those rights have never been overborne by any landlord class arising over them, and were it not for the policy of some of our revenue-systems which were devised when the Bengal landlord settlement had been found to be fraught with troubles, and when a great desire to protect, if not to push forward, the humbler classes, began to be felt.

The phenomenon described—the change from rulership to landlordship—of which instances so often occur in Oudh and the North-West Provinces, is by no means peculiar to them. Many cases are traceable in the Panjáb. To this cause also must be ascribed the direct origin of the landlord tenures of Malabár so often alluded to. The military caste, called Náyar in that district, at one time furnished the

[1] Necessity has forced Rájputs and others to take to agriculture; but some still compromise with their old dignity by confining themselves to certain parts of the process of tillage, avoiding, for example, the actual handling of *a plough*.

ruling chiefs and filled the higher official positions over the land. But the historical fortunes of the country were strange; the rulership was lost, but still the Náyars maintained their claims (supposed to be quite an exceptional instance of 'private property' in land!) as landlords of the soil, including both cultivated land and forest waste, and then began to talk about their 'janmam' or birthright, as is the usual course.

In Bombay the joint or landlord villages of the Guzarát country, which are well marked exceptions to the (there) usual *raiyatwárí* type of village, are clearly traced to the decay or dismemberment of former Rájput chiefships. The descendants have retained a village here and a village there, or even small groups of villages, and all the families are more or less connected by community of descent. The sharers in these villages will all regard themselves as superior to the cultivators, and will probably be addressed by some honorific title or appellation, and are sure to speak of their 'birthright' in the soil.

We may now proceed to consider the remainder of the five suggested origins of landlord or joint villages.

§ 25. (3.) *Usurpation of Land-officers.*

We come to the third head, the growth (and often the usurpation) of Government officials.

As long as the Muhammadan Government was strong, it maintained, under changed names, but without real alteration, the Aryan or Hindu system of territorial revenue administration. But it was under this Government, in the days of its decline, that the local officers were gradually left with less and less control, to manage the revenues; ultimately they (and also non-official persons who had influence or capital) were recognized as contractors for fixed sums of revenue over defined or undefined areas. This brought them into closer managing contact with the land, and enabled them to become landlords, a process which they effected by clearing fresh waste lands, buying up others, and ousting the old cultivators. Sometimes this process extended over large areas, and resulted in the formation of great estates (known as those of 'Zamíndárs' and 'Taluqdárs'); but often also the contractor became landlord of one or more villages, and his multiplied descendants, in the course of a generation or two, formed landlord bodies or 'village communities.'

§ 26. (4.) *Effects of Revenue-systems.*

The fourth head is really the same thing, only in a more modern form. It is exemplified chiefly in the North-West Provinces. There, at the beginning of the century, the real condition of the village bodies was unknown, the single-landlord idea was the only one familiar to the minds of the Collectors, and the revenue management of villages was leased to one man; he might be a leading land-owner or headman, or he might be a capitalist or speculator. In time this person, whose name might have been recorded by some device and without any just title, had opportunities of putting himself forward and getting a Settlement which confirmed his position. In those days, too, revenue sales were common; directly any arrear of revenue occurred, the estate was put up to auction, very often at the instance of a designing purchaser, who had contrived the default by unknown but nefarious means. The auction purchaser of course became landlord, and his descendants now form the regular proprietary community, either holding the village jointly, or having divided it up into shares[1].

[1] In Holt Mackenzie's great Minute on the North-West System, there are many allusions to this subject. He complains of the tendency there was to refer merely to records and see whose name was down as the nominal holder of a village, and consider him as the owner irrespective of facts (§ 414). And, speaking of the Revenue farmers, and other persons who claimed to be owners, some of several villages, others of single villages, he says (§ 406), 'Some of the moderate-sized estates were doubtless fairly created, by the successive purchase of individual villages from their original owners, or by the extension of cultivation by means of contract-cultivators, in districts having a large proportion of desert waste. But the origin of others was of a more questionable character. . . . He appears to have engaged in a constant struggle for the extension of his "zamíndárí" property; and as he generally had the hand of power and a preponderating in-

Under this head I ought to mention the Central Province villages. As they came under our rule they were certainly *raiyatwárí* villages, but it was, in pursuance of the North-West System, desired to treat them as if they were joint landlord villages, and make a village Settlement for one sum of revenue. This, as we shall learn more in detail in the chapters on the Central Provinces, could not be carried out; and the Government *determined to confer on the pátels or headmen, or the revenue-farmers* (called 'málguzár' under the Maráthá rule) *the proprietary title.* Since those days the original grantee-proprietor has often given place to a body of descendants who now form a landlord community. Only that in this case Government repented, if I may so say, of what had been done, and therefore early took steps to secure the rights of the original village cultivators, on whom, speaking generally, it conferred the privilege of an occupancy tenure with rents fixed by the Settlement Officer for the term of Settlement, leaving to the landlords the free control only of such lands as were in their own direct cultivation (called in revenue language their 'sír' lands). The Central Provinces thus exhibit the somewhat curious spectacle of villages held by artificially created landlord bodies, but with a 'tenantry' whose land is for the most part held quite independent of any contract with the landlords and beyond the reach of their interference.

§ 26. (5.) *Colonization and conquest.—Individual and tribal Settlements.*

The fifth head is one which is of great importance, as under it several varieties of origin may be collected.

The matter may be stated thus: the result of the Aryan immigration all over India was the fusion of the Aryan and Dravidian races, and the general establishment of

fluence with the "'Amil" (local Revenue officer), the various villages of the farm or *taluq* were too frequently converted by force or fraud into one *Zamindári* estate.'

smaller and larger rulerships or States, whose component units were village groups. These villages were owned, not by joint bodies, but by aggregates of separate families of landholders. In the course of time, as the rulerships broke up, and new conquering chiefs established themselves, the villages fell under the power of new families who soon formed joint-communities claiming the whole village—either single villages or groups. This did not take place over the whole country, but sporadically or occasionally, leaving large areas with the villages in their former condition. But in the Panjáb (more especially) we find that there were tracts of country where, at a later date, other tribes established themselves, and where small bodies of adventurers found a home: and *these*, from the first, formed joint bodies claiming the entire area of their settlements. This state of things is markedly illustrated by the Panjáb frontier districts.

All over the North-West frontier we shall find the districts occupied by comparatively small tribal and family groups who conquered or took possession of the land at a late date, not before the twelfth and as late as the fifteenth and sixteenth centuries, before which time the history of the land is a blank. It is known that in these cases the land was at once allotted into villages, sections, and family holdings, so that, as far as we know, the groups always regarded the *whole* area as theirs, and thus formed virtually a proprietary body over each village. It is possible indeed that their own theory may have been different; but as our revenue system, borrowed from the North-West Provinces, at once assumed these village bodies to be joint and entitled to all the land inside their local village area, and as the feelings of the people evidently fell in with this position, it is impossible to suggest any antecedent condition and any subsequent growth of a landlord class, or gradual development of landlord claims. Most of the tribes brought with them camp followers, dependants and inferiors of various sorts, who became tenants—however privileged in some cases—and there never was any doubt about the superiority and landlord spirit of the conquering tribesmen, whatever levelling effects later misrule may have had, and whatever equitable claims the other castes may have been able to urge. On the frontier this is extremely marked, and the evidence is clear and beyond dispute.

The same is hardly less true of the Central Panjáb, though the origin of the villages is often more remote and therefore more obscure. Indeed, for the Panjáb generally, I am unable to suggest that the joint or landlord village arose *over* an antecedent type in the way it did in the North-West Provinces and Oudh.

§ 27. *Panjáb Tribes.*

The Panjáb exhibits quite a peculiarity in this respect; we know that originally the Aryans did not occupy the plains; their kingdoms were only along the Himáláyan range. And where we now find 'Aryan' Rájputs, it is probable that they always represent later settlements, the result of what I may call a reflex immigration of single adventurers or small bodies. But it is also certain that the Gújars and Jats were tribes who entered the country independently, and established villages which, as I have said, were, owing to tribal sentiment, always landlord or joint villages. In Campbell's *Modern India* (p. 8) it is said 'we are not without a historical glimpse of the facts. We have very good and accurate accounts of Northern India as it was in Alexander's time, and we find that in addition to the Hindu kingdoms . . . he found settled or encamped in the Panjáb, great tribes of a purely republican constitution, far more warlike than any others which he encountered. The best account of this is to be found in Heeren, in the volume on the Persians (p. 310). Heeren represents their constitution as aristocratic or under the government of their optimates.' And when Alexander treated with 300 deputies of such tribes, the author goes on to say (what is doubtless true), that these were the 'pancháyats' or councils of the elders of the villages [1]. I cannot help concluding, then, that while in other parts of India joint villages arose in the various ways described, a number of joint villages in the Panjáb are due to the special customs of the particular tribes which—distinct from the Aryan race that overspread India—settled there. That is unquestionably the case with the later tribes in the districts on the North-West frontier, and it is probably the case with some of the Gújar and Jat tribes of earlier origin, and some of the less familiarly known castes also. The Jats and the Gújars I distinguish because they went beyond the Panjáb and formed settlements in Hindustán also, and are therefore better known [2]. The name 'Jat' becomes 'Ját' in Hindustán.

[1] The allusion is to *Historical Researches into the Politics, &c., of the principal nations of Antiquity*, by A. H. Heeren (translated from the German), vol. i. The Persians. Oxford: Talboys, 1833, p. 310. The author's account is very noteworthy. He distinctly shows that there were states under the Rájás in the North Panjáb—i. e. near the hills, where the Aryans (Rájputs) settled; and mentions that one of them, called Porus (perhaps this word is 'Purushá' and is only a title (confer. Dow's *Hindostan*, i. 24), was at enmity with the Takka or people of Taxila—who, as I remarked, were still earlier Dravidian settlers. There were also *kingdoms* along the Indus (which exactly corresponds to what we know of the early history of Sindh). 'When,' he says, 'Alexander crossed the Chináb (Acesines), he fell in with other nations not living under the rule of princes, but possessing a republican constitution. These Indian republics occurred in the country between the Acesines and Hyphasis (Chináb and Biás, i. e. Central Panjáb), or on the east of the province of Lahore.' He mentions the Cathœi, Adriaticae, and (in the South) the Malli and Oxydraceae of the Greek writers. Heeren's attempt to identify these tribes is less happy; for in his time nothing was known about the Panjáb tribes. No doubt many of the races—who really were our Jats, Gújars and other tribes—became afterwards Sikhs, but they cannot be identified with either Rájputs or Maráthás. It is true that among them, *some* clans, for whatever reason, never had Rájás, but lived under their elders in groups of equal right. And it was clans who did this that originated the form called 'bhaiáchára,' village, as distinct from the ancestral-share or 'pattidárí' villages. But this fact does not identify them.

[2] I cannot discuss the origin of Jats, but it is remarkable that Panjáb Jats are distinct from the Játs of other provinces, and in South-east Panjáb we have both Jat and Ját tribes physically unlike each other. I can only conjecture, following local tradition, that some were really Rájputs who lost caste by making mixed marriages, &c., others are a distinct race. A great number of the Panjáb tribes, Awáns, Khokhars, Aráíns, &c., may be mixed races, formed by the union of the original Takka and other tribes with Rájputs, or with later tribes colonizing from beyond the North-West frontier.

§ 28. *Colonies multiplied from individuals or small groups.*

But in any case a large number of joint villages are due to the multiplication of villages from single centres. There are numerous local traditions of scions of Rájput and other 'noble' families who, dissatisfied with their prospects at home (the parent stock had then found a home in Hindustán, Bikanír, &c.) turned on their steps and obtained land in the Panjáb, where doubtless it was abundant. Single adventurers or small parties thus established themselves, and spreading and multiplying founded village after village, over which of course the descendants are regarded as the landlord communities. Traditions to the effect are too numerous, coherent, and intrinsically probable, to be set aside. We may often distinguish villages of this class by their adhering to *ancestral fractional* shares in holding the land. Such shares show descent from a common ancestor, the colonizing founder or conquering chief.

There are no doubt a large number of villages where the co-sharers now hold on the basis of actual separate possession. Many of these are true landlord villages, only the accidents and the fortunes of the times have destroyed the ancestral shares. Others may have originally been of the *raiyatwárí* type. But if so, the example of numerous landlord or joint villages round them, and the fact that when our Revenue Settlement began, they were treated as joint and the waste adjoining made over to them,—either of these may have induced them to accept the lump assessment and the (nominal) joint responsibility without demur. We know this to have been the case with the Kángra district villages, and how far it may have been the case with others it is impossible to say. In fact it is now hopeless to argue what the original constitution may have been [1].

[1] I have spoken before of the failure of the attempt in Bombay and elsewhere to force the joint constitution on raiyatwárí villages; but it might always happen that, locally, owing to the force of example, or to the value of the joint-waste conferred when the village was settled by the Revenue officers, or from other causes, the joint con-

In the south-east Panjáb we shall also find villages, which have accepted the joint constitution, whose origin is clearly traceable to voluntary associations of different individuals and families, who applied to a local ruler for permission to settle, and thereon founded villages, only within the present century.

And the mention of this form of *co-operative* colonization leads me to speak of the survival of joint or landlord villages in Madras.

The Presidency of Madras affords another instance of the occurrence of landlord villages only in some places, or sporadically, as it were, among villages of the *raiyatwárí* type. In most cases it is a mere trace of such villages that now survives. The details will be given in the chapters devoted to Madras; but I may here give a brief outline of the events which led to the discovery of such traces, and notice how they illustrate the subject we are now considering.

When the failure of the first attempted Settlements in Madras caused an enquiry to be made (about 1814) as to the constitution of villages, with a view to determining what form of revenue-settlement could best be adopted, it was discovered that a number of villages existed, in which a class of landholders, generally known by the Perso-Arabic name[1] 'mirásdár'—holders of the 'mírás' or inheritance right—was found. A selection from the rather voluminous evidence on the subject has been reprinted in an official collection of papers issued in 1862. The conclusion to be drawn is, that the villages with a *mirásdár*, or landlord class, where they existed, were survivals of some high caste families who by conquest or grant had obtained the over-lordship. But in the neighbourhood of Chingleput the villages of this class were more continuous, and evidence was

stitution would be accepted without question. It is quite certain that in the Kángra district (a hill and partly submontane district) 'landlord' villages, or indeed villages of any kind, did not exist, and so in the dry tracts in the South Panjáb; yet the grant of the waste and the practical non-enforcement of any real joint revenue-liability, made the people accept the system without demur.

[1] The people had their own names; for instance, 'Káni-átchi' expresses *birthright* or inheritance.

forthcoming to show that they were due to the fact that there had been a great colonizing party sent out by one of the Dravidian kingdoms of Southern India; they had advanced into what was then an unpeopled forest country, and having cleared the land and established villages, the different leaders of the colonist groups became the landlords. In time the original founder or founders were succeeded by a numerous body of descendants who divided up the land into shares. This body, deriving their rights from a special emigration and colony planting, naturally regarded themselves as entitled to a superior kind of right; all others were their tenants, namely the low-caste cultivators and others who were either admitted at a later period, or represented the descendants of dependants and followers who were called in to aid at the original founding, which was a work of great labour requiring as many hands as possible. And I may here remark that at the present day we hear less of claims by 'conquest,' than of those derived from the 'founding' of the village, though in many cases the latter may be a euphemism for conquest or usurpation.

Especially in the Panjáb I have noticed the landlord class always claiming superiority as the descendants of the 'original founders' (bánián-gáṅw).

§ 29. *Conclusion regarding two types of Village.*

This brief sketch will now, I hope, have made it clear that we are to distinguish two distinct types of village: one is where the landholders are disconnected aggregates of families each claiming nothing but its own holding—the RAIYATWÁRÍ OR NON-LANDLORD TYPE; the other is where a class in the village, or it may be the entire body, claim to be a superior order, descendants of former rulers, or colonizing-founders, or conquerors, or grantees, or, later on, of revenue-farmers and auction purchasers, who claim jointly the entire estate; and this is the JOINT OR LANDLORD-VILLAGE type[1]. The former type prevails over the whole of

[1] In the first edition of this work I essayed to distinguish the two types as the 'non-united' and the 'united' type respectively. The

Madras, Bombay, and Central India. The Central Provinces villages were, and would still have been, of this type, but for the action of our own Government in conferring the proprietary right, so that these villages have now passed into the landlord class. On the other hand, the landlord or joint village now prevails in the North-West Provinces and Oudh, and in the Panjáb. Probably, in the North-West Provinces and Oudh this type was originally only occasional, as elsewhere; there must have been many groups of old cultivators who had never been interfered with, and whose system of holding land is, and always was, according to actual possession only. But the revenue-system, from the first, treated all villages alike, and whether it was the descendants of a superior family or a group of cultivators who had no joint-claims, all became, by the grant of the waste and the (nominal) joint and several responsibility for the land-revenue of the entire village, equally compacted into bodies, the joint-owners, in name, of the whole area. It is certainly also the case that in more than one locality the present joint-villages are the creation of our own system, circumstances permitting the change to be accepted or not practically felt.

§ 30. *Importance of the distinction as regards the Revenue system.*

The existence of two types of village is a fact of primary importance to the Revenue student, apart from its interest

terms are not, however, satisfactory; they do not indicate the fact that in one type there is a superior, landlord, class, and in the other there is not; while there may be a certain *union* in villages where no superior chief claims the whole. The people, though each claims only his own holding or field, may very well be 'united' in another sense, under a common headman and with a common staff of artisans. Sir George Campbell, in his essay in the *Cobden Club Papers*, has distinguished the types as 'aristocratic' and 'democratic.' This has some advantages: the landlord class have certainly a strong feeling of superiority. But there are many villages where the truly landlord class acknowledge no chiefs, and, as among themselves, are 'democratic,' but this does not put them on an equality with the non-proprietary residents and cultivators. On the whole, I think that the terms, landlord or joint village for the one type, and non-landlord or *raiyatwári* for the other type, are, though not neat or compact terms, still expressive of the main difference.

as a matter of history and of the development of land-tenures. Wherever the villages consist of the loose aggregates of separate cultivators, it has been found advisable to adopt what we shall presently describe as the 'Raiyatwárí' method of Revenue management, under which each field or holding is separately assessed, and no holder is responsible for anything else but his own revenue, nor has he any common right in an allotted area of waste [1]. He is, of course, provided with certain privileges of grazing and wood-cutting, but the waste or unoccupied lands are at the disposal of Government, and given to whoever first applies offering to pay the assessment, when they are not reserved for any other special purpose. Where there are landlord villages, the 'North-Western' or 'Village' system of Settlement is followed; the waste is given over to the village; the entire estate so made up (waste and arable together) is assessed to one sum of revenue, for which the landlord, or landlord body, are jointly and severally liable, and which (in case of several co-sharers) they apportion among themselves to pay according to their customary method of sharing—i.e. according to the constitution of the body.

§ 31. *Question as to whether one type is not a decayed form of the other.*

Seeing then that *joint* villages exist all over the Panjáb, and largely in other parts, while in Central and Southern

[1] The adoption of this system was not accomplished without some struggle. The attempt was made in Madras and Bombay to form village settlements with the joint responsibility for a lump sum. But the plan failed, because nature and the social system were against it. Conversely, where circumstances are favourable, the joint system alone succeeds, and is accepted even where the villages are really *raiyatwári*. Where there is a strong landlord body, attempts to individualize property and fix the shares of each otherwise than according to local custom fail. There were joint villages in the once Hindu island of Java. When this island was under British rule (before its cession to the Dutch), M. de Laveleye mentions that the Governor (Sir Stamford Raffles, 1811–1816) attempted to individualize holdings by making separate assessments: but the people immediately clubbed the sums together and redistributed the total, according to their own notions of responsibility and family custom.

India they appear only sporadically among the *raiyatwárí* villages, it is not surprising that the question should have been raised—May it not have been the case that all villages were once joint, and that those which are now not so represent a decayed form of the other? I have already admitted that there are certainly cases where a joint village has decayed. For example, the ruler of the time imposes a very heavy revenue burden on a village: this necessitates an effort on the part of the co-sharers, and results in the richer ones taking more than their ancestral family share of the payment, and demanding to hold more land to make up. Thus the proper shares are upset; then the co-sharers fall into poverty, sales take place, strangers are introduced, and in the end each holder regards himself as a separate unit, and the memory of the original status is lost. Or, what is often the case, the leading families have fallen into decay, the more energetic but inferior caste cultivators come to the front, bear the revenue burden, and in the end cannot be ousted with anything like justice from at any rate the several but full proprietorship of their lands. But all experience shows that such is the tenacity with which the superior classes remember their rights, that the loss is rarely complete; and it is hardly possible to believe that the whole districts where nothing but *raiyatwárí* villages now exist, could have owed their present state to a wholesale loss of rights. Nor is it easy to see how in such a case *some* villages exhibit traces of 'mirási' claims and others not.

§ 32. *Illustrations of decay of Landlord claims.*

I should like here to allude more specially to the cases where landlord claims existed and were lost, to show at any rate that I do not leave them out of account. It is certainly the case that in Madras the 'mirási' claims had often become very faint, but it is equally certain that the 'mirási' or landlord right was not a uniform feature of all villages.

There is an interesting paper on tenures in the Bombay Dakhan, by Col. Sykes[1], in which it is clearly shown that, after the overthrow of the great kingdoms which had adopted the Buddhist faith, and to which the well-known cave temples of Alúra (Ellora) and Karlí are due, the races, which afterwards rose to power as the Maráthás, conquered the country. And Col. Sykes finds many traces of their allotting the land on landlord-shares. The shares of families were called by the now forgotten Hindi term 'thal' (perhaps the same as the *túla* or *tola*). But fortune had not favoured them; and most of the holdings, at the time when Col. Sykes wrote were found in a decayed state, described as 'gat-kul,' i.e. the 'family' (*kula*) is 'lost' (*gata*). Where the landlord families had survived, the Muhammadans called them 'mirásdárs,' and there were also successors who had purchased the 'mirás' right. But it was evident that these cases represented estates appropriated here and there, by conquering families; and very likely were the result of the break-up of larger overlord estates of early Maráthá rájás or chiefs. This case does not lead to the conclusion that the landlord type was once universal and that the raiyatwárí type is merely, as a general rule, the decay of it.

In Bengal again, *all* village rights have been generally obliterated. This is due to the arrangements made in the decline of the Mughal rule for the management of the State Revenues. This we shall describe presently. Here I am only concerned to remark that the destructive influence did not change one kind of village into another but destroyed all alike.

§ 33. *Résumé of the position.*

In short, when we consider the evidence we have that the earlier races, and the lower castes, among the Aryans, all

[1] Published in 1835, *Journal of the Royal Asiatic Society*, vol. ii. p. 206. The holder of the 'thal' was called 'thalwái,' and the ancient lists of shares, which survived, were 'thal-jára.'

held land separately, by right of first clearance[1], and that we can in so many cases trace distinctly the growth of landlord rights in villages *over* an older race of cultivators who always had certain tangible rights in the soil; when we can prove that landlord villages (as we see them) are due (in the Panjáb) to special movements of colonizing bodies, who occupied virgin soil independently; and in the North-West Provinces and Oudh, to the dismemberment of kingdoms and ruling families, and also largely to later acquisitions of title by revenue-farmers and purchasers; we must come to the conclusion that the two types of village are due to original independent causes; and though in individual cases, a joint village may decay into a *raiyatwárí*, or a village of the latter type may be formed, by revenue administrative measures, into a joint village, such a transformation is local and occasional: it is not the general and everywhere operative cause of there being two types of village.

§ 34. *Differences and common features of the two types of Village.—The Village artisans.*

Let us now glance at the characteristic differences between the 'raiyatwárí' and the 'landlord' village.

Certain features, however, both have in common. In both there is an area of cultivated land and an area (very often) for grazing and wood-cutting[2], though the title, and the method of using that, are of course markedly different. In both there will probably (but not always) be a central residence site, and surrounding it, an open space for a

[1] And be it always remembered, the leading members of the higher castes would not themselves touch a plough. Hence they who furnished the landlord class were always rulers, military chiefs, or state officials in some grade. Humbler members of high caste, whom necessity compelled to take the plough and spade, fell to the lower level, and contented themselves with the same sort of tenure as the humbler cultivating classes.

[2] It is most unfortunate that in these days, when such an area has been given over absolutely to the (landlord) village they have been tempted to break it up for cultivation, and now are hard pressed for fuel and grazing, unless there are Government forests or fuel reserves and grazing grounds in which they can find a supply.

pond, grove, cattle-stand, &c. &c. In both there will be the arable fields with their boundary marks, and their little subdivisions of earth ridges made for retaining the rain or other irrigation-water. Under both forms, the people require the aid of certain functionaries, artisans and traders. They need a village messenger and night-watch, as well as some one to guard the crops: if it is an irrigated village probably some one will be required to distribute the water, to stop this channel and open that, when, according to the village custom of sharing the water, the different parties have had their due share. A potter will be required to furnish the simple household utensils or to make waterpots where the Persian wheel is used in wells. A seller of brass or copper pots will also be found in larger villages. A cobbler will make the village shoes and the plough harness or gear. A carpenter will fashion the agricultural implements and help in the housebuilding. A money broker will be needed, and some one to sell tobacco, drugs, salt, flour, spices, oil and other necessaries of life. Sometimes a dancing girl is attached to the village; always a barber, who is the agent for carrying marriage proposals, besides his functions as barber and also surgeon. Sometimes there is an 'astrologer' and even a 'witch-finder.'

The staff varies in different places according to locality. In Central India we find this staff, theoretically twelve in number, called the 'bára bulautí.'

In England such artisans in a village would casually settle where the prospects of trade invited, and would indifferently accept work from any comer, being paid by the job. But in India,—and this applies equally to both forms of village,—the village community invites or attracts to itself the requisite bands of artisans, finds them almost exclusive employment, and does not pay by the job for services rendered, but establishes a regular income or customary mode of annual payment, on receipt of which, every village resident is entitled to have his work done without further (individual) payment. In Central India, where the system of remuneration by 'watan' or official holdings of land found most favour, we find not only the headman or pátel and the accountant (kulkarní) with their official holdings of land, but also petty holdings rent-free for the potter, the sweeper, the water-carrier, &c. In other places the more common method was to allow the artisans certain definite shares when the grain was divided at the harvest; besides which they received periodically certain perquisites, in the shape of blankets, shoes, tobacco, or sugar-cane juice. It is not necessary for me to quote any detailed account of the village servants. Elphinstone has taken his well-known account from Central Southern India, Malcolm has given the detail from Central India. The numbers and names of the artisans of course vary in different parts[1].

[1] See Elphinstone (Cowell's 6th edition), page 69 and notes, and Malcolm (the reprint of 1880), vol. ii. p. 16, Phillips, p. 23. The following is a list of village servants as recorded for the Gujránwála district of the Panjáb. This will serve as a fair general sample of how these people are paid. Their occupation, as well as the right to serve the village, is often hereditary. The villages here spoken of are landlord villages.

1. The blacksmith (lohár). His dues are one bhari or wheat-sheaf in each harvest, one pai in money on each plough, two seers of molasses (gûr), and also one jar of sugarcane juice daily, while the press (belna) is working; and he is allowed to have one day's picking at the cotton-field at the end of the season.

2. The carpenter (tarkhán). He makes the well woodwork, handles for tools, beds (chárpai), stools, &c. His dues are much the same as the lohár's.

3. The kumhár or potter, who makes household utensils and also pots.

4. The 'rera' or grass-rope maker; the ropes are necessary to form the bands over the well-wheel which carry the water-pots. He gets one 'bhari' and four topas of grain per well.

5. The 'chúhrá' or sweeper. He cleans the corn, cleans the cattle-sheds, and makes the manure into cakes for fuel: a place for drying these cakes is often a recognized common allotment outside the village site.

6. The 'mochí' or cobbler and chamár, who also has a right to appropriate the skins of the cattle that die.

7. The 'hajjám' or 'nái.' He is the barber, but also carries messages and proposals connected with marriages and betrothals, and serves also at funerals.

8. The 'dhobi' or washerman.

9. The 'jhewar' (this is a local term), equivalent to 'bihistí' or water-carrier.

Besides there may be the village astrologer and musician (mirási) and various religious office-holders—the purohit, or brahman, a faqír who keeps the takyá or village place of assembly; the 'maulvi' for the mosque service, a 'bhái' at a temple called dharmsála, a 'sádh' at a thákurdwára, a pujári at a shivála (temple of Siva), and a mahant of a 'dévidwára' (other temple).

§ 35. *The Headman.*

Having noticed what the villages have in common, we may proceed to describe the points in which they differ.

If I had to select a characteristic difference between the two types of village, I should find it in the 'headman.'

When the village consists of a number of loosely aggregated cultivating occupants, it is very natural that they should choose or recognize some one of their number to be their headman. Possibly this man is, or represents, the leader of the original settlers, or is in some other way marked out as a trusty and privileged person. He is referred to to decide local disputes, to allot lands when cultivation extends, and so forth. And when the village comes under a definite State organization and pays a revenue to the ruler, most naturally that ruler looks to the headman for the punctual realization of his rights. His importance and dignity are then enhanced because he becomes vested with a certain measure of State authority, and is probably remunerated by the State. His office is hereditary, or becomes so, and the State does not interfere, except in some case of manifest personal incompetence, and then probably another member of the family is selected, at any rate to the practical functions of the office [1].

Where the headman is (as in Central India) allowed an official holding of land—his *watan*, as it is called—the office becomes still more desirable. In these parts it will generally be found that the 'pátel' owns the best land; he is also the owner of the central site in the village, frequently an enclosed space of some size, fortified perhaps by mud walls; and within this only members of the family, all of whom will be addressed as 'pátel,' reside, when other houses are situated around and below. We shall

[1] Some trouble must have been felt in former days when (in Central India) the pátel's family multiplied. They seem to have regarded the headman's office as jointly held, and exercised the functions in a sort of rotation, one member for one year (or whatever it might be), and then the next.

afterwards hear of great princes being anxious to hold the 'pátelship' of villages and the 'watan'[1] land pertaining to it, because of the permanence and stability of this form of right.

Now in the landlord village, naturally the *headman* as such, did not exist. The proprietary families were too jealous of their equal rights to allow of any great degree of authority residing in one head. *Their* system was to manage village affairs by a council of the heads of families called 'pancháyat.'

It is true that in landlord villages, either one headman, or one headman for each division is now to be found; but that is an appointment of the State, and for administrative purposes. In former days such a single headman selected to answer for the revenue and deal generally on behalf of the villages with the State officers, was called 'muqaddam[2].' In our own times, such a headman has received the name of 'lambardár' (the representative whose name bears a separate 'number' in the Collector's register of persons primarily responsible for the revenue), and this modern term at once marks that, in the landlord village, the headman is no part of the original social system. The State now usually recognizes his right to office as hereditary, and desires to make it to some extent elective also. But this is with a view of popularizing the institution. It is essentially an administrative addition to the village. Where a landlord village is united, it still keeps up its pancháyat, and where the institution is falling into discredit and the patwárí or some energetic 'lambardár' begins to dominate, we may be sure that poverty and decay are affecting the body.

[1] See remarks on the *watan* in the next section.

[2] In the Central Provinces they still keep the name 'muqaddam' (or in the Hindi form Mukádam) as well as lambardár, the former expressing the executive functions, the latter the direct duty of paying in the revenue. This is because under the particular circumstances of these provinces, it is possible that the functions of office may be divided between two persons.

§ 36. *Other Village officials.*

Just as an artisan staff is found (necessarily) under either form of village, so the accountant ('patwárí' in Upper India, 'karnam' in the South, 'kulkarní' in the West) is found. Originally in non-landlord villages, he was a State officer, and in the others more the servant of the proprietary body. But now, of necessity, he is a Government servant pure and simple, paid, controlled and appointed by the State, and subject to certain tests of efficiency. To popularize the institution, the office is allowed to be hereditary, supposing a next heir is fit, and is sent to school to qualify himself.

The village 'watchman' is also an important officer in both, as he is utilized and often controlled by Government as a sort of village policeman.

§ 37. *General statement of differences.*

I may perhaps best show at a glance the differences between the villages by arranging in parallel columns a list of characteristic features.

RAIYATWÁRÍ OR NON-LANDLORD VILLAGE (*Bombay, Madras*).	JOINT OR LANDLORD VILLAGE (*Panjáb, North-West Provinces, Oudh, and Central Provinces*).
1. The revenue is assessed on each field or holding. No responsibility of one man for another's default.	1. The revenue is assessed on the village as a whole, and the burden is distributed by the co-proprietors themselves. Village co-sharers are jointly and severally liable for the whole.
2. The village site is not owned by any one landlord, except as far as each occupant householder is owner of his site. The pátel has often a large central residence.	2. The village site is owned by the proprietary body, who allow residences to— (1) the 'kamíṇ,' the artisan class, farm labourers, and menials. (2) The tenantry.

	(3) The traders, money lenders, &c. These probably pay some small dues, according to custom; and if they leave the village may have no right to dispose of the site, and only in some cases to remove the roof timbers and other materials.
3. The waste outside for grave-yard, cattle-shed, pond, grove, &c., &c., is Government land, the area of which is allowed to the villages for these purposes, and this land cannot be diverted from such purposes. No waste area is granted jointly to the village. Probably the use of some available land for grazing, &c., is allowed; and if there are waste numbers which may be cultivated, they must be applied for (and revenue paid thereon) to the land authorities.	3. The waste is allotted to the village, forms part of the estate, and if wanted for cultivation, is partitioned among the share-holders.
4. The headman is an important functionary and part of the original constitution.	4. The village government is by the pancháyat or group of heads of families. The headman is called 'lambardár,' and is (as the name indicates) a later addition, and exists chiefly for revenue and administrative purposes.

5. The accountant (patwárí, &c.), watchman, messenger, artisan, and labourer staff are common to both forms.

§ 38. *Constitution of the Raiyatwárí or Non-landlord Village.*

Naturally there is little to be said about the constitution of the non-landlord village.

There is no room for any variety in tenure; for each man is master and manager of his own holding. Modern law defines his tenure as 'occupant,' or leaves it undefined as the case may be, and there is no question of sharing on this principle or that. Nor have I heard of anything like a common account of expenses chargeable to the whole village and which is rateably levied on the members.

All that we could have to say about the village would be to describe the routine of cultivation, of how the headman acts if his intervention is called for, and how once in the year there is the settling up (*jamabandí*) with the State officer as to what revenue is chargeable, what fields have been held, what taken up, and what, if any, relinquished, and what remissions are claimable (if the particular system allows this). But such a description would be one of social life or of revenue administration, rather than of land-tenure, and I shall dismiss the subject by quoting a pleasant account of the raiyatwárí village (as found in Southern India), which I read in the *Godávarí District Manual*:—

'Each village[1] constituted in itself a perfect whole. Unheeding the changes which may have taken place in the Government above them, the cultivators of the ground quietly continued their daily avocations. They yoked their bullocks to the plough, and followed them in their uneven course. They drew the scanty supply of water from the neighbouring stream or tank, and wrangled over the precious liquid. They cast their seed into the saturated soil, and transplanted the tender sprouts of the growing paddy. They gathered in the harvest, and tended their bullocks as they trod out the grain. The simple household routine went on as quietly and swiftly then as now. The women met at the village well and joined in the petty gossip of the day. The only excitement occurred on the

[1] *Godávari District Manual*, p. 247. This is a 'wet' or irrigated village chiefly cultivating *rice*. Rice is not the staple food of India, as is sometimes supposed. Throughout the North and North-Central India wheat, barley, and millets are the staples. Rice villages are mostly found in South and West Bombay, in East Bengal, in Madras, and in a few other localities on a smaller scale. It is the food of only a very limited portion of the population.

occasion of some feast in their own or a neighbouring village, or of a journey to the festival at some sacred shrine. The village shopkeeper sat cross-legged behind his store and offered loans at an extravagant rate of interest. The village scribe and accountant were employed in writing the accounts on palm-leaves, or drawing up the simple bonds and documents executed by the ryots, and in assisting the village magistrate in his rude administration of justice under the spreading branches of the village tree, where all trials were held and business transacted.'

§ 39. *Constitution of the Joint or Landlord Village.*

There is much more to be said about the landlord village, because it is in the nature of things that there should be changes in its course of existence. Suppose, for example, that the village is gained by a single grantee as landlord; before long his sole tenure—whatever its limits—will be replaced by the joint tenure of a body of heirs[1]. Suppose, again, that the village has from the first been founded by several 'landlords' jointly; it is improbable that they will long remain joint; they will divide the land wholly or partially, and then the shares will, from some cause or another, become altered or lost sight of. Moreover, as we have seen, there are joint or landlord villages where from the first, the principle of sharing is not that of the inheritance law, but some other.

Evidently then there are many points to be dealt with before we have done with the joint or landlord tenure of villages. The Revenue books have adopted, for the North-West Provinces, some terms which describe the various conditions of jointness, or division (or partial division) in which the landlord village may be found. They are unfortunate terms; and we shall presently see, from a

[1] I take it for granted that the reader is aware that by the Hindu law, and by custom also, the succession of heirs is joint Even by the Muhammadan law also it is, though the strict law is not largely followed by agriculturists. *Primogeniture* only applies to succession to royal or ruling chief's titles and their appanages. This subject is enlarged upon in the concluding section.

quotation which I shall make, how they mislead people; but it is necessary that they should be understood.

Where there was a landlord claim over the village, such as that of a revenue farmer who had become proprietor, or of some chief or other high caste personage who had, many generations ago, acquired the superior title, they expressed the right by the term 'zamíndárí.' I suppose it was meant that the landlord in his small estate had that sort of not very definite '*holding of land*' which is indicated by the native term, and which was also applied to the much larger estate-holder called 'Zamíndár' in Bengal.

§ 40. *Meaning of Zamíndárí Village.*

If the landlord were a single person, the term indicating the tenure was 'zamíndárí k͟hális' = simple or sole landlord tenure. When however the original grantee or acquirer of the village had died and was represented by a *family* who as yet remained joint, they called it 'zamíndárí mushtarka' —the joint or co-sharing landlord tenure. It ought to be needless to remark that the term *zamíndárí* by itself conveys no suggestion of *jointness* or *common-holding* in any way whatever. But whether it was that the full phrase 'zamíndárí *mushtarka*,' was too long, or whether it was that so few villages had a *single* landlord, and so many a co-sharing body, I cannot say; but in practice, writers came commonly to use the word 'zamíndárí village tenure,' as if it meant the *tenure of a still undivided joint-body.*

In joint tenures, as long as the body could agree together, they would remain undivided. In such cases the land was generally leased out to tenants; or only certain fields cultivated by one or more of the landlord body, for which rent was credited to the community. One of the family would act as 'manager,' and keep an account of the rents received and any other profits, and would charge against this the Government revenue and cesses, and the charges debitable to the village as a whole—cost of alms, of entertainment of strangers, &c.—and finally would distribute the surplus according to shares.

§ 41. *The Pattidárí Village.*

But very often—in quite the majority of cases indeed—the family agreed to divide; so that many joint villages are found in a state of division or severalty as regards the cultivation and enjoyment of the land. This may have existed only since a few years, or it may have been so from 'time immemorial.' Ordinarily, when the family is descended from some single village 'founder,' the shares will be mainly those of the ancestral 'tree,' and follow the law of inheritance. A sharer here and there may be holding a few (or many) acres more or less than his share; but the general scheme is easily traced and is acknowledged by the co-sharers. When this is the case the village is said to be 'pattidárí,' because the primary division, representing the *main* branches of the family are called 'pattí.' It will be borne in mind that 'pattidárí' properly means not only a village held in severalty, *but also held in shares which are wholly* (or at least in part) *ancestral*, i.e. *those of law of inheritance.* Some villages will be found where the primary division is into 'tarf,' and the tarf is divided into pattís; but where that is the case it may imply some ancient union of two or more distinct bodies who settled together or some other cause operating later in the history of the village. I know of villages where one 'tarf' consists wholly of Hindus and the other of Muhammadan converts, or where one is of one caste and the other of another. This is obviously a special or exceptional state of things. So that in the typical village body descended from a common ancestor, the 'Pattí' is the main-branch division. The 'pattí' is sub-divided into 'thúla' or 'tola' or 'thôk' (three various names), and then into 'beri[1].'

[1] I am not sure of this word. I find it variously written 'behri,' 'bheri,' and even 'bhari.' Wilson's *Glossary* does not give it, nor Elliott's.

Below the 'beri' come the 'khátá,' or individual holdings. This will be clearer from a diagram (which I have adapted from that in the *Selections from the Records of Government, North-West Provinces (Revenue) for* 1818–1822). It will be observed that the fraction held by each is here represented by the *biswa*, or twentieth of the 'bíghá,' which (in the North-West Provinces) is the usual land-measure. But sometimes it is expressed in 'annas' and 'pai'—fractions of a rupee regarded as the unit or whole.

In order to count up to the smallest of the sub-divisions, custom has established, in various parts, minute fractions far below the 'biswa' or the 'anna.' Instances will be found detailed in the chapter on North-West Provinces tenures. Thus we have the *anna*, not only divided into *pai*, but the *pai* into *kauṛi*, and the *kauṛi* into *gandá*, &c. In the present case, the whole estate consists of 2000 bíghás of land; accordingly this area represents the *whole*, or 'bíghá.' Then, a man who owns a four-biswa share, owns four-twentieths (one-fifth) of 2000, or 400 bíghás, and pays one-fifth of the revenue; so, if the revenue is Rs.1000, he will hold 400 bíghás, and pay (one-fifth of Rs.1000 =) Rs. 200[1]. In the example it is evident that the 'pattís,' which are here the primary shares, represent a state of the property when the family consisted of two brothers (A and B) in one branch, and three brothers (C, D, E) in another branch, in parity of descent. The fathers of these two branches were equal; for A and B have half (4 + 6 biswas) between them, and C, D, E (5 + 3 + 2 biswas) the other half, between them. Observe that A and B ought to have five *biswas* each; but, owing to some inequality of value—some sale or other accidental circumstance—one has four, and the other six. So, too, the shares of A's sons have become unequal. Under each share I have marked the area (in

[1] If we were counting by fractions of the rupee, a man who held 400 bíghás out of 2000 and paid Rs.200 out of Rs.1000 revenue, would be said to hold a '3⅕ anna share' of the estate. Probably in an estate counted by fractions of a rupee the shares would be in even numbers, as 1 anna, 2 anna or ½ anna, ⅛, &c. Such a fraction as 3⅕ annas would only occur if the share had become varied by sale, &c.

bíghás and biswas), and the share of the revenue paid in money.

VILLAGE X { Area 2000 bighás. Land-Revenue assessed Rs. 1000.

	(might form a 'tarf').		(might form a 'tarf').			
	Pattí A.	Pattí B.	Pattí C.	Pattí D.	Pattí E.	Grand total.
Share.	6 'biswas'	4 bis.	5 bis.	3 bis.	2 bis.	= 20
Holding.	600 B.	400 B.	500 B.	300 B.	200 B.	= 2000
Paying.	300 Rupees	200 R.	250 R.	150 R.	100 R.	= 1000

[These may all be subdivided in the same way: or in one or other branch all the descendants but one or two may be dead, and the whole *patti* be held by the survivors.]

Pattí A is divided into:

Thôk I. 3½ biswa share. 350 B. 175 R.

- Beri 1. (Each) ⅞ of a biswa. 87 B. 10 b. R. 43 as 12.
  - Divided into (say) 4 equal 'Khátá' or individual holdings.
- Beri 2. &c.
- Beri 3. &c.
- Beri 4. &c.
  - (Beri 2, 3, 4:) Remain undivided perhaps.

Thôk II. 2½ biswa share. 250 B. 125 R.

- Beri 5. 1¼ biswa. 125 B. R. 62 as 8.
- Beri 6. &c.

There may, or may not, be the last division (khátá). Possibly the 'beri' may be enjoyed by some sons or grandsons jointly. But the sharers will be on the list, with their fractional interest recorded. So that the individual proprietors are called, in Revenue language, the 'khátedárs.'

There are many villages in which, as far as we can tell, a separation of 'pattís,' and perhaps some minor subdivisions, have existed from the first colonization, foundation, or acquisition of the village.

§ 42. *The Bháiáchárá Village.*

But one of the curiosities of tribal history in India is that, owing to whatever cause, all tribes, clans, or families did not adopt the same system—indeed, I believe it is the case that different sections of the same tribe adopted different methods. Some tribes had no Rájás or greater chiefs, and all the families were exactly equal under their several heads or elders; and on settling in a new place they adopted a different method of allotting the land. One of the first forms of joint village to be discovered (in Benares) was a form of village called 'bháiáchárá'—i.e. held by the *custom* (áchárá) of the brotherhood (bháí). There is no sort of question that these villages were of the joint type, i.e. they were held by castemen of the higher orders, and that they formed close communities, regarding themselves as landlords and superior to all other people on the estate; but still they did not adopt any system of sharing based on the place in the ancestral 'tree,' but started (when the village first was founded) with an equal division of land, often adopting curious area-measures or standards for dividing, which were not the ordinary land measures or 'bíghás,' but were 'bháiáchárá bíghás,' measures of a larger size, and arranged so as to consist of several plots of the different qualities of land; or to be small in the best soil and larger in the inferior. The other distinguishing feature of this tenure was that the holders did not merely undertake the share of the revenue burden which corresponded to their fractional interest in the estate[1], but they distributed so that the payment should always correspond to the holding; and in many of the villages (notably in the Bundélkhand districts) there was a system of equalization known as 'bhéjbarár[2],' which consisted sometimes in exchange of holdings, but more especially in a redistribution of the payments, according to the actual holdings; so that if one sharer in the course of time found his holding diminished or its productive power fall off, he could—or rather, when things were ripe for it, the

[1] In a regular *pattidári* or fractional estate two men hold one-fourth each, let us say: each pays one-fourth of the revenue of the whole. But one man's one-fourth may become extraordinarily profitable by irrigation, &c. and the other one-fourth might remain as it was and even deteriorate. Still each would only pay one-fourth of the revenue, although this was out of all proportion to the real value of the land.

[2] The papers are collected in *Selections from the Records of Government, North-West Provinces*, Part VIII, No. 34 (Report by H. Rose, Collector of Bánda).

community could—procure a readjustment of the burdens according to the actual state of each holding and the relative value of them.

§ 43. *Extended use of the term Bháiáchárá.*

But the term 'bháiáchárá' soon got to be used not only for a special class of tenures, but for all tenures of co-sharers when there was no *ancestral system of fractional* shares, but when some other principle of distribution had always been followed, or where, if a fractional system had once been followed, it had *fallen into disuse.*

In many cases where the village was due to a body who joined forces to colonize and settle, they divided the area of which they became the landlords, not by family-shares, but by the number of ploughs each brought; or simply, land being abundant, each man took as much land as he wanted or could manage, and that became the measure of his interest in the entire estate; or a certain number of wells were sunk and a certain area was commanded by each well, and then shares in the irrigation became the measure of interest;—either shares by inheritance from one original well-sinker, or shares depending on the capital expended by several who joined in the sinking.

And it is to be remembered that a great number of old villages over which no landlord claims had ever arisen (or had disappeared), and in which the really individual holders had no system of sharing, exist in Oudh and the North-West Provinces, and probably in the Panjáb. Such villages would have remained *raiyatwárí* in form but for the revenue-system. In them the holder speaks of his field as his 'dádilláhi,'—the Divine gift, and has no idea of shares.

All these forms, owing to the absence of any fractional ancestral share scheme, *became equally confused under the common name of* 'bháiáchárá.'

The same thing happened with villages where ancestral shares once existed, but had been lost or allowed to fall into abeyance. A long course of oppressive assessments, the results of efforts to meet the burden (the proprietors earnestly striving not to lose their land), long absence of some co-sharers [1], poverty of others, the necessity for sales, and the voluntary surrender of unprofitable lands,—all these accidents might cause the old shares to be forgotten or given up, and to substitute a new scale of possession out of harmony with the rules of descent. In some cases, while the shares were lost as regards the land, they were adhered to in dividing minor profits of the estate, or in dividing out the waste. Where this is the case, it is proof positive that the village was once an ancestrally shared estate. Such cases are equally called 'bháiáchárá' in reports.

The subdivision of all kinds of bháiáchárá estates is into 'pattí,' 'thok,' 'berí,' &c., as in the other form; and the major division into 'tarf' is commoner.

The student will pardon my repeating once more that the term 'bháiáchárá' now includes:—

Real landlord villages.

(1) Villages where some special form of division or occupation at founding was adopted.

(2) Villages once ancestrally shared, but where the shares have been (wholly or partly) lost or upset.

Properly raiyatwári villages become joint under the Revenue system.

(3) Villages never shared at all—each man's possession is the measure of his right.

§ 44. *Partition of joint Waste under Bháiáchárá method.*

Where there is no real system of sharing, or where shares have been completely lost, and the partition of the waste included in the estate by the North-West Revenue System is called for, it will be distributed in the same proportion as the original holding bears to the whole.

[1] 'Absentee rules' were well known in our early Settlements, and the records constantly specified the village custom as to what was to be done if an absentee returned and claimed his share. Some would allow it unconditionally, others would fix a term of years, or impose conditions. Often too a man would get back, but only to a small portion of his share.

For instance, a man's actual possession is 50 acres out of a village of 2500 acres, all told. In fact, he is owner of one-fiftieth; so that on dividing the waste, he will get one-fiftieth of the area whatever it is.

Or, if the acres of the principal or original holding are valuable, and so pay a higher proportion of the revenue-assessment, it may be that the waste will be allotted according to the proportion of the total revenue paid; and then if the man pays (say) not one-fiftieth, but one-twentieth of the revenue, he will get one-twentieth of the waste area[1].

§ 45. '*Perfect*' and '*imperfect*' *forms of Shared Village.*

It is usual in the Revenue reports and returns to find a further classification heading—'imperfect pattídárí' or 'imperfect bháiáchárá.' These terms, however, merely call attention to a feature which is of no importance whatever from the tenure point of view. They mean nothing more than that when the estate was divided, whether according to ancestral-fractional shares (pattídárí), or according to some other method (bháiáchárá), the co-sharers did not care to *divide up the whole*, but left a part still joint. This might (and commonly did) happen, as there was an obvious convenience in it.

Suppose, for instance, that a considerable part of the village is held by or let out to tenants, or perhaps held by irremoveable, privileged tenants. It may be that the *rents* they pay suffice, wholly or partially, to pay the revenue. I have known many villages where this is the case, especially in sugar-cane growing villages, which command a high rental. In that case there is no object in dividing; the part that is separately enjoyed is held then by each sharer virtually revenue free. If the rental of the undivided portion does not happen to cover the revenue, then the

[1] This form of partition is then said, in revenue language, to be 'ḥasb rasad khewat,' or in proportion to the actual interest shown in the 'Khewat'—a list of share-holders and their payments made out for every estate.

deficit is made up by a rateable charge on the co-sharers according to their constitution. There may be other reasons for not dividing the whole estate, but the example is intelligible, and represents an extremely common case. This may be realized by looking at their statistics in the chapters on the North-West Provinces and Panjáb.

§ 46. *A better principle of classification required.*

It is unfortunate that these old terms are still made use of in the Imperial returns: they were useful enough in their day as office distinctions when village tenures were just beginning to be understood. But they are as inefficient now as the Linnæan system is to the modern botanist. They distinguish matters that are of no importance, and confuse together things that it is essential to keep separate.

A more suitable classification could be easily adopted, and I have ventured to suggest one which will be found in the chapter on the North-West Province tenures, and which is based on the distinction of cases where (1) the ancestral shares are followed wholly, or (2) partly, or (3) are theoretically allowed and recorded, but not acted on in practice, or (4) where some other plan of sharing is recognized, and (5) it might distinguish cases in which individual possession is the only measure of right, and where there is no *plan of sharing* at all, and never was.

§ 47. *The Proprietor's 'Sír' Land.*

Before leaving the subject of the joint village, I should like to explain the term 'sír.' It constantly occurs in such phrases as 'the proprietor enjoys his sír land practically without payment,' or 'the proprietor is never ousted from the occupation of his sír, except,' &c.

It refers to the home-farm or land which the landlord or co-sharer holds directly in his own management, either cultivating it himself, or by his farm-servants or personal tenants.

The distinction arose out of the fact that the landlord's right was so often superimposed on older rights. A *modus vivendi* had to be found; it was so, partly in the method of sharing produce, but chiefly in this, that while the landlords had certain rents from the whole estate, they left the actual management of a great part to the old 'tenants' of the village, who naturally held on somewhat easy terms; and each proprietor took for his own direct farming and profit such area of—usually the best—land as his share and other circumstances entitled him to. That was called his 'sír'= his 'own'[1]. Even if there should be no ancient rights on the estate, still the owners may be non-agriculturists and be obliged to lease out the greater part to tenants, retaining only special lands, the entire produce of which (or rather a larger share of it) goes to themselves.

Legally speaking, the term has become of importance, because under all Revenue systems based on the North-West Provinces model, there are certain privileges connected with the 'sír.' For instance, if by default in payment of revenue, or on refusal to engage, a co-sharer is put out of possession, he still retains his *sír* on a tenant-right. And a tenant who proves that he has fallen to that grade, being an 'ex-proprietor,' has always a privileged occupancy tenure of his former 'sír.' So also (in the Central Provinces) occupancy rights conferred by law on certain classes of tenants do not apply to 'sír' lands, and it becomes of importance to define in the tenant law exactly what is to be regarded as 'sír' and what is not[2].

In *raiyatwárí*, or non-landlord villages, there is, of course, no room for any such distinction. The 'watan' lands of the pátel (where such a system prevails) are the analogue of the 'sír' in the landlord village. Though we are here concerned only with villages, I may nevertheless take the

[1] In the Panjáb, where the proprietors are so very often themselves of the agricultural class, we hear much less frequently this term 'sír' land.

[2] In the Central Provinces difficulty had arisen from the definition of 'sír' that was in force, and one of the amendments of the law in 1889 was directed to correct the definition.

opportunity of remarking that in *any* form of landlord estate, the landlord will, or may, hold 'sír' land. Thus with the greater landlords called 'Zamíndár' in Bengal, or Taluqdár in Oudh, they had 'sír' lands which were sometimes exempt from paying revenue under the name of 'nánkár,' and were also exempt from all those privileges of *occupancy to tenants* which accrued on the ordinary lands of the estate[1].

§ 48. *Present state of the Joint-Villages.*

In the North-West Provinces the sentiment of joint-landlordship seems to be decaying. Some of the villages were, as I said, never really joint at all; they became so under our system; hence a strong principle of coherence is hardly to be looked for. Of those that are really joint, many are owned by families descended from an ancestor who was once ruler, conqueror, or grantee; and a great many from revenue-farmers and auction-purchasers. None of these had any attachment to land as land, since they did not belong to castes *who themselves cultivate the soil.* I believe I am right in saying that the individualization of land and the loss of the joint interest is proceeding apace. The *panchàyats* and lambardárs have little influence: the landholders apply for leave to pay their own revenue direct to the local treasury instead of through the headman of their 'pattí' or their village, as the case may be. 'Perfect' partition, which not only divides the land, but also completely severs the revenue responsibility, is allowed. The result is the growth of independent petty proprietors, but still more of capitalist landlords, who buy up first one field and then (availing themselves of the right of pre-emption) another. They are not men of the agricultural class, but must employ

[1] Supposing a 'Zamíndár' has leased his land to an indigo planter. The tenants hate growing indigo, and the lessee can therefore only compel its growth on such land as is absolutely under his landlord's control, i. e. on the Zamíndár's 'sír' land. Hence the importance of distinguishing the 'sír.'

tenants; these naturally are found in the old land-owning classes, whose *status* is thus slowly changing.

In the Panjáb the conditions are more favourable to the joint-village: there is a total absence of communities deriving their origin from the revenue-farmer or auction-purchaser[1]. The villages are almost everywhere due to foundation by colonists or tribes of superior strength and character, most of whom are agriculturists; and they seem to have retained more than elsewhere the sense of union and the power of maintaining their original *status*. Governed still by custom, they have hardly emerged—at least in many districts—from the stage when the feeling that land belongs as much to the family as to the individual is predominant. The law does not allow of perfect partition, i.e. dissolving the joint responsibility, except at Settlement and under special conditions. There is a rather strong law of pre-emption which generally enables any one in the village body to prevent an outsider purchasing land. The customary law still restricts widows to a life tenure, and prevents them alienating; while in many tribes a childless male proprietor cannot alienate to the prejudice of his next heirs without their consent. There is also in many parts a strong 'clannish' feeling which keeps villages together. Nevertheless, the power of free sale and mortgage is producing its results: non-agricultural capitalists are buying up land, and estates slowly undergo a change. Strangers are introduced; the village site enlarges, and the non-proprietary classes successfully resist the payment of dues to a proprietary body, and claim the right to sell their houses and sites; and gradually the old landlord body sink into oblivion. If large estates accumulate in the hands of individuals, they will again become joint if the heirs are numerous, and then, as the property will be not in one village, the *estate* will more and more cease to be synonymous with the *village*.

[1] The Panjáb was not annexed till after the days of revenue farming and harsh sale laws.

§ 49. *The Mahál and Village.*

Indeed I ought to explain that, though for convenience I often speak of the Revenue Settlement of villages, and the assessment of villages, strictly speaking this is not correct. The lump assessment is on what is called in revenue language the 'Mahál,' or lot of lands held under one title. This may, and does very often, coincide with a 'village'; but partitions and sales will always tend to make it less so. Supposing, for example, three villages come to be owned by a community of eight sharers, and they completely partition their estate: eight estates or 'Mahâls' may then arise. Sometimes a part of one village is a separate estate. And there are also peculiar customs of allotment of shares, by which the sharers in a large estate of several villages may get their land, not in compact lots, but some fields here and some there in different villages. In time these may form separately assessed 'Mahâls.'

When the partition of an estate results in compact lots, the estate is said, in revenue language, to be 'pattibat,' and when by scattered areas 'khetbat.' There are other local terms, but these are the common ones.

§ 50. *Some further quotations regarding Villages.*

We are now in a position to appreciate some of the standard descriptions of the 'village community' which have been usually copied from book to book without any question.

Here is one, which has become almost classical[1]:—

'The village communities are little republics, having nearly everything they want within themselves, and almost independent of any foreign relations. They seem to last when

[1] Sir C. T., afterwards Lord Metcalfe. In a minute of 7th Nov. 1830, No. 84, in the App. to the Report of Select Committee of H. C. (1832), cited in Elphinstone's *History of India*, 5th ed. p. 68.

nothing else lasts. Dynasty after dynasty tumbles down; revolution succeeds to revolution; Hindú, Pathán, Mughal, Maráthá, Sikh, English, all are masters in turn; but the village communities remain the same. In times of trouble they arm and fortify themselves. An hostile army passes through the country; the village communities collect their cattle within their walls and let the enemy pass unprovoked. If plunder and devastation be directed against themselves, and the force employed be irresistible, they flee to friendly villages at a distance; but when the storm has passed over they return and resume their occupations. If a country remain for a series of years the scene of continued pillage and massacre so that the villages cannot be inhabited, the scattered villagers nevertheless return whenever the power of peaceable possession revives. A generation may pass away, but the succeeding generation will return. The sons will take the places of their fathers; the same site for the village, the same positions for their houses, the same lands will be re-occupied by the descendants of those who were driven out when the village was depopulated: and it is not a trifling matter that will drive them out, for they will often maintain their post through times of disturbance and convulsion, and acquire strength sufficient to resist pillage and oppression with success. This union of the village communities, each one forming a little state in itself, has, I conceive, contributed more than any other cause to the preservation of the people of India, through all the revolutions and changes which they have suffered, and is in a high degree conducive to their happiness and to the enjoyment of a great portion of freedom and independence.'

This passage does not define, or even describe what the village is: it states certain characteristics, and there is, of course, a considerable amount of truth in it. But it should be remembered that there is quite another side to the same picture, or rather it should be said that the delineation is only true under certain conditions. The circumstances of the country necessitate the aggregation of cultivation in groups, and often encourage the fixing of a central and even defensible site for residence. But as to 'little republics,'—in a large number of villages, in most provinces, and at one time or another, individual headmen and farmers of the revenue have ruled with almost undisputed power[1]. As to the villages being unchangeable, their constitution and form has shown a progressive tendency to decay, and if it had not been for modern land-revenue systems trying to keep it together, it may well be doubted whether it would have survived at all. No doubt there are cases in which villages have been re-established by the descendants of a former body driven out by disaster; cases have been recorded, for instance, in Central India, where certain families who have held particular lands in virtue of hereditary office, and being strongly attached to the dignities therewith associated, have had a strong motive to return, as well as, in the sentiment of the people, a strong claim to do so; but the invitation of the ruler has much to do with the return: he desires to re-establish deserted estates for the sake of his revenue; and old landholders are the best; while an old headman family has an obvious capacity for inducing cultivators to restore the village[2]. When villages are refounded, it is however just as often by totally different people.

And let us take another feature in the account quoted. Mughals and Sikhs, we are told, are masters in turn, but the village remains the same. Does it? The village changes as much as, in the nature of things, a group of lands or an aggregate of houses, can change. Let us picture to ourselves an easily recognizable case. At first the village was a settlement founded in the virgin waste. Here a leader or headman started and directed the cultivation; each cultivator brought his own plough and oxen, and felt that the plot he cleared would be his own; he had no connection with other holdings save that he obeyed the common headman, availed himself of the village artisan's services, and had to share his grain-heap with them and with

[1] See for example Mr. (now Sir C.) Crosthwaite's remarks on certain villages in the *Settlement Report of the Etáwá district* (chapter on North-West Provinces Tenures).

[2] And it is sometimes the case that when the disaster occurred which broke up the village, the destruction was not complete, but a *nucleus* was left behind. John Lawrence, when Collector of the Sirsa district, noted villages there as exhibiting this characteristic.

the Rájá, and had to unite with his fellows whenever common defence was necessary. Then let us suppose the Rájá's cousin receives a grant of the village and becomes landlord, taking most of the waste to himself; as his family multiplies, they form a joint body and soon get the lion's share of the land, the old 'clearers' becoming tenants. Next, the landlord family quarrel, or otherwise determine to divide the land; in this state the village will be called in the revenue books a *pattídárí* village. Next, the proprietors get into debt, and sell their shares. Strangers thus get in, and a new order of things commences; for the purchasers are very likely of a non-agricultural caste and must employ tenants: some perhaps prefer the old landowners, others take new men who offer better terms. The remnants of both the older family groups run a good chance of going to the wall altogether. Lastly, the body comes under early English revenue-management, before it had become adapted to the true requirements of the case; the village once more changes hands. It is now sold for arrears of revenue, and passes with a clear title into the hands of an auction-purchaser, or falls under the tender mercies of a revenue-farmer who drives half the already heterogeneous population out, to make room for good Kurmi, or Saini, or Aráiṇ cultivators (according to the province we are thinking of), in order that he may clear off the balance and fulfil his object of making a profit for himself. And this is the village that never changes while dynasties tumble down, &c.!

Of course there is a true side to the picture; for all these changes do not alter the facts of situation: the methods of cultivation are the same, the fields remain—*et superest ager*; the customs of ploughing and of resting, the dealings with the money-lender, the daily gossip of the women drawing water at the well, or sitting over their cotton spinning; these and all other features of village life remote from the rumours of the world, will continue, no matter who is managing the estate. But we must not attempt to make a general picture of *the* 'Indian village' by either taking a partial and one-sided view of things, or by throwing together a variety of dissimilar facts till we get a sort of undistinguishable mixture of them all. Still less must we make a hasty generalization from a few imperfectly understood facts, and complacently adapt them to the latest theory (however admissible in itself) of ancient institutions or the development of ideas of property.

There are distinct varieties of villages in the different countries of India, and they are none of them (that I know of) at all like the Russian *mir*, or the Sclavonian house-community or the Swiss *allmend* or common holding, in the concrete. They have, or had, some *features*[1] *which can be traced back*, in all probability, *to those elements in early tribal life which are common to all races.* But the identity of some forms of Indian village with the 'Mark' or the tribal holdings in Ireland, is only 'identity' in the sense in which the German, Greek, Lithuanian and Latin tongues could be called 'identical' with Sanskrit or Zand.

§ 51. *Features of the Joint Village misapplied.*

One more instance must be given of the 'generalized' method of disposing of the features of Indian villages. This will now be intelligible, because I have explained the revenue terms applied to the landlord village of Northern India and the Panjáb—indicating that the village is enjoyed jointly, or has been wholly or partially divided for separate enjoyment. It is an extract from a valuable

[1] And I desire not to underrate these facts. In the frontier districts of the Panjáb, when the conquering tribes allotted the country into 'iláqas,' and then into villages, *Kandis*, &c., we have many features which recall the 'mark' or the Anglo-Saxon 'vill': and the reader of Mr. Joshua Williams' *Lectures on Rights of Common* (London, 1880), especially lectures 4, 5, and 6, might think he was reading a North Panjáb Settlement Report; and so with Mr. F. Seebohm's *English Village Community* (London, 1884, 3rd ed.). Some of the village customs of measuring and dividing land, the 'bulks,' the 'shots,' the 'lynches,' the holdings made up of scattered strips (though the reason is not the same), pp. 7, 113, the 'lœnland' as compared with the Rájá's or chief's *grant* (p. 169),—these and many others suggest interesting points of comparison.

standard text-book known to all Indian lawyers as Mayne's *Hindu Law and Usage*.

Thus Mr. Mayne writes [1] :—

'The village system . . . presents three marked phases, which exactly correspond to the changes in an undivided family. The closest form of union is that which is known as the "*Communal Zamíndárí* village." Under this system "the land is so held that all the village co-sharers have each their proportionate share in it as common property without any possession of or title to distinct portions of it; and the measure of each proprietor's interest is his share as fixed by the customary law of inheritance. The rents paid by the cultivators are thrown into a common stock with all other profits from the village lands, and after deduction of the expenses, the balance is divided among the proprietors according to their shares." (Quoted from Boulnois and Rattigan's *Panjáb Customs*, 1876.) This corresponds to the undivided family in its purest state. The second stage is called the *pattidárí* village. In it the holdings are all in severalty, and each sharer manages his own portion of land. But the extent of the share is determined by ancestral right, and is capable of being modified from time to time upon this principle.'

. . . .

The third and final stage is known as the *bháiáchárá* village. It agrees with the *pattidárí* form inasmuch as each owner holds his share in severalty. But it differs from it inasmuch as the extent of the holding is strictly defined [not at all *strictly*, very often there is a strong trace of the ancestral scheme besides] by the amount actually held in possession.'

This again reads convincingly; but if we hold the writer to the *strict* sense of the vernacular terms used, it would not be far wrong if we were to say that the real process of change or development is almost exactly the reverse of that described. If we look to the order of village development

[1] *Hindu Law and Usage* (Higginbotham, Madras) 4th ed. § 200. Of course the whole extract would lose some of its general inapplicability if by '*the* village system' we understand, the particular form of village in which first a single landlord and from him a joint-body of descendants, is found, and if allowance is made for a very inaccurate (but perhaps popularized) use of the terms *pattidárí* and *bháiáchárá*; but the author suggests no such restriction.

on the basis of such evidence as actually exists, we find a large number in which an allotment (liable, in certain places, to be periodically revised) was made from the very first; not necessarily on the principle of ancestral shares, but sometimes on this plan, sometimes on one totally distinct, according to tribal sentiment. We also find other villages over which we may suppose one chief or head of a family originally ruled, and his family at some very remote period divided it on ancestral shares.

It is quite an unnecessary abuse of terms to represent the 'bháiáchárá' as a *stage* beyond 'pattídárí.' As far as 'bháiáchárá' is (incorrectly) used to indicate villages where the shares have been lost, it is a matter of taste whether we call it a 'stage' of any process whatever. To my mind the pattídárí is just as complete an individualization of holding as that which is maintained when the *theory which governed the extent of* the separate lot is forgotten. But, considering that 'bháiáchárá' (and that correctly) also indicates a special plan or method of division existing alongside of the pattídárí[1], it is positively incorrect to say that it is a stage beyond pattídárí in a process of change or development. Once more; if 'bháiáchárá' is given its widest sense, it includes many villages in which, as far as we know, there never was any joint holding at all. In fact, if we put aside the special case of the Panjáb frontier and other immigrant tribal family settlements, it would be quite as correct (for a general paragraph) to say, that the first stage is when a number of colonists settle together, each working at his own holding and claiming it in severalty, the only bond of union being that of locality and a common government; that in the next stage a landlord arises—not merely a distant ruler, but—a claimant to the actual village acres, and that he is succeeded by a body of descendants who jointly enjoy the estate for a time; that they then divide almost always on *ancestral* shares; and that, lastly, the strict shares are lost or modified by circumstances.

[1] And the co-existence of these *diverse* methods of allotment and several enjoyment, is of exceeding value and interest, and one not to be obscured or left out of count.

And it would be proper to add, that in many cases villages are known where, though the feeling of joint right to an entire area was strongly recognized, some special method of equal allotment was *always and from the first* practised, while a portion of the area might or might not remain undivided, either for common grazing, or to support a tenantry, or from some other motive.

§ 52. *Forms of Village in the different Provinces.*

It will probably be of use to the student if I now give a list of the provinces treated of in this book, and state briefly and in abstract, what sort of 'village' is (chiefly) to be found in each.

BENGAL. In what is called 'Bengal proper,' the village tenure is of comparatively little importance: it has become overshadowed by the tenure of great landlords. In the Bihár districts, however, there are clearer traces of villages —of the landlord type—and the headmen have often become petty 'Zamíndárs.' In East Bengal there are peculiar tenures, the result of settlements in the jungle; and there are special survivals of peculiar villages in the Santál parganas, Chutiyá Nágpur, &c. Shifting cultivation in the hill tracts is also common.

ASSAM. In the Sylhet and Cachár districts there are some peculiar tenures. In the Assam valley the villages are peculiar and not of the landlord type, but practically *raiyatwárí*. There is much 'Júm' or shifting cultivation in the hills of Central, Northern, and Southern Assam.

NORTH-WEST PROVINCES. Mostly joint villages; many formed by families of revenue-farmers, &c., who acquired the landlord right at the beginning of the century. Many were really *raiyatwárí* villages, but have become 'bháiáchárá' under our system.

OUDH. Many villages of the old (*raiyatwárí*) type; in many, landlord claims have grown up by the grant of Rájás, or by the dismemberment of old estates of chiefs, &c.

But over all, the Taluqdár landlords have grown up: and they have reduced the villages to a subordinate position.

THE PANJÁB. In the Frontier districts strong landlord villages of immigrant conquering tribes. In the Central districts, landlord villages, some of immigrant tribes, some of associated bodies of settlers, some resulting from the multiplication of families of single or associated adventurers. In the hill districts real villages do not exist, and so in the Southern River districts; the now recognized village forms are there the result of Settlement arrangements.

AJMER. Joint villages, the result of our Settlement. Originally the old Hindu organization was complete.

THE CENTRAL PROVINCES. The villages would be, as a rule, of the *raiyatwárí* type, but Government conferred a landlord right on heads of villages, so that their descendants form landlord communities, but with rights much limited by legal reservation of rights to the old cultivators.

A considerable area is held by larger estate holders, who are the surviving representatives of the old Gond chiefs of the Dravidian-Hindu era.

BOMBAY. Mostly *raiyatwárí* villages:—a few survivals of landlord (shared) villages in Guzarát. In the coast (Konkán) districts a peculiar landlord tenure of 'Khots' over groups of villages, will be found.

MADRAS. Mostly *raiyatwárí* villages. Traces of landlord villages (mirási), now only surviving in a few special privileges or adaptations under the Raiyatwárí Settlement system. In Malabár and South Kánara no villages properly so called, and special tenures. So in the Wainád division of Malabár, and in the Nílgírí hills.

COORG. No villages properly so called, special tenures.

BURMA. Villages *raiyatwárí* in principle, but of a special type.

SECTION III. LAND-TENURES ARISING OUT OF OFFICIAL POSITIONS OR LAND-REVENUE ARRANGEMENTS AND STATE GRANTS OF THE REVENUE.

§ 1. *Early organization of territory for Revenue purposes.*

When the earliest regular kingdoms that we have any evidence of, were established—whether Dravidian, or Aryan, or of other immigrant tribes—there was always some organization of the territory, which was especially adopted with a view to ensuring the realization of the revenue. And under every form of government with which we are acquainted, a revenue from land was the chief thing.

The village grouping of cultivators or colonizers, which we have just considered in detail, being *the* feature of the agricultural constitution of society, naturally we find a State-recognized headman in each village aided by an accountant; not unnaturally too, we find the village government repeated in form but over a wider area, till we come to the governor or chief-regnant himself. First above the headman of a single village, we find an officer over a small group of villages, called a náik or náyak: this probably descended to the Muhammadan government as the 'tappa.' A larger group (Col. Sykes speaks of its containing eighty-four villages [1]) was the charge of a 'désmukh.' This also was adopted by the Muhammadans, and the territorial division is still well known under the familiar revenue name of 'pargana' (pergunnah) [2], or taluka. Over

[1] In his paper above quoted. Traces of 'Chaurassis,' or groups of eighty-four villages are found in various parts, also of 'beálisí' and 'chaubísí' (forty-two and twenty-one, the half and quarter charge respectively). These may have been the extent of major and minor chiefs' estates, or the jurisdiction of officers. I have seen suggestions however that they may represent the areas conquered or occupied by clans and sections (according to their size) of tribes. A long account of Chaurassis will be found in Beames' Elliott's *Glossary*, s. v. *Chaurassí*.

[2] The pargana is in Upper India almost everywhere preserved. It is too small for our administrative system and has therefore given way to the 'tahsil'—a subdivision of a district. The ta'lluqa (or in Hindi form Taluka) division is still in use in Bombay and Madras.

this area there was necessarily also an accountant called 'déspándyá.' The still larger, or what we should call 'district' charge, was not so permanent, nor has it survived so well. Our predecessors do not seem to have very much cared for a charge intermediate between the small *pargana* and the province of the Governor. But in some places, and at some time or other, there certainly existed such charges; and the title 'Sirdeṣmukh' implies a supervision of several *desmukhs* or pargana officers. This administrative organization is more fully described in the next chapter; I only state here what is necessary with a view to our immediate purpose.

§ 2. *The 'Watan' lands.*

One of the most ancient tenures, directly arising out of this series of official grades, is the service-tenure, called 'Watan' in Central India. From the fact of its localization in the very home of the old Dravidian (Gond, &c.) kingdoms, I am inclined to suggest that it is a direct survival of that system, and is therefore of great interest.

The Dravidian scheme of revenue seems to have included (if it did not originally confine itself to) the plan of making allotments of *land* as royal farms, for the payment of officers, and even for the more petty remuneration of village artisans, and for the priests. The produce of these lands went wholly to the king or the official as the case might be; while special arrangements were often made for their cultivation. I am not aware that any local name for this tenure has survived, a fact which points to a remote antiquity, and perhaps to some degree of localization. The name 'watan,' now applied to it, is Arabic, and is traceable to the Muhammadan kings of the Dakhan, before their overthrow by the Mughal empire of Delhi. We know that these kings were wisely careful of indigenous institutions, and they evidently preserved the 'ex-officio' holding and gave it a name. It comprised not only the holding of lands, but also a right to the 'mánpán,' i. e. various dignities, and precedence[1] on official or public occasions. In Central India, where this institution has long survived, the dignity of Pátel (headman), or of Pándyá (accountant) with the 'watan' attached, is such, or perhaps the security of the tenure is regarded as so complete, that rights in the form of 'watan' are eagerly sought after, and what is more, the pettiest 'watan' originally attached to some menial office is *bought* up and held by great men[2].

The *watan*, besides being heritable, is also saleable; moreover, as the whole family of the hereditary officer succeeds jointly, all hold it and may afterwards divide it.

We may find traces of the 'watan,' or something analogous to it, elsewhere; but I must not give more space to a tenure which is now extremely localized in Nimár, Central India and parts of Bombay[3].

[1] Such as the Pátel being entitled to walk first on certain ceremonial occasions; being the first to throw the sacred cake into the fire at the Húlí festival; having the right to have his cow's horns first gilded on a certain festival, and so forth. Col. Sykes gives a most curious account of these as they appeared on the occasion of a settlement (by a 'panch' or arbitrator) of a dispute regarding a Bombay 'pátelgí' or headmanship, in which certain shares had been sold, so that not only the *land* of the watan had to be divided between the claimants, but also the different 'precedences' and dignities. It was settled by allowing one claimant to be first in a certain number of ceremonial occasions, and the other at a number of others; the 'panch' trying to make the list of 'occasions' as desirable to each as possible, so that the rank might be equal. I have unfortunately mislaid my reference. The paper I allude to is in the *Asiatic Soc. Journal*, but later than vol. ii.

[2] In the *Berár Gazetteer* Mr. (now Sir A.) Lyall notices how in Western Central India the 'watan' is more prized than anything else. Berár is a purely Dravidian country—part of the ancient Gondwána. Speaking of the Sindkher chief (in the south-west corner of Berár), he tells us that the family had held large jágír estates in the sixteenth century. In Upper India he would on this basis have developed to a great 'zamíndár' or 'taluqdár'; but in the Dakhan he was content to be the 'deṣ-mukh' of a dozen parganas, the 'pátel' of fifty villages, and in his own town of Sindkher the pluralist holder of all the grants attached to menial services—washing, shaving, sweeping, &c. The family had let go its jágírs, yet had seized every sort of 'watan' on which it could lay hands (p. 101). Sir J. Malcolm (ii. p. 16) writes: 'The rights of the native hereditary officers of a village are much respected in Central India; and never did a country afford such proofs of the imperishable nature of this admirable institution. After the Pindárí war every encouragement was held out for the inhabitants to return. . . . In several districts, particularly those near the Narbada, many of the villages had been waste for more than thirty years. . . . Infant Potails (Pátel the second and third in descent from the emigrator, were in many cases carried at the head of their parties.'

[3] In the Central Provinces we do not find it till we come to Nimár,

§ 3. *General tendency of Hindu system.*

I am not aware that we can fairly attribute any other existing tenures to the Hindu State organization, or to the development of the position of its land officers, so long as the system remained in its pristine vigour. Indeed, in some parts, as in the Native States of Rájputána and in the Hill States of the Himáláyá, the old organization survives to this day, and though the present Rájás and subordinate chiefs, called Ráná, Thákur, &c., claim to be the owners of the soil, this is a much later claim, which all the more recent Oriental governments put forward. Even this is perhaps more a theoretical than a practical claim; except in so far as it results in the State owning (and drawing profit from) all waste land not held or cultivated by any one, and securing a certain fee on the rare occasions of a transfer of land. Otherwise there has been no great tendency to modify the tenures. The traveller in the hills can still see the villagers paying revenue in an actual grain-share, and notice in the larger villages the Rájá's 'kothí,' a great square building which forms a local head-quarters. Here the grain from the neighbourhood is stored, and here too (when needed) the 'kárdár' or other local official holds a rude kind of court for disposal of public business.

The introduction of Hindu officials when they came as foreigners, in some of the Chutiyá Nágpur States and in Orissa, produced some confusion, and originated landlord tenures in the end; but it would be hardly correct to refer to these cases as directly illustrating tenures arising out of revenue administrative arrangements.

§ 4. *The Muhammadan Empire.—At first changes are slight.*

The first influence on tenures caused by the accession to power of the Mughals, was by their reducing or conquering

which had been under the Muhammadan rule. May it have been that the Maráthás destroyed it in Nágpur?

the Rájás of the small states which then were the great feature of the country. As we shall state presently, the treatment of these States was a noteworthy feature in the Mughal rule. They conquered the Rájás, but only took from them the *land-revenue*, leaving the local taxes, and customs duties, and the administration of justice, as they were before — these latter being the very attributes of sovereignty which a modern government would have thought it its first duty to undertake and regulate.

But in fact the Mughals closely conformed to the old Hindu system. Their own ideas of right over conquered peoples, and of taking 'Khiráj' or tribute and capitation tax from them, were modified, or perhaps naturally fell in with the system of the land-revenue payment already in force [1]. Names were changed, but the administrative divisions of the country, and the official charges, were virtually retained.

§ 5. *Changes begin with the decay of the Empire.*

Except then for the change that was inaugurated (and that without intention or foreseeing the result) by reducing the Rájás, the influence of the Muhammadan rule on tenures, may be said to have been chiefly felt in the changes that occurred in revenue-management, when the empire fell into decay. Perhaps I ought not to say this without remembering also the influence of the change made when a money-revenue was substituted for a grain-share; and that was not in the decline of Empire, but when it was at its best. During the latter half of the sixteenth century, the Emperor Akbar made a revenue-settlement, under which (at first optionally) a money-payment was substituted for the grain-share. No doubt this was the beginning of a great change; still it was one which only indirectly affected land-tenures. It pre-

[1] The 'Khiráj' (*vide* chapter on the Land-Revenue System) naturally became the land-revenue. As to the 'jaziya' or capitation tax, we only occasionally hear of it, when one or other of the Mughal emperors in a fit of zeal, attempted to impose it on the Hindus, and were much hated in consequence.

pared the way for what followed, and for gradual changes in the relation of landlord and tenant, and many other modern features of land-tenure. The land-tenures were really directly affected when the Mughal government began to decline. Then it was that viceroys like those of Oudh, Bengal, and the Dakhan (Hyderabad) threw off their allegiance and became independent kings. Then too it was that the extravagant claims of the *ruler to be universal owner of land* were first heard.

The independent kingdoms did not have a very prosperous course. Before long, decay and corruption began to invade every department of the State. Under such a state of things honesty was hardly to be looked for in the local revenue collectors; and the land-revenue fell off. No doubt the Central government—as from time to time it fell into the hands of a more vigorous ruler—made desperate efforts to reassert a proper control over the district collectors, but in vain. The device, to save trouble and secure at least a certain revenue, was to employ local agents over greater or less areas of country, and to contract for the revenues of those areas. At first such agents were carefully appointed, and with much form; lists were made out of the villages in their charge; and they were bound to account for all they collected; except that they were allowed certain lands revenue-free, certain items might be deducted for special charges (as office expenses, alms, and police), and a certain share, usually one-tenth of the total revenue, as their own remuneration—denominated nánkár, that whereby they made (kár) their bread (nán).

But as time went on, these agents were less and less controlled; and they soon became mere contractors for fixed total sums; and the local officers had no power whatever over them, and finally disappeared before them. No one in fact knew (or cared) what was actually wrung out of the villages, so long as the contract sum was paid into the treasury. Nor was this sum a fixed one. Whether or not the strict ideal of Hindu or Muhammadan law was that the Revenue Settlement, once made, ought to be unalterable, it is quite certain that in practice it never was so; but instead of a careful re-survey of extended cultivation and a re-valuation of lands, the rough expedient was adopted of adding 'cesses' (abwáb) to the sum demanded from the agents, and so raising the total. These cesses were called by various names indicating the pretext under which they were levied [1]. The agents of course had in their turn, to make good the additional demand from the villages, and took the opportunity of adding a number of further cesses for their private benefit, on the strength of the example thus set them.

It should not be supposed, however, that this system of farming the land-revenue was altogether, or in all cases, due to the decay of the Government system. There is one important fact to be considered. The Muhammadan government succeeded by conquest to a number of Hindu states, such as I have described, where Rájás and minor chiefs already were receiving the revenue (grain-share) and governing the country. These Rájás in some cases had been slain in battle; in others had fled to the hills and there established new estates in the comparative safety of the distant and unoccupied country. In other cases their domains broke up, and the members of the ruling families seized on particular villages and became landlords, submitting to pay revenue to the Muhammadan treasury. But a number of the old chiefs, in certain provinces at any rate, though not able to hold their own, were quite strong enough to give trouble, and to reappear and head a rebellion on the appearance of the least opportunity. Hence it was matter of policy to conciliate them by giving titles, &c., and still more by leaving them in all their dignity, and with the power of administering justice locally, provided they would consent to pass on a large share of the land-revenue they collected, to the Imperial treasury. Such local magnates were well acquainted with the resources of the country, and had often a strong quasi-feudal hold on the people. True they would not like

[1] For details the chapter on Bengal tenures must be referred to.

parting with so much revenue; but provided the Imperial treasury only demanded a fixed sum, they could soon find means to make the villages pay more—in the process, be it observed, drawing nearer to the land, and becoming more and more like real landlords, more in actual managing contact with the villages.

The change from revenue-manager to landlord was accomplished in about a century or rather more; and it soon came to be as noticeable in the case of the former officials, and speculators who were allowed in many cases to contract for the revenue, as it was in the case of the old Rájás or chiefs.

§ 6. *Extent of the Revenue-farming system.*

The system we are speaking of was rampant in Bengal, and was adopted in the northern districts of Madras; it also extended to Oudh, which had been what I may call a stronghold of the Hindu State organization; it was very common in the North-West Provinces, though subsequent historical circumstances prevented its final development in these districts. It never extended to South or Central Madras (where the Muhammadan rule was never fairly established), nor to the Dakhan and Bombay, because there the Muhammadan kings never adopted it; and though their rule was overthrown in the end, by the Delhi emperors, the latter were in turn overthrown by the Maráthás before their influence was much felt. As to the Maráthás themselves, their revenue ideal never encouraged farming at all, if it could be helped; and only *ex necessitate* the governors farmed single villages or small groups of land, as in the Nágpur State. It never extended to the Panjáb, because the Mughal rule passed away from that province before its ultimate decline; and local circumstances never would have favoured the system.

§ 7. *The Zamíndár in Bengal.*

It is perhaps an important coincidence that the system of revenue-contracting by Rájás or others, who alike received the name of 'Zamíndár[1],' should have been specially developed in Bengal, the very province where our own revenue experience was to be gained, and where our first lessons had to be learned.

In Bengal the farm-system seems to have been like a plant which, originally introduced for some special purpose, has taken root, and can never afterwards be got rid of,—overrunning everything else. By the year 1765 the system had so far borne fruit that the Zamíndárs had really become very like landlords. It is to be remembered that Lord Cornwallis, no less than the preceding administrators of the first twenty years of British rule, had come to India with no other idea of land-holding but that of 'landlord and tenant,' as they had known it at home. Even if the Zamíndárs had been less like landlords than they really were, it was almost inevitable that a system should have shaped itself in the minds of our legislators, by which some one person would be recognized as landlord. So strong was the effect of prevalent ideas, that years afterwards, when the tenures of village bodies in the North-West Provinces, and their peculiar constitution, were discovered, our public officers could with difficulty realize this state of things; and they kept on writing as if some one person in the village must be *the* proprietor. It is easy for us, who have now been made familiar with early tenures, primitive institutions and ideas of property, and the like, to form hasty judgments of Lord Cornwallis's measures. But such knowledge did not exist in his days; and if it had, I must repeat that the *Zamíndárs' growth had in the course of events, and in fact, gone too far* to

[1] The term 'Zamíndár' means simply 'holder' (dár) of 'land' (zamín), and in its primary and generalized meaning indicates any-one who holds land—a member of the cultivating or landowning class at large. But as applied officially by the Muhammadan rulers, it was essentially a vague term and probably was meant to be so. Oriental governments rarely define rights, and care nothing for consistency or symmetry. Hence the word has got to apply to a number of different things. No doubt a large number of the local meanings include some idea of a managing or landlord control over land; but that is all that can be said. I have endeavoured to simplify matters a little, by always writing the capital Z when I refer to a 'Zamíndár' in the Bengal sense.

make any plan which ignored their rights, feasible. For, on various grounds, the Zamíndárs had been distrusted, and repeated efforts had been made to get rid of them, and such efforts invariably failed. Exactly the same thing happened in Oudh. The king had made many of the old Rájás (and some others) into revenue-agents, under the local name of 'Taluqdár.' When (more than sixty years after the Bengal Settlement) our administrators tried to deal with the villages direct, and ignore the Taluqdárs, they found it could not be done[1]. The events of the Mutiny compelled the acknowledgment of the Taluqdárs as owners.

Thus the Mughal revenue-system is the direct cause of the (unforeseen) growth of the Zamíndár landlord of Bengal and the Taluqdár landlord of Oudh. Indirectly, also, it has resulted in all those special tenures under the landlords, which have been recognized in both provinces, with a view of doing justice to all parties. And this is not the only result; for all the long controversy about landlords' rights and tenants' rights, which have so long engaged attention in Bengal and elsewhere, have really originated in the same causes[2].

[1] These facts should be borne in mind when reading such general criticisms as those of M. de Laveleye, where he says (p. 117) 'L'hérédité de la terre fut établie en faveur des *Zamindárs* et des *Taluqdárs* par les Anglais : *et cet article de loi* opéra ainsi instantanément une transformation dans l'ordre social que ne s'est accomplie en Europe que par une évolution lente de plusieurs siècles.' Without being hypercritical, it may be pointed out that the law by which the Zamindár was recognized in the legal position of landlord, was made in 1793, and that by which the Taluqdárs were recognized was some sixty-five years later (1858), under a totally different state of things—at a time when the Government policy was dead against landlords,—and was forced on them by the stern logic of facts. The law in either case effected no instantaneous change; it merely fixed and defined a change which had been gradually brought about during more than a century. What it did do was suddenly to render possible all sorts of difficult questions about tenant right under the Zamíndár, which could only come to notice when rights received a sharp legal definition.

[2] In the North-West Provinces when persons were found in the position of Zamindárs or Taluqdárs over a number of villages, they were, if their claims could not be got over, settled with but subject to the temporary settlement and tenant laws. But the policy was to set them aside wherever possible and deal direct with the village bodies. Many Taluqdárí claims were got rid of (some writers maintain, with considerable injustice) by granting a cash allowance of ten per cent. on

§ 8. *Revenue-free Grants and Assignments.*

Whether the Muhammadan government consciously imitated the Hindu system of appointing certain chiefs to manage special territories—especially frontier and mountain-tracts—I cannot determine; but at a very early stage they adopted the plan of granting to court-favourites, to ministers of state, and to military officers, the right to collect the revenue of a certain area of country, and to take the amount collected, either to support their state and dignity, or—in the case of military chiefs—to equip a body of troops, to be available for the royal service.

The Mughal empire recognized a definite portion of its dominions as that which was directly managed by the emperor's officers, and another area as that available for the assignment of the revenue spoken of. And when certain offices or titles were conferred, a fixed grant went with them as an appanage. Such grants were called 'jágír[1].' They were at first always for life, and resumable with the office. Nearly all later governments have adopted the 'jágír,' but chiefly to support troops, or to reward a service of some kind. They are still granted by our own Government, but as a reward for services in the past, and not with the obligation of military service. In time it was thought below the dignity of the ruler to resume, and so the grant became permanent and hereditary. Possibly this stage was hastened by the fact that the governments—both Hindu and Muhammadan—had always been accustomed to grant smaller holdings of land, free of revenue, to pious

the revenue. No doubt the policy of the day had much to do with making Settlement officers keen to detect the survival of right in the village bodies; but apart from that, the villages were universally stronger and better preserved than those of Bengal: and consequently Zamíndárs and Taluqdárs were much less firmly rooted. Some of the districts of the North-West Provinces (Benares Division) had been permanently settled under the Bengal law: and here there are Zamíndárí estates, but with rights of the lower grades fully recorded and protected by the Tenant law.

[1] Contracted from 'jái-gír' = place holding.

persons, to support temples, mosques, schools, or bridges and tanks, and these were called ''inám,' or 'muá'fi,' and were usually hereditary and permanent (as long as the object was fulfilled). As the 'inám was permanent, so the jágír grew to be in many cases. Possibly, also, it was the decline of power which caused jágírs to be irregularly granted, and thus to become permanent. When a disorganized government desires to reward a worthy servant (or an unworthy), it generally has its treasury empty, and the easiest plan (though true policy would suggest a cash pension for life or lives) would be to give a man a grant by way of assignment, and allow him to collect what revenue he could off the area.

A great number of assignments of revenue in this way grew into landlord-tenures, very much as the 'Zamíndárí' estates did. This was much facilitated by the fact that the grantee was allowed, and indeed expected, in many cases, to conduct the revenue-administration in his own way, and of course he had (or assumed) the full right to all unoccupied or waste land in the *jágír*, and had many opportunities of ousting refractory land-holders—buying up their lands, taking them as security for arrears of revenue, and so forth. 'Jágírs' were sometimes granted with the express object of the grantee settling the waste; and then, naturally, he would be looked on as the landlord of the whole.

§ 9. *Ghátwál.*

I can hardly exclude from notice here, the tenures which arise in some parts of India, where officers or chiefs were granted the revenues of certain hill-districts commanding the passes into the plains, on condition of 'keeping the marches,' repressing robbers, &c. The ghátwálí tenures, arising from arrangements of this kind, will be found described under the head of Bengal tenures.

§ 10. *Girásiya* (*Grassiah*).

I should also mention under this head, a curious tenure[1] of Central India, which arose on the overthrow and dispersion of the Rájput local chiefs by the Muhammadan and by the Maráthá powers. Deprived of their regular estates, these persons prowled about with small bands of followers and harassed the villagers. In time, the village bodies or the Government officers were glad to purchase immunity from attack, by agreeing to pay over to the chiefs a certain fraction of the revenue, called 'gírás' (*lit.* a mouthful), which was regularly entered in the revenue accounts. In some cases this was commuted for a small grant of land; and we find 'grassia' tenures recognized in some places, and still surviving. It is analogous to the 'chaháram' right acquired by the Sikh adventurers in the Ambála district of the Panjáb.

SECTION IV. THE MODIFICATION OF TENURES BY THE SUPERIMPOSITION OF NEW INTERESTS IN THE SOIL BY CONQUEST, &c.

§ 1. *View of the Subject.*

It is a noteworthy feature of most Indian provinces that they have been the theatre of repeated tribal immigrations, and of military conquests in later times; besides undergoing a great many minor changes in the case of petty states breaking up, and changing hands, and particular individuals rising to local power. The course of history is like a continually shifting panorama or procession. First, the Aryan races overcome, or enter into relations with, Dravidians and Kols that were before them. Then Scythian and other immigrants gain the mastery, and great kingdoms professing the Buddhist faith, for a long time prevail over

[1] See Malcolm, *Memoir of Central India*, vol. i. p. 508 (original edition of 1824).

a great part of the country. The Brahmanic Hindus again assert themselves, and the Buddhist states disappear. Then come the Muhammadan conquests; and when a strong Muhammadan rule was established—a system of administration based on the old Hindu ideal—it lasted for a century, and then began to fall into decline, after many local wars and disruptions of territorial rule. The Maráthás of West India then rise to power, and introduce many ideas of their own. In the north, the Sikh confederacies overthrow the rule of Patháns from the frontier, and finally are united under a central government, once more of the old Hindu type, but with many of the features, and much of the nomenclature, of the Mughal revenue-system retained.

Lastly, the British power supervenes; and while its appearance arrests in one direction the further change of landed interests, and the loss of rights of all classes, in another direction it inaugurates a new change, by its own policy of recognizing rights in a certain category and then more or less logically deducing consequences from this recognition. By calling some men landlords and others tenants, and then enacting laws on this basis, the position and prospects of more than one class have been affected. No one can doubt that the change by which a local Rájá became, first, an estate-agent or revenue-farmer, and then a landlord of many acres, was great; but it was hardly greater than the changes which followed logically from the simple definition by legislative enactment, of the title of the 'Zamíndár,' although the definition was undertaken not with any intention to produce a change, but rather with the idea of preserving rights *in statu quo*.

§ 2. *Nature of the changes.—The Muhammadan rule.*

I have already remarked on the comparatively small ostensible changes that resulted from the Mughal empire. It was wholly a case of creating fresh interests in the land over the heads of the pre-existing ones. The 'Zamíndár' in Bengal and the 'Taluqdár' in Oudh have been so much discussed, that the consequences of their growth have come to appear greater, and the change made by the Muhammadan system more sweeping, than, relatively, it really was.

§ 3. *The Maráthá Conquest.*

The Maráthá power arose with Siváji in the latter half of the seventeenth century. These rulers were thrifty: they did not make many State grants of land, but allowed existing revenue-free lands or 'watan' holdings, sometimes imposing a 'joḍi' or quit-rent on them, which was heavy enough. When their power was well established, they recognized the advantage of dealing direct with the villagers through their hereditary headmen, and rarely employed middlemen and farmers, who, they knew, would always manage to intercept a good part of the receipts. No doubt, individual cultivators were ejected and changed, but the general customs of land-holding were, perhaps, less affected by Maráthá domination than by any other. The truth of this is proved by the exceptions; for there were districts where the Maráthá rule was never more than that of a temporary plunderer, and where it was perpetually in contest with powerful neighbours. In such districts it was necessary to farm the revenues of certain villages, and then the 'málguzár' (or the 'khot' of the Konkán), as is always the case, grew or worked himself into the position of proprietor of the village, crushing down the rights of the original landholders. There are districts in Bombay where the 'khoti' (landlord) tenure is to this day a regularly recognized one, being really nothing but a sort of managing right over certain areas, which has now become fixed in the families of *khots* or persons originally put in to farm the revenues.

Throughout the Central Provinces, where village revenue-farmers were employed, their families grew into the proprietary position, and were, whether rightly or otherwise, ultimately recognized as proprietors of the villages at our Revenue Settlement.

§ 4. *The Sikh Conquest.*

The Sikh Government cared nothing for the land-tenure, and only for its revenues. Where the village community, so universal in the Panjáb, was strong, it paid up the demand, and its customs were intrinsically unchanged. Nothing is commoner in Settlement Reports than to find allusions to the confusion introduced by the grinding Sikh rule into the land-tenures. This is true, however, rather of the holders of the land than of tenures. No doubt, in many districts and throughout the village estates, one man was ousted and another put in, without any regard to title, and only for the sake of getting the revenue, in the most arbitrary way. Afterwards, perhaps, the old ousted proprietors would come back, and get on to their land again as privileged tenants, or would be allowed some small rental or málikána in recognition of their lost position: and thus many cases of 'sub-proprietary rights' under a superimposed new proprietary layer, arose; but I am not aware that any new form of land-tenure owes its origin to the Sikh dominion—anything like the growth of the Zamíndárí or Taluqdárí tenure under the Mughal system.

When the Sikh rule became centralised under Ranjít Singh, all the smaller chiefs, as a rule, were absorbed, and became the proprietary holders of villages merely, or were regarded as 'jágírdárs' (for the Sikh system recognized the 'jágír'). Some few States survived under the suzerainty of the Mahárájá. This does not apply to the cis-Sutlej States, where the smaller Rájás retained their independence under British protection. At first a number of these exercised almost sovereign powers, but they were afterwards reduced to the condition of jágírdárs.

In the cis-Sutlej territory (Ambála district) a curious survival from the early Sikh incursions is noticeable. A number of the marauding clans passed over the district, and would have succeeded in establishing either a general rule or a landlord right over individual villages. But the communities were strong; and they often succeeded in making a bargain, giving one-fourth of the share of the ruler to the marauders. Sometimes two or more chiefs would contend together for a village and obtain the '*fourth*' share between them. When the district became British, the growth of these overlord rights, which might in time have become proprietary, was arrested. But the right of 'Chahāram,' or the fourth, was so well established, that the Government recognized the families as 'jágírdárs' entitled to one-fourth the revenue. The principle of joint succession affected these tenures in the usual way. The revenue fourth became divided among a number of shareholders; and Government had to make rules as to when the share should pass to collateral heirs and when lapse. And, apart from the joint succession, the revenue was often shared among the members of the clan according to their grade. Thus the original 'jágírdár' was the leader or chief of the 'misl' or fighting corporation; and every member of the misl (misldár) was entitled to some share in the profits. In jágírdárí villages, a 'sirkarda' collects the rents or dues of the jágírdár, and distributes them among the graduated ranks of the body, first to the chief, and next to the 'zaildárs,' or subordinate chiefs, whose families form so many 'pattís' receiving each the proper fractional part of the zail share; below them, the 'rank and file' (the tába'dár) are entitled to some still smaller fraction of the revenue.

§ 5. *Smaller Conquests.*

I have taken notice, it will be observed, only of the main conquests marked in the history of India. Smaller local incursions, like those of the Pindárís in Central India, and the Rohclás (or Rohillas) in Rohilkhand, produced only local effects, and they were chiefly destructive, either depopulating villages or changing the owners. No doubt as a consequence of these disasters, many villages fell into the hands of capitalists and revenue-managers, who became in time the landlords; but such changes affected rather the individual than the form of tenure.

§ 6. *Result of the changes.*

It will now, I think, be apparent, that while the customs of village landholding were originally simple, the effect of the different forms of rule has been partly to obliterate old tenures and create new ones, and partly to introduce confusion among the persons entitled to the tenure right, by *successively displacing the older proprietary bodies and allowing later and more powerful successors to lord it over them.* In either case the result has been to leave a series of proprietary strata, in which the upper ones have become, *de facto*, the proprietors, but the lower ones each in his turn, have certain claims, which ought not to be ignored. When all the facts are taken into consideration, it will appear that the attempt to provide legally for the proper position of these various shades of proprietary right in our modern Indian law, is no easy task.

In some cases no overlord has grown up, and we have only the direct occupant to deal with, and the interest he has in his own field or holding is defined by law without much difficulty. It has been practically and simply laid down by the Revenue Code, in Bombay; and in British Burma it has also received definition, though a somewhat complicated and technical one.

It is in countries (like Bengal, Oudh, and the Central Provinces) where we have to deal with a series of concurrent interests, that the greatest difficulty arises. And it is easy to see that the different parties may have preserved very different degrees of right. In some cases the now dominant proprietor may have clearly distanced all rivals; the people under him have sunk, past revival, into being tenants. But in others, the claims of the present and former proprietor may be very evenly balanced, and it may not be easy to say who is really best entitled; or again, granted a clear predominance of one, there still may be so much to be said for the other, that some practical form of recognition is equitably a necessity, though under what name, may be doubtful.

§ 7. *How the concurrent interests subsist.*

It will be observed that this concurrent existence of several interests in the soil, is rendered possible by the fact that property or interest in land is more concerned with the *produce and with dividing it*, than anything else. Suppose, for instance, an old group of village cultivators with several rights: each takes the produce of his own fields, after allowing the village menials and officers their customary share, and after the State officer has taken the king's share. Suppose now a chief obtains a grant of the village or annexes it. He simply takes the Rájá's share and whatever else he can impose. His family after him do the same. Next, the Sikh Government (let us say) succeeds and imposes its revenue, taking a share alike for the landlord family and the old cultivators. In process of time the Sikh governor grants an interest in the village to a capitalist who proposes to spend money in irrigating the village. He takes his share theoretically out of the State share, but as the produce is now largely increased by the water, the actual amount taken by the grantee is an extra. Lastly, some pious person establishes a shrine, and the governor grants him a 'mu'áfí' of some fractional share of the State Revenue. He then goes to the villagers and all concerned, and arranges with them how his share is to be collected. In the course of time the 'mu'áfídár,' if not checked, will begin to claim and to cultivate the waste, to oust indigent or lazy villagers, and to grow into landlord of the whole. The case just given is a real one, observed in the neighbourhood of the Jihlam River in the Panjáb.

§ 8. *Grades of interest in the soil under British law.—State-Landlord tenure.*

When British rule began, it was recognized alike by the authorities on the spot and by the Home Government, that to grant or recognize a secure title in land was the best way to protect rights and at the same time to secure the Government revenue. It was in pursuance of this policy that the Bengal 'Zamíndárs,' of whom I have so often spoken, were recognized as proprietors or landlords. There was no doubt about their being distinctly in the uppermost grade of interest; and in the Regulations but little was said as to what was to be the name and nature of the rights below them.

A certain number of these rights indeed provided for themselves. Some of the stronger holders had managed to get from the State officers certain titles (locally known as *taluqs*) which entitled them to separate themselves from the Zamíndárí and become proprietors themselves: and in our early Bengal Settlement proceedings, a considerable number of persons succeeded in getting the Collector to record them as 'independent' of the 'Zamíndárs.' But nothing definite was settled about any other class.

§ 9. *Taluqdárí or Double Tenure.*

In other provinces it was in many cases found to be more questionable who (among several possible claimants) should be deemed the 'actual proprietor,' to be recognized as such by law, and to be responsible for the land-revenue payment. When once the village constitution prevalent in the North-West Provinces was understood, the policy of Government set strongly in the direction of recognizing the village co-sharers. As already mentioned in a note, when some overlord appeared, if the claim was so strong as to amount to the proprietorship, it was recognized; but in many cases the overlordship was held to be sufficiently provided for by a cash allowance, and the villagers were treated as owners, and with them the Settlement was made. These cases are the 'double' or 'taluqdárí' tenures of the North-West Provinces reports. The term implies that both parties have retained something of the landlord character, and that the proprietary benefit is divided between them. Most commonly the one gets a cash percentage on the revenue, and the other the management and other profits of the land. This tenure is confined to Upper India. It must not be confused with the tenure of the Taluqdárí landlords in Oudh[1]. These latter are sole landlord tenures, and the rights under them may be, some of them, 'sub-proprietary,' as the phrase is, or else in the form of tenant rights. The landlord is the person with whom the Revenue Settlement is made, and in cases where the others are protected, it is by a 'sub-settlement' or by record of their rights.

The Oudh Taluqdár, in fact, is a landlord very much like the Bengal Zamíndár, only that the extent of his interest and the amount of his profits vary in different estates, according to the greater or less degree in which the rights of the villagers (or others) have been preserved or have grown up; and it might be the case that most of the villages had strong rights, or it might be that the villages were much broken down and had no claims to any higher position than that of tenant, perhaps having occupancy rights claimable in one plot or another. In one case the Taluqdár would be little more than the holder of a rent charge on the estate; in the other he would be a nearly unfettered proprietor. As a matter of fact, the 'sub-settlement' villages are not numerous, but other (lesser) rights are; and the Taluqdár's position is something between the two extremes.

[1] Of course as regards any particular village which had retained strong rights under a Taluqdár, so that the latter's interest was a mere rent-charge, the tenure would be *quá* that village—an instance of the taluqdárí or double tenure. But I am speaking of the Taluqdár's title in the abstract.

§ 10. *Instances from the Panjáb—The 'alá málik.*

In the Panjáb again, where the overlord's right was found to be weak, or very ill-founded in origin, it was invariably set aside by the grant of a percentage on the revenue, while the villages 'hold the Settlement' with Government direct, only paying a somewhat higher rate to provide for the superior's allowance. But in not a few cases—in villages near the frontier and in the south for example—there is an individual or a family having the superior right over the village, which has not extinguished the right of the body below. In such cases the one party is called the ''alá málik,' and the other 'adná málik,' in revenue language. According to circumstances, the former may have little but a rent-charge or a share in the produce, while the other body have the water rights, and the management, and the waste, &c.; or else the ''alá málik' body may have the right to the waste besides other privileges.

Again, in some villages, where the present proprietary bodies are sufficiently well established to be the sole holders of the Settlement, certain ancient cultivators, or persons themselves once, in bygone times, the superiors, may nevertheless have such claims that a tenant-right is hardly enough for them. In that case they are called 'málik maqbúza,' i. e. sub-proprietor or 'proprietor of the holding'; implying that while this class does not manage the estate as a whole, or share in the waste or the profits, still, as regards their individual fields or holdings, they are proprietors; they pay nothing but the State revenue, and of course possess a heritable and alienable right over which the proprietary body (of the village) have no control whatever. In this instance we do not treat the case as one of double tenure, though obviously it is a sort of transition between the double tenure and the mere landlord and tenant tenure.

§ 11. *Meaning of 'Settlement' and 'Sub-settlement.'*

The person who is the 'actual proprietor,' whether he has or has not under him some subordinate proprietors of one kind or another, is the person whom Government looks to as responsible for the land-revenue assessed on the estate; because he is the person who enjoys the bulk of the profits which remain after it is paid. So that when there was more than one interested party, and it became a question for decision who is the 'actual proprietor,' the decision of that also disposed of the question, with whom shall the Settlement be made—who shall 'hold the Settlement' (as the revenue phrase is).

When it was determined that a given individual or body was to hold the Settlement and be the actual or principal proprietor, it might be necessary to protect the rights of a grade below, by making what is called a 'sub-settlement,' or in the older books a 'mofussil (mufassal) settlement.' This proceeding not only established the inferior's rights by record, but fixed the amount he was to pay to the superior, so that there was no question of the latter treating him as tenant and trying to enhance the rent or eject him.

§ 12. *Grades of Proprietary Right.*

We see then that, as evolved from the train of historical circumstances, the 'right of the proprietor' is only in some cases a simple thing. There are in fact *grades of proprietary right*, a series of persons, each with some of the characteristics of landowner, as Western nations understand the term. And consequent on this superposition of proprietary interest, all proprietary tenures can be brought under one of four classes:—

I. The Government itself may be the direct owner: as of waste land which it does not sell out-and-out; of a village which has been forfeited for crime, or has lapsed for want of heirs, &c., or has been sold for arrears of revenue and bought in [1]—here the cultivators become tenants properly so called. This latter class of estates is mostly found in Bengal, and but rarely in Upper India, the system there

[1] Land so held is said in revenue language to be held 'k͟hás' or 'k͟hám,' or to be a 'k͟hás estate.'

being unfavourable to the retention of such estates as a rule.

Of course all public forests, large areas of available waste, and other public property, may be brought under this class; but I am speaking of cultivated and appropriated lands, which would otherwise be in the hands of some other owner.

II. The Government recognizes *no* proprietary right between itself and the actual holder of the land (i.e. it creates or allows no proprietary right in a village or other larger area over the heads of the actual landholders). This is the simple form of raiyatwárí holding under the Bombay and Madras systems, and in Burma, Assam, &c.

III. Government recognizes *one grade* of proprietor between itself and the actual landholder. It settles for its revenue with this proprietor and secures the rights of the others.

IV. Government recognizes *two grades* of 'proprietor' between the landholders and itself. This is the taluqdárí tenure[1]. In the Panjáb and North-Western Provinces the Settlements get rid of this where possible by dealing direct with the villages, and granting to the person possessing the taluqdárí, or superior right, a cash allowance; but the tenure exists in Upper India.

§ 13. *Remarks on these Classes.*

The full understanding of these forms of tenure cannot be attained till progress has been made in the study of the local development of the system in each province; but I hope that what is here said will serve to introduce, as it were, the terms which will be constantly in use in the sequel.

The *first* of these proprietary tenures is only occasional, and presents no difficulty in understanding it.

The *second* we shall meet with in Madras and Bombay, where it is the natural tenure resulting from the old or non-

[1] There may possibly be more than two grades: but in such (rare) cases the analogy is exactly the same.

landlord village, the constitution of which had never been seriously interfered with by the Maráthá and other conquerors, except in some special cases, where a landlord having grown up, a single or double proprietary tenure arose in consequence[1].

The *third* of the classes finds its most perfect exemplification in the Zamíndár of the Bengal permanent Settlement[2], and in the málguzár or village proprietor of the Central Provinces, in both of which cases we find a new proprietor —the result of the revenue system, recognized over the original village-holding. The village communities of the North-West Provinces and the Panjáb are brought under this class, perhaps more theoretically than practically. Each landholder who has his share secured to him by record, or actually divided out to him in severalty (as is so often the case in these communities), is really owner of the share and pays the revenue on it, as independently as does the 'registered occupant' of a separately numbered lot or holding under the Bombay system; but the form is not the same: the Government does not settle with the individual sharer for any revenue, but agrees with the whole body through its representative, for a lump sum, and regards the whole body jointly as proprietor. The several holders are only bound to pay the share which custom or personal law directs; but that is a matter of internal concern to the village, not to the Government. As regards Government, and the liability for revenue, the *village body is the (ideal) proprietor* intermediate between the individual landholders or sharers and the State.

[1] Wherever there is only one class of separate field or farm holders paying revenue to Government direct, they are never called 'landlords' of their fields. They are always spoken of as 'occupants' —or something similar—probably owing to the lingering idea of Government being in some sense the superior lord, and they the 'tenants' *in a sense*; but probably, owing to the natural associations which cling to the word 'landlord' in India; we always instinctively think of some one who has gained or been granted, or has conquered or usurped the right *over* some earlier body of cultivators. A 'Jumma raiyat' of Coorg would hardly be called 'landlord' of his fields, although his tenure is a favoured one, and, as its name implies, is his 'birthright.'

[2] And in the Zamindári portions of Madras.

The *fourth* form is found in cases where the overlord's right has not developed so far as to make him sole landlord and all others mere tenants. In that case we have to count both the superior and the secondary interest as terms in the scale, so that we get (1) the taluqdár, (2) the village proprietary body or the individual landholder; or, in cases where there is an ''alá málik,' over the village body (adná málik), we should count up (1) the alá málik, (2) the inferior proprietary body (*as a body*), (3) the individual co-sharers.

§ 14. *Diagram of Proprietorship.*

It will perhaps aid in fixing these facts in the memory if I give a diagram showing the *series* of proprietary interests at one glance.

Government the only owner.	Between Government and the soil 0.	One Grade.	Two Grades.
Government is itself the direct owner. *Examples* :— Waste lands (not leased, &c.) Khás estates. Escheats. Forfeitures.	No one over the actual occupant, who may or may not be called 'proprietor' *eo nomine*. *Example* :— All Raiyatwárí villages in Madras, Bombay, and in Burma, Assam, &c.	*One* landlord over the soil cultivator or 'tenant' occupant. *Examples.*— Bengal Zamíndár. Oudh Taluqdár (in some cases). Joint body owning a village (as *represented* by their 'lambardár'). An auction purchaser at a sale for arrears of revenue. All persons once grantees, revenue farmers who have become *de facto* owners and are so recognized at Settlement.	1. An overlord—Taluqdár or Rájá, whose right may be represented by a mere rent charge, or may be more considerable. 2. The landlord, individual, or joint body of village sharers. 3. The actual occupant or co-sharer in the body. *Example*—Taluqdárí tenures in N. W. P. and Panjáb only consisting in a 10 per cent. interest. Taluqdárí in Oudh, where there is—(1) a Taluqdár; (2) a village *birtiya* or grantee landlord, subordinate, but protected by sub-settlement; the actual village soil occupants.
The 'Khás' or tenure by Government.	The Raiyatwárí tenure.	The 'zamíndárí' or landlord tenure.	The Taluqdárí or double tenure.

§ 15. *Grades other than Proprietary.—Difficulty of classing them.*

I have hitherto dealt with cases where an incoming conqueror, usurping grantee, or revenue agent, has become the superior landlord, and where the people, who *but for him* would themselves have been in the landlord or first rank, have been reduced but still have retained rights *which in their nature* are considered to be 'proprietary.'

But it is in the nature of things that the process of growth of what I may now call the upper layer, has been more or less complete, and may have reduced the rights below to something so indefinite, that it is matter of great doubt how to class or define them.

In Bengal the rights that remained after all *proprietary* rights were made independent of the Zamíndár, were not recognised as *sub-proprietary* or by any similar term. At the same time it is not easy to call them 'tenant-rights.' They have been called 'tenures' for convenience. No attempt has been made to *define* what is a 'tenant' right and what a 'tenure' right, though the modern tenant law draws the distinction and allows very important privileges to the 'tenure' over and above what it allows to the 'raiyat' or tenant.

In other provinces, after such rights have been allowed as are fairly called 'sub-proprietary,' or those of 'inferior proprietor,' all others are frankly treated as *tenant-right* in some grade or degree, and are protected under the law of landlord and tenant.

Every provincial law will be found to have its own series of tenants as defined for the purposes of the law; each series has certain greater and lesser privileges, as we go to the top of the scale (where the occupancy-tenant is hardly inferior to an owner) or to the bottom, where he is almost (or quite) a tenant dependent on contract with a landowner, or is a tenant of a tenant, which again is a mere matter of contract.

We must, in short, in India, everywhere be prepared to find 'tenants' so called in one place who are undistinguishable from those recorded as 'inferior proprietors' in another. The want of theoretic uniformity is however of no consequence, as long as practical security of enjoyment is given. So also we must be prepared to find 'tenants' whose position *owes absolutely nothing to any contract with the landlord*, or owes it to such contract, solely in its present shape. Hence the law has taken large powers to limit the landlord's power over the tenancy.

It should also be borne in mind that, in nearly every case (in some cases more markedly so than others), the landlord *owes his position to the grant or to the recognition and adoption of the British Government.* The Government in fact virtually limited its own demands and interests, and thus created valuable estates in land with a permanence and security that never really existed before. Being in that position, the Government had every right to say, 'we shall not give all the benefit to one party; we shall distribute the interest in the land so that some of its value shall go to the landlord class and some to the soil-holders, whom, for want of a better name, we call tenants.'

The reader who is tempted to regard as very great the privileges allowed under such law as the Central Provinces Tenant Act (for example) should always, as a corrective, recall to mind the fact just stated.

SECTION V. THE RELATION OF LANDLORD AND TENANT.

Let us now devote a brief attention to the classes of right which have been provided for as *tenant* rights or interests. And let me once more repeat that the continual changes that the succession of conquests and governments, and the successive grants, usurpations, and other acquisitions of interest they have given rise to, have left different classes of rights in different stages of decay or preservation. The first result is that, as already remarked, not a few of these 'tenancies' are totally independent of any contract or grant of the present overlord or landlord.

§ 1. *Cases of Natural Tenant Right.*

And the commonest instances of a 'natural' tenant right of this kind are the following:—(1) We may be certain that once the 'resident tenants,' whose home has been in the village for generations, were once individual soil-owners, perhaps first-clearers,' with the right which we have so often alluded to as asserted by Manu. Perhaps even they are members of a family that once flourished as village landlords, but have fallen into poverty and decay, and been obliged to handle the plough and accept the tenant position. But (2) there may be resident tenants who were always inferiors in the village, humble dependants (e.g.) of the original founders, who were privileged as helping in the first work of colonization; or they may have, for many years, been made to pay exactly as if they were owners, by the governor of the province. In the Panjáb, under Sikh government, it was almost universally the case that the tenants were made to bear just the same burdens as the landlords; the governor in fact drew no distinction.

§ 2. *Tenants in Bengal.*

There can be no doubt that when the Zamíndárs were legally recognized, and such persons as could show a right to hold independently of the Zamíndár were acknowledged, all the other cultivators became raiyats or tenants; and inevitably, in the minds of English officers, and in the law-courts, this suggested a right to *enhance* the payments of the tenants and to *eject* them if they would not pay.

No doubt the intention was to protect tenants, but the framers of the law did not know how to do it: it was thought that to prohibit the levy of extra *cesses* was an effective mode of protection; and it was supposed that, by making it legally binding on the landlords to grant *pattas* or written leases, there would be an end to uncertainty and extortion. No doubt a few influential persons, who could secure a fixed rent and permanent tenure, possessed such documents: but the common tenantry refused to take leases; in some cases, doubtless, because they feared that, by such acceptance, they might be held to admit an inferior position; but chiefly because they would bind themselves absolutely to pay without a chance of throwing up the land in a bad year, or to pay an amount which they knew the landlord would enter in his own terms—and these they could neither read nor understand. No other protection was provided: the law was silent as to any rule or limit of enhancement; it defined a small class of persons whose tenure was already known by Persian names implying fixity of possession and a permanent rate of rent, and that was all.

But in Bengal, as elsewhere, if we regard the entire scale of rights below the landlord, we shall find, at one end of the series, the small class just alluded to, and at the other end of the series, the real tenants, people who were cultivating the landlord's private lands, or who had been located by him on his own waste. It might be reasonably said that no special protection was needed for these: land was then abundant, and owners were only too anxious to get and to keep tenants, at any rate those who paid full rents[1]. Had any serious oppression been attempted, tenants of this class would have resisted and gone off to the next estate, where the owner would probably have welcomed them. But between these first and last members of the scale, there is the large class of permanent resident cultivators to whom it is no light matter to break up home, leave the acres they have held for generations and move on to another estate. They are distinguished in our earlier revenue books by the (Persian) term 'khud-kásht.' That all were equal in point of right is not to be supposed, though very many of them must have been, or have represented, the original soil-owners—that is a matter of detail: one thing

[1] It is said that, at the date of the Permanent Settlement, one-half to two-thirds of Bengal was uncultivated.

was quite clear,—*they* were in *possession absolutely independently of any contract with the Zamíndár.* The law could not, however, lay down that they *never* were to have their rates enhanced, though phrases verging on that may be quoted from official opinions and minutes; for it is to be remembered that, even if they had remained as proprietors, the State could, and would, have periodically revised their payments, and therefore it could not be supposed that the Zamíndár was denied a similar power when the cultivator's payments were handed over to him. But some rule of enhancement was clearly needed; and unfortunately no definite idea was entertained as to what should be done. Meanwhile, the necessities of punctual revenue-collection and the inevitable result of the introduction of the European idea of 'landlord' and 'tenant,' both worked directly against the old 'khud-kásht' tenant, though of course not designedly.

§ 3. *Effect of Revenue-realization Laws.*

The Government had always said that if the Zamíndárs did not or could not pay up the revenue, it must look to the estate to do so, and that the estate would be sold *at once,* if any arrears accumulated. And, as will appear fully in the sequel regarding Bengal history, circumstances brought about a vast number of *sales for arrears of revenue* during the first ten years[1]. These sales, of course, necessitated the purchaser being given the estate free of 'incumbrances' created by the defaulter; if it were not so, all sorts of fraud would have been perpetrated; a careless man would have raised all the cash he could on his estate, and then defaulted and let it go. But not only definite incumbrances such as mortgages

[1] The revenue at first is admitted by good judges to have been heavy, with reference to the circumstances, and especially with reference to a recent famine (1772), of which such a graphic account is given in Hunter's *Annals of Rural Bengal.* As time went on, matters rapidly improved, and sales became less and less frequent. The revenue is now, as I have stated before, extraordinarily light.

had to be avoided, but also existing contracts about the rental; and little by little the position of the old resident cultivators was forgotten, and the right of the purchaser to enhance even *their* rents came to be acknowledged.

§ 4. *And of Laws to facilitate Rent-collection.*

At the same time also the Zamíndárs complained of difficulties in realizing their rents; and Regulations (notably those of 1799 and 1812), which have become locally famous, were framed to help the landlord, fairly as it was thought, and without injuring the tenant; but as they threw on the tenant the burden of proving that the rent demanded by the landlord was *not* the proper rent, the effect was, as has been said, to commence proceedings with a 'knock-down' blow to the tenant.

§ 5. *The Zamíndárs begin to farm their Estates.*

Then, too, arose further complications—the Zamíndárs took to creating renting-interests over fractional parts of their estates: in other words, as soon as they became well enough off, they divested themselves of the trouble of directly managing and collecting their own rents, by accepting a proportion of the rent-total, and living on that, leaving to a farmer or lessee the duty of collecting the whole and running up the rent-roll to what he could for his own benefit. The rental of an estate was, say, Rs. 50,000 at a certain date, that being the total the Zamíndár had himself fixed. The Zamíndár then created a tenure called a 'patni,' and in effect said to the holder of the patni, 'Pay me Rs. 30,000 and realise the balance (and whatever else you can raise) for yourself.' This directly stimulated the further raising of rents[1], till at last the position of the tenants

[1] And when the contractor or patnidár had so run up the rental (partly, be it observed, by *bona fide* and large extensions of cultivation of the abounding waste, or by improving lands) that he again could afford to retire, he would *sub-let* his farm to another man (and he in turn to another in succession).

grew so bad that, after long discussions, the drafting of a tenant law was seriously taken in hand in 1859. The subject has thenceforth continuously been kept in view, till the Act of 1885 has furnished a (perhaps not final but) greatly improved *modus vivendi*.

Thus, under the one head we have so far been attending to, arose a fine crop of troubles and legislative anxieties out of that benevolent blunder, the Permanent Settlement. This sketch of the history of the tenant troubles in Bengal was worth giving at such length, because it illustrates throughout the ways in which indirectly, and in some degree insensibly, complications of tenure arise out of measures that in themselves seem necessary or unobjectionable.

Let us now turn to the provinces later acquired.

§ 6. *Other Provinces—Definition of Tenant right.*

In all provinces, according to the varying circumstances of each, the law has found it necessary to *classify* tenants according to the facts of their origin and position. The mistake made in Bengal was not repeated. Each class, as defined, is respectively secured in certain privileges, which are naturally greater according as the class is higher (more nearly approaching to a proprietary interest), or lower (approaching more nearly to a contract-tenancy). The first and most important thing is to define the circumstances which make a tenant of this class or that. Usually, when the proof of the facts would involve going back to a remote date, but it is found that certain conditions have been maintained for a long time—say twenty years—the law (as now in Bengal) will aid the tenant by raising a presumption that what has subsisted for twenty years is the ancient *status*, and will accordingly throw the burden of proving the contrary, on the landlord. It is then possible to define the circumstances which give rise to each class of occupancy right. In the Panjáb all the privileged classes of tenants are thus defined with reference to certain easily understood facts of tenure.

§ 7. *Where definition is more difficult.*

But in Bengal and the North-West Provinces, the history of the resident tenants was so obscure, that it was impossible to say definitely what were the facts of the tenure, so as to place any tenant in this class or in that. The Gordian knot was therefore cut rather than untied, and provision was made that any tenant who has continuously occupied land in the village for twelve years, is an occupancy-tenant[1]. This well-known 'twelve years' rule' was invented in 1859, and certainly under such conditions as those prevailing in Bengal, it was a fair rule; for while it secured all persons justly entitled, it could only occasionally have benefitted persons not entitled; and if it did so, it was hardly to be regretted, when we reflect what a long period of suffering tenants had gone through before the question of their rights was understood. But the rule was not invented in Bengal; it was proposed for the North-West Provinces, and was originally a compromise between the opponents of tenant right and those who wished to give an occupancy right to *all resident* village cultivators, and who further would have called all tenants settled for three years 'resident.'

§ 8. *Nature of the Privilege.*

The 'occupancy-right' has, of course, various forms and conditions in the different laws; but, speaking generally, all laws give a protection against *enhancement* without order of a Court—on specific grounds; and protection against *ejectment* without a decree. Either provision would be useless without the other. It would be of no use to say a tenant cannot be ejected, if at the same time his rent could be so raised as to make his position unprofiable; it would be of

[1] At first certain restrictions were placed on the rule: the tenant must have held the *same fields* for twelve years, and this is still the law in the North-West Provinces. The fear is that the landlord might defeat the law, by shifting the tenant from one holding to another, without incurring the *odium* of ejecting him altogether. Some of the laws have abandoned this distinction, and made it suffice to hold *any* land in the village.

no use to limit enhancement, if the landlord could give the tenant notice to quit. And all tenant laws further regulate such matters as distraint for arrears of rent; date for paying rents; the division of payments into seasonable instalments; and the grant of receipts for rent paid. Provision is also made for the division of the crop, in provinces where rents are still paid largely in kind (e.g. the Panjáb).

A very important matter also is the subject of improvements—what they are, and who is to make them, and what compensation, if any, is to be paid on ejectment of a tenant who has 'an improvement' to his credit.

§ 9. *Controversy as to the general Twelve-years' Rule.*

Notwithstanding the necessity for *some* protection to tenants in the shape of occupancy rights, the question, especially the general application of a twelve years' rule, evoked a sharp controversy. It raged in Bengal, and was renewed when it was found that the ordinary twelve years' rule was not sufficient; it raged in the Panjáb in consequence of the adoption of North-West Province forms in recording rights, the record of tenants of twelve years' standing as 'maurúsí' or hereditary tenants[1], and the attempts later made, to modify this record.

The tenant rights controversy in the Central Provinces was on somewhat different matters.

§ 10. *The Case stated on both sides.*

There have been able officials ranged on either side; since on either, a plausible argument may be advanced, both as to the facts and as to the policy. Those who favoured the landlords' view would urge that it was unfair to the Zamíndárs and other proprietors now saddled with the responsibility, strict and unbending, for the revenue that

[1] The occupancy-tenant is commonly spoken of as 'maurúsí káshtkár': but in legal parlance he is 'muzár'a mustaqil' (fixed or permanent cultivator).

was to be paid in good years and bad alike, to tie their hands, and to refuse them the full benefit of their lands by creating an artificial right in their tenantry; such a rule would be to virtually deprive the landlord of the best share of his proprietary rights. If it was wise of Government to recognize the proprietary right at all, it must be wise also to recognize the full legal and logical consequences of that right. True it might be, that in old days tenants were never turned out, but that was the result of circumstances, not of right; and if the circumstances have changed, why not let the practice of dealing with tenants alter too? The proprietors are the people we designed to secure, in order to make them the fathers of their people, to whom we looked for the improvement of the country at large, and for the consequent increase of the general wealth. Why should we doubt that they will act fairly in their new position? Let any tenant who can prove definitely a certain claim, have it by all means; but do not give rights *en masse*, in the hope of including all real cases, while also granting them to many not at all equitably entitled.

On the other side the advocate of the tenant would reply: The new landlords confessedly owe their position to the gift of Government; why should they get all? why should not the benefits conferred be equally divided between the raiyats on the soil and the 'proprietors'? The raiyats are the real bread-winners and revenue-makers, more quiet and peaceable, less liable to political emotions, and more interested in the stability of things as they are. Many of the tenants we know to have been reduced to that condition from an originally superior status. And if it is not so, the landlord ought to be able to show definitely that *he* originated the tenancy, and had not let it run unquestioned for a long period—twelve years—which in the case of 'adverse possession,' under the Law of Limitation, was the term which would give a title. And even if the tenant had no such original position, as far as his history can be traced, still the custom of the country is all in favour of a fixed holding.

In old days, if a powerful man ousted a cultivator, it was by his mere power, not by any inherent right, or that the public opinion supported him in so doing. But as a matter of fact no cultivator ever was ousted; he was too valuable. In the rare cases in which he was ejected, it was either because he failed to pay or to cultivate properly (which is still allowed as a ground for ejection), or else it was to make room for some favoured individual, which of course was an act of pure oppression: why should not the law still protect the tenant from such evictions?

The question is in truth not one which can be theoretically determined, because the idea of landlord and tenant, as we conceive the terms, and the consequences which flow from it, have no natural counterpart in Indian custom.

We have a double difficulty to deal with:—the vast number of 'tenants,' who have a valid claim to be considered, because their position (however difficult to define and formally prove), does not depend on contract, and also the case of tenants whose origin is not doubtful, but whose position has been seriously affected by the new order of things—a competition for land instead of a competition to get tenants and keep them. All we can do is to make the best *practical* rules for securing a fair protection to all parties.

The principle of the twelve years' rule was adopted, reasonably enough as regards the Zamíndárí estates that were settled under the old Bengal system, and probably equally so as regards the North-Western Provinces, where village communities of landlord families had grown up.

In the Central Provinces Act X[1] was put in force, under certain special conditions, but is now replaced by a special law. In the Panjáb and in Oudh it was never adopted. There, it was sufficient to provide for the special case of those tenants who had a 'natural' or customary right to be considered permanent.

[1] This Act is now generally repealed, and only remains in force in a few districts of Bengal; but the twelve years' rule has been retained in the Acts which superseded it in the different provinces.

§ 11. *Tenancies in Raiyatwárí Provinces.*

In the provinces where the Government deals directly with the occupants of the land, tenant right has given no trouble. But of course tenancies exist. A man may contract to cultivate land as a tenant-at-will or he may have something of a hereditary claim to till the land, as much under a raiyatwárí system as any other. But the question of subordinate rights never becomes as difficult of solution in such countries, as it does in those where the recognized proprietor is a middleman between the cultivator and the State.

SECTION VI. THE NATURE OF 'PROPERTY IN LAND.'

§ 1. *Introductory.*

When the tenures of land in India first began to be studied, it was not so much because of their great historic and social interest, but because of the more prosaic but practical reason, that without understanding the way in which the people held land (and felt it ought to be held), it was impossible to determine who should be responsible for the payment of the Government land-revenue, and consequently should, as 'proprietor,' benefit by the remainder —and a large and valuable remainder it would become— when once the Government demand was properly limited. It is hardly surprising therefore, that at the commencement of the enquiries, a large part of the early reports and minutes was occupied with two questions, which were connected together, or rather, one of which arose out of the other. The first question was, whether Government was or had become, in the course of historical changes, the actual owner or universal landlord of all land, or whether there was, in India, any real private property in the land. The second was whether Government took its land-revenue as a *rent* for the use and occupation of land, or as a sort of *tax* which represented a share in the produce converted into money.

There can be no doubt that in the latter part of the eighteenth century, when British administration began, the different native rulers who preceded us, had asserted rights as the universal landowners. That being the case, our Government succeeded, legally, to the same claim and title.

If it were determined that Government might be justly regarded as owner of the land, then of course what it took from the actual cultivator might be regarded as *rent*; and Government was further entitled to take the whole of the remaining produce of land, after allowing the cultivator the costs of cultivation and the profits of his capital. If not, it was rather a question of words whether the Government revenue was a rent or a tax.

It will, then, be proper for us to consider (1) What, according to the ancient authorities, Hindu and Muhammadan, were the established ideas regarding the right to land as vested in the State and the private individual respectively. (2) What the actual custom and practice were. (3) What practical solution was adopted by the British Government. (4) And what is the consequent true view of the modern land-revenue?

§ 2. '*Proprietary Right.*'

The first thing that will strike the student is the use of the term 'proprietary right' in these pages and in Indian Revenue books generally. It does not occur in text-books on English law or jurisprudence. I presume that the use of such a phrase is due to the feeling that we rarely acknowledge anything like a complete unfettered right vested in any one person. The interest in the soil has come to be virtually shared between two or even more *grades*, the cause of which we just now discussed. It is true that, in many cases, only one person is called 'landlord' or 'actual proprietor,' but his right is limited[1]; the rest of the right, so to speak, is in the hands of the other grades, even though they are called 'tenants,' or by some vague title such as 'tenure-holders.' In many cases, as we have seen, this division of right is accentuated by the use of terms like 'sub-proprietor' or 'proprietor of his holding.' 'The proprietary right' seems then a natural expression for the interest held by a landlord, when that interest is not the entire 'bundle of rights' (which in the aggregate make up an absolute or complete estate) but only *some* of them, the remainder being enjoyed by other persons.

§ 3. *Existence of Property in Land in India.*

The older writers often raised a discussion on this subject; some maintaining that the law and custom of the various countries of India always acknowledged a real ownership in land vested in private persons; others maintaining the contrary.

But such a discussion, except for the information that is elicited in the course of it, cannot be a fruitful one, because there is no natural or universal standard of what 'property in land' is.

In English law, for example, there is no such thing as an absolute ownership of the soil vested in any private person. Dr. Field remarks[2], 'As a matter of fact no one ever did or can own land in any country, i.e. in the sense of absolute ownership—such ownership as a man may have in moveable property, as e.g. in a cow or a sheep which may be stolen, killed and eaten, or in a table or a chair which may be broken up and burned at the pleasure of its owner.' And the author refers to Williams (*On the Law of Real*

[1] For instance, in the case of the Bengal Zamíndár, whose origin we have sketched (and shall discuss more in detail in the chapters on Bengal), he is called 'landlord'; but, as one of the High Court Judges remarked in his judgment in the great Rent Case of 1865, 'The Regulations teem with provisions quite incompatible with any notion of the Zamíndár being absolute proprietor.'

[2] Field, p. 509.

Property. pp. 1, 20), 'who after remarking on the erroneous notions too generally entertained . . . . on the subject of property in land, goes on to say—"The thing that the student has to do is to get rid of the idea of absolute ownership. Such an idea is quite unknown to the English law: no man is, in law, absolute owner of lands; he can only hold an estate in them."'

Estate properly means the interest owned by an individual (as 'estate for life,' 'estate in fee simple,' &c.). But in popular phrase 'estate' is applied to the land itself, and it is so used in the Regulations (XLVIII of 1793, XIX of 1795, &c.).

Sir George Campbell (*Essay on Indian Land Tenures*, Cobden Club Papers), well sums up the subject as follows:—

'The long-disputed question, whether private property in land existed in India before the British rule, is one which can never be satisfactorily settled, because it is, like many disputed matters, principally a question of the meaning to be applied to words. Those who deny the existence of property mean property in one sense; those who affirm its existence mean property in another sense. We are too apt to forget that property in land as a transferable marketable commodity, absolutely owned and passing from hand to hand like any chattel, is not an ancient institution, but a modern development, reached only in a few very advanced countries. In the greater part of the world the right of cultivating particular portions of the earth is rather a privilege than a property,—a privilege first of the whole people, then of a particular tribe or a particular village community, and finally of particular individuals of the community.

'In this last stage land is partitioned off to these individuals as a matter of mutual convenience, but not as unconditional property; it long remains subject to certain conditions and to reversionary interests of the community, which prevent its uncontrolled alienation, and attach to it certain common rights and common burdens.'

§ 4. *Absence of any standard idea of 'Property.'*

If the old Indian writers, and any universal opinion of the people, had formulated private rights in land in any particular way, it would be easy to determine the fact and definitely state the principle, by examining the prevailing practice, the declarations of the books, or the forms of ancient title-deeds. But an examination of those sources of information does not enable us to gather any generally accepted theory of property in land. Even the Muhammadan law-books, which are of a comparatively late date, and written after the Roman law was known, do not define —they speak of 'ownership' (*Milkíyat*, and the owner *Málik*), but do not say what constitutes ownership.

In Elphinstone's *History of India* it is remarked [1], 'Property in land seems to consist in the exclusive use and absolute disposal of the powers of the soil in perpetuity; together with the right to alter or destroy the soil when such an operation is possible. These privileges combined form an abstract idea of property which does not represent any substance distinct from these elements. Where they are found united there is property, and nowhere else.'

It must be remarked that this is really the Roman ideal —the *usus, usufructus, abusus et vindicatio*—rather than an Eastern formula; and it may certainly be denied that any such abstract ideas ever prevailed in India. But at the same time we must be prepared to find particular claims to land expressed with great force. In the chapter on Malabár (Madras Tenures in vol. iii), I shall notice an ancient deed which seems to sell or grant every kind of right from the centre of the earth to the sky above: but it is doubtful how far this is oriental verbiage, or what is really meant by it, for in that country we find the *produce shared*, as elsewhere.

[1] Cowell's ed. p. 79-80. Baillie (*Muhammadan Law of the Land-Tax*, p. 20) says that the holder of land who pays to the ruler the 'khiráj muwazifa' or tribute in the form of a share in the produce, has a right in the land which is owing to the productive power of the soil, without which the cultivator would not be able to meet his liability (to the tribute). See also Phillips, p. 47.

§ 5. *Two principal ideas of landed right.*

All we can assert as undeniable is, that both Hindu and Muhammadan authorities have always recognized a strong right in land of *some* kind.

(1) From very early times a right was asserted in favour of the person who *first cleared the land*—had undertaken the great work of removing the dense jungle and contending against tropical nature, till the land was won for the plough.

Probably also the fact that *land* so long as it is covered with jungle, in some cases, or without water in other cases, is valueless, caused the productive power of the soil—or the produce of soil—to be regarded as the real subject of ownership. This is illustrated by the minute attention everywhere paid to *sharing the produce*; and also by the great importance, in special districts, of rights in water. No one cared how much *land* a man chose to plough up; but let him try, contrary to established custom, to seize a share in the water of a tank, or a mountain torrent, to water the field, and he would be instantly resisted. I have already noticed how the possibility of the land bearing a series of concurrent interests, depends on the fact that the several parties only determine how the *produce* is to be divided, and leave every other question in abeyance.

I make these remarks in connection with the 'right of the first clearer,' because it seems that this right ultimately depends on the fact that this man has made the land *productive* (and he has therefore a special interest): he has converted land from being worthless to being a 'property,' in the sense that *produce* can now be enjoyed.

(2) I have already alluded to the strong claims put forward by the high-caste families and descendants of conquering or colonizing chiefs. But here again we are left to put our own interpretation on the terms as suggesting any *theory* of ownership.

The nearest approach to a soil-claim that I know, is quoted by Colonel Tod in regard of the conquering Rájput owners of Mewár (Udaipur State in Rájputána)[1]. The author indeed connects this with the principle of the 'first clearer' when he says: 'He has nature and Manu in support of his claim, and can quote the text . . . that cultivated land is the property of him who cut away the wood, or who cleared and tilled it. . . . *In accordance with this principle'* (the italics are mine) 'is the ancient adage, not of Mewár only, but of all Rájputána:—

"Bhográ dhani Rájhú
Bhúmrá dhani májhhú"

'(The share (revenue share of the grain) is the wealth of the Rájá, the soil (bhûm) is my wealth.)'

But the author also tells us that in this case the soil-right is that of the conqueror and the superior family, and is spoken of as being his 'bápotá' or patrimonial inheritance. I therefore doubt whether the Rájputs (as landlords) laid so much stress upon the *first clearing*, as upon another equally widespread idea, that land *conquered and inherited* by the next generation, is a very firm possession.

§ 6. *Prevalence of certain terms for inherited Land.*

And I have once more to call prominent attention to the fact that all over India we find the same thing. The conqueror's descendants, whose title is might—'the portion won by my sword and my bow'—is spoken of by some term implying 'inheritance' or 'birthright.' For some reason, which I cannot explain, the convenient Arabic terms for 'heir,' or 'inheritance,' have been frequently adopted even by Hindu castes. Thus we have already had occasion to notice that in Madras the vague rights of the superior (landlord) classes or villages are called 'mirási' rights, and the claimants 'mirásdár.'[2] The Muhammadan Government in Western India called the claims of the old Marátha con-

[1] Tod, vol. i. p. 424.

[2] Mirás is obviously, even to a reader ignorant of Arabic, derived from the root 'wirs,' inheritance, from which come also wáris (heir); wárisí, the right of an heir; wirásat, the inheritance or 'estate,' &c. In Madras there were native terms, as 'Káni-átchi,' for birthright, &c.

quering families 'mirási' claims. In the Simla states the leading families call these holdings 'wirásat' (not *milkíyat*, the Muhammadan law term for ownership). And in the Kángra district the landholders call their land their 'wárisí.' The old chiefs of Malabár (the military caste) in the remote past seized on estates of limited size, of which they are now recognized as owners, and they call these estates their 'Janmam,' a term perhaps (but doubtfully) implying birthright. So the Coorg or superior caste landowners call their land 'jamma' lands, which is the same word in a localized form.

I notice that the strong village communities of the Panjáb proper have not familiarized themselves with the word 'wirásat' for landed estates, but most commonly speak of their 'mál' and 'milkíyat'—their idea is, however, just the same.

In Ajmer we shall find 'allodial' holdings called 'bhúmíyá' tenures. Here once more we have a term referring to the *soil*; but all its features are just like those of the Rájput 'patrimony.' Princes are said to be glad to acquire 'bhúmíyá' rights, because they are so safe. The *prince* may be deposed from his throne, and his State rights may disappear, and he be driven into exile and into private life. If afterwards he reappears in his former kingdom, he will not attempt so hopeless a task as to reclaim his State rights, but as holder of a bhúmíyá plot of ground, public sentiment will probably restore it to him at once [1].

The Rájput landholder, says Colonel Tod, 'compares his right to the "ákhái dhúba"—the ineradicable *dhúb* grass which no vicissitudes can destroy.'

§ 7. *These two principles alone form the basis of property.*

I have examined a great number of authorities, and with some confidence it may be stated that the outcome of all is that, whatever may have been the ideas entertained regarding the *nature* of property—and it is most probable that

[1] Tod, vol. i. p. 426.

no speculation was ever entered into on the subject—two grounds or bases of claim to hold land and enjoy its produce, and generally to alienate it, certainly to inherit it, were universal: (1) The right—held by any class—consequent on first clearing and reclaiming the waste; (2) the right claimed by the military and superior caste or ruling races, in virtue of birthright or *inheritance*, which really meant that the land had been obtained by conquest, grant, or some form of superior *might*, and that the descendants who inherited it regarded it as their 'birthright.'

§ 8. *Further details.*

There are other matters, however, to be considered in connection with 'property.' I have already had occasion to say something about the *stages* of property in the history of human development, and here we must notice, in more detail, the idea that property resides in the *family* rather than the individual.

§ 9. *The joint succession.—Primogeniture.*

Though Manu speaks of an 'owner' in the abstract, he elsewhere fully recognizes the principle of family right and joint succession. Indeed the Muhammadan law, though it determines different fractions for different classes of heirs, is in principle a law of joint-succession. And in India it will be found that many agricultural tribes, who are Muhammadan by faith, follow a customary succession which is just the same as in the (nominally or really) Hindu tribes. While we are on the subject of succession, it may be mentioned that the law and custom of primogeniture only apply to certain things. In a Rájá's domain the right to the 'gaddi,' or royal seat, and the appanages of authority, are indivisible, and go to the eldest only. But in ordinary families all property is divided, and only in some instances do we trace an idea of primogeniture in the local custom of 'jethánsi,' by which the eldest son gets a slightly larger share, or some extra articles at a division of the family goods. Indeed, in families which are not noble, but yet are above the common rank, it is often difficult to say whether primogeniture obtains. It is a matter of family custom. We shall see cases where families have divided and then have *agreed* to divide no further.

It is obvious that this joint-succession is the cause of many peculiarities in land custom. Nor is it without effect in the case of individual or *raiyatwárí* holdings; for when a raiyat dies, his sons jointly succeed; only that if the estate or holding is small, it commonly happens that some of the sons of their own choice, go away and seek service or other means of livelihood. In many cases Nature herself puts a limit to subdivision [1].

The question, whether primogeniture and indivisibility is or is not accepted, often has an important effect on the land-tenants. For instance, suppose an indivisible Rájáship. If the family is dispersed and the Rájá slain in battle, the overlordship may simply disappear, and the village tenures below remain unaffected. But where the chief's estate is divided, then the several members seize on one or two or more villages each, and are sure to become landlords, obliterating the rights below, and founding landlord communities. We have seen how many joint villages owe their origin to this circumstance, and a brief allusion will here suffice.

§ 10. *Female succession.*

In agricultural castes, daughters and other females do not usually get a share in land, or sometimes only till marriage. This is a sure mark that property is in the 'family' stage: it means that the daughter on marriage goes into another family, and that if she got a share, she

[1] And if a village body or a family persists in subdividing beyond rational limits, the body is sure to fall into hopeless poverty and decay, when in all probability they get into debt and sell their land. Many of them then become mere tenants under the purchaser, who by virtue of his sale-title reaggregates the various shares he has bought up.

would take it away with her. Widows are allowed a life-tenure, but cannot devise the land or alienate it without 'necessity.' What constitutes 'necessity' is a question for each case as it arises [1]. In the Panjáb so strong is the feeling that land belongs to the family, that a childless male proprietor is, in many tribes, not allowed to alienate any ancestral land without necessity, nor can he will it away; his power to disappoint natural heirs by *adopting* a son, is, in some tribes, limited by custom [2].

§ 11. *Authorities on the subject of property in land.*

We may now proceed to consider the statements of ancient writers on the subject of property in land.

It will be interesting to quote both from Hindu and Muhammadan authors. But it will be found that, in spite of the weight of law-books and commentaries, we shall end, in India, with finding that, as already stated, the King or the State claimed to be the only owner or landlord of all land. At least that certainly had come to pass by the end of the eighteenth century.

§ 12. *Hindu authorities.*

If we date the *Institutes of Manu* about the fifth century B.C.[3], and also assume that what is said about landed interests is hardly a new idea of the author, enunciated for the first time, but more or less represents accepted ideas on the subject, it will be obvious that a right (of whatever nature) in the land is a very ancient idea. It is also represented as attaching to the individual, or rather to the family, of which the individual was only the head, the manager, or the representative.

[1] And there are of course many judicial rulings or precedents as to what is 'necessity' and what is not.

[2] In the Panjáb the custom of adoption is very different from the law of the Hindu text-books.

[3] Burnell would have placed it later. See Hunter's *India*, pp. 113, 114.

In Manu we read[1]:—'The sages declare a field to belong to him who first cleared away the timber [Kulluka Bhaṭṭá's gloss on this is, 'who cleared and tilled it'], and a deer to him who first wounded it.' This right, as before remarked, is still constantly asserted. In the Panjáb, tenants who never heard of Manu or any other Hindu law-book, and who admit that they have no direct landlord claim, will urge a right to occupy on the ground of 'búta shigáfi'—having broken up the land and cleared away the jungle.

It is, however, curious to note that Manu's standpoint is that of a very settled state of things. He knows absolutely nothing[2] about a landlord or a joint body claiming the whole of a village lands in a ring-fence, as their 'inheritance.' His standpoint is a settled government under a Rájá, who takes his revenue share from every village. Villages are known groups of land. Each has its headman. This officer is allowed a certain remuneration; several villages are united into a superior charge, and a number of these again into a larger charge or district[3].

In Chap. VIII (v. 237) we read of the case of one man sowing seed in a field 'which is owned by another.' In the same (v. 239) we hear of the 'owner of a field' enclosing it with a thorny hedge, over which a 'camel could not look,' and 'through which a dog or a boar may not thrust his nose.' Again (v. 245–63) we have detailed rules for settling and laying out the boundaries of estates or holdings; and in v. 264 a punishment is provided for taking wrongful possession of a field or a garden. There is also reference to the formalities of sale (among them the sale by pouring out water, which is noticeable among the ancient deeds collected in Logan's *Manual of Malabár*).

[1] Chap. ix., v. 44 et sq., and confer De Laveleye, p. 53.

[2] I have elsewhere alluded to this subject, and to M. de Laveleye's suggestions thereon.

[3] The king is no conquering lord, driving the 'aborigines' into the hills or making serfs of them. 'He is created as the protector of all those classes and orders of men who from first to last discharge their duties' (Manu, viii. 35). Regarding the last officials and their remuneration, see vii. 115–119. I have spoken in Chapter III of the king's revenue share (vii. 129, 130). The king is to draw moderate taxes from his realm, 'as the calf and the bee take their food, little by little.'

The reader can draw his own conclusions as to the state of feeling on the subject of interests in land involved in these references.

The king is, no doubt, invited to fine the cultivator who neglects to sow the field; but that is because the revenue is endangered; it need not detract from the notion of right in the soil. Colonel Wilks also argues that this text refers to the cultivator or tenant, not to the owner [1].

It seems to me extremely probable that in Manu's time the conquering race of Aryans had been long established. The ruling tribes were in possession as Rájás, chiefs, and 'lords of ten villages, twenty villages, and a hundred villages,' and content with their overlordship and the revenue; while the actual settlers were either the 'rank and file' of the immigrant race, their lower caste (Vaisyás), or mixed castes (Sudrás). Possibly all original cultivators who were not peaceably let alone, had been driven out, or reduced to 'serfdom.' In the Southern kingdoms we have ample evidence of lands cultivated for the nobles by slaves, and it is quite possible that this may have been generally the case. But the field-owners contemplated by Manu are clearly either Aryans or others established in possession as freemen.

§ 13. *Muhammadan Authorities.*

The original theory of the Muslím was that conquered races were to be offered the option between adopting 'the creed,' or death, or slavery. But, as has been justly remarked, this theory very soon gave way to the more practicable one, that conquered races, if they submitted and agreed to pay tribute (khiráj), were to be let alone. 'Respect tributaries,' said the prophet; 'for they are entitled to the

[1] See Wilks' *History of Mysore* (reprint), p. 79, 80. Sterling, in his account of Orissa (*Asiatic Researches*, vol. xv), must have been thinking of the state of things produced by successive conquests in that country when he wrote, 'It is a nice question whether under the old Hindu system the actual occupants of the soil were considered to possess any subordinate title of ownership' (i.e. to the Rájás, chiefs, &c.).

same rights and subject to the same laws as the Moslems[1].'

The author of the *Hidáyá* (a text-book of Muhammadan law) lays it down that if a prince conquers a country, he is at liberty either to divide the land among his soldiers, or to leave it in the possession of the inhabitants, on their agreeing to pay capitation (jazíyá) and land-taxes; in the latter case, the right of property remains with the inhabitants.

Colonel Briggs[2] quotes Abul Hassan Aḥmad bin Muhammad—a Haníf doctor of the fourth century of the Hijra—who states the same doctrine; and he quotes from the *Siráj-ul-Wahháj* to the effect that, if the ruler allows the land to remain with the conquered people, on their paying tribute, 'the land is the property of the inhabitants; and, since it is their property, it is lawful for them to sell it or dispose of it as they choose.' Other authorities to the same effect might be quoted[3]. The author of the *Hidáyá* also has adopted the same rule as the law of Manu asserts, viz. that land is the property of him who first clears it; and Colonel Vans Kennedy says that 'all Muhammadan jurists agree that the person who first appropriates and cultivates waste land becomes *ipso facto* the lord of the soil[4].'

There is no doubt, however, that the prince remained entitled to the *unoccupied* land; and the only difference among the doctors seems to be as to whether an intending cultivator need ask leave to begin his work. The prince

[1] See Col. Vans Kennedy on the Muhammadan Law, *Journal Asiatic Society*, vol. ii. p. 105. The infidels who submitted and paid tribute were called 'Zimmí,' in distinction to the 'ḥarbi,' those who were in arms.

[2] Briggs, p. 109.

[3] It is noteworthy that while this reasonable doctrine is that of the earlier authorities, all the later kings and nawábs of the country claimed larger rights, as we shall presently see. The doctrine of European international law, that conquest does not interfere with private rights, is quite a modern development (see Broom, *Constitutional Law* (ed. 1866), p. 21, and *Campbell* v. *Hale*, *State Trials*, vol. xx, 322. Col. Briggs has collected, at p. 128, other authorities, showing that by Muhammadan law, khiráj-paying land is the property of the person who pays the tax, even though he is conquered. See also Patton's *Asiatic Monarchies*, p. 339.

[4] Paper quoted above, p. 108, and Briggs, p. 112.

can, however, certainly make a gift (or grant) of the waste [1].

§ 14. *Later Claims of the Ruling Power.*

Though the early doctrine—both Hindu and Muhammadan—is beyond doubt, it is quite certain that, as time went on, the local princes and governments with whom we came in contact, or who had immediately preceded us, had come to claim, not only the waste, but a right of ownership in all land whatever, and treated the 'raiyats' as their tenants, except in the case of such claims as those of holders of *watan*, or other special cases [2]. In the first place, it should be remembered that most of the later governments were either powers which had recently thrown off allegiance to the Mughal government, or other chiefs, like the Peshwá of the Maráthás and the Mahárájá of the Sikhs, who were recent conquerors, and therefore had extravagant claims. Moreover, history shows that the native rulers in later times all adopted more or less oppressive revenue assessments, and this tended to make land a burden, so that private rights were hardly asserted.

Then, too, the right of the State to waste or unoccupied land was never doubted, and this would be an element in forwarding a general claim to the soil.

It is noteworthy that in 1668 (A. D.) the Emperor Aurangzeb's orders show that a private right was then recognized. And as late as 1715, when the Company applied for a grant of the 'taluqdárí' of thirty-eight villages near their Bengal factory, they were told they would have to purchase the rights of the owners [3]. And, when Mr. Shore put rather a leading question to Ghulám Hassan, the historian (author of the *Sayyar muta,ákhirín*), assuming the right of the ruler, and asking whether, therefore, he ought to pay for

[1] Idem. The *Institutes of Timurlane*, as quoted by Col. Briggs, are to the same effect.

[2] As for instance grants to pious persons and religious uses, in which a permanent right was everywhere acknowledged: and special grants under title-deeds which it would be beneath the dignity of a ruler to ignore or to revoke.

[3] Briggs, pp. 128, 134.

land he required to take possession of, the author replied, 'The emperor is proprietor of the revenue; he is not proprietor of the soil.'

I cannot acquit our own authorities of some exaggeration at the time of the Permanent Settlement. For instance, Mr. James Grant, who had resided at the court of the Nizám, in 1785, wrote: 'It would be a most dangerous innovation (diametrically opposite to the letter and spirit of all Oriental legislation, ancient and modern, devised by conquerors) to admit, either in theory or in practice, the doctrine of private individual landed property by inheritance,—free or feudal tenures extending beyond one life.' The *ancient* authorities do not support Mr. Grant at all.

And so in the preamble to Madras Regulation XXXI of 1802 (since repealed), it is said that the property in land belonged to the Government by 'ancient usage.'

Certainly, however, the governments of that time *did*, and the native governments of the present day *do*, make a claim to be landlords of all land—but they should rather base such a claim on conquest and the disorders of later times, than on any of these *ancient* authorities. Putting aside the obvious mistake about 'ancient usage,' it is hardly possible that Mr. James Grant, and Colonel Munro, and many others, could have been mistaken about the fact that *in their time* all governments *did* claim to be landowners; and, as I said, it is quite certain that the Nizám and other rulers make the same claim now.

Regulation XXV, of 1802, of the Madras Code—which did not commit itself to any theory—correctly stated that the Government had the 'implied right and the actual exercise of the proprietary possession of all land whatever.' And with reference to Regulation XXXI of 1802 (above quoted), it should be noted that the legislature only professed to assert this general right as a *locus standi*, from which it proceeded to *confer a title* on the Zamíndárs.

Colonel Briggs, who is very averse to admitting the growth of the rulers' claims, is unable to make out anything in the Nizám's dominions, except that *watan* lands were saleable (i.e. were private property)[1], and that the weight of taxation on ordinary lands prevented 'the existence of real property' in them.

Mr. Elphinstone (Governor of Bombay) thought that all land belonged to the Maráthá government, when it did not belong to 'mirásdárs,' or to government grantees (and the mirásdárs were either scions of Maráthá families or successors to their rights); and he noted that 'Bájí Ráo (the Peshwá), when he had occasion *for Mirásí land*, paid the price for it.'

Colonel Malleson says: 'It has been stated, and, I believe, truly, that throughout Holkár's dominions no private individual possesses permanent heritable or alienable rights in land; every cultivator is a tenant at will of the Mahárájá.'

This is, perhaps, rather strongly worded; but certainly a similar claim is made by the semi-dependent Rájás of Chamba, Kashmír, and those of the Simla Hill States. They respect occupancy-rights of old cultivators, and certainly admit the heritable nature of the right; but they do not allow of alienation, without permission and payment of a fee, or 'nazarána,' to the chief[3].

[1] Briggs, p. 75. And the rulers very often respected special rights of this kind.

[2] *Native States of India*, p. 197 *note*.

[3] By the courtesy of Mr. W. Coldstream, C. S. Superintendent of the Hill States, I have seen a number of interesting papers bearing on the rights of the State of Bághát near Simla, from the records of the Superintendent's office. In a letter (No. 219, 28 Feb. 1866) I find it stated that 'the chiefs are the only proprietors,' the occupiers of land are only cultivators but mostly hereditary. The chiefs have certain lands of their own which they call 'láná,' and cultivate by their own farm servants.

The following were the Ráná of Bághát's rights:—

(1) His revenue or grain-share.

(2) Offerings on a marriage in the chief's family.

(3) An 'offering' of 100-200 bútás or cobs of Indian corn, when the harvest is ready.

(4) When the *landholder* has a marriage in his family he gives the chief a goat, and the chief returns a sword (talwár) as a present to the bridegroom.

(5) Certain days of 'begár' or unpaid labour on State buildings or roads, but the chief gives flour for the day's bread.

(6) A 'nazar' or fee from every raiyat who asks for *waste* to cultivate.

§ 15. *Causes of the later State Claims.*

While, however, it is conceded that the real 'ancient' usage, or theory, of both the Hindus and Muhammadans, expressly discouraged the idea that the ruler was absolute owner, or owner at all, of *all* land, and certainly acknowledged private rights, there were in the books the germs of principles which easily recrudesced into new claims; and there was always the feeling of the conqueror, the successful adventurer, and the ruler who has asserted and gained independence, that his will is the only law, that he has conquered, and everything is his, to dispose of as he will.

The doctrine, for instance, that the Muslím conqueror only took tribute as an act of favour, and *might* have destroyed the conquered, or have dealt with the land in any way he pleased, and actually *did* so deal with all waste land, was very apt to make conquerors forget the *dicta* which should have moderated their pretensions. The very idea that the tribute, or khiráj was a mild substitute for slavery or death—however it may have been softened by the comments of jurists—was only too likely to recur to the mind of a conqueror disposed, for his own profit, to exaggerate his claims.

The author of the *Hidáyá* (Book ix. chap. 7), speaking of the limit of the khiráj being one half the produce, says: 'But the taking of one half is no more than strict justice, and is not tyrannical, because, as it is lawful to take the whole of the persons and property of infidels, and to distribute them among the faithful, it follows that taking one half their income is lawful *à fortiori*.' The later ruler, in the chronic emptiness of his treasury, was apt to act on this reflection, and arbitrarily increase the demand on the land to such an extent that no *valuable* property in it remained.

Indeed it is not easy to dispose of the reasoning. If the law is that a king acquires everything by conquest, surely he may claim the land, allowing only a liberal user—even a hereditary user of it—to the people; and the amount of his demand for revenue is a matter for his will and conscience only.

That such a claim was made by all the later sovereigns, is perhaps natural: and under the circumstances, we cannot wonder that the British authorities on succeeding to their place, were not perfectly consistent in their declarations, nor very well satisfied as to what they ought to do. In strict right, they succeeded to the position of the outgoing ruler; and if they found that this position—logical indeed, but morally ill-advised—had been taken up contrary to the earlier legal authorities, it was certainly a nice question, what was the proper claim for the British Government to assert.

§ 16. *Claims how far adopted by the British Government.*

I think, on the whole, what was meant by the various declarations in the Regulations and elsewhere, was this; that the Government claimed to succeed to the *de facto* position of the preceding ruler, only so far as to use the position (not to its full logical extent but) as a *locus standi*, for re-distributing, conferring, and recognizing rights on a new basis.

And the outcome of the action taken by the Government was this—that it at once recognized certain rights in private individuals, and only retained such rights for itself as were necessary.

The power to make this distribution was no doubt based on the *de facto* power of the Government to dispose of all land.

I may exhibit the main features of the disposition of landed rights made by Government under five heads.

(1) Government used its own eminent claim as a starting point from which to recognize or confer definite titles in the land, in favour of persons or communities that it deemed entitled.

(2) It retained the unquestionable right of the State to all waste lands; exhibiting however the greatest

tenderness to all possible rights either of property or of user, that might exist in such lands when proposed to be sold or granted away. This right it exercised for the public benefit, either leasing or selling land to cultivators or to capitalists for special treatment; thus encouraging the introduction of tea, coffee, cinchona, and other valuable staples. Or it used the right as the basis for constituting *State Forests* for the public benefit, or for establishing Government buildings, farms, grazing-grounds, and the like.

(3) It retained useful subsidiary rights—such as minerals, or the right to water in lakes and streams. In some cases it has granted these away, but all later laws reserve such rights.

(4) It retained the right of escheat; and of course to dispose of estates forfeited for crime, rebellion, &c.

(5) It reserved the right necessary for the security of its income (a right which was never theoretically doubtful from the earliest times), of regarding all land as in a manner hypothecated as security for the land-revenue. This hypothecation necessarily implies or includes a right of *sale* in case the revenue is in arrears.

§ 17. *Remarks on these Heads.—Head I.*

Each of these five heads requires a few words of comment.

The first is exemplified by the declaration made in conferring the proprietary title on the Zamíndárs in Bengal, and on other classes declared entitled, in the several Regulations and Acts of the Legislature, which we shall study as we come to each of the provincial systems in turn.

The Government conferred no absolute or unlimited estate on any one person or community: the landlord or the proprietor was the person or community that had the first or superior position and the major part of the rights.

But others might share it; either expressly as when they were called 'sub-proprietors'; or practically, where, as 'tenure-holders' or 'occupancy-tenants' their interests were secured by special provisions.

§ 18. *Right in the Waste.—Head II.*

There never has been any doubt that in theory, the 'waste'—that is, land not occupied by any owner or allotted to anyone—was at the disposal of the ruler to do what he liked with; in short, was the property of the State.

In ancient times, such as those referred to in Manu, the king certainly granted such lands to the cultivators. No doubt it is contemplated that the villagers should have a right to use the grazing, and to practise wood-cutting in the waste adjoining their cultivated holdings; and probably no king would think of making grants of land in such a way as to put any village to real inconvenience in this respect.

In the old kingdoms of Oudh we find the king levying his tolls on wood-cutting, at least on outsiders, and granting clearing-leases.

The Muhammadan law authorities (already quoted) declared the waste to belong to the ruler, and the right has always been exercised by making grants [1].

Land is not 'waste,' if it has been *occupied*, even though left uncultivated. When, for example, a noble family acquired the 'zamíndárí' right in a village in Oudh, or a family founded a village in the Panjáb, they understood themselves as entitled to a certain area within certain boundaries (however defined), whether the area was under the plough or not. When the British Government con-

[1] In early days, when waste was very abundant, the rulers were far too anxious to see it cultivated, and so increase their revenue, to make any objection to its being broken up, or to make any regulations about asking leave to take it. But that proves nothing. The whole subject of the right to waste is discussed in the 'Kánara Forest Case' (*Indian Law Reports*: Bombay series, vol. iii, p. 583), especially in Mr. Justice West's elaborate judgment. The subject is also gone into in detail in my *Manual of Forest Jurisprudence*.

ferred estates on Zamíndárs or any other sort of proprietor, it of course contemplated that an area of waste for expansion should (wherever nature permitted it) form part of the estate; because by such means the estate would grow in value, and the revenue burden become lighter and lighter. For this reason, the waste that adjoined the villages in the North-West Provinces, was fairly adjudged to belong to the estate[1], while excess waste *not* occupied, was always treated as belonging to Government. In Regulation III of 1828 the right of the State is expressly declared[2]. In after times, in Bengal, attempts were made to recover or 'resume' excess waste; but as there were no surveys showing boundaries of estates, the resumption was often a difficult task, and was only successful in certain localities. In the Panjáb and the Central Provinces, where there were large areas of waste, a certain proportion was included in the villages at the survey which preceded Settlement, and the rest marked off for Government.

In Malabár, unfortunately, the claims of the 'janmam' holders had so long been allowed, that it is to be feared all the forest land has, by prescription, become the estate-holder's, and is not now likely to be recovered[3].

In *raiyatwárí* villages, while certain provision is made for *user*, i.e. grazing rights and wood-cutting, the waste 'numbers' are all recorded as belonging to Government, and may be available for cultivation, to applicants, or may be retained, according to circumstances.

Whenever Government desires to allot waste, or convert it to any use, there is an Act (XXIII of 1863) which enables a notice to be given, and claims to any *right* to be settled. This Act clearly proceeds on the principle of the State right; so do the Forest Acts, which contemplate 'waste'

[1] Except, of course, large tracts of forests and waste in the Hills or in the Jhánsi district, which were left as Government waste.

[2] The preamble speaks of Commissioners appointed 'to maintain and enforce the public rights in different districts in which extensive tracts of country . . . . . being still waste belong to the State.'

[3] In North Kánara, where similar claims on the part of the estate holders were attempted, the Government successfully resisted them in the case already alluded to in a previous note.

lands being taken up for forest purposes subject to a 'forest Settlement,' i. e. a determination and separation of the rights of private persons and those of the State[1].

§ 19. *Waste Land Rules.*

In all provinces 'Rules for the lease of waste lands' are in force. The policy has from time to time varied, and the rules have been amended. At one time the idea was to sell the land out and out, with no revenue claims; then the policy changed; and seeing the great and rapid growth in the value of land, it began to be felt that to sacrifice the State rights so readily was a mistake. The policy now is rather to lease the land for a term of years, and only to allow the conversion of the title to one of ownership (and that subject to paying land-revenue) when the lessee has shown that he is in earnest and has really made proper use of the grant.

The rules sometimes draw a distinction between the lease of small areas for the purposes of ordinary cultivation, and the grant of larger areas to capitalists, for the purposes of commercial cultivation of tea, coffee, chinchona, or other staples on the large scale.

The chapter on Bengal Tenures will afford some illustrations of this subject.

§ 20. *Subsidiary Rights.—Head III.*

The reservation of a right to mines, minerals, and earth-oil, hardly concerns us in this manual; nor does the right to water in lakes and rivers. It is enough to mention that the latter is the basis of the Canal Acts, regulating the construction of canals and the distribution of the water.

[1] The *ownership* of the unoccupied waste may reside in the State, though certain *servitudes* or rights of user may be claimable by other persons, which latter have to be provided for or compensated, before the State can exercise any complete control. But no amount of mere *rights of user* can amount to ownership. Unless a claim be decided on its merits, to be one of proprietary occupation and title, not to a mere user, it does not destroy, however much it may hamper, the State ownership. The distinction is important.

§ 21. *Right to lapsed Lands, &c.—Head IV.*

It has happened that estates were forfeited for rebellion after 1857, or may be forfeited for crime under the Criminal Law. Such lands then became State property. The law of escheat of lands that had no heirs, was known to the old Hindus under the name of 'gáyári.' The Muhammadan law term 'nazúl' is also applied to escheated lands. But it is very commonly applied to lands or houses that were owned by the former government, and therefore became the direct property of the succeeding government.

§ 22. *Hypothecation of the Land.—Head V.*

This is really almost the only vestige of any 'universal' State claim to land. It is obviously necessary to the security of the land-revenue. The revenue is, in fact, an absolute first charge on all land, and must be satisfied before any other claim; and the land can be sold, by the Bengal law, at once, and by other laws in the last resort, to recover arrears.

When Government sells land, and no one buys it, the land remains (as in Bengal) on the hands of Government, as what is called in revenue language, a Government estate, or a 'khás mahál.' Should a proprietor decline the terms of Settlement, he may be excluded from the management for a time; but the estate, even though farmed or managed direct by the Collector ('held khás' as the phrase is) for a time, does not become the property of Government.

§ 23. *Government the 'universal Landlord.'*

After Government has so distinctly conferred proprietary rights in land, any later use of the term 'universal landlord,' as applied to Government, can only be in the nature of a metaphor, or with reference to the ultimate claim of Government alluded to in the last paragraph, or that which arises in case of a failure of heirs.

The only *function of a landlord* that a Government exercises, is the general care for the progress of the estates; making advances to enable the cultivators to sink wells or effect other improvements; advancing money for general agricultural purposes (under special Acts); suspending or remitting the demand for revenue owing to famine or calamity of season.

§ 24. *Land-Revenue whether a Tax or Rent.*

The land-revenue cannot then be considered as a *rent*, not even in *raiyatwárí* lands, where the law (as in Bombay) happens to call the holder of land an 'occupant,' not a proprietor. The reason for adopting this term will be noticed in the chapter on Bombay tenures. Here it is enough to say that the special definition does not entitle Government to a true *rent*. Nowhere and under no revenue system, does government claim to take the 'unearned increment,' or the whole of what remains after the wages of labour, or cost of cultivation and profits of capital, have been accounted for.

If we cannot be content to speak of 'land-revenue,' and must further define, I should be inclined to regard the charge as more in the nature of a tax on agricultural incomes.

CHAPTER V.

A GENERAL VIEW OF THE LAND-REVENUE SYSTEMS OF BRITISH INDIA.

SECTION I.—INTRODUCTORY.

THIS chapter, in which I have endeavoured to present an outline of the various LAND-REVENUE SYSTEMS OF BRITISH INDIA, and to show how they originated and how they are connected together, will contain much that is already familiar to every Indian official; and readers in India may therefore regard as unnecessary many of the statements and explanations offered. It seemed, however, desirable to deal with the subject from the point of view of the general reader, and accordingly to avoid assuming that he possesses a fund of knowledge to start with. It is necessary, then, to begin from the beginning, and not plunge *in medias res*, or at once make use of terms of revenue-law, familiar enough to officials, but certain, until duly explained, to appear mysterious, if not repulsive, to others.

I may, however, assume, to start with, a single item of knowledge, which, indeed, has been to some extent explained in the last chapter. The rulers, Rájás, and emperors of the successive governments in all parts of India, have at all times raised the greater part of their State income, by levying a charge on the land. Whether this was an Aryan institution, or was learned from the Dravidians, or was a natural method, adopted independently, I leave the reader to form the opinion which best satisfies him. But, as a matter of fact, it came to be an universally-acknowledged principle, that the king, Rájá, or chief of a territory, had a right to a SHARE IN THE PRODUCE OF ALL CULTIVATED LAND. In time, as might be expected, this revenue came to be no longer taken in kind, but in the form of a money payment, made at certain seasons when the harvests had been realized.

I have to remark on this generally, that the early authorities are naturally concerned only with discussing whether the king's share shall be a sixth, a fourth, &c. Nothing else was needed. It was early recognized that the share might be increased in time of war or special necessity, but that is all. As a matter of fact, while the early Rájás are supposed to have taken no more than the *sixth*, it is quite certain that all or many of the later ones demanded the *half*. So tenaciously is old custom clung to in India, that in many native states the ruler still takes his revenue in kind. On the whole, he is not a loser; for there has been a steady rise in the value of grain; and this, perhaps, compensates him to some extent for the want of any regular system of periodical revision of assessment.

But when the time came for the Government (it happened under the Mughal rule) to change the grain-revenue into cash, the first idea was to roughly estimate the standard share as yielding so many 'maunds' of grain[1] for each crop on each kind of soil, and then to value it at an average price. The early methods of fixing the grain-value were, however, so rough, that practically it was but an arbitrary process, effected with moderation, and with reference to the ability of the cultivators to pay easily. The change from a grain-revenue to a cash-payment had one important consequence: from that time forward it has been recognized as a general rule—certainly it was so by the Muhammadan governments—that the money-payment needed to be revised from time to time, i.e. after the lapse of a suitable term of

[1] The 'Maund' (man) is the usual weight for reckoning solids. It varies in different places; but the general standard is 80 lbs. = 1 maund. The maund is divided into forty seers (sír) of two lbs. each, and the sír into sixteen chhaták (chittack) of five tolás each. The tolá is the weight of the current silver rupee; approximately two and a half of them go to the ounce *avoirdupois*.

years. In the days of the later Mughal rule, the revenue was revised, not by any regular process of re-valuation, but by the expedient of adding on 'cesses' to the existing totals. These cesses were called by various names, which indicated either the name of the governor who imposed them, or the pretence under which they were levied. In the Bengal chapters we shall hear a great deal about 'cesses.'

But under our own Government such a device was not likely to be followed—at least, not as a means of enhancing the land-revenue [1]. It became necessary, then, to devise some plan of fairly assessing the land-revenue.

The process by which the Government officials determine the amount of land-revenue payable, is called a SETTLEMENT (of land-revenue); and the person or the body whom Government recognizes as entitled to be proprietor, subject to the revenue-payment, is said to be 'settled with,' or to 'hold the Settlement.' Who the 'proprietors' were and are, we have discussed in general terms in the last chapter.

Our first experiment was made in the province which first came under our rule—viz. the 'Bengal, Bihár, and Orissa,' of A.D. 1765. Here the plan was to find out what lump-sums the several local revenue contractors *had* been paying, or were, in the accounts, shown as bound to pay. Such corrections and adjustments as were possible were then made in the totals, and the persons responsible were told to pay that amount; and by law it was declared that they should *never* have it enhanced.

So *in Bengal*, the process of fixing the revenue-payment having been gone through once for all, under pledge that no future increase would be demanded, it was called the 'PERMANENT SETTLEMENT.' We shall, of course, have much more to say about this hereafter.

[1] I shall afterwards explain that by law the Government levies certain 'local rates or cesses' for *special purposes*, distinct from the land revenue, which is *Imperial* or general. The district roads and district schools are so provided for; and Government levies a rate to enable it better to meet the expense of periodical famines—a rate which gives rise to very mistaken notions about what people are pleased to call a 'Famine Insurance Fund.'

But when we began to administer other provinces—like the North-Western Provinces, or the districts of Madras (with exception of the northern part)[1]—it was found, as we have seen, that the land-tenures were wholly different, and that there were no 'Zamíndárs' to hold the Settlement. Moreover the inconvenience, and injustice to the public, of fixing the revenue for all time, regardless of changes in the value of produce, or the rise and fall of agricultural incomes, were soon recognized. Therefore different plans of making a Settlement were devised and worked out for the different provinces, according to the requirements and local conditions of each.

These plans have been gradually modified and improved up to the present day. They retain certain general distinctive features, but all have a certain common basis. Speaking generally, all the methods commence with a careful survey, and with a classification of the soil; and then begins the Settlement-Officer's difficult task, viz. to find out money-rates *per acre* which Government can fairly charge, as its cash revenue, on the 'proprietors' for each kind or class of soil.

According to the system in force, the Revenue is either assessed in a lump sum on a whole estate—which may be a considerable area, or a whole group of villages, or a single village (or parts of villages), or it is assessed on single fields or holdings surveyed, numbered, and marked out on the ground. When the estate is in the hands of a great landlord, like the Zamíndár of Bengal or North Madras, we call it a ZAMÍNDÁRÍ SETTLEMENT; and in these two instances it is also a PERMANENT SETTLEMENT.

In Oudh we have a TALUQDÁRÍ SETTLEMENT, with great Taluqdár landlords, but under peculiar conditions, and not 'permanent.'

When it is a single village (or some part or parts of villages) settled with a landlord body or community, we

[1] The Northern part was in some respects conditioned like Bengal, and a Permanent Settlement was made for it with Zamíndárs very much on the Bengal lines.

call it a VILLAGE (or rather a 'Mahálwár') SETTLEMENT[1]. And as this system is prevalent in North-Western India (and the Central Provinces) it is frequently spoken of as the 'North-West System'—for it was devised in the North-Western Provinces.

In the Central Provinces, we have seen that in each village, Government conferred the proprietary right on a person called the 'Málguzár'; this Settlement is therefore often spoken of as the MÁLGUZÁRÍ SETTLEMENT of the Central Provinces, though in all essentials it is a Settlement on the North-West model.

Wherever the system assesses each field separately (as in Bombay and Madras, and parts of the Central Provinces, and in Berár) we have a RAIYATWÁRÍ SETTLEMENT.

That is the very briefest outline of what we are now going to look into a little more in detail. But let me add one thing more of this general character.

The theory of the land-revenue being, that it is a *share in the produce*, that share to be fixed by the State itself, it might be supposed that all modern systems of assessment would aim at finding out the average weight or quantity yielded by the share (of each principal crop on each class of soil), whatever the share might be,—one-half, one-third, or two-thirds, and then valuing it in money at a price which would (naturally) be the average harvest price of a series of years. In fact, in our very first Settlements (putting aside the case of the Bengal Zamíndárs), something like this was actually attempted. But it was too difficult and uncertain; and they next tried to make a calculation of the 'assets' of the estate. They counted up the total produce in gross, and tried to find out the costs of cultivation, wages of labour, profits of stock, &c., and, deducting the latter from the former, they took a fraction of the balance as the revenue or share of the 'assets.' But this also proved impracticable, and so they gradually perfected other methods

[1] See remarks on this in Chap. IV. p. 170. The village is very often the unit, but the group of land held under one title, assessed to one sum of revenue, is, in revenue language, the 'Mahál' for assessment purposes.

which it will be my object to make plain in the sequel; but here I wish only to make it understood that modern assessment methods have departed further and further from the plan of valuing in money an actual share in produce. Certain systems, however, still retain some vestiges of the idea: some more than others.

SECTION II.—THE ORIGIN OF THE LAND-REVENUE.

§ 1. *The 'Law and Constitution' of India.*

In introducing the subject of ancient revenue systems, and quoting authorities as to what was the king's proper share, I must remind the reader that all this was matter of *custom*—that curious and often undefinable feeling that things ought to be in a certain way because they always have been so. The *custom*, however, has always to give way before the necessities of the ruler; and that is why, in spite of all that can be quoted from law-books, we find that, in modern times, all Native States claimed, and still claim, to be *de facto* owners of every acre of soil in their States, and have taken as much land-revenue as they could get without seriously starving the people. Yet, in spite of the facts, we find writers—especially the early ones—talking about the 'law and constitution of India'; and at least one book (Colonel Galloway's) has been published under that title. As a matter of fact, there never has been anything resembling a 'law and constitution' for any one of the diverse countries included in the geographical term 'India' (let alone for the whole), in the sense in which an English reader would ordinarily understand the term.

Possibly, in Colonel Galloway's time, Indian history was not accessible to the same comprehensive or panoramic view of it that, thanks to the labours of Sir W. Hunter and others, is now open to us. How it was likely that a series of loosely-connected States, always at war with one another, overrun from age to age by Dravidians, Greeks, Northern

Buddhists, Rájputs, Játs, Gújars, Afgháns, Mughals, and the rest, *could* ever have possessed any general and authoritative law entitled to be called the 'law and constitution of India,' it is not easy to understand.

I do not, however, ignore the fact that, under all this series of dynasties, there were some indications of uniform ideas and principles. In the absence of any other force, CUSTOM has had a potent influence on the rulers and conquerors no less than on the people. All that were in any way Hindu, or Hinduized, had certain common feelings; and the Muhammadan conquerors of later days, over whom the law-texts of Arabia or of Bág͟hdád never had any great hold, knew that their only chance of success was to conform as much as possible to the custom of their Hindu subjects.

The early Hindus never had anything that could be called a code of practical law. It is absurd to suppose that Manu, or any other author's collection of legal maxims, (especially in matters of government) was 'in force' as statute law is in England or France. The Muhammadan law-books were, perhaps, somewhat more generally referred to in matters of criminal and civil law between subject and subject; but as regards Government and its rights, they were only quoted (when convenient) with a certain respect; their phraseology was also adopted, especially by the more religious of the Emperors; but in reality the legal ''ashr,' and 'k͟hiráj,' and all the rest of it, according to the Musalman theory of conquest and taxation, had nothing more than a nominal or theoretic relation to the land-revenue as actually levied in India.

In this is one of the great contrasts between Oriental and European rule. The moment a modern Englishman gets into a district, his law-abiding soul looks for some Act or rule, or some 'Circular' by which he may be guided. Doubtless the 'paternal' District Officer dislikes the 'section 10, sub-section 3,' that prevents him making the order that he thinks needed for the particular case before him, and he abhors the pleader, with his niceties and technical difficulties; but, all the same, he desires a substratum of plain and solid authority on which to rely. He will have some kind of standard and keep to it; he will be content with nothing less, and he will sternly prevent any one from exacting more. His revenue-demand shall be assessed according to law, under the supervision of Commissioners and Boards, with the one idea of making it equal, just, and easily borne: but once fixed, it must be paid in full, regularly and to the day.

The Oriental administrator, on the contrary, avoids rigid rules, and rarely attempts definition. That is why every Indian institution connected with landed rights or proprietary interests, often presents seemingly contradictory and irreconcileable features; a man is what we call a landlord in one aspect, and something quite different in another aspect. This is distraction to the European ruler. To the Oriental mind it is highly satisfactory;—to the ruler, because it enables him to do what he pleases; to the ruled, because it discovers a way of escape: neither can be caught between the bars of a rule and made to feel—'You cannot do this because it is illegal,' or (on the other hand) 'You must be bound to submit to so and so, because your legal position as a "proprietor" or a "tenant" (or whatever it is) necessarily involves such and such a condition.' He can turn one face or the other to the outside, and act on this presentment of the case or on that, as it suits him, caring nothing for legal consistency or definiteness of principle.

As soon as circumstances compelled the ruler to exchange his grain-share for a money payment, the earliest methods were quite hap-hazard. Great rulers like Akbar, and wise ministers like Todar Mal or Malik 'Ambar (in the Dakhan) no doubt endeavoured to propound a fixed, equitable rule for assessing land; but they could not bind their successors.

We consequently find the later rulers enhanced the land-revenue from time to time as they pleased; and it is absolutely absurd to say that by 'ancient law and constitution'—or what not—they *could* not do so. We are no doubt credibly informed that in early days the Rájás contented themselves with their 'sixth'; and no doubt, as long as there was peace, and cultivation went on prosperously, there was little or no temptation to take more. But in more recent times it has always been the fact that the native rulers have taken to the full as much as they could get. But how?—by an arbitrary, elastic, method of alternate squeezing and loosing. Native rulers have always been ready to take the whole in good years, but have rarely shown themselves wanting in a perfectly unsystematic but practically-working sense of adaptation which does not let the pressure be overdone in a bad year[1]. Any definition or straightness of 'law' would have militated directly against this most obvious and characteristic feature of native rule.

And in all cases the restraint of '*custom*' was felt by all classes, both ruler and ruled. The 'Ámil or other collector knew exactly how far the golden eggs could be multiplied without killing the goose that laid them.

When, therefore, we refer to Manu for Hindu ideas, or to the *Hidáyá* and other Muhammadan text-books, it is not because these have, or ever had, any authority as practical statute-books—at any rate in the realm of *public* or constitutional law—but because the books of a time must more or less reflect the ideas of the people, and because, of course, a pious Hindu or a religious Muhammadan prince would always, to some extent, allow the value, as guides, of books written by sages or doctors of his semi-sacred law.

We may, therefore, quote the books, but remember that the only general 'law and constitution' of India was, that the people did what was the *custom*, and the king did what he *chose*, at least within the limits of the possible—limits which the elastic Oriental mind has ordinarily well known how to keep.

[1] I speak of course of the average fair-dealing ruler. There have been tyrants here and there, who seized everything and left depopulated villages and ruined provinces; but these were exceptional.

§ 2. *The Hindu State organization.*

Now let us turn backward, and place ourselves, in imagination, in the days when a regularly established Hindu State was in working order, in very much the condition which is indicated rather than described in MANU'S *Institutes.*

The whole country occupied by the tribe or clan who selected and conquered the locality, was first divided out into large territories or divisions, and the central and largest (or at any rate the best) one was assigned to the head chief called 'Rájá [1].'

Round about him, other estates, graduated in size, were occupied by lesser chiefs, heads of tribal groups or sections. These would be represented by such titles as 'Thákur,' 'Ráná,' 'Ráo,' or 'Bábú [2].' Every one of these held his estate on certain terms of service to the Rájá, which I will pass over without more detail than to say that a fine was paid on succession; that homage was done; that, on summons, the chief had to attend with his force; that he was expected to aid with such contributions as were, in times of difficulty, required. In some parts the most distant of the 'estates' were in hilly country; and here the chief was more independent than the rest, and was expected to keep the passes, and prevent the descent of neighbouring hostile tribes and robbers to harass the dominions of the Rájá and his chiefs.

Inside the Rájá's domain or 'khálsa,' as the later Rájputs and also the Sikhs called it, the greater portion of the land was directly under the control of the king's officers—a graded series of district and village authorities—and a certain portion of it was held or managed under royal

[1] See Sterling's account of Orissa kingdoms in *Asiatic Researches*, vol. xv. p. 220. 'In every part of India, it would seem that under the Hindus, the *domains* reserved for the Crown constituted, if not the largest, at least the most valuable and productive shares of the whole territory.'

[2] This term, now commonly employed to designate a clerk in office, really applies to a native gentleman of wealth and position, and primarily (in some places) indicates the sons, nephews, &c., of the Rájá or other chief.

grant or assignment, by courtiers, ministers of State, chief judges, and military officers, as well as by the younger sons and dependants of the royal house.

The Rájá enjoyed two main sources of revenue :—

I.—The first was the throne-right (spoken of as the 'gaddí' or state cushion) with a right to certain tolls and taxes, transit duties on trade, excise, rights in the forests (if there were any) [1], and taxes from the artisan and trading classes.

It is possible that if the other chiefs were not powerful, these royal rights might extend over their domains as well.

This group of rights was indivisible, or went to the successor of the Rájá,—always the eldest son or next heir-male.

II.—The second source of revenue was the share in the *grain produce* of every bíghá of cultivated land, already spoken of.

It will be observed that just as the Rájá took this share for his own 'khálsa' or demesne lands, so did the separate chiefs in their estates: the Rájá took no grain-share *in them* [2]. Exactly in the same way, where the Rájá made a *grant* (or in later days a sale) of a part of his own demesne lands to a courtier or a general, &c., the *grantee* took *the share* (and perhaps some of the other taxes and tolls) which would otherwise have gone to the king.

This fact is at the bottom of a great deal connected both with land-tenures, and the land-revenue. And we have already seen how, from the Rájá's grants and from the break-up of the territories, village landlord communities have arisen.

Of course the fate of the ancient Hindu States has been very various. The smaller ones have often fallen out of rank; the 'Royal' family has quarrelled; the estate has split up like those just mentioned, and dissolved into a

[1] See Chap. IV. p. 128.

[2] The reader will bear this in mind, because forgetfulness of it has been the source of a great deal of nonsense written in former days about there never having been any Royal revenue-share levied, as in Coorg, Malabár, &c., the fact being that the mistake arose from looking at lands which formed chiefs' estates, from which the Rájá as tribal chief never did take a royalty, whether in Malabár or in *any other country* where Rájás existed.

number of village-landlord families, only known from the rest of the village cultivators by their higher caste and memories of a more dignified origin in the remote past. In other cases the old Hindu kingdoms were either subdued or destroyed before the conquest,—whether of the Afghán, the Mughal, the Maráthá, the Sikh, or the armies of Clive or Wellesley or Lake.

In this case, the Rájá's *grain-share* passed on to the conqueror, or succeeding power. If the Rájá had been killed in battle, or had fled, there was no one to share or diminish it; it was simply collected by the State machinery of the conquering king or emperor; if the Rájá survived under the conqueror as a subordinate noble, he was probably installed by royal grant as a 'Zamíndár' or 'Taluqdár'; and continued to collect the grain-share as before, *but* had now to pass on a portion—perhaps the greater portion[1]—to the treasury of the conqueror; and he made his own wealth by *other* privileges which in the end left him richer than before; he was allowed to cultivate the waste, and take the profits for himself; he was gradually allowed to bargain with the State for a fixed revenue payment and keep the difference between that contract sum and what he could collect from the 'raiyats.' Then it was that the idea of the right of reassessing the revenue-share from time to time, ill-defined as that practice was, inevitably occurred to him; and when, under our own rule, the title in the land was secured to the Zamíndárs, the power of raising the assessment soon developed into the 'landlord,' and his right of 'enhancing' the 'rents,' which proved such a source of burning discussion for after years.

But this is to anticipate; we must first consider how the Hindu Revenue Administration was conducted, and how the system fell in with Muhammadan ideas, and was adopted by the Mughal conquerors, and has come down, in a modified form, to the British Government.

[1] When, in later days, in Bengal, the emperor's deputy allowed the surviving Rájás (as well as modern officials and farmers) to collect the local revenue, the theory was (and at first the practice) that nine-tenths of the whole collections were passed on to the State treasury.

§ 3. *The Internal Administration.*

Taking what was probably the most regularly governed territory, we may look within the Rájá's demesne to see how it was managed. The initial grouping of lands is of course the 'village,' and to this unit attention was mostly paid, because if the grain collection went wrong there, nothing else would go right. In the last chapter we have fully gone into the question of the origin of villages, and shown how cultivation could only be done by aggregates of men who were united in some sort of bond for mutual society and protection. Whether the villages were actually primæval settlements of tribes, allotting the lands according to custom, or whether they were later foundations by colonists and settlers, it was natural that some one man should take the lead as the representative of the village; and as the collection of the king's share at the threshing-floor required watching, that headman was naturally drawn more and more into connection with the State, and became in fact a State officer. No wonder, then, that the office soon assumed an hereditary character, and that, what with the importance his State connection gave him, and the emoluments which he was allowed to enjoy, the headman became an institution so useful, that he survived where many other institutions gradually disappeared. The fact that every village from which the king drew a share, had a headman—alluded to in the early books as the 'grámádhikár,' and later on by a multitude of names ('pátel,' 'mandal,' 'pradhán,' and later still, 'muqaddam' and 'lambardár')—became a recognized universal fact of village organization.

But the headman required the assistance of a person who could write and do sums and keep the accounts of the collection, and register facts regarding the land and its cultivators; so that a village 'patwárí'—the 'grámalekhak' (village-writer) of ancient days—became equally a necessary part of the system.

The natural land-unit of the revenue system being the

village, its administration furnished the pattern for all the rest. The village official *personnel* was, for Government purposes, simply repeated in wider and wider circles, first over a smaller area, and then again, over a still larger area such as we now call a *district*.

As regards the 'district,' there are allusions in Manu to 'a lord over 1000 villages'; and we have traces, in parts of India, both of the ancient districts and of the officers who presided over them, still remembered in later Hindu dialects as 'sirdesmukh' (chief head of a 'des'); with him an accountant of the district was also recognized. But the most generally used and best known division was that which was smaller than a 'district' and comprised the charge of eighty-four villages or some similar group. It is better known to us by the later (Muhammadan) name of 'pargana.' It was always adopted by the Mughal system, and the *parganas* into which the country was then divided, are almost everywhere known to this day. In Maráthá countries, and by the Sikhs, the same division was known by the name 'taluka[1].'

The pargana or taluka official staff just repeated that of the village, only in the larger jurisdiction. There was the 'desmukh' or pargana headman, and the 'des-pándyá,' or desái, who kept the pargana accounts. The former, as we shall see, became the 'chaudhari' of later times, and the latter the 'qánúngo.' Directly under these were the *villages*; unless indeed for certain purposes, a circle of villages was locally recognized and called a 'tappa,'—intermediate between the *pargana* and the single village.

It seems that from very early times these officials were paid (wholly or partly) by *holding land revenue-free in virtue of their office*, which is exactly the 'watan' it afterwards came to be called in Central India and Bombay[2]. 'Let the lord of ten villages,' says Manu, 'enjoy the produce of two plough lands (or as much ground as can be tilled

[1] This was the Arabic word 'ta'alluqa,' but as it was adopted as a Hindi word in the form *taluka*, I write it so.

[2] See Chapter IV, on Land Tenures, p. 180.

with two ploughs), the lord of twenty that of ten ploughs, the lord of 100 that of a village, the lord of 1000 that of a large village.' Traces of this holding of service-lands (service I here use of official service as distinct from land held for *military* service) we shall meet with all over India; it extended not only to the village, subdivision, and district headmen and account-keepers, but to the watchmen, priests, and even artisans of the villages. The reason why the official holdings, as a direct origin of a peculiar land-tenure, survived so in Central and Western India, and to a lesser extent in the South, and disappeared in the North, is that in the former countries the Muhammadan kings were even more respectful to local institutions than the Mughals; and though the Mughal Empire at last extended over the Dakhan, its duration was brief and its hold imperfect. The Maráthá rulers, who followed the Mughals, were Hindu, and therefore imbued with the spirit of the universal Hindu system. Averse to revenue-free holdings as they were, they did not dare to interfere with such a deeply-rooted institution as the Hindu official's hereditary land-holding.

§ 4. *The Mughal Revenue-organization.*

How very generally the Mughals preserved the Hindu system, only with some attempt at definition and with the adoption of Perso-Arabic official terms for everything—terms that have come down to our own officers—is well known through the description given by Ab-ul-Faẓl (Akbar's minister) in his *Ayín-i-Akbari*, and through other historians.

The great provinces, like Bengal, Oudh (in later times), the Dakhan, Alláhábád, &c., were the grand divisions, and were designated 'Súba[1].' Each Súba was primarily divided

[1] Before the Mughal times, some of them, as Bengal and Jaunpur, had been independent Afghán kingdoms, and became Mughal Súbas. Again in the days of decline, the Náwábs or other governors (officially called Súbadár) threw off their allegiance and set up as separate States. Oudh, and the State of the Nizám of Hyderabad in the Dakhan, are familiar examples.

into districts (but larger than our present *districts*) called 'Sirkár[1].'

The Sirkár was divided into parganas (sometimes called mahâls), and these, for some purposes, were aggregated into contiguous groups called 'dastúr'[2] (or dastúr-ul-'aml)—a grouping which does not appear long to have survived, or to have had any great importance.

In the reign of Sháh Jahán, another subdivision was recognized, that of 'chaklá': it was a division of the Súba. Thus, in Bengal, in the time of Ja'far Khán, the Súba was divided into thirty-two Sirkárs or into thirteen chaklás[3]. We read of the Company being granted, in 1760, the 'chaklá' of Bardwán in Bengal.

In Akbar's time the important revenue officer was the ''ámil' (or 'amlguzár), who supervised the village collections of his district, and adjusted the assessments on the principles of the Settlement made during this reign. The 'ámil's jurisdiction was not determined by area, but according to the amount of revenue under his control. Thus it would happen that the charge would be small where the land was well populated and highly cultivated, and larger in a poor and barren country. The 'ámil was in after times called 'Karori'—the officer who collected a 'crore' (ten million = Karor) of 'dáms' (i.e. R. 2,50,000)[4]. Still later, the Karori's duty was restricted to revenue-collection, the assessments being made by another officer (amín-faujdár), in subordination to whom the Karori acted.

[1] Incorrectly written 'Circar.' Thus we read of the Northern Circars of Madras. It was suggested that each Súba should consist of twenty-two Sirkárs, and each Sirkár of twenty-two parganas, but this was only an idea never realised in practice.

[2] Beames' *Elliott's Glossary*, vol. ii. p. 20 et seq.

[3] *Fifth Report*, vol. i. 19, 389. Beames' *Elliott's Glossary* speaks of the 'Chaklá' as a division of a 'Sirkár,' somewhat larger than a modern 'district' but less than a Commissioner's division. It was known in Oudh, not in the North-Western Provinces. In Bengal certainly the Chaklá was not *part of* a Sirkár, but a larger district, as the numbers in the text show. The 'Chakládár' was the District Officer, and the 'ámil was under him for one or more 'parganas': the 'ámil might be alone, or there might also be a revenue-farmer at the same time. (*North-Western Provinces Gazette*, vii. 107 note.)

[4] The 'dám' was a small copper coin, of somewhat doubtful value; in Akbar's time, it is said, forty went to the rupee.

For each *pargana* there was a district accountant-registrar, called 'Kanungo' (Qánúngo = one who declares the rule or standard). He was the Hindu 'Des-pándyá.' The executive officer of the *pargana* was called Chaudhari, the old Hindu 'des-mukh.'

§ 5. *The Jágír System.*

One other feature of the Mughal system should be mentioned. Just as the Hindus divided the whole country into the royal domains and chief's domains, so the Mughals apportioned their territory into 'khálsa' and 'jágír' lands. The former was divided into charges, and managed by 'ámils and State officials, as just described. The rest was divided out into blocks, or estates, which were made over for life (the grants became hereditary at a later stage) to certain military commanders, ministers, and courtiers, who took the revenues for their own support, or that of a military force which they were bound to maintain. Probably the idea was copied from the Hindu system. Sometimes waste tracts were granted in 'jágír,' and sometimes outlying and troublesome districts. The jágírdár managed the whole, increased the cultivation, and applied the revenue to his own support, and to the expenses of the administration and the pay of troops. While a strict control lasted, the jágírdár was bound to take no more than the sum assigned; and if more came into his hands, he had rigidly to account for the surplus to the State treasury[1]. The system of assigning the revenues of a tract as a reward for good service, or the support of troops, is a regular Oriental method, and has been continued in our own times in a modified form.

[1] The system of Jágírs, which has also been touched on in the last chapter, is more fully explained in the chapter on Bengal Tenures.

§ 6. *Farming or Contracting Systems.*

The last phase in the administration was that which marked the later days of the Empire after the death of Aurangzeb.

I have already explained[1] how important it was for the Mughal rulers to conciliate, and if possible make use of, the old Rájás, who, though yielding submission to the conqueror, were only too likely to give trouble directly a chance of revolt occurred. This circumstance led to the appointment of Rájás to collect, or rather to contract for, certain defined sums of revenue required from their territories. I have also explained how, in days of disorder and feeble rule, such a plan of contracting for a fixed sum of revenue saved all the trouble of local control, and so was generally adopted; and then, not only old territorial chiefs, but speculators, courtiers, and *quondam* officials, were allowed to become *revenue-farmers*, either of *parganas* or of larger or smaller areas, according to their means and spheres of influence. Their territories were spoken of as the 'ihtimám,' or charge. A Rájá, a chaudhari, or a speculator with no title at all, thus appointed to manage the tract under his influence, would be equally designated as the 'landholder' or 'Zamíndár' of his territory, and would be so called in the '*sanad*,' or official warrant of his appointment. A person allowed a somewhat less important tract on the same terms (and sometimes made subordinate to a 'Zamíndár') would be called 'Taluqdár.' In Oudh, the title of 'Taluqdár' was applied, with no suggestion of inferior rank, to holders of estates of the first class[2].

At first, the duty of such a 'landholder' was strictly to gather the revenues of the villages, and retain only his own recognized share of the total, which was usually *one-tenth*,

[1] See Chap. IV. p. 185.

[2] Possibly it was that the Oudh Taluqs were not so large as the districts of Bengal Zamíndárs: but I think it likely that the term 'zamíndár' had acquired a special meaning in Oudh, and was applied to grantees or others who had the management of single villages.

besides making certain other deductions, all exactly specified and accounted for. But in time the strictness was relaxed, and the 'Zamíndárs' were simply required to make good a lump-sum, raised from time to time, and partaking more and more of the nature of a bargain. Under such a system, oppression of the country people was sure to follow. All regular assessments, and authorized revisions of land-revenues, were further and further abandoned[1]. The Treasury authorities of the province merely increased their demands on the 'Zamíndár' by adding extra *cesses*, giving them this name or that, according to the particular necessity or fancy that originated them. These amounts had, of course, to be got out of the villages—with a good deal more besides. In the days of decline, as we shall see, both in Oudh and Bengal, an occasional vigorous governor would make a desperate grasp at the reins of revenue-control; for a time the revenue-farming, or Zamíndárí management, would be set aside, and an attempt made to return to village collections through the pargana officials; but always without lasting result. Exactly the same thing happened in the first days of British rule. Zamíndárs were set aside, and other local collectors tried; but in vain. The Zamíndárí system had become the only one by which the revenues could be secured; at least, without an entirely new system, which would have involved a survey of the lands, and other steps, which were not possible at the time, even if anyone had thought of them.

[1] *Farming* the revenues (a bad example which was often copied in our first essays at management) was always the resource either of governments in their decline or of mere marauders like the Rohillas. The Maráthás adopted it also when their position was not secure. The Rohillas made farming the corner-stone of their financial system, and it is still in force in the small Rohilla State of Rámpur. '"Proprietors" were not recognized; the only favour conceded to landholders was permission to hold their "sír" (home-farm) at privileged rates.' The farmer, however, was bound to let the tenant's rates alone for the period of his lease. The Rohillas certainly succeeded from a financial point of view. They raised from Bareilly a sum nearly equal to sixteen lakhs of our currency in 1754, which is not far short of the assessment 120 years later. But after twenty-five years of the Nawáb Wazír's (Oudh) rule, the revenue had fallen to half that amount.—(*Review of Bareilly Settlement Report*, p. 5.)

How this contract system spread all over Bengal, and over the upper part of Madras; how, in a modified form, it was adopted in Oudh, and to a much less extent and in a different form, it prevailed in Northern India; how it was only allowed by the Maráthás to a limited extent, and for individual villages; and how, wherever adopted, it produced various effects on the land-tenures, I have already given some idea in the last chapter. Here I must return to the revenue-administration, and pass on to notice the changes that followed from the example set by the Mughal Empire, in later Hindu States—Rájput, Maráthá, and Sikh. Indeed, they were very slight. When we look to the organization of Rájput States, as we find them after the time of Akbar—whose policy had been to encourage and gain the support of the Rájput princes—we find a number of Persian revenue terms gradually introduced, but the administration essentially the same as that of the early kingdoms.

Exactly the same thing happened when Maráthá States rose on the ruins of the Muhammadan and Pathán kingdoms, and when the Sikh States took the place of the Afghán governor in the Panjáb.

§ 7. *Post-Mughal Hindu Administration.*

The Hindus always held to the system I have already described,—the allotment of the whole territory into tracts governed by the Rájá or overlord, and tracts governed by his 'feudal' chiefs; and I have before alluded to their recognition of estates called bhúmiyá—holdings which were virtually proprietary estates but of inferior rank, because the holders were proprietors, not governors. The direct management was by heads of districts, practically the same as the Muhammadan 'pargana,' and called taluka; under these were subdivisions called 'tappa,' and then came the villages.

The only remarkable fact is this, that the later Hindu

States adopted many Perso-Arabic terms derived from the Muhammadan system[1].

§ 8. *Maráthá Revenue System.*

For *central government* each Maráthá State had a Díwán or Minister. Under him was the Fard-navís, a sort of Financial Minister, and with him the Mazúm- (or Majmu'a) -dár, or Registrar. There was also a Chitta-navís (letter-writer or Secretary), a 'Sikka-navís,' who kept the Prince's seal, and a 'Pôt-navís,' or Treasury Officer. This group formed the 'Secretariat' or State Department.

In the *districts*, a considerable territory was in charge of a 'kamavísdár,' who had deputies in each subdivision. The deputy, again, in each patta, subdivision, or tappa, was aided by a 'kárkun' or agent. The minor subdivisions varied according to convenience. The Maráthás sometimes continued the use of the Muhammadan 'sirkár' and 'pargana,' and sometimes spoke of the 'taluka.' The 'tappa' used by them was larger than a pargana, and was subdivided into 'zilas[2].' But each district was not left to the kamavísdár alone: his authority was shared by an officer called the 'zamíndár.' Here we have another meaning for this Protean term. The zamíndár was, in fact, the old 'desmukh' with a new name; he was the executive head collector; and the kamavísdár was really put in as a spy or check on him to prevent his absorbing the revenue. Of course the kánúngo or district accountant was maintained, and he ranked next below the 'zamíndár.'

§ 9. *Later Rájput States.*

The later Rájput States had, and still have, an exactly similar system, only with different names: thus the díwán

[1] Just as the Sikhs adopted Persian for the official or Court language.

[2] Malcolm, vol. ii. p. 4. The term 'zila',' as here locally used, is different from the use later acquired, where 'zila'' was adopted in the Regulations, for the district embracing several parganas.

was called 'kámdár' = *chargé d'affaires*; the fard-navís was called 'daftarí,' and so forth.

It should be remembered that certain tracts were either held by renters or farmers, or by 'jágírdárs,' military and other assignees of the revenue of certain areas; and in these tracts the official collectors did not interfere.

The Maráthás, and the better Rájput chiefs, were careful of their territories. 'All ground,' says Sir J. Malcolm[1], 'be it ever so waste or hilly, is included in the divisions (pargana, tappa, taluka, &c.) which are marked by natural or artificial boundaries, such as rivers, water-courses, ranges of hills, trees, rocks, ridges, or lines between any two remarkable objects. The lands were measured, including the space occupied by banks, walls, houses, &c., in the time of the Mughal Government; and this record of measurement was lodged in the office of every *zamíndár* of a district as well as in the fard-navís' (State Secretary's) office. Several of these records have been saved; but where they are not, the ease with which the memory of the respective limits was preserved by the hereditary officers of the district and village to whom this duty belongs, is very extraordinary.'

§ 10. *Sikh System in the Panjáb.*

When the Sikh Government succeeded to the Muslím dominions in the Panjáb, they followed the same system. I may pass over the first short period when the confederate and equal chiefs (grouped in what were called 'misl') divided the country into a multitude of 'taluqas[2].' Soon the genius of Ranjít Singh prevailed, and he became King (or Mahárájá) and made the other chiefs 'feudal' lords and governors of districts under him. These governors he called 'Jágírdár, or 'Diwán,' or 'Názim,' as the case might be. Under these, again, were districts of manageable size (talu-

[1] Vol. ii. p. 5.

[2] The Sikh dominion commenced with a sort of confederacy of a number of equal chiefs. They of course quarrelled, and very soon they were reduced under one head. See Hunter's *India* (Gaz, vol. vi. p. 410, 2nd edition.)

qas), and 'Kárdárs' were the presiding officers, who assessed and collected the revenues.

§ 11. *Résumé of Native Systems.*

In short, the student will bear in mind that the Mughal system, as introduced by Akbar and his successors (before that organization was virtually replaced by the system of *revenue-farming*), was, in fact, the old Hindu model. The Hindu States always kept it up, only that they preferred several of the Persian names that the Mughal Empire had introduced. The fact was, that while the early Hindu system had been one without any survey or measurement, and without any records to speak of, the Mughal rulers crystallized it into more business-like permanence, by measuring and recording villages, parganas, and 'sirkárs' with their revenue assessment. Once fixed, the local hereditary officers became the depositaries of the measures, rules, and facts (qánúngo means the officer who 'declares' the 'rule,' measure, or law in revenue matters). All later Governments were glad to avail themselves of these records; and the old formal assessment of Akbar's date formed a sort of basis or fundamental assessment, remembered with almost superstitious reverence, though of course it was altered and increased according to circumstances, and no one really expected to be assessed according to it, unless he conceived a right to hold at fixed rates, which was thus expressed. Briefly, the essential features of all historic revenue-management, whether Rájput, Mughal, Maráthá, or Sikh, have been the following, under whatever variety of names:—

(1) the village, with its headman and accountant;

(2) very frequently there was an intermediate grouping of villages forming a 'tappa,' under a minor civil officer and staff; this is not always found;

(3) a larger district forming a pargana or taluka, under a district headman (kárdár, 'ámil, chaudhari, kaṛoṛí, &c.), and aided by an accountant (kánúngo);

(4) Several *parganas* united into a sirkár (or locally a chaklá) under a Díwán, Názim, &c.

Wherever revenue-farming arrangements were introduced in the late Mughal days, it was on a large scale; and the local magnate who became contractor, first atrophied and then obliterated the local revenue staff; whereas, when the Maráthás and Sikhs adopted farming it was chiefly by single villages or small taluqas.

SECTION III.—ANCIENT AUTHORITIES REGARDING THE 'KING'S SHARE.'

§ 1. *The Hindu Theory.*

I have called attention to the fact that the earlier races who preceded the Aryans—or, as I call them, Rájputs, according to their later and surviving name—did not originally accord their king a share in the grain-heap of every village in his dominion, but allotted him the entire produce of certain lands. In Chutiyá Nágpur, for instance, among the Dravidian races, and among the Gonds and others of Central and South India, we find distinct traces of the allotment of areas for the king, ministers, and so on, down to the village heads[1]. But even there the practice gradually grew up of taking a grain-share from the other lands also. And this practice became universal. The Hindu States always took a *grain-share* for the king in his territories, and for the chiefs in theirs.

The idea of a 'share' for the king seems to have been a very early one: thus Sir John Malcolm quotes the *Mahábhárata* as alluding to the origin of kings: 'Mankind' (says the author) 'were continually opposing each other, and they at last went to *Brahma* to ask him to appoint a king over them. Manu was directed to be their king. He replied, "I fear a sinful action: government is arduous, especially among ever-lying men." They said, "Fear not;

[1] See also the section on Chutiyá Nágpur Tenures (Bengal).

you will receive a recompense:—of beasts a fiftieth part, and also of gold, and we will *give you a tenth of the corn*, increasing your store,"' &c.[1] Manu (chap. vii. 127–130) says: 'Of cattle, of gems, of gold and silver, added each year to the capital stock [the king's share is] a fiftieth part[2], of grain an *eighth part*, or a *sixth* or a *twelfth*, according to the difference of the soil and the labour necessary to cultivate it.' In Chap. x, v. 118, it is admitted that the share may be raised to one-fourth of the crops at a time of urgent necessity, as in war or invasion; and so the tax on the mercantile classes may be raised. It was noticed that in Alexander's time the cultivators were already contributing one-fourth of the grain[3]. In the great southern Hindu kingdom of Bíjanagar or Vijáyanagar (which lasted till the seventeenth century), the Minister Vidyáranyá declared that a king who took more than one-sixth 'shall be deemed impious in this world, and shall be cast into hell-flames in the next[4].'

Colonel Wilks, in his *History of Mysore*, has given other instances of the southern kingdoms taking one-sixth[5].

Harihar Rái, who was one of the early kings of Bíjanagar (A.D. 1334–47), is said to have divided the grain thus: half, including the straw, to the cultivator; and the remaining half was made into three shares, one of which went to the king, one to the overlord or 'proprietor' of the village, and one-third to priests and the religious classes; but the latter *the king also took*, on the plea that he supported the priests[6].

From the many allusions in books, it seems probable that, as long as the old kingdoms were at peace, the *tradi-*

[1] Malcolm, vol. i. p. 231, note.

[2] Briggs notices that in the time of Tavernier the king took two per cent. of the gems found at Golkhandá (the celebrated diamond mines, then worked).

[3] Strabo, lib. xv. 1030; and Diodorus Siculus, ii. 53, quoted by Briggs.

[4] Briggs, p. 62.

[5] But it seems that the sixth was enlarged very easily. Thus, Colonel Wilks tells us of a Pándyan king invading Kánara in the thirteenth century, who made the people give him the sixth of *husked* rice, thus adding ten per cent. to the contribution at one stroke.

[6] See this more fully described, and the curious method of *calculating* the produce by a certain multiple of the seed sown, described in Sir T. Munro's Minute on Kánara, given in Arbuthnot, p. 61 of vol. i.

tional sixth was adhered to[1]. The king had no expanding administrations nor demands like those on a modern government; and as long as the revenue-share came in regularly, and as it was moderately increased by increase of cultivation and by the other tolls and dues which the king levied, he had no great temptation to raise the share, at any rate formally and openly. But there always comes a time when invasion and war and other difficulties disturb affairs; and in later days we shall find Hindu kingdoms, no less than others, raising the revenue freely.

In other places, the share of two-fifths was commonly levied, and the 'panchdo' is still a traditionally common proportion of grain-produce, now paid to a 'proprietor' who has intervened between the cultivator and the king.

The 'Fifth Report' gives many more details as to the extent of shares taken at different times[2]. What the Sikh demand was, will appear fully in the chapter on the Panjáb Revenue System.

It is unnecessary, however, to go into further detail, because, whatever was the early practice, and whatever its causes and its duration, it is quite certain, as Campbell remarks, that in later times the practice in all States—a practice that can be traced back before the end of the seventeenth century, at any rate—was to take a half of the grain in some cases, and in places where money assessments were levied, as much as could be got without driving

[1] Indeed, Abul Fazl, in the *Ayin-i-Akbari*, says the Hindu custom was to take *one-sixth* (of the gross produce). And see M. Williams' translation of the *Sakuntalá*, Act II. p. 49.

[2] Vol. ii. pp. 411, 462, 472-3; see also Hunter's *Orissa*, vol. i. p. 32-5; Campbell (*Cobden Club Papers*), p. 155. See also Sir T. Munro's opinion in a Minute at page 92 of Arbuthnot, vol. i. See also note in Phillips, p. 227, showing that there was no real limit on the share. It should be remembered with reference to the supposed moderation of the 'one-sixth,' that it really represented little more than a charge for the royal 'privy purse.' No public works, no army, and no police had to be maintained out of it. The army was supported by the estates on the feudal system, and so with the police as far as there was any distinct from the military force. And when the great tanks, bathing places, and other works which are now looked on with just admiration as showing the wealth, power, and wisdom of the old kings, were made, it was chiefly by unpaid labour, or at least by labour fed with food taken from the neighbourhood. All this cannot be ignored in comparing the modern system with the ancient.

the raiyats to abscond into the jungle, and by the carefully elastic mode of exaction which the old rulers were so clever in applying.

§ 2. *Muhammadan theory of Land-Revenue.*

I will now briefly allude to the Muhammadan law theory of the revenue—not, as I have already said, because the Mughals really understood it or carried it out, but because it was sometimes convenient for the orthodox to refer to it; and because, occasionally, fanatical rulers did impose some of the taxes *eo nomine* on the Hindus.

The theory was that the inhabitants of a country might be regarded as '*millí*,' or peaceful; '*zimmí*,' or subdued infidels; and '*ḥarbí*,' those in arms against the Muslím; and the treatment of a conquered country may be briefly described in the words of an author quoted in Colonel Galloway's *Law and Constitution of India* [1] :—'When the Imám (leader of the faithful) conquers the country by force of arms, if he permits the inhabitants to remain, he imposes the *khiráj* on their *lands* and the *jaziya* (correctly *jiziyat*) on their *heads*'; and he adds that the land then remains the property of the conquered [2].

Some authors considered *khiráj* to be of different kinds —the term in itself meant *the whole of the surplus produce after deducting the cost of production* [3].

But there was also the more lenient form of '*khiráj mukásima*,' or division of produce, by which the sovereign

[1] P. 32: the work is called Siráj-ul-wahháj.

[2] With the poll-tax or 'jaziya' we have no concern; but the reader will find some curious facts about it in Beames' *Elliott's Glossary*, vol. ii. sub voc. jaziya. Thus 'Alá-ud-dín Khilji is described as conversing with a learned Qázi—'From what description of Hindus is it lawful to exact obedience and tribute?' The Qázi replies: 'Imám Hanif says that the *jaziya*, or as heavy a tribute as they can bear, may be imposed, instead of death, on infidels; and it is commanded that the *jaziya* and *khiráj* be exacted to the uttermost farthing, in order that the punishment may approach as near as possible to death.' 'You may perceive,' replied the king, 'that without reading learned books, I am in the habit of putting in practice that which has been enjoined by the Prophet.'

[3] Quoted in Briggs, p. 115.

took one-fifth or so. This was, of course, the exact counterpart of the old Hindu grain-share.

The tax converted into money was called '*khiráj-muwazifa*,' or simply '*wazífa*,' and this was (originally) 'regulated by the ability of the cultivator to pay.'

On such general principles, it is not surprising that the Muhammadan rulers exercised considerable latitude in assessing their revenue; and that no particle of evidence can be adduced for the proposition that by 'law and constitution' of India, Akbar's Settlement, or any other, constituted a standard to which every one could appeal, and beyond which he could not lawfully be enhanced. As a matter of fact, in the best days of Mughal rule, moderation and control over collecting officers were duly observed; but no ruler ever dreamt that he might not from time to time (as he chose—there was no other principle) revise the assessment. Good rulers did so by a formal measurement and moderate additions. Indifferent rulers did so by the easier expedient of merely adding on 'cesses' (known in revenue language as '*ḥubúb*' and '*abwáb*'). Bad rulers simply bargained with farmers for fixed sums, thus both compelling and encouraging the farmer to raise the assessment on the cultivators, or, in other words, delegating to the farmer the proper functions of the State officer in revising assessments.

How the revenue-farmer exercised this power we shall see in the history of Bengal; it was the origin, of course, of his right of enhancing (what became) the *rent*. When the raiyats ceased to be dealt with direct by the State officers, they were, in effect, handed over to the Zamíndár, who in time became 'the landlord,' and they his 'tenants.'

Before the Mughal times, we find 'Alá-ud-dín (A.D. 1294–1315) imposing a *half* produce tax, or *khiráj*[1]. But the

[1] See Briggs' *Ferishta*, vol. i. 347. The reader will notice that this term, though not now used for the land-revenue, has entered into common use in the official term 'lákhiráj,' i. e. land which, by the grant of Government, pays no land-revenue, or of which the revenues are assigned to a grantee. The 'land-revenue' as an amount assessed is jama' = total; as a payment it is spoken of as '*mál*,' or in

practically useful history of land-revenue begins with the reign of Akbar.

Before, however, I speak of the Akbarian Settlement, of which the central feature was the commutation of the grain-share into a money payment, let me introduce to the reader the method of grain-division as it used to be employed, and as it is still locally employed, either between the native Rájá and his subjects, or between landlord and tenant, as in Bihár, the Panjáb, and other localities.

§ 3. *Practice of Grain-division.*

The earliest form of grain-division is the deposit of the grain in heaps on the threshing-floors and measuring it out with certain measures, which varied with the custom of the place. How complicated such a measurement can be made, and what varied forms of fraud can be practised on either side, it is not easy to realize. In the chapter on SINDH, I have made allusion to the elaborate practice followed in former days in some of the districts there; and in various other provincial sections I have given accounts of the curious local practices of division. Here I only give a general idea of the commonest forms, which were—(1) actual division; (2) estimating the standing crop and declaring a certain number of 'maunds' to be the king's share.

In order to save the trouble of dividing, sometimes—and this was perhaps a step towards dissolution of the system—a method of *estimation* would be allowed; a practised eye looked at a field, and judged, 'The reaping of such a field will give so many *maunds* of grain, of which so many go to the king'; and the officers took that amount of grain, whether more or less than was actually harvested.

I will ask the student to remember the vernacular terms: 'bháolí' (or 'batáí') by itself or in compound, is applied to

some provinces '*mu'amla*.' (In the Panjáb this use of the term is universal and the only one understood.)

actual grain-division: 'kankút' (or kan) is applied to the estimate.

§ 4. *In Rájput States.*

Colonel Tod thus speaks of the grain-share collection in Rájput States[1]:—

'There are two methods of levying the revenues of the Crown on every description of corn—"kankút" and "batáí": —for, on sugarcane, poppy, hemp, tobacco, cotton[2], indigo, and garden produce, a money payment is fixed, varying from rupees two to six per *bighá*. The *kankút* is a conjectural estimate of the standing crop by the united judgment of the officers of Government—the pátel (village headman), *patwári*—and the owner of the field. The accuracy with which an accustomed eye will determine the quantity of grain on a given surface is surprising, and should the owner deem the estimate overrated, he can insist on batáí or division of the corn after it is threshed. . . . In the batáí system the share of the Government is from one-third to two-fifths of the spring harvest[3], as wheat and barley; and sometimes even half, which is the invariable proportion of the autumnal crops. The "kankút" is the most liable to corruption. The cultivator bribes the collector, who will underrate the crop; and when he betrays his duty the "watchman" (one of the village establishment) is not likely to be honest: and as Indian corn, the grand autumnal crop of Mewár (Udaipur State), is eaten green, the Crown may be defrauded of half its dues. . . . There was a "barár" or tax introduced to make up the deficiency, which was in no proportion to the quantity cultivated, and its amount was at the mercy of the officers.'

§ 5. *A Modern Native State.*

The following is another picture of 'batáí' from one of the 'tappas' or groups of villages called Khairodá, in the Mewár (Udaipur) State[4]:—'Of the first crop, consisting of

[1] Tod, i. 431.

[2] Cotton in some places was shared in kind. In Chittagong certain of the remoter hill estates used to pay their revenue in cotton, and gave rise to the 'Kapás mahál,' or estate in the accounts, which paid in cotton.

[3] There are in most parts two harvests (see Chap. i. pp. 12–13). The spring crop is in Mewár called 'unálú,' and the autumn crop 'síyálú'; 'ún' = heat, 'sí' = cold; referring to summer and winter harvest time.

[4] Tod, vol. ii. 547.

wheat, barley, and *gram*, the produce is formed into heaps of one hundred maunds each; these are subdivided into four parts of twenty-five maunds each. The first operation is to provide from one of these the "síráno" or *seer* on each maund, to each individual of the village establishment, viz. the *pátel*, or headman; the *patwárí*, or accountant; the *shána*, or watchman (guardian of crops); the *bulái*, or messenger and general herdsman; the *háthí* (*alias* satár), or carpenter; the *lóhár*, or blacksmith; the *kumhár*, or potter; the *dhobí*, or washerman; the *chamár*, who is shoemaker, currier, and scavenger; and the *nái*, or barber-surgeon. These ten "sírános," being one seer on each heap or two and a-half maunds to each individual, swallow up one of the subdivisions. Of the three remaining parts, one share (twenty-five maunds) go to the Ráj or State, two to the cultivator, after deducting a "síráno" for the heir-apparent, which is termed "Kúṅwar-mutka" (the prince's pot).' An innovation of late years has been practised on the portion (two heaps) belonging to the village, by which no less than three maunds are deducted nominally for the prince, the Rájá's chief groom, and his grain-steward; so that the Government share in total becomes three-tenths instead of one-fourth. The autumn crop is also divided by heaps: out of every one hundred maunds, forty go to the Government and sixty to the village[1].

[1] I cannot forbear making one other extract describing *batái* in one of the old Sikh estates. I found among the records of the Ambála Commissioner's office a report on a lapsed estate of Sirdárni Dáyá Kúṅwar, dated 23rd May, 1824. It contains the following curious passage (which I transcribe exactly—capitals and all):—

'The Native system of making the collections may be termed threefold;—the kun (kan) [also called "kankút" and "típ"], batace (batái) and tushkhees (tashkhis), all of which had at different periods been adopted by the officers of the late Sirdarnee. The kun or appraisement [of crop before cutting], if skilful makers can be found, is the most simple and expeditious method, but requiring great Fidelity, Experience, and Judgment in the "kunneea" or appraiser, who should be chosen from among the oldest Zumeendars, and over whom the Tuhseeldar should keep a vigilant and circumspect Eye. In the case of a cultivator being dissatisfied with the appraisement of his field by the kunneea, an instant recourse should be had to the Practice of beating out a Beega or a Biswa of the grain on the disputed Field, and thereby ascertain the exact quantity to the satisfaction of both parties. It is obvious that a constant appeal to this principle ought

§ 6. *Maráthá System.*

In the Maráthá States the financiers had already replaced *batáí* by money-rates. Sir J. Malcolm[1] writes:—'The mode of realizing the revenue varied little as far as it related to the collections of the cultivators. *Batáí* or payment in kind is very unusual; except with the Rájput principalities, almost all the subjects in the Maráthá States pay in money. The basis on which Settlements were generally founded was a measurement of the kharíf or first crop[2] when it is cut down, and the rabi or second crop, when it is about half a foot high, and is renewed every third year. This measurement[3] is made with a coarse rope divided into yards.' In a note the author mentions that in Nimár no measurement had taken place since the Muhammadan rule, and that the people regarded re-measurement as an innovation, desiring to be held to what was in the kánúngo's books.

A village Settlement had to be made for each harvest with the headman, unless the village was farmed or rented. The regular assessment was said to be moderate, and was intended to amount to the money equivalent of twenty-five to forty per cent. of the produce after deduction of seed

to be avoided as tedious and vexatious, and it is seldom that the cultivator calls for its application, still less does the kunneea like to put his judgment to the Test.

'The butaee or division of grain on the spot seemed to present many objections. Three Heaps are made: one for the Sarkar (the Government), one for the Ryot, and the third for the Khurch, or village expenses; so that the Government receives only about one-third of the produce, which has led to the phrase "bataee lootaee" or Division is plunder. The grain has to remain in the field for a length of time, exposed to the Elements, ere it can be trodden out and winnowed, added to the expense of persons to watch the khulwara (khalwára) or stacks from the spoliation of the Zumeendars, who are tempted to remove portions of grain during the night season. Could these and similar Difficulties be surmounted, no mode offers such a show of justice to the Government and its subjects as dividing the Gifts of nature on the spot.

'The tushkees, or farm of an estate to the highest bidder, distresses the cultivator, however pleasing the lucrative receipts may appear for the first few years of the lease . . . .'

[1] Vol. ii. p. 24.

[2] I. e. counting the year as beginning before the rains, which is the plan of the *fasli* or agricultural year.

[3] In Central India they used the Akbari measure of one bíghá = a square of 60 *gaz* or yards, which will be explained further on.

and costs[1]. The moderation, however, was deprived of its advantage by the additional charge of '*tafrík*' or contingencies.

The system of management adopted by the Maráthás was not, however, uniform; in outlying tracts they farmed their revenues and did it cruelly; in other places they made no arrangement at all, but levied a 'chauth,' or fourth, as tribute. The Maráthá 'chauth' in Bengal became historic.

In the Settlement report of the large Dholká taluka, or local division of the Ahmadábád Collectorate of Bombay, I find the most curious account of the old assessments. Whether this was altogether due to the Maráthás or to the chiefs (called taluqdárs), remains of the Muhammadan kingdoms in the Guzarát province, I do not know; but the assessment consisted sometimes of a grain-division (bhágwatái), and sometimes of a cash assessment by area (always called bíghotí—rate on the bíghá). This varied with each crop, and was levied on all sugar-cane, garden produce, and vegetables. Then, besides that, there was a whole series of 'bábtí,' which is merely an old friend,—the Bengal 'cess' (abwáb) under a new name. Yet most of the assessment was levied on the *basis* or foundation of the moderate and recorded rates of the Settlement effected by the Muhammadan kings. The latter was called the *'ain* (the 'thing itself'); and when the Maráthás had levelled up the village *'ain* to what they considered as much as could be got, they called it the 'kamál' or 'perfect' assessment.

§ 7. *Certain Crops always paid in Cash.—Zabtí.*

In concluding this notice, I ought to allude to a fact which perhaps suggested, certainly facilitated, the change from a *grain* to a *money*-payment. When vegetables, sugar-cane, spices, and similar crops, not forgetting cotton, are largely cultivated, it is very difficult to divide them in

[1] Irrigated land for opium and sugar-cane was rented at R. 5 to 10 a bighá, and garden land nearly as high; the black soil was assessed at R. 1 to 1-8.

kind; the process takes too long and the produce is spoiled, or the determination of a yield, when the whole crop is not taken off the soil at once, becomes impossible. At a very early date such crops paid at customary rates in cash; and when in later times all crops paid in cash, these—more valuable—kinds of produce were charged at a higher rate. In revenue language they were called 'zabtí' crops, and paid at 'zabtí' rates[1].

SECTION IV.—THE BEGINNING OF REGULAR ASSESSMENT UNDER NATIVE RULE.

The first beginning of the change from a mere levy of a share of the grain to a regularly-assessed land-revenue, may fairly be traced to the Emperor Akbar's Settlement, begun in 1571 A.D. There had been some earlier attempts, but they were not systematic, nor have the details come down to us. There was another great Settlement at a later date carried out by the Muhammadan kings of the Dakhan, but that was almost wholly a copy of Akbar's Settlement. The astute emperor employed a distinguished Hindu Rájá, Toḍar Mal[2], to do the work conjointly with a Muhammadan official. It should be remarked that this Settlement did not at once *enforce* the method of cash payment; it left it optional with the raiyat to pay the old grain-share if he objected to the commutation price. Abul Fazl, in the *Ayín-i-Akbari*, describes the methods of grain-division as above detailed, showing that the methods have never varied in principle. He mentions the 'kankút,' or estimate of crops while standing; the 'bháoli' or 'batáí' being the actual division of the grain on the threshing-floors. And he adds another method called 'khetbatáí,' or taking a certain measured area of the standing crop of each field, the

[1] Zabt (A.) means 'sequestered,' set aside; hence special or exceptional.

[2] This name is found variously tortured in the older books: the *d* in Toḍar being the *palatal*, it is sounded something like *r*; hence the name appears as Torun Mall, Toren Mull, Tooral Mal, and Turymal (in the Fifth Report).

yield of which is assumed to represent the share of the whole holding; and one called 'lang-batáí,' whereby the cultivator piles the grain into as many heaps as there are shares, and the Government officer takes the heap that pleases him.

§ 1. *Akbar's Settlement under Rájá Todar Mal.*

In 1571 A.D. the survey was commenced; a standard, the 'iláhi' gaz, or yard-rod, was fixed, and a 'ṭanáb' or chain [1]. The Settlement extended to Bengal in 1582. The classification of land adopted was into (1) 'pulaj' [2] (or 'pulej'), which was land that was continually cultivated and did not require fallow; (2) 'phiráwati,' or rotation land that required a periodical fallow; (3) 'chíchar,' that lay fallow for three or four years, or rather that, being inundated or otherwise bad, could only be occasionally depended on for a crop; and (4) 'banjar,' waste that had not been cultivated for five or more years. The first three kinds were again classed into 'best,' 'middling,' and 'worst.'

The share of Government was one-third of the produce; and to ascertain an average, a bíghá of each kind was taken as a sample, and one-third of the aggregate produce was considered to be the *average* bíghá produce. One-third of this gave the Government share. Tables are to be found in the *Ayín-i-Akbari* showing the averge yield for various crops grown at each harvest [3]. Garden crops and *pán* (the aromatic betel-leaf used for chewing) were charged at certain money-

[1] The *gaz* was 41 fingers or 33 inches long; a square of 60 such yards (a 'jarib' each way) gives one bíghá. The standard bíghá of the Upper Provinces is then 3,025 English square yards (five-eighths of an acre). In Bengal it is 1,600 square yards, or about one-third of an acre. In other places it is various. We have still some means of testing the figures by the *minár* or 'mile posts,' which are still standing—a few of them—along the old imperial road from Delhi.

[2] This word is not in the glossaries. I suspect it is a corruption of the Persian 'pález'—garden-land, land that grows melons, &c.

[3] See Briggs, p. 126; and Field, p. 433. The names of the crops in both are so misspelt as to be unrecognizable; e.g. *adess* = *'adas*, the Arabic for *masúr* or lentils; *shaly mushkeen* is the Persian *Shál-i-mushkin*, or scented rice, one of the best kinds (bánsmatti); *moung* = *múng* is pulse (*Phaseolus mungo*); *lubyeh* is, perhaps '*lobiya*' (beans). What '*tyndus*,' '*kelet*,' '*berty*,' and '*kawdey*' are, I cannot even guess.

rates. For grain crops, the prices of nineteen years (from the sixth to the twenty-fourth of Akbar's reign), were collected by inquiry. This period was selected because nineteen years being a cycle of the moon, the seasons were supposed in this time to undergo a complete revolution, and so to exhibit all varieties of quantity. Mr. Elphinstone observes that the *Ayín-i-Akbari* gives no information as to how the comparative fertility of fields was ascertained, though it is probable that the three classes formed for each of the better soils were applied in consultation with the cultivators. There must, however, have been great inequality: for instance, if a man's holding were all of the 'worst' kind of pulaj, in that case the average rate ascertained as above described, would be too high.

The revenue on *phiráwati* land was calculated in the same way, but it was not charged in fallow years. *Chíchar* was allowed to be paid for in grain or kind according to its yield; probably the actual crop was looked to. *Banjar* was distinguished by progressive rates. In itself, waste or long-fallowed land might be of any class, and when brought under cultivation, it was allowed to pay only a *sír* or two[1] in kind for the first year, four *sírs* for the second, and so on till the full rate of the land, according to quality, was attained.

It was Mr. Elphinstone's opinion that the commutation rates above spoken of were *maximum* rates; and indeed this is probable, for they would have been both high and unequal; and there are other indications that besides the option the cultivator had of tendering grain, there was also the practice of allowing him to offer the money value of the grain *at the time*.

§ 2. *Akbar's Revised Settlement.*

But however this may be, some practical difficulty certainly arose, for after this, a new *ten years' money Settlement* was made[2].

[1] See note at p. 242, explaining the *man*, or 'maund' and its subdivisions.

[2] See the passage from the *Ayín-i-Akbari* quoted in Field, p. 437.

The rates of actual collection from the fifteenth year of the reign to the twenty-fourth (inclusive) were written down, and a tenth part of the total was accepted as the revenue for the next ten years.

§ 3. *Akbar's Settlement not permanent.—The Native Custom always contemplated variation.*

It is true that such was the fame of this last assessment, that the rates of it were often appealed to as a sort of standard; but in view of the frequent references in Aurangzeb's and other reigns, to other rates of collection, and to orders restraining the collectors from taking more than *one-half* the produce, it is clear that it can never have been regarded by the anthorities as unalterable.

Besides this, it is a matter of fact that reassessments *were* made from time to time. Mr. James Grant expressly insists that when the 'standard' assessment was referred to (called 'Asl túmár jama'—i. e. the land-revenue proper, without cesses or imposts) it was not Akbar's that was meant, but the *last authoritative recorded assessment* [1]. As I have already remarked, it is impossible to assert that, either by law or custom, the king or emperor was prohibited from reassessing or raising his revenue periodically [2]. The old law-books do not deal with the subject, because they belong to a stage when a share in the produee was taken.

[1] In his 'Analysis of the Finances of Bengal,' one of the appendices to the *Fifth Report*. See (for instance) p. 236, vol. i. of the Madras Reprint.

[2] I repeat this, because on the fact depends a great deal of the controversy about rent under the permanent Settlement. The 'tenants' of the 'landlords' were the people who had been the cultivators or *de facto* proprietors of the holdings on which Akbar's assessment was fixed. Had no proprietors been created by law over them, they would have submitted to reassessment, say after ten or fifteen or thirty years, according to the will of the governor, as prices altered, or as circumstances suggested. When, therefore, Government ceased to deal with the cultivators and made a fixed contract with 'Zamindárs' over them, it did not follow that the people had any claim that *their* payments should never be reassessed: Government *might* have made such a declaration, but it never did. The grievous defect was this, that the Government never devised any rule by which the revision and enhancement of what had now become *rent*, could be regulated, as it would have been, supposing it had remained *as revenue* under the direct orders of a good and considerate ruler.

Even the share varied according to State necessities; but putting that aside, it is in itself an increasing quantity, (1) because values rise; and (2) as more and more land is under the plough, the total of the king's share becomes larger.

§ 4. *Disadvantages of the Grain-division.*

The disadvantages of a grain-assessment are manifold. In the long run they outweigh the convenience which causes such methods to be still adopted in some places. They may be admitted to have some virtue in their application to precarious soils and climates, where it is impossible to calculate what the produce or its equivalent will be for even a short term of years. A payment in kind may here avoid the technical difficulties of a fluctuating cash-assessment.

But in fairly well developed districts, where irrigation secures the crops to a considerable extent, a grain collection becomes intolerable, and there is nothing to recommend it. It is a source of never-ending dispute: it is extremely troublesome for the State officer to manage. It affords the maximum of opportunity to the cultivator to pilfer and conceal on the one side, and to the officials and their satellites to peculate and extort, on the other. Moreover, when grain markets are well established, and values rise, the one party or the other suffers; a very slight accident may, in reality, double the assessment. The actual history of districts has shown that gradually, by the action of the people themselves, grain rates invariably, if slowly, give way to cash rates.

§ 5. *Causes of a change to Cash-payments.*

The change took place gradually, and was sometimes concealed by a fiction; as e.g. in the case of the 'Khot' villages on the West Coast, where the assessment was nominally in grain but was levied in cash by means of an artificial valuation. But in general the change forced itself on the notice of administrators directly the increase of population and the subdivision of farms made it impossible for the full grain-share of the State to be collected. Supposing that a farm of eighteen acres yields ten *maunds* of grain per acre. Let us assume that the cultivator needs one-third of this for his subsistence, that the king takes one-third, and that the remaining third covers the costs of cultivation and profits of stock. The king thus gets sixty *maunds*. But in time the farm is subdivided among an increased number of heirs of the original holder. The individual holding now becomes (say) six acres. The subdivision will doubtless promote increased care in tillage, and probably improved irrigation. Suppose these improvements double the produce. The total produce of the holding is still only one hundred and twenty maunds, and the king's share is forty maunds: possibly the proportions can be maintained, as prices will have risen, and the shares, though diminished in amount, will have become of greater money value. But there is a limit to this; for the rate of production will not go on increasing in the same proportion as the holdings diminish by subdivision. As the share required for the subsistence of the cultivator will not materially lessen, the king's share cannot be paid at the same rate. But the king does not like to diminish his share ostensibly, and the expedient which conceals the fact, is to take a sum of money instead. This will probably be calculated at some rate *per plough*, or so much for each holding on an average of what has been paid for a given period of years. The idea of acreage valuation, according to different relative productiveness, or the idea of competition rents, are alike unfamiliar, and among the people themselves are still imperfectly understood in many districts.

When at last a settled Government, with ideas of law and order, begins, it becomes necessary to devise some means of passing from arbitrary and unequal rates to an assessment that shall be—on some definite principle—just to the land-holder, while giving a full revenue to the State.

§ 6. *Need of periodical Revision.*

But the moment money assessments are established, then, as soon as there is a change in the value of produce, or in the value of money itself, as coined money becomes more plentiful, or, owing to improved communications, or to other causes, the assessments become locally so unequal that revision is called for on this ground alone. Again; every government—not excluding the best Oriental governments—regards the development of districts as one of its first duties; and the moment canals, railways, tanks, wells, agricultural-loans and the like, come under consideration, it is obvious that Government is entitled both to raise the means of expending capital on such works, and to reap its share of the largely increased amount and value of the produce obtained.

§ 7. *Reflections on the state of the Revenue-System to which the British Government succeeded.*

When, in 1765, British government began in Bengal, a land-revenue assessed in money was, and long had been, the principal source of the State's wealth.

It is quite immaterial to discuss whether such a system is good or bad in theory, because any such discussion would be based on European, not on Oriental ideas.

In the same way, in the last chapter (see Sec. vi, on Property) I deprecated the argument as to whether we should call our land-revenue a 'land-tax' or not. I know of no idler and less interesting war of words than such an argument, at least under existing conditions, when rights in land have been well established.

An Oriental institution is what it has grown to be, by the effect of custom and the wear and tear of historical events. To take it up, turn it round, and force it into the mould of any European definition or theory of taxation, is impossible[1]. The land-revenue is everywhere acquiesced

[1] Kaye, p. 141, has some excellent remarks on the difference between English taxation and Indian. In England we are always being taxed

in by the people, and paid without demur; it has the advantage of an immemorial prescription, which in the East is a matter of first-rate importance; and it is quite certain that no other means of raising an equal revenue could be devised, which would work with equally little trouble and interference with the people. The whole land-revenue machinery works as smoothly as possible—even the difficulties of such districts as Chittagong or Sylhet, in Eastern Bengal and Assam, are mere local problems which are approaching solution. Almost the only grave objection that could be raised to the system is the cost of, as well as the harassment of the people involved in, the work of a 'Settlement,' with its survey and record of the rights of landholders and tenants. But this our modern systems have tended greatly to reduce; and it is probable that before another thirty years have passed, the operation of revising the revenue will be a matter which will be carried out with hardly a perceptible ruffle of the quiet course of district and agricultural business.

SECTION V.—THE BEGINNING OF BRITISH LAND-REVENUE SYSTEMS.

We have now seen how a system of a land-revenue paid in money was ready made to the hands of our first administrators. Our laws have always avoided any theory on the subject of the origin of the right of the State, and the earliest Regulations of 1793 contented themselves with asserting just so much (and no more) as would serve as a sufficient basis for the system when reduced to shape,—namely, that 'by ancient law (custom would have been

and untaxed. The Minister of Finance has his budget proposals, and the reduction of one tax or the imposition of a new one is a perpetual subject for discussion all over the country. As a result of it, ministers may fall. But in India everything goes by custom; a tax is good or bad, not so much according to political economical theories, but according as the people take kindly to it and it can be realized without inquisition, without pressing hardly and unequally on certain classes. It is found better to trust to what people have long been accustomed to, than to devise new plans however theoretically perfect.

better) the Government was entitled to a share in the produce of every bíghá of land, that share to be fixed by itself[1].' As a necessary corollary, it has always held that the revenue is a first charge on the estate, to which all other charges must give way; and that, in effect, the land is hypothecated for the revenue assessment on it.

I have already explained that Government makes no claim to be the immediate or exclusive proprietor[2] of all lands; but it reserves to itself the ultimate ownership in default of any other owner,—as, for instance, in unoccupied waste lands, as in the case of escheat or forfeiture for crime. To secure its own revenue, which (as just stated) is a first charge on all land, it holds all land as hypothecated to itself for the amount of the revenue, and consequently it reserves the right to sell the land (under whatever conditions it may enact by law) if the revenue falls into arrear.

In order to protect its subjects, it also reserves the power to declare and to adjust the rights of all classes of rights and interests in the soil, and in some cases to divide the benefits of landed right, equitably between different classes.

It was the misfortune of our early administrators that they succeeded to Akbar's revenue system, not developed as it might have been by the practical wisdom of Oriental financiers, but as one which represented only a state of misrule and corruption. A thoroughly-developed native system might have been difficult to define or explain in a statute, but it would have been easily workable.

As it was, the administration had fallen into confusion beyond hope of remedy. Some theory or practice of revising the assessments, some customary *period* for such revisions, might have been expected, but none such was left us. We know that in Bengal reassessment had taken

[1] See preamble to Bengal Regulations XIX and XXXVII of 1793. The same phrase has been adopted in the modern Acts; for instance, see the Bombay Revenue Code, (B.) Act V of 1879, Section 45.

[2] Chap. IV. Sec. vi. p. 239.

place from time to time[1]. But the only principle that had settled down into continuance, was the hateful expedient of adding cesses or 'abwáb' to what was called the ''asl túmár' or standard sum still borne on the books as representing the last measurement and assessment. And the practice fell to a lower depth still; the State gave up all control, and merely bargained with local and influential men in certain tracts of country, for the largest sum they could reasonably expect to realize, and left *them* to get out of the people what they could. In such a state of things, our first officers did not well know what to do. They were not able to make a survey before Settlement: general inquiries had been carried out, but the machinery was too sparse and imperfect to enable the right sort of information to be gained. The reason of this remains to be stated.

The Zamíndárs, who had gradually, since the beginning of the eighteenth century, been allowed to contract for the revenue of large areas of country, were the only really well established revenue machinery which remained in existence. A century's growth had given them such a hold, that they had not only become virtually landlords, so that to ignore them would have been unjust from the point of view of private interest in the estate, but from the revenue point of view, their aid was indispensable. For, if they were not to be trusted to for the revenue, who was? The reader will be inclined to answer—'Why, the village cultivators, through their own headmen—people who were the real bread-winners and proprietors of the soil on which they had resided for generations, and which their forefathers had either conquered or colonized out of the trackless jungle.' This is very easy, and even obvious, to say now, with reference to modern conditions; it was not so in 1789. There was no local machinery to do such a work. Even if a complete district staff, with well-trained native subordinates, in subdivisions and parganas, had existed, even they could have only succeeded by making out

[1] For some details, see Field, p. 441.

village records afresh. For it must never be forgotten that the direct consequence of the growth of the Zamíndár was twofold. One consequence was the existence of a certain interest in the estates which demanded a special treatment at the hands of our administrators; but a still more important consequence was the gradual annihilation of the district control, and the atrophy of the official charges, which has above been described. The Zamíndár not only relieved the kánúngos and patwárís of all responsibility to the State, making them therefore careless about keeping up their records and accounts; but, more than that, when the Zamíndár was only liable, as in later times, to answer for his contract sum, and *not* for the details of his village and *pargana* collections, it became positively distasteful to him to have details of authorized rents and rights of raiyats entered in village records: the kánúngo, then, got no information; and the village patwárís were made merely to keep just such accounts as the Zamíndár wanted for his own purposes. In a word, the kánúngo became an official shadow, and the patwárís the bond-slaves of the Zamíndárs.

The few 'Collectors' of 1789, and their supervising Committees of Revenue, therefore, *could not have thought* of going to the villages as we now should.

§ 1. *Attempt at farming the Revenues.*

They did indeed try for several years an experiment which proved a failure. They had heard of the oppression of the 'Zamíndárs,' and they thought that, if they made *independent contracts with special farmers*, these would be more amenable to restraint. The process was tried with ever-increasing trouble and disappointment from 1770 up till the date when Lord Cornwallis came out in 1786. And then a system was adopted which restored the Zamíndárs, but gave them a new position, which it was expected would remedy all defects.

In the chapter on Bengal I shall fully explain that the

system which Lord Cornwallis introduced as the celebrated 'Permanent Settlement,' was emphatically not any new idea of his own. It was elaborated by Mr. Shore[1] and the ablest Civil servants, in communication with the Court of Directors at home, as the documents in the celebrated *Fifth Report on the Affairs of the East India Company to the House of Commons* will abundantly testify.

§ 2. *Outline of Lord Cornwallis's System.*

In effect that system recognized that the revenues must be collected by means of local men of influence and wealth, who took charge of considerable estates, larger or smaller, according to circumstances; and that, in order to give these persons confidence, they must be endowed formally with such an interest as made them legally and in name, what most of them were *de facto*,—'proprietors' or 'landlords.' The king's subjects, or 'raiyats,' then became the tenants of the new landlords. It was well understood that they were not ordinary tenants, in the sense that they were persons located by the Zamíndár on contract or lease. Some of them, of course, would be so—as, for example, when the landlord began to break up the waste and to form new colonies of cultivators; but others—the majority—would be the original and hereditary possessors of the village soil. It was intended to protect their rights, as we shall see; but unfortunately the intention was not practically carried out. The benefit to the landlord was secured; that intended for the tenant was not. As far as the revenue is concerned, the main feature of the system was the plan of *fixing in perpetuity* the sum to be paid annually for each estate. The details of that proposal I shall describe in the chapter devoted to Bengal; here it is enough to say that our first revenue system in Bengal involved (1) the acknowledgment, as landlords,

[1] Mr. Shore did not advocate, but strongly opposed, the particular feature of the Settlement which caused it to be 'permanent.' But he agreed with the others in securing the position of the Zamíndárs.

of persons found in actual charge of large areas of land, and (2) an assessment of such reasonable sum as could be discovered by comparing the accounts of actual payments in previous years; the sum so fixed being declared unalterable for ever.

SECTION VI.—THE MAIN PRINCIPLES OF THE BENGAL SETTLEMENT AND WHAT HAS RESULTED FROM THEM.

§ 1. *Special features of the Settlement.*

About this PERMANENT (Zamíndárí) Settlement, there are three things to be observed.

I. The system involved the presumption that for every local estate or group of lands there must be some person with whom Government should *settle*, or (in official phrase) who should 'hold the Settlement'; and further, that this person, or middleman between the *raiyat* and the State, should be vested with a proprietary interest in the land. The benefits and obligations in such an arrangement or contract were to be reciprocal. The *Government* was to have some one who was to be looked to as responsible, in person and estate, for punctual payment; *the person* was to be given the means of discharging his responsibility by having a *secure title* to the land for which he engaged. He was to be irremoveable (otherwise than temporarily, in the event of his not agreeing to the terms offered). He was to be at liberty to raise money on the credit of the land, to sell or gift it, or pass it on to his children by inheritance or bequest, as the case might be. In other words, he was to be declared and legally installed as *proprietor or landlord.*

This principle has always been followed, either in set terms or in some equivalent shape, in all Settlement systems.

In all systems which deal with a landlord, the middleman may be an actual person or an *ideal* person—a body or a community considered as one legal person, by means of a representative (as in the North-Western Settlements). In other systems, where there is no middleman, actual or ideal, the cultivator is directly settled with. In the former case, under whatever necessary limitations, the Zamíndár, the Taluqdár, or joint body of village co-sharers, is 'owner' or 'proprietor.' To say that a man is 'proprietor,' and that he is the 'málguzár' or revenue-payer, are, in our official literature, practically synonymous; to say that a man *pays four annas of the revenue*, means also that he is owner of one-fourth of the estate, fractions being commonly stated in so many 'annas', (sixteenths) of the 'rupee' (taken as the total). And even in Madras and Bombay, where (as explained in Chapter IV) no landlord body had grown up over the village cultivators, so that they could not be regarded as a jointly responsible proprietary of the whole, the individual occupants were nevertheless vested by law with a definite, transferable, and heritable right, subject to the revenue demand: and this, for most practical purposes, is undistinguishable from a proprietary title [1].

II. Another thing to be observed in the Bengal Settlement is, that the amount of revenue to be paid by the Zamíndár being once ascertained, that amount was fixed for ever under the law of 1793. Hence this first experiment in Settlements is called the PERMANENT SETTLEMENT.

III. The amount was determined, not with reference to any area-survey, any consideration, that is, of the number, various fertility, or productive power, of the acres held in each case, or of the influence of proximity to market and facility of communication, on the value of produce. Local scrutiny, as we shall see, was directly forbidden to the Collectors; they were directed to make the best estimate they could, of a fair lump sum for the whole estate, on a consideration of what sums had been paid in the past, and of the general prosperity of the owners.

[1] For remarks on the occupancy rights in Bombay, see the chapter on Land-Tenures in Bombay. The Madras raiyat has not had his tenure defined by statute, but is practically settled by judicial decision to be proprietor of his holding.

§ 2. *Remarks on the three features.*

These features demand some further remark, as having given rise to various and important results.

The *first* feature in itself needs no comment, especially in view of our immediate subject. But indirectly, the question of 'proprietor' and his 'title' have given rise to all those difficult questions about grades of proprietary interest and privileges of tenant-right, which have been such a source of controversy in India. An outline of the subject was presented in Chap. IV. Sec. iv. p. 196.

§ 3. *The second feature.*

This feature—the permanency of the assessment—has had a great influence. For a long time, and under other methods of Settlement, which we shall have to discuss, people thought that as soon as a fairly good method was elaborated, the resulting assessment might be declared fixed and unalterable. After the first Settlements of the North-West Provinces, for example, a great discussion arose, and was continued for some years; indeed, the question of a Permanent Settlement for *all* districts lingered on, till it received its *quietus* in a despatch of the Secretary of State in 1882. The history of this question is important, but will not be understood till some description of the other Settlement systems has been given. I therefore defer its further mention for the present.

§ 4. *Effects of Laws for the Realization of Revenue.*

But connected with this subject, though, perhaps, indirectly, is the law enacted for the realization of the revenue.

While the Government had conferred valuable rights on the Zamíndárs, it required of them (what they had been little in the habit of rendering) a prompt and punctual payment of the fixed revenue amount. From the first it was notified that if the instalments ('kist,' or properly 'qist') were not paid at due date, the estate would be sold. Government would not imprison the person of the landlord, nor take his private goods and chattels [1]; that would be an indignity. As will appear more fully in the sequel, circumstances brought about a vast number of sales for arrears of revenue [2] during the first ten years. And as these sales introduced a purchaser who necessarily had a *clear title*, another *bouleversement* of the tenant relations resulted. This last is a question of tenures, and does not now concern us; but the subject of 'sale-law' is here mentioned, as it is a distinctive feature of the old Bengal revenue-administration.

§ 5. *Remarks on the third feature.*

The fact that the Permanent Settlement was made without any survey, and without any record of landed rights and interests, has proved more fraught with evil consequences than perhaps any other feature of the Settlement. It is difficult now to say what Lord Cornwallis really thought when he prohibited any detailed scrutiny of the estates; but his first object was to be liberal to the Zamíndár, and to make him feel secure as to the intentions of the Government; and to do this it seemed important to prohibit all minute inquisition into his affairs or rents, and to fix a lump assessment on general considerations. For the same reasons, it was impossible to harass him with conditions about his subordinate tenants and with vexa-

[1] The law is spoken of as the 'Sunset law' The Deputy-Collector would sit in his Treasury office on 'Kist-day'—the latest date for payment of the revenue instalment—till he saw the sun go down. Then he closed the doors. The man who rushed up with his bag of money after the door was shut, would be too late.

[2] The revenue, though permanently fixed, was not at first very light: it is admitted by good judges to have been the reverse, especially under the circumstances of the terrible famine of 1772, of which such a graphic account is given in Hunter's *Annals of Rural Bengal*. The country had not recovered from it in 1789. But as cultivation extended, peace bore its fruits, and prices rose, the assessment became lighter and lighter; and sales of course became less frequent. At the present day it is extremely light, probably not more than one-third or even one-fourth of what it ought to be.

tious interference in his dealings with them. It was supposed that the newly-acknowledged landlord would extend cultivation, and thereby enlarge his own receipts; that he would improve the class of crops grown; and, as differential rates were always acknowledged for richer and poorer crops, it was vaguely supposed that rentals would rise in this way. Whatever the process, the landlord would certainly become rich; on the other hand, he would employ and liberally pay, more and more labour; everywhere he would be known as the benevolent landlord of a contented tenantry; he would abstain, under the strict orders of Government, from levying 'cesses' in addition to the rents, which latter, it was supposed, would settle themselves by the good understanding of both parties; he would always grant a 'patta' (pottah) to his tenants, and so have it definitely on record what land they held, and what rent they were to pay. Lastly, as both classes grew rich, though the land-revenue would not alter, other revenues would increase; for wealthy people demand more and more in the way of foreign imports and articles of luxury, and the custom-house would reap the benefit in the shape of duty. All these expectations have been rudely disappointed, with some rare exceptions; the Zamíndárs, as a class, did nothing for the tenants but rack-rent them, or hand them over to 'patnidárs' or rent-farmers, who did so still more. They made no improvements; and their wealth did not augment the general revenues by income from other sources of indirect taxation. All the while, the want of a survey (for revenue purposes) has been seriously felt. Agricultural statistics, which are available for other provinces, are wanting in Bengal. But even to enumerate the inconveniences, the difficulties under the tenant-law, and the endless litigation, that the absence of an authoritative record of subordinate rights may cause, would occupy more space than I can here give. In short, some day a district cadastral survey and a record of rights and rents *must* come; and the sooner it is commenced, the better it will be for the province.

SECTION VII.—RESULTS OF THE ACQUISITION OF OTHER PROVINCES.

§ 1. *Different conditions occur.*

But, whatever may have been thought of the *method of assessing* the revenue in Bengal, the continuance of that method in other provinces which came under British rule was rendered practically impossible by the totally different circumstances of those provinces. I would here invite the reader to refer to the coloured map, in which, by means of tints, each referring to a certain year or group of years, I have shown how the different districts and provinces gradually were added to the East India Company's dominions.

§ 2. *Madras.*

The first grant was that of the districts in the north of MADRAS, called the 'Northern Sirkárs[1].' In these districts there were local chiefs who had the management of the revenues, and were, in fact, Zamíndárs, like those in Bengal. But in other districts of Madras that fell to our lot as the result of escheats, and the wars with Mysore in 1791 and 1799, *there were no Zamíndárs.* In some districts there were, indeed, chiefs called 'polygars' (pálegárá). In origin, they were frontier chiefs—relics of that Hindu organization which I have described. Under favourable circumstances, they would all have been recognized as Zamíndárs and landlords, and, indeed, some few of them were so recognized; but the majority of them chose to resist and to rebel, and the 'polygar wars,' as the books call the military campaigns necessary to put them down, have added not a few stirring pages to the military history of Madras.

[1] Sirkár (or Circar as the popular form is) was the Revenue division or district of the Muhammadan system already described, p. 256.

§ 3. *Permanent Settlement ordered.—Its failure.*

By the time the Madras territories were fairly consolidated, Lord Cornwallis's principles were in full force; a Permanent Settlement was ordered and carried out (though with some improvements as to the 'tenant's' position) in North Madras, and in the case of certain peaceable 'polygars.' But how was it to be effected for Chingleput, Salem, and Tanjore, and the 'Ceded Districts,' where there were no Zamíndárs? The unhappy idea that occurred to the authorities was to *create* landlords, by making the villages into large groups or parcels, called muṭṭhá (*mootah* of the old reports), and selling the Settlement rights to the highest bidder! The real Zamíndár, in his natural growth of a century and a half, was bad enough; but what could be said for an auction-room landlord? Of course the system failed miserably.

§ 4. *Commencement of a new method.*

Meanwhile, the Madras authorities were making a new departure. They had not civil servants enough to undertake all the district Settlements, and they determined to employ some of the ablest of their military servants, who had gained familiarity with the languages, localities, and people, in the course of their military duty. New men have new ideas; and if these are only based on a real acquaintance with the people in their village homes, they are likely to be valuable. It is enough to name CAPTAIN MUNRO (afterwards Sir Thomas Munro, Governor of Madras) as among the ablest of these Settlement officers. In the Madras chapters I give all details, but here I may shortly mention that MUNRO developed, if he did not originate, the idea *of surveying the districts and dealing direct with the village landholders.*

To advocate and to defend this system, he wrote many able minutes, and conferred with the Court of Directors at home in 1807: the result was the authoritative adoption of the system known as the 'RAIYATWÁRÍ' Settlement.

§ 5. *Circumstances which led to the new system.*

The villages of the Madras districts were, as we have seen, mostly of the non-landlord, or *raiyatwárí* type. And even where high-caste families or colonizing adventurers had once established themselves as landlord communities, the results of later Hindu conquests, and of the Muhammadan rule, where it had extended, had been to destroy such rights, and to reduce the village cultivators to a common level. There were, here and there, more or less vague recollections that some of the villagers held a superior position; they claimed *mirásí* rights (rights by ancient inheritance), and so forth; but this was exceptional: speaking generally, the villages were only aggregates of separate cultivators, held together under a common headman, each man regarding himself as only responsible for, and connected with, his own land. On the whole, it was clear that a system of dealing with the individual occupants of the land would be best. The system now proposed, was to commence with a survey of fields, to classify these according to soil, and then, by various means, to determine a sum of money to which each should be separately assessed. Claims to the waste, or other vestiges of privilege belonging to a once superior class, would be practically adjusted, within the lines of the system.

§ 6. *Features of the Raiyatwárí system.*

The effect of former misrule in many of the districts had been to inspire a great dread of a fixed revenue responsibility. But few of the cultivators cared to be *bound down* (so to speak) to their farm or holding; if they could not make it pay, they would give it up rather than owe the revenue—so thoroughly, in a large number of instances, had private property in land been broken down. It was therefore a principle of the new system that each man was free to hold his land, subject to payment of the assessment, or to give notice and relinquish it if he pleased.

The waste (and abandoned) fields were not given over to villages, except a limited area for pasture. The waste 'numbers' were retained in the hands of the State, as a means of extending cultivation and increasing the revenue, when better times came, and land was more in demand. Any man (with a certain preference in favour of old cultivators) was at liberty to apply for a vacant or waste number, on agreeing to pay the revenue which would become due on it according to its class.

In order, therefore, to know what land every cultivator had actually held in each year, what he was to pay, and what to receive remission for, an annual account was made out, under a simple system; this process, known as the 'annual jamabandí,' is characteristic of the system of Madras and of Bombay also.

§ 7. *The Mode of Assessment.*

It was long before any definite mode of assessment was adopted. The first Settlements endeavoured to find out rates for the different classes and kinds of soils adopted for assessment purposes; and in doing so, regard was had to existing rates; perhaps I ought to say great reliance was placed on them. It was known that under the late rulers, certain sums were paid for certain fields, and were shown in the accounts. But these rates were probably very high, and moreover had to be adjusted and equalized, to give soil-rates. Then too, there was free recourse to consultation with the people and comparing one village with another. Rates, in short, were founded partly on old accounts, and partly on estimates based on general considerations and the local officers' sense of fitness.

The local officers, I suspect, were much inclined to lower the rates; but the necessities of the Government in those days rendered reduction an unpalatable proposal, and hence they did not venture to be as liberal as they would have wished. Whether this is so or not, the fault of the early Settlements certainly was, that the rates were pitched too high. They worked so badly (in that respect) that the history of our revenue-administration, as found in the *District Manuals*, is chiefly an account of revisions and remissions, and of devices for mitigating over-heavy assessments [1].

It was also a common practice in the earlier Settlements, to discover the *produce* of an acre of each class of soil, to value that produce—of course a low average quantity—at an average price deduced from a number of yearly price-tables, and then to calculate out the costs of cultivation and profits of stock, and take a fraction—never exceeding fifty per cent.—of the balance. This method is still recognized in Madras, to some extent at least, and especially as a test for checking rates arrived at in other ways.

As a method pure and simple, it is an impossible one; the 'average produce' never can be ascertained; the circumstances of localities—even those near together—are too unaccountably various; and the costs of cultivation may be calculated by the most experienced officers at widely different figures for the same areas.

The modern system of Madras assessment has developed more in the direction of making simple and accurate the classification of soils, and applying a comparatively simple scale of rates to the soils, than in any novel method for fixing the rates themselves.

The soil classification is both simple and neat; and it answers every purpose. A different classification and grouping are adopted in 'dry lands,' i.e. those cultivated by rain, or by wells, and those—chiefly rice-lands—which are 'wet,' or habitually irrigated by tanks. First of all, there is the usual grouping of villages according to position; for it is obvious that, given a certain kind of soil, the same

[1] The accounts too, bristle with technicalities and the most heart-rending local vernacular phraseology, which gives the Revenue history an air of mystery and difficulty which does not really belong to it.

rate may be too high if the village is in a remote inaccessible group, and too low if it is in command of a good market and close to an important line of communication. Soils are naturally divided into certain *series*—'black soil,' 'red soil,' &c., &c. But each *series* will have several *classes*, according to the proportion of the mineral material which gives the character to the soil. This is technically called 'clay.' Every *series* may show a soil (I) nearly all 'clay,' (II) half clay and half sand, (III) mostly sand. These are the *classes* of the *series*. And once more, each *class* of each series may differ within itself; there may be a 'good' *sort*, or 'best,' 'ordinary,' or 'worst,' &c., of the same class. As the I, II, III *classes* belong to the first *series*, and the IV, V, VI to the second, and so on, the Roman numeral used for the *classes* suffices also to include the *series*. The *sort* is indicated by an Arabic numeral. Thus, having a standard table in use, there is no occasion to write out at length, series, class, and sort, but only the two numerals. Thus 'IV. 5' by the table, indicates 'Regar' *series* of the mixed or loamy *class*, and of the 'worst' *sort*.

It is not necessary to have a separate rate of assessment for each separate class and sort, because it is obvious that the same rate which suits one kind in one *group* of villages will suit other kinds in other groups.

Hence lists of rates are made out, called 'taram.' In all, let us suppose, that *twelve* rates will cover XIV classes, with their sorts. Then the first, or highest, *taram* will apply (in dry soils) to the best land in the first group; the second *taram* of the first group will be the *first*, or highest, of the second group; the third will be the highest of the third group, and so on; the lowest, or twelfth, taram will probably not be used in the first group, and only in the second and lower groups.

The actual taram-rates per acre are ultimately based on a calculation of an average produce of one or two 'standard' grains, valued at a low average price.

The grains selected as the 'standard' are always food-grains, and are ascertained by referring to the statistics of a *taluka*, and seeing what food-grains are most largely cultivated.

The costs of production are calculated and deducted, and fifty per cent. of the balance—not more—is taken as the Government revenue per acre.

There are special charges and allowances made where the land bears two crops in the year; but for such details the chapter on Madras must be consulted.

But though this calculation of average produce duly valued, and the deduction of costs, and the taking a fraction of the balance, represents the theory[1], as a matter of fact existing rates (as these have been in the course of years modified till they work well) are much looked to, and they can be altered on general considerations, and without a lengthy re-calculation, when necessary.

Thus, when a calculation on the produce-basis has once been made, and prices have steadily risen since; the rate can be raised, at a revision, by a simple percentage addition. And so with the calculation of costs made to get the net balance. It is rarely that a new investigation has to be made; figures are taken from neighbouring districts, or other talukas similarly situated, and the use of these is justified in various ways.

It is also a feature of this system that certain *remissions* for loss of crop are regularly allowed at the annual *jamabandi*; this is not found in any other system.

[1] Here is an example given briefly and in abstract:—Suppose a taluka has 13 per cent. of 'Rágí' cultivation, and 13 of 'Varagú,' and these are the highest of the food-grains. Other grains approximate in value, so that we can treat them practically as if they were Rágí and Varagú, respectively. Thus we may let the whole produce be fairly represented by 48 per cent. 'Rágí' and 52 per cent. 'Varagú,' or roughly, half and half. Then, taking a class and sort of soil (say IV. 2) in the first or best group of villages, the outturn of grain is found to be 320 Madras measures of Rágí and 440 Varagú. Roughly each acre has 50 per cent. of each, or 160 + 220, and the value by the price table is R. 7.1.7 + 6.1.11 = 13.3.6. Suppose the costs of cultivation to be R. 6.3.6; then the *net* produce is 7.0.0. 50 per cent. of this is R. 3.8.0, which is the *taram* (or revenue rate) applicable.

§ 8. *Rates not permanent.*

In the early days expressions may be found in many of the official minutes, to show that it was then thought possible to fix *rates* once for all; so that though the revenue would rise by new lands being brought under cultivation, the *rates* would not alter. But the Settlements, as I have said, made before the modern system was developed, worked so badly, that the rates had to be again and again revised; doubtless this had its effect in showing how unwise it is to talk about a permanent Settlement, while information as to rates is not perfect, or while conditions are in any degree undeveloped.

The tendency, in revision Settlements, not to alter rates found to work well, is distinctly visible in Madras. Indeed it is laid down as a principle, that at revision, no change is to be made, except on the ground of a general rise in prices.

§ 9. *'Ceded' and 'Conquered' Districts in Upper India.*

While the Madras *Raiyatwárí* system was being worked out and discussed in letters from home (which I quote in the Madras chapters), there had been important ADDITIONS to BENGAL. Passing over the Benares province, which was permanently settled in 1795–96[1], we come to the year 1801, when a number of districts were 'ceded' by the Oudh Government, in order that the revenue might pay for troops to defend the King of Oudh from his many enemies. And two years later (1803) the result of Lord Lake's campaigns had been to wrest from the Maráthás a number of districts adjoining the former (and extending into what is now the Panjáb Province) known as the 'conquered' districts. The same campaign also added to Lower Bengal the districts

[1] The ordinary law and practice were followed; but the tenures were somewhat different. Moreover, being soon annexed to the other North-West Provinces, the Benares districts were in time surveyed, all rights recorded, and management carried on exactly as in the rest of the province, with the one special feature that the assessment is unalterable.

of Orissa. The student will remember that when the Emperor granted, in 1765, the civil government of Bengal to the Company, it was, in form, the grant of 'Bengal, Bihár, and Orissa.' The 'Orissa' of those days meant the district of Midnapore (Mednipur), exclusive of the Patáspur pargana beyond the Subarnrekhá river. The 'Orissa' conquered in 1803 was described in the Regulations passed for the Settlement, as the pargana of Patáspur and the Cuttack (Katák) province (now Púri, Balasore, and Cuttack).

In all these districts, both of the North-West and of Orissa, there were but few Zamíndárs. I may pass by Orissa, as it did not present any such features as led to a special theory of Settlement: the law ultimately passed for the Settlement of these new territories, was, in reality, framed chiefly with reference to the North-West Provinces.

§ 10. *Absence of Zamíndárs.—Strong Village Communities.*

In the North-West Provinces *the* feature that brought about a revolution in Settlement ideas, was the fact that, though here and there there were native Rájás who had become revenue 'Zamíndárs' and Taluqdárs of great estates, their growth was not in all cases equal[1]; and whether there were overlords or not, the village-bodies had (except in parts devastated by the Rohillas) preserved a vitality which soon attracted attention. There were, in many of them, bodies claiming descent from a chief or other notable who had founded the village or obtained it on grant. They were now numerous and frequently had divided the village into shares called 'patti'; but they had a strong claim over the whole area, including the site on which the village dwelling-places clustered, *and* a certain extent of waste and pasture-ground beyond. They had never been ground down to being 'tenants' under any Zamíndár, or if the process had begun, it was not difficult to arrest it.

I do not mean, of course, that all villages were like this;

[1] They had not, in fact, grown into the very nature of things as they had in Bengal.

but this was *a* salient feature among them. There were, no doubt, many villages which were only of recent growth. Throughout Rohilkhand, for example, the Robillas had destroyed all rights, and such villages as had revived, now mostly contained groups of ruined tenants; and a 'proprietor' had arisen in the person who had come forward to pay the revenue, and re-establish the cultivation[1]. Other villages had really passed under the power of Taluqdárs and Rájás, and formed part of their estates. This brief *résumé* will, I think, be quite sufficient after what has been said in the last chapter.

§ 11. *Early Regulations did not comprehend the position.*

At first, however, the Settlement Regulations still suggested by their language that the Bengal system would apply. They appear to suppose that there *must* be *a* landlord over every estate to be settled with; and the permanency of the Settlement was contemplated. As a preliminary measure, contracts were made with *farmers* who undertook one, or a few, or many villages; and this was productive of great mischief. The Regulations directed that a Settlement should be made for a term of five years and then renewed, and then renewed again for a short term; and that when the fourth Settlement was complete, it should be PERMANENT (*if sanctioned* by the home authorities). This, it was thought, was a cautious plan, allowing ample time for collecting information, and for testing by practice the effect of the Settlements—five years was long enough to reveal errors, and not long enough to stereotype them. But the design was only partly carried out.

Two things followed: *first*, the authorities at home were by this time thoroughly aware of the danger of fixing a permanent assessment on imperfect data, and for districts not yet developed; they therefore prohibited the per-

[1] In the course of a few generations the descendants of such a person became a joint or a divided body (as the case might be) of *proprietary co-sharers*.

manency of the Settlement; and a new Regulation had to be passed announcing that the assent spoken of in the first Regulations was withheld. *Second*, the inquiries gradually made, showed that the true titles of those who held interests in villages had been greatly overlooked, and that rights had been destroyed by the farming system, and that all sorts of frauds in selling villages for arrears of revenue had taken place; this was an additional reason for not hastening a *permanent* Settlement which would have necessitated the irrevocable determination of who was the *proprietor*. (See Sec. VII. § 1.)

§ 12. *The Result of Settlement Inquiries.*

When the time for the Fourth Settlement came round, a very capable Commission was appointed to make it with all care and circumspection.

This Commission, with its Secretary, was so useful that it was afterwards made permanent, and developed into the Board of Revenue or chief controlling authority in revenue matters, over the north-western districts of Bengal. The districts themselves were, as I have explained, separated from Bengal in 1834–6, and formed into a distinct province under a Lieutenant-Governor.

The labours of the Commission were concluded by a report to Government on which Mr. Holt Mackenzie wrote a long and most valuable minute dated 1st July, 1819[1].

§ 13. *Holt Mackenzie's Minute.—Regulation VII of* 1822.

This minute strongly protested against all artificial creation of landlords, forcing farmers of revenue and headmen, who were mere representatives of the body, into the position of landlord; and finally urged the *survey of the districts and the complete record of all rights and shares and interests* in the village lands.

[1] This invaluable paper, which is to the 'village Settlement' system what Mr. Shore's minutes were to the Bengal Settlements, is reprinted in the *Revenue Selections*, North-Western Provinces, 1818-20. Calcutta, 1866.

The result was the passing of the celebrated Regulation VII of 1822, which long remained the central law of the TEMPORARY SETTLEMENT system[1].

Under this system, certain principles soon developed. The aim was to restore, and even perhaps unduly restore, the rights of the village owners; recognizing their landlord character, they were settled with, *not* individually, but as a *joint body*. That body was jointly and severally liable for the revenue, and was entitled to the whole area determined by the survey as appropriated to the village, *whether cultivated or waste*. There were some cases where villages were clearly owned by Rájás or others; and here while the Rájá (as Zamíndár) held the Settlement and was 'proprietor' *par excellence*, the villagers became 'subordinate proprietors,' in which case their rights were protected by a sort of secondary Settlement, called (formerly) a 'mufassal Settlement[2]': this determined, for the whole period, what they were to pay to the overlord, just as the main Settlement determined what *he* was to pay to the Government.

§ 14. *Policy of setting aside the Overlords.*

But a policy soon developed itself, of setting aside the overlord with a 'taluqdárí' money allowance, and settling direct with the villagers. This resulted from the law which prescribed that where there were several parties with interests in the land, the Settlement Officer should determine, under the orders of superior authority, with

[1] The term 'temporary' has been always used to indicate Settlements that are not permanent. It is not a very happy choice, as it suggests the idea of something that is a make-shift or to be replaced by something else. That is not the meaning. All that is denoted is that the assessment is fixed for a period, usually thirty years (sometimes less), after which the rates may be revised, and the records of rights also, if they need it.

[2] I may repeat an explanation of the term. The Arabic mufassal means 'separate' or distinct. Hence the 'mufassal jama' is the subordinate revenue payable to the overlord as distinct from that which the latter pays to the Government. The term 'mufassal' (or commonly mofussil) is applied also to the districts as distinct from the capital or 'sadr.'

which party the Settlement was to be made, and how the interests of the others were to be recognized.

§ 15. *New principle of Assessment.*

The next principle was that the assessment was to be on a different plan from that pursued in Bengal. The Governor-General ordered:—

'It seems necessary to enter on the task of fixing in detail the rates of rent [revenue] and modes of payment current in each village, and applicable to each field: and anything short of this must be regarded as a very imperfect Settlement.'

The revenue was, in short, to depend upon inquiry into the actual produce of all varieties and classes of land. From the gross produce was to be deducted the calculated amount of the cost of cultivation, the wages of labour, &c.; and the net result, added to any profits derived from the produce of grazing and waste lands (and the prospective value of waste when brought under the plough), was spoken of as the 'assets' of each village or other estate. The Government revenue consisted of a fraction, at first ordered to be two-thirds, and afterwards about one-half, of this sum of 'assets[1].'

§ 16. *Duration of the Temporary Settlement.*

As the law said nothing about the duration of the Settlements, the Government fixed from time to time, from motives of policy and convenience, such term as was thought fair. The object was, to give the village body or other proprietor the benefit of a solid property, encourage improvements by securing to him the benefit of all increase during the term of Settlement; avoiding, also, the trouble and expense of a too frequent repetition of the elaborate process of assessment. The term of thirty years

[1] In the Bengal chapters I have discussed at some length the origin of the fraction of the estate assets taken by Government.

was fixed, not by law, but by executive order, for the first 'Regular Settlement.' And this term has become very general for Temporary Settlements. In some cases, a period of twenty or even ten years, has been preferred. The special considerations bearing on the subject in each case, must be reserved to the detailed chapters.

§ 17. *Explanation of 'Regular' and 'Summary' Settlement.*

I may mention that when it is necessary in a new province, to fix a preliminary amount of revenue, pending a more exact adjustment, and pending arrangements for a survey and record of rights, such a Settlement is called a 'summary' Settlement. When the full operations required by law have been gone through, it is a 'first Regular Settlement'; and subsequent Settlements are called 'Re-settlements,' or 'Revision' Settlements.

§ 18. *'Temporary' Settlements are also, in the North-West Provinces, village or mahál Settlements.*

The Regulation VII Settlements are spoken of as Settlements under the TEMPORARY system, and also as under the VILLAGE, or, more correctly, the MAHÁL, system, because, in the bulk of cases, the village is the estate or unit. But this is not always the case, for it may be that part of a village or parts of several villages *are held under one title*, and therefore form the *unit* of assessment, or, in Revenue language, the MAHÁL. Sometimes the Settlement is said to be 'zamíndárí,' not because there is any great landlord or 'Zamíndár' as in Bengal, but because the principle is maintained that the Government deals with a *landlord*, not with the individual raiyat; only that in this case the landlord is not (or not usually) a single individual but an *ideal body*,—the village community jointly liable for the revenue, and regarded as a corporate unit represented by its 'lambardár,' as the headman is called in the North-West Provinces. (See Chap. IV, pp. 152–3.)

§ 19. *Failure of the first method of Assessment.—Modification of the Regulation VII system.*

For the first eleven years but slow progress was made with the North-West system, as I may shortly call it. The machinery was insufficient for the purposes of such an inquiry into produce as I have indicated. The Government repeatedly complained of want of progress; and the Board were compelled to admit that they could record little or none. The fact is, the villages in the North-West Provinces, as a rule, are not 'raiyatwárí'; there are landlord classes in the villages, even where there are not great landlords, and they did not facilitate such inquiries. The result was (as we shall see in more detail in studying the North-Western Provinces) that a Committee was assembled, over which the Governor-General presided in person; and Regulation IX of 1833 was passed, which improved the official machinery and abolished the minute inquiry into the produce of fields and the costs of production.

§ 20. *Tenants and Cash Rents.*

By this time the use of coined money was so general, that in the older districts, land was not only largely held by *tenants* (the co-sharers not themselves cultivating), but the rents were commonly paid in cash, not in grain; and thus it became possible to adopt the system of Settlement which has been gradually perfected into the modern plan. I should defeat my present object by going into detail (which is given elsewhere), but I may say generally, that the beginning of the new system was first to ascertain a general lump sum which each estate could afford to pay; and this lump sum was tested by seeing how it would fall as an acreage rate on the lands, and how such rates would compare with what the Settlement Officer calculated were fair and proper rates for the different sorts of land. Later on in revenue history, the fixing lump sums was discarded, and attention was given to classifying soils carefully and determining acreage rent-rates independently for each.

The village system being strong, either the original body, or one of later origin (the descendants of a grantee, village-founder or revenue-farmer) had usually maintained their lands and their privileges; and, as a natural consequence, village institutions—the headman and the patwárí (with their records and accounts)—had not suffered the decay that marked them under the different historical conditions that had arisen in Bengal.

Hence it was possible to ascertain from the village records (as compiled and formulated in the Settlement operations) what rates of revenue, and to some extent of rent, were proper. But at first the system demanded a great deal more reliance on what ought to be, and would be, than what actually was. And it must be admitted that village accounts were often purposely framed to represent the rents as lower than they really were; and the Settlement officials had to 'correct' them by bringing them up to what (by inquiry and the application of various test calculations) they supposed them really to be and likely to become. Moreover, much land was held by the proprietors themselves, and, of course, paid no rent or only a nominal sum for village account purposes. This land had, therefore, to have its full rental ascertained and recorded; so too there were lands, held rent-free in charity or for religious purposes, which the land-owners granted, not the Government, and these had also to be valued. By thus ascertaining an ideal or corrected rent for every acre in the village, a new total 'assets' sheet was made out. It will be remembered that at first, owing to the difficulty of finding out the real, actual, rents, the plan adopted was to make allowance for what it was believed, on general considerations, *the rates would be raised to in the years immediately succeeding the Settlement.*

§ 21. *Proportion of the total rental Assets taken by Government.*

The early rule was to take two-thirds of what were roughly calculated to be the 'assets' of each estate. But after twenty years of gradual growth in the methods of Settlement, this proportion was reduced. When, under rude methods, we take the assets at a very low figure, it is morally certain that in reality they are very much greater; and if we take as much as two-thirds of such lowly-calculated assets, we are really taking a moderate share. But the more our system approaches to ascertaining the *full* income of an estate, the more moderate must we be in the proportion.

In 1855 it was determined that the Government share should be reduced to about fifty per cent. of the assets.

§ 22. *Principle of the later North-West Assessments.*

The later systems of assessment in the North-Western Provinces are really successive attempts to perfect the methods of calculating the rental assets; and they have twice been modified. The first modification consisted in a simpler and better soil-classification and in attending *more* (but still not entirely) to *actual rents.* The latest modification may be briefly described as attending *only* to *actual* rents,—refusing all speculative additions, though of course carefully correcting the village records, by additions to supply manifest under-statements, or to fix rental rates for lands for which either privileged rates, or no rents at all are paid, and which are not entitled to escape assessment. Then we speak of the 'corrected assets.'

§ 23. *The Proprietor's 'Sír.'*

I have already explained (Chap. IV. sec. ii, § 47) the term 'sír,' and I must ask the student to familiarize himself with it. When the bulk of lands in any estate[1], whether in Bengal or the North-West Provinces, is rented out, certain lands, often the best, are kept in the hands of the co-sharers (or the sole proprietor as the case may be), and are cultivated as the home-farm, by hired labour, or even by the family itself. Such land is called 'sír.' It sometimes happens, if the revenue is light, that the landlords are able to pay the whole out of the proceeds of the rented lands, supplemented by grazing fees from common lands and other miscellaneous sources of income: and then each enjoys his 'sír' for his sole personal benefit; or, if the income is not sufficient to meet the Government demand, the proprietor (or each co-sharer) may have to make up by a rate or rent on his 'sír,' what is deficient. The importance of the sír land in estimating the 'assets' of the estate is very great. The revenue being a fraction of the 'rental assets' as estimated, it is obvious that, in order to get at a fair rental value for the entire estate, rent-rates must be assumed for all 'sír' lands, because these are not actually rented, and do not appear in the rent-roll of the village (or if they do, it is at nominal or privileged rates). If, therefore, the 'sír' be valued at full rental rates, the revenue of the whole estate will be much higher than if some lower rates were fixed. And as a matter of fact, the holder of 'sír' was greatly benefited by the successive changes in the assessment rules. But this is a point of detail which I must reserve for the special chapters devoted to the North-West Provinces. I will here only mention that the last modification allowed the *sír* to be valued at twenty-five per cent. below the full rates as calculated for tenants. In future revisions, however, this allowance, which is certainly over liberal, will be reduced to between ten and fifteen per cent.

There are also certain other privileges attached to 'sír'

[1] Any estate, that is, where it is not a mere farm or holding worked by an (agriculturist) landlord, as in the Panjáb. In the provinces named in the text, the landlords are mostly of non-agricultural castes, and the bulk of their land is held by tenants who represent the old cultivators before the 'landlord' came.

land. For example, it may happen that the estate is sold for arrears of revenue; the proprietor will not be turned out of his 'sír,' but be allowed to remain in possession as an 'exproprietary tenant': and the same thing would happen if the proprietor declined the terms of Settlement and Government gave the estate, for a time, to some one else.

When the tenant-law grants occupancy-right, with its attendant rental limits, on ordinary land, it always exempts the proprietor's sír from such burdens. It thus becomes a matter of importance to see that, under colour of any legal definition of 'sír,' a proprietor is not enabled to get the best part of the village lands into his own hands and so defeat one of the most important rights of the village tenantry. It was (among other things) to prevent an incipient danger of this kind, that the Central Provinces Land-Revenue Act was amended in 1889.

This general sketch (and it is not exhaustive) will at once suggest the importance of the term 'sír' which crops up again and again in revenue literature; and it should be remembered accordingly.

§ 24. *The Panjáb Territory and its Settlement.*

The history of our territorial acquisitions already given, will have informed the student that (exclusively of the Delhi districts) the Panjáb was acquired partly in 1846, and as a whole in 1849. The Delhi districts in the region of the Jamná, and forming part of the 'Conquered districts' of the year 1803, were at first under the North-West Provinces, and afterwards (1858) were added to the Panjáb owing to the events of the Mutiny.

The Panjáb Settlements were made entirely on the North-West model, which was easily copied because the villages were of the landlord or joint type and in a still more perfect state than in the North-West Provinces. From causes which I cannot here examine, no Rájás and Taluqdárs had, as a rule, survived, over the communities of Jats, Rájputs, Aráíṇs, and others. The Sikh rule had placed jágírdárs over many of them, these being in fact the chiefs of territories holding estates in 'feudal' subordination to the Mahárájá on the usual Hindu model. It was rarely, however, that such overlords had grown into 'actual proprietors.' The 'superior' claims were almost all disposed of by grant of cash allowances; and in the overwhelming majority of cases, the village joint-body was the immediate or actual landlord. The landlord families were mostly of the agricultural castes, and consequently the land was largely cultivated by the co-sharers themselves, and only held by tenants to a limited extent: these tenants pay grain-rents in most cases. Moreover, there had been no farmers and revenue sales to speak of, so that new proprietary bodies (descendants of the farmers and purchasers)—and nearly always persons who do not themselves cultivate—had not grown up over the villages.

These features at once necessitated a different mode of ascertaining the *assets* of estates for revenue purposes. As cash rents paid by tenants were the rare exception, the *rental*-asset plan above described could not be adopted. At the same time the method of working out produce rates, and calculating costs of production, was hardly more feasible in the Panjáb than it was in the North-Western Provinces.

The method actually adopted was that also at first used in the North-West Provinces (and especially for districts where grain-rents were common), namely, the calculation of lump sums of revenue to be distributed over the holdings, and called the 'aggregate to detail' method. It consisted in looking to former revenue-payments, and then, with the aid of local knowledge of the growth and prosperity of a pargana or other circle (adopted with reference to similarity of market advantages, soil, irrigation, and other conditions), determining a lump sum for the whole area, which it was supposed would be fair. This was tested by distributing it over the villages; and once more, by dividing the village totals over the holdings, it could be seen whether these were fair. Produce-estimates were often made use of, and by turning into money a sixth, a fifth, and so on, of the gross produce it was seen how the rates would compare with those first assumed. Then, perhaps, *some* lands did pay money-rents, and these could be made use of for comparison; and so also could *plough-rates*, when the people made use of certain rates for each 'plough' possessed by the village-body. Fair rates being thus got out and submitted for sanction, a total was again made out for each village, and the total would be finally modified with reference to the class of cultivators, to prospects of utilising the waste, or to profits from grass. A village jama' would thus be arrived at; and this would be distributed over the holdings in consultation with the co-sharers. These latter always well understood such an operation (called making the 'báchh'); and then the whole business was concluded. It is of no use for my present purpose to describe the latest rules for assessment: they prescribe a more exact but simple method of soil classification and the direct calculation of *revenue-rates per acre*, which rates are one-half the rental rates as ascertained on a basis of actually observed facts of payment, in specimen, or standard, areas. These rules will be noticed in detail in the chapters on the Panjáb.

§ 25. *The Central Provinces System.*

In order to complete the series of developments of the 'village or mahál system,' I will pass over what ought, in point of time, to have been mentioned before—the Bombay system—and so proceed to notice another development of the North-West system. The Northern districts (Ságar, Dámoh, and Jabalpur) of what is now called the 'Central Provinces' were early settled on the North-West plan, not without some considerable difficulties, the record of which must be reserved. But when the rest of the province was added, and the whole formed into a Local Administration (under a Chief Commissioner) in 1862, there was some discussion as to what sort of general Settlement should be made. The villages, except a few in the North, were not of the landlord or joint type, but represented aggregates of cultivators, each claiming his own holding and nothing more, like the villages of Bombay and Madras. There is no doubt that a *raiyatwárí* Settlement, as in Madras or Bombay, would not only have been possible, but highly advantageous. However, the North-West Provinces principles were in the ascendant, and a village Settlement was ordered. But the jointly responsible body was rarely to be found; and the Maráthá system, which had long prevailed, had also produced its natural results. That system was one of keen financing; it was as opposite as possible to the lax system of the later Muhammadan rule; a Maráthá governor rarely (in such of his territories as were firmly in hand) farmed out the revenues of large tracts or made reckless revenue-free grants. He went straight to the villages, caring nothing for individual rights, and made the *pátel* or headman responsible for the village total assessment. Where the local hereditary *pátel* was inefficient, or some interested person could get the preference over him, he was superseded, and the person who obtained the farm of the village was spoken of as the *málgúzár* or 'revenue-payer.' The persons thus employed and trusted must have had large and undefined powers; and they consequently grew in influence and gradually acquired a *quasi*-proprietary position. It is no doubt a matter of opinion to what extent these headmen and farmers (whom we now generically call 'málgúzárs') had really become proprietors. The progress made in that direction varied in different districts and under different local conditions.

§ 26. *Málgúzárs recognized as Village proprietors.*

However that may be, it was determined to make these 'revenue-payers' 'proprietors,' and the Settlement was made with them. There might be one 'málgúzár,' or there might be several descendants of one; but the individual or the body jointly was recognized as proprietor; and this fact gave the peculiar character to the Central Provinces Settlement which has caused it to be popularly called the 'MÁLGÚZÁRÍ' Settlement; and it has had curious results.

§ 27. *Features of the Settlement.*

As regards the first assessments, there is nothing particular to record. They followed the 'aggregate to detail' method; and the interesting system of soil rent-rates elaborated for the present Settlement (since 1881) must be reserved for description at a later stage.

A number of estates have been left in the hands of Gond and other chiefs with the usual designation of Zamíndárí; but the noticeable peculiarity of the more or less artificial position of 'málgúzár' proprietors is, that Government never abandoned the village-holders as it did in Bengal. Nor did it acknowledge the 'málgúzárs' everywhere. In the Central Provinces we have some tracts which are frankly *raiyatwárí*[1] (where there is no over-proprietor or landlord); and in the málgúzárí villages there are a considerable body of sub-proprietors and a large number of original tenants, *over whom the landlord has no power as to eviction and enhancement; their rents are all fixed by the Settlement Officer for the term of Settlement.*

§ 28. *Oudh Taluqdárí System.*

There is one other form of Settlement with a middleman landlord;—I refer to the Oudh Settlement. The province was annexed in 1856. The neglect of the local native administration had resulted in the abandonment of all real control over the revenue, and in the adoption of a system of settling different tracts of country by bargain with local magnates for a fixed (but from time to time enhanceable) sum total of revenue. The moment such a tract, called a 'taluq,' came on to the State-books, all note of the villages composing it was dropped, and only the taluq and its annual total recorded.

This course was certainly facilitated, if not initiated, by the earlier history of Oudh. The province had been the

[1] And so recognized by the Revenue law as amended in 1889.

very centre of the old Aryan dominions. To this day the limits of a number of petty kingdoms—Gondá, Atraulá, and many others—can be traced; and Mr. Benett has told us, in more than one excellent Settlement Report, how these kingdoms were organized and managed, and how village communities grew up out of their dismemberment and decay. The petty kings were probably once united in a confederation under some great Mahárájá; but at the Muhammadan conquest they were not strong enough to resist the Great Mughal, though still able to give him much trouble, if not conciliated and made use of. Naturally enough, they were allowed to contract for a revenue-payment for their old dominions (or such part of them as remained), and then were called 'Taluqdárs.'

The plan being profitable, it was extended. Other persons, namely Court favourites, bankers, and speculators, occasionally obtained similar grants of 'taluqs' and became 'Taluqdárs'; but the marks of origin long survived in the ominous distinction of 'pure' and 'impure' Taluqdárs.

How far in the century between 1750 and 1856 the Taluqdárs had by purchase, by violence, or by founding new villages, really worked themselves into a proprietary position, I cannot here examine. Opinions still vary on the subject; and it is obvious that the process, which undoubtedly *did* go on, must have reached very various stages in different places, and under different conditions, especially with reference to the character and caste of the village bodies.

§ 29. *Circumstances necessitated the recognition of Taluqdárs.*

Here I need only note that, under the North-West policy of ignoring the overlords and settling direct with the villagers as proprietary bodies, the first plan of 1856 was to settle with the villagers under the North-West Provinces law, though it must be admitted that, even under that plan, Taluqdárs were much more recognized as *de facto* owners, than is sometimes supposed.

Scarcely, however, had the Settlement begun, when the Mutiny broke out, and the Taluqdárs, with a few exceptions, revolted. What had been done towards Settlement, in the matter of records, perished. The people voluntarily returned to the Taluqdárs and paid their revenue to them.

When the pacification of 1858 ensued, views had changed; the great body of the Taluqdárs were amnestied, and a Settlement was made with them. This necessitated an elaborate series of provisions as to the protection to be afforded to villages in the taluqs. Some had so far preserved their integrity that they were entitled to a 'sub-settlement'; others had not, but various degrees of occupancy-right and rent-limitation were acknowledged; all these measures have been the subject of much criticism. Besides that, the general question of tenant-right left a long legacy of trouble which has only found its end (for the present at any rate) in the tenant-law of 1886.

There is nothing to call for remark as to the method of Settlement which was based on the earlier North-West Provinces system. This Settlement is distinctively spoken of as the TALUQDÁRÍ Settlement.

§ 30. *The Bombay System.*

Such has been the development and the variation of Temporary Settlement systems originating in Regulation VII of 1822 and Regulation IX of 1833.

We must now retrace our steps to look to Western India. The Bombay territories (speaking generally) were acquired between 1803–1818, as the result of the defeat of the Maráthá power. For a long time no progress was made in the revenue-administration. A system of farming the revenues, on the basis of the Maráthá or other preceding assessments, was pursued, and with very unsatisfactory results.

There never was any appearance of great 'Zamíndárs,' so that the Bengal system could not have been thought of. The bulk of the villages in the Dakhan districts were of the *raiyatwárí* type, though in certain parts there were a few 'narwá,' 'bhágdárí,' and other estates jointly held by communities connected by a tie of descent. In Guzarát, also, the immigration of martial tribes of the Rájput type, and the government by chiefs, had left traces of an 'overlord' or taluqdárí tenure over the villages; while in the Konkán, 'khots,' or revenue-farmers of the Maráthá rule, had acquired rights over the villages, of a somewhat peculiar character.

A portion of these territories had originally been settled by Malik 'Ambar, the best representative of the power of the Muhammadan kings of the South in their palmy days[1]. This minister had been at much pains to secure and acknowledge a proprietary right, and this tended to preserve the ancestral communities, where they existed; since ancestral holding is, in all Eastern countries, the strongest form of connection with the soil. In his time, village assessments in the lump, were apparently the rule; and although the Maráthá system had superseded that of Malik 'Ambar, and was essentially a raiyatwárí system, it had not obliterated the traces of the former system. It is therefore not wonderful that the opinion should have been advocated that, in Bombay, the existing status of the *raiyatwárí* villages was in many cases, if not universally, due to the decay of an earlier landlord or joint constitution, rather than inherent in the nature of the groups themselves[2].

At first, indeed, the matter did not come prominently to notice, because, during the early years of our rule, the territories were provided for by the usual tentative arrangements for farming the revenues on short leases. A twenty years' experience, however, during which grievous hardships were inflicted on the districts, sufficed to make us at once, and for ever, discard the farmers, and set about finding a better plan.

[1] He also settled most of Berár.

[2] Details about the faint survival of 'mirásí' claims will be found in Vol. III. (Bombay chapters). At best, the Dakhan *mirás* right was too shadowy for practical revival.

§ 31. *Attempt to introduce a system of Settlement with Villages jointly.*

The raiyatwárí system was then much in vogue, consequent on Sir Thomas Munro's action in Madras. But Mr. Elphinstone, the then Governor of Bombay, took the view above alluded to, about the joint system, and was anxious not only to maintain it wherever it could be found, but even to create it in the case of those communities where no landlord claims survived; securing, indeed, the rights of each cultivator by record, but establishing a joint responsibility, and settling with the original 'pátels' or headmen of the village as *representatives of the body*.

It is no easy thing, however, to create a joint responsibility where it does not in fact exist. Although long years of custom may have taught the cultivator to submit to an annual adjustment of his individual burdens and liabilities by the headman, it has never laid him under any responsibility in case one of his neighbours failed [1].

[1] The account of the Bombay system in Campbell's *Modern India* (1858), though giving a good description of Mr. Elphinstone's views, is now too much out of date to be otherwise useful; for the Bombay system has since been altered and perfected in a way that has completely outgrown a description penned more than thirty years ago. The account is also to some extent marred by the author's apparent prejudice in favour of the joint responsibility and village settlement with which he was familiar. His objections to the Bombay system (notably the costliness of the village officials and the recognition of rights to rent-free holdings) affect mere accidents of the place, they do not touch the principles of the system. As a matter of fact, many of these evils have been removed or greatly mitigated. He also speaks of the joint responsibility as if it was an easy thing to introduce. But in fact it is not so. To establish it artificially over whole districts, and tell the people 'the system is convenient to your rulers, and when you are wiser you will see that it is also calculated to promote your own interest,' is beset with such difficulties as to make it impracticable. The people positively decline to undertake that the solvent members shall be responsible for the defaulting ones. What becomes of your system then? I need hardly point out the futility of *comparing* revenue systems in point of inherent merit, because every system may be good or the reverse according as it fits the *facts*. But even admitting the superior facilities which the joint-village system offers to revenue-management, the originators of the Bombay system claim for it certain counterbalancing advantages. By breaking up the land into small holdings, and allowing every occupant to keep as many of his 'numbers,' or give up as many, as he thinks desirable, the small farmer is enabled to contract his operations or enlarge them according to the capital and stock at his disposal. The revenue

The plan of settling for a lump sum with the village as a body used to be advocated because it was said to facilitate revenue-management; it enabled Government to deal with fewer units. The Bombay officers do not, however, admit that there is any difficulty in dealing with thousands of separate cultivators[1]. The difficulty only seems great to those accustomed to deal with one or with a few revenue-payers. At any rate, if there is difficulty, it is obviated by a perfect survey, a clear and complete record of each lot or field and the revenue assessed on it, and by a thorough control over the

being fixed for a long term of years, the farmer gets all the benefit of a long lease without its disadvantages. Nor does the Government really lose; because taking its revenue, not from one estate, but from the whole country, that revenue must, under any system, fluctuate with the circumstances of the country at large. With farmers of large capital, the long fixed lease may answer best; but with those of small means, the risk and responsibility which have to be set off against the security of profits, are more to be considered, and such risks are avoided by giving the villager the right of holding his land from year to year only, if he pleases.

In the North-West Provinces every village is allowed an area of waste, which it can bring under cultivation without the total assessment of the village being increased. Under a raiyatwárí system, any uncultivated number that is taken up has to be paid for; but in practice this does not interfere with the extension of cultivation; and as a matter of fact, though the North-West assessment does not increase when the waste of the village is made to yield crops, still that assessment is originally fixed after taking into consideration the capabilities of the estate, and the probable average yield *of the whole*, for the entire term.

It is also urged that the village officers collect the revenue from each separate holder just as easily as they do from a joint body, who, though together responsible, still ultimately pay separately according to known shares; and as under the Bombay system every occupant is furnished with a receipt book, which the patwárí (pándyá or kulkární) is bound to write up, there is no room for fraud. To any one who wishes further to study the *pros* and *cons* of both systems, and the improvements which the Bombay authorities made on the Madras system to remove objections, I cannot do better than recommend the perusal of the able 'Appendix I' to the *Official Correspondence on the Bombay Settlements* (reprint of 1877: Bombay Government Press).

[1] In the Bombay and Madras Presidencies the number of raiyats and average size of holdings are as follows (*Govt. Ind. Statistics*, 1886-7):—

Presidency.	Number of raiyats.	Average size of holding.	
Madras	3,955,788	. . . .	7·5 acres.
Bombay	1,284,238	Northern division 8 acres Central „ 32 „ Southern „ 23 „	21·5 „

village accountants and revenue-officers of small local subdivisions of districts.

It was no doubt this inherent difficulty of creating a joint responsibility where it did not, naturally or in fact, exist, that led to the abandonment of the design to make village-Settlements, and to the adoption of the separate field or 'raiyatwárí' system. As a matter of fact, a sort of joint responsibility is kept up in certain villages where the rights of co-sharers have survived to this day.

§ 32. *Progress of the system in Bombay.*

The defects of the survey-Settlement, as at first worked (up to 1835), acted as a warning to the authorities; and a new departure was then made. An experimental re-survey of the Indápur taluk having proved successful, the same method was followed elsewhere. In 1847 three of the ablest Settlement Superintendents met and were able to formulate the results of practical experience, in the shape of a complete scheme for the survey and assessment of village lands. It was not till 1865 that a local Act was passed specifically legalising the system. This Act has in its turn been repealed; and the whole law has now been completely revised in the Land-Revenue Code (Bombay Act V of 1879). There is but little mention of a *Settlement* (although the term does occur in the Code); there is really a survey and assessment only. There is no procedure like that of Upper India,—proposing a certain sum as the assessment on the whole village, discussing the matter with the village proprietary body, and perhaps making a reduction and coming to terms with the representatives, who then sign an agreement to be responsible. Under the Bombay system, every acre is assessed at rates fixed on almost scientific principles, and then the occupant must pay that assessment or relinquish the land.

§ 33. *Outline of the Bombay System.*

The system will be described more in detail in the sequel, but here I may generally indicate the outlines of the procedure.

A certain convenient unit of division is selected to form the 'survey number' or 'field.'

Every field or lot is surveyed, and then the work of classification begins. The soil-classes are noted, and each field is examined and a sort of diagram of it made, which shows not only its soil, but any defects which reduce its value. It is thus ascertained for every field what is its *relative* value; in other words,—taking the maximum rate for the class as one whole or sixteen annas (on the Indian method of reckoning),—whether the field can be assessed at the maximum or at something less,—at fourteen annas, at twelve annas, and so on, down to a minimum. The department charged with this work becomes highly experienced in the process, so that it can be performed with the greatest accuracy and fairness. Cultivation is usually classed into wet and dry: the process just described treats land only on its dry aspect; if there is irrigation, then an additional rate may be charged, which will be higher or lower according to the goodness and value of the source of irrigation; the rate is only applied to such land as is really capable of irrigation from the source in question[1].

Next, the Settlement Officer begins his work as assessor of actual rates; he has before him the facts of soil classification on its unirrigated aspect, and the details of the means of irrigation where they exist; he has to fix what are to be the full or maximum rates for dry soil, and what are to be the additional rates for irrigation. These rates he

[1] Wet cultivation is rice land, or land that is always flooded for cultivation. A 'dry' field may have a well or other means of partial watering, that does not make it 'wet' land. *Wells* are not now charged for directly, but a certain addition may be made to the rate, on account of an easy supply of subsoil water regarded as one of the qualities of the soil.

calculates with the aid of all the data he can collect, regarding former history, the general situation, climate, proximity to market, &c. Having thus arrived at the *absolute* or full rates, the field diagrams, which show the *relative* values, at once enable the rates to be applied. A sixteen *anna* field pays the full; an eight *anna* field the half, and so on.

In Bombay (just as in Madras) the occupant of such a survey number holds it on the simple terms of paying the revenue; if he admits that he is (or is proved by a decree of Court to be) holding on behalf of some one else, as a tenant, or in an inferior position, then the 'superior holder's' name is entered in the register, not his: he becomes the 'inferior holder,' and it is the superior who is entered in the register as the 'occupant' responsible for the assessed sum. Any one who is recorded as the responsible holder can simply resign (if he does not like to pay the assessment) any field in his holding. The assessment is fixed for a period of thirty years, so that a man who elects to hold continuously, knows for certain that, during that long period, *all* the profit he can make will go to him.

At the beginning of each year, he can signify to the mámlatdár (or local revenue officer of a taluká subdivision) what fields he wishes to hold and what he wishes to give up: as long as he does this in proper time, he is free to do as he pleases. If he relinquishes, the fields are available for any one else; if no one applies for them, they are usually auctioned as fallow (for the right of grazing) for the year, and so on, till some one offers to take them up for cultivation. Nothing whatever is said in the Revenue Code about the person in possession (on his own account) being '*owner*' in the Western sense. He is simply called the 'occupant,' and the Code says what he can do and what he cannot[1]. The occupant may do anything he pleases to *improve* the land, but may not without permission do any-

[1] The 'right of occupancy'—*the right to be* an occupant—is itself declared to be a *transferable* and *heritable property* (Code, section 73); but that is quite a different thing from saying that the occupant is the proprietor of the soil. In the official language of the Presidency, the occupant is said to hold on 'the survey tenure.'

thing which diverts the holding from agricultural purposes. He has no right to mines or minerals.

These are the facts of the tenure; you may theorize on them as you please; you may say this amounts to proprietorship, or this is a '*dominium minus plenum*'; or anything else.

The question of tenancy is just as simply dealt with. I have stated that if it appears that the occupant is in possession in behalf of some one else, that some one else is recorded as the 'superior holder,' and he becomes the 'inferior holder.' What sort of 'inferior'—whether a tenant or on some other terms—is a simple question of fact and of the agreement or the custom by which he holds [1].

If an occupant dies, one (the eldest or managing) heir must be entered as the succeeding occupant who has to pay the revenue; for there can only be *one* registered revenue-payer for each field or recognized share of a field with a separate survey number; though of course there may be several sharers (joint-heirs of the deceased owner, for instance) in it. Which of them is so entered depends on the agreement of the members of the family, or on the result of a Court decree, if there is a dispute. Sharers can always get their shares partitioned, recorded, and severally assessed, as long as there is no dispute as to what the shares are.

I should here add that BERÁR was settled on the Bombay system.

§ 34. *The Revenue-Systems of other Provinces.*

The retrospect just brought to a close embraces all the older, and most of the larger, provinces of India. The others that have special systems really need but little pre-

[1] There is also no artificial tenant right. In Bombay, as in all other provinces, there are jágír and other 'inám' holdings which are revenue-free, or only lightly assessed, and occasionally other tenures in which there may be a superior holder drawing a revenue from the estate; there the actual occupants are sub-occupants, not tenants, as they do not hold in consequence of any contract with the superior.

fatory comment. ASSAM, of which a small portion only had been permanently settled, when it formed part of Bengal; the little province of COORG, and the great and growing province of BURMA, are all of them managed under local systems of Land-Revenue Settlement which have this great advantage;—they are free of all theories and artificial creations, with all that has elsewhere necessarily followed from such creations. They are (in this manual), therefore, classed as varieties of the RAIYATWÁRÍ system.

But they have little or nothing in common with the systems of Bombay and Madras, except this one thing, that there is no middleman—landlord, or overlord, or ideal corporate body—between the actual soil-occupant and the State.

In the map, which indicates by different colours the area which each Settlement system I have been reviewing occupies, I have ventured to give the same tint to Madras and Bombay and Berár, because the systems differ only in detail; but I have given a different tint to Assam and Burma, though I have endeavoured to indicate their connection with the raiyatwárí system by making it a different shade or tint of the same *colour*.

SECTION IX.—THE MACHINERY OF BRITISH LAND-REVENUE ADMINISTRATION.

§ 1. *Modern organization of Territory.*

Perhaps I ought next to devote some space to describing how the various British revenue systems are worked; how the records are preserved; how the land-revenue is collected; how questions of revenue-law and matters of executive management are disposed of under each system, and in each province. But, as a matter of fact, each province must, in the sequel, have a separate chapter on this subject, and it would be of little use to present a series of provincial abstracts in this place. Some of the most essential matters of management must also be further discussed in another connection in the remaining sections of this chapter. I will therefore here offer only a brief outline of what, with some slight modifications, is the general framework or basis of constitution COMMON TO ALL PROVINCES, as regards their land-revenue administration.

In all provinces the *district* is the starting-point. The Magistrate and Collector, as he is called in the Regulation Districts, and Deputy Commissioner, as he is called in the rest, is the head of the district: and he is supported by Assistants and Deputies, who are either general assistants or are in charge of subdivisions of the district, in which such assistants are practically chiefs, only acting under the general control of the district head.

Of the multifarious duties of the *District Officers* I am not here going to speak; they are described elsewhere [1].

In all provinces but Madras [2], a varying number of districts forms a *division*, which is presided over by a 'Commissioner.' The duties of this officer are those of inspection and general control in the districts; to hear appeals in any case from district orders; and to be the channel of communication between the district and the higher revenue authorities and the Government.

At the head of the revenue-administration in Bengal, Madras, and the North-West Provinces, is a Board of Revenue; in the Panjáb there are two Financial Commissioners with Secretaries, who in fact, though not in name, form a Board. In Burma there is a Financial Commissioner instead of a Board. In the Central Provinces, Oudh and Assam, the Chief Commissioner is himself the chief revenue authority.

Under the district there are now, in all provinces, small local subdivisons, which are to our administration, what

[1] See, for instance, the Bengal chapter on Revenue Officers; and especially see Sir John Strachey's *India*, Lect. X, and p. 263 et seq.

[2] In Madras, the Collectorates or Districts are larger and are subdivided; the Collector corresponds directly with the Board of Revenue, which (as reorganized in 1886) consists of 'Commissioners' for several departments of duty who are aggregated in the Board instead of presiding over local areas of territory.

the pargana was to the Mughal system. But they are, for convenience, usually made larger than the old pargana or taluká, and sometimes consist of several such areas combined.

In Bengal for a long time, as there were only a certain number of district Zamíndárs to deal with, local centres of revenue-management and collection were not thought of; but of late years, as the estates subdivided, Government estates became more numerous and business generally increased, a system of subdivisions of districts has been adopted, and these subdivisions are usually under Sub-Deputy Collectors, and are, in fact, very much like the tahsíl subdivisions of other provinces to be next mentioned.

In all Northern and Central India, the district (which, if large, may have one or more primary subdivisions) is always subdivided into 'tahsíls,' which are groups usually consisting of several parganas of the older system. The head (native) official who receives revenue at his local or tahsíl treasury, is called a Tahsíldár. This term is in use in certain districts of Assam, all over the North-West Provinces, Oudh, the Central Provinces, the Panjáb, and in Madras. In Bengal, the Tahsíldár is only known as a minor official in certain special cases, as in Government estates, or where there are numerous small holdings. The Tahsíldár is usually assisted by a Náib or Deputy Tahsíldár.

In Burma there is a somewhat similar system, of course under Burmese nomenclature.

In Bombay the same system obtains, except that the local areas are called 'talukás,' retained, I believe, without aggregation from the older system. The officers in charge are called 'mámlatdár' aided by subordinates called 'kárkun.' In Madras, the Mughal administration was not sufficiently generally established to make its divisions well known. The district subdivision is the 'taluk,' and the native officer is (as stated) the Tahsíldár.

The object of this universal local subdivision, in its

slightly varying forms, is the same. The local officer—vested with small criminal, and sometimes with civil-court powers—has to receive the revenues of the local area, to keep a close watch over the agricultural and social condition of the sub-district, and to see the village officials are doing their duty. For this purpose the Tahsíldár (or whatever he may be called) has not only an office and treasury establishment, but also a staff of kánúngos (or Revenue Inspectors), one of whom usually remains at the tahsíl headquarters to compile statistics and see to the despatch of the proper returns to the district headquarters, while the others constantly move about, check the work of the village patwárís, and see that they do their duty in keeping a record of all changes in the maps, and in the proprietary interests as they occur by inheritance, gift and sale (and to some extent by mortgage), as well as in keeping the statistics of crops sown, and other matters which local rules require.

The Agriculture and Land Record Department aids the district officer, especially in seeing that this important duty is carefully and punctually fulfilled, as it is on the proper performance of it that several important features of district administration depend.

Some of these duties of the local establishments are of modern introduction; they may be reckoned as among the results of the Famine Commission of 1879, but success is already beginning to be attained. And in the North-West Provinces, where the system has been longest in operation, the improvement in the records and statistics has already been very considerable. Indeed, though we have not yet arrived at the wished-for ideal of revisions of Settlement being carried out by the district staff absolutely without extraneous aid, a step in that direction has been taken. The cost of the latest revisions will hardly be one-third of what it used to be; and both the labour involved and the duration of the work will be greatly curtailed.

As far as the general working of the system is concerned,

—the collection of the revenue, and other branches of general duty,—it is a matter of fact, for years past, that these local agencies have worked well. Sales of estates for revenue-arrears are now rare, and coercive processes seriously carried out are also rare. In most cases the issue of notices ('dastak') or very temporary detentions at the tahsíl, are quite sufficient.

§ 2. *Other branches of the Revenue Officer's duty.*

I have purposely avoided mentioning other branches of work for the district staff; many, such as Excise, Stamps, and Registration of Assurances, are foreign altogether to my purpose. But even those directly and indirectly connected with land-revenue can only be enumerated. These are first, the disposal of matters connected with the collection, recovery of arrears, and the suspension and remission of land-revenue; next, questions of boundary, and those matters of land-revenue law which require to be dealt with by revenue-officers. In some provinces cases between landlord and tenant as to enhancement, ejectment, improvements, and the like, are heard by Revenue Courts. In all provinces, the registration of transfers of proprietary interests; the making of partitions of estates; the management of estates of which Settlement has been declined, or which are under direct management by reason of default in revenue payments; the management of estates of minors and others under the Court of Wards; the special Settlement of *alluvial* areas, or measures taken for reduction by reason of *diluvion*; assessment of revenue-free areas when the estate lapses, or the assignment for life or lives falls in; acquisition of land for public purposes; making loans for agricultural improvements, and to aid cultivators for general agricultural purposes;—these are all matters of a Land-Revenue officer's duty. There may be also work in connection with the law under which certain cesses are levied for roads and schools and to meet the costs of famine relief, and in Bengal in connection with embankments[1] and special surveys. The Land-Revenue Administration has also to watch the effect of the Settlements, whether the assessments work well or bear hardly, and to take note of the condition of the people, as evidenced by the frequency of mortgages and sales of land, and to study the general question of indebtedness of the agricultural classes. Irrigation questions and appeals regarding rights of water, and right of taking water-channels across land, also occupy no little time in canal districts; while (in the Panjáb, for example) schemes for the construction of canals in districts where the soil is good, but the rainfall is so scanty that canal irrigation is the only condition under which husbandry is possible, have led, of late years, to questions of colonization on an extensive scale, and of the location of villages under appropriate rules. Lastly, in certain districts, the results of local mistakes in Settlements of past years, or of the improvidence of certain classes, or both combined, may have also left us a legacy of duty in securing relief from hopeless debt, in the shape of several 'Encumbered Estates Acts,' or 'Raiyats' Relief' Acts.

The mere enumeration of these matters will show how the land-revenue administration of an Indian district is in fact the central part of Government, and how it comes into contact with almost every other branch of administration which can be named.

SECTION X.—RÉSUMÉ OF THE PRINCIPLES OF LAND-REVENUE ASSESSMENTS.

§ 1. *Objects of Settlement.*

The duty of making or revising assessments of land-revenue is a separate branch; it may be undertaken by the Collector, and will be more frequently so in the future; but

[1] Embankments, i. e. by which floods are kept out of culturable lands. This work, always laid on local authorities from ancient times, is of great importance in many parts of Bengal proper.

hitherto, a special Settlement officer (or Settlement Collector) aided by a special staff, has been employed. The object of a Settlement, I may repeat, is,—(1) to assess the Land-Revenue; (2) to furnish the officer responsible for its collection with a correct list of the persons by whom it is payable; (3) to give those persons a secure title, and at the same time to secure the rights of those who hold on shares with them, or those who hold under them.

At the risk of some repetition, I shall here briefly resume the general principles of assessment as they are developed in the several provinces.

It will be observed that, while the modern land-revenue assessments trace back their origin to the old principle of the Rájá's share in the produce, and derive their authority from that ancient custom, the actual levy of a share, or anything representing it, has long since been abandoned; the old theory and the actual practice have been sundered widely apart by the changing circumstances, both of different provinces and different eras of history.

If all land-tenures had remained unaltered, or had presented uniformly the features, say, of an ordinary Madras village, where each cultivator deals direct with the State officers, responsible for no one but himself and for the crop his own labour has raised, then no doubt the revenue might long have remained, in true theory, a share of the produce valued in money. And, indeed, in Madras the land-revenue is still professedly in theory, and to some extent in practice, based on the value of a share in the *net* produce of land. (See Sect. vii. p. 296.)

In Bombay, though in principle the same direct dealing with the cultivator is adopted, the plan has been, ever since 1847, frankly to abandon the practice of produce-calculation. At the same time, the conditions of land-holding do not afford any possibility of finding out a rental value. In Bombay there is the usual preliminary division of villages into similarly situated groups. For each group certain maximum, or full, or standard, cash rates per acre of certain determinate kinds of soil, are worked out. The rates are based on a number of practical and general considerations, reference being had to what has been paid in the past, to the present increase in cultivation, general prosperity and rise in prices of produce: such full rates being made to vary in each group with reference to the relative advantages of each. But, before applying these full or standard rates (for each group), every field is classified by a skilful and practised staff, and valued *relatively*, according to its kind, and according to various circumstances which add to or diminish its value individually. The result is that the value of each field is nicely graduated on a scale extending from a minimum up to the full rate: the scale is expressed in 'annas' or fractions according to the common practice. Supposing, then, the 'full rate,' applicable to the group, is, for a given soil, as above, R. 3: then a field belonging to such order of soil, and of such depth, and so free from accidental defects that it ranks as '16 annas,' its rate will be R. 3; but should the soil be of less depth, or of an inferior grade, and subject to defects, then it may only rank as '4 annas,' and therefore pay only one-fourth of the R. 3. That is the plan of valuing land as land watered only by the rain of heaven. If in such land there is irrigation from a tank or by 'lift' from a river, or by well, such irrigation-advantages may be taken into account by rates charged in excess of the 'dry-rate'; if it is 'garden' land,—i.e. brought by long culture, manure, and watering, up to a high standard,—it will pay rates of its own; and so if it is permanent 'wet' or rice land.

In the Temporarily Settled provinces, where the whole village is dealt with as the unit, the assessment is in one sum, which is, however, distributed among the co-sharers according to their constitution; so that the separate payments are just as well known as under the raiyatwárí system.

The first Settlements date from a time when the 'aggregate to detail' method of assessment in use in the North-West Provinces, and advocated in Thomason's well-known *Directions to Settlement Officers* was the common one. In practice, a lump sum was estimated for the 'pargana,' or a *circle* of similarly-situated villages (assessment-circle), and then this sum was divided so as to give the amount for each village. There were three real grounds for fixing this sum—*first*, the knowledge of what sums had been paid in the past (with the additional fact that they had been paid with ease or the reverse); *secondly*, the rise in general prices, population, increase of advantages in the matter of wells, roads to market, &c. These considerations suggested that the total might be increased, or maintained as it was, or possibly diminished. *Thirdly*, there was the general sense of a locally experienced officer that such a sum would be fair, the estimate having been arrived at after careful inspection, inquiry among the people, and consultation with experienced native subordinates. These grounds, however, had to be more elaborately justified in the *Assessment Reports*, in which various rate calculations were set out, tending to check and to illustrate or justify the general totals proposed.

The proposed village totals would then be worked backwards into the form of rates on the acre of each different kind of soil (according to a fixed classification), and the rates would be justified by comparing them with rates got out by estimating produce, and valuing one-sixth[1] of the gross produce at average prices, by calculating a fair rate on the number of ploughs in the village, and so forth. Under this method, the revenue was not absolutely divorced from the old idea of a share of the produce, and it is confidently believed (in the Panjáb, for example) that our land-revenue can be stated to represent not more than the traditional sixth at the outside, probably in many cases not more than a tenth or twelfth, of the gross produce.

[1] One-sixth, because it was roughly estimated, that of the total produce two-thirds represented the cultivator's and one-third the landlord's share: so that the Government revenue share was fifty per cent. or one-half of the latter.

§ 2. *Later Methods of Assessment.*

But in the North-West Provinces, Oudh, and the Central Provinces, a totally new element had gradually been introduced. In these provinces the landlord classes were largely non-agriculturist, and in consequence the land was mostly cultivated by *tenants*, and the rents thus realized from the land came to be more and more commonly paid in cash. At the present day the cases where grain-rents are paid are insignificant (and the means of ascertaining a cash-rate by comparison are easy); so that the system is not altered by such exceptional cases.

The growth of tenant-cultivation and the use of cash-rents were very important changes in the constitution of agricultural society. And gradually they affected assessment principles. In fact we may reckon four stages of assessment rule development. The first was marked by the attempt to value *produce*, which I have alluded to as characteristic of the *early* working of Regulation VII of 1822; it was, in fact, a clinging to the idea of finding out a proper share of the produce and valuing it in money. The year 1833 marks the *second period*, when the produce idea was given up, and an attempt was made to obtain a direct cash valuation of the estates, with more or less reference to the rental value. This was the old 'aggregate to detail' method, and consisted in roughly calculating out a *gross rental* of the estate, and taking two-thirds of it as the revenue.

The third period is marked by a great improvement in the method of classifying soils, and in an attempt to fix more scientifically the rent-paying capacity of each class. This I may call the *stage of scientifically estimating what rent ought to be*, and taking a share —reduced to fifty per cent.—of the ideal 'rental.'[1]

[1] I quote the following from an able article in the *Pioneer* (June 21, 1884). Speaking of the 'ideal' rent system, the author says :—

'The individual rents actually paid were, in theory at least, disregarded. The main feature of the Settlement . . . was that the process employed in the preceding Settlement was exactly reversed. Rent

The *fourth* and last stage I shall speak of when I come to mention the latest policy of the Imperial Government regarding future revisions of Settlement,—viz. those now in progress, or, speaking generally, since 1881. It will be sufficient here to state briefly that it abandoned the *ideal* rent for the natural or *actual* rent.

The abandonment of the elaborate method which is associated with the honoured names of C. A. Elliott and other eminent Settlement Officers of the last North-West Provinces Settlement, does not imply any disparagement of the skill and ability of its authors.

'It is owing' (writes Mr. Fuller, himself the author of an improved method of assessment in the Central Provinces) 'to their (the Settlement officers') labours and to their ability that assessments were made which were an immense improvement on what preceded, and under which the country has generally prospered. But the circumstances on which the value of land depends are so numerous, so diverse, and often so occult, that, however great be the talents or energy of the Settlement officer, it is impossible that he should not occasionally slip into error: and a single error on a point of detail may vitiate a whole assessment. It is notorious that past assessments have from the outset pressed unequally on the people. No sooner has a Settlement been completed than it has become a matter of common report that such and such a village has fared badly, whilst others have got off very lightly—the all-sufficient explanation to native minds lying in the temper of the Settlement officer (*hākim kī mizáj*).'

rates were based on the actual rents found to be paid by cultivators in the neighbourhood, and were then applied to the lands of each village, which had been minutely classified, so as to correspond with the various rates of rent which were, or were supposed to be, paid for each kind of soil. Crop rates were still worked out on calculations of the gross produce and its value, but they were not professed to be used except as checks on the rates based on actual rents, and in fact they were hardly used at all. They were merely the atrophied relics of a disused theory. Each then of these three Settlements rested on a different basis,—the first on the produce and its value; the second on gross rents assumed for large areas; the last on special rents paid for individual fields; and each successive stage was an approximation to the true theory of our present land-revenue, namely, that instead of dealing with the cultivator we deal with the proprietor, and instead of taking a share of the produce we take a share of a natural rent.'

§ 3. *The latest system of Assessment.*

The North-West Provinces districts that are now being settled have, of course, been settled several times before. Therefore, in most of them very little in the way of re-survey or record of rights is required. But the revision of the assessment is now conducted solely on the basis of the rents actually paid. The account has, of course, still to be completed, by applying rent rates to the proprietors' *sír* lands (with an allowance of from ten to fifteen per cent. below full tenant rates); by applying rents to lands held at favourable rates, or at no rent at all; and by correcting any manifest defects or errors in the rent-roll.

Provision is also made for cases where the recorded rent-rolls fraudulently misrepresent facts, or are otherwise inaccurate or unreliable.

In short, though the assets are now to depend on the actual rental, irrespective of allowance for extension of cultivation, or anticipated enhancements, still it is to be an actual rental, not one which represents imaginary rents, below what are paid, or excludes land from the account without showing any rent at all.

In the *Panjáb*, the latest method of assessment still remains different from this. We cannot make use of *rentals* of the estates, because the bulk of the land is not rented,—and what is rented pays 'batáí,' or rent in grain. At the same time, the old plan of assessing the aggregate revenue first, and then distributing it, and the subsequent practice of relying on the valuation of one-sixth of the produce, is completely given up. The assessing officer has therefore to determine *for each class of soil*, in each assessment circle, *rates per acre, which are direct revenue rates.*

These have to be sanctioned before being made use of in actual assessment, and when so made use of can be modified to meet peculiar requirements of individual estates,—requirements, that is, of a special character, and not already provided for by the grouping into circles for assessment purposes.

There is still no method of finding out the rates which dispenses with personal opinion and sense of fitness; but the rates that are proposed can start with the basis that there are existing rates, and *primâ facie* these are to be raised (or it may be lowered) on a consideration of the history of the circle and its prevalent prices since the last Settlement.

Then again, rates that first suggest themselves are tested by a variety of calculations; and it is worthy of remark that the rules of 1888 now distinctly direct that as a test of rates, an average tenant holding in each soil-class should be selected, and the rent, if it is in cash, accurately ascertained; or, if it is paid in grain, then the grain is to be valued in money at a fair average price. On this basis estimates of the landlord's share, or produce rent (and the Government half) per acre, are drawn up for each of the different soil-classes. This shows that circumstances are beginning to admit of tenants' rents being made more use of, in calculation; and it is also to be pointed out that such estimates have one great value—they afford a good idea of the *relative* value of different soils or different modes of cultivation.

But perhaps the most interesting development is that of the assessment method devised for the Government Settlements in the Central Provinces.

It may be observed, that in the North-West Provinces, though the Settlement officer calculates tenants' rents in order to obtain his valuation of estates, in *theory* he had nothing to do with fixing rates that the tenants were actually bound to pay. That was supposed to be done by the consent of the parties, and by recourse to the Rent Courts under the Tenant Law. As a matter of fact however, the Settlement officers *did* do a very great deal, though informally, to help the people to a settlement of the rents consequent on the new assessment. But in the Central Provinces the law has so limited the rights of the proprietors of villages as regards the old tenants, that it also was necessary by law to provide that the Settlement officers should formally and legally determine fair rents. Hence it was desirable to strike out a method which should fix tenants' rents equably, and at the same time enable the Government share of the rental-assets to be assessed without further trouble.

Unfortunately it has been the great difficulty of all Settlement calculations, that rates, however carefully tested, *will* fall unequally. The surveyor and classifier can take note of palpable differences of situation, and distinct kinds and varieties of soil; but besides these, there are a hundred other circumstances which affect value, some of which defy explanation. It was desired to see whether some steps could not be taken to *compare* the rents paid in one village with those paid in another, so that there could not only be a positive increase (or decrease) where needed, but also an equalization of one estate with another.

Mr. Fuller, B.C.S., who had been assistant to Sir E. Buck in the North-West Provinces, was appointed to direct the new Settlements in the Central Provinces, and he devised a system which is working very well. This system is described in detail in the proper chapter of the sequel; here I can only generally indicate its principle.

The *actual rents* paid in different villages on different classes of soil are first carefully ascertained; and, so far, it can at once be seen (individually) whether they are too low or too high; and if too low, up to what they can fairly be enhanced. For we can compare the rates within the village, with what, under the circumstances, they might be expected to be. For instance: the present rental is found to be only very slightly in excess of what it was at the beginning of the expiring Settlement: yet during the period, cultivation has extended 200 per cent., and prices (suppose) have doubled; here, unless there are special reasons, the rental may be considerably raised. But this does not enable us to compare the rents of one village with those of another; in order to do this, the soils of both must be reduced to a 'common denominator'; for we could not compare the results (taking an all-round rate per acre) unless the villages were alike in classes of soil, and in the proportion of each class of soil in each village area, which, of course, is rarely or never the case. But if we can ascertain that one class of land stands, as regards its productiveness, in a certain relation to another, then we can reduce the area of a village to a number of 'soil-units' of equal value. Suppose, for instance, a village *A* consists of 1000 acres and pays a total rental of R. 1000, and that a village *B* has the same acreage and same total rental :—

	Acres.	
But *A*'s area consists of	{ 300 'black' soil 700 'red' ,, }	= 1,000
B's area consists of	{ 600 'black' ,, 400 'red' ,, }	= 1,000

Now, by observation, careful experiment as to actual produce on calculated areas, and inquiry, it is found that the productiveness of 'black' to 'red' is as 20 : 12—

So that in *A*	{ 300 × 20 =	6,000
	700 × 12 =	8,400
		14,400 soil-units of equal value.
And in *B*	{ 600 × 20 =	12,000
	400 × 12 =	4,800
		16,800 ,, ,, ,,

We can now compare how the equal rental of R. 1000 falls; for by dividing R. 1000 by the total *soil-units* of each, we find that *A*'s rate per soil-unit comes out 1·11 anna, while *B*'s comes out at 0·95 anna. The difficulty is to work out the proper 'soil-factor' or number by which each acreage of class of soil must be multiplied to reduce it to a common denominator of equal productivity.

But this factor can be calculated for an entire *tahsíl* and can then be used by slightly modifying the results to provide for special and local features in individual villages or groups of villages.

The tables prepared for the villages in each circle, will show the actual incidence per soil-unit; the unit-rate as it ought to be on general considerations, in comparison with other villages; and the actual unit-rate adopted with reference to any peculiarity in the village itself. In many tables I find this last is something less than the second, because of the caste or condition of the tenants, or some other special consideration of the kind. Thus, for instance, we may have an actual incidence *per* soil-unit of 0·65 anna; but with reference to increase in assets (extended area of cultivation, rents having risen, &c.), the incidence might fairly be 0·80; but from considerations of the actual state of the tenantry, the Settlement Officer will recommend 0·70 as the rate to be adopted. Of course, given this rate and the soil-factors, it is a mere matter of arithmetic to take out the actual rent per acre of each soil in the village as shown in the map and field index.

§ 4. *Element of intuitive calculation in Assessment work.*

With all these different methods, it is apt to be supposed that, after all, Settlement is very much a matter of individual taste and opinion, and that the elaborate tables and calculations do not produce much but expense and long report-writing. There is, no doubt, in every assessment, a point where it comes to taking a certain figure, which implies an element of personal judgment—the intuitive conclusion of a trained mind accustomed to the work. But such conclusions are *tested* after they originate, so that they are practically satisfactory.

All Settlement systems of a modern kind depend on having an accurate survey of every field—grouping of villages into 'assessment circles'—or something equivalent—according to general similarity of position and advantages, and a complete classification of soils whereby every field can be referred to a certain class, for which an appropriate rate is worked out.

What that *rate* is to be, is calculated under the different systems in different ways. In a country rented by *tenants*, it depends on the rent actually paid, correcting the record where it is not a real or full rent that is shown; and supplying a proper figure where the land does not pay rent. In other places, it is a rate derived from general considerations of past payments in relation to subsequent rise in prices and improved condition, generally checked by estimates of produce or rental receipts. In others again it approximates more to a rate representing the half of the actual 'net produce' (produce after allowing for all costs and profits of labour). In most systems the acreage rate represents rather the net income, than an actual net produce valued in money; and the general rule is that from 45–55 per cent. of the calculated *net* income is the Land-Revenue.

Originally the person responsible for the revenue was content to pay ninety per cent. and retain ten per cent.; he made his profit in other ways. Even when under British law, he was first called 'proprietor'—and it might seem that a proprietor was hardly to be so called if he had to pay so heavy a share to the State,—it must be remembered that the *proprietary right was a pure gift of which one person (or one body) was not to get the whole benefit*; and further that the 'assets' of which he gave up ninety per cent., did not really represent anything like his whole receipts. As the systems became more searching in their calculations, the percentage was reduced, at first to sixty-six per cent. or two-thirds, and then lower still [1].

But, to return to the calculation of assets or the rates which represent assets per acre. There must necessarily be a point where estimation—guess-work if the term is preferred—comes in. No *rule* can possibly be laid down as to whether a certain soil should pay 1 R. or 1 R. 8 a. or 1 R. 10 a. per acre: a sense of fitness under all the conditions of the case, arising in the mind of a practical officer who has carefully inspected the land map and note-book in hand, must begin the work; but if the figure is not justifiable, its error will surely appear when we come to apply the rates

[1] And where, as in some cases in Bengal, it still remains at seventy per cent., it is where the person holding the Settlement is really only a nominal proprietor, and glad to collect at a remuneration of thirty per cent., while the tenantry get a larger share of the total.

to the whole village or circle, and compare the results with existing payments and test them in various ways. And in Bombay the test is mainly applied by having the relative value of fields fixed on certain definite principles, so that if the full rate is at all accurate, the individual valuation of fields is almost a matter of arithmetic.

All systems insist on the rates being reported and justified, before actually put into force; and therefore, though the rates may be *initiated* to some extent by more or less arbitrary methods, they are not *used* till their resulting totals are tested and examined on *data* which are quite sound and satisfactory, while the results are made to conform to principles of equitable taxation laid down by Government.

§ 5. '*Cesses.*'

Properly speaking, we are concerned only with the 'land-revenue,' but it may be convenient to explain that in many Settlement Records another charge will be found entered. The co-sharer in a village, for example, is entered as paying for his field say 15 rupees, of which 13 R. is 'mál' or land-revenue, and 2 R. is 'siwái' or cesses. The cesses were from an early date levied to pay for certain public works which benefited the locality only, and were not, therefore, properly a charge against the Imperial Land-Revenue[1].

The 'cesses' are levied at the present day under local Acts.

SECTION XI.—THE MODERN QUESTION OF A GENERAL PERMANENT SETTLEMENT.

Before I pass on to some other matters of importance connected with land-revenue administration, I feel that it is almost unavoidable to give some further detail regarding

[1] The land-revenue proper is, for budget purposes, divided between the Imperial treasury—to meet Imperial or general charges, like the army, home charges, &c.,—and the local treasures of the different provinces, for *general* provincial expenditure.

the proposal to assess the land-revenues of provinces once and for all. Probably there are now very few persons of Indian experience who are likely to entertain any such proposition with favour; and for official purposes the question is dead and buried. But from time to time such questions recrudesce; and dressed up in showy and plausible arguments, they are made use of to the bewilderment of persons to whom the facts of the case are not familiar. I believe that a few pages devoted to the actual history of the question during the last twenty years, and to a plain statement of some of the leading considerations on the merits of the discussion, will not be without their use, nor wholly devoid of interest, especially to the non-official reader.

§ 1. *Official History of the Question.*

This question arose for the second time with reference to the Settlements of the North-Western Provinces[1].

When the thirty years' Settlements made under the Regulations of 1822 and 1833 began to fall in, the country was still suffering from the effects of the disorder produced by the Mutiny, and by the famine and cholera of 1860. Under such gloomy circumstances, the districts came up to be re-settled for a new term. The report on the famine of 1860–61 by Colonel Baird Smith, struck the key-note of praising the moderate assessments of the past Settlements, and treating them as an instalment of a gift which would be completed by making the moderate assessment *permanent*. The light assessments had enabled people to bear up against the famines in the last year better than they had done in the famine of 1837–38; and it was urged that if the assessment was made, not for thirty years but for ever, it would achieve still greater success. This report received, at the time, a good deal of commendation. There is, however, no

[1] I am indebted throughout to Mr. (now Sir A.) Colvin's admirable Memorandum on the Revision of Land Revenue in the North-Western Provinces, 1872 (Calcutta: Wyman and Co.). A collection of official papers regarding the Permanent Settlement was also reprinted in 1879.

sufficient reason to assume that the permanence of a Settlement has anything whatever to do either with the improvement of the land or the happiness of the people. And there are other considerations which the Report ignored. But the pendulum of general and official opinion swings in a long course from side to side in these revenue-administration questions,—permanency, tenant-right, and so forth; and at that period it was again on the descent towards the Permanent-Settlement side. It also happened that, in 1861, attention had been attracted to the unexploited *waste lands* of India. Forest conservancy had not then come under the public notice, and even if it had, the area of waste available for cultivation was large. Lord Canning, then Governor-General, wrote a minute on the subject; and it was argued that if the lands were sold free of any revenue demand, it would encourage their occupation and draw capital to this source of expected profit.

And naturally, from the question of occupying waste lands free of revenue charge, the Governor-General's remarks passed on to the possible advantages of a general *redemption* of the land-revenue on estates already occupied. The redemption was to be effected by paying up in one sum the prospective value of the revenue demand. On this, the Board of Revenue in the North-West Provinces advocated *a permanent settlement* (for, of course, the revenue must be permanently assessed before it could be redeemed). The Secretary of State, however, in 1862, rejected the policy of a redemption of land-revenue, but said he would listen to proposals for a permanent Settlement.

It needs no lengthened explanation to understand that so long as a district is not fully cultivated, and there is any serious prospect of alteration in its economic position, an assessment hastily made permanent must be ever after regretted. The form the problem took in 1862 was—What are the conditions which must be fulfilled *seriatim* before a district can be fit for a final revision of assessment, so that there need be no further change? At first it was assumed that when a careful revision of the existing (and then expiring) rates had been effected, and when no considerable increase of cultivation in future was probable, a permanent assessment might be practicable.

In 1864 the terms were formulated by the Government of India (and were modified at home in 1865). The condition was laid down that eighty per cent. of the culturable area should have been brought under cultivation, and then that the rate of permanent assessment need not be as low as fifty per cent. of the net assets (the rate at which the revenue demand had previously been fixed by the ordinary Settlement rules). But this was not satisfactory; and in 1867 another condition was added, regarding the probability of canal irrigation being extended to the lands in the next twenty years. This, of course, largely alters the rate of produce and the value of the land.

Then, it seems, officers were set to work to find out what districts or parts of districts could be permanently settled under these conditions. But in 1869 some cases came up (in the course of the inquiry) in which it was demonstrated that—although the conditions were satisfied—there would be a great prospective loss to Government by making the assessment permanent. Accordingly a third condition was recommended. The Government of India, in concurring, went so far as to say, what practically amounted to this, that a permanent Settlement should be deferred so long as the land continued to improve in value by any causes which were not the direct result of the occupant's own efforts.

It does not seem to have occurred to the supporters of the idea of a permanent Settlement, that it would be possible to secure all or nearly all the advantages, whatever they are, without the disadvantages of fixing a limit which—no matter what new combinations the future may produce—can never be altered. Still less did it seem to them necessary to be very cautious (in India) when we prophesy what *will* be the results, in the future, of any given proposal. For instance, let us refer to the difficulty which arises when a cash assessment is fixed for ever, and a fall in the value of money occurs. The reader of the present day will peruse with something like amazement, the remark in Sir Charles Wood's despatch of 1862, that the 'fall in the value of money was not of sufficient moment to influence the judgment of Her Majesty's Government to any material extent. Prices were unlikely to rise greatly: even if they should rise, the Government of India might easily find sources of income other than the land[1].'

But to continue: the practical outcome of the discussion at the time, was (as I have said) that a searching inquiry into the condition of districts was to be made, to see really what districts were in a condition that would satisfy the requirements of the case. Before this was completed, the very difficulty which Sir Charles Wood treated so lightly, actually overtook us;—the increasing depreciation of silver had begun seriously to embarrass the Indian Government; and the financial position afforded unmistakeable proof of the danger of attaching permanency to a money-assessment. For a time the subject dropped. But in 1882, it finally came up again in connection with the Resolution which the Government of India issued on the subject of reform in the procedure of Settlements. The key-note of this was, the possibility of securing the advantages derivable from a permanent Settlement, without abandoning the unquestioned claim of Government to share in the increase resulting from improvements made by itself, and from a general rise in prices.

As far as a question of permanent Settlement (pure and simple) is concerned, the Government of India despatch

[1] As a matter of fact, nothing is more difficult than to 'find the other sources.' While provision has now to be made for making an increasing charge in the Budget for loss by exchange, the subjects of taxation are extremely limited. The Income-tax, or a tax on trades and professions, is the main alternative, but it presents great difficulties. Nevertheless, it is interesting to mark that, as *Manu* contemplates the king taking a share from the produce of land, so also he gives him a share of the increase of the merchant and the manufacturer. (Chap. vii. 127–131; x. 120, &c.) The land-revenue becoming more and more in effect a tax on agricultural income, the tax on other incomes is its direct and logical counterpart. However this may be, it is certainly *not* easy to find other sources of revenue.

elicited from the Secretary of State a reply[1] which, after admitting the difficulty of finding other sources of revenue, noticing the change that had come over the financial position, and acknowledging that the anticipations of benefit from the permanent Settlement in Bengal had not been realised, concluded:—

'I concur with Your Excellency's Government that the policy laid down in 1862 should now be formally abandoned.'

And in writing to the North-Western Provinces Government the Government of India said[2]:—

'It is sufficient for present purposes to announce that Her Majesty's Secretary of State has now definitely agreed with the Government of India in rejecting the policy of a permanent Settlement pure and simple.'

§ 2. *General reflections on the principle of permanence.*

It is no part of this work, intended for practical purposes, to enter into discussions of principles. I desire to give the results rather than the details of controversies. At the same time, in a matter like this, which has so often been misrepresented, I may be pardoned for adding a few remarks. It would be difficult, in a thorough and unprejudiced inquiry which went beyond mere phrases, to discover any real argument for a permanent Settlement—I mean an argument in which the perpetuity of the assessment is the essential point—except the *one* that all future costs of re-settlement and all harassment to the people would be avoided. All other arguments (as far as they are not merely prophetic of imagined results) *may at once be admitted*, only they are equally true of any Settlement for which a fair term of duration is provided. And as regards the one argument which is real, the benefit is surely far outweighed by the admitted sacrifice of revenue, when it

[1] Despatch No. 24, dated 28th March, 1883.

[2] No. 525 R., dated 9th May, 1883.

is remembered that the process of re-settlement *can*, by judicious arrangements, be so carried out as to be very slightly, if at all, vexatious, and its cost reduced to a minimum.

As regards the 'prophetic arguments'—the hoped-for creation of a prosperous middle class, the improvement of the land and the growth of other sources of State income, expected from the permanent assessment, the experience (under most favourable conditions) in Bengal and Benares, shows that as a fact, though the assessment has become *very* light, nothing of the kind has happened[1]. As regards the greater encouragement to agriculture, and to the expenditure of capital on irrigation and other landlords' improvements, as a matter of fact, in no single province or district has a permanent Settlement been known to have any such effect.

In the first place it may be asked (with one of the Collectors in the North-Western Provinces)—as to improvements made by landlords, where, as a rule, are they? Generally, they are made at the expense of the cultivating tenants, at any rate in the end. And certainly where landlords do make improvements, little difference can be detected between permanently-settled and other estates. Here and there, a landlord makes improvements, because

[1] Nothing can be more curious than the results of a low assessment, whether fixed for ever or not. In one large district, at least, where a low assessment was secured for thirty years, the result has been, not that a wealthy class has arisen, but that simply all restraint has vanished, and the poor population has multiplied to such an extent that the wealth accumulated is not more able to support the increased mass of people than the former resources were to feed the then existing numbers. In other words, ten men have not grown rich by the rise of their income from R. 1000 to R. 10,000, but a thousand persons have appeared instead of ten, to live on the increased amount. Moreover, under native custom, properties become subdivided and again subdivided, till their value is frittered away; the money-lender steps in, and land again begins to aggregate in the hands of a class alien to agricultural knowledge and interests. All these economical questions, interesting as they are, are necessarily beyond the scope of my book. I must only add the notorious fact that in well-managed Native States, where the revenue is double, perhaps four times as high as in the British districts, the people are apparently as prosperous: only that, to be sure, their power of transferring their land is very limited, and there are no pleaders and few law courts!

he is an enlightened man, but it depends on the *man*, not on the supposed security[1].

Mr. J. R. Reid, Secretary to the Government, North-Western Provinces, giving his personal experience, wrote in 1873:—

'According to theory one should find estates like these (permanently settled) in the most flourishing condition, with all manner of improvements introduced, and landlords very well to do, and most liberal to their tenants. But, in fact, in riding through these villages, and through the *parganas* generally, you would not detect anything in the appearance of the people and land, in the number of wells and other means of irrigation, the kind and look of the crops, the size of the houses, the air and condition of the people and cattle, to make you suspect that the (permanently-settled) land-owners enjoy a different tenure from their neighbours of similar caste[2] and condition in temporarily-settled estates. There is as much capital laid out and industry bestowed on the land in the one set of estates as in the other.'

I could multiply testimony to the same effect; but the fact does not really admit of dispute.

This matter of improvements is connected directly with another question, which is not usually noticed by the advocates of a permanent Settlement. Does any landholder really believe in or realize, *permanency*? For example, will any one seriously contend that, looking at all the ups and downs of history, a Zamíndár in 1793 *realized* that the Government would last for ever, or even for a long period of years? Would not a promise of fixity for thirty or

[1] I would call attention to the curious case noted in the chapter on North-Western Provinces tenures, of the great improvements made by a Rájá of Benares, in the pargana of Bárí (Alláhábád), of which he was merely the auction-purchaser at a sale for arrears of revenue in 1820. Not only was there no kind of permanence about his Settlement, but the question of inquiry into revenue sales was then in the air, and this very sale was ultimately upset by the Special Commission, as an unjustifiable one. Yet the Rájá, during the years he held, made improvements on the most liberal scale, which doubled his rental.

[2] He mentions similarity of *caste*; because, for purposes of comparison, if the *caste* is altogether different, the result might be put down to that. Some *castes* are by nature good thrifty cultivators; others slovenly and bad: there is no ignoring the fact.

twenty years, even then, have seemed to him a period longer than he could count on? And at the present day, do the mass of unlettered but hard-working petty landowners ever think of anything so remote as fifty years hence, still less realize the idea of permanency, and act upon it[1]?

But even if it were otherwise, what possible right has one Government to bind (and seriously embarrass) its successors for all time? The effect of a permanent Settlement is practically this, that the Government of the day selects a certain class of estate or a special province, and says—'*You* shall never be called on to bear more than a certain share of the public burdens, no matter what your neighbours pay.' Of course, I am aware that other, and especially indirect, taxes may be imposed, but practically, in Bengal for instance, what are they? It is a fair estimate to make, that at present, for no conceivable reason, the class of Bengal landlords is contributing (proportionately) to the public expenditure, less than one-third of what any one else pays[2].

On the whole, therefore, it is impossible not to conclude that in theory, as binding future Governments and exempting certain classes from part of the burthen of taxation,

[1] As the Collector of Gorakhpur remarks '*Revenue-free* estates (in many the revenue is altogether remitted, be it remembered, *in perpetuity*) are as secure as they can be, but I do not find that this security adds to their selling value. Revenue-free and revenue-paying estates alike sell according to their immediate profits.'

[2] On this subject I may quote Mr. Justice H. S. Cunningham in an article on Indian Finance in the *Asiatic Quarterly Review* (April 1888). He says:—

'The question has sometimes been asked whether a compact so inherently inequitable as the Permanent Settlement, can be maintained under the altered conditions of succeeding times . . . A certain expenditure being, in existing circumstances, indispensable, it must be paid by some class or other, and no historical justification can get rid of the essential injustice of an arrangement by which those who benefit most by the administration should contribute least to its cost.'

It is interesting to note that as early as Col. Wilks' time (*The History of Mysore* was published about 1817) this aspect of a Permanent Settlement was not unperceived. Thus Col. Wilks wrote (*History*, p. 123), 'An English Chancellor of the Exchequer who should presume to pledge the national faith to an unalterable tax, might captivate the multitude, but would be smiled at by the financiers of Europe; yet principles do not alter in traversing the ocean.'

and not applied universally, the declaration of a permanently fixed land-tax is inadmissible. Further, that in practice, a general, unchangeable, assessment has no advantages which are not equally to be secured by a *moderate assessment* for a fairly long term of years. What that term should be, depends on a variety of considerations, local, as well as of principle; and though a certain concurrence of practice has resulted in thirty years or twenty years as an usual period, Government has wisely refused, by either legislative enactment or otherwise, to stereotype any rule. The circumstances of the Central Provinces have only recently demonstrated that periods from twelve to twenty years for the new Settlements, will be practically the best.

As to imaginary or anticipated encouragements and advantages to agriculture, it is idle to refer to them in the face of nearly a century's experience of what *has* happened in provinces where the experiment has been tried, and tried under very favourable circumstances. It certainly is high time that this 'policy' should now be regarded as 'formally abandoned.'

SECTION XII.—THE DEPARTMENT OF AGRICULTURE AND REVENUE.

Having thus sketched the development of the provincial land-revenue systems, the remainder of this 'General' chapter will deal, without reference to particular provinces (unless they are expressly named), with certain important matters of modern revenue-administration, which have of late years come into prominence—chiefly as the result of the inquiry into the whole subject of land-revenue administration which was made by the Famine Commission in 1879. It is hardly needed to point out that, except in limited tracts, the failure of the summer or autumn rains (as the case may be) brings famine as the great scourge of agricultural life in the Indian provinces. Serious famines in 1866 and in 1877-78—not to speak of others—led to the most earnest desire, *first*, to perfect a system of organized relief when famine actually occurs, and for this purpose to compile 'Famine Codes' giving the results of experience as to what is to be done and how to do it; but still more (in the *second* place) to see what could be done to put the administration in a state of preparedness against the occurrence of bad years. To effect this object the entire land administration machinery had to be overhauled, and all agricultural conditions reviewed. If I were asked to summarise, in a few words, what has been the most useful outcome of the reforms recommended, I should say,—the perfection of the *local* official machinery and of the records of fact which their work makes available for administrative purposes.

Without this knowledge of facts, you cannot have the difficulties of re-settlement overcome; you cannot have famine warning; you cannot have any agricultural improvement; and you cannot have good revenue-administration.

In order, therefore, to organize agricultural inquiry and record, and to improve revenue-administration, two things were necessary. A series of *Provincial Departments* charged with this special business, and an Imperial Department to guide and direct the general aims of each local centre of administration, without, of course, derogating either from the responsibility or the power of the Local Governments. Provincial Departments require a systematizing and controlling head; their necessary supplement is an Imperial department; and it may be justly said that one is of little use without the other.

I do not undervalue the importance of the labour which has given us a *Famine Code*; but that is outside the scope of this manual. And therefore I may seem to ignore one part of the Famine Commissioners' work, and only put forward what they intended to be a secondary object.

The Famine Commission was naturally more directly concerned with famine, its prevention and cure. It was therefore proposed that the Agricultural Department in each province should have three primary objects,—agricultural inquiry, agricultural improvement, and organization of famine relief. But it is obvious that there are other duties which the Government, looking beyond the single subject of famine, must require. In the first place, famines are not universal, and are happily only occasional, even in provinces subject to them. There are some whole provinces (like Assam) and parts of others, where anything like real famine is hardly known; nevertheless, there is ample scope for an Agricultural Department. Moreover, 'improvements in agriculture' cannot be effected in a short time. Too great a zeal is apt to cost much and come to very little. Before we can 'improve,' we must have full information as to facts. Agricultural *inquiry* must precede agricultural *improvement*.

And agricultural inquiry is equally important for famine purposes. 'The success of an Agricultural Department would mainly depend,' said the Famine Commission, 'on the completeness and accuracy with which agricultural and economic facts are collected in each village, and compiled in each subdivision and district throughout the country. Without a perfect system of local information, the warnings of approaching troubles are lost or misunderstood; and the liability of different parts of the district to calamity,—the weak points, on which a watchful eye has to be kept, are not known; and relief, in the shape of remissions and suspensions of the revenue demand, even when there is no widespread famine, is apt to be given imperfectly and with the least benefit.'

The branch of reform which it comes within my province to speak of, is therefore one which is by no means of secondary importance.

§ 1. *The Imperial Department of Revenue and Agriculture.*

An Imperial Department of Revenue and Agriculture had for some years past been in contemplation; and under Lord Mayo's viceroyalty one had been formed in 1870. But this was abolished in 1876[1], partly for financial reasons and partly because the measure was not successful, owing to its not being supported by corresponding departments in each province. It became, in fact, only an additional Secretarial Department, with a miscellaneous burden of public business; so far relieving other offices, but not effecting its own special object, because it had no corresponding machinery under each local government to give effect to its recommendations.

Sir John Strachey, however, when Lieutenant-Governor of the North-West Provinces in 1875, formed a local department on a new basis. The principle of action was that which I have already briefly indicated as the necessary preliminary, as well as the complement, to any direct method of preventing and remedying famines. The credit of clearly perceiving this principle and applying it in practice, is due to Mr. E. C. (now SIR EDWARD) BUCK, then serving under the North-West Provinces Government. The attention of the Revenue officers was directed first to the perfecting of the Land-Records and Agricultural Statistics, while agricultural improvement was kept in mind as a secondary, or

[1] The causes of failure are briefly alluded to in § 2 of the Resolution (Government of India) of 8th December, 1881. An undue amount and variety of subjects was thrown on the new Department; but what really prevented it effecting its special object, was the fact that no agency existed in the provinces with similar objects.

It was not till the discussion of the Famine Commissioners' Report, in 1880, that the scheme was again considered under better auspices. The branches of work actually taken up by the Revenue and Agricultural Department are—

Revenue.
Agriculture.
Famine.
Fibres and Silk.
Cattle-Breeding and Cattle-Disease.
Meteorology.
Fisheries.
Minerals.
Museums and Exhibitions.
Land-Trade and Agricultural Statistics.
Surveys (including Geological).
Emigration.
General.

rather as a subsequent, object. This may not be the most popular, but it is certainly the only practical ideal of an Agricultural Department in the present state of affairs. The maintenance of maps and land-records in a state of continuous correctness, not only leads to economy in the future, and facilitates re-assessment of the revenue, but provides a useful basis of agricultural statistics, and a knowledge of the peculiarities of the different districts. Without these, agricultural improvement cannot be attempted; it would be working in the dark, and spending money in vain on experiments that had no basis to start from.

The success of the system in the North-West Provinces has been marked; and when action was taken on the Famine Commissioners' Report, it was wisely determined to organize for each province a department on the same basis. The Imperial Department could now be reconstructed with every prospect of permanent utility, and the sanction of the Home Government was accordingly given; naturally Sir EDWARD BUCK was selected to be the first head[1].

The Imperial Department pays primary attention to the Land Administration, and to improving the system of assessing and collecting the land-revenue in each province. But the department is not unmindful of agricultural improvement, the introduction of valuable staples, the development of trade in Indian products, and the conduct of useful experiments in cultivation. It will, of course, supervise operations connected with famines when they occur. But the chief feature in the new arrangement has been the utilization, under efficient control, of the local agency in each village, for the purpose of maintaining maps, statistics, and records, correct and up to date each

[1] The head of the Department is, officially, one of the Secretaries to the Government of India (Department of Revenue and Agriculture). This plan was preferred to appointing a 'Director' of the Department. The Secretary is enabled, however, to spend part of his time on tour, and thus can arrange on the spot, or in conference with the local authorities, many matters that could not be so quickly or so well disposed of by correspondence.

year. The economy thus effected in the cost of Settlements has been estimated[1] to have already secured a saving of two hundred *lakhs* of rupees; and it is likely to realize, in the future, an annual saving of from twelve to sixteen *lakhs*.

§ 2. *The Provincial Departments.*

In order to emphasize the importance of that part of the scheme which is directed to perfecting, and keeping correct, the Agricultural and Land-Records, it was officially determined that the heads of the Provincial Departments should be called 'Directors of Land-Records and Agriculture[2].' The departments have many other duties which I cannot here describe, and which, of course, must vary according to the requirements and local conditions of the several provinces. The conduct of agricultural experiments, the care of veterinary schools, and model farms (where these exist), are among the most obvious[3].

The Resolution of the Government of India (8th December, 1881, on Agricultural Departments) concludes :—

'The views of the Government of India may be summed up by saying that the foundation of the work of an Indian Agricultural Department should be the accurate investigation of facts, with a view of ascertaining what administrative course is necessary to preserve the stability of agricultural operations.

[1] See the Finance Members' Budget Speech (1888) in the *Gazette of India*. The *lakh*, I may remind English readers, is 100,000,—a lakh of rupees is £10,000 conventionally, i.e. if the rupee is two shillings.

[2] Resolution Government of India) Financial No. 608, dated 9th February, 1887.

[3] The establishment of Agricultural Departments had not long proceeded before a financial inquiry was made as to whether they would be successful. Fortunately, this has resulted in a satisfactory verdict. But, in fact, these Departments are defensible in the highest degree, on their own merits. The 'District Officer' has, by the legislation of the last twenty years, had an almost continually increasing burden thrown upon him; and the Land-Records Department gave sorely-needed relief and help in a matter of peculiar importance. In discussing the financial question, such a consideration is necessarily left out of sight; but if the Agricultural Departments resulted in less saving than is actually the case, the enormous good done by the improvement of land records would amply justify their existence. I know of no ono administrative measure of greater benefit to the country than the establishment of these Departments.

. . . The primary efforts of the Department should . . . be devoted to the organization of agricultural inquiry, which has been shown to comprise the duties of gauging the stability of agricultural operations in every part of a province, of classifying the areas of the province according to the results of careful investigation, and of deciding what method of administrative treatment is suitable to each so as to maintain agricultural operations at the highest standard of efficiency possible under present conditions. . . . From a system . . . of inquiry thus conducted will follow the gradual development of agricultural improvement.'

SECTION XIII.—REFORM IN PROCEDURE FOR RE-SETTLEMENTS.

The establishment of Agricultural and Land-Record Departments, it is hardly too much to say, alone rendered the real simplification of the Settlement work of the present and future possible.

Already, by Resolution in October 1881[1], the Government of India had called attention to the fact that when the Settlements fell in, it did not follow that a re-settlement, in any shape, was to be undertaken as a matter of course. The sanction of the Government of India was required to new Settlement operations; and it was to be considered, in all cases, whether any such increase in the revenue was probable as would make it worth while to undertake them. Four points were especially to be noted—the probable cost of the operations, the time they would take, the increment of revenue expected, and the incidence of the existing revenue on the individual landholders.

If there could be no increase (or less than one which represented a profitable rate of interest on the total anticipated expenditure), revision should ordinarily not be

[1] No. 144, dated 4th October, 1881. It did not apply to the Governments of Bombay and Madras; though of course similar principles would be recognized in those presidencies.

undertaken, unless, indeed, a revision was needed because of the inequality of incidence of the last assessment.

§ 1. *New System of Land Records and their Maintenance.*

But this 'Resolution' only touched the fringe of the subject. The whole question of re-settlements, and the means of reducing their cost, and depriving them of all their inconveniences to the district population, is one of such importance that it is desirable to explain at some length how the work of the Land-Record Departments affects it. The sketch given in preceding sections will have shown how very gradually the work of assessment has been reduced to a method, or rather to different methods, suited to the varying circumstances of each province. There remained still the difficulty that, however 'scientific' the method, hitherto the work of a new Settlement has been very costly and very troublesome; and the more elaborate the method, the more costly and prolonged the operations. The difficulty arose from the fact that it has hitherto been unavoidable, in making a Settlement, to have a special staff of Surveyors and Settlement Officers, with all their subordinates and office staff, to record facts, compile statistics, fair out records, and so forth. Such a staff, in the nature of things, during the whole of its stay, harasses the people not a little[1], and it upsets all the regular work in '*tahsíls*' and of the *kánúngos* and *patwárís*. But suppose that at last the work is at an end; the Settlement records are all faired out and bound in volumes, and the maps mounted; the originals are deposited in the Collector's Revenue Record Office; the copies disposed of at the tahsíl and in the patwárí's office or 'patwár-khána' in the village. How soon these records, correct as they may have been at a given

[1] To say nothing of the petty demands that subordinate officials always make when they are in camp, in the shape of supplies, grass, firewood, and such like; even if the foolish landholders do not think it necessary to pay fees and *douceurs* to secure more or less imaginary benefits. It is impossible wholly to prevent such things, when the entire population practises and tolerates them.

date, cease to correspond with facts! New fields are added to the cultivated area out of the waste; old fields change shape or boundary; they are aggregated or divided. New wells are sunk, new roadways are substituted for old ones, and many other such changes take place. Then, again, proprietors are continually altering; a certain number of sales are notified, and the usual applications for mutation of names are made and allowed; but whether the fact has ever found its way into any such record that the Settlement list could be corrected, is another matter. The result of all this (and much more could be said if space permitted) is that, hitherto, when the thirty years (let us suppose) of Settlement expired, the whole of the records, prepared originally with so much care, have proved out of date, and more or less useless. There is, then, nothing for it but to re-survey the whole area, and to make out fresh maps and records, putting the whole district once more—for several years—into the state of unrest already described, to the great detriment of agriculture, as well as of administrative and social well-being.

If only the separate records could be abolished; if only a certain set of necessary papers—the large scale-map showing every field and every detail of the estate, the index-register to this; the list of proprietors, their shares and interests, and the revenue they pay; the list of tenants and their rents; and any such supplemental statistics as local rules might require,—if only these could be placed in the hands of a village patwárí, tested and signed as correct up to a given date, viz. the commencement of a new Settlement; and if thenceforward these maps and statements could be continually corrected, fresh fields plotted in, and statements periodically recopied and kept up to date; when the term of Settlement expired, the 'Record-of-rights' would be found as correct and conformable to facts as when it began. Then the Collector himself, or perhaps a specially-deputed officer, could soon make out the necessary schedules for revising the assessment, and the 're-settlement' would be over.

But to secure such an ideal procedure, several things are necessary. First, the staff of village *patwárís* and inspecting *kánúngos* must be well taught and made competent to do the survey work that the maintenance of village maps involves. Next, their work must be continually inspected, tested, and corrected, till the machine works without friction and failure.

Next, the rules for assessment, applicable to future revisions, must be reduced to the greatest simplicity.

The first of the steps above indicated has everywhere been taken. Schools have been opened for the instruction of *patwárís* and their sons in surveying and other necessary branches of education. The whole staff has been graded and organized, and rules made for its appointment and control.

Speaking generally, each *patwárí* has a circle of three or four villages, and the inspecting officers or *kánúngos* are continually moving about and testing the measurements and the accuracy of entries in the books made by the *patwárí*. There is also what is called a *Registrar kánúngo*, at the head-quarters of the *tahsíl* or local subdivision, who keeps the books and compiles the village returns into corresponding subdivisional returns. To give a general idea of how the village staff is manned and supervised, it may be mentioned that in the North-West Provinces (excluding Oudh) the number of *patwárís* is about 20,000, the field inspectors or *kánúngos* number 450, or one to every 45 *patwárís*. The average area of a *patwárí's* circle is 1,130 acres (cultivated), so that the local inspecting officer looks after above 50,000 cultivated acres; the whole establishment costs somewhat more than 23·75 lakhs of rupees, the reorganized establishments and their supervision costing about two lakhs more than the old establishment of *patwárís* and *kánúngos*.

It will be seen, then, how this improvement will increasingly render possible the greatest reform of all in re-settlement operations,—namely, the carrying out of revision operations without an elaborate re-valuation of lands, and by the aid of the ordinary district staff, with the smallest possible addition of special establishments. Instead of having elaborate volumes of special records, prepared and put into an office to become totally useless at the end of thirty years, and another set of village and pargana accounts increasingly out of correspondence with the first, we shall have one set of simple maps and records attested as correct for a given date and thenceforward kept up, because papers in exactly the same forms will be in the hands of the staff to be continually corrected from day to day [1].

I need only add, that the records will not only help the work of revision of Settlement; they will affect every branch of revenue-administration, for they will, in time, put us in possession of what I may call *analytical knowledge of the districts*; the knowledge, as regards each estate and group of lands, whether it is fully developed, well cultivated, and secure from famine, or only partially so, and what estates must be treated as 'precarious.' This knowledge will be the very key to famine prevention and relief, as well as to management of estates in the matter of granting timely suspensions and remissions of revenue in bad years, and to the adoption of a more elastic system of

[1] This is what Sir Alfred Lyall wrote on the subject :—

'It is hoped that, under the regular inspection and supervision now given from year to year by the district establishment, and subject to certain checks and corrections, a body of statistics can, during the currency of existing Settlements, be got ready for each estate, upon which, without minute inquiry, a summary and fairly accurate estimate of the rental assets might be made. This system would, it is thought, provide the best possible method of securing for Government its full share of enhanced rentals. It would, moreover, provide, from time to time, for a tolerably equal distribution of the land-tax, a point on the propriety and expediency of which much stress is laid by those consulted. It would put an end, in districts already properly settled, to all formal and minute valuations of the land; it would, in great measure, do away with the systematic enhancements and levelling up of rents that formed part of the duty of the Settlement Officer, and by the keeping up, along with the other statistics, of a careful record of improvements made by landlords and cultivators, the profits of these improvements might be secured to them. The body of statistics under collection from year to year could at any time be made open to the scrutiny of the proprietors of the land, who might thereby be able to forecast, with a certain degree of assurance, the revenue for which they would become liable.'

fluctuating assessments for precarious tracts, and, ultimately, to really beneficial schemes of agricultural improvement.

§ 2. *The principles of reassessment or revision of Land-Revenue.*

The Government of India, on the 17th October, 1882, issued a Resolution indicating certain principles on which re-assessments should be made. I wish to state the plan propounded as a whole, but at once premising that it was a tentative proposal, and has not been adopted in its entirety. The original scheme was (1) that *enhancements* of revenue should only be allowed on the ground of—

(*a*) rise in prices,
(*b*) increase in cultivation,
(*c*) improvements made at Government expense.

This proposal eliminated, as a general rule, *all fresh attempts to value land.* The fact is, the majority of districts have been thoroughly surveyed, and soils classified; and if the local establishment do their duty in keeping the Records, and the maps on which they are based, up to date in the manner above described, there should be only in exceptional cases any necessity for further valuation.

The 'rise in prices' principle (*a*) was to be applied with two very important limitations. In the first place, to guard against the effect of small or uncertain fluctuations, small rises of prices were to be disregarded; nor need the enhancement be in full proportion to the rise, but so as to leave a margin with a view to meeting any increase in the cost of agriculture, and of providing for a rise in the standard of living.

In the second place, enhancement, on the ground of rise in prices, was also to be limited to fifteen per cent. on the former rate.

For the purpose of calculating prices, years of scarcity were to be eliminated, for prices are then abnormal. Certain staples and certain market localities, it was suggested, might be taken for the purposes of calculation, and the prices of, say, the decade before the current Settlement, should be compared with those of the concluding decade.

(2) In order to give landowners immediate assurance of their future position, an assessment should, except in backward districts, be declared for each estate as soon as possible, which the Resolution called the 'initial assessment,' which should not be altered when the re-settlement began, except on one or more of the above grounds.

This point has, however (in particular) been given up, as it was found impracticable.

(3) That measures should be taken to secure to tenants the same protection against enhancement of their rents, as would be offered to landlords in respect of the revenue.

These proposals were generally and in principle agreed to by the Governments of Madras and Bombay. In the North-Western Provinces, however, they met with elaborate criticism; and the Secretary of State [1], while approving the general object of the Resolution, also felt doubts about the details.

The arguments about the inequality of the incidence of the revenue-demand under existing Settlements, and therefore the difficulty of fixing an 'initial assessment,' may be passed over, as this portion of the scheme stands abandoned.

The principal objection in the North-Western Provinces, was on the question of enhancing solely with reference to *rise in prices*. It must be admitted at once that the application of the principle of a rise in prices is easier in a *raiyatwárí* province, or in the Panjáb, where the revenue approximates more to a money sum representing a share in the produce obtained by the cultivating proprietor. But in the North-Western Provinces the land is cultivated by cash-paying tenants, and the revenue is now a certain share of the rental; and the objection was

[1] No. 24, dated 22nd March, 1883.

stated that in the North-Western Provinces 'prices do not affect rents immediately or otherwise than at long intervals.' Under any circumstances, the prices looked to should be prices at the *pargana capital*, where produce is sold by agriculturists; and harvest prices, not averages of other months, should be taken. It was also urged that rises in prices could not be counted on as permanent, and that if they fell naturally after a revision made on the strength of what appeared at the time, there would be no remedy but to resort to remissions of the revenue, which would be unsatisfactory.

There were minor objections, such as that the system would benefit different tracts unevenly, and that in consequence of the varying proportion of staples in different tracts, there would be some difficulty in adjusting any calculation of what the rise in prices was, which would be fair to all. The Government of India admitted that any rise in prices counted on ought to be widespread; that it was not to be one affecting small areas but whole provinces, while it would be easy to allow for an additional demand on any particular district or tract where a new railway or canal had produced a durable and marked local effect on prices. It was also admitted that the difficulty about existing rents not following prices, was a serious one; but reference was made to a possible change in the tenant law, by which enhancements would necessarily be brought about almost wholly with reference to prices; and if so, revenue enhancement would follow the same rule[1].

[1] Briefly, I may explain that in the North-West Provinces, occupancy-tenants' rents are in practice enhanced only on the first of the grounds allowed by the law (Section 13, Act XII of 1881); i. e. they are enhanced up to the 'prevailing' rate, which, in effect, is the rate assumed as fair by the Settlement Officer in his calculations. Occupancy-tenants must now have held the *same* land in the village for twelve years, therefore they are a minority; and the ordinary tenant is, by competition, paying more than the 'prevailing' rates, as above explained. But should the law be changed to allow all tenants having held *any* land in the village for twelve years, to claim occupancy, then the majority would become occupancy-tenants, of whom the older ones would soon become equalised as to rates, and the new ones would be already paying *above* these rates; so that the application for enhancement on the ground that the 'tenant was paying below

It is unnecessary to go into the subject further, as there is no present prospect of the tenant law of the North-Western Provinces being altered so as largely to increase the number of occupancy-tenants.

§ 3. *The present state of the question.*

In a despatch of 16th August, 1884 (No. 16), the Government of India reviewed the objections of the North-Western Provinces, and informed the Secretary of State that they had abandoned the plan of framing initial revenue assessments, and they continued:—

'We shall have no objection in the more recently assessed districts, to the entire exclusion of new land from assessment on any estate in which the increase could be proved to be below a certain percentage. We would divide *districts*, not estates, into two classes:

'(1) those in which the revenue is fairly adequate, which would include the majority of districts assessed within the last twenty years; and

'(2) those earlier assessed districts in which rentals have considerably outgrown the revenue.

'The *latter* should be re-assessed according to the method proposed by Sir A. Lyall (Lieutenant-Governor of the North-Western Provinces) [i. e. the latest Settlement rules under which the *actual* rent-rolls, corrected only to supply positive errors, and to give rents for non-rented land liable to assessment, without prospective and calculated additions, are made use of]. The *former* (should be re-assessed) on the principles stated in our first despatch, subject to the modifications now suggested; one of the conditions would be the fifteen per cent. maximum (enhancement). The rise in prices would be determined primarily by a consideration of the prices in the whole province, subject, perhaps, to a further scrutiny in particular districts of the effect on them of improved communications.'

The Secretary of State replied in a despatch (No. 4, Revenue) of 8th January, 1885. It was observed generally

the "prevailing rate" for other tenants of the same class,' &c., would cease to be operative, and *then* the second ground allowed by the tenant law—rise in prices—would be the chief one.

that some of the objections to the original scheme were admitted, and that others depended for their removal on an alteration of the tenant law, which was not regarded as practicable; but that much remained which might be usefully carried into practice. As the despatch gives the final orders on the subject, I may now sum up both the discussions which I have been describing, and the general subject of the *latest rules for the simplification of the procedure in the re-settlements*, by giving the actual principles sanctioned :—

(1) The permanent Settlement idea is formally abandoned;

(2) the State shall still retain its claim to share in 'the unearned increment' of the value of land to which there is a tendency in a progressive country;

(3) that a general and permanent rise in the prices of produce is one of the principal indications and measures of this increment;

(4) that it is nevertheless desirable to modify the existing system of revision of the temporary settlements of land-revenue with a view of rendering it less arbitrary, uncertain, and troublesome to the people;

(5) that the modification should be effected at least in the following particulars :—

(*a*) repetition of field operations (survey, valuation, minute inquiries into assets, and the like) which are considered to be inquisitorial and harassing to the people, should be, as far as possible, dispensed with;

(*b*) enhancement should be based mainly on considerations of general increase in the value of land;

(*c*) the assessment will not be revised *merely* with a view to equalizing its incidence with that of the assessment of other estates;

(*d*) improvements made by the land-holders themselves should not be taken into account in revising assessments; but improvements made at the cost of the State should be taken into account, and also, to some extent, increase of cultivation.

As regards more detailed rules, the Secretary of State observed:—

'It is not desirable that I should attempt to lay down, for the guidance of the Local Governments, rules for the revision of Settlements. But I may state the general principles upon which, in my opinion, such operations should be conducted, subject to the conditions specified' [viz. the Nos. 1 to 5 above given].

'All tracts (whether whole districts or parts) which were in a backward condition [when the existing assessments were framed, and where the subsequent process of development has produced inequalities so great and numerous as to make the application of any general uniform rate of enhancement unadvisable and unfair [1]] will be excluded from the scheme, because the present assessment would evidently afford no proper basis for the future assessment. These tracts must be left for regular [re-]settlement.

'As regards other localities, when a Settlement is about to expire, a summary inquiry should be made into the condition and resources of the tract . . . and upon the results of this inquiry the Local Government, with the approval of the Government of India, should determine the general rate of enhancement to be applied to the tract. The factors to be taken into consideration would be, general rise in agricultural prices, in actual rentals, and in letting-value and sale-price of land; and care would, of course, be taken, that the increment determined on should be such as would not unduly raise the revenue, certainly not in any case beyond fifty per cent. of the "apparent assets" [i.e. the assets obtained by consideration of the factors above mentioned, of which the 'actual rental' was the amount which the assessing officer, on a consideration of the estate or tract, was led to consider the *proper actual rental* [2]].

[1] This explanation was approved by the Secretary of State in a later despatch.

[2] The term in the despatch is 'apparent assets' which was explained to mean what I have put in brackets; the proper 'actual rental' does not include, be it remembered, any prospective rise in rent or (in this class of estate) any increase in the cultivated area (Revenue Despatch, Secretary of State, No. 65, dated 30th July, 1885).

'There is no necessity for determining beforehand what shall constitute the unit of area . . . to which the same rate of increment will apply. That must depend on local conditions. It might be a whole district, or, when the conditions of progress vary, different sections of it. Within that area, the rate of increment, as determined by the Local Government, would, as a rule, be applied by the Settlement officer rateably all round. But it should be in his discretion to treat special cases exceptionally. There may be tracts, or groups of estates, to which a rate higher than the average rate should be applied, —such, for example, as have benefited by improvements made at the expense of Government, or where there has been an unusual increase of cultivation or rise of rental. There may very probably, on the other hand, be estates in which, from over-assessment or other cause, it may not be expedient to take the whole increase, or any part of it, or in which possibly even a reduction of the existing demand may be expedient. And objecting proprietors might have the option . . . of a regular revision.'

The practice now is, under these orders, to draw up a programme of Settlement work with reference to supervision of survey operations and other considerations; and the Government lays down instructions for the Settlement of each district[1].

[1] For example, I may abstract the 'Jaláun' district instructions (December, 1884) in a few words:—

1. No new survey or soil-classification or records (except in seventeen villages for special reasons).

2. Revision to be an actual recorded rent-roll corrected (1) to put a rent on 'sír'; (2) to correct fraudulent concealments of rent; (3) correct rent for fields held rent-free or at 'manifestly inadequate' rents. The actual rentals to be average of six years (from 1878-1883-4). Instructions go on to explain how the rent-rolls should be verified, and it should be tested what area really *is* 'sír,' and what held by tenants of this class and that; what is to be done when a particular village has a fraudulent or wholly inaccurate rent-roll. Observations are added about fraudulently inadequate rates as distinguished from those allowed at favourable rates on customary grounds; and about determining the area that is really 'sir.' The question of 'imposing fixed *maxima* of enhancement' is reserved.

The Government of the North-Western Provinces have also issued general rules for assessment (under Act XIX of 1873), which I have spoken of in detail in the chapters on the North-Western Provinces.

§ 4. *Instalments of Land-Revenue.*

Another subject of consideration has been the fixing of the most convenient dates for the payment of the Government revenue. This payment could not be conveniently made in one sum for the year, nor on any purely calendar arrangement of quarter-days, &c. In some Settlements it is expressly provided that it shall be paid in a certain way. It is obvious that this matter requires attention, and that the power of the people to pay without difficulty, largely depends on the suitableness of the time of demand.

In places where the revenue-payers are landlords or employers of tenants, their power of payment depends on their first having time to collect their rents. And in its turn this depends on the power of the cultivators to find the money for the rents. Rent, again, cannot be paid till the harvest is realized; and this condition applies also to the *raiyat*, who pays revenue direct to the State, and to the petty cultivating proprietor who does the same, indirectly.

Here there are usually two harvests to be considered; some pay most of their revenue from the 'rabi,' or spring harvest; others, from the autumn, or 'kharíf'; others part from both. If a principal part is demanded when the harvest relied on is not yet got in, the payer must borrow the money at high interest; and though, when the produce is presently sold, he may pay back to the money-lender a portion of the debt, he will not be able to repay the whole. If, on the other hand, the date for payment is so fixed that the cultivator has got in his money by sale of his produce, and yet the village headman will not receive it, he is very likely to spend this sum, or lose it in some way, before the time comes for the revenue payment [1].

[1] In a very able paper on Instalments in Berár, Mr. W. B. Jones mentions the difficulty of getting into the districts the requisite amount of silver money to pay the revenue:—

'It is the weak point in our system that by concentrating the payments of land-revenue on one or two dates it adds enormously to the difficulties of the cultivator. For a small province like Berár to pay thirty lakhs of silver rupees into the treasury on the 15th Janu-

On this important subject the Government of India issued a Resolution (No. 15 R., dated 3rd May, 1882).

The leading idea is to establish a 'normal proportion between the amount of revenue collected and the amount of produce gathered at harvest'—to establish a closer connection between current liabilities and current assets [1]. And it is not only for whole districts that this has to be seen to; agricultural circumstances vary within much more limited tracts. 'Attention has lately been drawn to the case of three adjacent villages, in one of which the cash of the agricultural community is principally obtained from rice at the end of the rainy season; in the second, from a sugar-harvest in January; in the third, from cereals in spring. Yet for all these villages the same dates were fixed for the payment of rent and revenue.' Attention was also drawn to the matter I have alluded to in a foot-note: 'The sudden demand for large quantities of silver money on certain dates, causes prices to fall (because of the withdrawal of silver) while the rate of interest rises; grain has to be thrown into a slackened market, and loans must be negotiated on usurious terms.'

The result has been to call for an inquiry in each province as to the practice. The North-Western Provinces Government has issued rules on the subject.

ary, and thirty lakhs on the 15th March, is a stupendous financial operation—an operation which causes violent fluctuations in the price of produce—fluctuations which give the *baniya* (grain-dealer and money-lender) his opportunities. If we could but make these vast sums flow into the treasury in equal monthly amounts, the benefit to the cultivating classes would be great indeed. For they would then be able to raise the loans they require to pay the revenue at the true market rate. As things now are, the enormous demand which takes place all at once, enables, I might almost say compels, the *baniya* to ask exorbitant interest.'

[1] The Famine Commissioners remark (*Report*, Part II, Chap. iii, Sec. 3. § 2):—

'Where one crop is mostly reserved for food, and another mostly sold, if the circumstances of the people require it, larger instalments should be made payable upon the crop which is raised for the market, and smaller instalments upon that which is raised for food. The dates for payment should also be fixed so as to allow of the produce being harvested and sold before the instalment is collected, so as to avoid the losses which the landowner would suffer if he were compelled to raise money on an unripe crop, or sell it hastily in an overstocked market.'

SECTION XIV.—REMISSION AND SUSPENSION OF LAND-REVENUE.

§ 1. *Suspension—when sufficient, and when not.*

Another subject of great importance is the granting of relief when a bad year, or a succession of bad years, occurs.

Ordinarily, the revenue is calculated at rates which are fair for the average of years, good and bad together; so that, speaking generally, if one crop fails outright, but the next is good, the cultivator ought to be sufficiently relieved by the *suspension* of the demand for the instalment of one crop, payment being demanded only on the occurrence of the *second* of two successive good harvests. But sometimes there comes a more serious calamity, and suspended revenue has to be remitted altogether. This causes disturbance in the estimates, which is often embarrassing.

§ 2. *General considerations.*

The principle of the Native governments, which cared nothing about estimates and financial equilibrium, was always to be elastic; they ran up the nominal revenue to a high figure, which they perhaps rarely exacted to the full. But, from the first, our system has been to fix a very moderate revenue, and demand an exact payment; failing this, in Bengal, the sale of the estate is at once ordered, and in other provinces, various coercive measures.

Fortunately the progress of the country has been such, that the land-revenue is collected with remarkable facility, and the issue of coercive processes is mostly confined to the minor forms—mere notices or threats to the careless, rather than serious action against defaulters; but still there is a rigidity about our system that, whatever its justification, is not always acceptable to the Oriental mind [1].

[1] The following remarks in the BANDA Settlement Report (p. 150) by Mr. A. Cadell struck me:— 'Our system of Settlement and land-revenue collection is logically a good one, and is theoretically

There is also much difficulty in dealing with districts—of which Gurgáoṅ in the Panjáb occurs to me as an example—where, sometimes for three or four years together, if there is a sufficient rainfall, the qualities of the prevalent soils are such, that excellent, and more than excellent, crops are obtained. Then come a series of bad years: the rain fails, and lands that were before fertilized by a deposit of soil washed down from the low hills (dahrí), are left untilled: or again, if rain is in irregular excess, they may be over-flooded and water-logged. Unless we adopt variable or fluctuating rates, *any* fixed assessment can hardly work. If it is very low, it will sacrifice revenue needlessly in good years; and in bad years, even then it will not be easily, if at all, paid. It seems hardly possible to manage such areas, except on the plan of allowing the *Collector a power of immediate action in bad years.* In this matter, we should take a lesson from the best Native governments. It will be seen that their principle was always to keep up the assessment pretty high, but allow of an immediately-acting and thoroughly elastic system of easing off in bad years. Our system, it is true, tends to make the land-revenue partake, somewhat, of the nature of a *tax*; and rigidity and certainty are the necessary features of a proper tax-administration: they have their advantage in compelling thrift and habits of forethought. But land-revenue is not wholly a tax, and cannot be effectively treated wholly on the principles of one.

just and fair; we fix a demand based neither on the abundance of good seasons nor on the poverty of bad; we argue that the proprietor who gets more than his due in bumper seasons can afford to pay more than his half share of the rental in unfavourable years. But, unhappily, it is as true now as it was sixty years ago when Mr. Holt Mackenzie made the remark, that "men, especially men so improvident as the natives of India, do not live by averages"; and the attempt to collect a revenue, in itself not excessive, through good years and through bad, has been the great motive of the irregularities which in Bundélkhand, more than elsewhere, have disgraced our administration. Theorists may argue that if men do not put by money in good seasons they deserve no mercy; but the same argument pushed a little further would condemn the improvident to death as well as ruin, when the next period of scarcity arrives.'

§ 3. *Government orders on the subject.*

The Government of India's Resolution issued on the subject in October, 1882, was intended to indicate the lines of a policy rather than issue hard-and-fast orders. It suggested that, in order to enable the Government officers to know how to act, and in order to systematize knowledge, five principal measures should be taken in hand :—

(1) the classification of agricultural land according to the security or insecurity of its yield;

(2) the adaptation of the system to the character of each class;

(3) the extension of relief granted to landlords, to the tenant class also;

(4) an investigation into the outturn of every harvest;

(5) the making more definite the authority of local officers to act at once.

It was suggested that estates (and even parts of estates might require to be noted in this respect) should be classified into those (1) which are, to a great extent, *secure* against failure of crops, by having a fair proportion of their area irrigated; (2) those in which, in abnormal seasons, suspensions, or ultimately remissions, are likely to be needed (called *insecure* areas); (3) areas in which cultivation is so uncertain in its result as to render an annual adjustment requisite: these may be termed 'fluctuating areas.'

As to the first and fourth measures noted above, it is sufficient to remark that the improved land records and statistics, subject as they are to constant inspection and testing, ought in time to secure good results, whether in the form of village and pargana note-books, containing an account of each estate, or in the form of specially-coloured maps and tabulated lists of villages and estates,—as provincial circumstances may suggest. The second head indicates that in 'secure' estates, suspensions or remissions would only become necessary in the rare case of some special plague of locusts, hail, or other calamity. 'Insecure' areas would

B b 2

require a ready power of suspension, which has to be systematized by indicating the duty of the District Officer and the Commissioner, and their respective powers to act on their own authority; defining the cases in which reference to the chief controlling authority and to Government is requisite[1].

Whether suspension is temporarily granted, or is more formally sanctioned for a definite period under orders of higher authority, the ultimate grant of *remission* depends on the orders of Government; and where the remission aggregates ten per cent. of the entire land-revenue of the province, the previous sanction of the Government of India is required.

§ 4. *Fluctuating Assessments.*

The plans for 'fluctuating assessment' vary according to circumstances. In principle they proceed more or less on the lines of assessing at fixed *average rates* (for different qualities of soil), and charging those rates only when, after the crop is or ought to be mature, it is known what acreage was actually productive. An account of a special 'fluctuating system,' applied in the recent Settlement, will be found in the chapter on Ajmer-Merwára.

In several parts of the Panjáb, including riverain villages liable to violent and extensive changes by river action, as well as tracts liable to flood or where the rainfall is extremely small and uncertain, fluctuating assessments are also employed. Speaking generally, the basis of the method is, to fix certain differential rates for classes of land bearing crops, which rates are levied on an annual (or a harvest) measurement of the land which actually bore a crop. Partial failure in the yield is allowed for by deduction in the total. Newly cultivated land is always

[1] A certain graduated scale of powers, according to the greater or less fraction of the crop lost, was suggested, but is too much in detail to be practised. The rules under which Collectors and other officers can act in the North-Western Provinces are stated in the special chapter on Administrative business.

allowed a reduction for the first year or two. In some cases, besides the fluctuating rate, a small fixed acreage rate is levied on account of the value which the land has as waste or grazing ground even when not cultivated.

§ 5. *Relief to Tenants.*

As regards the benefit of revenue relief granted to landlords being passed on to tenants, that is a matter which is provided for in some of the Tenant Acts [1], and is then a question of law; otherwise it may be a matter of conditions annexed to the grant of the relief.

It may be added that the Secretary of State has decided against the principle of charging *interest* on revenue dues *suspended.*

SECTION XV.—CONCLUSION.

Conspectus of the Systems.

I conclude this introductory and general sketch, first with a diagram which will recall the chief features of the development of our revenue systems, and next with a table taken from the Government of India's printed 'Statistical Returns, 1886-87,' which will give some idea of the general effect and results of land-revenue Settlements.

As an *appendix* to the chapter, I also reproduce an able and instructive *résumé* of the financial aspects of Settlement work contained in the Honourable J. Westland's Budget Note for 1888–89 [2].

[1] See, for example, Section 23, Act XII of 1881; Act IX of 1883, Sections 65 and 73.

[2] I may remind the reader that, to save useless printing of figures, it is customary to print not 'Rupees' but 'Rx,' i.e. ten rupees, and then to omit *three cyphers.* So the Rx 27 means 2,70,000 rupees.

(A.)—Settlement with Landlords, or Joint-bodies.

The Bengal system of 1790–93 (seeks to declare some person to be landlord or proprietor, and secure his position, between the cultivator and the State).

Permanent Settlement with Zamíndárs as proprietors, (1793,) with no survey, no record of rights, and no defined method of assessment.

Improved system of Regulation VII of 1822 and Regulation IX of 1833; non-permanent Settlements with survey and record of rights and prescribed method of assessment.

- Settlement with *proprietary joint communities*, through a representative; **North-Western Provinces: the Panjáb and Ajmer.**
- Settlement with *Taluqdárs* over the communities; **Oudh.**
- Settlement with *málguzárs* over the individual occupants of villages; **Central Provinces.** Tenants' rents fixed as well as the proprietor's revenue payments by the Settlement-officer.

(B.)—Settlement with Raiyats or Individual Occupants.

The Bengal system first applied to Madras, but afterwards prohibited; still survives as regards some of the estates. Attempts in some districts to make joint-village Settlements.

Madras Raiyatwárí system (1820); occupants regarded as proprietors. Settlement for thirty years; uniform system of assessment with annual remissions. Re-settlements confined by rule to alterations resulting from a rise in prices—no general Revenue Code.

Bombay Raiyatwárí system of field assessment; no theory of ownership; occupant has right defined by law. Settlement for thirty years only: system of assessment uniform and defined by rules. A complete Revenue Code enacted.

Other systems, in principle Raiyatwárí (no middleman) of **Assam, Burma, Coorg, &c.**

APPENDIX.

Extract from the Supplement to the Gazette of India.

(*March 31st*, 1888.)

'*Land-Revenue during the twelve months ending September 30th.*

(In thousands of Rx.)	1881.	1882.	1883.	1884.	1885.	1886.	1887.
India . . .	99	91	88	96	110	110	116
Central Provinces.	608	609	612	613	613	615	619
Burma . . .	1,036	1,060	1,099	1,166	1,133	1,137	1,222
Upper Burma .	...	...	...	...	...	39	235
Assam . . .	385	379	396	404	410	420	401
Bengal . . .	3,687	3,880	3,801	3,680	3 915	3,799	3,736
North-Western Provinces and Oudh.	5,653	5,848	5,782	5,769	5,809	5,784	5 798
Panjáb . . .	2,112	2 099	2 075	2,058	2,153	2,157	2,146
Madras . . .	4,777	4,556	4,721	4,779	4,492	4,807	4,864
Bombay . .	3,119	3,095	3,083	3,407	3 316	3,342	3,373
TOTAL .	21,476	21,617	21,657	21,972	21,951	22,210	22 510
See Note .	665	694	677	676	734	811	880

The figures in the lowest line are the alienated Land-Revenue of Bombay, which, in the system of accounts of that province, are added on the Revenue side, and charged again as expenditure under Assignments, Land-Revenue, and Police. The amounts are neglected in the statement itself.

It will be remembered that a portion of the total receipts of Land-Revenue is in the accounts shown under the separate head of irrigation.

'33. Although the growth of revenue shown in the above figures has been very steady, it can hardly, from a financial point of view, be said to be satisfactory in amount. It has been less than one per cent. a year, and is on the whole a poor return for the money which Government has spent, in the form of railways and of canals, in improving its estate.

'But the fact is that the period covered by the above statement represents, in a general way, the close of the thirty years' Settlements in several of the provinces, and the Government is only now beginning to reap its share in the advance of the past two or three decades. Settlement operations are at present being carried on on a more extensive scale than at any previous time, and we have every reason to expect a handsome increase of revenue under this head.

'NEW SETTLEMENT SYSTEM.

'34. During the last four years (and in a great measure in preparation for this re-settlement of revenue) a very great improvement has taken place in Northern India in the administration of this important head of revenue and in the means adopted by the Government to assess and settle from time to time that share of the produce of the land which has in all ages been the main source of the revenue of the sovereign powers in India.

'As no systematic review has recently been published of the position and prospects of this our most important head of revenue, I propose to take up the subject in some detail, both from an administrative and from a financial point of view, the materials having been supplied to me by Sir Edward Buck, the Revenue Secretary to the Government of India, to whom personally is due by far the largest share of the credit of the improvements effected.

'35. The system of land-assessment has hitherto, in every province, involved the complete survey, field by field, of every village—an operation which was rendered necessary by the absence of correct maps at the commencement of the thirty-year period. The object of the system now introduced is to preserve, and to correct up to date, the records upon which the surveys and Settlements are based, so that the re-settlements, when they fall due, may be made upon existing records, and may not require an elaborate investigation *de novo*. The maps which have been provided by the great cadastral survey which has now almost drawn to an end, are in future to be corrected up to date from year to year by permanent establishments in which the patwárís or village accountants occupy the most important place. In the same way the Settlements now being completed have involved a complete revision of all records-of-rights, including details of the occupancy of every field, and these records, like the maps, are in future to be maintained from year to year by the permanent establishments. The assessment included also the valuation of the soil and productive powers of every field; but the valuation made during the past thirty years will in future revisions of Settlement be accepted without material alteration. Three important elements of expenditure have thus been eliminated from future Settlement operations, viz. the cost of periodical field surveys, of revisions of records-of-right, and of soil valuations. The introduction of the new system is made possible both by the more complete maps and records which have been supplied by the operations of the past thirty years, and by the creation of Agricultural Departments which are permanent Departments of Survey and Settlement.

'36. An examination of the cost under the old and new systems has recently been made in pursuance of the inquiries of the Finance Committee with the object of ascertaining the financial effect of the new arrangements and the probable cost of future Settlement operations. This investigation is not complete, but it points to a maximum expenditure, in future, of R. 100 a square mile, including the cost of additional establishment, and in some provinces to a considerably lower figure. The comparative results are shown in the following table, in which a maximum rate of R. 100 is applied to all provinces :—

PROVINCE (EXCLUDING ASSAM).	Rate per square mile under the old system at rates recently prevailing.	Average expenditure per annum at rates in preceding column.	Average expenditure per annum at the maximum rate of R. 100 per square mile.
	R.	Rx.	Rx.
North-Western Provinces and Oudh	350	115,000	30,000
Panjáb	200	50,000	25,000
Central Provinces	220	35,000	15,000
Bengal	350	17,500	5,000
Madras	440	70,000	15,000
Bombay	260	65,000	25,000
TOTAL . .	303	352,500	116,000

showing an ultimate annual saving of Rx. 237,500.

'The above table is based on an estimate of the maximum cost which may be incurred in the revision of assessments when the new arrangements have been completely established. In the meantime some saving has been already made by their partial introduction and by measures which have recently been taken to accelerate the current revisions of Settlement. Under the programmes which have been arranged in recent conferences with the local authorities, there has been effected a saving either in the expenditure on survey and Settlement, or in the more punctual recovery of increments of new revenue, which, in three provinces—the Central Provinces, Panjáb, and Madras—is estimated at a gross amount of Rx. 2,000,000 during the next ten years, or an average of Rx. 200,000 a year during the next decade. In these and other provinces the new increments of Land-Revenue to which the Government is entitled will henceforth be assessed and collected up to date, while hitherto they have in many cases come into force only several years after the date of the expiry of the old Settlement.

'37. The general growth of the Land-Revenue is exhibited in the following table:—

Table showing growth of Land-Revenue (including Permanently-settled Tracts.

(The figures are thousands of Rx.)	Receipts, 1856–57.	Receipts, 1870–71.	Average annual growth (14 years).	Percentage of increase (14 years).	Receipts, 1886–87.	Average annual growth since 1856–57 (30 years).	Percentage of increase (30 years).	Receipts, 1890–91 (rough estimates).	Average annual growth since 1870–71 (20 years).	Percentage of increase (20 years).
North-Western Provinces	3,920	4,130	15	5	4,390	16	12	4,560	21	10
Oudh	970	1,320	25	36	1,410	15	45	1 470	7	11
Panjáb	1,840	1,970	10	7	2,150	10	17	2,210	12	12
Central Provinces	570	600	2	5	620	2	9	650	2	8
Bengal	3,540	3,760	16	6	3,740	7	6	3,800	2	1
Madras	3,800	4,400	43	16	4,860	35	28	4,900	25	11
Bombay (*a*)	2,150	2,950	57	37	3,370	41	56	3,450	25	17
Assam	80	210	10	162	400	11	400	420	10	100
Lower Burma	410	600	14	46	1,220	27	197	1,230	31	105
Minor Provinces	20	20	—	—	120	3	500	120	5	500
	17,300	19,960	190	15	22,280	166	29	22,810	142	14

(*a*) Excluding Alienations.

'The figures show actual collections both of Land-Revenue and of miscellaneous items classed as Land-Revenue, e. g. sale-proceeds of waste lands; water-rates in Madras; nominal revenue assessment on lands assigned for service in Bombay; capitation-tax and receipts from fisheries in Burma and Assam.

'38. Three periods are taken, viz.:—(1) the first fourteen years after the mutiny, during which the growth was at the rate of Rx. 190,000 a year; (2) a period of thirty years from the mutiny to the present time, during which the growth was at the rate of Rx. 166,000 a year; (3) a period of twenty years (partly estimated) from 1870–71 to 1890–91, during which the growth is at the rate of Rx. 142,000 a year.

'39. It will not fail to be seen that, while the fourteen years preceding 1870–71 showed an annual increase of Rx. 190,000, the rate of increase in the twenty succeeding years has averaged only three-fourths of this. The reasons for this are, that the first period was, in many parts of India—Oudh and Orissa for example—a period of active re-assessment and Settlement, and that, therefore, during the second there was less of the growth of revenue which comes in from Settlement operations; that a large accession of land-revenue occurred after the mutiny in consequence of confiscations; and finally, that there was, between 1860 and 1870, a rapid increase in the cultivated area of the provinces of Bombay and Madras, in which the system of land-settlement is such that newly-tilled land comes under annual assessment, and in which the demand for cotton during the American war gave a powerful impulse to cultivation. On the other hand, a corresponding check to cultivation occurred in the same provinces during the last of the three periods in consequence of the drought of 1877–78.

'40. Notwithstanding these causes of exceptional growth in the beginning of the post-mutiny period, it may reasonably be expected that the capital outlay which the Government has recently devoted to irrigation and railways will, during the next few years, bring to it a larger return from the land, by reason of the great improvement of its produce, both in quantity and value, by the agency of canals and the opening-out of communications. In these accessions to the landed income of the State strict regard will be had to the principles which have invariably been followed by the Government of India in the assessment of the land, its guiding policy having always been the lenient consideration of the proprietary classes. During thirty years of peace and progress, the rentals of tenants have, through the cultivation of new fields or the imposition of new rents by landlords, been continually expanding, and, in some of the most fertile areas of India, the landlords themselves have, without the intervention of the Government, materially enhanced the rent paid to them, while at the same time that proportion of it paid by them to the State has been continuously reduced to lower and more definite limits. In the same way, a lenient consideration is extended to the agricultural community in provinces where the cultivators or cultivating proprietors are assessed by the State itself, so that in these also the percentage of produce paid as land-revenue has been constantly decreased.

'The growth of land-revenue, therefore, which is to be anticipated will be a growth due to that peace and prosperity which directly spring from a lenient and careful administration rather than to any direct action of the Government in the direction of raising rentals.

'A brief review of the position in each province will now be given.

'REVIEW BY PROVINCES.

'41. *North-Western Provinces.*—The old system comes to a final end within the next two years. The greater part of the province is held by tenants on small holdings of a few acres paying rent to landlords who are charged with a payment of 50 per cent. of their assets to Government. The advanced condition of the province led the Secretary of State to inquire, so long ago as 1863, whether a permanent Settlement could not be introduced; but a final consideration of the subject between 1882 and 1884 ended in the adoption of the system already described, under which annually revised maps and records are made the basis of assessment.

'The rate of growth of land-revenue in the North-Western Provinces since the mutiny year has, however, been moderate. In the first fourteen years it was only 5 per cent. (say ·35 per cent. per annum), but it has in the current period of twenty years risen to 10 per cent. or ·5 per cent. per annum. There was in the North-Western Provinces less room for extension of cultivation than in most parts of India. Lying mainly in the fertile alluvial plain between the Himáláyas and the high-lands of Central India, the province attracted a large population at an early historical period, and it was at the period of the mutiny highly assessed. But the large amount of State capital spent since that time in the form of railways and canals, and the contemporaneous rise of prices has given a fresh impulse to agricultural wealth, and the province is now in many districts as lightly, as it was formerly heavily, assessed. A considerable amount of relief was given at the commencement of the thirty-years' period of Settlement now expiring, by the reduction of the standard of the State demand from 66 per cent. of assets to 50 per cent.—a change which was, however, somewhat counterbalanced by the high valuation of assets made under the rules which governed the operations of the Settlement Officers. The relief is now made complete by the elimination of soil valuation from the assessment system which, except in cases of suspected fraud, requires that the recorded assets should be accepted as a basis of assessment. Rentals are in many districts still growing at a rate of about 1 per cent. per annum, and in certain tracts the growth is likely to be so great that even under the lenient system now adopted, some difficulty may be anticipated in taking the Government quota in full at the next Settlement from the landlords, on account of the large and sudden increase which would be involved in such an assessment.

42. *Oudh*, with the exception of a closely populated tract between Lucknow and Benares, came under much later development than the North-Western Provinces. Its revenues were not, until after the mutiny, brought under the effective administration of the British Government, who applied to it the same system of Settlement as that which prevailed in the North-Western Provinces. The tenants of Oudh have less positive rights than those of the adjacent province, as in the latter the greater number are more securely protected by statutory rights against unlimited enhancement of rent. There is, therefore, a prospect of a larger growth of rental, and also of revenue, in Oudh than in the North-Western Provinces. The land is rich, the climate favourable, and although since 1860 the extension of cultivation has been very large, considerable areas still remain to be brought under the plough. Competition for the land is likely to increase, and with it the enhancement of the rents by the landlords, who have in Oudh practically a free hand. The development of the province

under British rule has been very great, and is still, with the extension of railways, progressing at a rapid rate. The province will come under re-assessment, on the new or economical system, between 1892 and 1906.

'43. In the *Panjáb* there is a large proportion of dry sandy soil which is only capable of development under the influence of irrigation. Subsoil water is generally too far from the surface for wells, and the growth of revenue depends mainly on the expenditure of State capital on canals. The revenue-payers are for the most part cultivating proprietors paying direct to Government, no part of the produce being intercepted by middlemen. A large amount of State capital has been in recent years invested in the province in railways and canals. Under these circumstances the growth of the land-revenue, which has since the mutiny been slow, should now progress at a rapid rate.

'The revision of Settlement has, under the old system, involved, as in the North-Western Provinces, a high rate of expenditure and protracted operations, but only a very few districts now remain to be completed under that system, and measures have recently been taken to expedite their assessment. The whole province will then come under the operation of the new rules which require the Settlement to be based on annual maps and records.

'44. The *Central Provinces* have shown a very small development of land-revenue since the mutiny. They have been to a great extent cut off from the railway system and have at the same time been lightly assessed. The revision of Settlement takes place during the current decade commencing with the first year of the present Provincial Contract, 1887–88, and it is estimated, after nine years, to yield an increase of Rx. 180,000. Owing to the backward state of the province, the low rates now paid to Government, and the new development of the railway system which is taking place, it has been determined to make the new Settlements for terms varying between twelve and twenty years, so that the reassessment of the province will recommence shortly after the termination of the existing revision.

'The revision of Settlement is being made at present partly on the old and partly on the new system, but at a low cost not exceeding R. 100 a square mile. The same necessity for a complete series of maps and records has existed in this as in other provinces, but owing to the circumstance that the revision of annual records was commenced, with the creation of the Agricultural Department, five years before the old Settlements began to expire, there has been more time than elsewhere to utilize the village and district establishments in the work of preparing for Settlement. Arrangements were made under which a large number of parties of the Survey of India have covered the surface of the provinces with a network of triangulation available both for topographical and revenue purposes. These are filled in by the village officers under the supervision of the local Revenue officers, and they provide sufficiently good maps as a basis for future revisions of assessment. The revision of the record is also primarily effected by the permanent establishments, leaving only the valuation of soils and general supervision to be effected by a special staff. At the close of the present revision, nine or ten years hence, the new system will be introduced and the cost be brought considerably below the new maximum of R. 100 a square mile.

'The land is held, as in the North-Western Provinces and Oudh, by cultivators of small holdings paying rent to proprietors from whom the Government takes revenue. But whereas in those provinces the landlords have the power, which is freely used, of raising rents contemporaneously with increase of competition and rise of prices, they have no such power in the Central Provinces. The growth of rent and, therefore, of revenue, entirely depends, except in land newly taken into cultivation, on the periodical assessments of rent made by the Government at the time of Settlement. The existing rents are, in most parts of the province, an unusually small fraction of the total value of the produce; while, in consequence of the rising prices due to the extension of the railway system, the disproportion is continuously becoming greater. The area of culturable land still to be brought under the plough is exceptionally large. The province is one, therefore, from which a material growth of land-revenue may be looked for.

'45. Thus far the provinces dealt with are those popularly known as the 'temporarily-settled zamíndárí' or 'landlord' provinces. I will next refer to *Bengal*, which is recognized generally as a 'permanently-settled landlord province.' But there are in Bengal not less than about 14,000 square miles which belong to the temporarily-settled landlord class and of which the old Settlements will shortly fall in. In respect of this tract preparations are now being made for punctual assessment on much the same plan as in the Central Provinces, and at equally moderate rates of cost, by the Agricultural Department of the province.

'The area in question comprises large tracts in Orissa and Chittagong, and several Government estates. It will hereafter come entirely under the new system. An increment of land-revenue of 20 per cent. would in this area be equivalent to a fixed addition of ten lakhs a year to the annual demand.

'46. The province of *Madras* must be divided into two sections—the permanently-settled zamíndárí or landlord area, and the temporarily-settled raiyatwárí or tenant-proprietor area. The first is about 48,000 square miles and the second about 93,000 square miles, or roughly one-third and two-thirds respectively. The Settlement on the old system, which required a complete series of field maps and a valuation of soils, is now drawing to a close and is being hastened by assistance lent to the local Survey Department by the Government of India. In a few years the whole province will, in accordance with the intention which for some time has been declared by the Madras Government, be permanently relieved of special Settlement and Survey establishments.

'The growth of land-revenue in the tenant-proprietor tracts takes place in two different directions. There is the periodical growth due to the increase of rent-rates at the end of every thirty years' period, and the annual growth due to the gradual increase of the area brought under cultivation. For in Madras all tenant proprietor waste land has an annual rate attached to it at the time of assessment which is applied and collected whenever the land is occupied. The periodical growth (that is, the increase of rates between the last Settlement and the one now being completed) is roughly estimated at from 5 to 7 per cent. and the annual increment due to increased cultivation at Rx. 10,000 per annum. The rate of increase under this latter head will necessarily fall off as less land becomes available.

'47. In *Bombay* the same general conditions prevail as in the raiyatwárí or tenant-proprietor area of Madras. The growth rate, however, is not checked by the presence of permanently-settled land, and has, as in the temporarily-settled section of Madras, a double growth, the one being due to the periodical increase of rent-rates every thirty years, and the other to the annual occupation of fresh land at the revenue-rates which were attached to it at Settlement.

'The whole province has in recent years undergone a thorough and searching revision of assessment which is now drawing to a close. This revision has been in the hands of a separate Survey Department which will within five or six years be gradually broken up and absorbed in the new establishments, and the province will then come permanently under the new system. It may be noticed here that both in the Madras and Bombay Presidencies the holdings or small farms of tenant-proprietors have had their boundaries fixed once and for ever by the Survey Department, and that instead of, as in other provinces, the map requiring annual revision in order to keep it in accord with changing boundaries, it is here necessary to maintain the boundaries in accordance with the map as originally made. This duty, as well as that of the maintenance of the statistical record, is on the close of Settlement operations in each district made over to the Agricultural Department.

'The growth of land-revenue has been more satisfactory in Bombay than in any province. It began in a marked degree with the impetus given to cotton production at the time of the American War, and has been continued under the influence of rising prices, extended cultivation (and in Sindh, extended irrigation), supplemented by a careful system of assessment.

'48. In *Assam* the very backward state of the province and the absence of communication with the seaboard in the years immediately succeeding the mutiny, have made the growth of revenue in the later years appear to be exceptionally rapid. A part of the province (about 9,000 square miles) is, however, under the permanent Settlement system of Bengal, and the growth of revenue depends on the remaining area which is temporarily settled, chiefly with tenant-proprietors, at rates which are practically fixed, as there is hardly any competition for land on account of the great extent of waste area which can be taken up. The most fully-occupied portion has been revised on the system employed in other temporarily-settled provinces, and this revision is nearly completed. The remainder will probably be surveyed and settled on a cheaper system under the direction of the Agricultural Department, and the whole province will thereafter come under the new arrangements. As in Bombay and Madras, there is an annual growth (estimated at from Rx. 8000 to Rx. 10,000 per annum) which is almost solely due to new occupation, as there is here no periodical growth due to increase of rates.

'49. *Lower Burma* has been undergoing for some years a regular revision of Settlement, of which about one-fifth, or nearly 10,000 square miles, is completed. Each district, when it leaves the Settlement officer's hands, is made over to the permanent care of the Agricultural Department, which will henceforward be responsible for maintaining the maps and records. The land is held by tenant-proprietors, and there is again in this province a double growth due to annual increase of occupation and to periodical increase of rates. The annual assessments are complicated by the release of all fallow land from payment of any but a nominal revenue, but there is a steady extension of cultivation which, supplemented by the effect of a careful survey and assessment, has resulted in a growth of from two to three lakhs a year on a comparatively small total revenue. Lower Burma is practically a large rice-field formed by the alluvial deltas of the river systems, and at present it yields only 1 per cent. of other produce. About 37,000 square miles, or 84 per cent. of its cultivable area, are still uncultivated, and there is room for further growth both by extension of cultivation and by the improvement of the agricultural system through the introduction of other crops. The soil is rich.

'50. *Upper Burma* is composed of high-lands, the agricultural value of which is under examination. The land-revenue is, like that of all border provinces on first-occupation, initially small; but there is an equal promise of the same steady growth in the future which has taken place elsewhere.

'51. The increase of revenue in minor provinces under the direct control of the Government of India is mainly due to the re-assessment of the little district of Ajmer and the addition of Quetta.'

BOOK II.

THE LAND-REVENUE SYSTEM OF BENGAL.

SKETCH MAP
of
BENGAL.
English Miles.
0 20 40 80 120
Railways thus
NEPAL
SIKHIM
BHUTAN
ASSAM
BURMA
CALCUTTA
Darjeeling
Patna
Gya
Benares
ALLAHABAD
LUCKNOW
Fyzabad
Gonda
Basti
Jaunpur
Mymensingh
Comillah
Agartalla
Jessore
Bogra
Maldah
Burdwan
Hooghly
Midnapore
Sambalpur
Bilaspur
Raigarh
Pooree
(Jagannath)
Ganjam
Akyab
CHOTA NAGPORE
CENTRAL PROVINCES
CENTRAL INDIA AGENCY
MADRAS PRESIDENCY
Tributary States
SANTAL PERGUNNAHS
Mouths of the Ganges
BAY OF BENGAL
Longitude East 84° of Greenwich

CHAPTER I.

GENERAL HISTORY OF THE PERMANENT 'ZAMÍNDÁRÍ' SETTLEMENT OF BENGAL.

SECTION I.—INTRODUCTORY.

§ 1. *Early History of the Presidency.*

THE limits of this work make it necessary for me to plunge somewhat abruptly into the history of the Bengal Settlement. But in this chapter, and in that which afterwards describes the Revenue Officers and their duties, I shall go into more detail than elsewhere, regarding the early history of our administration. The reason for this will be already apparent from the introductory chapter (Book I. Ch. V.) in which I have explained how the Bengal system is the parent of all others. To this day the district staff,—the Collector and his assistants,—by whatever other titles they may be locally known, exist on the model, and with many of the characteristics, of the original Bengal institution. And the principles which underlie the Bengal Settlement have not been without their influence on the later systems which in many respects depart widely from the old Bengal ideal. The strong conviction of the advantages of a *recognized landlord with a secure title*, which moved the Government to make, and to congratulate itself upon, the Zamíndárí Settlement of Bengal, resulted indeed in a reaction which produced (after no little conflict) the *raiyatwárí* systems of Madras and Bombay; but it survives in the modified systems—lying midway, as it were, between *raiyatwárí* and *Zamíndárí*—that prevail in Upper India.

Still our detail must be of a practical character, and I must therefore pass over many interesting phases of the history of the administrative system developed by the East India Company when it was changed from a trading corporation into the ruler of a great Empire [1].

I will only briefly recall certain salient points.

BENGAL, which in the end became the first among the provinces, was at the outset the lowest in rank as well as the latest in origin. The 'President' at the factory of Surát was originally the chief representative of the Company in the East. Madras was erected into a Presidency in 1653, and Bombay—though still subordinate to Surát—in 1668. The Bengal Presidency was not formally constituted till the next century had begun.

Our trade with Bengal, no doubt, was established much earlier. It began practically with the factory at Bálásúr in 1642. But our permanent establishment—following on the grant made in gratitude for some remarkable cures in the Imperial family effected by Surgeon Gabriel Boughton—may be said to date from 1652. Sultán Shuj'á (one of the sons of Sháh Jahán) was local ruler or Súbadár of Bengal, and was favourable to the English and allowed a factory to be opened at Húghlí. But that privilege was liable to all the changes and caprices of Oriental rule; and it so happened that Sháh Shuj'á's successor took a dislike to the traders, with the result that, after the affair of Job Charnock in 1686, the settlement was put an end to. But this was only for a time; four years later, a reconciliation was effected (as the loss from the cessation of our

[1] A succinct sketch will be found in Phillips, *Lecture* vii. Also in the Historical Summary of the *Bengal Administration Report for* 1872-73; and in Kaye, pp. 57-108: and Field, chapter xix.

trade was considerable), and Charnock returned and founded Calcutta in A.D. 1690. Permission was obtained, in 1698, to buy out the rights of the landholders in the vicinity of Calcutta; the Company thus became holder of estates, spoken of in the official language of the day, as 'independent *taluqs*.' In 1699 Sir Charles Eyre was sent out to build the fort which was called after the reigning sovereign, and has given the name to the Presidency—'Fort William in Bengal.' In 1707 this Presidency was formally recognized[1]. After this, nothing that is here noteworthy, occurred till the outbreak which culminated in the 'Black Hole' tragedy, and the battle of Plassey (Palásí), on the 23rd June, 1757. Affairs then took a new turn; instead of the Company's officers being the humble dependants of the Mughal power, they became the real arbiters of affairs. The local governors or Súbadárs, were in fact created by the authority of Clive. By treaty the Company then became 'Zamíndár' of the town of Calcutta and the territory around known as 'The 24-Pergunnahs.' Afterwards the grant was made revenue-free[2].

In 1760 the 'Chaklás' or districts of Bardwán, Midnapore (Mednipur), and Chittagong (Cháṭṭágráoṅ) were granted revenue-free. Lastly, in 1765 (12th August), the grant of the 'Diwání,' or right of civil and revenue-administration of Bengal, Bihár, and Orissa, was made to the Company, on condition of payment to the Emperor of a fixed sum of twenty-six lakhs annually, and of providing for the expense of the 'Nizámat,' i.e. the criminal and military administration[3].

[1] See Harington, vol. i. 2; and Phillips, p. 231. Kaye gives 1715 as the date, pp. 67 and 76.

[2] For the Sanad see Aitchison's *Treaties*, vol. i. 15. The nature of the Zamíndár's office under the Mughal government has already been sketched (see p. 184); and we shall presently study the subject more in detail. But this grant shows it was a position which then implied something very like the landlord's right; and doubly so when no revenue had to be paid to the Imperial treasury, but everything was managed, and all dues appropriated, by the grantee.

[3] The Diwání means the office or jurisdiction of Diwán—the civil minister, as the Nizámat was of the 'Názim,' or military governor. Hence the term 'Diwání' is still used to mean 'civil' as in the phrase Diwání 'Adálat, or Civil Court; and 'Nizámat' was long used to mean 'criminal,' the chief

This put the Company into virtual possession of the three provinces,—the Orissa of 1765 including only the present Midnapore district, with part of Húghlí, not the whole of the country now called by the same name.

§ 2. *Commencement of British Rule.*

For some time no interference with the native officials was contemplated [1]. It was soon found, however, that the uncontrolled acts of local officials under a corrupt and effete system, produced results little short of intolerable. In 1769, 'Supervisors' were appointed in the hope of improving the administration. They were directed to acquire information as to the revenue-history of the province, going back for the purpose to a given era when good order and government had been universal; they were to inquire into the real limits of 'estates' held by the Zamíndárs, the quantity of land they ought to have revenue-free, and the real 'rents' or payments which the actual cultivators of

Criminal Court being called Nizámat 'Adálat. Now the term 'Faujdárí' is used for Criminal Courts. But both terms indicate that the military and criminal jurisdictions were considered as one and the same. The grant of the Diwání did not *theoretically* give the whole rule of the country, but it did practically. (See this explained in Cowell's *Tagore Lectures for* 1872, pp. 26, 27.)

[1] Motives of policy, natural but short-sighted, impelled Clive to leave the actual administration in the hands of the old native functionaries to be carried on in the name of the Súbadár. In 1767 Clive wrote to the Select Committee :—'We are sensible that since the acquisition of the Díwání, the power formerly belonging to the Súba of these provinces is totally, in fact, vested in the East India Company; nothing remains to him but the name and shadow of authority. This name, however, and this shadow it is indispensably necessary that we should venerate ..... To appoint the Company's servants to the offices of Collectors, or indeed to do any act by any exertion of the English power ..... would be throwing off the mask, would be declaring the Company Súba of the province. Foreign nations would immediately take umbrage,' &c.—See Kaye, p. 78. Mr. Kaye is, I think, much too severe on this policy: there was very little 'gorging ourselves on the revenue and leaving the responsibility.' As to the revenue, no system could well have brought in less to the Government; as to the form of administration, Clive had to consider the susceptibilities of the French—a very present danger;—and it was with no desire to shirk responsibility that the government was let alone, but in a perfectly genuine belief that the native rule was best, as it was most politic. The Company had only a staff of merchants and writers, barely enough to manage their commerce, and quite unequal, as Mr. Verelst wrote, to civil administration.

the soil ought to make in each estate. Various other improvements were hoped for; and especially illegal revenue-free holdings were to be properly assessed and made to pay. The cultivators were to be protected from the exactions of the Zamíndárs, and leases or 'pottahs' (pattás), specifying exactly what each man had to pay, were to be granted[1].

The intention thus to supervise and control the native revenue-administration was no doubt excellent, but it entirely failed of realization: and on the 28th August, 1771, the Court of Directors at home announced their intention 'to stand forth as Díwán, and by the agency of the Company's servants to take upon themselves the entire care and management of the revenues.' In India a proclamation to this effect was issued on 18th May, 1772, and Clive took his seat as *Díwán*, or Minister of State charged with the Civil and Revenue administration of the Province, at the annual ceremony (punyá) for settling the year's revenue, held near Múrshidábád. That was the beginning of our direct revenue-control.

But the idea of a Settlement and a recognition of the proprietary right in land, had not yet occurred to the Company's government. This is hardly to be wondered at. The whole theory of Indian land-revenue was absolutely strange to the English authorities. They could not tell who owned the land and who did not; nor in what category to place the different native officials they found in the districts. Everything had to be learnt by slow experience. There was no guide to the system, and no principles of law to which it could be referred; nor were the Company's servants fitted by their training and antecedents to prescribe systems or devise administrative forms. As Mr. Kaye says, 'The Company's servants were dead hands at investments, but they know nothing of land-tenures.'

[1] This proposal should be noted, as showing that from the first, the idea of protecting the rights of the cultivators was in the mind of our administrators; and also as showing how the belief originated, which was not abandoned till many years after, that those rights would be efficiently protected by the issue of definite written leases.

§ 3. *Sketch of the early Revenue system.*

In 1772 the affairs of India had for the first time attracted such attention as to be mentioned in a Royal Speech to Parliament; the result was that the 'Regulating Act' of 1773 was passed, and this (insufficient in detail as it afterwards proved) established the Governor-General and Council in Bengal with a power of supervision over the other Presidencies, and laid the foundation of a system of Courts of Justice, as well as of a series of written and published Regulations for the guidance of the authorities in India.

Warren Hastings became Governor-General in 1772, and under him, reforms were at once undertaken. The mercantile element in the Company's service was gradually replaced, or supplemented, by men who could become civil administrators, and the Collectors and assistants were given more reasonable salaries instead of being expected to eke out a merely nominal subsistence allowance by profits of private trade, and by other more questionable means. It was not to be expected that while such changes were in progress, a Revenue Settlement system could all at once come into view. The plan first adopted was to give out the revenues in farm for five years. Each 'pargana' was separately farmed; unless indeed the pargana gave more than one *lakh* (100,000) of rupees revenue, in which case it was divided. 'Collectors' were for the first time appointed (instead of Supervisors) to receive the revenue[1]. A native Díwán was associated with them, and they were superintended by Revenue Councils at Múrshidábád and Patná.

The existing Zamíndárs (who managed the revenue under the Native rule) were not necessarily to be displaced by this arrangement; but they often refused to contract for the total sums demanded, so that other farmers were appointed, and in some cases injustice was done.

[1] In the chapter on Revenue business and officials, the history of the Collectors, Commissioners, &c., will be more fully gone into. Details about the five years' system of 1772 will be found in Field, pp. 477 et seq.

Stringent orders were given to prevent the farmers robbing the cultivators or *raiyats*, and to make them adhere to the 'hast-o-búd[1],' or lists showing the rents which it was customary for the raiyats to pay, and to prevent illegal cesses being collected.

Notwithstanding the best intentions, and that the members of the Central Revenue Committee went on circuit to arrange details, the new farming system proved a failure, as such systems always do. They required the utmost honesty in the lessees, and that honesty did not exist. They required also that the amounts bid for should be really fair, and fixed with reference to the real resources of the estates; they also required local supervision based on a minute knowledge of details, neither of which requirements can be said to have been attainable. The leases were arranged too much in the auction-room[2]; the *data* for real assessments were wanting. And if the total amounts could not be checked, any detailed watchfulness over village collections was impossible; officers were too few, their knowledge too imperfect, and the local machinery—the *kánúngo* and the *patwárí*, which our best modern systems have developed and instructed—were either wholly wanting, or existed only in name,—the holders of the offices being persons under the absolute control of those whose object was to deceive[3]. But perhaps the greatest cause of the failure of the farm system, was the widespread and decimating famine of 1770, on account of which enormous remissions of revenue had to be made[4]. It was not without reason that the Court of Directors wrote in 1773 (speaking of the failure of the system of Supervisors

[1] Literally (Persian) 'is and was'; in fact, the actual and customary rent-roll without arbitrary additions to it.

[2] The farmers in many cases were mere speculators who bid up the leases, hoping to get an uncontrolled power to take what they liked. Excellent *orders* were issued to prevent this. Nothing was to be taken from the raiyat beyond what was in his *patta*, and a heavy penalty and the cancelment of the lease should follow extortion; but there was no one to enforce these provisions. See Field, p. 481.

[3] See pp. 256, 284.

[4] What that famine was in one district—Bírbhúm—has been told in piteous and graphic language in Hunter's *Annals of Rural Bengal*. As to the remissions, see Kaye, p. 168, note.

before 1772): 'Every attempt for the reforming of abuses has rather increased them, and added to the miseries of the country we are anxious to protect and cherish.' As a partial remedy it was determined, under instructions from the Court of Directors, to abolish the agency of Collectors, and try again the 'Ámil' or Native local Collector of the first Mughal system. Had a strong district staff kept watch over these agents, the results might have been different; but unfortunately, the local Collectors were abolished and the only direct supervision was given by *Councils* placed at distant points of the province. For this purpose the country was divided into six divisions with a Provincial Revenue Council for each. Five of these sat at Bardwán, Patná, Múrshidábád, Dinájpur, and Dákhá (Dacca). The central Revenue Committee at Calcutta, which had a general control over the whole, also undertook the direct management of the sixth division, which was the Orissa of those days.

When the period of five years' farms was about to expire, Warren Hastings was carefully considering what system should next be followed. But unfortunately, at this time, the opposition of Francis, and the unseemly strife which resulted from the imperfect constitution of the Governor-General's office in relation to the Council, were at their height[1]; otherwise there can be no doubt that Hastings' advice was good. To gain information about the land tenures; to protect the *raiyats*, whom he perceived to be the real ultimate producers of revenue; not to commit himself to Settlement with any class for a long period, without fuller knowledge;—these were the points on which he insisted.

[1] Francis at that time had the benefit of John Shore's advice, who wrote his minutes for him. 'The Councillor seasoned those minutes with the necessary amount of acrimony, and then served them up as his own.' When Shore fell sick, Francis, it is said, was silent, and Hastings smiled grimly at the ludicrous discomfiture of his foe (Kaye, p. 170). It is satisfactory to know that Shore lived to repent of his association with Francis, and became the friend of Hastings, as he afterwards was President of the Revenue Board and the trusted adviser of the Marquis of Cornwallis.

It was not, however, till the death of Colonel Monson had given Warren Hastings a majority, that (in 1776) his designs could be given effect to. Meanwhile the farming-leases expired, and the Court of Directors did not exactly agree to any plan sent home, while they did not offer any substitute of their own, beyond directing *annual leases to the Zamíndárs* whenever possible. These instructions are, however, noteworthy, because in them for the first time it was ordered that if the Zamíndárs fell into arrears they should be liable to be 'dispossessed, and their Zamíndárís, or portions of them, shall be sold to make up the deficiency [1].'

Meanwhile, under Hastings' orders, a commission was issued to three officers to travel about and collect further information. They made their report in March 1778. During this period annual Settlements were made, i. e. in 1777, 1778, 1779, and 1780. In 1781 several 'Regulations' were enacted [2]. Notably, the six Provincial Committees were abolished, and a Metropolitan 'Committee of Revenue' (four members, of which the chief was Shore, afterwards Lord Teignmouth) was appointed. This Committee at once proceeded to report on a mode of Settlement, and recommended that the plan 'most convenient and secure for Government, and the best for the raiyats and country, is, in general, to leave the lands with the Zamíndárs, making the Settlement with them.'

Meanwhile the annual Settlements were continued. We now come to the eventful year 1786, when, in the autumn, the *Swallow* arrived bringing Lord Cornwallis, and with him John Shore, who had been appointed (as just stated) to the Board of Revenue. It should be noted, that in this year it was found (as might have been expected) that the

[1] Kaye, p. 172.

[2] The reader will recollect that the provisions for Regulations in the Act of 1773 were insufficient. The defect was partially removed by an Act in 1781; but even then the Regulations made, which were afterwards reconstructed as the Bengal Code in 1793, were not in exact accordance even with the powers given, so they had afterwards to be finally legalized by the Act of 1797 (37 Geo. III., sec. 142).

Collectors were indispensable, and they were reappointed to the number of thirty-six (afterwards reduced to twenty-three). In this year, also, the Central Committee became the Board of Revenue.

I should also mention that, in 1782, a definite attempt was made to regulate the holding of lands revenue-free, and to 'resume' or charge with revenue, those that were held without authority: the office for registration and inquiry was called the 'ba'zí-zamín-daftar' (office for certain lands).

The yearly Settlements (latterly with Zamíndárs always, unless expressly disqualified) continued till 1789.

Two things will here strike the reader; one is how little in a hurry Lord Cornwallis was to take action. The other is, how all attempts to dispense with the *Zamíndár* failed, and that in spite of repeated efforts to be free of him.

It is also instructive to note how little use central control proves when the local agency is defective.

The Board, far removed from the actual scene of operations, knew nothing of the real state of affairs, and the díwáns and local officers combined with the Zamíndárs and others to deceive them.

§ 4. *A.D.* 1786.—*Plans of Lord Cornwallis.*

Before Lord Cornwallis arrived, Parliament had passed the Act 24 George III., cap. 25, in 1784. And Lord Cornwallis came out with instructions for carrying this Act into effect.

The law indicated, as the means for ensuring a proper Settlement, an inquiry into the real 'jurisdictions, rights, and privileges' of Zamíndárs, Taluqdárs, and Jágírdárs under the Mughal and Hindu governments, and what they were bound to pay; it also directed the redress of the grievances of those who had been unjustly displaced in the course of the earlier tentative and imperfect revenue arrangements. The Court of Directors suggested that the Settlement should be with the 'landholders,' *but at the same time maintaining the rights of all descriptions of persons.* As for the revenue, it was desired that there should be a durable assessment, based on a review of the Settlements and actual collections of former years. It was thought that the various inquiries which had been ordered ever since 1765 would have resulted in a sufficient knowledge of the paying capacity of the estates, and therefore a *Settlement for ten years* was ordered. The Court then thought that a fixed period of ten years would be better than promising a 'dubious perpetuity'; but they directed that, on completion of the arrangements, the whole matter should be fully and minutely reported on, so that they might have an opportunity of settling the whole question, without necessity for further reference or future change.

As I have said, while these arrangements were in progress, the Settlements continued to be annual, and Lord Cornwallis was so little in a hurry to carry out any scheme of his own, that he continued seeking for fuller knowledge. 'No efforts,' says Mr. Cotton, 'were spared to increase the store of information.' The vast body of opinions thus collected was declared by the celebrated *Fifth Report* to be 'too voluminous to lay before the House [1].'

§ 5. *Issue of Regulations forming a legal basis for a Decennial Settlement.*

Meanwhile, the rules for the decennial Settlement were being elaborated. They were issued on the completion of Mr. Shore's celebrated Minutes of 1788, and of June and September, 1789 [2]. The rules for settling Bengal, Bihár, and Orissa (as then constituted) were separately issued between 1789 and 1790 [3].

[1] See Cotton's *Memorandum on the Revenue History of Chittagong* (Calcutta, 1880), p. 50. Unfortunately, however, they consisted chiefly of opinions and masses of detail about accounts, which did not in the least suffice to solve difficulties when it came to a question of assessing individual lands or estates, still less of fixing the *raiyats'* payments on an equitable basis.

[2] The Minutes of 1789 are printed in the appendix to the *Fifth Report*, but not the elaborate Minute of 1788 with its appendices, giving Shore's information about the rise and growth of the Zamíndárí title, and its becoming proprietary. This latter is consequently given *in extenso* in Harington, vol. iii. (and in the Reprint).

[3] As to the rules, see Harington,

When Lord Cornwallis commenced the codification of the Regulations in 1793, these rules (amended and completed) formed one of the forty-three Regulations passed on the same day, and have since been borne on the Statute-book as Regulation VIII of 1793.

This is the law under which the 'decennial Settlement' of Bengal was made.

§ 6. *Result reported to the Home Authorities.—The Permanent Settlement.*

When the inquiries had been completed, report was made, as ordered, to the Court of Directors at home. Lord Cornwallis was for making the Settlement permanent at once. But the Court of Directors, knowing that Shore and other able advisers deprecated the immediate declaration of permanence, deliberated for two years, and it was not till September, 1792, that they sent a despatch consenting to the proposal. On receipt of this, Lord Cornwallis, by proclamation of 22nd March, 1793, declared the decennial Settlement to be 'permanent.' This proclamation was also included in the Statute-book of 1793, as Regulation I of that year[1].

The student will then bear in mind that the Bengal Settlement has two main features, which must not be

vol. ii. p. 171. The dates were :—
Bihár . . 18th September, 1789.
Orissa . . 25th November, 1789.
Bengal . . 10th February, 1790.

Having undergone alteration and received additions, they were issued with translations on 23rd November, 1791, and in this form are given at length in Colebrooke's *Digest of the Regulations*, vol. iii. p. 308. Still further improved, they were ultimately legalized, as above stated, in Regulation VIII of 1793. It is to the provisions as they appear in Regulation that reference is made in the text.

[1] The proclamation, after reciting that the Governor-General in Council had been empowered by the Court of Directors to 'declare the *jumma* which has been or may be assessed upon their lands . . . fixed for ever,' went on to say: 'The Governor-General in Council accordingly declares to the Zamíndárs, independent taluqdárs, and other actual proprietors of land, with or on behalf of whom a Settlement has been completed, that at the expiration of the term of the Settlement [ten years] no alteration will be made in the assessment which they have respectively engaged to pay, but that they and their heirs and lawful successors will be allowed to hold their estates at such assessment for ever.'

confused. Either one might have been adopted without the other. They were—

(1) That the Zamíndárs were settled with; and as they could not fulfil their obligations to the State, nor take an interest in their estates without some definite legal *status*, they were declared proprietors of the areas over which their revenue-collection extended. That proprietary right, however, was a limited one; it was subject, on the one hand, to the payment of revenue to Government, and to liability to have the estate sold *at once* on failure to pay; and it was subject, on the other hand, to the just rights of the old and original cultivators of the soil, the *raiyats*, dependent taluqdárs, and others. The Zamíndár was accepted as the person to be settled with, not as a matter of chance, but as one of deliberate policy, and on administrative grounds.

(2) The other main feature was that the assessments fixed in the manner presently to be described, were declared to be unalterable for ever.

From these two features, the Settlement of 1793 has acquired the name of the PERMANENT Settlement, also (sometimes) that of the ZAMÍNDÁRÍ Settlement of Bengal.

§ 7. *General reflections on the Settlement of* 1789–93.

Let me here pause to correct one of the common misapprehensions about the Permanent Settlement with Zamíndárs. Let me ask whether it was possible for the English administrators to do anything else than acknowledge them?

In the first place, I have already explained in a general way (and shall give some further details in the sequel), that *some* of the Zamíndárs were old Rájás who had a very close connection with the land, and on whom the people greatly depended.

In the next place, there was the strong practical argument that every attempt to dispense with the Zamíndárs had been a failure; injustice had been done, and the Statute of 1784 had insisted on the 'ancient immunities and privileges' of the Zamíndárs being respected. All previous experience had shown that it was impossible to dispense with their agency[1]. Even when each enormous district (as it then was) had its one European Collector, it would have been quite impossible for him to deal with thousands of detailed holdings; how much more would this apply before that date, when, as from 1772–79, there had been only councils or committees for controlling revenue matters —at one time six of them for all the districts included in Bengal, Bihár, and what was then Orissa!

Against these forcible facts it was of little use to take the opinions of experts and historians[2] as to what were the origin and design, or the limitations, of the office of Zamíndár. The *theory* is probably much clearer to us, with all the authorities at hand, than it was to the Collector of 1789; but what he was concerned with was not the true theory of origin, but the practical position at the end of the eighteenth century.

There was no hand-book of ancient law to guide the Collectors in understanding the history of landholding, to direct their attention to the origin of *villages*, the units

[1] This is very instructive. In Akbar's time, the whole country was divided out into 'Sirkárs,' and these into parganas, each with its vigilant revenue 'ámil, and the parganas even had recognized subdivisions under petty revenue officers. As long as this system was kept working by a powerful Government, the revenue was not intercepted, the people were not oppressed. The moment the Government became too weak to control the machinery, the subdivisions disappeared, and then the revenue *could only* be collected by the agency of great farmers, who undertook to pay a fixed sum for a certain portion of territory, saving the Government the trouble of going into any detail. This was the system our early administrators found already long established. In the position they were placed in, it was utterly impossible for them to have restored the 'Akbarian' method, as we have now restored it in Northern India. The 'tahsíldárs,' and all the host of local officials trained and able to carry out such a system, are the product of a century of British rule. In 1789 no such persons could have been found.

[2] This was freely done. See the series of questions and answers appended to Mr. Shore's *Minute* of 1788.

composing the great estates, or to explain what those aggregates of cultivators meant, in the light of a comparative study of early customs and institutions. *Their* only conception of landholding was embodied in the English landlord with his tenants. And it is impossible to deny that the Zamíndár was more like a landlord than anything else[1]. True it was that the tenants' holdings were not valued like English farms and offered to tenants at the consequent rent, to be taken or left at the tenants' pleasure. Even in England tenants had been on farms for generations. The superficial differences were not greater than what differences of race and climate would account for; and the deeper but minuter differences were unperceived, because land-tenures had not been cleared up as they have now. The Zamíndár was more oppressive than an English landlord, therefore measures of protection were required for the tenantry: that seemed the chief, if not the only thing.

Grievous as the failure of the Permanent Settlement has been, its failure is not due to the fact that Zamíndárs were confirmed, or that, in the unavoidable necessity of defining and securing their position in English legal documents, they were called and made, landlords. The evil consisted in this, that their right was not limited with regard to all the older raiyats, leaving new-comers to be in principle (with such detailed conditions as might be advisable) contract-tenants. The other evil—that of assuming to a legislature the power of binding all future lawgivers, and permanently exempting a certain class of proprietors from their due share of the State burdens at the expense of other people and provinces—that is a matter quite unconnected with the grant of proprietary rights or the protection of tenants.

I shall point out in due course, the ample evidence there is, that from 1769 onwards, the rights of the *raiyats* were

[1] At any rate he must have appeared to combine the landlord and collector in a fashion which could not explain itself to the Company's servants of 1789.

never intended to be forgotten; but it is easy for us now, after half a century of inquiry and discussion about tenant right, and with the experience gained in many provinces and their Settlements, to criticise our predecessors of 1790. At that time no one knew what practical steps to take. Collectors knew that village rolls—'hast-o-búd,' 'raibandí,' or whatever other name they were known by—existed, showing the sums payable by *raiyats*; but how these sums were ascertained and how far they could be altered periodically, and on what principles if any, they did not know. 'Pargana rates' were talked of rather than actually adopted or enforced; for re-assessments were periodically made, or rather, virtual additions to the old rates were covered by the irregular expedient of 'cesses' and 'benevolences' (abwáb, &c.). With this knowledge, it is hardly wonderful that they should have thought the one and sufficient remedy to be the *compulsory* issue of '*pottahs*' or *leases* to the tenants, setting forth what the payment was, and hoping that vague traditional 'pargana rates' would be, or could be, respected. It was not foreseen that the 'pattás' would not be generally granted, and that no machinery existed for seeing that they were granted; still less was it suspected, that, as afterwards proved to be the case, the pattá would be turned—when used at all—into an engine of extortion.

Another point must be mentioned, and that is that the Zamíndárí Settlement was not Lord Cornwallis's idea. It was distinctly ordered in April, 1786, by the home authorities: it was advocated by all the chief revenue authorities in Bengal. Shore, though he deprecated the hasty assessment of the amount of land-revenue *in perpetuity*, never hesitated in recommending the grant of a secure estate to the Zamíndár. Mr. Thomas Law, Collector of Bihár, was indefatigable in writing in favour of a Zamíndárí Settlement. Mr. Brook of Sháhábád was also urgent in its support. The Settlement was then, as Mr. Kaye says truly, the work of the Company's Civil servants. No doubt it fell in with Lord Cornwallis's views, because, as I have said, *no one* at that time could have thought of imagining a theory of village communities or of village Settlements. It was not till some years after, that the existence of villages, with all their customs in full force, in Benares, attracted the attention of Mr. Duncan, the Resident, in 1795-6. Even then it is only necessary to read the report to see how completely the landlord theory—as the only one realized—was in the mind of the writer [1].

When Lord Cornwallis, supported by the general opinion, had made up his mind—and he deliberated carefully from 1786 to 1793—that the *Zamíndárí* Settlement was the right thing, he further considered that it would be useless unless the assessment was also declared *Permanent*.

In this one point Lord Cornwallis may be charged with haste—he might have let the originally ordered ten years run out, and then see what it was best to do. His arguments in favour of permanency of the assessment—some of them based on grave mistakes of fact [2]—hardly answered the objections of Mr. Shore.

It is worthy of note here, that while Shore thought it right to declare the Zamíndárs proprietors, he held that time would be required to settle what, under the circumstances, was really meant by the proprietary right conferred [3]. He did not observe any specific rules for the security of the raiyats; he well knew 'the difficulty of making them, *but some must be established*. Until the variable rules adopted in adjusting the rent of the raiyats, are simplified and rendered more definite,' he added, 'no solid improvement can be expected from their labours upon which the prosperity of the country depends.' With true foresight Mr. Shore further predicted that 'if the

[1] Instances of this will also be seen even in the minutes made thirty years later, when the North-Western Provinces villages were beginning to be understood (Revenue Selections, North-Western Provinces, 1818-22).

[2] As, e.g., what Dr. Field calls the 'cardinal' mistake—it vitiates everything—of supposing that the raiyats paid rents by *agreement* with the Zamíndárs. See Field, p. 490, &c., quoting the minute of 18th June, 1789, and Lord Cornwallis's reply.

[3] Mr. Shore's own words will be found quoted further on.

Zamíndárs were left to make their own arrangements with the raiyats without restriction, the present confusion would never be adjusted.' The system, in short, had not *defined the relation* of the new 'landlord' to his 'tenant'; would it not be better to introduce a new system by degrees than to establish it at once beyond the power of revocation?

On the other hand, it may be urged that probably the consideration which most weighed with Lord Cornwallis, was one that would not take long to mature. He was certain he had done the right thing in making the Zamíndár proprietor; he believed that legislation would protect the raiyat; but that if the Settlement, as a whole, was not closed for ever, a revision might occur, which would shake the Zamíndár's position, and so at any moment, all his benevolent work might be undone. In this, of course, he was wrong: reassessment based on just principles of growth in the cultivated area and rise in prices, has nothing to do with unsettling fixed rights of property, any more than a revision of income-tax renders the capitalist's position as a man of property insecure. But that was not understood. It will be remembered that the Zamíndár's revenue, as fixed in 1793, was not a light one under the circumstances. It was certainly supposed that many of the raiyats would pay *fixed rents*: and it was thought that if the Zamíndár was to be secure and prosperous, his revenue *could not* be raised. True, he would cultivate more waste which would bring in new rents; and in some undefined way, *some* rents would rise by improved cultivation [1], but that would only be his legitimate profit; he would become rich and would then import luxuries, live at ease, and enrich the treasury by the indirect taxation he would pay on import of commodities [2].

[1] And so they would. It was a question of paying rent in kind. A bad tenant gets three-hundred seers of wheat off an acre, and the landlord gets one half. A good one gets five hundred, and the landlord benefits thereby, though the rent is not raised. Whatever the truth may be, expressions occur in the early minutes *alluding to a rise in rental, just as often as those which imply fixity of rents.*

[2] 'Every man,' wrote Mr. Law, 'will lay out money in permanent

All this seemed at the time, and backed by Mr. Law's glowing periods about the gratitude of ancient Zamíndár and jágírdár families restored to opulence, to point conclusively to the *permanence* of the *assessment*, as well as the *security of the landlord's title.*

Unfortunately, facts, as they afterwards developed, could not be foreseen; the necessity for punctual payments involved a severe law for recovery; the *sale laws* had from the first suggested themselves without question; and indeed the law would have acted with much diminished harshness if it had not been for the characteristics of the landlords. They were indolent and extravagant; they did nothing for the land; and even when there was no glaring personal defect, the climate and the habits of the country unfortunately suggested that the proprietor should save himself trouble by *farming* out his estate to any one who would give him the largest profit over and above his revenue-payment. And as the proprietor's farmer in time grew rich,—what with freedom from war, and security, and the daily increasing value of land,—so he too farmed his interest to others, till farm within farm became the order of the day, each resembling a screw upon a screw, the last coming down on the tenant with the pressure of them all. But who could have foretold this in 1790?

We must now return to the direct narrative of the progress of the Settlement.

§ 8. *Procedure of Settlement.—Absence of a Survey.*

One of the first things that will strike the student is that the Settlement *was made without ascertaining the boundaries of the estates and without a survey.* The cost

structures, as such works enhance the value of his estate and promise future benefit. If a scarcity happens the landholders will forego demands, and encourage cultivation to preserve their tenants, who become a part of their necessary property. The increasing independence will raise a class of native gentlemen proprietors, who will gradually have established themselves in good houses with the various comforts of life.' (See Kaye, p. 178.) See also par. 32 of Revenue letter to Bengal, 1st February, 1811; Field, p. 544.

of survey would have then been great, and the requisite establishment such as could hardly have been contemplated with equanimity; moreover there were visionary advantages in abstaining from measurement and inquiry which then commanded much attention.

The direct consequence of admitting the Zamíndár to the position of an English landlord, was a desire to leave him in the enjoyment, as far as possible, of the independence dear to an English landholder. What need was there, the rulers of those days thought, to harass the proprietor we have established and now wish to encourage, by surveying or measuring his lands and making an inquisition into his affairs? Fix his revenue as it has all along been paid, or correct the recorded amount if it is wrong; sweep away illegal taxes, resume what land is unfairly held without paying revenue, and then leave the proprietor in peace. If some neighbour disputes his boundary,—if there is room to believe that he is encroaching,—let them go to law and decide the fact.

Besides this feeling, there was another, which at first made a survey unacceptable. Strange as it may appear to European ideas, measurement was looked on with great dread, both by Zamíndár and raiyat. Whenever the raiyat had to pay a very heavy rent, or the Zamíndár to satisfy a high revenue demand, both were glad to have a little (or often a good deal) more land than they were in theory supposed to pay on.

It was always found an effective process under the Mughal rule, to threaten a raiyat with the measurement of his lands; for his 'rent' was fixed at so much for so many *bíghás*. If this rent was oppressive, as it often was, his only chance of meeting that obligation was that he really held some *bíghás* in excess of what he paid for, and this would be found out on measurement. But that was not the only danger; the landholder well knew that even if he had no excess whatever, still the adverse measurer would inevitably *make out* the contrary. By raising the 'jaríb,' or measuring rod, in the middle, and by many other such devices, he would make the *bíghá* small, and so produce a result showing the unfortunate raiyat to be holding more than he was paying for; and increased rent for the alleged surplus was immediately exacted. In the same way the Zamíndár, even though the Settlement law was explicit, thought it on the whole safer to have the details of his estate as little defined (at least under the eyes of the Collector) as possible.

Of course, the want of survey and boundary demarcation led, as we shall afterwards see, to great difficulties; and various enactments have been since passed to provide a proper register of estates and a survey to ascertain their true limits; but it is not difficult to understand why a survey was not at first thought of. At that time nearly all the occupied parts[1] of the districts were divided out into 'Zamíndárís.' In a few instances in Bengal, but more commonly in Bihár, the estates were called 'jágír,' and some estates were held by grantees called 'taluqdárs.' But whatever the title, the actual allotments of land forming the settled estates were those mentioned in the native revenue records. As before stated, there were no maps or plans or statements of area; the boundaries of the estate were vaguely described in words, and a list of the villages included was given; but the limits of these were very imperfectly known, especially where a large portion was waste. Each Zamíndár held a warrant, or 'sanad,' under which the Emperor or his deputy had created the 'estate'; and that specified the revenue that was to be paid, and declared the Zamíndár's duties; but the limits of the estate were only indicated by the string of names of villages or parganas.

[1] I say 'occupied parts,' for at that time a majority of the districts, especially those near the hilly tracts, had large areas still waste, but nevertheless forming part of the Zamindárí, or at least claimed as such. Lord Cornwallis stated that one-third of the Company's possessions was waste at the time when the Settlement work began. The object of the Settlement of 1793 was to recognize *all the land*, waste or culturable, in each Zamindárí, as the property of the Zamindár; but no doubt at that time there was very little certainty as to what was really included in the estate. See *Fifth Report*, vol. i. p. 18.

§ 9. *The Property made transferable.*

It is hardly needed to remark that the 'property' granted to the Zamíndárs was made transferable, which, it was expressly stated, it previously had not been. The 8th Article of the proclamation sets forth—

'That no doubts may be entertained, &c., the Governor-General in Council notifies to the Zamíndárs, &c., that they are privileged to transfer to whomsoever they may think proper, by sale, gift, or otherwise, their proprietary rights in the whole or any part of their respective estates without applying to Government for its sanction to the transfer; and that all such transfers will be held valid, provided that they be conformable to the Muhammadan or Hindu law . . . and that they be not repugnant to any regulations now in force which may have been passed by the British Administrations, or to any regulations that they may hereafter enact[1].'

§ 10. *Selection of Zamíndárs.—Joint Estates.—Refusal of Settlement.*

Some curious restrictions were at first placed on the selection of persons to be Zamíndár-proprietors. It was at one time attempted to exclude from Settlement not only minors and females incompetent to manage their estates, but also persons of 'notorious profligacy' or 'disqualified by contumacy.' These grounds of exclusion, being of course impracticable to prove satisfactorily, and being sure to give rise to great scandals, owing to the necessity of an inquiry in Court, were ultimately given up[2]. As regards estates of minors and others unable to take care of their own rights, they were placed under the Court of Wards, and managed on behalf of the incompetent owners.

When there were several shareholders in an estate, there was at first a rule to make them elect a manager. This

[1] The subject is further mentioned in the preamble to Reg. II of 1793.

[2] See Reg. VII of 1796. Reg. X of 1793 (Section 5, clause 4) had attempted to lay down the method of charging, defending, and establishing such objections.

failed, and after a time the law was altered, and they were left to manage as they pleased, but were held jointly and severally responsible for the revenue. The law, however, permitted a partition and a complete severance of responsibility if the sharers wished it.

When there were cases of doubtful or disputed boundary, possession was looked to; and if possession could not be ascertained, the estate was held by the Government officers (held 'k͟hás' as the revenue phrase is) till the dispute was legally settled.

If the Zamíndár declined Settlement (i.e. objected to pay the amount assessed and the proper authorities refused to reduce it) the lands were farmed or held k͟hás, and the ex-proprietor got a 'málikána,' or allowance of 10 per cent. on the Government assessment.

I may add that such refusals were rare, for though some refused the terms for the decennial Settlement, they accepted when the proclamation of perpetuity was issued.

§ 11. *Dependent and independent Taluqdárs.*

The Regulation prescribed that the Settlement was to be made with 'Zamíndárs, taluqdárs, and other actual proprietors'; that implies that the Zamíndárs were not the only persons entitled to be recognized as proprietors.

I have mentioned that there were grantees of the State called taluqdárs. These were sometimes separate grants, outside and 'independent' of the Zamíndár's estate[1], in which case they paid revenue direct to the treasury. Sometimes, being of an inferior order, they were found inside the estate, and were then 'dependent' on the Zamíndár, and paid through him. Rules were laid down for determining when the taluqdár was to be settled with separately as proprietor, and when he was considered as subordinate to the Zamíndár.

[1] Called also 'Huzúri' taluqas, i.e. paying revenue direct to the Huzúr, or headquarters of the Government authority; or 'k͟hárija,' i.e. outside, or without, the Zamíndári estate and control.

This was a matter of no little importance. Every one who could get himself treated separately, became an independent proprietor with his revenue settled for ever. A taluqdár who could not establish his right to be separate, though he might have substantial privileges as to his tenure and the non-enhancement of his rent, still was only a subordinate—a raiyat, or as he is now called, a 'tenure-holder.'

The Regulation also mentions that there were taluqdárs who had purchased or obtained their title by gift from the Zamíndár. These were independent; so were persons who held grants direct from the Government, also taluqs which had been created before the Zamíndárí. A rule was also made that if the Zamíndár was proved to have exacted more than was due, any taluqdár might ask that his estate should be separated. On the other hand, leases granted for clearing waste, and called 'jangalbúri-taluqs,' were treated as only subordinate.

As to the origin of these various *taluqs*, I must defer details till we come to Chap. III. Sec. iii, where the matter is regarded from the tenure point of view, whereas here we are dealing with the question of Revenue Settlement only.

There were also grants known as 'aímá' (of which hereafter). If these had been granted free of all payment, they were treated as independent properties; but if only granted at a quit-rent, or with the annexed condition that the holder was to clear the waste, they were subordinate tenures.

When the taluqs were granted by the Native Government under the denomination of 'muqarrarí' or 'istimrárí' (or both terms together), they were independent. Of these terms, the former means 'fixed' as regards the rent or revenue, and the latter 'firm' or 'in perpetuity' as regards the tenure.

Such a grant implied that whether the grantee were or were not proprietor, the whole rent or assessment would go to him, and only the fixed (muqarrar) proportion be passed on by him to the Treasury. This sum of course was much less than the full assessment. Here clearly the grantee was independent of any Zamíndár. If his grant was not istimrárí, in perpetuity, but only for life, then on its expiry the succeeding holder would still be entitled to separation, as clearly he had not had anything to do with the Zamíndár, but only with the authority which made the grant.

It will be remembered that there are tenures under these same names 'muqarrari,' &c.—but *granted by the Zamíndár*, not by the State: in that case they are only subordinate tenures, though the *rents* may be 'fixed,' and the right to hold be 'in perpetuity.'

The Collector's duty is limited to determining the question whether the 'taluq' ought to be independent or not. He had nothing to do with the validity of the title itself if that was disputed[1].

It was hoped that the process of inquiry would be terminated with the Settlement, but it seems that for some years after, people kept on filing applications for separate recognition, and it became necessary to give a year's grace for such applications, after which no further requests would be listened to[2].

These remarks will not make clear the *nature* of the tenures spoken of, but they are intended to indicate how that besides 'Zamíndárís,' there were *many other* estates

[1] Of course if a Zamíndárí estate was held jointly and the sharers separated, each would become a separate independent proprietor.

Mortgagees in possession were settled with, the mortgagee taking the place on redemption.

The Settlement was also always made with the person *in possession*; a claimant out of possession must go to the Civil Court, and, if successful, the Settlement would be transferred to him.

[2] Harington mentions that about three thousand taluqs were separated by him in the Zamíndári of Rájsháhi alone. A summary inquiry was made in every instance as directed, in the presence of the Zamíndár's *vakil* (law-agent), and one appeal only is known to have been afterwards made to the Civil Court. When the Zamíndár had previously engaged for the revenue of his Zamindárí, including the taluqs, he was allowed an abatement to the amount separately assessed on the latter as previously stipulated with him. Of course, all this applied only to taluqs existing or created before the Settlement. Any *new* taluq would only be treated as separate if properly registered and applied for under Regulation XXV of 1793, which provided for the partition of Zamíndári estates and the allotment of the *jama* on the divided portions. If this was not done, Government would take no notice of the taluq, if the estate were sold for arrears. See also *Fifth Report*, vol. i. p. 34.

which were treated as entitled to separate Settlement, and their holders to be (equally with the greater Zamíndárs) 'actual proprietors.'

§ 12. *Basis of the Assessment.*

The Settlement rules of 1789–93 laid down separate principles of assessment for Bengal, for Bihár, and for Orissa. In Bengal and Orissa the actual revenue of the preceding year, or some year nearly preceding (which was to be compared with the accounts, and tested by the information which the Collector had acquired), was to furnish the standard of assessment. In Bihár, the standard was to be the average produce of land in any ordinary year, which would give a fair and equitable assessment. If any land had paid the same revenue for twelve years past, that was to be accepted as the Settlement rate.

With the single exception, then, of Bihár, where in many cases former accounts were not forthcoming, and where consequently an estimate of the produce of an ordinary year had of necessity to be made, there was nothing required as the basis of assessment, but a reference to old accounts, with such adjustment and consolidation of separate items and abolition of objectionable ones, as the declared principles of the Government rendered necessary.

I may repeat that, in order to determine the assessment of each estate, no inquiry was made (as under the later Settlement procedure) either what the value of the estate was, or what the produce was, or what the 'rents' were as paid by the raiyats. Reference was simply made to the old records of the lump assessments under the native rulers; and these were roughly adjusted in cases where such adjustment was needed, and the Zamíndár or other owner was directed to pay this sum.

The following description occurs in an article in the *Calcutta Review* by Mr. Thornton, reprinted in 1850:—

'The Collector sat in his office in the sudder (headquarter) station, attended by his right-hand man, the kánúngo, by whom he was almost entirely guided. As each estate came up in succession, the brief record of former Settlements was read, and the dehsunny (dah-san, ten years) book, or fiscal register for ten years immediately preceding the cession or conquest, was inspected. The kánúngo was then asked who was the Zamíndár of the village. . . . Then followed the determination of the amount of revenue. On this point also, reliance was chiefly placed on the *daul*, or estimate, of the kánúngo, checked by the accounts of past collections and by any other offers of mere farming speculators which might happen to be put forward.'

Such an assessment must have been almost pure guess-work; for, as the *Fifth Report*[1] says,—

'The lights formerly derivable from the Kánúngo's office were no longer to be depended on: and a minute scrutiny into the value of lands by measurements and comparison of the village accounts, if sufficient for the purpose, was prohibited by orders from home.'

The *Report* goes on to explain how Mr. James Grant's *Analysis of the Finances* raised expectations, and how Mr. Shore's Minute (June 18, 1789) removed many misconceptions; and it continues:—

'A medium of the actual produce to Government, in former years, drawn from the scanty information which the Collectors had the power of procuring, was the basis on which the assessment of each estate, whether large or small, was ultimately fixed.'

By such a process, the assessment was not so likely to be fixed at an excessive rate, as the rights of individuals to share in the profits left by its moderation, were to be overlooked.

Scrutiny was, as I have said, prohibited, for fear of making the Zamíndárs distrust the promise of a Permanent Settlement, and think that the information supplied would be used to enhance the revenue afterwards. The evidence adduced by Dr. Field[2] proves that, even so far back as the

[1] Vol. i. p. 22. [2] Field, p. 469 note.

time of Warren Hastings, the orders to collect information contemplated that it should be general; there was not to be any 'vexatious' extraction of details. The influence of this fear can still be clearly traced in Regulation VIII of 1800 (Secs. 3 and 7)—the first Regulation for compiling a formal register of revenue-paying and revenue-free estates (for the Collector's purposes). The Regulation explains how the information is to be acquired, and prohibits inquiry into rents and measurements of individual 'málgúzárí' (revenue-paying) lands.

It is evident also from what Hastings wrote in 1776, that the revenue accounts exhibited by the kánúngos were generally believed to be much better kept and more reliable than they really were. It was believed that we had only to go to the *pargana* abstracts (checking them, when necessary, by reference to the village rent-rolls) to get all possible information. But, in fact, nothing about the real value of estates was found out; only the attempt was made to distinguish the revenue figures from the abwábs or cesses which had overlaid them[1].

§ 13. *Origin of the Revenue Accounts and Registers.*

Before we can understand the nature of the pargana and village accounts of revenue which existed, we must take a brief retrospect of what the native system had been in Bengal.

In a general chapter (V) we have already gained some knowledge of the Mughal system of administration, and also of the Settlements made under Akbar. It may therefore be at once stated that it was under Rájá Todar Mal that the first Settlement of Bengal was made about 1582 A.D. The assessment was exclusive of Orissa, and some of the territories in Eastern Bengal that were only added to the province at a later date.

We have no evidence of any formal change in this assess-

[1] See Field, pp. 483-4. Whole sets of accounts were often fabricated to suit particular purposes.

ment till A.D. 1658, when Shuj'á Khán, Súbadár of Bengal, revised it by raising the total from nearly 107 lakhs of rupees to about 131 lakhs. The next rise was under Ja'far Khán (surnamed Múrshid Qulí Khán). This revision is curious, because it exhibits one of those changes which are always observable in the Mughal kingdoms. An energetic ruler soon feels the loss to the treasury which contracts with Zamíndárs and others cause. They save trouble, but they intercept too much of the income. Ja'far Khán, therefore, put aside the Zamíndárs and collected by his own 'ámils and officers[1]. About this time other countries in Orissa and Eastern Bengal were annexed, and came under assessment. Shuj'á-ud-dín, who succeeded, raised the assessment in 1728, to over 142 lakhs. But in his time (as indeed in his father's) the impost of abwábs or 'extras' had begun. We then find the assessment continually raised: the last assessment before cession to the British power, was Qásim 'Ali Khán's, which was said to be over 256 lakhs; but there is some doubt whether this amount was ever realized[2]. It was calculated that the regular assessment had increased about 33 per cent., but that the increase of the Zamíndárs' exactions from the raiyats could not be less than 50 per cent.

There can be no doubt that for many years of the later rule, assessments were habitually increased, not by a Settlement or any new land valuation, but by imposing cesses which were openly added to the payments required from the Zamíndárs or other collectors. The local kánúngos doubtless long preserved the original or last regular land-assessment,—spoken of as the 'túmár' or ''asl'; as well as the subsequent reassessments; and they had also the 'taksím' or division of the total sum over the villages. But the progress of events destroyed the practical use of such

[1] He employed Hindus always as his Revenue officers. He divided the country into thirteen collectorates called 'Chaklá,' and the officers put in charge afterwards became Zamindárs in many instances. The whole history of the assessment is stated in Shore's Minute, §§ 13 39 and § 63 (*Fifth Report*, i. p. 103, et seq.).

[2] Minute, 18th June, 1789, § 141.

accounts. Warren Hastings, no doubt, was quite right when he wrote—

'Under the old Government, the distribution was annually corrected by the accounts which the *Zamíndárs* or other collectors of the revenue were bound to deliver into the office of the *kánúngo* or king's Register, of the increased or diminished rents of their lands and of the amount of their receipts: but the neglect of these institutions, the wars and revolutions which have since happened in Bengal, have totally changed the face of the country, and rendered the *túmár* rent-roll a mere object of curiosity. The land-tax has therefore been collected for these twenty years past (i.e. since 1756) *upon a conjectural valuation of the land formed by the amount of receipts of former years, and the opinions* [estimate or '*daul*'] of officers of the revenue; and the assessment has accordingly been altered almost every year.'

This account is also borne out by the *Fifth Report* [1].

Hence in the decennial Settlement, as Mr. Thornton described, the estimates were really based on the payments made by Zamíndárs in past years, increased or diminished according to the opinions of such local experts as were at hand.

It will appear hereafter how very uncertain were the raiyats' payments, owing to this system. The idea that the whole body of raiyats had any guarantee under native rule for payment at fixed rates for ever, or that the law, when the Permanent Settlement was made, could have easily defined such rates and made them permanent too, is quite untenable. The custom varied from place to place and pargana to pargana, according to the character and influence of the revenue-collectors.

I do not say that it would not have been impossible to ascertain the traditional 'túmár' rates of Akbar's, or some other later Settlement, but would those rates have been reasonable at the close of the century? [2] Had the task been

[1] Vol. i. p. 19, at the bottom.

[2] Mr. Phillips gives a perfectly accurate account of the Zamíndárs' dealings with the raiyats at p. 171. For whatever the Zamíndárs' *sanads* required, the raiyats were annually

seriously undertaken, it would have been necessary, as was found in the Central Provinces, to *fix* the *raiyats'* rates on the basis of local inquiry by a Settlement officer after a survey and registration of fields; and such a proceeding no one could have dreamt of in 1790.

§ 14. *The Síwáí or Abwáb.*

This is the place to introduce a description of the additions by which the native Governments were accustomed to raise the demand from the Zamíndárs. The *cesses* were called 'síwáí' (*lit.* 'extra,' 'besides') or 'abwáb' (plural of 'báb,' the *heads* or subjects of taxation[1]). Sometimes the Arabic term ḥubúb (plural of ḥab) is used. The common Hindí or Bengálí name is 'máthaut.' They were calculated on the same principle as the *jama'*, at so much per bíghá, or so many seers in the maund of grain. The ruler's local deputy levied them on the Zamíndár, who was authorized to levy them on the cultivators. When such extras got numerous and complicated, there would be a sort of compromise; the account would be re-adjusted so as to consolidate the old rate and the cesses in one; and this would become the recognized rate, till new cesses being imposed, a new compromise was effected[2]. In this way, therefore

settled with (*Land Tenure by a Civilian*, 1832, pp. 65, 66). There were lists kept by the patwárís and kánúngos, of village and pargana rates, called 'raibandí' or 'nirkh.' But then the abwáb or cesses were added, and from time to time consolidated with the original rates See also p. 178, where Mr. Justice Campbell, describing the system of additions, is quoted. On the subject of the practical existence of the old Akbarian assessment, I may refer to the undeniable authority of Mr. Shore's Minute quoted in the *Fifth Report*, vol. i. p. 139 (Minute, § 218). 'The assal jumma established by him does not now anywhere exist.'

[1] They were called after the name of the ruler inventing them, or after the nature of the tax. Thus we find the first cess imposed by Ja'far Khán called 'khásnavísí, a tax to support the Government writers of 'sanads,' &c.; 'nazarána muqarrarí,' a rate to enable the Deputy or Governor to send his customary annual present to the Emperor; the 'faujdárí, to maintain police; zar-i-máthaut,' comprising several items; 'chauth-Maráthá,' a tax to meet the loss caused by the cession of part of Orissa to the Maráthás, &c., &c. An elaborate account of cesses will be found in Phillips, p. 176 et seq.

[2] See Mr. Justice (Sir G.) Campbell's judgment in the great Rent Case, *B. L. Reports*, Supplementary volume, p. 256.

the revenue would periodically rise, and the rates exacted from the cultivators rise also, with more than corresponding frequency. The revenue actually realized was thus composed of the ''*asl jama*' *plus* these extra charges (síwáí), and was collectively called the 'mál.'

The Zamíndárs naturally enough, not only raised the rents of the *raiyats* to a sum sufficient to cover the whole assessment, but imitated the example by levying private cesses for their own benefit, in addition to the 'mál.'

§ 15. *The Sáyer.*

Besides the land-revenue there were other imposts only indirectly connected with the land, and called 'Sáír,' or, according to the Bengálí writing, 'Sáyer.' These were taxes on pilgrims, excise, transit and customs duties, taxes levied on shopkeepers in bazaars (ganj) and markets (hát), tolls, &c. They amounted usually to about one-tenth of the land-revenue; they also included charges on the use of the products of the jungle (*ban-kar*), on fishing (*jal-kar*, produce of water), and on orchards and fruit-trees (*phal-kar*[1].)

It is easy to understand, then, that the total revenue which each Zamíndár had to account for to the State consisted of two kinds,—the 'mál' (above described) and the 'sáír.'

The sum under each head payable in total for the different 'mahals' or estates included in the Zamíndárí, was placed on record, and noted also on the *sanad* of appointment.

[1] The *Fifth Report* (vol. i. p. 26) describes the *Sáyer* as consisting in 'land customs, duties and taxes, and *whatever was collected on the part of the Government* and not included in the "Mehaul" (meaning "mál" or land-revenue.)' But the Sáyer also included the charges on produce above mentioned. I may here mention that (as regards the mistake of mahál for mál in the extract) that the report (the original as well as the reprint which exactly follows it) is *full* of mistakes or misprints of native terms. Many of them are quite unrecognizable.

§ 16. *Disposal of these items at Settlement.*

The British Government abolished all extra cesses or 'abwáb' as they existed when its rule began; and naturally it required the Zamíndárs, under penalty, to abstain from levying such cesses from the raiyats.

As to the *sáyer* dues, those which were in the nature of separate taxes—excise, and the like—the Government took into its own hands, severing them entirely from the land-revenue account. Others, which were oppressive, as transit duties, taxes on pilgrims and the like, it gradually abolished. Such dues of this class as represented payment for the use of produce of land or water, the Government handed over to the landowners to augment their legitimate profits.

The good intentions of the Government as to freeing the raiyats from liability to vexatious cesses imposed by the Zamíndárs for their own benefit, were never carried out, at least fully. Even at the present day such cesses are paid by the raiyats, partly under the inexorable bond of custom, and partly from a sense of helplessness. For though the authorities would at once decide against the exaction, still the Zamíndár could always either conceal the fact or colour it in some way, or else make things so unpleasant for the raiyat, that he would rather pay and hold his tongue[1].

[1] The private cesses, as distinct from the authorized cesses of old days, were legion. A few names will sufficiently indicate their nature; thus, we find the 'mángan,' a benevolence to assist the Zamíndár in debt; 'nájái,' a contribution to cover the loss when some of the cultivators absconded or defaulted; 'porvani' or 'parbani,' a charge to enable the Zamíndár to celebrate 'parva,' or religious festival days. There were also levies for embankments (púlbandi), for travelling expenses of the Zamíndár, &c., &c. As regards the modern levy of cesses, I cannot do better than quote from the Administration Report of 1872-73. Those who care to go into more detail will also find, following the extract I make, a list of cesses, showing the variety and ingenuity which their levy displayed.

'The modern Zamíndár taxes his raiyats for every extravagance or necessity that circumstances may suggest, as his predecessors taxed them in the past. He will tax them for the support of his agents of various kinds and degrees, for the payment of his income-tax and his postal cess, for the purchase of an elephant for his own use, for the cost of the stationery of his establishment, for the cost of printing the forms of his rent receipts, for the payment of his

The Regulation XXVII of 1793 gives a somewhat detailed account of the abolished *sáyer* duties[1]. It refers to the *Ayín-i-Akbari* (vol. i. p. 359), as showing that Akbar had rescinded some, and that 'Álamgír (Aurangzeb), 'the last Emperor who maintained the full authority of the Mussulman government,' abolished seventy others. The abolition of all transit duties and marriage taxes, having been at an early time of the Company's administration enjoined (viz. in 1772), was to be maintained. But so anxious were the Government not to injure the Zamíndárs,

lawyers. The milkman gives his milk, the oilman his oil, the weaver his clothes, the confectioner his sweetmeats, the fisherman his fish. The Zamíndár levies benevolences from his raiyats for a festival, for a religious ceremony, for a birth, for a marriage; he exacts fees from them on all changes of their holdings, on the exchange of leases and agreements, and on all transfers and sales; he imposes a fine on them when he settles their petty disputes, and when the police or when the magistrate visits his estates; he levies black-mail on them when social scandals transpire, or when an offence or an affray is committed. He establishes his private pound near his cutcherry, and realizes a fine for every head of cattle that is caught trespassing on the raiyats' crops. The abwáb, as these illegal cesses are called, pervade the whole zamíndárí system. In every zamíndárí there is a náib; under the náib there are gumáshtas; under the gumáshta there are piyádas or peons. The náib exacts a 'hisábána' or perquisite for adjusting accounts annually. The náibs and gumáshtas take their share in the regular abwáb; they have also their own little abwáb. The náib occasionally indulges in an ominous raid in the 'mofussil' (the plain country away from the town or headquarters). One rupee is exacted from every raiyat who has a rental, as he comes to proffer his respects. Collecting peons, when they are sent to summon raiyats to the landholder's cutcherry, exact from them daily four or five annas as summon fees.' (P. 23, *Body of the Report.*)

On the other hand, it should not be forgotten that all this need only continue as long as the people themselves choose; but in fact it is the ingrained custom and is submitted to as long as it is kept within customary limits. Every petty native official is born to think that 'wasíla' (pickings and perquisites) are as much a part of his natural rights as air to breathe or water to drink. Nor will the public seriously object as long as he does his duty fairly. When he tries to take too much and does 'zulm' (petty tyranny), the people will turn on him, and a conviction for extortion is more or less attainable, according as the culprit still has friends or is generally in the black books.

There is also a bright side to the question: an amicable understanding with a raiyat for some cesses will often obviate a good deal of litigation about rent enhancement. This was the case in Orissa. In Macneile's *Memorandum on the Revenue Administration* (1873), an interesting notice of the subject will be found. The people complained of certain cesses, and the Zamíndár immediately responded by bringing suits under the Rent Act for enhancement, and by *measuring their lands* (see p. 408).

[1] See Markby, Appendix, pp. 144–148, and authorities quoted.

that where the remission of *sáyer* caused a real loss (by taking away from them the tolls on roads and ferries, or the taxes on bazaars and markets established on their lands), they were compensated.

§ 17. *Other Allowances.*

There were other charges and allowances to be taken into account in the process of consolidating the Zamíndárs' revenue liabilities into one sum. Allowances which had been made *to* the Zamíndár, for expenses of collection, office charges, and the like, were of course duly considered and deducted in making up the totals, where the expense would continue to fall on the Zamíndár. Other payments which he formerly had to make and received allowance for, were now made by the State direct, so that no deduction had to be made on account of them. Thus the payment of pensions and allowances to Muhammadan law-officers called Qázís, other pensions, and the salaries of *Kánúngos*, were now to be paid direct by the treasury, and the Zamíndár was not concerned.

Nor under the revised arrangements, was it necessary to make the Zamíndár any allowance of land free of revenue as remuneration of office—he had now become proprietor of all, and his remuneration was amply secured in other ways. Such lands as were formerly held as nánkár, or by other similar name, were not excluded from assessment [1].

§ 18. *Resumption of Invalid Revenue-free Holdings.*

When the calculation of the assessment on each estate was, so far, provided for, there was still another important and very troublesome matter to be disposed of. If in any Zamíndárí, a large portion of the land was held 'revenue-free' by landholders on the estate, owing to royal favour

[1] But if the Zamíndár refused to engage, he would continue to hold such land revenue free, if he could show a good title (Reg. VIII. 1793, secs. 37–39).

and grant, it is obvious that the Zamíndár could not be called on to make good the revenue to the treasury. But in some cases the Zamíndár himself had made such grants, and then he had to make good the State claims as a matter of course; the grant he made operated against himself, not against the State.

It was however known that in the disordered state of the late Government, a great number of claims to hold revenue-free were really invalid, and so the land was liable to be assessed, or as it is technically called, 'resumed.' This subject demands a somewhat fuller notice. It may now seem a matter of dry detail, but at the time it affected the livelihood of many hundreds, or indeed thousands, and involved a vast amount of Government revenue.

When a Government is strong, it is very careful about titles assigning the revenue of lands away from the treasury, and about granting lands to be held revenue-free. It was no doubt reckoned a pious duty to make such grants for mosques, temples, schools, dharmsálas (or rest-houses), or to the families of reputed saints or men of eminent piety and learning. But it is also an easy thing, when the treasury is empty through waste and corruption, to assign revenue-free lands to favourites or to persons to be rewarded, who ought properly to have received cash pensions or life-grants. In short, though there is a legitimate use of revenue-free grants which the oriental mind approves, still it is easy to abuse the institution and to forget that in all cases they mean freeing one set of persons from taxation at the expense of others who have, in the end, to make up the loss. In the decline of the Mughal empire, not only were such grants multiplied, but a great many of them were made by subordinate officials who had no real authority: not only so, but a considerable number of grants were held under no authority at all, or were supported by forged title-deeds.

It was therefore necessary in the proclamation of 1793, to announce that a scrutiny of revenue-free claims would be made. 'The Governor-General in Council will impose such assessment as he may deem equitable, on all lands at present alienated[1] and paying no public revenue, which have been, or may prove to be, held under illegal or invalid titles.' The grants are spoken of as 'lákhiráj' grants; and the lands were 'lákhiráj' lands. The name is derived from two Arabic words, 'lá,' the negative, and 'khiráj,' revenue or land-tax.

These grants had been either made by royal authority (bádsháhi), in which case they were dealt with under Regulation XXXVII of 1793, or 'hukámi' (incorrectly hukmí), i. e. made by authorities other than the king, called in the Regulations 'non-bádsháhi,' and these are dealt with in Regulation XIX of 1793. It was the latter class that were the most likely to be doubtful in origin; properly speaking, they were all invalid. The Regulation recites that if a Zamíndár had made such a grant (in past days) it was considered void. On the subject of grants assumed to be made by 'officers appointed to the temporary superintendence of the collection of the revenue, under pretext that the land was for pious or charitable uses,' some were no doubt *boná fide*; but, says the preamble, '*in general*, they were given for the personal advantage of the grantee, or with a view to the clandestine appropriation of the produce to the grantor,' or were given for a money consideration to him. Government settled the Zamíndár's estate *jama'* without reference to such grants and exclusive of them. Consequently it was at liberty to 'resume,' i.e. to impose an assessment on, all that were invalid. In determining to do this, Government generously enough said *that if the grant was less than* 100 *bíghás in extent, the assessment would not be for the benefit of Government but for the estate* —would be in fact claimable as *rent*. It is said that both these Regulations failed,—as might be expected in the

[1] This phrase 'alienated' is commoner in Bombay and Madras than elsewhere; it refers rather to the *alienation* of the revenue from the treasury than to the land itself. Of course Government might have land at disposal, and grant both it and the revenue due on it; and in that case 'alienation' would be used in an ordinary sense. But where the land did not belong to Government, 'alienation' referred to giving up the revenue demand, and the consequent lien or ultimate title, which Government has over, or to, all land whatsoever.

absence of a survey and any sufficient land records; for I suppose that by 'failing' it is meant that the claims did not come to light. The law was accordingly revised by Regulation II of 1819, and again by Regulation III of 1828. This latter enactment appointed a Court of 'Special Commissioners'; and after they had done what they could for many years, they were abolished by order of Government in 1846. The more modern procedure of Registration and Certificate, which will be described in the sequel, have at length done everything that is wanted.

The Zamíndárs who were thus empowered to 'resume' all the petty estates for their own benefit, were long loath to do so. No doubt where the 'mu'áfi' was for a pious purpose, it would have been contrary to the public feeling to resume; but if many were created, as asserted, either as a means of raising money or otherwise irregularly, it is not so easy to see why they should have been tenderly dealt with; at a later date, when the Zamíndárís changed hands, successors were not so particular, and resumption suits became common [1].

§ 19. *Principles of Resumption.*

In order to simplify matters, *all* grants made previous to the 12th August, 1765 (date of grant of the *díwání*),

[1] See this explained in Markby, p. 7. I take occasion to observe that I do not quite follow the learned author in his remark that the Regulations gave an extraordinary facility to the estate-holder to resume, or that they laid the burden of proof on the persons claiming to hold free in a manner contrary to the usual rule; but perhaps the remark is due to the confusion, which undoubtedly is traceable in the law, between *assessing* revenue or *rent* (as the case might be) and *ejecting* the claimant from the land. As far as the claim to rent is concerned, the rent was only what had before been the State revenue demand; every acre of cultivated land is bound to pay this; consequently, everybody asserting a grant or claim *not* to pay, is surely most naturally the person who has to take the burden of proof and produce his exemption. It may be that he has no grant, but has been allowed to go free so long, that now it would be hard to charge him; but that is a matter of the nature of his title; it is beside the question of who should take the burden of proof in the first instance. On the other hand, if it was a question of ejecting from the *land*, then the burden is, of course, the other way. The man in possession on an apparent title is to remain until some one else proves his superior title or proves that the other has no business there.

were recognized as valid without question, by whatever authority they might have been made, and whether in writing or without it: the only condition was, that the claimant (or his predecessor) should have actually, and *bonâ fide*, obtained possession of the land so granted previous to the date mentioned, and that the land had not already been declared liable to pay revenue by the officers, or under the orders, of Government.

Grants subsequent to 1765, and before the date of the decennial Settlement (taken as December 1st, 1790[1]), were invalid (with a few unimportant exceptions). So also were grants *after* December 1790.

The provisions of both Regulations refer only to the revenue question, not to the right in the soil, which, if disputed, could be settled in the Civil Court.

§ 20. *Terms of Settlement for such Lands.*

When a grant lapsed to Government or was resumed, the Settlement was to be made, *in perpetuity*, with the person entitled to hold the land, which became an independent 'taluq'—a separate proprietary estate.

In the case of grants made between 1765 and 1st December, 1790, Section 7 of Regulation XIX of 1793 contemplated certain differences as to amount of assessment, which are rather complicated; and it is now of no importance to go into them. These rules applied also (Section 8) to grants resumed in favour of Zamíndárs, but with certain directions as to ascertaining the revenue without expense to the grantee.

The Government seems to have been more anxious to facilitate the resumption by the *landholders* of the invalid lákhiráj grants of less than 100 bíghás, than it was to secure *to the State* the larger invalid grants. Section 10 invalidated *all* grants since December 1790; so that if the Zamíndár himself, or a predecessor, had made the grant, he

[1] 1198 Fasli era of Bengal (see Book I, chap. i. p. 13).

could undo his own act[1]. The grant was invalid as regards the revenue (become the *rent*), and as regards the soil also, if it purported to include the latter: 'and no length of possession shall be hereafter considered to give validity to any such grant.'

§ 21. *Procedure.—Limitation.*

The Settlement-holder (or manager, should the estate happen to be held '*khás*') was empowered to levy rent (or to eject an unentitled holder of the land) without any action in Court or notice to any Revenue Officer; but this applied only to invalid grants dating *after* 1790. In order to assess, or to eject from a grant *previous* to 1790, a regular suit was at first required (Section 11).

Section 30 of Regulation II of 1819 endeavoured to facilitate resumptions of grants previous to 1790, by saying that the application to resume might be presented direct to the Collector, or if presented to a Civil Court, should be referred to the Collector for an opinion; but this was found inconvenient and was repealed in 1862 (Bengal Act VII).

It should be remarked that the landholders at no time largely availed themselves of the summary power given in Section 10 of Regulation XIX of 1793, but preferred to resort to the Civil Court even when the practice of resumption became more general[2]. In consequence, Section 30 of Regulation II of 1819 was frequently misapplied: it was not intended to apply to cases under Section 10 of Regulation XIX (regarding which no suit at all was needed, and therefore if one was filed it was the landholder's own pleasure); it was designed to facilitate inquiry as to grants *before* 1790, for which a suit *was* needed; but it got applied

[1] The motive for this was the principle—which is not unknown in other revenue laws—that the revenue-payer ought not to be allowed (or encouraged) imprudently to give away his lands free of the revenue (which now became his *rent*), and so *contract himself out of the power* of meeting his own revenue engagements to the Government.

[2] See Markby, p. 8, and the cases there quoted.

to both, till the Privy Council ruled that it could not legally be so.

The power given under Section 10, above referred to, was, however, taken away by Act X of 1859, and the land-holder was required to file his suit, which, however, lay to the Collector as a Revenue Court: and when this Act was repealed by Act VIII of 1869, the reference was re-transferred to the Civil Court, as in all other matters.

It was also ultimately ruled by the Privy Council, that notwithstanding the terms above quoted, the Government right to resume was subject to the *law of limitation*, and that, by parity of reasoning, so was the Zamíndár's [1]. The modern limitation law (1877, Act XV) sets the question at rest, since Article 130 of Schedule II expressly gives twelve years as the limit for a private resumption suit; and all suits by the Secretary of State are limited to sixty years.

§ 22. '*Thánadári Lands.*'

Among other '*resumptions*' it may be proper to mention that the Zamíndárs were relieved from the responsibility of maintaining police forces, and so lands held free under the name of 'thánadári,' to provide for them, were resumed and assessed. The 'chákarán' lands held for village service—i.e. for village watchmen or 'chaukidárs' and 'buláhirs'—are not included in this. Sec. 41, Reg. VIII of 1793.

§ 23. *The Waste Lands.*

Although we gather, from the early reports and histories, that, at the date of the Permanent Settlement, a very large proportion of Bengal was uncultivated and covered with jungle, the matter attracted no definite attention.

[1] This was because, in the limitation law then in force (Regulation II of 1805), it was provided that 'nothing . . . in *any part of the existing* Regulations' should be held to authorize a suit barred by the various periods prescribed; so that the terms quoted above, out of Section 10, Regulation XIX of 1793, were over-ridden.

Perhaps it was less prominent in the central districts that formed the important revenue-paying tracts.

At all events, it was assumed that the boundaries of Zamíndárís or other estates were known. And all that was within the boundary belonged to the proprietor, whether waste or cultivated; so that many fine 'sál' forests and other such lands have become included as private property, though, in the absence of any detailed survey or register of fields, it was quite impossible, in most cases, for any one to tell whether the waste was *really part of* the 'estate' or not.

That *some* waste was so, goes without saying; for the extension of the Zamíndár's income, by bringing under the plough lands that were uncultivated, was one of the means most frequently spoken of, by which his wealth was to be assured.

I do not find any mention of 'excess waste lands' (i.e. not included in any one's estate) till Regulation II of 1819. Even then nothing is said about the want of title of persons who had squatted or occupied; only it is said such lands were liable to be assessed to revenue. The Regulation referred especially, as instances of such lands, to—

Reg. II of 1819 sec. 3.

(*a*) lands cultivated in the Sundarbans[1] (these were chiefly on the higher parts of the delta—better protected from inundation, and probably extensions or encroachments from the permanently cultivated estates inland);

(*b*) 'chars' and islands formed in rivers; and other alluvial accretions since the decennial Settlement;

(*c*) lands which did not come under the Settlement specially let out on clearing leases by Collectors.

The assessment was to be on the 'principles of the General Regulations,' and therefore permanent (see Section 6 of Regulation I of 1793).

[1] A vast tract of forest intersected by myriads of tidal streams and creeks, and forming the southern or delta portion of the districts of 24-Pergunnahs, Khúlná and Bákirganj, between the main mouth of the Húghlí on the west and the Megná river on the east.

The matter was better provided for at a later time. Regulation III of 1828 recites in the preamble that—

'Commissioners have likewise, from time to time, been appointed, under the orders of Government, to maintain and enforce the public rights in different districts, in which extensive tracts of country, unowned and unoccupied at the time of the Permanent Settlement, are now liable to assessment, or, *being still waste, belong to the State.*'

This is the first legislative declaration I have found on the subject of the title to waste lands (see Chap. V, p. 236). And while it also follows from this that all lands 'owned' and occupied were liable to be assessed (and that permanently), no *others* could claim a Permanent assessment. In other words, the benefit of the Regulations extended to estates then occupied, even without title, not to all that might thereafter be created by new occupation and cultivation.

We shall have occasion to notice how waste lands were disposed of in several instances in the sequel. Here it is sufficient to notice what the Settlement Regulations intended on the subject.

§ 24. *Résumé of the Zamíndár's Position under the Permanent Settlement.*

The result of these various provisions may now be summarized.

(*a*) The Zamíndár was only required to pay *one* sum, with no extra cesses on the land.

(*b*) The '*abwáb*' were abolished; and he was not allowed, in his turn, to levy such charges on his *raiyats*.

(*c*) The 'Sáyer' were not charged in the revenue: some items were left to benefit the estate, others were abolished, and others (excise, road-tolls, &c.) were taken out of the land-revenue account altogether and separately collected by the Government.

(*d*) The Zamíndár was not allowed to have any deductions from his sum total on the plea of private lands revenue-free as 'nánkár' or subsistence allowance.

(e) Nor to claim deductions on the ground of grants of land revenue-free made by the former Government or by its officers, unless these were valid on the terms prescribed by law. All others were 'resumed' and assessed. This did not affect the Zamíndárs if the 'resumed' grant was over 100 bíghás, because such were treated as *separate estates* and assessed. But, as regards smaller grants, the Zamíndár got the benefit of the resumption, and it was left to him to resume or not, under the prescribed procedure, as he chose.

(f) The Zamíndár was not allowed deductions for pensions, pay of *Qázís*, or of *Kánúngos*, or for police lands—because the State no longer required him to meet any such charges.

§ 25. *Profit left to Zamíndár.*

The Settlement thus made with the Zamíndárs for one consolidated lump sum of revenue, was supposed, *in theory*, to represent nine-tenths of what they received directly in rent from the raiyats, the remaining tenth being allowed to them for their trouble and responsibility[1]. In reality,

[1] See Regulation VIII of 1793, Section 77; and Whinfield's *Revenue Law and Practice of Bengal* (1874), p. 11. That was also the theory under the native rule. The Zamíndárs were to pay in the whole of their collections, less only a percentage allowed them for the trouble (called mushahara), together with some allowances (called 'mazkúrát'), for charitable and religious purposes—to keep lamps at the tombs of saints, to preserve the 'qadam rasúl' or foot-prints of the Prophet, to give khairát or alms to the poor, to pay the village or minor revenue officials, to support the peons or messengers, to keep up the office, &c., &c.

If anything is wanting to show how utterly unlike a 'landlord' the Zamíndár *originally* was, this will supply the want. He got *nothing in the nature of rent from the land*. The raiyat took the balance of its yield after paying the Government share (the balance to him being often small enough), and the Zamíndár had to account to Government for the whole of his collections, getting back only such allowance as the State made him to keep up his office, &c., and to remunerate him for his trouble. Whatever he made

the Zamíndár, when made landlord, got all the increase of rents (as the raising of rents gradually came to be understood), and, in any case, he got the *benefit of all extension of cultivation*, as well as all the 'sáyer' items from fisheries, fruit, grazing, &c., and the benefit of all invalid grants (under 100 bíghás) which he chose to resume. And with all these sources of income, it very soon came to pass that the revenue payment was nothing at all resembling nine-tenths of the total receipts from the estate.

§ 26. *Settlement Arrangements regarding the Zamíndárs' dealings with the Raiyats.*

The Settlement procedure certainly involved very little action with reference to the raiyats,—the great body of agriculturists,—now reduced to a secondary position under the Zamíndárs. The Regulations may be said to have hoped much and provided little. What they did, however, though it might, in some respects, be conveniently noticed here, had better be passed over, for the reason that I must recur to the subject (of landlord and tenant) at a later stage, and it is an object to avoid repetition. I will therefore simply reserve the provisions of the Regulation regarding raiyats or tenants to a subsequent chapter.

§ 27. *Registration of Landed Estates.*

It will next be asked, what attempt was made to prepare registers of estates and records of other rights under the Permanent Settlement?

As there was no survey or demarcation of estates, the only thing that could be done was to prepare a descriptive register, showing the names of estates and the villages, and local subdivisions of land included in it. Regulation

for himself was derived from revenue-free land,—that held as 'nánkár,' or from the levy of unauthorized cesses. In time, it is true, he *came to get* something very like rent. When the later Native rulers contracted with the Zamíndár for a fixed sum, this soon came to be regarded as something apart from the total rents paid in by the raiyats.

XLVIII of 1793 contemplated a general register of estates paying revenue immediately to Government. Each estate was to be described by name, and it was to be mentioned whether it consisted of a *village*, a *tappa* (group of villages), or a *pargana*; whether it was a *jágír* grant, or a *taluq*, or any other special form of grant (of which we shall hear when we come to the chapter on Tenures). If the estate had been partitioned, the shares were to be specified. And should portions of estates lie in different districts, the term 'qismat' (section or fragment), was to be prefixed.

The registers were also supposed to show the local name and the (nominal) area of each village and *pargana*, with the names of the landlord, farmer of rent, &c.

The registers were to be renewed every five years; and a register noting intermediate changes in the proprietorship, partitions and other like occurrences affecting the estates, was to be kept up.

To facilitate this work, the Civil Courts were to send copies of all decrees which affected land, and the Board of Revenue were to notify sales made under the Revenue Recovery laws. Registrars of deeds were also to send notices, and proprietors were to give due information of transfers of property, failing which they became liable to penalty.

Separate registers were kept up of revenue-free estates, and of those which, being invalid, were resumed and assessed to revenue.

These rules were first revised by Regulation VIII of 1800, which mentions the failure[1] which had occurred, and

[1] I do not mean, by the failure of the early records, to imply that the authors of the Settlement purposely neglected the work. On the contrary, 'The original intention,' says Sir G. Campbell, 'of the framers of the Permanent Settlement, was to record all rights. The kánúngos and patwáris were to register all holdings, all transfers, all rent-rolls, and all receipts and payments; and every five years there was to be filed in the public offices a complete register of all land-tenures. But the task was a difficult one: there was delay in carrying it out. English ideas of the rights of a landlord and of the advantage of non-interference, began more and more to prevail in Bengal. The Executive more and more abnegated the functions of recording rights and protecting the inferior holders, and left everything to the judicial tribunals. The patwáris fell into disuse, or became the mere servants of the Zamíndárs: the kánúngos were abolished. No record

directed, among other changes, that the registers should be kept by *parganas*. There is no occasion to go into detail, as the rules have long since been repealed. They never were, or could have been, fully carried out, so impossible is it to manage Records of rights without a survey.

§ 28. *Registration of Under-tenures.*

But no registration of under-tenures, or record of the nature and extent of the rights of cultivators and lessees subordinate to the landlords, was made. And this was a serious want, because after all the 'taluq' grantees and others had been 'separated' (and so recorded as estate-holders on their own account), there must have remained a large number of '*dependent*' taluqs, 'muqarrari' and 'istimrárí' lessees, and others (of whom we shall afterwards hear), whose rights were certainly above those of tenants, and ought therefore to have been recorded. The Settlement Regulations, however, though by no means ignoring such rights, or wishing to destroy them, thought it enough to assume that there were fixed terms of the grant by which the tenure originated, and to declare these binding. The want of proper authoritative registers of such tenures and their holders long continued; and it is only of late years that the registration has been put on a better footing. A notice of the present practice, however, belongs to a later stage of our study.

§ 29. *The means of recovering the Revenue.—Sale-laws.*

I have already alluded to the first indication of the SALE LAWS. The Government had dealt liberally with the Zamíndárs; it had given them a valuable property, and secured them by a permanent limit to the State revenue demand. It was, therefore, thought only fair that, in

of the rights of the raiyats and inferior holders was ever made; and even the quinquennial register of superior rights, which was maintained for a time, fell into disuse.' (Sir G. Campbell's *Land System of India—Cobden Club Papers*, p. 148).

return, the State revenue should be paid with the unfailing punctuality required to meet the pressing needs of the treasury; and it was held, without question, that if the landlord did not or could not, pay, he must be removed at once, by the sale of the whole or a part of the estate, as circumstances should indicate. In those early days, the Revenue instalments were payable *monthly*; and it was held that failure to pay any month's due justified an immediate sale[1]. But in 1799 the rule was relaxed. Regulation VII provided that no sale should take place till the *end of the year*, and thus give more time. And, as the landlord was dependent on the recovery of his rents for his ability to pay, a summary power of distraint for rent was given him. The sanction of the Board of Revenue was also required before a sale was ordered; and only such part of the estate as would suffice was actually sold. Interest was not charged on arrears; and this is still the law.

The law of summary distraint was oppressive to the raiyats, but we are not concerned with that here, but only with the law for recovery of arrears of revenue and its effect on the system. As the revenue got lighter and lighter, and the landlords had more and more power against the rent-payers, it is hardly to be wondered at that the provisions against revenue default should have been made more stringent. The next Regulation of importance was Regulation XI of 1822, which made it no longer necessary to issue process of attachment or try any arrangement for direct collection, before putting up the estate (or part of it) to sale.

This law lasted till 1841, when Act XII replaced it; this in its turn was repealed in 1845; and Act XI of 1859 began what I may call the 'modern sale law'—to which reference will be made in the chapter headed 'Revenue Business and Procedure.'

[1] Kaye, p. 185. As a matter of fact, the first Regulation, XV of 1793, prescribed the ordinary process against debtors, viz. the imprisonment of the person, and the sale of his property. Regulation III of 1794 abolished the imprisonment of the defaulting proprietor, and substituted a power of immediate sale of his estate.

§ 30. *Voiding of existing encumbrances when the Estate was sold.*

One feature of the sale law, which was early allowed to be necessary, deserves to be mentioned. Besides the under-tenures, which existed in the shape of dependent taluqs and other privileged holdings, it became the custom with the landlords to divest themselves of the trouble of management, by farming out portions of their estate. The detail of this will appear later on, but it is obvious that the result was to create, on most estates, numerous under-tenures. All these were so many encumbrances on the estate; and if, when the landlord's interest was sold for arrears, all these remained valid, the net interest saleable would, in all probability, not fetch enough at auction to realize the arrear. As early as Regulation XLIV of 1793, we find that when an estate is auctioned for arrears— Reg. XLIV of 1793, sec. 5.

'all engagements which such proprietor shall have contracted with dependent taluqdárs whose taluqs may be situated in the lands sold; as also all leases to under-farmers, and *pattás* to raiyats [with certain exceptions] . . . . shall *stand cancelled* from the day of sale, and the purchaser . . . . shall be at liberty to collect from such dependent taluqdárs, &c., whatever the former proprietor would have been entitled to demand, according to the established usages and rates of the pargana, &c., had the engagements so cancelled never existed.'

This did not apply to absolute alienations (e.g. to reverse a sale actually made), nor to leases to Europeans, of lands for dwelling-houses, gardens, or manufactories; nor did it interfere with the assessment imposed by the Permanent Settlement[1].

But this wholesale avoidance of contracts made by the defaulting landlord, was soon recognized to be excessive. We gradually find new Regulations softening the terms.

[1] So that, when the estate was sold, the Collector could not offer it at a new assessment, otherwise the Permanent Settlement would, in many instances, have been got rid of.

First, Regulation I of 1801 protected arrangements that might have been concluded during *the year previous* to the date of sale. Next, Regulation XI of 1822 modified the general rule. It no longer provided that such leases, &c., '*stood cancelled*,' but only that they *were* '*liable to be annulled*' by the purchaser: and it was also expressly allowed that five classes of persons who had an heritable and transferable interest, or raiyats who had a right of occupancy, could not have their engagements annulled. This was perhaps *implied*, but not stated, by the earlier law.

The Sale laws of 1841 and 1845 are very much the same in these respects, but expressly declare the right of the purchaser to enhance the rents of all under-tenures and (after notice given) to eject tenants, subject to exceptions, five in number.

Nothing further was changed till 1859. The only interest these earlier provisions now have is as illustrating how the revenue system grew, and how ideas regarding sales, under-tenures, and enhancement of rents, were gradually modified. But it is to be remembered that titles to existing property may still depend on the laws which were in force at the time when the sales, under which they arose, took place, and therefore the early laws cannot be omitted altogether from notice.

How many difficulties have arisen out of this principle of sale, and the necessary 'clear title' which goes with it, and how those difficulties had been met, belongs to a later section, where we shall deal with the modern law in its practical application.

§ 31. *Effects of the Permanent Settlement and its Laws.*

Having now taken a general retrospect of the principles and practice of the Permanent Settlement, as regards the persons settled with, the nature of the revenue, the method of its assessment, the treatment of the waste land, the registration of estates, and the recovery of arrears of revenue, we may proceed to make a general retrospect of what the effects of the Settlement have been.

The decennial Settlement, made permanent in 1793, extended to Bengal, Bihár, and Orissa—the Orissa of these days being (I may repeat) the tract between the Rúpnarain and Subarnrekhá rivers, now in the Midnapore district [1].

In general terms, it may be said that it disappointed many expectations and produced several results that were not anticipated. It has been stated that, at first, the revenue levied from the Zamíndárs and others made proprietors, was heavy; but as the effects of British peace and security made themselves felt, and as the value of land and its produce rose, and waste lands were brought under the plough, the assessments became proportionately lighter and lighter [2]. And it must be borne in mind that every estate at the time of its original assessment contained considerable,

[1] The land-revenue, though permanently fixed in 1793, was liable to be increased by causes which had nothing to do with the assessment of the original estates; for example, the Zamíndárs were relieved of police charges, and the lands held free for the purpose would be called in and assessed as the arrangements were completed. Then the gradual resumption of invalid revenue-free tenures caused an increase, as well as the assessment of land held in *excess* ('taufir' in revenue language) of the proper estate (Reg. II of 1819): and there were other causes. This is exclusive of the revenue of temporarily settled estates, or lands held by Government. The Permanent Settlement Revenue was about R. 2,85,87,722. In 1828–29, the demand had risen to Company's R. 3,04,27,770, in 1846 47 it was R.3,12,52,676, and in 1848 49 R.3,40, 96,605. In 1856-57 it appears at the slightly reduced figure of 3,37, 38,783. In the following year it rose to R. 3,39,10,632. In 1882–83 it was R. 3,62,78,355: the increase during the ten years previously had been more than a lakh a year. In 1888–89 the permanently Settled Revenue was R. 3,22,90,777 (*Rev. Adm. Rep.* p. 2). These figures are calculated for the whole of the districts in the old Permanent Settlement, excluding Chota Nagpore (Chutiyá Nágpur), which had not then been settled (*Report*, 1883).

[2] The revenue assessed in 1790–93 being, as just stated, Company's R.2,85,87,722, or under three millions of pounds, the Zamíndárs were estimated to get, as their profit, a sum equal to about a tenth of the total assessment. They no doubt got more; but even if we say a fifth, instead of a tenth, the rental or profit would be under a million. At the present day, judging from the valuation for road-cess (made in respect of the rent paid to landlords by tenants and tenure-holders of all classes, *plus* the value of land in the direct possession of the proprietors), a fair estimate of the rental made it thirteen millions, and it must have largely increased since that date. The revenue they pay now is about three and a-quarter millions. So that even on the rule of 'half-rental assets = the revenue' prevalent in Northern India, they pay less than half (probably less than one third) of what other landowners have to pay.

often very large, areas of culturable waste of great value; and as this was entirely unassessed, all the immense subsequent extension of cultivation was so much clear profit to the owner[1].

Before, however, these changes began to tell, the assessments were heavy enough to necessitate diligence and prudence; and the landlords were not able at once to keep pace with the inflexible demand. The consequence was a very widespread default. As just now explained, the law practically stood to enforce a *sale* of the estate (or part of it), directly the owner was in arrears, and it followed that large numbers of estates were put up to sale.

'In 1796–97,' says the late Mr. J. Macneile[2], 'lands bearing a total revenue of Sicca[3] R. 14,18,756, were sold for arrears, and in 1797–98 the *jama'* of lands so sold amounted to Sicca R. 22,74,076. By the end of the century, the greater portions of the estates of the Nadiyá, Rajsháhí, Bishnpur, and Dinájpur Rájás, had been alienated. The Bardwán estate was seriously crippled, and the Bírbhúm Zamíndárí completely ruined. A host of smaller Zamíndárís shared the same fate. In fact, it is scarcely too much to say that, within the ten years that immediately followed the Permanent Settlement, a complete revolution took place in the constitution and ownership of the estates which formed the subject of that Settlement.'

One effect of the 'Sale Law' was to reduce very greatly the size of the Zamíndárís, for up to 1845 they were sold piecemeal. The making into separate estates of taluqs, the owners of which established a claim to be dealt with sepa-

[1] Government, no doubt, afterwards resumed, and assessed separately, some large areas of waste, but it was waste improperly or fraudulently annexed to the estate. Many, if not most, estates had a great deal of waste which was confessedly included in their boundaries.

[2] *Memorandum on the Revenue Administration of the Lower Provinces of Bengal* (Calcutta, 1873), p. 9.

[3] The 'Sikka' was the first rupee struck (in 1773) by the Company at Murshidábád, but still bearing the name of the Mughal Emperor Sháh 'Álam. In Regulation XXXV of 1793, it was enacted that this coin was to be legal tender, and was to bear the 19th year of the Emperor's reign for uniformity sake. Speaking roughly, three 'Company's rupees' equalled two *sikka*. The sikka contained 176·13 grains Troy, and the rupee afterwards introduced in 1835 as the 'Company's,' 165 grains, of pure silver.

rately from the Zamíndárs, and the effect of partitions, had also tended to the same result. The tendency to *subdivide* estates is also great, and especially in Bihár. In twenty years, the number of estates was doubled in Patna division, and in Tirhút (Muzaffarpur and Darbhanga districts) was more than trebled. Taking the figures for 1882–3, out of a total number of 110,456 estates borne on the roll of 39 districts of Bengal proper and Bihár, 457, or 0·41 per cent. only, are great properties, with an area of 20,000 acres or upwards: 12,304, or 11·1 per cent., range from 500 to 20,000 acres; while the number of estates which fall short of 500 acres, is 97,695, or 88·4 per cent. of the whole [1].

In Chittagong, however, the estates were always small, and in Bihár there never were any very large Zamíndárís.

§ 32. *Districts affected by the Permanent Settlement.*

The Permanent Settlement extended over the following districts in Bengal, as the districts are now constituted:—

BENGAL.

Bardwán.	Nadiyá.	Maimansingh.
Bankúra.	Murshidábád.	Farídpur.
Bírbhúm.	Dinájpur.	Bákirganj.
Hooghly (Húghlí).	Málda.	Chittagong (Cháṭṭágráoṅ).
Howrah (Haura).	Rájhsháhi.	Noacolly (Nawákháli).
24-Pergunnahs.	Rangpur.	Tipperah (Tiprá).
Jessore (Jasúr).	Bogra (Bagurá).	Dacca (Dákhá).
Khúlná.	Pabná.	

BIHÁR.

Patná.	Darbhanga*.	Purneah (Parniya).
Gáyá.	Sáran.	Bhágalpur.
Sháhábád.	Champáran.	Monghyr (Munger).
Muzaffarpur*.		

* These two form the old Tirhút District.

SANTÁLIA.—Part of the Santál Pergunnahs adjoining the Regulation Districts.

ORISSA.—Mednipur (Midnapore), except one pargana which was settled along with Káták (Cuttack).

CHOTA NAGPORE (Chutiyá Nágpur). Parts of all the districts.

[1] *Report*, 1883, p. 4.

Some estates in the Mánbhúm, Singbhúm, Lohárdagga, and Házáribágh districts (now in the Chutiyá Nágpur Division) came under Permanent Settlement, though they are 'non-Regulation districts,' because they were then included in collectorates which formed part of the Bengal or Bihár of that date.

The part of the Jalpáigúrí district south-west of the Tísta river, also was permanently settled under the same circumstances. A glance at the 'Settlement map' annexed to this volume will show the whole matter.

A portion of Sylhet was permanently settled, but the Settlement did not extend to Jaintiya, nor did it touch anything but the lands under cultivation at the time. This district will be alluded to under the head of Assam, in which province it is now included. Part of Goálpárá (also in Assam) was included in the Permanent Settlement[1].

§ 33. *Proportion of Permanent and other Settlement Revenue in Bengal.*

It may also be convenient here to notice the proportion of Bengal revenue which is permanently settled to that obtained from estates not so settled. The total land-revenue, as stated in the Board's Report 1888–9, is, in round numbers, R. 3,81,00,000, of which R. 3,23,00,000 comes from permanently-settled estates and R. 58,00,000 (or 15·2 per cent. of the whole) from estates which are temporarily settled, and from estates of which the soil is owned by Government, *together*.

[1] The results of the Settlement, and the condition of the tenants under it, both in Bihár and Bengal, as questions of social economy, are well stated in Mr. (now Sir H. S.) Cunningham's *British India and its Rulers* (p. 166 et seq.). Such questions, interesting as they are, are evidently outside the scope of a Revenue manual, and I can only make this brief reference to the subject.

CHAPTER II.

THE TEMPORARY SETTLEMENTS, INCLUDING THE RENT-SETTLEMENTS OF GOVERNMENT ESTATES.

SECTION I.—INTRODUCTORY.

§ 1. *Lands not Permanently Settled.*

IN this chapter we have to treat of two different classes of lands, which must not be confused together: (1) lands held by persons recognized as proprietors, but not under the Permanent Settlement law; (2) lands which do not belong to proprietors, i.e. in which no proprietary right other than that of Government exists.

In the first class there is, of course, a Settlement of land-revenue, only that it is not under the Permanent Settlement Regulations, but under later laws which contemplate the assessment being raised periodically, and the making of a Revenue-survey and record of the rights of all parties.

In the second class there is properly no *Settlement of land-revenue*, because Government being itself the owner, the *revenue* is merged in *rent* taken by the Government as owner. Nevertheless 'Settlement operations' are spoken of as applicable to both classes of estates, under a view of the matter which I will presently endeavour to make clear.

In the first class of lands,—proprietary estates temporarily settled,—the law is chiefly contained in Regulations VII of 1822 and IX of 1833, and some special Acts which will be noticed more in detail hereafter.

In the second class, or Government estates, two methods

of management may be adopted: either the tract is kept 'raiyatwár,' i.e. Government deals as landlord directly with its tenants[1]; or a farmer or some kind of middleman (who is in no sense a proprietor) may be employed on certain terms, to collect and pay in the rents of the tenantry, for which he receives a certain emolument by way of deduction from the collections. The present tendency is, however, against the employment of such persons; it is preferred to deal direct with the tenants[2].

The origin of these two classes of lands has to be explained.

§ 2. *Temporarily-settled Estates.*

To this class belong—

(1) Territory annexed by treaty or conquest at a date subsequent to 1793. In these Government recognized existing proprietary rights, but the Permanent Settlement Regulations did not apply; as (speaking in general terms) in the districts of the modern Orissa (Katák, Bálásúr, and Púrí). To this we may add districts exempted, for special reasons, from the operation of the Regulations;

(2) Resumed and lapsed revenue-free (lákhiráj) lands,—not in permanently-settled districts, but held by persons who are recognized as proprietors[3];

(3) Alluvial accretions to temporarily-settled estates, which, under the law, may belong to the estate-owner, but be liable to pay revenue.

[1] The student will mark this, and not confuse the 'raiyatwárí tracts' of modern Bengal Reports with the raiyatwárí districts of Bombay, Madras, &c. In the latter, Government treats the raiyats *not as its tenants*, but as individual proprietors—whether called in law 'proprietors' or 'occupants'—and assesses their holdings to land-revenue properly so called. The term 'raiyatwárí tract' in the eleven Bengal districts in which it occurs, means that there is no proprietor but Government, and that Government acts directly as the *landlord*, taking *rent* from the tenants, which rent it enhances, &c., just as any other landlord does under the law.

[2] See post, § 6, page 449.

[3] Invalid or lapsed revenue-free holdings *in a permanently-settled district*, when 'resumed,' are entitled to be permanently settled, but no others.

§ 3. *Government Estates.*

To this class belong—

(1) *Waste lands.*—In the first place the Permanent Settlement Regulations extended only to estates of Zamíndárs and other actual proprietors *as they existed at the time.* These estates, no doubt, were very loosely defined, and all included a good deal more land than was actually cultivated at the time, and were intended to do so; but there were districts in which the area of waste was so large that no claim to it was made, not even by squatters or persons encroaching beyond their own adjacent estates. This is notably the case in such districts as Goálpárá and Sylhet (described under Assam) and Chittagong; and again in the tract known as the Sundarbans between the mouths of the Húghlí and Megná rivers (part of the districts of the '24-Pergunnahs,' Khúlná and Bákirganj), in the 'Dáman-i-koh,' or hilly tract of the Santál Pergunnahs. In all such waste lands, until (under 'Waste Land Rules') Government leased or granted the proprietary right, the ownership remained vested in the State.

(2) When estates or parts of estates were sold for arrears of revenue and Government bought them in, either because no bidders appeared, or because satisfactory terms were not offered[1].

(3) Thánadári lands, or lands formerly allotted to Zamíndárs for keeping up 'thánas' or police stations. The Zamíndárs were exonerated from this duty, and the lands were resumed by Government. Reg. I of 1793, sec. 8, cl. 4.

[1] At one time it was supposed that if Government parted with the proprietary right in estates originally permanently settled but sold for arrears, the proprietor so acquiring was only entitled to a temporary Settlement: but this is not so. Whenever sold, the purchaser would acquire a Permanent Settlement right under the Regulations. See *Boards Rev. Rules*, vol. ii.

(4) Islands and 'chars' formed in rivers or on the sea-shore—not being accretions by alluvion to existing estates, which by the law or custom (Reg. XI of 1825) belonged to the estate to which they accreted—were liable to a separate Settlement. With such a vast river-system as Bengal possesses, this head is not devoid of importance.

(5) Lands escheated in default of legal heirs or claimants.

(6) Lands forfeited for any State offence, e.g. the Khúrdá estate in Púrí.

(7) Lands which were acquired by conquest in cases where the lands were not already owned, and the Government did not see fit to confer any general proprietary title: as, e.g. the Dwárs of Jalpáigúrí and the Darjíling District [1].

§ 4. *Official Classification.*

The existence of these variously-originating estates necessitated a recognized official classification. Such a classification was adopted under Sir G. Campbell's administration in the district Revenue Rolls for 1876–77 [2]:—

CLASS I. (All) permanently-settled estates—

(1) At the decennial Settlement (1789 to 1791);

(2) Resumed revenue-free settled permanently;

(3) Estates formerly the property of Government, but the proprietary right in which had been sold to private persons subject to revenue fixed in perpetuity.

(4) Ditto, ditto, subject to a revenue liable to periodical revision [3].

[1] I need hardly add an eighth class —Land acquired under the Acquisition Act—for such lands will usually be applied to a special purpose; but such lands are sometimes taken, and not being needed, are either re-sold or kept as Government lands.

[2] And lands were described according to it in the Board's Report, 1874-75. See *Report*, 1883, p. 3.

[3] As a subhead of Class I, No. 4 seems a little contradictory: I sup-

CLASS II. Temporarily-settled estates, the property of private persons—

(1) Settled for definite periods, including (of course) such estates, when—

(2) Farmed } Owing to refusal of the proprietors to
(3) or managed direct. } accept the terms of Settlement.

CLASS III. Estates the property of Government, however acquired, and whether settled (i. e. the rents are made over to a responsible collector, who is allowed a remuneration), or whether managed direct: but this class has been for convenience subdivided so as to give a further—

CLASS IV. 'Raiyatwárí tracts,' i.e. large Government estates with an area of not less than 5000 acres, where the Government deals direct with the cultivators, settling and recording their rents, and collecting them itself.

A glance at the table of estates and revenue at pp. 470–1 will show how these are distributed.

The orders contemplate the 'Daman-i-koh' of the 'Santál Pergunnahs,' being classified as a single raiyatwárí tract.

The Khúrdá and Noánand estates in Orissa are, however, entered as Government estates under Class III, because, though in some respects raiyatwárí (all rents and rights being recorded), the collection is managed by responsible 'sarbarákárs,' who are allowed a sort of Settlement.

Government lands called 'Jalpái' lands in Midnapore[2] are not treated as 'raiyatwárí' unless the tract is 5000 acres or over—notwithstanding that the raiyats pay direct.

In Chittagong, farms of circles, and 'nauábád' taluqs or holdings, are in Class III, because they are Government property as far as the right in the soil is concerned.

pose it refers to cases where the Settlement has been made once for all, but at progressive rates.

[2] Mentioned in the chapter on Tenures. They cover 76.835 acres (*Statistical Acc., Bengal, Midnapore*—vol. iii. 86–100). They are lands for producing the fuel used in boiling brine to make salt. Government resumed these lands under the Salt laws, and compensated the owners or holders.

§ 5. *Certain Districts without any Revenue System.*

In concluding this introductory explanation, I should take occasion to observe that I omit from consideration certain territories which are under Government control in the Political Department, and have no regular revenue-system. Such are—

(1) The portion of the Chittagong district known as the Chittagong Hill tracts.

(2) The portion of the Tipperah (Típrá) District known as Hill Tipperah belonging to the Mahárájá of Tipperah.

(3) The Chiefships known as Tributary or 'Peshkash' States of Orissa.

(4) Chiefships in the Chutiyá Nágpur Division (those of the old 'South-West Frontier Agency').

§ 6. *Policy as to Retention or Disposal of Land.*

It will next be asked, Under what principle does Government sell or retain and farm or manage direct, the lands which became Government estates? To this question I can best reply by an extract from the Report of 1882–83 on the Land system in Bengal, Bihár, and Orissa (p. 6):—

'The Government estates were originally either permanently settled or sold outright. The policy was changed in 1871, since when, temporary Settlements only have been allowed, and, where sales have been considered expedient, the estates were first settled for a term of years, and then sold subject to a revision of the Government revenue on the expiration of the term of Settlement. The above procedure, however, appeared to be of questionable legality, and in 1875 the Government, at the suggestion of the Board of Revenue, ruled that an estate should be considered as qualified for direct management—

(1) If it was of sufficient extent and cultivation to support a tahsíldári [special collecting] establishment;

(2) If, though not yielding a revenue sufficient to cover such expense, there was reasonable expectation that its gross rent could be increased by improvements, extended cultivation, or otherwise, to that amount;

(3) If, though not sufficient in extent or rental alone, to find employment or funds for a separate establishment, it was so situated as to be capable of being incorporated with one or more similar 'khás-maháls,' so as to form a compact tahsíldári circle[1];

and that smaller isolated estates might still be retained under direct management, if their situation near the headquarters of a district or a subdivision was such as to allow of their proper supervision by the Government officers. Smaller estates not admitting of such supervision were to be sold after survey and Settlement, in which the rights of all classes of cultivators were to be recorded; and the estates so sold, were to be transferred to their new proprietors, with the revenue fixed in perpetuity, except in Orissa (a temporarily-settled province), where the sale should be made subject to revision of the *jama'* on the termination of the general Settlement of the province. The above orders are still in force. Farming is adopted only in very exceptional cases, or as a last resort, when every other mode of disposing of the estate has failed. Direct management, though more troublesome, and probably not less expensive, is preferred to farming, because it enables Government officers to gain a practical knowledge of the progress of agriculture, of the extent to which the productive powers of the land have developed, and of the increased money-value of the produce, which, in Bengal, it is difficult to obtain in any other way.'

[1] I may repeat the explanation that, in revenue language, when any land was managed directly by the Collector's establishment (without a farmer or lessee) it was said to be held 'khás.' Government estates were therefore called 'khás mahals,' and the term is commonly used in Revenue Reports.

SECTION II.—THE TEMPORARY SETTLEMENT LAW AND PROCEDURE.

§ 1. *Origin of the Settlement Law.*

When the first extensive additions to the Company's territory occurred on the annexation of the 'Ceded' districts (1801) and the 'Conquered' districts (1803), the Permanent Settlement and its methods had already come into discussion in connection with the Madras Settlements, as I have stated at length in the chapters devoted to Madras. Both the Ceded Provinces in the North-West, and Orissa, presented special features which did not invite a repetition of the Permanent Settlement; and notably there were few, if any, 'Zamíndárs' of the Bengal class. I will state presently some particulars about Orissa, but here I only wish to touch on certain salient points.

The result of the discussions, and of Mr. Holt Mackenzie's [1] Minute, was the passing of the Temporary Settlement Regulation, No. VII of 1822, which applied to the 'Ceded and Conquered Districts'—the Orissa Districts (called in the preamble 'Katák, Patáspúr, and its dependencies') being among the latter. Now this law, instead of proceeding to an estimated lump-sum Settlement without survey or inquiry into details, expressly directed a survey and an inquiry into the rights in every village and field, which was to be followed by a valuation of the 'net produce' of land —i. e. (briefly stated) an inquiry into the actual produce on various lands, of various crops. From the gross produce valued in money, the cost of production, wages of labour, &c., were to be deducted, and the result was the *net* produce, of which a certain fraction, never fixed by law but

[1] This eminent civilian was, if I may say so, the prophet of the Temporary Settlement system of Upper India (and Orissa), as Mr. Shore had been in 1788-89 of the Zamíndárí Settlement of Bengal. Mr. H. Mackenzie's great minute of 1819 in the North-Western Provinces, did for the system there, what Mr. Shore's minutes of 1788-89 did for Bengal. (See the chapter on N. W. Provinces Settlements.)

determined on principles of fair dealing and expediency by the executive power, was to be taken as the State share or land-revenue. But (as more fully detailed in the chapter on the North-Western Provinces Settlement, vol. ii) the task of finding this 'net produce' of every field proved an impossible one; and by Regulation IX of 1833 it was abandoned in favour of one which aimed at determining the 'net assets.' This practically meant (or rather came to mean as experience widened) the total receipts from the land in the shape of *rents*. Putting it shortly, all modern methods of Temporary Settlement which trace their origin to the Regulations of 1822–33, tend more and more to aim at discovering what is the *actual rental* of land, correcting the sum total of rents paid, by adding in the estimated rent (calculated on the *data* afforded by the neighbourhood) of lands which are enjoyed rent-free or are cultivated by the proprietors themselves. In other words, the ascertainment of the *income from rental* and personal enjoyment of cultivated lands, is the basis of Settlement. Now, in Bengal, for temporarily-settled districts, a certain proportion of this 'corrected rental' is the *land-revenue*. But in Government estates, the State as landlord, has also to fix the whole *rental* which it takes as owner. In both cases, therefore, a *public officer has to ascertain the rent*: and it matters very little whether it is only ascertaining what that rent is, with a view to taking a portion as revenue, or whether it also involves (in disputed cases), adjusting, equalizing, raising or reducing, rents, with a view to taking the whole as landlord[1]. A rent-inquiry of some kind is at the basis both of temporary Settlements and of managing Government estates.

The reader will then understand why we are able to put these two dissimilar classes of estates under one chapter, and why 'Settlement operations' are conveniently, if not quite logically, spoken of as applicable to both.

[1] Or the whole rental less such percentage as it allows in case a middleman is employed to collect the rents.

§ 2. *Settlement and Rent-settlement Law.*

The law for the *Settlement of Rents* is now contained in the tenth chapter of the Bengal Tenancy Act (General), Act VIII of 1885[1], and, when that Act does not apply, in other Acts, as will be presently noted.

The same principles apply to the adjustment of rents in Government estates and raiyatwárí tracts, as in those cases, in private estates, in which the Tenancy law contemplates the interference of public authority to settle rents.

And for all matters connected with the *Settlement of the Land-Revenue*, other than the adjustment of rents, Regulation VII of 1822 (amended in 1825) and Regulation IX of 1833 are still the law, except for the 'Scheduled districts,' in which there are special laws for the Land-Revenue administration.

Act VIII of 1885, sec. 189.

Rules under the Tenancy Act (which have the force of law), and instructions as to Settlement issued by the Board of Revenue, are the natural and necessary supplement to both kinds of Settlement law.

The Tenancy Act of 1885 does not, however, apply (unless extended specially) to the districts of Orissa (Katák, Bálásúr, and Púrí) nor to the 'Scheduled Districts.' Hence, *in those*, we have three sources of rent and Settlement law: (1) the Regulations and instructions above mentioned; (2) Bengal Act VIII of 1879 (not repealed in districts to which Act VIII of 1885 does not apply); (3) any special laws or Regulations relating to particular districts as far as those touch on rent or revenue matters. The law in force under these three heads may be thus exhibited[2]:—

[1] The magnitude of the interests involved, and the contest there was, as well as the bearing of the Act on other laws framed in the Imperial Council, rendered it necessary that the Act should be passed in the Legislative Council of India, and not in the Bengal Legislative Council.

[2] R. and F. Tenancy Act, p. 176. B. Act VIII of 1879 refers to Settlement officers' powers, and will not be confused with VIII of 1869 (the old Tenant Act) still in force in those districts.

DISTRICTS.	
Bálásúr, Katák, and Púrí.	Regulation VIII of 1793[1]. (For Katák) Regulation XII of 1805. Regulation V of 1812 (not applicable to Katák); Regulation XVIII of 1812. Regulation VII of 1822 (and amendments in 1825). Regulation IX of 1833. Bengal Act VIII of 1879.
Darjíling, Jalpáigúrí (south of the Tísta).	Bengal Act VIII of 1879.
Jalpáigúrí (the Bhután or Western Dwárs).	Bengal Act VIII of 1879. Act XVI of 1869.
Santál Parganas.	Regulation (33 Vict., Cap. 3) III of 1872.
Chittagong Hill Tracts.	Act XXII of 1860. (See Bengal Settlement Manual, 1888, page 4.)
Chutiyá Nágpur Districts— Mánbhúm, Hazáribágh, Lohárdaggá, Singhbhúm.	Bengal Act VIII of 1879; and see Bengal Acts II of 1869 and I of 1879.

Under these laws, according to circumstances, different kinds of Settlements can be made: e.g. if it is desirable merely to settle a lump sum of revenue without recording tenants' rents or rights, it can be done under the Regulations. This is seldom the case. If (as is usually the case) the more complete Settlement with a record of rights and an enhancement of rents (where necessary) is desired, then in districts where the Act of 1885 does *not* apply, the Regulation, aided by Bengal Act VIII of 1879, will give the needful authority. The Act is, in fact, the supplement of the Regulations of 1822–33. The latter only enabled the Settlement Officer to declare what he considered a fair rent, and this was only presumed to be correct till set aside by a regular civil suit; but Act VIII of 1879 empowers rents to be enhanced under circumstances therein stated.

In cases where the Act of 1885 *is* in force, then, if it is desired to have a complete record and adjustment of rents, the Act must be followed; but if it is supposed the en-

[1] Applicable to a number of estates, intermediate between the semi-independent 'Tributary' States or Mahâls and the periodically-settled portion. These were granted a Permanent Settlement for special reasons; and they occupy a considerable portion of the districts—Katák especially.

hancement is not necessary, and that Settlement will be made without readjustment of rents, or with such a readjustment as can be made by agreement (e.g. the enhancement not being in excess of two annas in the rupee[1]), then there will be no occasion to proceed to notify the tract under the Tenancy Act, but the old Settlement procedure will suffice.

§ 3. *Certain operations even in permanently-settled Estates.*

It should be remarked that even where no re-assessment of land-revenue is possible, i.e. in permanently-settled districts,—some of the operations of a Settlement may require to be carried out.

The Local Government, *with* the sanction of the Governor-General in Council, may order a survey and a record of rights to be prepared for all lands in any local area. This power has not yet been exercised except experimentally. In time it is to be hoped that every district will ultimately be so provided for[2].

Without the supreme sanction, such orders can be issued in cases where a large proportion of either landlords or tenants desire it and deposit the amount (or security for the amount) of expenses, as directed by the Local Government; or where such a proceeding is calculated to settle or avert a serious dispute between landlords and tenants; or where the estate is being managed by the Court of Wards. This is in addition to its application (before alluded to) to all Government Estates (where, indeed, legal sanction would hardly be necessary); or where a Temporary Settlement of land-revenue is to be made.

Act VIII of 1885. sec. 101.

[1] That being the limit under the Act to which enhancement by contract is valid. (Sec. 29, &c.)

[2] The reader will learn hereafter that in the North-Western Provinces permanently-settled districts (those that belonged to the Benares Province and were ceded in 1795), though permanently settled, have now all been cadastrally surveyed, and a complete record of rights prepared. In Bengal an attempt —which I am afraid I must call abortive—has been made in one of the Bihár districts, but the day *must* come when the work will be carried out.

[3] F. and R. Tenant Act, p. 174, where the orders are quoted.

This remark practically covers the whole ground, because in territories to which the Act of 1885 is not as yet extended, the existing law enables the same thing to be done, at least to a certain extent.

§ 4. *Operations of Settlement.*

In any ordinary Settlement under the Regulations of 1822–33, measurement, I have said, is contemplated by the law; or, if proceedings are undertaken under the Tenancy Act, a survey is specially authorized. There is also a General Survey Act (Bengal Act V of 1875), under which the Lieutenant-Governor may direct that a survey may be made of any lands, and that the boundaries of estates, tenures, 'mauzas' (villages), and fields, be demarcated and surveyed.

The following processes are therefore ordinarily comprised in Settlements of land-revenue, and in other Settlements of rent, so far as may be necessary[1] :—

1. Demarcation of lands and adjustment of boundary disputes.
2. Measurement and testing the same.
3. Fixing and recording of rents.
4. Recording rights and interests in the soil.
5. Settling any provision for police expenses, village patwárís, allowances of the nature of *málikána*, &c.
6. In land-revenue Settlements, fixing the terms of Settlement, and who is to be settled with.

§ 5. *Demarcation.*

The Collectors or the Settlement Officers are empowered, by the Regulations and Acts mentioned, to enforce the attendance of the proper persons to point out boundaries and give the necessary information. They are also empowered to decide boundary disputes generally, on the usual basis of

[1] The student will do well to have for reference the Board of Revenue *Settlement Manual* (Edition of 1888 : Calcutta Secretariat Press).

possession, leaving disputes of title to be settled in the Civil Court. But where the proceeding is under the Tenancy Act, the Settlement Officer is wisely endowed with the power of settling disputes of title as well[1].

Act VIII of 1885, sec. 106, 7.

§ 6. *Survey.*

I may take this opportunity of giving a *general* account of the Bengal Survey system. The *Report* of 1883 gives the following account:—

'Almost the whole of these provinces has now been surveyed so as to show the boundaries of each village and estate; but there has been no field-measurement except in a few limited tracts. There is a demarcation department whose business it is to define the boundaries of villages and estates, and to make a compass-and-chain survey of them. The ordinary scale of the maps prepared from this survey is sixteen inches to the mile. All disputes regarding boundaries are decided by the demarcation officers.

'Where the whole of a village belongs to one estate, nothing but the outer boundary of the village has to be defined and surveyed; but, in a very large proportion of cases, there are lands of more than one estate in the village, and the lands of each estate are frequently scattered about the village and not situated in one compact block. Thus, there may be lands of ten estates in a village, but they may be contained in forty, fifty, or even double that number of separate plots. Each of these plots has to be separately defined and surveyed by the demarcation surveyor. It is the extent to which plots of land belonging to different estates are thus intermixed that renders the demarcation of a Bengal district such a lengthy operation. To take Hooghly as an example, there were in round numbers 4000 village circuits demarcated; in about 1000 of these the whole of the village belonged to one estate, and no interior measurements were necessary. In the remaining 3000, no

[1] Act VIII of 1885, secs. 106–7. In Section 108 it is enacted that the Local Government shall appoint a special judge (or more than one) to hear appeals in such cases. Both suits and appeals are heard (speaking generally) under the Civil Procedure Code, and there is a second or 'special' appeal (on a point of law only, with certain special additions, Sec. 109) to the High Court.

less than 80,000 plots had to be surveyed, owing to the intermixture of lands of different estates.

'The demarcation has been followed by a professional survey-staff, whose business it is to make a scientific survey of the village boundaries, and also a map (usually on a scale of four inches to the mile) showing the geographical and topographical features of the country. The whole of the work, both of the demarcation and professional survey, has been carried out at the expense of Government, although the Government derives no additional revenue and no direct advantage from the process. The surveyors, in making the survey of the village boundaries, were guided by the marks put up at time of demarcation at every bend and turn of the boundary. Unfortunately, there were no permanent marks round the boundaries of villages or estates in Bengal, and no provision then existed for compelling landholders to set them up and keep them in order. The consequence was that the marks have been obliterated and the use of the survey for practical purposes has been greatly impaired.'

§ 7. *Special Survey of Alluvial Lands.*

'The surveys of Ganges alluvion and diluvion, in accordance with the provisions of Act IX of 1847, were commenced in the Patna division about 1863, and brought to a close in the Rájsháhí division in 1871–72. The operations were afterwards continued in the Dacca division. The object of the law was to obviate the effects of the changes constantly going on in the banks of rivers and adjacent lands. By these changes large portions of land are often washed away—sometimes suddenly, sometimes by slow degrees—from one side of a river, while an accession of land takes place on the other side. It was thought advisable, for the security of the land-revenue, that some provision should be made for allowing to a proprietor whose estate had suffered diluvion, an abatement of revenue corresponding to the extent of his loss; and, on the other hand, for assessing the proprietor whose estate had gained land, with an additional revenue, proportionate to the amount of his gain. The law accordingly enacts that in districts of which a revenue survey has already been made, Government may, whenever ten years may have elapsed from the date of approval of such survey, have a new survey made of lands on the banks of rivers with a view to ascertain the extent of the changes since the last survey. Having ascertained, by inspection of the new survey map, which estates have lost and which gained land, a corresponding abatement from, and addition to, the revenue assessed on the estates respectively losing and gaining, is to be made.

'The Settlements made were formerly permanent, except when the proprietors of some of them refused to take the engagement, in which case the lands were let in farm for periods of from three to ten years; but, latterly, orders have been issued by Government prohibiting further permanent Settlements, and temporary Settlements are made.

'In the course of the six years, 1877–78 to 1882–83, the banks of the chief rivers of Eastern Bengal—namely, the Ganges and Megna, with their principal branches down to the Bay of Bengal, the Dhaléshwari, the Brahmaputra, and the southern portion of the Jamuna—were surveyed. The total area of the tracts of country surveyed in Dacca, Furreedpore, Backergunge, Tipperah, Noakholly, and Mymensingh, is 5,682·74 square miles, at a total expenditure of R. 1,59,430. The cost per square mile of country surveyed has therefore been R. 28-6-10. This survey has been made in the same scientific manner as the survey conducted by the Revenue Survey Department, and the accuracy of the work has been tested by connections made with eighteen tower stations of the Great Trigonometrical Survey.

'The total area of land added to estates since the survey of the districts, ascertained by a comparison of the new maps with those of the previous survey, was nearly 479 square miles. Out of this area, 273 estates, measuring 120·5 square miles, have been assessed and settled under the provisions of section 6, Act IX of 1847, yielding an annual revenue of R. 59,461-2, including málikána; 128 estates, measuring 51·2 square miles, with a rental of R. 23,848, are pending Settlement. In 113 cases, 57 square miles, with a rental of R. 45,084, have been left unassessed under orders passed in appeal by the Commissioner or the Board; 151·3 square miles have been left unassessed as being (1) less than ten acres, (2) accretions to temporarily-settled estates which are not liable to assessment until the Settlements of the estates expire, (3) washed away between survey and Settlement, and (4) included in estates sold or permanently settled by Government on a revised assessment since the first survey of the districts, and therefore not liable to reassessment. In 165 cases, covering an area of 99 square miles, with a rental of R. 48,765, the proceedings have not yet become final, as objection cases are pending before the Superintendent or in appeal.'

§ 8. *Surveying Agency.*

In large areas—generally speaking over fifteen square miles—the area is professionally surveyed under the Survey Department of the Government of India. In areas less than that, the ordinary district staff carry out the detailed work (as more fully described in the chapters on North-Western Provinces). With the aid of skeleton maps in which main points and traverse lines have been laid down for them with scientific accuracy, they survey both the outer boundaries and field- and holding-boundaries, and plot them. With the detailed map, a field-index or register called (as usual) a *khasra* is prepared. This shows the details of area, crop grown, irrigation, and class of soil. The area is given in standard (Bengal) bíghás [1] (of 14,400 square feet or 1600 square yards).

The *khasra* ordinarily names the raiyat working the field, but does not attempt to record his *status* or his rent. In order to group the different fields held by the same man together, the surveyor prepares from the *khasra*, abstracts (called 'khatián' or 'jamabandi') showing this. The record of the *status* and the determination of the *rent payable* come afterwards.

§ 9. *Fixing and recording Rents.*

Assuming that the particular law under which the Settlement is proceeding allows it, the rents will be adjusted, wherever required by the circumstances under which the Settlement is being made. The surveyor hands

[1] And the bíghá is divided into 20 cottas (katthá), the biswa of other parts; and that into 20 gandá (the biswáṇsi of other parts). The gandá contains 4 'kauṛi.' This last subdivision is equal to 9 square feet or 1 square yard.

over his maps, with the index-register and abstracts, to the Settlement Officer, who has then a basis to work upon. I assume also that the *status* of all existing tenants has been recorded and the incidents of their tenancy. What the status is, is a matter concerning land-tenures and will be described in a later section.

'Generally speaking[1], it may be said that the determination of rents includes the ascertainment of existing *rates* of rent which may be applied to the areas ascertained by measurement' (and of course this may be something different from the actual sums paid hitherto), 'and the enhancements of such rentals as may be legally possible under Bengal Act VIII of 1879, or the Tenancy Act, or other special Act under which the officer is working.

'The first object is therefore the ascertainment of existing facts. For this purpose the Settlement Officer calls the parties together, attests the entries made by the surveyor regarding areas and occupation of lands, and records the *status* of tenants and tenure-holders, and their existing rents. He at the same time disposes of such disputes and objections as may arise.'

§ 10. *Enhancement of Rents under the Act of* 1879.

When Settlements (involving rent adjustment) are being made under the Regulations, supplemented by Bengal Act VIII of 1879, Sections 6 and 7 of the Act explain the grounds of enhancement, which are—(1) that the rate of rent is below that paid by raiyats of the same class for land of a similar description in the vicinity; (2) that increase is justified by an increase in the productive power of the land which has taken place otherwise than at the expense of the raiyat; (3) that the value of the produce has increased otherwise than by the agency of the raiyat; (4) that the quantity of land held is greater than that for which he has been paying rent. In order to legalize an enhancement on these grounds, the record must be published with a

[1] The inverted commas refer to a memorandum prepared by the Director of Land Records and Agriculture, to which I am indebted for much of the information on details in this chapter.

notice to each raiyat specifying exactly the grounds on which the demand is based. The raiyat may, within a period of four months, contest the enhancement by suit in the Civil Court. Under this law, also, the sanction of the superior revenue authorities is required to increase of rates or rentals.

§ 11. *Enhancement of Rents under the Act of* 1885.

Under the Tenancy Act (1885) in Government estates, the landlord (Government) may apply for an enhancement. The application is dealt with as a civil suit. The legal presumption under the Act is that the existing rent is fair; granted then, that the existing rent is ascertained, the claimant must show justification for increase on one or other of the grounds mentioned in Sections 6, 30–37, 46, &c. (as the case may be). These grounds are briefly—(1) that the rate is below the prevailing rate paid for the same class of lands by occupancy raiyats in the village; (2) that there has been a rise in the average local prices of staple food-crops during the currency of the present rent; (3) that the productiveness of the land has been increased by improvement effected by the landlord, (4) or by river action; (5) that the area of the holding has been increased, new land having been brought under cultivation for which rent was not previously paid.

The same principles apply to private estates when an adjustment of rents has been ordered.

§ 12. *Duration of Rents so settled.*

Under the Tenancy Act, 1885, when an *occupancy raiyat's* rent is enhanced, it cannot be again enhanced for fifteen years; and when an *ordinary tenant's* rent is raised, no further increase can take place for five years: it follows that the effect of a Settlement is to fix rents for fifteen and for five years respectively. Act VIII of 1885, sec. 37. Id. sec. 46, cl. 7.

Under Act VIII of 1879, any rent fixed will be for ten years, or for the period of Settlement, whichever expires first. Id. sec. 113. Act VIII of 1879, sec. 13.

§ 13. *Remarks on the policy of the law.*

In the 'Papers relating to the Bengal Tenancy Act, 1885,' at page 424, the following explanatory remarks are made—

'What has been done has been to give the Revenue Officer in the first instance power to settle all disputes that may come before him. Where no dispute arises, and it does not appear that the tenant is holding land in excess of or less than that for which he is paying rent, and neither the landlord nor the tenant applies for the settlement of a fair rent, the Revenue Officer will record what he finds,—he will not alter rents, and his entries will only have a presumptive value (will be presumed to be true—Section 109—until the contrary is proved) in cases afterwards brought before the Courts. When a dispute arises, or it appears that the tenant is holding land in excess of or less than that for which he is paying rent, or either of the parties applies for the settlement of a fair rent, the Revenue Officer will decide a dispute or settle a fair rent, as the case may be, on the same grounds, by the same rules, and with the same procedure, as a Civil Court. His decision will be liable to appeal to a special Judge, who may or may not be the Judge of the district, and will be subject to a further special appeal to the High Court. In appeal the High Court may settle a new rent, but in so doing, is to be guided by the other rents shown in the rent-roll. In other words, there can be no second appeal to the High Court merely on the ground that the rent has been pitched too high or too low; but if a second appeal is preferred, as it may be, on the ground that the special Judge, owing to some error on a point of law, has (for example) found the holding to comprise more land or less land than it actually does comprise, or has given the raiyat a wrong status, and the appellant succeeds, the High Court can, without altering the rates, reduce or increase the rents, as the case may be.'

§ 14. *Sub-tenants or under-raiyats.*

In addition to settling the rents of raiyats (i.e. tenants not being tenure-holders), the Settlement Officer is bound to record (that is all—for the rent payable is matter of contract) the rents payable by any sub-tenants, or under-raiyats as the Act calls them.

§ 15. '*Tenures.*'

In many districts the 'sub-infeudation,' which I have before alluded to, has taken place; i.e. the landlord has contracted for the management and collection of his rents with a patnidár or other 'tenure-holder,' and he again with a sub-tenure-holder, and not infrequently he again with a third. Thus there may be quite a chain of interests between the superior landlord and the actual rent-paying cultivator, when rent has been settled in the manner described. And there are other kinds of tenure-holders (not being patnidárs) who are above the grade of ordinary tenants.

The rights of these tenure-holders must be defined and recorded. It may also be necessary to declare them invalid and to set them aside.

If these tenures are found to be binding against the landlord or against Government, it is necessary (unless they are rent-free) to determine the relations in the matter of payments between them and the superior. This is ordinarily done by determining the portion of the total of the cultivating rentals under them which they are entitled to retain and not pass on to their superior or landlord. This deduction must be at least ten per cent., and may be as much more as the Revenue Officer thinks proper under the circumstances of the case (see Section 7).

It is to be remembered that no tenure which has been held rent-free or at a fixed rent since the Permanent Settlement, can now be assessed to rent or enhanced; nor in any case where the facts are such that a suit for resumption in a Civil Court would be held barred by limitation.

§ 16. *Publication of Rent-rolls.*

When the record of rents is complete, if under the earlier law, only so much of it as includes enhancements must be published for *four months*, during which period a civil suit to contest the orders may be filed. Under the Tenancy Act, 1885, the *whole* roll has to be published for *one month*, within which objections may be filed (as civil suits) before the Settlement Officer.

B. Act VIII of 1879, secs. 9, 10.

§ 17. *Record of Customs, &c.*

In all important Settlements, a record is made of village customs regarding rights of pasture, and waste land, forest, fisheries, and customs as to payment of village officials, and the like.

§ 18. *Assessment of Land-Revenue.*

Where we are dealing with lands that have a recognized proprietor other than the State, there is an assessment of land-revenue, and the Settlement is one strictly so called.

The Government revenue (as above explained) is a proportion of the 'assets,'—i.e. the total rents of raiyat lands, or of tenures which are recognized as binding on the Government[1], *plus* any income from fisheries, jungle, or fruits, or mineral profits (if there are any) belonging to the proprietor.

§ 19. *Proportion of Assets taken by Government.*

The proportion fixed for Settlement-holders (properly so called) is 70 per cent. to Government and 30 to the Settlement-holder.

Where there are, as in Orissa, sarbarákárs or village headmen, who, though Government servants, contract for the revenue of the villages, the amount of the allowance is

[1] Where there are no 'tenures,' the whole rent of the raiyats is taken of course by the proprietors; where there are, the proprietor gets only so much less than the full raiyati rent as the grants of the under-tenure-holders indicate. And if the under-tenures are recognized as binding on Government, the sums received accordingly are recognized as the assets; if the under-tenures are invalid, any deductions are the proprietor's concern. His assets are then regarded as the rents of the raiyats irrespectively of the unrecognizable under-tenure.

regulated by special order of the Board of Revenue in each case.

In Government estates managed direct (khás), or where the raiyats pay direct to Government (raiyatwárí tracts), there is, of course, no question of dividing the proprietary assets between the proprietor and Government, because they are merged in one.

But should Government in any estate make an arrangement for its rental with a tenure-holder, or with one or more of its principal tenants, the rule is to make an allowance of 20 per cent. on the total rental for expenses of collection and farming profits [1].

This is a convenient place at which to offer some remarks on the percentage taken by Government. It should be remarked that the 'proprietor' who gets only 30 per cent., is in reality a person with no strong claims, who is well remunerated by such a proportion of profits. In a letter (N. 1917 Government to Board of Revenue), dated 8th Sept., 1874, it was inquired whether 30 per cent. was not too much, and whether 10 per cent. for expenses of collection and 10 per cent. for profit was not enough. In the Board's office is an excellent printed note (dated 4th June, 1874) on the whole subject. The origin of the percentage was the one-tenth, i.e. 10 per cent. originally allowed (as already stated) by the Native Governments to the Zamíndárs as collectors of the revenue. When the proprietary position of the various kinds of landholder was recognized, naturally it was desired to be a little more liberal, so when Regulation VII of 1822 was passed, section 7 (clause 2) mentions 20 per cent. as the *minimum* profit exclusive of costs of collection. In Bengal 20 per cent. remained the rule, and a circular of 1836 pointed out[2] that the 10 per

[1] It may here be mentioned that when a person entitled to a Settlement refuses the terms, and so the estate is held in farm, 20 per cent. is also allowed to the farmer, and 10 per cent. as málikána to the excluded proprietor for the term of his exclusion. Málikána means anything paid to a proprietor (or oftener ex-proprietor) in recognition of his (lost) right.

[2] The 20 per cent. was supposed to represent 10 per cent. costs of collection *plus* 10 per cent. allowance for profit.

cent. from profits was to be on the balance *after* allowing for 10 per cent. as costs of collection. All this depended on the fact that the so-called proprietor was really a very artificial creation—a mere farmer called proprietor. In other provinces, where the person called landlord was one who had a strong natural right in the land, his profits were larger. He had at first to give 66 per cent. on his assets, very loosely calculated, and when these assets were more closely ascertained his revenue payment was reduced to 45 to 55 per cent. of the *net* assets.

§ 20. *With whom the Settlement is made.*

In temporarily-settled estates there is always some one recognized as proprietor, and he is settled with; and so in the case of resumed or lapsed revenue-free estates. Where it was a Settlement for land that was in excess of the holder's proper estate (in some cases under Regulation II of 1819), the Settlement was made permanent, because at the time no other law existed. But no law declared *all* 'taufir' land to be entitled to such a benefit. Hence, when the Temporary Settlement Law was passed, such lands would be settled under it, and with the person who could prove a title. When it is a Settlement for alluvial accretions to existing estates, which accretions under the law are liable to be separately settled, the Settlement is of course made with the owner of the estate, who is under the alluvion law (Regulation XI of 1825) entitled to the accretions.

§ 21. *Alluvial Settlements.*

I shall not go into details about the special rules regarding 'Deára Settlements,' as they are called—the Settlements of alluvial accretions. They apply to river flats and islands (chars) and to alluvial lands which are not accretions but are the property of Government; they also contain special directions regarding the survey (Deára Survey). They can be read in the Board's 'Settlement Manual,' 1888.

§ 22. *Duration of Settlement.*

For temporary Settlements there is no rule fixing twenty years or thirty years or any other period; the term depends on the circumstances of the estate, and is usually fixed with reference to the period for which occupancy rents are fixed (fifteen years or ten years, according to the law in force). And the periods are further ordered so that they may fall in in successive years in the different divisions, so that Survey and Settlement establishments may proceed from one district to another as their services are required.

§ 23. *Records of Settlement.*

When the record of rents, &c., has been published and has become final, clean copies are prepared for deposit in the Collector's office. Under the Tenancy Act copies or extracts are also given to the landlord and tenants. An abstract or 'tírij' (written also 'terij') is made out, showing, in a convenient form, all the main features of the estate or holding with the owner, tenure-holders, raiyats, &c., and the payments due from each [1].

A general report is then prepared (either for each village or for the whole tract, as may be ordered). It shows—

(*a*) the number of tenants of each class;

(*b*) the area and classification of the village lands according to the Survey and Settlement, and also according to the landlord's own *jamabandi*, if known;

(*c*) the rental according to Settlement and according to the landlord's *jamabandi*, with explanation of increase or decrease, amount of Government revenue, and comparison of rent with revenue;

(*d*) the rates of rent prevailing, with history of past enhancements;

(*e*) proximity to markets;

[1] Called also 'Sadhárán-khatián.' See No. 10 in the Appendix to the Settlement Manual.

(*f*) facilities for irrigation ;
(*g*) village customs, including payment of village officials ;
(*h*) arrangements made for maintenance of records ;
(*i*) other matters deserving of notice which do not find a place in the record of rights.

Besides these particulars, the report will describe the whole tract as regards—

1. General features of the tract.
2. Its fiscal history.
3. Statistical results.
4. Comparison of condition of the tract as regards rentals before and after the Survey.
5. Final results, including approximate division of expenses under the heads of—
   (*a*) Survey.
   (*b*) Record of rights.
   (*c*) Preparation and distribution of records.

The report also makes proposals as to the parties to be settled with, and notices arrangements existing, or to be made, regarding the instalments of rent and revenue, which must be adapted to local circumstances, seasons, and harvests.

§ 24. *Sanction of Settlements.*

When whole districts or large areas are settled, the sanction (as usual) of the Local Government and of the Government of India is required. But many Settlements are of single or limited estates. The following are the powers of sanction in that case :—

Temporary Settlements up to a rental of R. 500 ...	The Collector.
From R. 500 to R. 10,000...	The Commissioner.
From R. 10,000 to R. 25,000 ... ... Also when the Settlement will be permanent under a statutory right	The Board of Revenue.

§ 25. *Supervision.*

The Director of Land Records and Agriculture supervises all Settlements in which the agency of the Survey Department is employed or which are made under the Bengal Tenancy Act; and his services are available for other Settlements at the discretion of the Board. He exercises, in respect of all these Settlements, the powers of a Commissioner, save in matters in which power is by law vested in the Commissioner himself.

§ 26. *Conclusion.*

It may be necessary to repeat here, that for matters of detail, the Acts and Regulations quoted require study, and also the Settlement Manual. The object here (as in the chapter on Revenue business) is not to furnish a complete handbook of details, but an introduction or *general guide to the principles and leading features of the system*,—preparatory to such a detailed study as will be necessary for officers who have actually to take their part in district duty.

§ 27. *General Conspectus of Estates.*

Such being the general principles on which Temporary Settlements are made in tracts owned by private proprietors, and on which Rents are fixed in Government estates (whether raiyatwárí tracts or managed otherwise), it will be desirable, before proceeding to an account of special Settlements in certain exceptional districts, to give some particulars about the general results of Settlements and the distribution of the different classes of estates.

The general map, showing the prevalence of the various Settlement systems, indicates, as far as Bengal is concerned, the Permanent Settlements in one colour, and those districts which are as a whole temporarily settled—i. e. the districts of Orissa—in another colour. An attempt has also been

Division.	District.	Permanent Settlement.		Temporary Settlement.		Government Estates.		Raiyatwárí Tracts.		Remarks.
		No. of Estates.	Revenue in Rupees.	No. of Estates.	Revenue in Rupees.	No. of Estates.	Revenue in Rupees.	No. of Estates.	Revenue in Rupees.	
BARDWÁN	Bardwán	4838	76,87,377	30	4,609	141	4,631			
	Bankura.........	890		—	....	19	913			
	Bírbhúm	1001		1	156	1	125			
	Midnapore......	2696		29	4,82,759	224	48,105			
	Hooghly with Howra	3615		72	5,213	245	38,420			
PRESIDENCY	24-Pergunnahs	1588	44,45,113	122	66,521	67*	1,93,484	1	83,322	* There is one Government estate in *Calcutta* included here.
	Nadiya	2197		160	50,262	102	18,667			
	Jessore	2437		50	4,845	95	3,252			
	Khúlná	759		26	7,740	172	1,31,820			
	Murshidábád...	2315		65	29,333	67	27,736			
RÁJSHÁHÍ	Dinájpur	747	4 84,081	2	8	10	285			
	Rájsháhí	1365		31	2,590	27	14,335			
	Rangpur.........	613		19	2,208	6	354			
	Bogra	670		...	....	8	38,945			
	Pabná............	1714		73	28,335	49	3,099			
	Darjíling	1		...	....	107	24,990	5	91,799	
	Jalpáigúrí	82		...	....	...	....	5*	2,77,144	* The Bhután Dwárs.
DACCA......	Dacca	8181	26,42,749	287	39,233	152	37,403			
	Farídpur	5647		153	96,073	164	31,421			
	Backergunge...	3015		212	1,35,091	358	2,34,605	1*	1,02,438	* The Túshkhálí estate.
	Mymensingh...	6645		193	63,928	70	19,340			

CHITTAGONG	Chittagong......	28927	19,29,359	3	9,085	5*	3,85,290			* The whole of the Naubád holdings are shown as aggregated into five *estates*, 45,000 plots=1,187,600 acres.
	Noakháli	1546		43	31,311	185	1,18,171			
	Tipperah.........	1850		92	25,628	128	88,513			
	BIHÁR.									
PATNA	Patna	9368	77,69,473	21	15,735	60	64,082			
	Gayá	5828		23	14,117	43	1,04,914			
	Sháhábád	6317		280	70,212	183	1,12,806			
	Muzaffarpur ...	17111		24	10,393	64	2,908			
	Darbhanga ...	10481		2	547	8	12,375			
	Sáran	4403		59	12,596	18	1,781	11	4,881	
	Champáran ...	1094		6	1,177	1	72			
BHÁGALPUR	Monghyr	6691	30,22,496	41	33,814	27	18,016	2	47,276	
	Bhágalpur	4383		3	662	75	9,146	1	22,094	
	Purneah.........	1618		9	751	44	2,858	1	1,852	
	Málda	553		15	15,859	26	16,926			
	Santál Pergunnahs	459		18	1,559	15	2,578	1*	1,69,495	* The *Dáman-i-koh*.
ORISSA	Cuttack	23	1,46 4	3930	7,16,789	5	64,779			
	Pooree...........	3		453	3,03,192	8	2,67,626			
	Bálásúr	148		1333	3,52,367	20	22,742			
CHOTA NAGPORE	Hazáribágh ...	68	1,63,365	...	....	302	76,295			
	Lohárdagga ...	56		...	....	6	64,138	3	12,724	
	Singhbhúm ...	1		2	18,189	...	....	1	46,054	
	Mánbhúm	24		2	1,669	...	....			
	Grand Total...	157968	3,22,90,777	7884	26,54,561	3307	23,08,688	32	8,59,079	

made to indicate by a third colour the larger *raiyatwárí* and Government estates; but it was not possible to show *all* such tracts, on account of their (often) small size and the way in which they are scattered about in the districts.

In the Board of Revenue's Annual Reports it is now the practice to insert district-maps which show the Government estates.

Taking the Report for 1888–89, Appendix II gives (A) the permanently-settled estates; (B) the temporarily-settled estates; and (C) the Government estates, separating the raiyatwárí tracts under (D).

The Government estates in (C) all appear as either settled for definite periods or occasionally 'farmed' or managed direct owing to recusancy of the proprietors[1]. The table on p. 470 is an abstract of this Appendix II, designed to give the student an idea of the distribution of estates in those general classes[2].

The numbers of permanently-settled estates vary by reason of *partitions*, which are most numerous in the Patna division districts: the temporarily-settled estates also vary chiefly by reason of alluvial accretions.

[1] These cases of recusancy, I believe, are where the lands are unproductive and the holders do not care to undertake the Settlement responsibility.

[2] Under those *general* classes the individual estates may be in great variety of origin as the result of the operation of different laws and circumstances. For example, in the Tipperah (Típra) district the following details appear (*Statistical Account of Bengal*, vol. vi. pp. 400-440):—

	No. of Estate.
1. Permanently-settled Estates of 1793	1262
2. Resumed Revenue-free of 1793	98
3. Islands, &c., excess ('taufír') lands settled under Regulation II of 1819...	103
4. Estates sold for arrears and then permanently settled (Section 6 of Regulation VIII of 1793).	167
5. Tenures temporarily settled (this includes Government Estates)	241

Section III.—The Orissa Settlements.

The three districts of modern Orissa—including the Patáspur pargaṅa—were acquired after the Maráthá war in 1803, so they did not come under the Permanent Settlement Regulations. That Settlement only affected, more or less, the Midnapore district which (excluding Patáspur) was the *old* Orissa of 1765. Midnapore is not *now* spoken of as 'Orissa' at all.

These districts were originally the seat of Hindu kingdoms—'Rájputs,' who at a remote period invaded, conquered and ruled over the Kolarian and Dravidian population. The conquest probably only extended to the level and culturable districts, for the Kolarian and other tribes in the hilly country were found following their own customs, but little if at all changed. The incursion of the 'Yávanas,' and other events, detailed in Hunter's *Orissa*, cannot now be traced in any effect they may have had on the land-system, and so I pass them over.

The Rájputs were in the end overthrown by the Muhammadan king of Bengal; and Orissa was finally swept into the dominions of the Mughal Emperor. But in the middle of the eighteenth century, the Maráthás succeeded to a short-lived domination. Neither of these later powers had therefore the time and the opportunity to modify very deeply the land-tenures; and we do not find any 'Zamíndárs,' in the sense of contractors for the revenue, like those in Bengal.

The Rájput kingdom was organized here as it was elsewhere; for the remains of this organization are still manifest.

The country consists, roughly speaking—(1) of a marshy tract on the coast, full of swamp forest like the Sundarbans; (2) a belt of rice-land and other cultivation; (3) a hilly tract beyond, going up into the hill ranges of the 'South-West Frontier.'

As might be expected, the chief Rájá had his 'khálsa' or

demesne lands in the best and level parts, and the hill tracts were the territories or estates of his feudal chieftains, who held them and took the revenue on condition of keeping the country quiet. With the estates of these chieftains the Mughals appear not to have interfered, but the rice-tract (2) was called the 'Mughalbandí,' and was regularly assessed to revenue.

The Maráthás in turn assessed the chiefs to a tribute or quit-rent. On the British annexation in 1803 the chiefs' estates were maintained. Some have been recognized as 'tributary chiefs'—the 'Tributary Mahály' of Orissa. These are not subject to any regular Settlement and Revenue system; they are managed in the Political Department, and this work is not concerned with them.

There were nineteen of them formerly; but two were confiscated,—Angul in 1847 for the rebellion of its Rájá; and Bánki in 1840, the chief having been convicted of murder[1].

A certain number of the chiefships nearer the plains were, though not placed in the first rank, favoured so far that they were granted a Permanent Settlement, and this fact accounts for the permanently-settled estates shown in the table under the Orissa districts. These estates were called 'qila'' (i.e. forts—territories surrounding and protected by the chief's residence). The estates were treated as in the position of full-rated permanently-assessed Zamíndárí estates. At first, fifty such estates were proposed to be constituted. The rest of the province was left to the ordinary (temporary) Settlement.

On the 15th September, 1804, a proclamation regarding the Settlement was issued; and this was afterwards embodied in the Regulation XII of 1805. The plan was first to settle for one year, then to grant a three years' lease. Then a four years' lease was offered at an increase to be

[1] Angul and Bánki now form 'Government Estates'—Angul as part of the Púrí district, Bánki in Katák. The remaining seventeen states consist of 15,187 square miles, with a population of nearly a million and a half. They pay a tribute of £3,322 to the British Government. This tract was called 'Rájwára' or Garhját, as opposed to the revenue-paying plain called 'Mughalbandí.' The chiefs were locally known as 'Khandáits.'—Hunter.

obtained by adding two-thirds of the net increase of any one year of the three years' Settlement, to the total assessment amount of that lease. At the expiration of the four years it was announced that for such lands as then were in a sufficiently improved state of cultivation, a Permanent Settlement would be concluded on such terms as the Government considered fair and equitable.

The Regulation next refers to the 'Tributary Mahals,' which it exempts from the Regulations. Of the second class of estates above mentioned, eleven were selected; the *sanads* granting a permanent assessment to nine of them, which had been issued by the Board of Commissioners (appointed to manage Orissa, or the Katák province as it was then called), were confirmed. Khúrdá[1] and Kaniká were directed to be treated in the same manner hereafter. These eleven estates however differed only from the rest of the district in having the assessment fixed for ever.

The history of the Settlements is briefly as follows:—

Certain changes as regards the revenue (of no importance now) were made by Regulations X of 1807 and VI of 1808; and when the last or four years' Settlement became due, a Special Commission was appointed to make it with due care: for it was supposed it would be made permanent if the Home Government approved. But the Home Government by this time had seen the evil of hastily concluding Permanent Settlements; they did *not* approve[2], and Regulation X of 1812 was passed to declare the fact, but (as was done in the Upper Provinces) still held out the hope of a permanent assessment *when* the state of the lands

[1] Khúrdá soon afterwards (1804) was confiscated owing to the rebellion of the Rájá. The titular Rájá was hereditary guardian of the Jagan-náth temple, and he was maintained as such, as a pensioner. But the holder of the title in 1878 was convicted of murder and deported. The estate of Khúrdá, which gave some trouble in 1804 by rebellion, and again in 1817–18, is now a large and well-ordered, and indeed a model, Government estate.

[2] See Kaye, p. 239. It will be observed that the *principles* adopted for Orissa were exactly the same as those in the Regulations of 1805 for the North-West Provinces. It is instructive to note the prevailing ideas on revenue matters, as exhibited by the Regulations of this date, and how they had begun to be doubted at home.

was such as to recommend it. Regulations of 1815 and 1816 made some further provisions which are now of no interest.

In 1818 disturbances occurred, due in great measure to the operation of the Sale Law[1], and a Special Commissioner was appointed (Regulation V of 1818). In the same year Regulation XIII extended the existing Settlements for three years, so as to afford due time to the revenue officers to collect the materials necessary for the formation of a new Settlement on proper principles.

Though the 'materials' were not ready, the outlines of the new Settlement system—imperfect, but in the right direction—had been determined on. Regulation VII of 1822 was passed for Katák (i.e. the Orissa districts), certain parganas (Patáspur, &c.) which are part of the Midnapore district, and for the districts of the North-Western Provinces.

The history of this Regulation, and of the recognition of its defects and their removal by Regulation IX of 1833, is stated more fully in the account of the North-Western Provinces (vol. ii.).

The Regulation (Sec. 2) once more extended the existing Katák Settlements for five years, and Act VI of 1837 declared that the Settlement should continue until a new one was made. The first regular Settlement, with a survey and record of rights, was made in 1838–45.

In 1856 a revision was undertaken. In 1867, Bengal Act X again extended the Settlement; this time for thirty years; so that there will be no further revision till 1897[2].

The Settlement was made with various kinds of estate-holders, either individuals or joint families,—málguzárs (as Act VI of 1837 calls them), who had grown up over the villages—as we shall see hereafter.

[1] Field, p. 681, note.

[2] There is an abstract of the history of the early Settlements in Mr. Stack's *Memorandum on Temporary Settlements*, 1880, p. 579. In the Selections from Bengal Records, No. III. 1851, is a minute on the Province by the Commissioner (A. J. Moffat Mills, 1847); and Macneile's *Memorandum on Revenue Administration in Bengal*, 1873, also contains ample information.

The estates were then assessed village by village; and there were in most cases subordinate tenures or interests of headmen and village-managers who collected the proprietors' rents; these were entitled to a certain allowance representing their own interest, so that the Settlement is spoken of as 'mauzawár.' As a matter of fact, all the village lands were cultivated by 'tháni' (i.e. resident) raiyats, or by 'pái' (i.e. non-resident) raiyats, and some were held as the village headman's 'sír' or free holding in virtue of his office (a relic of the former Dravidian organization).

The plan of settling a lump sum of revenue for the village—the 'aggregate to detail method,' and then distributing this sum over the holdings—was rejected. The Settlement Officer determined separately the rents of the holding of each raiyat, and, putting a value on the 'sír' land, added the whole together. The total revenue was 60 to 70 per cent. of the rental assets so ascertained. But the nominal landlord did not get even the 30 or 40 per cent. which remained; for there were the village-headmen or managers, who directly collected the village rental and had certain rights—almost like sub-proprietors—in virtue of which they received a percentage, 20 to 25 per cent. if a mukádam or pradhán (hereditary headman), 15 to 20 if a sarbarákár (manager).

§ 1. *The Khúrdá Estate.*

This estate, occupying a considerable portion of the inland side of the Púrí district, is one of the Government estates, managed as a 'raiyatwárí tract.'[1] For some years after the confiscation in 1804, separate survey-Settlements were made by 'maháls' or groups of land, with local managers called sarbarákárs; but in the last quinquennial Settlement, care was taken to make the *sarbarákárs* give the raiyats leases at rates fixed for the whole term. In 1836, a regular—virtually raiyatwárí—Settlement was

[1] There is a printed volume of *Selections from the Correspondence relating to the Khúrdá Estate*, 1879.

made, at rates ascertained for classes of soil and applied by measurement. Sarbarákárs were, however, charged with the responsibility for the revenue of the whole area. In 1853, some three years before the expiry of the term of Settlement, a renewal was offered to the sarbarákárs at the old rates, *plus* the assessment recorded for the culturable waste fields, on the supposition that they had been, or would soon be, all taken under the plough. This proposal was declined; consequently actual measurement of the extended cultivation was made. And the Settlement so made expired in 1880. Preparations for the revision that then became due, began in 1875, and the estate was cadastrally surveyed. The produce of fields was ascertained by declaration of the raiyats themselves, and an acreage produce rate being thus established, villages were classified into homogeneous tracts, ranked into grades, and revenue rates applied accordingly. The Government share had been fixed at one-fifth [1] of the average gross produce. The sarbarákárs still collect the revenue, and are allowed a deduction to cover their risk and expenses. Joint bodies of sarbarákárs are avoided, and it is arranged so that each sharer in a family gets a separate village. Mr. Stack compares the sarbarákár, who is thus a paid collector, not a proprietor, to the 'mauzadár' described under the Assam system. The Settlement shows a considerable increase of revenue and works admirably. The raiyats' holdings are generally small. The average of 172 test villages gives no more than 1⅓ acre to each raiyat. The raiyat's rent is fixed for the term of Settlement; but there is no relinquishing and taking up lands, and consequently no annual 'jamabandi,' as under other raiyatwárí systems, is necessary.

[1] The proposal was one-fourth, but it was ultimately fixed as stated.

SECTION IV.—THE WASTE LAND RULES.

§ 1. *Importance of the Subject.*

This subject seems one which demands a certain detail in treatment. The economist, and perhaps also the capitalist, may be interested to know how (for example) the 'tea-estates' of Darjiling and Assam had their origin; and perhaps to inquire how land for cultivation of imported staples can still be obtained. The whole system of dealing with *waste* lands depends on the principle developed in Chapter IV of Book I, that waste and unoccupied land is at the disposal of the State.

In Bengal, as already stated, the Permanent Settlement only extended to the estates actually possessed, or to alluvial accretions which (though separately assessable) were afterwards formed upon their boundaries. In tolerably settled parts this gave rise to no difficulties; but where there were large tracts of waste it was otherwise. In 1819, it seems, the subject first came under notice, but that notice did not extend to the question of *ownership*; the Regulation II of that year only declared the lands *assessable*. The authorities of the day were perhaps only too glad to see waste taken up, and seemed to think that if it had been occupied *de facto*, no matter how, they might accept the fact, treating the occupier as lawful owner; what was more essential was to provide for his duly paying land-revenue.

Regulation II of 1819 specially mentions the case of the Sundarbans [1],—the forest tract on the delta between the Húghlí and Megná rivers. The waste lands there occupied were in fact temporarily-cultivated lots known as 'patítábádí taluqs,' and were encroachments from the regular estates inland. Hence arose the practice of calling these irregularly-occupied lands 'taufír' or excess, i.e.

[1] As to the early attempts to issue clearing leases, see article 'Sundarbans' in *Imp. Gaz.*, vol. xiii. p. 110. They date back to 1782. In later times, grants began to be asked for in 1807, and up to 1872 nearly 1087 square miles had been brought under cultivation.

assuming that they were extensions of regular estates. On this ground perhaps such lands were treated as entitled to be permanently assessed[1]. At any rate, this was the practice till after the Temporary Regulation (1822) had become law. The Regulation did not, indeed, in terms, apply to anything but the 'Ceded and Conquered' Provinces; but obviously, if the land was not entitled to a permanent assessment, the Government could assess it for a term.

A particular instance of this occurs in the case of the districts of Sylhet and Cachár; but as these districts, once part of Bengal, were attached to Assam in 1874, the history of them—and it well illustrates this section—must be looked for in the chapters relating to Assam.

In 1828 (Regulation III) further and more definite provision was made regarding assessment, and it was then declared that the 'waste' was Government property.

§ 2. *The Sundarbans.*

In the Sundarbans, the first occupied lands (higher up on the delta) appear all to have been recognized as having proprietors[2]. But in time 'Waste Land Rules' were provided, and then there was an end to irregular occupation. A part of the area is now taken up as State forest; it is the great source of fuel-supply to Calcutta, besides yielding many valuable woods for building and for industrial purposes. Waste land rules for the Sundarbans had been issued as early as 1825, but they were ineffectual (Macneile, § 173), and the first useful code seems to have been that of 1853. Under these rules 1773 square miles were granted. The land was held subject to a revenue payment which was

[1] Mr. Macneile's Memorandum (§ 167) mentions that the squatters were so fully treated as owners, that in cases where they refused the 'taufír' assessment they were allowed málikána like excluded proprietors on regular estates.

[2] In one place indeed, the Regulation distinctly declares the Sundarbans to be State property, although parts of it had been occupied before 1819. This led to various orders and legal contests (see Macneile's Memorandum, §§ 166-70). The right of Government was affirmed; but in the end, hard cases were allowed, and the occupiers recognized as proprietors.

progressive. In 1889, 474,080 acres (of which the maximum revenue would be R.137,231) were still held under the terms of the rules of 1853. But the rules themselves were superseded by the *Sale* Rules of 1863.

These rules were made after Lord Canning's Minute of 1861[1] on the disposal of waste lands. As regards the Sundarbans, they did not prove successful. Only a few lots were sold; and seven out of twelve fell in for default in payment of the purchase-money. For a time recourse was had once more to the rules of 1853. In 1871 a committee reported on the whole subject, and in 1879 another set of rules was issued.

'The rules of 1879[2] differ from the rules of 1853 in providing a rent-free period of only ten years, and in laying down only one clearance condition, viz. that one-eighth of the entire grant should be rendered fit for cultivation at the end of the fifth year. This condition may be enforced either by forfeiture of the grant or by the issue of a fresh lease, omitting the remainder of the rent-free period, and requiring payment of rent at enhanced rates during the term of grant.

'The rules also provide for gradually increasing rates of assessment after the expiration of the rent-free period, and varying rates within different tracts according to the rent-paying capabilities of the land. It is further provided that there shall be constantly recurring renewals of the lease on re-settlement. The term of the original lease is fixed at forty years, and re-settlements are to be made after periods of thirty years; maximum rates being laid down for each re-settlement.

'The limits within which lands may be held for leasing are fixed in consultation with the Forest Department. An accurate definition of boundaries is provided for. The maximum area of grants is restricted to 5000 bíghás, the minimum being 200. Cultivation must not be scattered all over the area of the land, but proceed regularly through the blocks; and leases are to be sold at an upset price when there is only one applicant, and to the highest bidder when there are more than one.

'The leases confer an occupancy right hereditary and transferable. Survey fees are payable by the applicant, at the rate

[1] This minute is described further on.

[2] Quoted from the *Report*, 1883, page 22.

of four annas an acre, as also a deposit of R. 16 for notices to objectors. Refunds and adjustments of fees deposited are permitted. Rights of way and water and other easements are reserved. The right of using all streams in any way navigable, and the use of a tow-path not less than 25 feet wide on each side of such stream, are also reserved to the public; while Government reserves to itself the right to all minerals in the land, together with rights of way and other reasonable facilities for working, getting, and carrying away such minerals. No charge is made for timber on the land at the time it is leased, nor for any cut or burnt to effect clearances or used on the land; but a duty is levied on any exported for sale.

'Forms of preliminary grant called 'amalnámas—for plots of land below 200 bíghás—are given to small settlers, guaranteeing them a formal lease for thirty years if the lands are brought under cultivation within two years. The thirty years' lease allows a rent-free term of two years, and then progressive rates of rent on the cultivated area, fixed with reference to the rates paid in the neighbourhood by raiyats to landholders for similar lands.

'If available, an area of unreclaimed land equal to the cultivated area is included in the lease, and in addition the lessee can bring under cultivation any quantity of land adjoining his holding which he may find *boná fide* unoccupied. The holding is liable to measurement every five years, and all cultivated land in excess of the area originally assessed can be assessed at the same rate. After thirty years, renewed leases can be given for thirty years' periods, and rates of assessment can be adjusted at each renewal with reference to rates then prevailing in the neighbourhood. The tenure is heritable and transferable, provided that notice of transfer is given to the Sundarbans Commissioner within one month, and no holding is to be divided without his permission. No charge is made for wood and timber on the grant, nor for any cut or burnt in making clearances, or used on the land; but a duty is levied on any exported for sale.

'These rules are reported not to have worked well, as when the time comes to grant leases those who hold *'amalnámas* wish to be recognized as under-tenure holders, of the class (to be described hereafter) called hawaládárs; and they refuse to take leases as raiyats. It has been decided, therefore, to grant hawaládárí rights.'

§ 3. *Statistics of Occupation.*

It may be interesting to give a few statistics of the occupation of land in these delta forests.

The result of the recognition of squatters under the early law of 1819, was that in 1874 there were 98 holdings recognized as estates permanently-settled, and amounting to 255,849 bíghás in the '24-Pergunnahs' district, 93,695 in Khúlná, and 134,709 in Bákirganj. There were also a number of 'resumed' plots and other estates kept in the hands of Government [1].

As to the lands sold or leased under the Rules, as they now survive, the Board's Revenue Report of 1888-9 gives the following figures.

It will be seen that a certain number of persons are content to hold under the ordinary Temporary Settlement and not under the special rules.

Kind of Estate.	Number of leases.	Acres.	Revenue payable.
			Rupees.
Under ordinary Settlements.	31	46,238	15,240 (will eventually rise to 16,782).
Capitalists' rules of 1879	21	28,590	—20,641.
Petty cultivators' rules..	129	3.375	2,216—10,049.

§ 4. *Waste Lands in other parts.*

The Waste Land Rules have found application (besides the Sundarbans) chiefly in Jalpáigúrí and Darjíling (hill estates for tea), and in Chittagong: a few leases have been granted in Lohárdagga.

[1] Among them the Túshkháli Estate of 22,754 *acres* in the Bákirganj district, which became the property of Government in 1836. It was settled as a 'raiyatwárí tract' in 1875.

The following account of the Rules is once more quoted from the *Report on the Land System*, 1882–83:—

'Lord Canning's Minute of the 17th October, 1861, laid down three main principles on which grants of waste lands were to be made in future. These were, *first*, that "in any case of application for such lands they shall be granted in perpetuity as a heritable and transferable property, subject to no enhancement of land-revenue assessment"; *second*, that "all prospective land-revenue will be redeemable at the grantee's option by a payment in full when the grant is made, or, at the grantee's option, a sum may be paid as earnest at the rate of 10 per cent., leaving the unpaid portion of the price of the grant, which will then be under hypothecation until the price is paid in full"; and, *third*, that "there shall be no condition obliging the grantee to cultivate or clear any specific portion after grant within any specific time." The minimum price for the fee-simple was fixed at R. 2-8 per acre, so that by paying 10 per cent. of this, or four annas per acre, a title was obtained. Moreover, many large tracts were obtained by speculators in anticipation of measurement, for a merely nominal payment. A despatch from the Secretary of State subsequently required in addition to these provisions that grants should be surveyed before sale, and that all sales should be by auction to the highest bidders above a fixed upset price.

'In granting waste lands under the above rules, some abuses were unfortunately allowed to occur. There was a great rush upon tea-planting; speculators bought upon credit Government wastes wherever they could get them, and Government officers were so far carried away by the mania, that they relaxed the rules as to surveying wastes before they were sold, and in other particulars. It followed that large areas of waste were sold to jobbers, who transferred them at a profit, or threw them up if they could not transfer them; while in many cases cultivated lands not regularly settled were sold as "Government waste lands" over the heads of the occupiers. In other cases, lands beyond the British border, in others again valuable forest lands, were sold under the Waste Land Rules. Before Sir George Campbell came to Bengal, attention had been directed to this matter, and, in Chittagong especially, mistakes had been recognized. There had in more than one instance been risk of grave disturbance with frontier tribes on account of ill-judged sales of waste land in the occupation of border people. To prevent complications, the Lieutenant-Governor published *ad interim* rules, which received sanction; and orders were passed that no more land should be sold revenue-free in perpetuity without the previous sanction of the Government of India, excepting such small plots, not exceeding ten acres in extent, as might be required for buildings or gardens.

'In 1874, revised rules for the sale of waste lands, superseding all previous rules for the sale and lease of waste lands within the Lower Provinces, were issued. The formation of the Chief Commissionership of Assam had, by that time, withdrawn the districts in which the chief transactions in waste lands used to occur, from the control of the Bengal Government; and, in the districts left to the Lower Provinces in which there are waste lands, these sale rules remained inoperative, the terms having failed to attract applicants; and eventually, in May 1879, the *sale* rules were withdrawn, and the only rules now in force in Bengal are those under which waste lands are *leased* for certain terms of years.

'Waste lands capable of being leased exist in the Sundarbans. the Western Dwárs of Jalpáígúrí, Darjíling, Chittagong, the Hill Tracts of Chittagong, in Palámau, in Lohárdaggá, and to a very small extent in Sháhábád. The tea lease-rules for the Dwárs of 1875 were at first extended to Palámau, but were found inapplicable, and applications for waste land there require to be dealt with on their own merits. For the other districts there are different sets of rules. It may be here observed that one feature in the Sundarbans and Chittagong is that the leases are sold by auction.

'There are two classes of lease-rules—

'(1) Those for large capitalists wishing to grow special crops. as tea, coffee, or cinchona.

'(2) Those for small capitalists for ordinary cultivation.'

§ 5. *Rules in Darjíling and Jalpáígúrí.*

'The main features of the rules of the first class, as applicable to Jalpáígúrí and Darjíling, published on 10th October, 1878, are the following:—

'Declared forest-reserves and land having valuable timber in compact blocks, lands in which other rights exist, lands lying within sixty feet from the centre of any public road, and lands expressly exempted by Government, are not to be granted. Each lot must be compact, and not contain more than 800 acres. Inquiry and survey at the expense of the applicant must ordinarily precede the grant of a lease. A preliminary five years' lease is granted rent-free for the first year, and at progressive rents for the rest of the term. The rights conveyed are heritable and transferable, provided that the whole lot is transferred, that clearance conditions are observed, that the transfer is registered, and a registration fee paid. The right of Government to minerals and quarries, and to payment for valuable trees on the grant, and the right of the public to fisheries, and a right of way along the banks of navigable streams, are reserved, while provision is made for the construction and maintenance of proper boundary-marks, the presence of the lessee himself or of a resident manager on the grant, and for acquisition by Government of any land required for public purposes free of cost, except by proportionate reduction in the rent and by the payment of the value of any improvements in the land taken up. If, after inspection during the term of the preliminary lease, 15 per cent. of the total area shall have been brought under cultivation and actually bears tea-plants, the lessee is entitled to renewal for a term of years, and to similar renewals in perpetuity, provided that Government may fix the rent on certain specified conditions on each renewal; that the renewed lease be heritable and transferable in so far that only the whole may be transferred, and that only with the consent of Government; and that all the other conditions of the preliminary lease hold good. Failure to comply with any of the conditions renders the lessee liable to forfeit his lease; and failure to apply for a renewal before the expiration of his preliminary lease reduces him, if he is allowed to continue, to the status of a tenant-at-will till other arrangements are made. Grantees can club or amalgamate their grants by transfers, duly registered, on payment of the prescribed fee.

'The second class of rules for small capitalists, as applicable to the Dwárs, published on the 23rd June, 1879, correspond in the main with the rules for the grant of leases for tea-cultivation. The differences are briefly these: Ordinarily the lot must not be less than ten acres or contain more than 200 acres[1]. The survey fee is to be three annas an acre, and no further sum will be demanded nor any refund made, while in the case of tea-leases the fee is fixed at one rupee an acre and the applicant is entitled to a refund of any surplus, or, if the expenses exceed the deposit, has to make good the deficiency. Renewal of the preliminary lease is conditional on one half of the total area held being occupied by homesteads, or cultivated or left fallow, according to good husbandry, or otherwise fairly turned to account for agricultural purposes. The periods of renewals are to be conterminous with the period of Settlement of the district, current at the time of renewal. Sub-infeudation in the first degree only is allowable[2]. The sub-tenant is, however, to have from the lessee the same promise of renewal as the lessee himself has from Government, and the sub-tenant's rent is to be determined by the Deputy Commissioner. Rates of rent on renewal of lease have been fixed both in the case of tea-leases and of leases of arable lands. Where half the area of the grant of the arable land has not been brought under cultivation, the renewed lease shall ordinarily include an area of waste land equal to the extent of land brought under cultivation during the currency of the preliminary lease, but in such cases the Deputy Commissioner has the power, under certain restrictions, of refusing renewal altogether, or of allowing it on special conditions. Each description of land—tea, bastoo, rupit, &c.—is charged at the rate fixed in the pergunnah wherein it is situated. In the case of tea-leases in the hills of the Darjíling district, an all-round rate of one rupee an acre will be imposed on renewal of the lease, subsequent to the expiration of the preliminary lease.

'For small capitalists it has been decided that no rules are necessary for Darjiling.

'In consequence of re-adjustment of the boundary between Darjíling and Jalpáigúrí, the issue of orders which have indirectly affected the rules, and the grant of certain concessions on the part of Government,—such as extending the term for renewed leases, reducing the fee to be charged on transfers,

[1] Grants under these rules are heritable, but not transferable during the term of preliminary lease. It has been the local custom not to allow tea to be cultivated on land leased under these rules; but there seems to be no reason for such a restriction.

[2] The grantee may farm out his rights of management, &c., to one person, but that person may not create a farm of a farm.

and permitting partial transfers,—the tea-lease rules of 1878 are under revision; and it is at the same time proposed to revise the Dwár arable land-lease rules of 1875.'

§ 6. *The Chittagong Districts.*

'A set of rules for the grant of leases for tea cultivation in the Chittagong Hill Tracts, based on the tea-lease rules for Jalpáigúrí and Darjíling, was published by Government on the 30th June, 1879. No charge is made for trees on tea grants, though the right to levy tolls on forest produce exported either by land or water is reserved.

'There are no rules for leases to large capitalists in this district. Government are averse to granting waste lands in Chittagong proper for any other purpose than ordinary native cultivation. Here and there may be large tracts of waste land better fitted for the cultivation of tea than for anything else, and a special grant may be made of such blocks, if necessary, on special terms.

'For small capitalists, the waste lands are broken up into compact blocks of fifty acres each, and the lease of each lot sold by public competition. There is no restriction as to the kind of crops that may be grown.

'The whole of the waste lands are not thrown open at once for sale, but the leases of the surplus waste-land blocks in one village at a time are put up to auction on a given day on the established terms.

'The leases are heritable and transferable. The rates are fixed with reference to the quality of the land. A measurement and assessment after ten years, and another after fifteen years, is provided for; and in the case of lands exposed to salt-water inundation, and requiring the protection of embankments, a larger area than fifty acres, up to a maximum of 200 for a single applicant, or fifty acres each to several applicants jointly, may be granted. The other provisions generally follow the rules for the grant of tea-leases in Jalpáigúrí and Darjíling.'

SECTION V.—THE REVENUE-SYSTEM OF CHITTAGONG[1].

Chittagong is one of the eastern districts of Bengal between the sea-coast and the hills which separate Bengal from Burma. The soil is rich, but in 1793 a large portion was, as might be expected, still covered with luxuriant and tangled jungle, the clearance being chiefly in the level plains suited for rice-lands. There had been no natural opportunity, save in exceptional cases, for the growth of large Zamíndárí estates. The different settlers formed groups or companies, and each cleared one plot here and one there. The leader of the company was required to be the collector of the revenue from as many of the settlers as chose to pay through him, and therefore came to be looked on as the superior owner of the whole of the scattered group of holdings which paid through him. The group was called a 'taraf,' and the person who was at the head (or his descendant) was called 'tarafdár.' It also happened that settlers were called on by the Muhammadan conqueror for help and feudal service, and

[1] Properly Cháṭṭágraoṅ or Cháṭṭagrám.

The text refers to the regular district and not to the hilly portion known as the Chittagong Hill Tracts. In these the only revenue is a tribute paid by the chiefs. Formerly it was taken in kind (cotton), according to the population; this was afterwards converted into a money payment. This revenue was consequently shown in the old accounts as derived from the 'kapás mahál,' and became fixed by custom.

By Act XXII of 1860 the Hill district (as defined in a schedule to the Act) was removed from the operation of the General Regulations and put under a Deputy Commissioner. Simple rules regarding judicial procedure have been drawn up under the Act, and no revenue Settlement has been made. But there is a capitation tax payable by householders to the chiefs, and the latter pay the 'tribute' or quit-rent (or whatever it is proper to call it) above alluded to.

The cultivation is still chiefly of the temporary kind called 'júm,' so natural to all semi-barbarous people in tropical hill countries, and an attempt has been lately made to record in a simple way (so as to gradually get them fixed) the rights and interests of the different clans or tribes and their chiefs and headmen. The record is called the 'júm book.'

There are a certain number of estates in which lands are permanently cultivated, and these may be under a Settlement under the ordinary law. A portion of the district called the 'khás mahál' is reserved from the jurisdiction of the chiefs, for the purpose of making land grants to settlers. There are also State forests in this tract.

were then recognized as jágír-grantees of their land, holding it by *stated area*. So also 'tarafs' were founded by the military force sent to defend the province, and these tarafs were also held in jágír in lieu of pay. The consequence was, as early as 1764, *all the occupied lands* (which alone came under Settlement) having been granted by area, had been actually measured[1]. The Permanent Settlement then *extended only to the measured lands as they stood in* 1764.

All land cultivated subsequent to that, is locally spoken of as 'noabad' (nauábád=newly cultivated). And the ways in which this nauábád came to be cultivated were various. Under Regulation III of 1828, such cultivators would have no title whatever; but this was not at first looked to: assessment was the main object.

In the first place the 'tarafdárs' began to encroach on the waste all round, and extend all their cultivation without authority. This led to repeated re-measurements on the part of the authorities, and to a great deal of oppression and bribery, owing to the action of informers and others who threatened to expose the encroachments, if not paid to keep silence. A great number of other persons, mere squatters, also cultivated lands.

§ 1. *The Noabad Taluqs.*

All the 'nauábád' lands could claim nothing but a temporary Settlement. It happened, however, that one of the old estate-holders laid claim by virtue of a *sanad*, which afterwards proved to be forged, to have had *all the waste in the district* granted to him in 1797. An immense correspondence, ending in a lawsuit, followed, and lasted for nearly forty years[2]. The result was that Government

[1] See Chapter III (on Tenures) for some further remarks on the 'taraf.' See also Cotton's *Memorandum on Revenue Administration of Chittagong* (1880), pp. 7, 8, 10.

[2] When the fraud was discovered, Government dispossessed him of the whole, without discriminating those lands to which he had a just title, from those fraudulently obtained. The Sudder Court decreed in his favour for the *original* estate, but gave Government the rest. (Macneile's *Memorandum*, Chapter IV.)

recovered its right, but had to allow the Zamíndár so much land as really belonged to his original estate. This could not be found out without a survey, and the opportunity was taken to survey the whole district, with a view to the proper separation of the old permanently-settled lands of 1764 from the nauábád lands. The process took seven years to complete (from 1841–1848), and the Settlement was made by Sir H. Ricketts. All the 'nauábád' lands were surveyed, whether held by squatters or taken as encroachments by the original tarafdárs; but each plot separately occupied was, as a rule, formed into a separate 'taluq,' though some few were aggregated: 32,258 little estates were thus formed, called in revenue language, the 'noabad taluqs.' A small number (861) of these, that paid R. 50 revenue and upwards, were placed directly under the Collector, and the host of smaller ones were grouped into 196 blocks, each of which was at first given out to a 'circle farmer' who was to be responsible for collecting the revenue. The system was afterwards abandoned in favour of khás management by the aid of local revenue officers, on the analogy of a *raiyatwárí* management.

Nor was this the only trouble in Chittagong. The invalid revenue-free grants, to which I have already alluded as liable to resumption and assessment, were peculiarly numerous and intricate; even after relinquishing all cases in which the holding did not exceed 10 bíghás, there were still 36,683 petty estates of this class separately to be settled. Many of these had to be permanently settled under the law alluded to previously (see page 427).

There were also a large number of small grants or leases made by the revenue authorities under the designation of clearing or 'jangalbúrí' leases[1].

Thus the Chittagong district consists of a mosaic of petty estates; here a plot of old permanently-settled land, next a jangalbúrí plot, then a recovered and assessed encroachment, next a resumed lákhiráj holding, and so forth.

[1] There were 1290 of them, of which 1002, settled originally for twenty-five years, gave only R. 2,475 revenue between them.

The table already given will show how the estates are now grouped under the head of 'permanently settled,' 'temporarily settled,' and Government estates [1].

The work of revenue collection in the petty estates will now be facilitated, inasmuch as recent orders have resulted in the issue of a proclamation [2] notifying that, for the term of one year, petty estates permanently settled and paying less than one rupee *per annum* may be redeemed on a payment of ten times the annual *jama*'.

The question of how to deal with the nauábád lands or taluqs, was for a long time in suspense. At one time a Permanent Settlement was offered, but on such terms that but few accepted it. It was then determined, generally, that the nauábád taluqdár was a tenure-holder on an estate belonging to Government. The Settlement of 1848 was made for fifty years in the case of *taluqs* which had their cultivation fairly fully developed, and for twenty-five years in jangalbúrí-taluqs, where much land was still waste. In 1875–76, the re-settlement of these latter began, and the measurements are now complete. A question then arose as to whether some of these *taluqs* (and some resumed revenue-free *taluqs*) were legally liable to re-settlement at all. An order also had been obtained that 4913 tarafs of the Government estate were not liable to re-settlement. In respect of all these, it has ultimately been determined that they *are* liable: but it was agreed not to re-settle the 4913 estates till the fifty years' leases fell in in 1892 [3].

[1] In the *Revenue Report* (1888-9) the map of Chittagong shows how the Government and private estates are intermingled, and the 'Settlement' map appended to this volume endeavours to show (though only roughly) the same condition. The real number of the Government estates is about 45,000, but for management purposes they are grouped into five circles, each circle being called an estate, and bearing a name as the Town khás Mahál, the Ranjan Mahál, &c., &c. (*Report*, 1883, p. 29.)

[2] *Revenue Report*, 1887–88, Section 55.

[3] *Revenue Report for* 1885 86, Section 114.

SECTION VI.—THE CHUTIYÁ NÁGPUR DISTRICTS.

We shall have more to say about these districts under the head of *Tenures*, because it is in them that we have certain relics of one of the original village-systems,—that of the Kols and kindred tribes, Hôs, Mundás, and also of the southern or Dravidian Uráoṅs.

Here, however, we are concerned with the Revenue Settlements.

A portion of each of the present districts that was formerly attached to the old Collectorates of that date, came under the Permanent Settlement.

§ 1. *Mánbhúm.*

Nearly all *Mánbhúm* is permanently settled by treating as 'Zamíndár' (with a fixed revenue) the chiefs over *parhás* or groups of villages, which the old native tribal organization originated. There are but two temporarily-settled estates in the district.

§ 2. *Singhbhúm.*

The northern portion consists of the permanently-settled pargana of Dhálbhúm formerly attached to Midnapore, and of two chiefs' estates (Sarái-kaláṅ and Kharsáwáṅ) under political control, and one estate permanently settled and two temporarily settled in the subdivision of Dhálbhúm.

The rest of the district consists of the tract called Kôlhán [1] (1905 square miles) occupying the whole south-west portion of the district, and forming a 'raiyatwárí tract' and the confiscated estate of Parahát [2].

In both these districts and in Mánbhúm, lands are never sold for arrears of revenue; and *all* sales and mortgages of land require the sanction of the Commissioner.

[1] Kôlhán is sometimes called Ho-desam—the settlement of Hos.

[2] There is a history of the Parahát (or Porahat) estate in *Government of India* (Rev. and Agr.) *Proceedings for February*, 1889.

§ 3. *Hazáríbágh.*

Here there are four principal subdivisions according to the different Settlement arrangements :—

(*a*) *Rámgarh* was originally a single estate; but it has since been split up into four separate estates, one being the Government estate occupied by cantonments, &c., around Hazáríbágh, called (the 'Government enclosure' or) 'Sirkári-háta'; the second being the Zamíndárí of Kodarmá, confiscated in 1841, and now a Government estate, the third the remaining part of the Zamíndárí of Rámgarh; the fourth the Kenduá estate,—a Government 'taufír' estate made up of resumed surplus lands and farmed for twenty years.

(*b*) The Kundá pargana and estate.

(*c*) The Kharakdihá estates, one of which is permanently settled, one is revenue-free, and others are Government estates.

(*d*) The Kendí pargana, which is permanently settled.

The whole district is composed of 68 permanently-settled and 186 Government estates.

§ 4. *Lohárdagga.*

The Palámau subdivision, occupying the north-western portion of the district, is a Government estate or 'khás mahál' shown partly as 'Government estate' and partly as 'raiyatwárí tract.' It contains some good State forests. The rest of the district is settled with the Mahárájá of Chutiyá Nágpur as a sort of permanently-settled estate, but it is looked upon rather as a tribute-paying chiefship, and has never been held liable to sale for arrears of revenue.

§ 5. *General Remarks.*

In the Chutiyá Nágpur districts there are some curious subordinate tenures, provision for the record and declaration of which has been made in the Bengal Act II of 1869. These tenures will be dealt with in the chapter devoted to the subject of tenures.

But as regards Settlement arrangements, it must here be mentioned that the Act contemplated the appointment of one or more special Commissioners, who were to have exclusive jurisdiction to try and determine all disputes regarding tenures in the estates, and to make a record (which was final and authoritative), regarding the right to the different lands and the privileges attaching to each. The fact that a chief had been recognized as Zamíndár, or that the Government was the superior owner, did not prevent this.

The tenures were based on the peculiar arrangement (already alluded to) that besides, or rather anterior to, the plan of allotting a *share* in the produce to the chief or overlord, the ancient system was to set apart certain lands for the king or the chief. Thus in every village these lands were called (majhhas) and in later times became the Settlement-holding proprietor's lands, whoever he might be—a descendant of the chief, a purchaser, or a person with a merely prescriptive title. Certain other lands were, on the same principle, allotted to the original founders of the village who held the office of headmen, &c., others to the priest for himself and for the worship of various deities; others were taken by the mahto, or collector, who was (at a later period) put in by the chief to look after his interests; others, again (called beṭ-khetá) were assigned, in lieu of wages, to the labourers who cultivated the once royal or *majhhas* lands.

Such a system, in later days, gave rise to great facilities for wrong-doing. The more powerful would annex lands and drive out the feebler. The object of the special record was to restore the rightful holders (who had had possession within a reasonable limit fixed by the Act), and to secure, by record, these rights with the privileges attaching thereto, in the *majhhas* lands and in lands in which rights of the original founders (bhúíṅhár) existed.

SECTION VII.—SANTÁL PERGUNNAHS [1].

A glance at the map shows this district to consist of a central hilly portion which begins in the north and extends downwards; this is the Government estate, or 'Dáman-i-Koh': below this, on either side, and at the south, is plain country which was permanently settled.

Regulation III of 1872 applies to the whole district, and gives certain rules for the fixing of the cultivators' rents; so that in fact the Permanent Settlement only affects the right in the soil and the fixity of the Government assessment on the landlords.

The Santál Parganas were first removed from the operation of the ordinary law by Act XXXVII of 1855 [2], which provided for a special superintendence. And this Act has been continued and amplified by the Regulation III of 1872 which declares the laws in force. It is important to remember that Act XXXVII declares that no Act of the Legislature, either past *or future*, shall apply to the Santál Parganas unless they are expressly named in the Act. This is why the Forest Act of 1878 does not apply, nor has it yet been extended under the Regulation of 1872. The old Forest Act of 1865 was specially extended, and consequently still remains in force, but will probably be repealed.

Part of the plain or old-settled tract, is regularly cultivated, but part of it is hilly and still much covered with jungle. This portion is largely peopled and cultivated by Santál immigrants. These brought their village institutions with them and settled, each village paying rent to the existing Zamíndár landlord. Practically, all the village tenures are permanent and alienable—subject only to the superior landlord's rent. As a rule, the landlord gets his rent, not direct from the raiyats, but through a village

[1] The limits of this district are described in a schedule annexed to Act X of 1857.

[2] The schedule to this Act has been replaced by the revised schedule in Act X of 1857.

headman; so that in fact the Zamíndár is really more like a pensioner drawing a rent from the land, but not, as a rule (for there are some lands under his direct management), interfering in the cultivation or management of the villages.

§ 1. *The Dáman-i-Koh.*

As early as 1780 A.D. the tract known as the Dáman-i-Koh was withdrawn, by an act of State, from the general Settlement, and was made a separate 'Government estate[1].' This, however, practically meant that the Government took the tribes under its own immediate management and did not recognize any Zamíndár, or intermediate landlord, as having any hold over this wild region.

The Santáls are not the original inhabitants of this tract, but two or three Kolarian tribes, now indiscriminately known as 'Pahárias.' The Pahárias cultivate chiefly by 'júm,' or shifting cultivation, already described. At first there was no Settlement; or rather the usual order of Settlement was reversed; the people did not pay anything to Government, but the Government paid them an annual grant to support their headmen and tribal officers. These officers seem to be the relics of the old days when the hills were nominally within the adjacent Zamíndárí estates. There were local divisions of the separated tract, described by the imported term 'pargana.' Over such a division there was a 'sardár,' with his 'náib' or deputy; while the headman over a village was the 'mánjhí.' The pargana division has long fallen into disuse; but the sardárs and others survive, drawing their pensions. This is a relic of the old Kolarian plan of village government with nothing above it but the chief of a group of villages. The old terms were lost, and the present equivalent Persian names of office were adopted.

The Santáls then seem to have immigrated in consider-

[1] I am indebted for this information to the kindness of Mr. W. Oldham, the Deputy-Commissioner, and to a *Memorandum on the Santál Settlement* by Mr. C. W. Bolton, C.S.

able numbers, and cultivated all the valleys and lower slopes, so that the wandering Pahárias, with no settled cultivation, became confined to the hillsides; since that time, the Pahária headmen have begun to claim specific properties in the hill-tops and slopes, which, however, Government does not theoretically recognize, it having all along claimed the region as a 'Government estate.' No interference with these people is, however, contemplated; and they have, of course, wofully abused and destroyed the forest. It has been long a question whether part of the forest could not be put under regular conservancy; and quite recently it has been determined to enforce simple rules in a portion of the area.

§ 2. *The Settlement.*

The Settlement arrangements of the cultivated villages of the Santál Parganas are governed by the Regulation III of 1872, the mánjhí or headman of each village collecting and paying in the rents to Government or to the owner, as the case may be, and being allowed 8 per cent. as his 'commission.' The Regulation contemplates the record of all classes of interests in land and fixing of all rents (those in Permanently-Settled estates not excepted), whether payable to a proprietor or to Government; these rents are to remain unchanged for at least seven years.

SECTION VIII.—JALPÁIGÚRÍ AND DARJÍLING.

§ 1. *Jalpáigúrí.*

That part of the district which is south-west of the Tísta river is all permanently settled, having been formerly part of the old Rangpur Collectorate. The remaining part of the district, north of the Kuch-Bihár (tributary) state, and extending to the borders of the Goálpára district of Assam, comprises the Bhután (or Western) Dwárs [1].

[1] In a notification, No. 308, dated 3rd March, 1881 (*Gazette of India* March 5th, 1881), the laws in force in Jalpáigúrí and Darjíling (besides

The district as a whole is called a 'non-regulation' district, but the whole body of ordinary law is in force in the 'regulation portion,' to which the Permanent Settlement extended.

The Dwárs lie along the foot of the hills, and were taken from the Bhútiás in 1865. In 1870 the country was settled for ten years, and again in 1880 for ten years more. The whole constitutes a Government estate managed as a 'raiyatwárí tract.' The Settlement is made with the soil occupants called 'jotdárs,' whose tenures are recognized as fixed tenancies, with a rent unalterable for the term of Settlement. The 'jot' is saleable for arrears of revenue [1].

In some of the 'girds' or parganas (of which the Dwárs contain nine in all) the Settlement was made with farmers without proprietary rights, who were allowed 17½ per cent. on the revenue, as their remuneration and profit. When the Settlement is with the jotdár, the revenue collection is made by 'tahsíldárs,' who are remunerated by an allowance of 10 per cent. on the revenue.

§ 2. *Darjíling.*

This district also may be described as divided into several different tracts:—

(*a*)[2] { (1) In the north-west corner a large estate (115 square miles) has been granted on a perpetual rent to the Chebu Láma.

(2) The old Darjíling territory ceded by Sikkim in 1835—a long strip of 138 square miles, extending down to the Tarái near Pankhábárí.

(3) Two strips on each side of this, acquired in 1850, bring the district up to the Nepál frontier on one side and to the Tísta river on the other. }

Act XIV of 1874) have been declared. All the 'Regulation' laws apply to the Jalpáigúri district up to the Tísta river. The Western Dwárs are separately provided for.

[1] Some further details will be found in the chapter on Tenures.

[2] By the Notification of March 3rd, 1881, the laws in force in Darjíling are specified. For this purpose the district is divided into three portions—(*a*) the hills west of the Tísta; (*b*) the Darjíling Tarái; (*c*) the Damsong subdivision (east of the Tísta).

(*b*) The Tarái below Pankhábárí, also annexed in 1850.

(*c*) The Damsong subdivision, or hill portion of the Bhútia territory about Dalingkot, taken in 1865 (east of the Tísta, west of the Jaldáha, and north of the Western Dwárs in the Jalpáígúrí district just alluded to).

Nearly all the territory in (*a* 2 and 3) seems to have been dealt with under various 'waste-land rules' and now to consist of—

(1) Estates sold or granted or commuted into 'fee-simple' or revenue-free holdings.

(2) Estates 'leased,' i. e. granted to persons who pay revenue according to their lease.

(3) Government estates appropriated to forests, to station-sites, military purposes, &c., and waste not yet disposed of.

In the tract (*b*) there were some lands at first settled for short terms (three years) with Bengalis, the Settlement-holders being called chaudharis of 'jots' or groups of cultivation. The chaudharis were, however, abolished in 1864, and the Settlement was made with the jotdárs, or cultivators of the *jot*.

In the upper Tarái are also Settlements for short terms, made with Mech and Dhimal caste-men, who pay a certain rate on each 'dáo' or hoe used for cultivating. Some jungle-clearing leases for five years were also given. In 1867 there was a survey and Settlement under the modern procedure for thirty years.

In the Damsong subdivision (*c*) at first only a capitation-tax was collected; the tract will probably ultimately be surveyed and brought under temporary Settlement[1].

[1] The map in the *Revenue Report* colours the whole district as 'Government estates' except the Chebu Lámá's (P. S.) estate in the north: this is hardly satisfactory.

CHAPTER III.

THE LAND-TENURES.

SECTION I.—GENERAL REMARKS.

THE task of writing, in moderate compass, an account of the LAND-TENURES OF BENGAL is a difficult one, for two reasons. In the first place, it is not easy to hit upon a grouping or classification which is suitable; and yet some classification, based on an intelligible principle, is indispensable. Otherwise the tenures will only be presented to the reader in a haphazard catalogue. Most of our books adopt this latter method, with the result that, while the memory is bewildered over a string of names that often are not worth remembering, those real distinctions and actual varieties of land-tenure which are based on custom and on feelings and ideas about landholding, and are therefore worth remembering, are undistinguished and forgotten. The second difficulty arises from the enormous mass of records and authorities. But little attempt has hitherto been made to digest it. The *Fifth Report to the Committee of the House of Commons* of 1812 is a great mine of information, but neither classified nor arranged. In Harington's *Analysis*, again, is a formidable collection of papers. Mr. Phillips, with his usual industry, has given, in the *Tagore Lectures* (1875), a mass of information scattered through various lectures, but in a rather bewildering fashion. Dr. Field has collected all the best authorities in his *Land-holding in Various Countries.* In an anonymous work called *The Zamíndárí Settlement of Bengal*[1] another vast

[1] 2 vols. Calcutta: Brown & Co., 1879.

mass of authorities, of very various value, is piled up. And these are only the more accessible of the references; I have not mentioned Special Reports, Notes, and Monographs, whose name is legion.

In this chapter I have therefore to make the attempt to present the student with a classified account of tenures, and in doing so, not merely to re-quote the authorities *en masse*, but to rigidly exclude all that does not appear to be of real importance and weight. This should enable a reader to dispense with a reference to bulky and inaccessible volumes, except in case he wishes to make some special study and go into 'original sources [1].'

In dealing with Bengal tenures, I propose to relegate to separate sections the tenures observed in the Santál Parganas, Chutiyá Nágpur, Orissa, and Chittagong. There are special historical features about these localities which fit them for separate notice; but they are full of interest, and indeed it is in these places that we find survivals which are of the highest importance in connection with the early history of land-customs.

Taking, then, the districts of Bengal proper and Bihár, we shall find that the original village organization has too far decayed to enable us to start from it as a basis of land-tenure investigation; what traces of it survive in headmen's privileges and grants of land for village service, will now and again come to notice as we explore the peculiarities of the landlord's right, and the origin and nature of the tenures under him.

In a word, in Bengal the Zamíndár has become the central figure, and our study must start with him and with the 'independent' landholder, jagírdár, and other 'actual proprietor,' whom the Regulations placed on the same footing.

The 'actual proprietors,' to state the matter in other words, may be great Zamíndárs, or they may be lesser

[1] The labour of this task has been much lightened by the excellent *Memorandum on Land-Tenures* which Mr. J. S. Cotton, C.S., has prepared.

estate-holders, all equally now raised to the status and legal privileges of the Regulation proprietor.

In close connection with proprietary tenures paying revenue, are the lákhiráj holdings allowed as valid. They *may* be mere assignments of revenue, but often include the ownership of the land as well. Some of these have become landlord-estates; other smaller ones have remained *under* the proprietor, and therefore fall into the class of subordinate 'tenures,' just above the grade of 'raiyat.'

As we pass out of the class of fully proprietary tenures, we enter on a border-land, which in Bengal is a most curious one,—I refer to the region of tenures which we cannot classify as *proprietary*, and are yet not exactly *tenancies*.

The latest attempt of the legislature to deal with the subject has not resulted in a complete definition; but it has given us the term 'tenure' for this class of rights; and we can describe their peculiarities and privileges, if we cannot frame a definition.

Some of these tenures practically represent relics of older rights which gave way beneath the growth of the *Zamíndárí* right, but still showed some traces—as we can see the remains of the original tree under its overgrowth of the many-rooted *Ficus* in an Indian forest. And even where the holder of such right possesses a document in the nature of a grant from the Zamíndár, or some other authority, it by no means follows that the right really originates in contract, or in an act of pure donation by the superior. Other such tenures (as already indicated) are due to the desire of the landlord to disembarrass himself of the direct management of the whole or part of his estate; he creates tenures in favour of persons who will pay him a fixed sum, and make what they can out of the land. Other such tenures are again due to the desire to encourage the bringing of the waste under cultivation, for which purpose a fixed tenure and favourable terms are needed—backed, no doubt, by the strong and long-established feeling of right in favour of him 'who first cleared the land.' There are other tenures also originating in grants free of rent for the rendering of certain services.

Further detail would be here unintelligible; but what has been said will show that we have an ample supply of material for a separate section on '*Tenures*' (in the technical sense). When we come down to the lowest grade—'raiyat-holdings,' or cultivating tenancies—it is obvious that we have also much to consider. The whole battle of the tenant-question in Bengal is before us, and the history of the many attempts to define and secure different grades of tenant-right. These are the divisions of our chapters on Land-Tenures.

Section II.—The Zamíndár Landlord.

§ 1. *General Remarks.*

I have said enough in the earlier chapters to make the student familiar with the name Zamíndár. How the later and declining Mughal ruler adopted the plan of collecting his revenue through agents who, having contracted to find a certain sum for the Treasury, were left to manage the land as they pleased—that has all been described. The question what is the true nature of the Zamíndár's office or title has been discussed in various books. But in point of fact it is quite impossible to bring all the facts which were true about the Zamíndárs at one time and at another,—to bring all these facts to a focus and then to make them fit in with tolerable exactitude, to any definition of right or title to be found in an English law-book or dictionary. Looked at with reference to the circumstances of a certain period of Bengal history, and with reference to the terms of deeds of appointment, it is easy to say that the Zamíndár was only a revenue official—a tax-gatherer if you please. Looked at with reference to the practical position actually held, I do not think that any one who dispassionately considers what influence and hold over the land (and the raiyats) the Zamíndár really had in 1789, will hesitate to conclude that it was right to call him 'landlord,' *provided* the subordinate rights were adequately secured.

There are allusions to Zamíndárs even in Akbar's time, in the *Ayín-i-Akbari*; but certainly not to a 'Zamíndár' as holding an office or function created for the realization of the revenues of a certain tract, and charged with police and other duties. Indeed, the term was then used as synonymous with 'bhúmi' (evidently the Hindu term for the natural proprietor or lord of the soil). This alone should at once indicate what Ab-ul-Fazl meant. In one place certain zamíndárs are mentioned as having functions like jagírdárs, but *any* landholder might have been employed or granted allowances to keep a force of foot or horsemen to maintain order locally. I have already alluded to the fact that in most provinces where the Mughal power extended its conquest, there were found, as in Oudh, local Rájás or chiefs holding considerable areas of country as rulers [1], having both their own private lands and certain rights and dues, as ruler, over the whole country. Such chiefs could not resist the Mughal arms to the extent of maintaining their independence, but yet might give great trouble in outlying districts; it was, therefore, often a matter of policy to leave them in possession, on condition that they would pay over to the Imperial Treasury a certain proportion of the revenue collected from the villages. If a chief accepted—as he would be obliged to do—that position, unless he were expressly recognized as holding revenue-free, or as assignee of the revenue for special service, he would be called 'landholder'—Zamíndár. In

[1] 'Native leaders, sometimes leading men of Hindu clans who have risen to power as guerilla plunderers, levying black-mail, and eventually coming to terms with the Government, have established themselves, under the titles of Zamíndár, polygár, &c., in the control of tracts of country for which they pay a revenue or tribute, uncertain under a weak power, but which becomes a regular land revenue when a strong power is established. This is a very common origin of many of the most considerable modern families, both in the north and in the south. To our ideas, there is a wide gulf between a robber and a landlord, but not so in a native's view. It is wonderful how much in times such as those of the last century, the robber, the Rájá, and the Zamíndár run into one another.'—(Campbell's *Land-Tenures in India: Cobden Club Papers*, 1876, p. 142.)

the same way, when the authorities wished to show some local landholder of lesser *status*, some kind of favour, they gave him a grant of a local tract over which he was to collect the revenues; and this smaller grant they called 'taluqdárí.' According to the size of the estate and the influence of the holder, the grantee was allowed to be in direct relation with the State, or was placed in a privileged position, but made to pay through a greater 'Zamíndár.' An instance of this is afforded by the case of many village headmen in Bhágulpur and the petty landholders of Chittagong, all of whom were vaguely called 'taluqdárs.'

Let us confine ourselves here to the *Zamíndár*.

I do not think that the student need trouble himself with anything more than can be gathered from a few really authoritative sources. There are the minutes of Mr. Shore and Lord Cornwallis, both based on very valuable native authorities of the time [1], and these give what I may call the landlord view. On the other side, the chief authority urging the 'official' nature of the Zamíndár's position was Mr. James Grant, who wrote a history of the 'Northern Sirkárs' [2] of Madras (where there were also Zamíndárs), and who afterwards became 'Chief Sarishtadár' under the Bengal Government, and published an *Enquiry into the nature of Zemindary tenures in the landed property of Bengal*, 1790 [3]. The opinion of Mr. Harington himself (his service extended from 1780 to 1823) is entitled to the greatest weight, as he was in the service all through the period when the inquiries were going on. I shall therefore quote it, as found in the *Analysis*, in some detail.

[1] A number of these, on which Mr. Shore based his minute of 1788, are given in Harington, vol. iii., and in the Reprint of Harington's chapter on the Rights of Landholders.

[2] *Political Survey of the Northern Circars*, dated 20th December, 1784; also an *Analysis of the Finances of Bengal* (April, 1786); Appendices to the *Fifth Report*.

[3] This was answered by Mr. C. W. B. Rouse, Secretary to the Board of Control, in a Dissertation concerning the Landed Property in Bengal. Mr. Grant was a good deal followed in Patton's *Principles of Asiatic Monarchies*, 1801.

§ 2. *Origin of Zamíndárs.*

Mr. Shore said that the origin of 'Zamíndárs' was uncertain [1]. There probably never was a time when a Mughal governor or emperor deliberately conceived the plan of creating an official collector of rents, or invented as a title, the word 'Zamíndár,' and making a decree or regulation defining the rights and duties. But, as already stated, persons who had a real estate of some kind or degree over villages and districts, were always, from the earliest times of Muhammadan rule, spoken of generically as 'zamíndárs'; and if they received a warrant or *sanad* from the ruling power, for any purpose, it would probably speak of them as being (official) Zamíndárs. If, as I have already stated, they were people of minor importance, they would be called 'taluqdár,'—holder of a portion of land—a 'dependency,' as the word implies, not a great and independent estate. Persons recognized as 'Zamíndárs' and some of the superior 'taluqdárs' were no doubt allowed to collect themselves, and to pay in direct, the revenue for their territories. The rest of the country was managed solely by State officers who collected through the heads of villages from the cultivators. The Mughal system, it should be always borne in mind (with the exception of the country held on service grants, or by such local magnates as it was politic to recognize), was essentially *raiyatwárí*; it went straight to the cultivator through the headman of each village. The original system then did not countenance farming the revenues; so that chiefs and others (recognized landholders) would not then have been known by any particular name or official status. Probably, the degree of actual power which the landholder had in managing his estate, varied with the wealth, respectability, and influence of each chief or grantee, and especially with his nearness to, or remoteness from, the centre of control. But it would seem that when the Emperor Farukhsíyar ascended the

[1] Minute of 2nd April, 1788.

throne in 1713 A.D., the decline of the Empire had already begun, and decline was always marked by relaxation of control, not only over the outlying provinces, but over the whole administrative machinery, and by the substitution of plans of *farming* the revenues of convenient tracts. Then it was that, besides the Rájás, chiefs, and ancient grantees, who had a real hold over the country, and were already spoken of as the Zamíndárs, other classes of persons were employed as farmers, and the same name and the same designation came to be applied to them also. As a matter of fact, we find ex-officials possessed of wealth and energy —'ámils, karoris, &c.,—also bankers and Court favourites, receiving the name of Zamíndár.

And such persons would, besides taking the name, also ape the dignities and importance of the older landholders.

This class of Zamíndár would commence with neither the *prestige* nor with the *customary* incidents of tenure which generations had established in the case of the others. The old Rájá, for instance, was already well established in his right to take a share of the produce, besides having a more or less definite claim to all waste land, and certainly the unquestioned right of bringing it under cultivation, for which purpose he made grants or located his own 'tenants.' He had also tolls and dues of all kinds from traders and artisans, fees from woodcutters in the forest, and transit duties. His estate was, of course, hereditary, and probably, if it was that of a Rájá or greater chief, the custom of primogeniture was established. Opportunities for getting the best lands absolutely into his own hands were not wanting. As the public authority declined, his opportunities increased; no wonder that in time he grew to be a landlord, and that, in 1789, he was recognized as such. The later class of revenue-farmers was originally in no such favourable position: they had certainly no right to succeed by inheritance, nor could they make a grant of any land except their own. They held a *sanad*, which professed to convey no property in anything, but merely to fix duties and require obedience and faithful service, and moreover they had to subscribe a recognizance for due observance, and a stipulation for the amount of revenue to be paid in, which was supposed to be the total rental, less a fixed allowance for the expense and risk of collection, usually one-tenth of the whole, with or without an allowance in money or land specially granted as 'nánkár' or subsistence.

It is quite certain that before the system of *farming* came into vogue, and Zamíndárs of this class were appointed, the village cultivators, where there were no chiefs over them, had a customary tenure, which was certainly, however decayed or weakened, a proprietary right, in their holdings. Therefore the Zamíndárs, when put over them, could not be proprietors in the sense of absolute owner, entitled to the *usus, abusus, fructus et vindicatio* of European law. Nevertheless, the 'Zamíndár' had some land to begin with; he soon bought up, took in mortgage, and otherwise made himself master of, other lands: he cultivated the waste with his own tenants, and it became his. And it is very likely that in these matters the lower order of men were more pushing and energetic than the old nobility; so that in the end, what with the growth of the modern estates, and the decay of the older ones,—for noble families die out, quarrel, break up, become bankrupt and lose their lands,—*all Zamíndárís came to be looked upon as one and the same*, and their ancient differences of origin ignored. In 1788 Mr. Shore said that most of the (then existing) considerable Zamíndárs might be traced to an origin within the last century and a half[1].

[1] The following passage is from Ghulám Husain, the historian (author of the *Sayyar-muta,ákhirin*, 'deeds of the moderns'). He was the son of a Názim or Governor of the Bihár province. He was one of those to whom questions were addressed regarding the history and status of Zamíndárs before the Permanent Settlement. 'Since the decline of the constitution in the reign of Farukhsíyar and the introduction of the farming system at the recommendation of Ratn Chand, when corruption pervaded every department of the State, the unprincipled *Zamíndárs*, by ingratiating themselves with the rulers for the time being, distressed the inferior zamíndárs (i. e. persons who had been recognized over smaller estates) by every possible mode, until they were reduced to the necessity of selling their *zamíndárís* to their oppressors, who thenceforward became . . . . the acknowledged proprietors of them.

§ 3. *Incidents of the Zamíndárí as it was understood after 1713 A.D.*

(A) *Hereditary Succession.*

The title, if it was that of a Rájá or other chief, who became Zamíndár, was *naturally* hereditary. Only the ruling power took care to keep the heirs in mind of their subordinate position, by exacting a fine or fee at each succession, as well as by renewing the *sanad* or grant. When Mr. James Grant says the office was not hereditary till after Nádir Sháh's time in 1739 A.D.[1], he is speaking of those revenue-farmers who had no natural connection with the soil, but got the official position.

One thing that helped the general recognition of the *hereditary* right, was the fact that many Zamíndárís were created for restoring cultivation or on condition of clearing the waste (jangalbúrí), and *these* were always recognized (from the first) as passing from father to son, because a single lifetime would hardly suffice to develop the estate; or, at all events, it would be most natural to continue it to the son, who would have local experience at the time when the estate was probably just beginning to be a settled and steadily-paying one[2].

(B) *The form of appointing Zamíndárs.*

To begin with, when the State affairs were still managed

Other Zamíndárs, having desolated their lands by mismanagement and dissipation, were obliged by the ruling power to dispose of them to more prudent and opulent Zamíndárs for the liquidation of their balances. The title of the purchasers of such lands was considered good and valid. Towards the close of the reign of Muhammad Sháh (Farukhsiyar's successor in 1719)... certain Zamíndárs by attaching themselves to these (certain State) officers acquired great influence, and either by force or under different pretences, unjustly possessed themselves of the estates of inferior (smaller) landholders, till at length becoming rich and powerful.... they declared themselves proprietors of the lands thus unfairly acquired.'

[1] *Fifth Report*, vol. ii. 156.

[2] The author of *Land Tenures by a Civilian* probably puts it correctly when he says (p. 72) that 'the *office of Zamíndár* could not be claimed as hereditary, though by long custom, and perhaps out of policy, the children of deceased contractors were very generally admitted as successors to their parents; they were not in all cases appointed, and sometimes were ousted.'

with some care and attention to detail, the Zamíndár who proposed to farm a considerable area, had to go through a somewhat formidable office-procedure. No doubt all this detail was not exacted from the 'Zamíndárs' of the old Hindu aristocracy, who simply accepted a *sanad* with a fixed sum entered in it. It was otherwise with the farmers, though even they, in time, ceased to receive the *sanad*, except in special cases, and then chiefly in case they sought it as a protection against rival claimants[1]. The original procedure was for the new Zamíndár to petition the provincial governor informing him that the office was vacant—let us suppose by death,—and adding that the petitioner desired favour as the heir or successor. The Governor would reply, in the case of a person of some consideration, by letters of condolence, &c. This prepared the way for the submission of the *'arzi*, or formal petition, offering to be responsible for the usual revenue total, together with any balance that might be outstanding. On receipt of this, the Government officer prepared a *fard sawál*—an abstract of the petition with necessary information as to figures, &c.,—and asked for the orders of his superior. On the orders being received, the proper officer made out an exact schedule of the villages or component parts of the estate, and of the assessment expected from each, the deductions allowed, and the balance payable to the treasury. This was the *fard-i-haqíqat* (or 'statement of the true facts')[2]. The expectant Zamíndár had then to give a sort of recognizance or 'muchalka,' a document[3] which acknowledged his responsibility for the revenue stated in abstract, and for the performance of the duty:—as Mr. Phillips puts it,—

'to observe a commendable character towards the body of the inhabitants at large, to endeavour to punish and expel the refractory, and to extirpate robbers; to conciliate and encourage the raiyats, and to promote the increase of cultiva-

[1] Harington, vol. iii. 337.

[2] It is an elaborate document in four columns, each filled up by the proper officer.

[3] Also called 'qabúliyat' or acceptance.

tion; . . . . to take care that travellers might pass in safety, and that no robbery or murder should be committed; and if any one should be robbed, he agreed to be responsible for producing the culprits with the property, or to make good the loss[1]; to repress drunkenness and all kinds of irregularity; to pay punctually the assessment, less the items of allowed deductions (mazkúrát); to transmit to the Government office the official papers required.'

Lastly, the Government office issued the 'sanad' (called also 'parwána') addressed to the Government officials in the limits of the Zamíndárí, and to the village accountants (patwárís), village headmen, who were called (in the Persian revenue language, but not, of course, by the people) 'muqaddam.' It recited the Zamíndár's duties, prohibited his levying *abwáb* or cesses without authority, and commanded the local officers and others to receive him as Zamíndár, and to take all pargana papers and accounts signed by him, as authentic[2].

It is quite obvious from the terms of such documents, that the holders of them, *as such*, were neither constituted soil-proprietors, nor treated therein, as in any such position. But then the executor of such a series of documents might have rights independently of them, and, what is of more importance, might in time easily *grow* into a new position. As a matter of fact, when we reflect on the emoluments and opportunities of the Zamíndár, his power of getting land by sale and mortgage, his 'right' of ousting obnoxious men, and by taking possession when an unfortunate owner absconded—perhaps to avoid exactions which had become intolerable, perhaps in his inability to pay his 'rent'—it is not difficult to perceive how the Zamíndár grew into his ultimate position. When this virtual ownership had gone on for several generations, and had become

[1] This is a very ancient custom in parts of India. In the Rájputána States it was common till quite of late years.

[2] Specimen sanads are given in Harington (Appendix 9 to Shore's Minute of April, 1788), and Phillips gives a translation of the sanad (of Muhammad Shah's reign) in A.D. 1735–6 granted to the Zamíndár of Rájsháhi.

consolidated, the fact of a formerly different *status* very naturally became little more than a shadowy memory. Our early legislators of 1793 could then hardly avoid calling the Zamíndár's right a proprietary one, and treating it accordingly; though, as I have already shown, they limited, or intended to limit, the right thus conferred, with a view to securing at least so much of the original right of the now subordinate village landowners as could still be established.

(C) *Power of Transfer.*

In one respect, however, the recognition accorded to the Zamíndár's right in 1793 was a material advance beyond what practice had hitherto sanctioned. Powerful as the Zamíndár became in managing the land, in grasping and in ousting, he had no power of alienating his estate; he could not raise money on it by mortgage, nor sell the whole or any part of it. This clearly appears from a proclamation issued on 1st August, 1786; the illegal practice 'of alienating revenue lands' is complained of; the 'gentlemen appointed to superintend' the various districts, are invited zealously to prevent the 'commission of this offence'; and the Zamíndár, chaudhari, taluqdár, or other landholder who disobeys is threatened with 'dispossession from his lands [1].'

But such a limitation was soon thought to be inconsistent with the 'proprietary right' which it was the policy of Government to secure and develop; and it was abandoned accordingly. Several of the Regulations allude to the power of alienation, as now for the first time conceded. (See, for example, Section 9 of Regulation I of 1793, quoted at p. 410.)

The right was unrestricted, provided only that transfers should not be inconsistent with the Hindu or Muhammadan law (whichever applied), or to any Regulation; that they should be registered before the Collector, so that the revenue liability might be known; and that the transferee would

[1] This proclamation will be found reprinted in Appendix F, p. 179, of Mr. Cotton's *Revenue History of Chittagong*.

be answerable for the revenue, or for a portion of the revenue, in case of sale of a part of the estate to which the revenue share was allotted on principles stated in the Regulation.

(D) *Emoluments of the Zamíndár.*

Originally the Zamíndár was bound to account for all he collected from the raiyats; these payments were not *his rents* but the revenue assessed by the State, and increased from time to time. He was to pay in all to the treasury, less a certain percentage and some cash allowances, which were carefully specified. But this strictness died out in time; for the very laxity of rule which induced the Governors to save themselves trouble by handing over the entire management to Zamíndárs, operated also to prevent any scrutiny into details. More and more, therefore, the Zamíndár got to be a mere contractor for a fixed sum, and able to make his own terms with the *raiyats*.

In the original accounts we find that the Zamíndár was allowed—

(1) His percentage called 'dastúr-zamíndárí';

(2) An allowance called nánkár (lit. bread of service): this was at first in cash (as a deduction); but afterwards *lands* called 'nánkár' were held revenue-free;

(3) The mazkúrát (or 'specific items'), being the charges of collection, such as headman's fees (muqaddamí), wages for servants and messengers (páíkán), expenses of office (daftar-band and sarinjámí), and a number of others;

(4) Fees (nimtakí—half a 'taká' (or *paisá* in the rupee) to the kánúngo;

(5) Charitable allowances, being remissions for 'aimá' and 'inám' holdings (plots left free to religious persons, teachers, village servants, &c.); qadam-rasúl, fees paid for preservation of 'footprints of the Prophet,' also (*khairát*) alms; and daily allowance to religious mendicants and others (rozína).

(E) *The Zamíndár's Private Lands.*

In many cases the Zamíndár had private lands called 'nij-jot' (the Hindí equivalent of the Persian 'khud-kásht,' and the same as the 'sír' of other parts)—i. e. lands of his family which he cultivated with his own labour or personal tenants. From these the State might or might not take revenue.

A large portion of the estates, in many districts, was waste, and the duty of the Zamíndár was to extend cultivation, not (originally) for his own profit, but with a view to revenue from additional fields profiting the Treasury. But when the Zamíndár's revenue came to be a lump sum fixed by bargain, it further resulted that all new cultivation was solely a benefit to him as contractor. Not only so, but as all the waste lands would be unoccupied and there would be no resident or ancient 'raiyats,' to claim any special terms, it followed that the land was cultivated by real contract-tenants, and of course was acknowledged to be the property of the Zamíndár under the name of 'khámár[1].'

A third kind of land which the Zamíndár came to hold was under the head of 'nánkár,' already mentioned. When this allowance was made up by granting certain lands free of revenue, the Zamíndár, very naturally, absorbed them as his own property[2].

This custom of 'nánkár' spread wide, and in the Northern

[1] 'Khámár' is an Uriya or Bengalí word meaning 'threshing-floor,' and indicates lands the produce of which is divided on the threshing-floor between the cultivator or the soil-owner. Naturally in new lands, where at first cultivation is precarious, liable to fail or to be destroyed by deer, pigs, and wild beasts from the neighbouring jungles, the terms of the tenancy are not a cash rent but a 'bháoli,' or division of produce. This saves the tenant from loss, as, if the crop fails, or is only a partial one, no demand, or only a limited one, can be made on him. The first mention of khámár lands that we have is in the *Instructions to Supervisors* (1769). The Revenue Committee remark that such lands have no natural tenants, and that the Zamíndár cultivates by contract, making advances to cultivators, and receiving back his advance with interest and a share in the produce (one-half to two-thirds).—(Colebrooke's *Supplement to the Digest*, pp. 182. 183.) At that date the Committee thought this was an encroachment, and desired that the waste when cultivated should be 'raiyatí' land—i. e. liable to pay to the State through the Zamíndár.

[2] Harington, iii. 320.

Sirkárs of Madras was found enjoyed under the local name of 'sávaram[1].'

§ 4. *Other Items.*

As the Zamíndár owned the waste in his estate, so he owned 'manorial rights,' such as fisheries, and produce from fruits or from grazing, and sale of jungle products. These were the 'sayer' items, already spoken of in another connection. The Zamíndár appears to have levied a small fee called 'parjot' (or in Persian 'muhtarfa'), on non-agricultural residents in the villages, exactly as the Panjáb village landlords do to this day. It may be likened to a kind of ground-rent for the house-site.

§ 5. *Málikána.*

This term so often occurs in Bengal (and indeed in all revenue literature) that I may take this opportunity to explain it.

The revenue responsibility being on the land, Government is entitled to exclude the proprietor who refuses what the authorities deem a reasonable assessment; but in such cases it grants a 'málikána,' or ex-proprietary allowance, to support the recusant during the period of his exclusion. This is not less than five nor more than ten per cent. on the revenue.

See Sec. 44, Reg. VIII of 1793; and Reg. VII of 1822, Sec. 5, cl. 2.

But the term málikána has also a wider application: it refers to any portion of the produce, or payment made in acknowledgment of a proprietary[2], or more commonly an ex-proprietary, right or title. It is well illustrated in Bihár; there the villages appear in many cases to have come under the landlord claims of men who were leaders

[1] A Telugu word obtained from the Persian 'Cháyar,' a certain measure of land.—(*Wilson.*)

[2] Thus the term is sometimes used to mean the portion of the total assets which, on a Settlement, Government leaves to the proprietor as his share or profit. It is also commonly used to signify the allowances paid to a person as having *some* claim, but not enough to entitle him to a Settlement. In this sense we often find it used in the North-Western Provinces and Oudh.

of troops and minor chiefs, or cadets of noble families, who so often, as we have already seen, established themselves as landlords over single villages and small estates. Small owners of this class cannot make terms with later conquerors, as large estate-holders can; and it came to pass that, under the Muhammadan rule, such petty landholders were displaced either by Muhammadan jagírdárs, who got grants over their heads, so to speak, or by other minor grantees (lákhirájdárs); further, under our own earlier revenue system[1], the country was farmed to outsiders, and in the end the new-comers had got so firmly fixed that the Permanent Settlement was made with them. But such is the force of custom, that the new grantees, and farmers, were always obliged to recognize the older ousted proprietors by making them a 'málikána' allowance. When our Government resumed a number of the lákhiráj estates and assessed them to revenue and settled with the present holders, the estate was often charged with paying the 'málikána' to the ousted proprietor.

§ 6. *Small Zamíndárís in Bihár.*

The mention of the small land-holdings of Bihár remind us that we must not suppose *all* Zamíndárs to have had *great* estates. The fact is that in Bihár, had it not been for the Bengal system, it would have been found that there were *village*-estates of *the landlord class* in a tolerable state of preservation. We have here actual tradition (see Chap. IV. page 123) how the Aryans advanced into Bihár; and there can be no doubt that the petty landlords of the Bábhan (the military or Kshatriya caste) alluded to by the older writers, were just the descendants of the chiefs and rulers who either originally, or by the breaking up of larger territorial rulerships, acquired the position of landlords over single villages or over small estates of two or three villages. In the course of time some of these small estate holders were superseded by 'jágír' grantees or farmers of revenue, as above stated, but many of them survived, and

[1] Mr. Shore's Minute of September, 1789, § 2.

the family chief or leading man among them, became the Zamíndár. (The system only admitted of *one* man bearing the title, unless several expressly agreed that they were co-sharers.) Some of these families, though they had dropped out of rank, and were not Zamíndárs in possession, were still so far recognized as to receive the málikána allowance as just now explained. Some of them, as we shall see presently, in the Sháhábád district, fell into the lower position of 'tenure-holders' (called guzáshta jot). But the case of Bihár is interesting as showing how, what in the North-West Provinces would have produced village landlord-communities, developed there into *small Zamíndárí* estates. The Monghyr district affords another instance of the existence of small estates caused by the subdivision of an original family grant or acquisition. I have alluded to it more particularly under the head of *taluqs* in the sequel, because the subdivision of the estate seems to have resulted in the formation of a number of taluqs, some of which paid their revenue direct to Government, and others through one of the larger estate-holders.

The rules by which 'taluqs' were separated from the Zamíndárís have been alluded to before: in Monghyr the result was that a number of small separate estates were recognized as petty Zamíndárís.

In Sylhet and Chittagong, the nature of the holdings of land was such, that, as we shall see, the 'Zamíndárs' in those districts were quite small landholders[1]. In Benares also, the 'Zamíndárs' actually settled with, were *village* bodies; for the Rájá, who would have been the great Zamíndár under other circumstances, had resigned his claims.

[1] Sylhet is treated of in another part of the book, because it is in Assam. Chittagong is separately described further on.

§ 7. *Authorities on the nature of the Zamíndár's Right.*

Mr. Harington's[1] definition (or rather description) of a Bengal Zamíndár is as follows:—

'A landholder of a peculiar description, not definable by any single term in our language—a receiver of the territorial revenue of the State from the *raiyats* and other under-tenants of land—allowed to succeed to his *Zamíndári* by inheritance, yet in general required to take out a renewal of his title from the sovereign or his representative on payment of a fine on investiture to the Emperor, and a *nazárana* or present to his provincial delegate—the Názím; permitted to transfer his *Zamíndári* by sale or gift[2], yet commonly expected to obtain previous special permission; privileged to be generally the annual contractor for the public revenue recoverable from his *Zamíndári*, yet set aside with a limited provision, in land or money, whenever it was the pleasure of Government to collect the rents by separate agency, or to assign them temporarily or permanently by the grant of a 'jágír,' or an 'altamghá'; authorized in Bengal (since the early part of the eighteenth century) to apportion to the *parganas*, villages, and lesser divisions of land within the *Zamíndári*, the *abwáb* or cesses imposed by the Súbadár (provincial governor) usually in some proportion to the standard assessment of the *Zamíndári* established by Todar Mal and others, yet subject to the discretionary interference of public authority, either to equalize the amount assessed on particular divisions, or to abolish what appeared oppressive to the *raiyat*; entitled to any contingent emoluments proceeding from his contract during the period of his agreement, yet bound by the terms of his tenure to deliver in a faithful account of his receipts[3]; responsible by the same terms for keeping the peace within his jurisdiction, but apparently allowed to apprehend only, and deliver over to a Musalmán magistrate for trial and punishment.'

[1] Dr. Field notices that Mr. Harington gave this opinion to Lord Cornwallis in 1789, and that he had seen no occasion to alter it twenty-eight years afterwards.

[2] This is more doubtful—see Phillips, p. 270. No doubt they assumed this power, but under the British rule this was at first disallowed, as stated at p. 513.

[3] This, of course, was not done in later times; or an account was rendered, framed just as was convenient for the interests of the Zamíndár.

§ 8. *Mr. Shore's Views.*

Mr. Shore speaks of Zamíndárs as proprietors of the soil, —to the property of which they succeed by right of inheritance; but he explains that a property in the soil must not be understood to convey the same rights in India as in England. We can only, under a despotic government, look to the general practice as acknowledging a sort of right [1].

In another place [2] he says expressly :—

'The relation of a Zamíndár to Government, and of a raiyat to the Zamíndár is neither that of a proprietor nor a vassal, but a compound of both. The former performs acts of authority in connection with proprietary right; the latter has rights without real property. . . . . Much time will, I fear, elapse before we can establish a system perfectly consistent in all its parts, and before we can reduce the compound relation of a Zamíndár to Government, and of a raiyat to a Zamíndár, to the simple principles of landlord and tenant.'

§ 9. *Lord Cornwallis's Views.*

Lord Cornwallis expressed himself satisfied with Mr. Shore's proofs that the Zamíndár, though not an absolute soil-owner, was yet entitled to be considered as a landlord and recognized with a secure title, and he added something that is important, as showing that the recognition of the Zamíndár was not founded on a mere abstract decision on historical evidence, but on a State policy of justice and the (supposed) welfare of the province. He says :—

'Although, however, I am not only of opinion that the Zamíndárs have the best right, but from being persuaded that nothing could be so ruinous to the public interest as that the land should be retained as the property of Government, I am also convinced that, failing the claims of right of the Zamíndárs, it would be necessary for the public good to grant a right of property in the soil to them or to persons of other descriptions. I think it unnecessary to enter into any discussion of the

[1] See Section 383 of the Minute of the 18th June, 1789 (*Fifth Report*).

[2] Minute of December, 1789.

grounds on which their right appears to be founded. *It is the most effectual mode for promoting the general improvement that I look upon as the important object* for our present consideration[1].'

§ 10. *Decision of the Court of Directors.*

With all these minutes and views before them, the Court of Directors came to a conclusion; and their final orders will naturally be regarded as of first-rate importance[2].

After stating that they had previously stated their views, but always felt that the materials were insufficient for a decisive opinion, the Court of Directors go on to say:—

'On the fullest consideration, we are inclined to think that, whatever doubts may exist with respect to their original character, whether as proprietors of land or collectors of revenue, or with respect to the changes which may in process of time have taken place in their situation, there can, at least, be little difference of opinion as to the actual condition of the Zamíndárs under the Mughal government. Custom generally gives them a certain species of hereditary occupancy, but the sovereign nowhere appears to have bound himself by any law or covenant not to deprive them of it; and the rents to be paid by them remained always to be fixed by his arbitrary will and pleasure, which were constantly exercised upon this object. If considered, therefore, as right of property, it was very imperfect, very precarious, having not at all, or but in a very small degree, those qualities that confer independence and value upon the landed property of Europe. Though such be our ultimate views of this question, our originating a system of fixed equitable taxation will sufficiently show that our intention has not been to act upon the high tone of Asiatic despotism. We are, on the contrary, for establishing real, permanent, valuable landed rights in our provinces, and for conferring such rights upon the Zamíndárs; but it is just that the nature of the concession should be known, and that our subjects should see they receive from the enlightened principles of a British Government what they never enjoyed under their own[3].'

[1] *Fifth Report*, vol. i. 591, quoted in Phillips, p. 276.

[2] General letter, dated 19th September, 1792, quoted by Dr. Field.

[3] Those who wish for further details will do well to consult the

§ 11. *Reasons for the difference of opinion as to the Real Status of the Zamíndár.*

It will thus be easy to see how, by singling out and fixing the attention on certain undoubted features of the farming system, we can argue (and that conclusively) that the 'Zamíndár' was originally only a revenue-farmer and an official. On the other hand, by doing the same in respect of other features, especially in the history of those Zamíndárs who were local chiefs and had been rulers under a previous organization, but who were employed in a sort of official capacity by the Mughal conquerors, we can, with equal justice, argue that the Zamíndár was nearer a *landlord* (in our sense) than anything else. Had the Settlement been made by Mr. Holt Mackenzie in 1822, instead of under Mr. Shore in 1789, it is probable that the *variety* of status would have found recognition. Some Zamíndárs of the old stock would certainly have been allowed as proprietors, and the villages protected by a sub-settlement; others would have been merely allowed a cash málikána. But, perhaps, in so saying, I am not allowing sufficiently for the fusing and equalizing influence of time; and that really all had come to be very much alike. However that may be, certainly no one in 1790 dreamt of making any difference. To find a general rule for all, was what was contemplated; and this leads me to repeat that what our administrators of 1790 had to do, was not to determine a historical and accurate theory of the Zamíndár's position, but to take facts as they found them after a century and a half of growth and development, and to confer on the Zamíndárs such a position as was best, not with reference to what they *once were*, but with what they had then practically become, when the prescription of years, I might say of generations, had covered original acts of illegality or usurpation.

opinions of the Judges declared in 1865 in the case known as the Great Rent Case (*Beng. Law Reports*, supplementary vol. 204). A good abstract will be found in Phillips, p. 312 seq.

It is very easy to write that the authors of the Permanent Settlement, with a few strokes of the pen, converted Muhammadan tax-gatherers into landed proprietors, and phrases of that sort; but they are far too summary to be accurate or just.

Moreover, from the authoritative declarations which I have above cited, it must certainly appear that no one intended to make the Zamíndár an absolute owner of anything, but to give him a certain *estate in land* (which is juristically a different thing), and that limited by a due observance of the rights of subordinate holders and cultivators. If, in effect, he got more than was intended, that was because the steps taken to secure the inferior rights were ineffective; it was not because the authorities were wrong in the view they took of the Zamíndár's position.

§ 12. *Modern legal view of the Zamíndár's Title.*

The actual right of the landlord, as it now exists, is an estate in the soil certainly less than a 'fee-simple' of English law, but freely heritable and alienable and available for mortgage, sale, gift, or bequest. It is, however, limited by the rights of tenure-holders and *raiyats* (i. e. tenants), when they possess such under the Tenancy Law, or other special law applicable to the case. And, of course, it is limited (like all other rights in revenue-paying lands) by the Government right to its revenue and the right of sale in case of default to make good, at due date, the full amount of that revenue[1]. The original intention most probably was to limit the landlord's demands on the raiyats much more than the later laws limited them. But there is no clear decision traceable as to whether all 'raiyats' (or any but a small class) were intended to

[1] Mr. Justice Macpherson put it well when he said in the Rent Case (p. 214), 'As regards the legislation from 1793 to Act X of 1859, it, in my opinion, shows clearly that the Zamíndár never was, and was never intended to be, the absolute proprietor of the soil .... for certain classes of *raiyats* have at all times had rights quite inconsistent with [his] absolute ownership.'

remain on for ever at fixed rents, or whether their rents could be raised from time to time. Sometimes we meet with expressions that imply the former or something like it; at other times with expressions that imply that rents (or some rents) may be altered and tenants evicted. And the legal powers actually put into the hands of the proprietors were such as to enable them in practice both to enhance and to evict; it soon came to be looked on as a matter of course, that in most cases, they had the full powers of an English landlord. Then came the revulsion of feeling which led to the legislation of 1859, and ultimately to that of 1885; but meanwhile the prescriptive position which had been growing steadily during seventy years, was so strong, that opinions were much divided, and the difficulty of legislating completely on the subject became enormous.

SECTION III.—OTHER PROPRIETARY TENURES.

I have mentioned that revenue-managing grants were not always of the rank or extent implied by the title Zamíndár. Such minor landholders were allowed (by *sanad* or otherwise) an undefined position of the same kind but of lesser importance, and were called taluqdárs—holders of taluqs, i. e. 'dependencies.' Degrees of importance were marked by the fact that some were allowed to pay *direct* to the Treasury, while others were made to pay *through* a Zamíndár.

§ 1. *Taluqdárs.—Holders of 'Taluq Estates.'*

Who were the persons so recognized? Some no doubt were persons who by ancient possession, or grant of the Rájás, or by purchase, had become landholders in some sense, and being recognized by the Muhammadan governors, got vaguely entitled 'taluqdárs.' Mr. Grant mentions that such taluqdárs existed by royal grant in Bengal near

Murshidábád and Húghlí, and that they were rich or favoured persons who, desiring to be free from the interference of revenue-agents and Zamíndárs, obtained grants for which they often paid a consideration or fee.

A number of such taluqdárs may have existed before the date of the Zamíndárí, others arose as fragments of a larger estate of which the holders managed to get themselves recognized as separate landholders[1]. In that case they were 'independent,'—that is, outside the Zamíndárí estate of any one,—and were called 'huzúri' or 'khárija': (huzúri, i.e. paying to the huzúr or headquarter treasury; 'khárij' means outside)[2]. But many of the smaller taluqs were either holdings which were not strong enough to prevent their being absorbed into Zamíndárís, or else had been tenures granted on favourable terms to conciliate influential persons,—or merely to save trouble, by the Zamíndár himself or some State official. These were called 'mazkúri,' or 'dependent' taluqs. They paid their fixed revenue through the Zamíndár, and were not liable to many of the interferences which mere tenants were subjected to. It was a question of the facts and merits of each case at Settlement, what taluqs were of one class or the other. If independent, they were allowed to hold a separate Settlement and were full proprietors; if dependent, they became 'tenures' under the landlord, however privileged in regard to fixity of holding or rent. I have already alluded to the rules in Regulation VIII of 1793 (page 411-13) for settling the question whether the taluq was a proprietorship or an under-tenure. Independent holdings were not always large

[1] E.g in the 24-Pergunnahs I find it noticed that the estates had been much broken up and portions separated or sold, or gifted. When the decennial Settlement came on, all estates that paid R. 5,000 revenue and more were called 'Zamíndárís,' and those paying less were called 'taluqs.' (*Statistical Account of Bengal*, vol. i. p. 262.)

[2] A good instance of the way in which estates might become 'independent' is afforded by the case of the 'nawára' estate in Jasúr (*Statistical Account*, vol. ii. p. 262). This consisted of some 1176 holdings of land (scattered over the district) treated as a sort of jágír in the Mughal days, their revenue being set apart for the maintenance of a river fleet. They were not of course included in any Zamíndárí; the holders fell into arrears and were sold up, and the purchasers became 'independent taluqdárs,' or petty proprietors holding the Settlement.

ones. Mr. Harington quotes a case in Bhágalpur where the headmen of villages—'muqaddams,' as they were called—had succeeded in working themselves into the position of proprietorship, and the Courts decided in their favour, separating them from the Zamíndárís. They were called 'málik-muqaddam' (proprietary-headman) and treated as 'actual proprietors' entitled to Settlement under Sections 4 and 5 of Regulation VIII of 1793. Here the muqaddams put forward 'bills of sale' to account for their rights, while the other side was a Zamíndár who had risen to this rank from being the 'chaudharí' of the parganas [1].

It was not always necessary that an estate which happened to be called 'taluq' in the Revenue-language of the day, should be held under a distinct grant. In the *Fifth Report* [2] a curious account of the Monghyr district is given, which well illustrates how taluqs might come into existence. Tradition asserted that on the Emperor Humáyun appearing at Monghyr (at the time of the Mughal conquest) two Rájputs, Hírá Rám and Rám Rái, obtained the appointment of chaudharí; and they ultimately became Zamíndárs. But the possession was regarded as a family right, and was divided up, exactly on the principles that any single ancestral village would be. 'Havelí Munger,' as the district was then called, was divided into eleven 'tarf' or divisions, for five sons of Hírá Rám, and six of Rám Rái. Of the latter, two had passed out of the family. Each of the 'tarfs' was further divided among the descendants of each branch, and the holdings formed so many *taluq* estates. Some of them gradually passed into the hands of other families. A

[1] It is probable that these 'muqaddams' were really minor chiefs or scions of families who had once either ruled or had obtained 'birts' or grants from the Rájá, and then, dividing up the estate, had come to hold each one or two or more villages of which they long regarded themselves as the landlords. The judgment of the Court quotes Ferishta's history, which alludes to these 'muqaddams' as well as the 'chaudharis' or State officers, as having ridden on horseback clad in armour or clothed in rich dresses, till the tyranny of Sultan 'Alá-ud-dín (fourteenth century) reduced them to being mere raiyats.'

[2] Vol. i. pp. 211–14. The account is full of misprints, but is very curious; it is followed by an account of the assessment and the various allowances to be made.

number of these taluqs, proprietary, were formed into separate estates as small 'Zamíndárís.'

Under the head of taluq estates I may also mention the 'invalid jágírs' found in this same Bhágulpur district (see Regulation I of 1804). They were grants—now permanently-settled estates—made out of waste land to pensioned or invalided soldiers of the Company's army. It is interesting to note that at the time the 'Zamíndárs' protested. Whether or not these lands (in the Kálgáoṅ or Colgong pargana) were really included in the known limits of any Zamíndárí I cannot ascertain; but, on the supposition that the Zamíndár was a mere revenue collector, his protest against the grant of certain lands and their revenue (and of course the revenue would be deducted from any demand made against the Zamíndár) would be preposterous.

In Chittagong, as in Sylhet also, the nature of the country was unfavourable to the formation of large estates which absorbed all the essentials of proprietorship; and there we find that the heads of parties of settlers were regarded as 'actual proprietors' though the estates were 'taluqs.' But I shall best describe the land system of Chittagong in a separate section.

The above are the estates—all known as *taluqs*—such as were allowed to be *proprietary*, and therefore mentioned here. Taluqs that were 'dependent,' and only formed '*tenures*,' will be dealt with further on: and it will be found (in their case) the *taluq* is only one of quite a number of local names.

This will serve as a caution, and prevent confusion in the mind of the reader.

SECTION IV.—LÁKHIRÁJ OR REVENUE-FREE HOLDINGS.

We have already noticed, from the Settlement-point of view, how the Collectors had to deal with tenures claimed by persons who were, or professed to be, grantees of land free of revenue; and we found that many of such grants were irregular or were wholly invalid. We have now to examine them from the land-tenure point of view. In early times the grants could only be made by the Emperor, or by recommendation of a few of the most important local authorities; in after-days all sorts of authorities used to make them. In speaking of the Settlement, we have already seen how the Regulations dealt with these cases; and that rules were laid down for testing the validity of the royal (bádsháhí) and subordinate authorities (non-bádsháhí or hukámí) grants. Whether valid and left revenue-free, or invalid and therefore assessed to revenue, *the holders were regarded as the proprietors of the land, if that were the intention of the grant*, as determined, in the case of dispute, by the Civil Court. Whether it was so, depended on the circumstances. For example, the grant may have remitted the revenue on a man's own holding, or on land (unoccupied) granted to the holder; in that case, the grant was originally called 'milk' (ownership grant), or later 'mu'áfí,' and constituted a clear form of property, because the Government had then *no* concern with the land, either with the soil or the revenue on it. But in many cases, as with jágírs, it often happened that the grant was merely of the revenues realisable from lands already held by other persons; but even in such cases, in the course of time, the grantee might have so developed his position as to become virtually landlord. A great portion of the estate may have been waste, and by his exertions brought under the plough; he may have bought lands, or ousted the original holders for default, and so forth.

As a matter of fact, I believe I am right in saying, that in Bengal the 'freehold' estates were, *or had come to be*, all or mostly, proprietary, whatever they might once have been. The grantee would become landlord by the same influences as caused the growth of the Zamíndár.

§ 1. *Jágírdárs.*

The institution of the jágír (jáí-gír=place-holder) was essentially a Muhammadan one, but was not dissimilar to the position occupied by Hindu chiefs in frontier territory. In effect, when a tract of country was distant from head-quarters and troublesome to manage, the State would appoint a jágírdár, who would collect and appropriate the revenues, and in return keep the country in order and maintain a body of troops for local or other service. From the *Ayín-i-Akbari* we learn that it was a regular part of the Mughal system to make life-grants of this kind to nobles and courtiers for the maintenance of their state, with a more or less nominal claim to service in return.

In Bengal, however, jágírs were rare. Mr. Grant, in 1797, said he only knew of three or four. But the old proprietary Hindu chieftains were stronger in Bihár, and many jágírs were there granted, besides other revenue-free gifts.

The jágír was originally only a *life-grant*[1]. Hereditary nobles did not exist under the Mughal Empire; the Emperor made and unmade dignities at will. When he wished to confer a dignity, he appointed the person as *mansabdár* of a certain rank, which was estimated according to the number of horsemen he commanded; the jágír was an appanage to the grant of a *mansab*, and the revenue was appropriated both for the support of the grantee and the maintenance of his troops, which might be from ten to ten thousand. At first the official forms of appointment were minute and carefully followed out. Mr. Shore gives a very detailed account of how the jágírs were granted[2]. This will be found *in extenso* in Harington (chapter on Rights of Landholders). I have said that at first jágírs were granted only by the Emperor or on recommendation of the governors of the most important of the distant provinces, as Kábul, Bengal, and the Dakhan. In the times of the decline, however, all sorts of local governors granted them[3]. Clearly, under such grants, the jágírdár was not in any

[1] Harington, vol. iii. 361, 413. Baillie's *Land-Tax*, xxiv, xxv.

[2] Minute on *Rights and Privileges of Jágírdárs* (April 2nd, 1788, the same date as the minute so often referred to). In the best days of the Mughal rule, the whole of the districts were classified, in the State accounts, as (1) available for grant (páibákí), or (2) charged with the king's revenues (khálsa muqarrarí).

[3] Jágírs were often granted in mere notes addressed to the local officials called 'tankhwá.'

sense proprietor of the land. Indeed, he was not allowed to collect more from it than the actual amount assigned according to his grade and the terms of the *sanad*; and had to account for all the surplus or 'taufír.' In course of time, however, the precautions and rules fell into abeyance, and the jágírdár was allowed to do much as he pleased; and then too it happened that the grant was not resumed on the death of the holder, as it ought to have been, and soon became hereditary. In short, the grantee in time came to be looked on as proprietor, unless there was any holder on the land strong enough to maintain his own position. The Regulations accordingly declared that the terms of the grant should be looked to, and that a jágír was not to be assumed to be a life-grant if the intention appeared that it should be hereditary[1].

§ 2. *Other Grants.—Altamghá; aimá; Madad-ma'ásh.*

Besides the jágír grants, which were eventually connected with *military or State service of some kind*, there were several other grants which involved the remission of the revenue, and in time came to constitute actual estates in land. One such revenue-free grant, or rather an assignment of the revenue of cultivated land, was called altamghá—grant by the royal seal or stamp (tamghá). The term was applied to *any* grant which was permanent and not revocable (except in case of misconduct[2]), and therefore hereditary. The grant of the 'Díwání' to the East India Company was called an 'altamghá';[3] where granted (as in Bihár) on estates already in the hands of a landholder, the grantee ousted the existing landlord, but felt obliged to pay him 'málikána.' This illustrates what I just now remarked about the growth of grantees.

Another was the 'madad-ma'ásh'—which was a 'milk' grant (i.e. included the soil ownership). As its name implies (help to livelihood), it was a subsistence grant, perhaps

[1] See, for example, Section 2, Regulation XIX, 1793.

[2] Colebrooke's *Supplement*, p. 238.

[3] Phillips, p. 199.

on condition of some service, but ordinarily to pious and religious persons; and it was hereditary. Mr. Phillips, on the authorities quoted in his note[1], says the grant was in practice revocable at the will of the sovereign.

It was always a proper thing to make grants to Sayyids and holy or learned men of family; and the class of grant made for this purpose was, in the official language of the Empire, called 'suyúr-ghal.' These grants were assignments of revenue only, not conditional on service, and were originally for life[2]. They were made by order or 'tankhwá,' and very naturally became hereditary, as the son was likely to follow the condition and vocation of his father. To the same class belonged another kind of grant known as 'aimá.' But it seems that there were 'aimá' grants which included the land also, and then there were 'milk,' not 'suyúr-ghal' grants. We hear also of 'aimá' grants given with a view to encourage the cultivation of the waste, and these were proprietary grants. They were sometimes merely holdings at a low or privileged rate of revenue payment, and were then called 'málguzárí aimá[3].'

§ 3. *Minor Service Tenures.*

I may include in this section some mention of a numerous class of tenures which here (as in other provinces) were either wholly free from revenue charge, or else assessed at a quit-rent. I allude to the 'chákarán' lands, by which village servants, the watchmen, the Zamíndár's guards, and others, were remunerated. A number of these were petty grants, and became subordinate *tenures* under the landlord, but it will be well to notice them here. They are all conditional on performing service. The nánkár or 'bread-lands' of the Zamíndárs were originally of this kind. Mr. Phillips says that there were 150,000 petty officers of all kinds—kánúngos, headmen, patwárís, guards and watchmen, &c., remunerated in this way[4]. In some cases the lands, though

[1] P. 197.
[2] Baillie, *Land-Tax*, xlviii.
[3] Harington, ii. 65.
[4] See Phillips, p. 208.

hereditary, were not allowed to be divided; so that the person who actually did the duty, enjoyed the holding.

Ghátwál lands were holdings of this kind—an institution which originated probably in the earliest times and was adopted by all classes of rulers. They were in fact a kind of jágír created in frontier territories, so that the holders might be 'wardens of the marches.' In such territories there often were hill-passes (hence the name *ghát-wál*), and incursions were to be feared from wild tribes inhabiting the hill country beyond, or from robbers who would make the inaccessible jungles their haunt. The State granted lands to be held free on condition of guarding the passes. In Bengal these holdings appear to have originated in Bírbhúm. They occur also in Bánkura, Mánbhúm, &c.[1], and we shall make a more detailed study of them hereafter.

SECTION V.—PROPRIETARY TENURES OF MODERN ORIGIN.

§ 1. *Waste Land Estates.*

I have already given the chief results of the 'Waste Land Rules,' and therefore here, in an enumeration of tenures, I have only need to recall the fact that out-and-out grants, whether with the revenue redeemed or not, may constitute a class of *modern proprietary* tenures. Many rights under Waste Land Rules, especially those designed for petty cultivators, as opposed to capitalists, are not proprietary but cultivating or *lessees'* rights under Government.

§ 2. *Proprietary Tenures with reference to the Settlement.*

Connecting the various forms of proprietary rights in land with the different Settlement laws, I may briefly

[1] And Regulation XXIX of 1814 relates to the Birbhúm 'Ghátwál Maháls,' declaring the estates transferable and heritable, and fixing the rent in perpetuity.

observe that *any proprietary* estate may be, according to circumstances—

(1) Permanently settled;

(2) Temporarily settled, as in Orissa; or in Bengal, wherever the original estate permanently-settled did not include the land in question, as in the case of excess waste.

(3) Not settled, by reason of the proprietor's refusal to accept the terms of Settlement: here the property is not lost, but the management is, for a term.

SECTION VI.—'TENURES.'

§ 1. *How they arose.*

I have already explained that the long-continued rule of the Muhammadan power tended gradually to overlay and ultimately to obliterate the original tenures, with the result that, in process of time, the chief proprietary tenures came to be those of the Zamíndár, the larger taluqdárs, jágírdárs, and grantees, who, under the terms of the Permanent Settlement Law, retained sufficient importance to be called and treated as, separate 'actual proprietors.' It follows almost necessarily, that there were a number of smaller tenures,—those of headmen who had obtained favourable tenures of lands, of ancient holders of land, of grantees who failed to resist the absorbing influence of the greater landholders, but who managed to retain a certain degree of recognition as 'dependent taluqdárs,' or otherwise,—all of whom became *tenure*-holders or subordinate holders *under* the recognized landlord. I have also quoted authoritative opinion to show (what might be expected) that when once those subordinate holders descend to the position of tenure-holders, it is impossible to draw any hard-and-fast line between them and the persons who have no pretension at all to proprietary right, and are therefore simply 'tenants.'

But every case stands on its own history and merits, and

therefore there are special provisions of law by which persons having certain facts found in their favour, are 'tenure-holders,' not tenants.

§ 2. *Classification of 'Tenures.'*

A very large class of land interests in Bengal is represented by the 'tenures' of this secondary order. For the purposes of treatment I can best classify them as (A) taluqs and other tenures of a heritable and transferable character, with or without absolute fixity of rent; these being of small area, or otherwise by their nature, were not recognized as separate, but remained 'dependent' or subordinate to some larger proprietor. It is impossible to separate these accurately, as to origin. Some of them may have been distinctly created by the Zamíndár since Settlement; others existed from before that date. If so, they are often *relics of former proprietary right.* Even when traceable to a grant of some preceding Zamíndár, they yet may be really due to an ancient proprietorship, which the strong fetters of custom had induced the Zamíndár to recognize (not *eo nomine* but) by granting a 'taluq.'

(B) In a second group I place tenures which arise from the desire of the Zamíndár *to improve his estate* by extending his income—the large margin between the taxed revenue and the possible rental,—and at the same time to divest himself of the trouble and responsibility of direct management. But such farming-tenures are not only due to the desire to save trouble, they are often advantageous when the landlord has no taste or capacity for estate management, and the employment of an energetic lessee will develop the capabilities of the estate.

When the farming-lessee manages well, he secures extended cultivation, founds new villages, and otherwise increases the rental (very harshly, it is feared, in some cases); and that being so, the margin between his contract sum with the Zamíndár and the collections becomes so large, that he can afford, as time goes on, to retire and to be content with a portion; he therefore, in his turn, gives up the trouble of management, and subleases to another contractor. More frequently, however, when there is much waste, the lessee is unable to bring the whole under cultivation, and so he sub-farms a portion with a view to more rapid extension of cultivation. In any case it often happens that the sub-lessee shares his liability with another, and yet another 'sub-sub-lessee.' This is what is meant by the 'sub-infeudation' spoken of in revenue reports.

(C) A third and important class of tenures has arisen—especially in Eastern Bengal and in the districts containing 'Sundarban' tracts—out of grants and contracts (sometimes antecedent to the year 1793), for *clearing and reclaiming the waste.* In the native mind, first clearing of the waste gives one of the strongest titles to permanent right in the cultivation, and it is not surprising that this sentiment should have given rise to many tenures, with (as usual) tenures under them created by 'sub-infeudation.'

(D) Lastly, as we find 'lákhiráj' (*revenue-free*) rights giving rise to estates of the first or proprietary order, so in the same way less important *rent-free* holdings, though remaining included within proprietary estates, have become 'tenures' of essentially the same origin. Village service grants, and especially grants in aid of temple-worship and for the support of holy men, represent this familiar class.

§ 3. *Absence of the Sub-proprietor or 'Proprietor of the holding' found in other Provinces.*

It will be noticed that in Bengal we have nothing of the '(sub- or) under-proprietor,' the man who is complete owner as far as his personal holding is concerned, but has no interest in the general profits of the estate. There is nothing like the 'málik-maqbúza' of Upper or Central India, in theory; though where a tenure-holder has a fixed rent, his position is, *quâ* his holding, about as good as a separate proprietorship; especially when, by registration or otherwise, his tenure is protected from being annulled on the sale of the superior estate for revenue arrears.

§ 4. *Difficulty of separating 'Tenures.'*

The terms adopted are 'tenure-holder' (or sometimes in books) under-tenure-holder.' It will be interesting to the student here to turn to the Acts and compare the definition of 'tenure' in the Recovery of Arrears Act (B. VII of 1868), and in Section 5, clause 1, of the Tenancy Act, 1885. But here I must add a word of apology. In dividing rights into *tenures* and *raiyat's tenancies*, it is hardly possible to escape the criticism that some rights which I have treated as tenures, ought to be regarded rather as occupancy-tenancies. I believe that absolute accuracy in drawing a line between the two is unattainable. The framers of the Act have not pretended that their definition is exhaustive. The Commission said that it was impossible 'to discover any principle of distinction between raiyats and tenure-holders or under-tenure-holders, which will hold good universally or even in a large majority of cases[1].' Actual cultivation is not a test, for a tenure-holder (like a small proprietor) may cultivate the fields himself, while a 'tenant' may have sublet the whole holding. The same would apply to the act of 'receiving rents'—the tenure-holder may be receiving rent from a sub-lessee in actual occupation. So some tenant rights are *heritable*, as much as in a *tenure*. Some tenant rights are also transferable, and saleable in execution of a decree for arrears. It is equally impossible to refer to the amount of rent payable, for some tenures are extremely petty, and some *raiyat* holdings pay considerable sums. The Act, however, has given some assistance by enacting that local custom and the purpose for which the right was originally acquired, have to be looked to, and that where the holding exceeds 100 bíghás (Bengal standard), the legal presumption is that it is a *tenure* till the contrary is shown.

Act VIII of 1885, sec. 5, cl. 4, 5.

[1] The whole passage may be read at page 23 of *R. and F. Tenancy Act*.

In these pages I shall follow the Act in treating all persons under the proprietor as equally 'tenants' *in class*. But, to avoid confusion, we describe separately the 'tenure-holders' and the raiyats [1]. The distinction is of some importance, because tenure-holders are only liable to *enhancement of their rent* under very limited circumstances, which will be noticed hereafter. The tenure may be also permanent by law or by contract (as the case may be), and if permanent it is transferable and can be bequeathed like any other immoveable property, subject to certain provisions of the law.

§ 5. *Remarks on the variety of local names for Tenures of the same kind.*

One other difficulty remains to be noted, and that is the tendency to give different names to tenures and forms of lease, although there is really nothing *essentially different*. In so far as the variety is due to locality and change of dialect, it is of course not to be wondered at. What is called 'jot' in Rangpur may be called 'gánthí' in Jessore. and so forth. But it will often be observed that in an elementary stage of civilization, languages are as rich in terms distinguishing things that need no such discrimination, as they are poor in terms for things and for conceptions that really do differ. In English, for example, we are contented with one word 'bracelet' for all ornaments of that class; or one word 'earring' for any ornament for the ear. Not so in the vernacular dialects; there are dozens of words for each kind and shape of bracelet or earring;—the pattern of ornamentation, or the number of stones set, often sufficing to alter the name of the article. And so it

[1] In a case reported in *Calcutta Law Reports*, IX. 449, the Court said: 'The only test of a raiyat's interest is to see in what condition the land was when the tenancy was created. If raiyats were already in possession of the land, and the interest created was a right, not to the actual physical possession of the land, but to collect the rents from the raiyats, the interest is not *raiyati* (in other words it is a 'tenure'). It is unfortunate that the use of the words 'tenure,' 'a tenure,' &c., is not uniform or precise in judgments and references. There is no remedy: all we can do here is to adopt the language of the Act and adhere to it.

is with tenures: a slight difference in the conditions of holding, in the rate or method of rent-payment, or in the fact that the area is measured or not, will give rise to a new name, as if the tenure itself were different. This gives at first sight an air of mystery and complexity to Bengal 'tenures' which they do not really possess[1].

(A) *TENURES DERIVED FROM ANCIENT RIGHTS.*

§ 6. *Dependent Taluqs.*

As all the estates separated at the Permanent Settlement from Zamíndárís and *originally* called taluqs (huzúri or kh̲árija[2]) are now landlord estates, the term 'taluq' *at the present day* is a restricted term, very vague, but always implying a subordinate *tenure.* In popular language, such a 'taluqdár' is said to be 'shikmí' (shikm, the belly—one within the other).

The tenure may be under a private proprietor, or, as in the taluqs of Eastern Bengal, may be under Government itself as proprietor.

Those dependant taluqs which have been in existence from the time of the Permanent Settlement, are not liable to be cancelled if the estate to which they are subordinate is sold for the recovery of arrears of revenue. They are heritable and transferable. The rent at which they are held cannot be enhanced except upon proof[3] (1) of a special right by custom to enhance, or (2) of a right appearing from the conditions of the grant, or (3) that the taluqdár, by accepting abatements, has (impliedly) subjected himself to increase;—if the lands are capable of affording it. If the rent has never been changed since the Permanent Settlement, it cannot now be enhanced; and in order to relieve

[1] For example, in Tipperah I find about sixty names for tenures or under-tenures in proprietary estates; one of these kinds—the taluq—is distinguished as 'mushakh̲si' (lump-rent for the whole), 'takh̲sisi' (particularizing rents), 'chauhaddi,' 'muqarrari,' 'qáimi,' &c.—all these words signifying, not any real difference of kind, but some incidental condition or feature attaching to the terms of the tenure.

[2] See pp. 411–13.

[3] See *Tenancy Act*, 1885, chapter iii.

the tenure-holder to some extent from the difficulty of giving proof extending over a period of so many years, the law provides that if it be proved that the rent has not been changed for *twenty years*, it shall be presumed, until the contrary be shown, that the tenure has been held at the same rent since the Permanent Settlement.

§ 7. *Guzáshta holdings.*

Among taluqs which represent a vestige of old proprietary right, I mentioned as a characteristic example, those known as 'guzáshta jot' in the Sháhábád district. It is not necessary now to allude to the difference of opinion that once existed, for there can hardly be a reasonable doubt that the term 'guzáshta,' which (in Persian) indicates something 'lost' or 'passed away,' refers to a proprietary right once held. Most of Bihár, as already stated, was held by small proprietors, who were descendants of military retainers and minor chiefs under the old Hindu kings; in many cases one of the family (or perhaps more than one jointly) succeeded in getting recognized at the Permanent Settlement; or else were found to have lost all their rights, except the málikána payment [1]. In Sháhábád, landlords of this class were found too strong to be put aside with a mere málikána allowance, and yet (from causes which we cannot now ascertain) were not considered entitled to an independent Settlement. They were placed *under* the great Zamíndár of Dúmráon, but so as to become tenure-holders at fixed rates; and this is now their true position: they are not mere occupancy raiyats [2]. It is quite clear that their position has nothing to do with any artificial rule under Act X of 1859, or any other law creating *occupancy* rights.

[1] In this fact the reader will recognize another proof of the strength of those old claims by virtue of conquest, which the descendants of the chiefs call 'birthright.' Though overridden, the incoming landlord is obliged to give *some* recognition to the ancient title, and he pays *málikána* accordingly.

[2] Cotton's *Memorandum on Tenures*, and Board's *Letter to Government of Bengal*, No. 1024 A, dated 22nd December, 1883.

§ 8. *Fixed-rent Tenures.*

Under this class I may consider the 'istimrárí,' the 'muqarrarí,' and 'maurúsí' tenures existing from before the Permanent Settlement. These Persian names have been noticed before: they give no clue to origin, and only describe certain incidental features; but it may be reasonably supposed that they originated in some closer and hereditary connection with the land, either independent of any contract with the Zamíndár, or such as to have won recognition in the shape of a special lease or tenure from the local authorities.

Properly speaking, 'istimrárí' refers to the stable or perpetual nature of the tenure, which is not voidable when the estate is sold for arrears. 'Muqarrarí' refers to the *rent* being 'fixed'; and a tenure might be either *istimrárí* or *muqarrarí*, or, more commonly, both. 'Maurúsí' merely means that the tenure is hereditary, and implies nothing about the fixity of rent. 'Mirás[1]' leases (mirás is only another grammatical form from the same root as *maurúsí*) are also found in Dacca and Eastern Bengal.

When such tenures are of modern creation, they are sometimes found to have been created in favour of relatives of the landlord's family, or to settle old claims by way of compromise[2].

In Rangpur and the adjacent Kúch Bihár territory, a tenure of this class called 'upanchaki' is found; it is a perpetual holding for religious services at a small rent.

The 'upanchaki' tenure of Rangpur is said to be the creation of the Zamíndár, and is the collective name for lands granted for the worship of deities, the keeping of lamps at shrines, &c., &c., under the well-known names of debottar, pírpál, chirághi, shibottár (see p. 542). They pay

[1] We shall again notice the term 'mirás' in Sylhet, and in other parts of Bengal.

[2] Mr. Cotton mentions that Rájá Silanand Singh, of Bhágalpur, granted a number of muqarrarí-istimrárí tenures to ghátwáls (p. 532) under him, in order to settle a dispute; and he revoked the condition of service, which of course attached to the *ghátwál* tenure as such.

a nominal quit-rent [perhaps connected with the 'fifth' (panchak) of the produce], are hereditary and transferable. If liable (rarely) to enhancement of rent, they are distinguished as 'majkúri[1].'

In the Bhágalpur division I find references to a tenure called 'ghorabandí[2].'

In not a few districts I find mention of a great variety of 'taluqs' and 'mirásí' (hereditary) tenures, distinguished by various names, which, however, mean nothing more than that there is some condition attached to their recognition by the landlord, or some special feature in their origin or terms.

In Tipperah, for instance, there is the 'zimma-mirás,' which means a tenure held originally by one person but made over in *charge* (*zimma*) to another; the 'az-mushakhsí mirás' or 'specific,' is a tenure recognized after measurement and assessment. There are also many tenures compounded with the now familiar term *taluq*; e.g. there is the 'takhsísi,' which means that the landlord has reserved the right to test and measure the area and reassess it at some future time. 'Tashkhísi,' again, means a *taluq* recognized *after* measurement. 'Bandobastí' *taluq*, is one granted after measurement and making out an account of expenses, allowance for 'málikána,' &c., and determining the resulting payment as rent.

All these details sound very complicated, but in reality indicate nothing that affects the nature of the tenure. To recur to the illustration already used (p. 537) of the variety of native terms for ornaments of different forms, these separately-named tenures are on the same footing. They are really no more difficult to understand, than would be the case if our language used a separate name for a lease with repairs and for a lease without repairs, or a lease terminable with notice, and a lease for a fixed period.

[1] *Statistical Account of Bengal*, vol. vii. p. 278.

[2] It is stated that this means a tenure where the rent is payable for a definite area, whether cultivated or not; but it is not enumerated in the *Statistical Account of Bengal* (vol. xiv) as a 'tenure.'

§ 9. *Rent-free Tenures.*

Just as Government has created certain revenue-free estates, so the landlords have in turn allowed certain rent-free tenures, known as 'brahmottar,' 'shibottar,' 'debottar,' 'píruttar,' and 'ḥazratdargáh,' &c., i.e. lands devoted to the worship of the deities, or to that of a saint (pír). They call for no special remark. In the same way some service tenures (chákáran) may exist under the Zamíndárs. Especially these will be noticed in the Santál Pergunnah, Chutiyá Nágpur, the Bardwán division, and in the Rangpur district [1].

(B) *TENURES DUE TO THE DESIRE OF BEING RELIEVED OF DIRECT MANAGEMENT.*

§ 10. *Origin of the Class.*

These tenures are due partly to the desire of improving the estates by handing them over to the more energetic management which a lessee would give, and partly to the effect of prosperity and the desire to be saved trouble. In either case a time came when the landlords began to create permanent subordinate-tenures; by this means they escaped not only the labour and risks attendant upon direct management, but were successful in bringing large tracts of waste land under cultivation. Many a Zamíndár, who had no taste for estate management, or had more land than he could manage, would by a well-considered *farm*, or sub-lease, greatly improve his income. Considerable portions of estates have been thus conveyed, in perpetuity, by Zamíndárs in consideration of a bonus paid down and of a fixed annual rent. This rent is calculated so as to leave to the lessee a margin of profit over and above the sum payable to the Zamíndár and the revenue payable to

[1] The Deputy-Collector mentions that most of the Zamíndárs remunerate village servants by small grants of this class (see *Statistical Account*, vol. vii. p. 283).

Government—a margin which it depends on the lessee's skill and ability to make more and more considerable[1].

§ 11. *The Patní*[2].

The commonest tenure of this kind is now the 'pattaní,' or *patní-taluq*, as it is usually written. At first under the Regulations,—for fear of endangering the power of paying the land-revenue,—the Zamíndárs had been prohibited from giving any lease for longer than ten years. This provision was rescinded in 1812; and gradually the practice of granting long (or perpetual) managing leases or farms, called *patní*, became so common, that it was not only legalized by Regulation VIII of 1819, but special provisions were made regarding it. The *patní* itself can be protected by registration (as will presently be explained) from being dissolved, should the Zamíndár fall into arrears to Government.

A *patní-taluq* is heritable and transferable, and all the rights of the Zamíndár are transferred by the grant. It is held at a rent fixed in perpetuity. The holder is required to furnish collateral security for payment, and for his conduct generally, though he may be excused from this obligation at the Zamíndár's discretion. But even if the original holder is excused, the Zamíndár may require this security from any

[1] Sometimes the creation of such *farms* has been the greatest benefit to the estate: sometimes it is the resource of mere laziness, and of a device to procure money at almost any sacrifice. Thus, for example, Government became the purchaser (for arrears) of fractional shares in the Bardhákát estate of Tipperah district (first, the '8-anna share' was sold, and then a '2-anna,-13 gandá,-1 kárá,-1 kránti' share). The details of the former management soon came out. The default had in fact resulted from the fact that the Zamíndár, to raise ready money, had sold so many taluqs or under-farms for 'salámi' or fees paid down (which he squandered), that he had disabled himself from paying the revenue. Fifty-two of these taluqs are now recognized as valid.—(*Statistical Account*, vol. vi. p. 401.)

[2] Whence the *patni* derives its name is uncertain. Wilson inclines to connect it with 'patta,' a lease. Had the land been usually waste, it would have been natural to suggest the Bengalí word *pathan*—colonizing or founding. Harington (vol. iii. 519) says it means 'established or settled,' but gives no word in the vernacular; and Wilson remarks that the term originated in the estate of the Zamíndár of Bardwán, and soon became common in other districts. The meaning is questionable.

new holder introduced by private transfer (by *sub-infeudation* as it is called), or by purchase at a sale of the *patní* for arrears due under it. A *patní-taluq* is liable to summary sale, upon application to the Collector, if the rent is not paid; and this is allowed to be due twice in the year. The effect of sale is similar to that of a revenue-paying estate; inasmuch as all leases granted and incumbrances created by the defaulting *patnídár* are voidable by the purchaser, who is entitled to take the estate in the condition in which it was at the original creation of the *patní*. Persons whose interests might suffer in this way by a sale, are authorized to protect themselves by paying up the rent due by the defaulting *patnídár*, and on doing so can claim to be put in possession of the *patní* tenure in order to recoup themselves. If they do not take this course, and the *patní* tenure is sold, they can only claim to be compensated out of any surplus which remains from the sale-proceeds after satisfying the rent due to the Zamíndár. If they are unable to obtain compensation in this way, they may bring an action for damages[1].

§ 12. *Sub-letting, or 'Subinfeudation.'*

The margin left to the patnídár is often so considerable—that is to say, the capability of the estates for improvement is such—that the patnídár can again divest himself of the management, and content himself with a fixed sum, sub-letting the actual rental to persons who are called 'darpatnídár' or 'darpatní-taluqdár.' This is, however, often done, not to save trouble, but simply because if there is much waste, the charge may be more than the original farm-holder can manage: and he at once sees the advantage of giving out waste portions, or outlying blocks, to a sub-lessee.

And another special feature in this tenure has to be noticed. It is not only the whole or some specific lands forming part

[1] For this account of the *patni* I am indebted to Mr. J. S. Cotton, C.S.

of the estate that are thus sub-let; often a *fractional share* of the whole estate (or of the first tenure) regarded as an undivided unit, is thus granted.

Mr. Cotton writes:—

'These [*dar-patnís* or sub-farms] again are sometimes similarly under-let to se-patnídárs; and the sub-letting in some instances has continued several degrees lower. In some places there are now as many as a dozen gradations between the Zamíndár at the top and the cultivator of the soil at the bottom. In these alienations, the proprietors, as a rule, have made excellent terms for themselves. It rarely happens that a *patní* is sub-let otherwise than on payment of a bonus which discounts the contingency of many years' increased rents. The descendants of the grantor suffer by this arrangement; because it is clear that, if the bonus were not exacted, a higher rental could be permanently obtained from the land. This circumstance has not, however, had much practical weight with landholders. And if the wide diffusion of the profits from land is in itself a desirable thing in the interests of the community, the selfishness of the landholding class is not, in this instance of it, a subject for regret. In one respect, however, the cultivators of the soil undeniably are placed at a disadvantage by the practice of sub-letting; for it is a peculiarity of the system that, although these tenures and sub-tenures often comprise defined tracts of land, a common custom is to sub-let *certain aliquot shares of the whole superior tenure*, and in consequence the tenants in any particular village of an estate are often required to pay their rents to two or more than two, and often to many different landlords [tenure-holders]. The desirability of correcting this state of things, so productive of confusion and of hardship to the rent-payers, is admitted, but it is not easy to find a remedy. The extent to which sub-infeudation has been carried in some parts of the country, the minute subdivision of shares[1] which exists in other parts, the claims of individual shareholders on the raiyats for personal service and consideration, and, most of all, the too common feuds and jealousies of copartners, while they are the main causes of the difficulty,

[1] In the estate of Katalipára, in the district of Farídpur, there are no less than 500 sharers, each of whom is in possession of an infinitesimal interest in the property.

are at the same time insurmountable obstacles to the introduction of any scheme having for its object to induce or compel joint-proprietors [tenure-holders] to act in concert.

'The enormous number of permanent holdings now existing in Bengal is due to the practice of sub-letting. The total number of perpetual leases registered in the offices of the Registration Department during the past fifteen years, is 1,221,417. More than half of this almost incredible number is furnished by the three districts of Jessore (273,892), Backergunge (192,514), and Chittagong (230,795). The gradual accession to the wealth and influence of small proprietors, almost all of whom are themselves cultivators, induced by this wide dissemination of a permanent interest in landed property, is evidenced by the comparative material prosperity of these districts.'

§ 13. *Temporary Leases.*

I do not propose to regard as *tenures* mere temporary agreements for a five years' lease or more. In the Bihár districts, where there are small landowners, there is no general creation of *patnís* or permanent sub-tenures, but a host of temporary farms, contracts, and leases, called 'ijára,' or 'thíka,' or 'mustájiri.' A farm of a farm is called 'katkina.' A 'zar-i-peshgí' ('money in advance') lease is common in parts: it is a grant of the rent-collections, either against an advance made at the time, or by way of repaying a debt already incurred[1]. The *analogy* of such contracts to tenures is obvious, but they are not tenures in the legal sense.

[1] Mr. Cotton notices a curious case of an estate (in the Kishnganj Subdivision of Parniya) which came under the management of the Court of Wards in 1874. The owners had let the whole estate out in circles, which they called taluqas, on five years' leases. Each circle or taluqa contained several villages, and the lessee was called 'mustájir' (the common Persian term for a revenue or rent farmer). These lessees had divided their circles into sections or 'qismat,' and let them out to sub-lessees called 'málguzár.' The *qismat* might again be subdivided into parts less than a whole village, and called 'gách,' held by a 'gáchdár' or ábádkár. This last would usually cultivate himself or by hired labour, but even he will sometimes once more sub-let to a 'kulait.'

(C) *WASTE-CLEARING OR JANGALBÚRÍ TENURES.*

We have seen already that from the days of Manu, the Hindu custom has always respected the title of him who 'first cleared the jungle.' Instances of this will continually occur in the land-tenures of almost every province. On the one hand, the rulers were naturally inclined to encourage such work, as it enlarged their revenue, and accordingly they—even the worst—afforded protection and favourable rates of rent or revenue payment to the 'ábádkár' (settler) on the waste; on the other, the sentiment of the people conceded to him a right in the holding of a permanent character[1]. A number of the *taluq* or tenure rights which we have been examining may very possibly have had their origin in rights connected with village-founding and clearance, though it is not so expressed, and they may have been wrongly classified in my account: if so, it will not really make much difference. But in this section we are concerned with those tenures which are professedly created on this basis only. They are all distinguished by locally different names, and there are, as usual, separate terms which indicate differences in the rate of rent, or the conditions of holding, which, while making these tenures apparently complicated and multifarious, do not really show any fundamental or structural distinctions.

The *commonest* terms indicating this kind of tenure are 'jôt[2]' in East Jessore, Rangpur, Jalpáigúri W. and the Dwárs; 'gánthí' in Jessore and the 24-Pergunnahs; 'hawála' (often written and pronounced hawalá or hawlá)

[1] 'In all tenures based on the right of reclamation, it will be found that claims exist and are asserted, with more or less tenacity, not only for the permanent character of the holding, but also very often for fixity of rates . . . and accordingly it is a principle always claimed in these provinces, though it is not always conceded, that a taluq or sub-proprietary right is vested or transferred, or conferred, as the case may be, on the person who reclaims jungle and causes waste land to be brought under cultivation.'—(Mr. J. S. Cotton.)

[2] I need hardly remind the reader that when the vernacular name of the *tenure* is given, the *holder* of it (as a person) is indicated by adding 'dár' (P) = holder. Thus the holder of a 'jot' or gánthi tenure is the jot-dár, gánthi-dár; just as the holder of a taluq is taluq-dár.

in Jessore, Backergunge, and Noákháli. In other places we have the 'taluq' of Chittagong, and the 'chak' in the Sundarban tracts. In Midnapore we shall find that the revenue-free grant already mentioned as 'aimá,' was there applied in favour of clearers of the jungle, and the 'aimádárs' of that district are tenure-holders.

Some remarkable features are presented by the Khúlná district, which, in 1882, was separated from Jessore. It might be supposed that the customary tenures, based on jungle-clearing, would be the same both in the northern and southern halves of the old collectorate. It is not so. In the Khúlná parganas Bághirhát and Náldi, the terms 'gánthí' and 'jôt' of North Jessore are not recognised.

§ 14. *Features of the tenures in Jessore, &c.*

We may commence our study with these districts—remarking that Khúlná includes a good portion of the delta tract we have already spoken of in connection with the waste-land rules—the Sundarbans.

The following extract from Mr. Westland's [1] Monograph on Jessore will give a good idea of these tenures; and Mr. Cotton remarks that this also describes the state of things in the Sundarbans generally.

'*Patni* tenures and farms are almost unknown, as the Zamíndár does not ordinarily transfer all his rights to others, constituting himself a mere rent-charger; but, on the other hand, he manages his lands himself. In the south of the district (i. e. in the present Khúlná district), in fact, it is the raiyats and not the Zamíndárs who take to creating tenures. The highest tenure is called a *taluk*, the talukdár holding and paying rent for a village or half a village; sometimes cultivating himself, sometimes not. The talukdár corresponds with the gánthidár of the older tracts (where the word talukdár [2] has a totally different application, and refers, not to the

[1] Westland's *Monograph on the District of Jessore* (pp. 198, 199).

[2] See p. 525 and note. It applied to the holdings in the 'nawára' estate.

raiyat series, but to the landholder series of tenures). The talukdár's rent is looked upon as a fixed rent. Under him comes the hawáladár, who corresponds with the jama'-holder farther north, and whose rent is also regarded as fixed. The hawála tenure may be created by the Zamíndár if he has not already created a talukdár, and in this case a talukdár subsequently created, will take position between the hawáladár and the Zamíndár. The right of a talukdár, however, includes that of creating *hawálas* within his own tenure; and the hawáladár, again, may create a subordinate tenure called 'ním-hawála,' and may subsequently create an 'ausat-hawála,' intermediate between himself and the 'ním-hawáladár.' In these subordinate tenures the holders are almost always of the pure peasant class, and engage personally in agriculture. They are always regarded as having rights of occupancy; but if they again let their lands, those who cultivate under them, who are called *charcha* raiyats, have no such rights, and regard themselves as only holding the land for the time.

'These tenures have their origin, I have no doubt, in rights founded upon original reclamation. A raiyat who gets a small piece of land to clear always regards himself as having a sort of property in it—an 'ábádkárí swatyá' or reclamation right. As reclamations extend, he begins to sub-let to other raiyats, and we have a hawáladár, with his subordinate ním-hawáladárs in a few years.

'The talukdárs above described are those who, in the pergunna lands, come between the Zamíndár and the raiyat proper, or hawáladár.

'In Sundarban grants[1], the word has another meaning, for the Sundarban grants are themselves called taluks, and their possessors are talukdárs. Among these talukdárs we find several persons holding considerable estates (zamíndárís) in Jessore, Backergunge, or the 24-Pergunnahs; but a great number of them appear to belong to the comfortably-circumstanced class of people residing immediately north of the Sundarbans. Many people there, who derive a competence

[1] The grants here referred to are those which have been made by Government under rules promulgated from time to time for the encouragement of reclamation in the Sunderbans. The lands covered by these grants are tracts of Sunderban waste which are not included within Zamindárís under the Permanent Settlement.—(H. J. S. Cotton.)

either from a tenure in land or from commerce, have also some taluk in the Sundarbans, and they form, for the most part, successful reclaimers. They have just enough money to enable them to carry on Sundarban reclamation with success; and they are not rich enough to leave everything in the hands of agents, and, by forgetting their direct interest, relax the enterprise. Many of them also have raiyats of their own in their older-settled lands, and can use them for their newer lands. It is to the class to which these men belong that the greater part of the agricultural improvements and extension since the Permanent Settlement, is owing, and the advantage of having men of this class as Sundarban talukdárs was strikingly shown in 1869. The raiyats lost very much indeed by the cyclones of that year; and the loss would have been sufficient to paralyze the whole reclamation scheme, but that these talukdárs, immediately connected as they are with the grants, at once came forward to give their raiyats the necessary assistance, drawing only upon the little surplus of money they had at their homés. Larger Zamíndárs require to have these matters brought home to them, and even then, expect their raiyats to settle matters themselves; these smaller men at once appreciate the whole case, and step into the gap.'

While the old-established 'jôt' and 'gánthí' of Jessore are founded on the clearing right, modern gánthís are now much connected with the Zamíndárs' arrangements for rent-collection; still the gánthídárs have much to do in the way of promoting cultivation and settling the villages. Mr. Westland says that these 'tenures are, whatever the law may say, understood by the people to be fixed.' Their right is so firmly established, that, according to Mr. Finucane, the Zamíndárs do not think of contesting it[1].

§ 15. *The hawála.*

The 'hawála' of the Sundarban tracts of Khúlná, Bákirganj, and Noákháli is so named from the Arabic word signifying something placed 'in charge of' or 'consigned

[1] There is a report on the jôt and gánthí of Jessore by Mr. Finucane in the printed selections from the *Correspondence on the Preparation of Tables of Rent-rates.*

tc' a person. The tenure implies the grant by a superior landlord, of a certain limited area of waste for reclamation. The hawáladár settles some cultivators on the land, advances them a little money wherewith to erect homesteads, buys ploughs and cattle, and advances seed for sowing; he then realizes rents from the cultivators and pays his own quit-rent to the superior landlord. The tenure is permanent, but the quit-rent is not absolutely fixed (unless there is a grant in set terms). Mr. Cotton says:—

'This point has been settled by the Courts and is admitted in many cases by the hawáladárs. But it so happens that the tenure of the hawáladár has often, either intentionally or through carelessness, been perpetuated . . . and that the hawála has been sold, re-sold, and transmitted by descent. . . . In such cases the hawáladárs naturally claim permanence of terms and fixity of rate.'

In the Noákháli district there are some considerable Government estates, and consequently the exact position of the hawáladár has come up for determination. Under the Settlement law of Bengal Act VIII of 1879, they were treated as 'occupancy raiyats.' Their rents were settled under Sections 5 and 6 of the Act, but not on the principle of charging them with the total of all the sub-rents, less a specific percentage deduction. Agreeably to this concession, they were to pay a certain lump sum to Government as determined by the Settlement officer, and are free to make their own contract arrangements with the actual cultivators. I presume that now, under Act VIII of 1885, the hawáladár will come within the meaning of 'tenure-holder.'

The extract from Mr. Westland's Monograph, given in the last paragraph, forcibly reminds us how, coming *under* permanent waste-clearing tenures, smaller sub-tenures also arise: the tenure-holder finds he has more land than he can manage, and he sub-lets a portion of the surplus; his sub-lessee, for the same reason, again sub-lets. The hawáladár creates an 'ausat-' (corruptly áshat) hawála, also called 'ním-' (or half) hawála. The sub-lease of this is the 'ním-ausat-hawála'; and then again a 'ním-ausat-ním-hawála' (fortunately shortened into 'tím-hawála')[1].

§ 16. *Taluqdárs of Chittagong.*

Under the head of tenures I ought to mention the taluqdárs of Chittagong. On the Permanent Settlement being made with the heads of groups or tarfdárs, the individual settlers or talúqdárs became tenure-holders under them. The position also of the 'nauábád' taluqdárs or new settlers who came in after the Settlement, has also to be considered; but as it would be inconvenient to break up the account of Chittagong into parts, I have put everything relating to that district under one section which follows.

§ 17. *Jalpáigúri Jóts.*

The cultivated land of this district is held by 'jôtdárs' who are described as descendants from original settlers who appeared as mere squatters on the waste and prepared a portion of it for cultivation. As land was more plentiful than labour, a large part of the holdings still remained under jungle; and now, as usual, the jôtdár sub-leases to tenants called 'chukanidárs'; and as these cannot manage it at all, they sub-lease to others called 'dar-chukanidárs.'

In the Western Dwárs Settlement, the jôtdár has been recognized as a tenure-holder under Government as proprietor[2]; but as originally his right was regarded as a strong one—a sort of quasi-proprietary right—he has been allowed an unusually large margin of profit by the Settlement.

[1] Original hawálas are distinguished by added names indicating any little peculiarity. Thus, in Tipperah (Típra), I find that an 'izhári hawála' means a tenure which is claimed by the holder but not recognized by the Zamíndár (who takes the rent all the same). 'Mirás hawála' will be one acknowledged as having been inherited; 'qáimi hawála' will be one with fixed rent; 'karári hawála' one with certain conditions attached; 'raiyati hawáli' one with express conditions for rent-enhancement. All these terms, therefore, formidable as they look, mean little or nothing from the tenure point of view.—See *Statistical Account*, vol. vi. p. 405.

[2] The tenure is heritable and transferable, but the power of sale is limited; the Bhután custom was that a sale could not be made to the prejudice of any one who would succeed in the event of the death of the 'jôtdár.'—*Statistical Account of Bengal*, vol. x. p. 284.

The rights of the sub-lessees are protected by a record of their rents, and the *pattas* provide that the rents are to remain fixed during the term of Settlement, unless and until the jôtdár can show that the payments to him have given him a less profit than 50 per cent. on the revenue he pays to Government, or the chukanidár can show that he is left a less profit than 30 per cent. on the rent he pays to the jôtdár.

SECTION VII.—CHITTAGONG TENURES.

§ 1. *Origin and growth of Tenures.*

Mr. H. J. S. Cotton, some years ago, published a graphic memorandum on Chittagong Revenue-history[1], and I cannot do better than substitute, for any abstract of my own, the paragraphs Mr. Cotton has himself put together in a recent printed memorandum on Tenures in Bengal.

The land-tenures, it will be observed, are—

(1) the proprietary estates of the petty Zamíndárs or tarfdárs who were the connecting links between the State and the families who cultivated;

(2) the subordinate tenures of those individuals and families whose rights—as usual in Bengal—are described as taluq holdings;

(3) the tenures of cultivators who came in after the Permanent Settlement, and whose cultivation was therefore described as 'new' (*nau-ábád*), and whose holdings are nauábád-taluqs.

Chittagong is certainly an instance of a country to which the ideals of the Permanent Settlement were wholly unsuited. Obviously enough *now*, the Settlement should have been *raiyatwárí* with the several taluq-settlers: not only does the 'tarfdár' proprietor bear more than usually strong marks of being a purely artificial landlord; but as the different taluqs under him are scattered one here and one there, his estate must be practically unmanageable, were it not for the strength of the individual taluqdár's position, which frees them from any direct interference.

'The origin,' writes Mr. Cotton, 'of the peculiar system of land-tenure in the Chittagong district has, in my opinion, been

[1] *Memorandum on the Revenue History of Chittagong*, 1880; Calcutta, Secretariat Press. By H. J. S. Cotton, Collector and Magistrate of Chittagong.

correctly stated by the Commissioner, Mr. Lowis, in a recent report submitted to the Board [1], as follows :—

'"During the turbulent times preceding the final Mahomedan occupation of the district, small settlements of 'khúshbásh' cultivators appear to have been formed in different directions. As soon as the Mahomedans finally established themselves in the country, the first step was to collect rents from these men, who, to save themselves from the annoyance and trouble of visits from the revenue underlings, attached themselves to some person having influence at the Nawáb's court, and paid their revenue through him ; hence these self-elected agents came to be called tarafdárs, from the Urdú word *taraf*—on the part of—a partizan [2]. Hence it is that each taraf is a mere aggregate of taluks, as these 'khúshbásh' holdings came to be called, the component parts of each being scattered in different villages and different thánas. Such a thing as a compact estate is unknown in Chittagong.

'"The taluqdárs must have chosen their own tarafdár, otherwise we would not find every estate, whether large or small, scattered piece-meal over the district. Had the tarafdárs obtained the land and settled taluqdárs, or had Government farmed out the collections to tarafdárs, it is quite clear that such a fragmentary division would have been avoided—opposed as it is to all facility for collection. Looking to the facts as they stand, it seems to me perfectly clear that the popular belief is the correct one, viz. that the taluks were the original clearances, and that for their own convenience these taluqdárs elected to pay revenue through the agency of certain individuals known as tarafdárs, an aggregate of such scattered holdings forming a taraf."

'In this manner the large tracts of jungle existing in Chittagong were taken up in the first instance by taluqdárs or jangalbúri [jungle-clearing] settlers, while the work of subsequent reclamation went on by the agency of the same class. I agree with Mr. Lowis that it was the intention of the Govern-

[1] No. 72 C.T., dated 8th December, 1882, paragraph 13.

[2] The term 'khúshbásh' (P., being at ease) is used all over India to indicate a tenant or settler invited to take up his abode at a place under promise of protection and favourable terms. The word *taraf*, it may be remarked, also means a section or 'side,' as when a village is divided into 'tarafs' or major sections in Northern India ; so that 'tarafdár' *may* also imply the headship of a group or section, i.e. of the cultivating settlers or taluqdárs.

ment of Lord Cornwallis to fix the demand against these taluqdárs at the time of the Permanent Settlement. In the correspondence[1] of the time, reference is made to the "fixed jamabandi raiyats," and the necessity of seeing that the Zamíndárs do not exact from them sums in excess of their engagements, is insisted on. In these allusions to fixed jamabandi raiyats there is no doubt that reference is made to the jangalbúri-taluqdárs, and it is evident that, in fixing the demand due from the Zamíndárs or tarafdárs, it was intended that the amount payable by the taluqdárs should be fixed also, and that all of that class should continue to enjoy the same privileges which we find enjoyed by them at the time of the Permanent Settlement.'

§ 2. *Change in the position of the Taluqdár.*

'For some time subsequent to the Permanent Settlement, the rights and privileges of the taluqdárs appear to have been respected; but the tendency of late years has unfortunately been in an opposite direction. Even at the present day, however, though bereft of some of the privileges which used to attach to it, the taluq is still a valuable holding, and its possession carries with it something of a proprietary title. It is always considered to be permanent, and is, in consequence, called *qáimi*, although the taluqdárs are frequently persuaded into consenting to some small increase of rent, which under our laws militates against the claim of fixity of rate. A taluq is transferable and heritable, and a taluqdár can grant permanent leases without question. Roughly speaking, the entire district is divided amongst these taluqdárs, most of whom cultivate personally.'

[1] An extract from Mr. Collector Bird's letter, reporting on the proposals for the decennial Settlement, dated 14th January, 1788, is as follows: 'The rates and rules of assessment do not vary in any part of this province, and the raiyats are immediately redressed wherever it is found that the zemindárs exact anything beyond the established jamabandi, with their different abwábs which are specified in the accounts annexed.' The whole of this letter, with the accounts, will be found at pp. 55-61 of the *Memorandum on the Revenue History of the Chittagong District*. The statement there given shows the nature of the assessment: first, the assul-jumma, with its component parts; then the abwáb, mahtot, and other demands added to the assul, until the Government demand on a droon of land amounted to Arcot R. 15, annas 5, gundas 19, and 3 cowries. This amount is equivalent to R. 15, annas 13, gundas 16, in Sicca rupees; and for convenience of calculation has always been reckoned as R. 16 of the Company's coinage.

§ 3. *Etmámdárs.*

'Where, however, the holding is of any size, or where a person owns more than one, a portion only is reserved as "nij-jot" (home-farm), and the rest is leased to cultivators locally called etmámdár (the term is a corruption of ihtimám—a trust). An etmám is like the taluq, *qáimi*, and the rent is not theoretically subject to increase; but in practice, if the taluqdár is persuaded by a new auction-purchaser or otherwise to consent to some small increase, he generally manages to get some corresponding rise in the rent payable by his etmámdár. The etmámdár is also generally a cultivator, but he enjoys the same power as the taluqdár of granting permanent leases to under-raiyats. Hence the creation of "dar-etmáms" and "qáimi raiyati" leases.'

§ 4. *The Nauábád holdings (subsequent to the Permanent Settlement).*

[All land that was not held by *taluqdárs* paying revenue though 'tarfdárs' who became the landlords, at the Permanent Settlement, was outside the scope of the Settlement, and remained the property of the State. But as time went on, squatters occupied it informally, and then naturally questions arose about their position. They called themselves *taluqdárs* like the older cultivators. This large area of land, shown in a separate colour on the maps, was collectively called the *mahál* or estate of Government, and distinguished by the term *nau-ábád*—newly cultivated. The following is what Mr. Cotton writes about it.]

'The taluqdárs of the Government nauábád mahál base their claims on exactly the same grounds as do the other taluqdárs,—viz. on original reclamation of the soil. When Chittagong passed into the hands of the English, the policy of encouraging the reclamation of waste land and of granting rights to the holders or taluqdárs, such as existed under the Mogul administration, was carefully adhered to. Accordingly in May, 1761, a proclamation[1] was issued, inviting people to take up waste and bring it under cultivation. The reclaimer was only required to record the amount of his reclamation and was to be assessed at the established rate. The immediate result of this proclamation was a considerable extension of cultivation which was claimed by one Joy Naráyan Ghosál as having been brought about by his efforts; and in the measurement of the district in 1765 the new nauábád taluqs were grouped and recorded under pattás granted by him, as "taraf-Joy Naráyan Ghosál." Subsequent measurements made from time to time recorded the increased area of land brought under cultivation. In 1796, the grant under which Joy Naráyan Ghosál claimed to be "tarafdár" of all new lands brought under cultivation, was declared to be a forgery, and his rights were confiscated by the State. But the rights and privileges of the nauábád taluqdárs were obviously unaffected by this action, and, as a matter

[1] An extract from the proceedings of the Chittagong Council, dated 12th May, 1761, is to the following effect: 'Taking into consideration the vast quantity of lands that have been laid waste for many years past from the dissensions between the people of this province and those of Arracan, and as an encouragement to every one who will undertake the clearing and inhabiting these lands again, agreed that a proclamation be put up and publicly declared throughout all parts of the province, that whatever persons will undertake the clearance of such lands shall for the first five years be excused all rents and taxes whatever; that at the expiration of that time their rents are to commence at the usual rate of lands in every other part of this country; and that a guard shall constantly be kept there to protect them from any insults of the Muggs or other foreigners: and to prevent hereafter disputes regarding the property of the land when cleared, every person who shall engage in the inhabiting and clearing of them shall first register his name in this office, and every month send an account of what quantity he has cleared, for which pottahs shall be immediately granted him.'

The effect of these orders is to create precisely a junglebooree taluq as defined in sec. 8, Regulation VIII of 1793, as follows: 'Taluqdárs also, whose tenure is denominated *jungalbúri*, and is of the following description, are not considered entitled to separation from the proprietors of whom they hold. The *pattá* granted to these taluqdárs in consideration of the grantee clearing away the jungle and bringing the land into a productive state gave to him and his heirs in perpetuity the right of disposing of it either by sale or gift; exempting him from payment of revenue for a certain term, and at the expiration of it, subjecting him to a specific *'asl-jama*, with all increases, *abwáb*, and *mahtaut* imposed on the pergunnah generally, but this for such part of the land only as the grantee brings into a state of cultivation. And the grantee is further subject to the payment of a certain specified portion of all complimentary presents and fees which he may receive from his under-tenants exclusive of the fixed revenue. The *pattá* specifies the boundaries of the land granted, but not the quantity of it until it is brought into cultivation.'

of fact, they were clearly recognized by the Collector at the time of the confiscation.

'It is impossible in this memorandum to describe the subsequent history of the nauábád taluqdárs. It has become the subject of an elaborate and intricate correspondence, extending over a period of ninety years, and a variety of conflicting orders have been passed from time to time by the highest authorities; the rights of the taluqdárs have again and again been emphatically asserted and they have been as emphatically denied[1].'

. . . .

'The Re-settlement of nauábád lands was ordered in 1872. It was then decided that the position of a nauábád taluqdár was that of a tenure-holder in an estate the property of Government. Under orders then passed, the Settlement has been based on the rents actually paid by the cultivators: no intermediate tenures have been recognized[2], the proprietary title has been held to belong solely to Government: and the taluqdár himself been treated as a sort of rent collector with little more interest in his holding than that possessed by a farmer.' . . .

'The Commissioner has now challenged the propriety of the conclusions at which the Government arrived, and on which it founded the orders on which the Settlement has been made.'

It has been decided (see section on Settlement, p. 492) that the holdings are liable to re-settlement, but it has been conceded that a number of these shall not be re-settled at present, which puts them on the same basis as other holdings to which a fifty years' settlement was conceded in 1848.

§ 5. *The Island of Kutubdia.*

'The title of the taluqdárs of the island of Kutubdia rests upon the same origin as that of the taluqdárs of the mainland. They were declared by the Settlement officer in 1834[3]—

[1] The subject is discussed by me at length, with full extracts from correspondence, in a note recorded in the Board's office, dated 7th February, 1883. A copy of this note was submitted to Government with the Board's letter No. 693 A, dated 18th August, 1883.

[2] Under orders passed by Government, paragraph 7, No. 993, dated 13th April, 1878, it was directed that certain intermediate holdings should be recognised; but these instructions were not properly carried out.

[3] Mr. Plowden's Report, No. 34, dated 29th September, 1834, paragraph 14. But of course if the

'"to hold a jangalbúrí tenure differing in no respect from the description of that denomination of tenure as laid down in Section 8, Resolution VIII of 1793. These dependent proprietors, under the above section, enjoy a permanent, hereditary, and transferable right of occupancy, privileges to which they have always considered themselves entitled; for whilst in some cases the original jangalbúrí taluqdárs are still in possession, others have become proprietors in right of succession as heirs of the original clearers of the land, whilst a third class rest their claim on the deeds of purchase or gift executed either by the original grantees or their heirs."

'In the recent Settlement of the island, the title of taluqdár has been retained, but practically the taluqdárs have been treated as occupancy raiyats, and the Settlement records do not contain any entries of the holding or rental of the actual cultivators. The claim to hold at fixed rates was strenuously asserted, but it has not been admitted. In one case only a taluqdár contested the principles of the Settlement in the civil court, but unsuccessfully, and the others appear to have accepted the situation.'

clearing had not been made in 1793 it did not follow that the settler would be entitled to any quasi-proprietary or permanently settled estate under the Regulation.

SECTION VIII.—THE LAND-TENURES OF ORISSA.

§ 1. *Early History.*

Only a part of what is now the Midnapore district constituted the 'Orissa' comprehended in the grant of the Díwání in 1765. For the purposes of this section, however, I include both the old and the modern Orissa: in other words, I go beyond the Subarnrekhá river which now forms (roughly speaking) the provincial boundary, as far as the Rupnarain river further to the north-east.

First, taking the modern Orissa only, as to its general features; I have before noticed that it consists

(1) of certain Tributary States furthest inland;
(2) of certain Permanently Settled Estates next beyond them towards the coast;
(3) of the flat, rice-growing country called the Mughalbandí, which was the chief seat of Temporary Settlement operations; and
(4) a swampy coast-line.

The 'Tributary States' are not properly part of British territory: they are the home of various relics of primæval tribes, the Kandhs (sometimes written Khonds), Sávars or Saurás, and others; they present great attractions to the ethnologist. The Uriyá people or Uráons (Dravidians from the south by origin) seem, at a remote period, to have conquered the whole country.

The primæval tribes were not altogether displaced by the Uráons, but the two races apparently co-existed. The Uráons in some parts left the aborigines alone in such fastnesses as the Bod State (where the Kandhs now are), or the hills to the south, where the Sávars are (or in Keunjhar, where the curious Bhúmiyás, who claim to be *autochthones*, and the leaf-wearing Jawangs are found). In other parts they took the ruler's place, seizing, of course, the best lands for their chiefs. Sir W. W. Hunter has extracted for us, out of the old official records of Orissa, a most interesting account of the Kandhs[1]. That I must pass over, merely remarking that the Kandhs exhibit the same peculiarity as other Kolarian tribes. They had no organization above that of tribal families in villages, these again being loosely grouped into circles under petty chiefs.

The Kandhs (as is the case with other tribes similarly situated) have hardly settled down from the nomadic stage, in which cultivation is practised by firing the forest and raising a crop or two by the aid of the ash-manure. Where they are more confined as to space, there the tribe has finally settled, and lays claim to the whole area occupied, while the families have their allotments which remain undivided until the death of the family-head[2]. It is this head of the family who is everything. There is, of course, the necessity for protection from enemies and wild beasts, which causes a number of families to group together; they arrange their residence like the people of Kánara[3], where the 'village' site is in fact a single street with houses on either side, and at the end the huts of the menial caste and artisans, who supply the needs of the residents. The villages are often divided by rugged peaks and dense forests, but the only organization is that as each village is under a headman, so a group of villages—probably the 'sept' or section of a tribe—forms a 'mutthá'[4]; and the chief of the sept is over the mutthá. This exactly resembles the village union called *parhá*, and the chief (*mánki*) which we shall notice in Chutiyá Nágpur.

The Uráons had a much stronger government; and, indeed, like those southern (Dravidian) states about which

[1] *Orissa*, vol. ii. p. 69.

[2] In their native settlements they change their villages once in about fourteen years. 'Priority of occupation forms the sole origin of right. No complicated tenures exist, every man tilling his own field and acknowledging no landlord. Where the population begins to press heavily on the territory of the tribe, they parcel out the waste for pasturage among the village hamlets.'—*Orissa*, ii. 77.

[3] Cf. p. 106, *ante*. In such a village a headman is a necessity, and becomes still more so when the tribe is brought into contact with a conquering Rájá or some one mightier. He is, however, elected and only partly hereditary, and has no particular emoluments or authority.

[4] *Orissa*, ii. 70.

we shall hear so much in the Madras Presidency, they had an organization which it is very hard to distinguish from the Aryan or Rájput. We find the same gradations of rank; first, a great chief over the whole nation, with his central demesne; minor chiefs on the frontiers, and a system of militia to guard the marches, and to keep the peace within.

At a remote period, however, Orissa became the scene of Rájput conquest; and the Jagannáth records, though Brahmanical, and naturally inclined to ignore everything non-Aryan, leave no doubt that the Rájput or Aryan settlement must have taken place long ago and assimilated the institutions of the villages and states of the non-Aryan tribes: so that the present state of things is due—(1) to the Dravidian organization; (2) to its modification by the Rájput system which supervened, and later by the Mughal conquest which tended to convert the Rájput fiscal, police and military officers into landlords; (3) the action of the brief and ill-established Maráthá rule, in arresting the growth of the landlords, and pushing forward the heads and managers of villages and smaller estates.

It has been suggested that the Aryans really copied and adopted the earlier system[1]. I must be content with merely noting the fact, adding that in Chutiyá Nágpur we clearly see how the Dravidians strengthened the Kolarian village system, linking it on to their own State organization of chiefs and courtiers, by adding to the village an *accountant*, or fiscal headman—the 'bhúíṅ' of Orissa, the 'mahto' of Chutiyá Nágpur.

§ 2. *The organization of the Orissa-Rájput Kingdom.*

As to the Rájput organization of Orissa, we find that the Rájá occupied the level and fertile plain as his demesne, or, as it would be called in Rájputána, his 'khálsa.' All round were the hilly frontier tracts which were held by chiefs called 'khandáits.' This term, derived from the

[1] See Chapter IV, p. 119, and *Orissa*, ii. 207.

Uriya 'khandá,' a sword, was applied not only to the great frontier chiefs who kept the marches, but also to the military chiefs of all grades who were located within the king's demesne. The hill states were protected by the 'forts' at which the chiefs resided, and hence the territories came to be known collectively in Muhammadan times as 'Garhját.' The estate-owners were called 'Qila'dárs [1].'

We may dismiss the Garhját chiefs from further notice; the Mughals and Maráthás never interfered with them beyond exacting a tribute and nominal allegiance: they have now become the 'Tributary States' or 'Maháls' of the Regulations, and are under political control only [2].

The 'demesne' itself was also portioned out into many estates; for there was a large military force to be maintained, and estates also called 'Qila'' were also formed on the margin, which estates became the 'Zamíndárís' and were admitted to a Permanent Settlement as noticed in the chapter on Settlements. The ordinary districts were divided for fiscal purposes into 'Bísí' or 'Khand'—territorial tracts under a Desmukh, Bissái, or Khand-adhipatí, aided by some military chief or 'Khandáit,' whose 'páiks' or military retainers were supported by small rent-free holdings. The district officer, who was to the district what the headman was to the village, had a district accountant (Bhúi-múl) to aid him, and a village accountant also was subordinate to him in each village. Every one of them had lands held in virtue of office (a Dravidian institution), which laid the foundation of those estates or tenures dealt with in our own Settlements at the beginning of the century.

But besides supporting the military chiefs, the king made grants within his demesne for the support of the priesthood [3], for his family, and for his ministers and courtiers. Some curious survivals of these grants are

[1] 'Qila'' means a fort in Arabic, as 'garh' does in Hindí.

[2] This was judicially decided. See *Indian Law Reports*, viii. 985 (Calcutta Series).

[3] The existence of the sacred temple at Púri ensured many lands being granted revenue-free for the worship of Jagannáth.

mentioned in the reports. They were called by fanciful names, perhaps representing the *titles* given to the holders; thus we have the grant of 'The Lion's Cub' (Chhuál Singh), that of Hari Chandan, of Sudhákár (the receptacle of nectar), Utsal Ránájit (grant of the exalted conqueror), 'Beg' (grant to some Afghán adventurer), and many others.

§ 3. *Effect of the Mughal Conquest.*

When the Mughal rule supervened, the district organization was scarcely changed, except by the substitution of Persian names: the 'khand' or district became the pargana. The military and civil heads remained on their own lands, but were called 'chaudhari,' and probably with ill-defined functions; the accountant became the kanúngo; and the village the 'mauza,' with its head or accountant variously named according to locality and the tribal origin of the village itself.

'Two centuries,' writes Sir W. Hunter, 'of conflicting usage followed (1567–1751). During that period of confusion and chronic rebellion, the Muhammadan governors were only too glad to secure the revenue for each current year without any nice scrutiny of the machinery by which they collected it . . . What they wanted was a body of powerful native middlemen who should take the trouble of dealing with the people off their hands, and who should have both the power and local knowledge enough, to enforce the revenue demands against the individual villages[1].'

The body of hereditary Hindu officials thrust into this position, soon came to act like landlords; if it had not been for the intervention of the Maráthá period, they would probably have become absolute landlords under the British system.

[1] *Orissa*, ii. 221.

§ 4. *Illustration of the growth of Land-officers into Landlords.*

Before noticing what relics of the 'estates' of the kanúngos, chaudharis, and others survive, I would call attention to the very instructive account which Sir W. Hunter gives of their *means of growth*; because this, though written of the Orissa districts, really explains the growth of 'Zamíndárs' and others everywhere in Bengal.

First of all, these officers were all *appointed*; but as soon as the Government became weak and relied upon the local knowledge and power of those who were its instruments, it followed almost necessarily, that the son, or other competent near relative of the last man, stepped into his shoes; and the right of *appointment* practically became softened into the right of *confirming* or issuing a 'sanad' to the new man, and perhaps taking a fee or present by the governor. In the end the 'sanad' was discontinued, and there was then nothing but a *tacit recognition* of the succession.

The opportunities[1], then, of these fiscal officers were, first, that they were practically hereditary; they were responsible for the revenue, and therefore had large powers in realizing it; they also had the right to retain a nominal percentage and various charges or heads of expense in collecting: really they kept whatever they could collect over and above the fixed sum they had to pay in to the treasury. They had their official holdings of revenue-free land; they had the profits of bringing new waste and abandoned lands under cultivation,—all the newly-settled cultivators of course looking to them as their direct head or 'landlord.' They had various dues and cesses, rights over fisheries, pasture lands, thatching-grass, bamboos, jungles, forests, transit dues, and the like. What wonder, then, that in time such officers should become landlords? And be it observed, all this process of growth is the more

[1] See *Orissa*, ii. 230.

possible because, in the *individual villages*, there is no strong proprietary right. The actual cultivators who are residents (tháni) are practically proprietors of their holdings, just as much as the Kandh families were of their lands; but the long-continued effect of the Rájá's rule, and the encroachments of the grantees and others who took the royal share within the grant, reduced the *resident* cultivator to being nothing more than a *permanent occupant with a hereditary right*: it was no one's interest, as long as government was settled, to reduce them lower than that. In North India we have seen that as the *grantee's* family multiplies and divides, it produces a number of individuals or families holding each perhaps a single village as the share of the estate; and then, in time, they appear as the actual proprietary body owning the village (which then becomes a 'zamíndárí' or a 'pattídárí' village of the text-books).

§ 5. *Circumstances limit the growth.*

In Orissa the process was arrested by the fact that there were certain greater fiscal chiefs who kept the Bissais (kanúngos) *subordinate* to themselves; but furthermore it was arrested by the fact that when the Maráthás came, they checked the growth of these incipient landlords. Wherever we come across a tolerably settled form of Maráthá government, we shall again and again notice that the Maráthá at once did two things: he imposed a quit-rent on revenue-free holdings—thus avoiding the odium of wholly resuming them; and he ignored the middleman system, went straight to the villages, and made use of the *headman* as the distributor of rents, holding him primarily responsible for their collection. It was only in the outlying tracts where the Maráthá rule was uncertain, that the governors granted large farms and took all they could grasp before the day of destruction. So it was in Orissa; the village heads were resorted to, with the result of greatly increasing their power: as usual, in many cases inefficient headmen were turned out and replaced by 'sarbarákárs' or managers; exactly as in the Central Provinces, a 'pátel' who did not give satisfaction was replaced by a 'málguzár' or revenue-paying manager.

§ 6. *First British policy.—Absence of great Zamíndárs.*

When our rule began in 1803, no attempt was made to introduce the Permanent Settlement or its laws. I have described the chief features of the Orissa *Settlement* before[1]: I have here only to speak of the *tenure of land.* It is unfortunate that our reports so often speak of 'Zamíndárs,' as if Orissa had been permanently settled, and as if such an institution had existed generally. There are in fact hardly any 'Zamíndárs' in the Bengal sense[2]. There were a few of the 'Qila's' or chiefs' estates lying on the edge of the royal demesne (which it will be remembered was the scene of our detailed Settlement), and a few of the greater fiscal officers, who had retained such a hold over the whole of the pargana, that our first administrators thought fit to acknowledge them as proprietors, and give them the benefit of a permanent revenue. Then there were a certain number of kanúngos' estates, and those of other chiefs and grantees (of which I have spoken). Of these some were regarded as subordinate to the greater estates, and others were allowed to be independent and were treated as proprietary.

The larger number recognized as 'landlords' were the headmen, 'muqaddams' or 'sarbarákárs' of *villages* (in some places the local names, 'pradhán,' &c., survived.)

As regards the class of large 'landlord estates,' the latest return I have shows only 174 such estates (permanently assessed), viz. 23 in Katák, 3 in Púri, and 148 in Bálásor[3],

[1] See p. 473.

[2] The proclamation of 1803 issued on annexation, spoke of zamíndárs, meaning 'landholders' generally. See *Orissa*, ii. 257.

[3] The larger estates are called Zamíndári in Regulation XII of 1805, and the sanads were so worded. I find, for instance, one of the Khandáit chiefs (Sakinda estate) giving his 'qabúliyat' or engagement setting forth that he

while the smaller village and other estates, temporarily settled, exceed six thousand.

§ 7. *Smaller Landlord Estates.*

Putting aside the few great estates called 'Zamíndárí,' the bulk of estates which came under Settlement were smaller properties,—holdings of kánúngos, chaudharís. courtiers, grantees, and revenue-free holders. They are described as 'taluq,' and are called after their origin 'taluq chaudharí,' the estate held by the chaudharí, and so forth. These estates should not be described as 'tenures,' as the term has a special or technical sense in Bengal. I may repeat that when we speak of 'holders of tenures' in Bengal we now mean interests of the second class existing *under* a recognized landlord. But in Orissa the larger number of the landholders we are speaking of became Settlement-holders direct with Government.

One of the results of the former rule had been a system of *selling* estates and villages, nominally, but not always actually, waste; and a number of those who had purchased such estates became 'proprietors' and their estates were called 'kharídadári,' 'patná,' and 'khárija' (i.e. lands outside any other recognized estate).

§ 8. *Revenue-free Holdings.*

There were also many revenue-free estates[1]. Some of these, of course, were petty rent-free holdings under other

had been 'appointed to the service of Zamíndár' in his Qila' by the Government, and that he would pay the revenue and keep the raiyats prosperous, &c. (see *Statistical Account of Bengal*, vol. xviii. p. 123). In Katák the old records showed that of 1779 proprietary or quasi-proprietary estates, 16 only were called 'Zamíndárí' and the rest 'taluq.'

[1] Mr. Stack mentions that the claims to *lákhiráj* decided by Deputy Collectors amounted to 277,925 (*Memorandum on Temporary Settlements*, 1880, p. 580). The Maráthás imposed a 'tankhí' or quit-rent on many such tenures, consisting of 1 tankhá or rupee of the time per 'bátí' of 20 'mán.' The Orissa 'mán' is closely equal to the English acre. A number of these tenures were settled at half rates under the British Settlement.

proprietors. The rule was that such holdings, when admitted as valid, were treated as proprietary estates if they exceeded 75 acres, and as subordinate (tenure) interests if smaller.

Among the smaller rent-free holdings figure many belonging to the 'páiks' or old militia; and some were called 'jágírs' or 'dográ' (literally 'stick-holder')[1].

§ 9. *Village Heads become Proprietors.*

In many cases the village heads, especially those who had *purchased* the villages, and others whose actual position demanded the step, were settled with.

§ 10. *But artificial Landlord rights rarely created.*

The Orissa officers, as is amply testified by the valuable notes they have left on the land-tenures, and which Sir W. Hunter has turned to such good purpose in his *Orissa*, were under no necessity for *creating* landlords: and, as Sir W. Hunter remarks, 'putting aside very quietly the theories of distant bureaucrats, the local officers proceeded laboriously to construct a system in accordance with the *actual facts*.' Hence the variety of estates actually recognized. But while a number of larger or smaller proprietary estates were recognized, and the owners held the Settlement, the mistake was not made of leaving undefined the power of the estate-holder, or letting the question of the rent-payments of subordinate holders be doubtful. The estate-holders' interest was strictly limited by the procedure at Settlement. The officers went direct to the villages and fixed the rents of the tháni raiyats (who really were the original individual proprietors—only, as I have explained, they ceased to claim so high a position). This done, there was a fixed total rental, of

[1] The *Statistical Account* notes that, in 1875, sixty-five of these existed in Katák district, covering 8339 acres.

which part went to Government and the rest to the 'proprietor.'

§ 11. *Grades of interest—how provided for.*

But though the proprietor was one, he had often to share the profits with other persons interested—as, e.g. *first* the *sarbarákár* of the village, *second* a dependent taluqdár.

In our Settlements, whether there was a proprietor over the village or not, the headman, muqaddam, sarbarákár, parsethi, pradhán, or whatever his local title, was allowed to collect the rents and manage the village and receive a percentage for his trouble; and so with the 'kharídadárs,'—headmen by purchase of reclaimed or new villages [1].

Practically, therefore, the difference between the nominal landlord and the inferior interests is represented by the larger or smaller share of the rental fixed at Settlement.

§ 12. *Protection of Tenants.—The Thání Raiyat.*

The cultivators are, as I said, protected by rents fixed for the term of Settlement, if they are 'thání' or resident; and the Rent Law of 1859, still in force [2], protects the *pahí* tenants who have fulfilled its terms.

The 'thání' cultivator is in fact a 'sub-proprietor' in everything but the name. 'Rooted to the soil,' wrote Mr. Sterling in 1821, 'he has a local habitation and a name, a character known to his neighbours, and a certain

[1] In the *Statistical Account* (vol. xviii. p. 307) will be found a discussion as to the origin of the 'sarbarákár' as distinct from the muqaddam or headman (the Muhammadan equivalent of barúá, pradhán, or other local names). As to the 'parsethi,' the explanation of his being a *town* headman (p. 134) is very unlikely: most probably he is the headman of a later colony, i. e. a village of modern foundation (see p. 310). The sarbarákár's right was the subject of judicial decision in 1859. The percentage he gets under the Settlement represents no right in the soil, but is a collection allowance only. But, as a matter of fact, the village total payment to the proprietor being fixed, the sarbarákár gets the benefit of an increase in the rental when alluvial land is formed and let out, or when waste in the village is occupied. The tenure may be (if so proved by custom) heritable and transferable, but the holder is liable to be removed for misconduct.

[2] See p. 452.

degree of credit thence resulting, which enables him to borrow from the maháján (money-lender) and secures him a settled market for the disposal of his produce.' He is exempt from demand of 'chándniyá' (a payment—chándina—made by outsiders for the use of a site in the village); he is allowed a bit of rent-free 'khánabárí' or garden-ground near his house[1], also a rent-free patch in his holding called 'talmundá,' or a nursery-ground for his rice-plants.

'A preference,' adds Mr. Sterling, 'is given to him in cultivating the lands of village lákhirájdárs (revenue-free,—the aimá, debottar, &c., lands, so often spoken of) when the holders do not themselves handle the plough; and his sons and brethren, and even he himself, may cultivate untenanted land as "pahí" raiyats in their own or any other villages.'

§ 13. *Midnapore.*

I include the district of Midnapore in this notice, though the greater portion of the district, being the old Orissa of 1765 (all in fact but the Patáspur pargana), came under the Permanent Settlement. The tenures now found in the district are those which are usually found described in Persian terms of the Mughal system and that of the Regulations, and again and again repeated in the *Statistical Account*. There is the usual array of Zamíndárís, the resumed 'lákhiráj' estates, and the 'baháli' [i.e. those not resumed, but that remained in (ba) their own state (hál)]. Under them are the usual 'taluqs' or *tenures*,—'patnís,' 'ijárás,' and the like. Of these no special mention is here required. A certain number of special jungle-clearing tenures (but sometimes granted out of favour) exist under the name of kámdurá. They are heritable and trans-

[1] The reader will also note the same custom in Assam. There is an exceedingly good account of the village (exactly resembling the villages all over Bombay and Madras) in *Orissa*, vol. ii. p. 241, and there the differences of *Brahman* villages are noted. As the Brahman could not plough, the whole cultivation was done by the aid of tenants, which resulted in some peculiarities.

ferable. I also notice favourable tenures called 'panchaki,' seemingly identical with the 'upanchaki' of Rangpur[1]. It is also worthy of notice that the revenue-free tenure or 'aimá' seems to have been here created, not for the support of religious persons, but as a favourable tenure for cultivating the waste. As it is not entirely free, it is called 'málguzárí aimá.' No rent is paid for some years, and then the rent progresses to the rate usually paid in the pargana for similar lands. Some of these tenures in pargana Balrámpur are said to date back before the Permanent Settlement; others, under the same name, are more recent.

To this class also belong what are known as 'mandali jôt' tenures in Midnapore, which are nothing more than the holdings of certain men who were set to reclaim the waste (ábádkár), undertaking that a lump sum of rent should be forthcoming. From time to time the terms of the bargain were readjusted. Naturally the ábádkárs became the *mandal* or headmen of the new villages. They had a higher status than ordinary resident raiyats; and they were entitled to make their own terms with their cultivators, thus getting a considerable profit out of the difference between the lump rent they paid and the total of the collections from cultivators. Their tenure became transferable by custom.

[1] See pp. 540 and 586.

SECTION IX.—CHUTIYÁ NÁGPUṚ TENURES.

§ 1. *Interest attaching to the Tenures.*

The tenures of these districts have a peculiar interest for us, because here (and in Santália) we have one of the centres in which we can trace pretty clearly one of the earliest native methods of landholding in relation to the State, which are so interesting. Just as Oudh and Rájputána, and to some extent Orissa, give us the best information regarding the Rájput or Aryan organization which has so profoundly affected the constitution of village communities, so Chutiyá Nágpur is a centre which enables us to reconstruct the organization of Kóls and Dravidians, the latter being great colonizers and conquerors, like the Rájputs; and this organization is probably identical with what once existed in Gondwána (now the Central Provinces and Berar) as well as in Southern India[1].

§ 2. *General Description of the Country.*

The Chutiyá Nágpur country covers an area of about 46,000 square miles. It consists of a series of table-lands rising in succession from 800 to 3500 feet above the sea-level.

On each terrace are well-cultivated plains, and the borders of each are scarped and forest-clad hills. The plains themselves are dotted over with wooded hills. In the east of the division are the tribes known as Mundas, Hos, and Santáls (Kolarian); in the west are Korwás (Kolarian

[1] The materials for this sketch are Mr. J. F. Hewitt's paper on Village Communities in *Journal, Society of Arts*, vol. xxxv. p. 613 (May 1887); 'Chota Nágpur, its People and Resources,' by the same author (*Asiatic Quarterly Review*, April 1887, vol. iii.); an interesting 'Official Paper' in the *Calcutta Gazette*, 17th December, 1880, on the Lohárdagga District; and the volumes of the *Statistical Account of Bengal*, relating to the Division.

also). The independent States along the frontier of the Central Provinces are Gond (Dravidian). There are Bhúyá tribesmen in the States of Gangpur and Bonai, and in the (British) Singbhúm and Mánbhúm districts. In some parts there are also Uráoṅs. These are all Dravidians.

It seems that the Kolarian tribes are the earliest inhabitants, and the Uráoṅs and Bhúyás are invaders; in fact, part of that great wave of conquest made by the Nágá (snake-worshipping) people, who advanced far up to the Ganges valley. The Santáls are Kóls; they moved from Orissa to Hazáribágh to escape the Maráthás, and then, in the middle of the last century, settled in the hills which are now known as the 'Santál Pergunnahs.'

§ 3. *Kól and Dravidian Organization of Land.*

Of these tribes some appear to have had but little organization, but to have lived by shifting or temporary 'júm' clearings in the forests[1]. But in the plains they formed settled villages with a headman over each (mundá). The Nágá races in their advance, where they did not drive out the weaker tribes, admitted them, as it were, into their confederacy, and the system became one—that is to say, the Kól village system was strengthened by the Dravidian military organization, which was very like that of the Aryans.

There were senior chiefs or Rájás of territories, who had a central domain, while all around, estates were allotted to the lesser chiefs and to the servants of the kingdom,—some, as usual, on the frontier, being charged with keeping the passes. The villages, as usual with all earlier colonizing systems in India, show no sign of a joint claim to a defined area of soil. Such a right appears, rather, to arise at a later stage, when some petty chief gets a hold over the village by grant or otherwise, and then claims to be, in that little circle, what the Rájá was in his larger domain. His claim is distinctly *territorial* and is focussed on a

[1] See p. 116, *ante*.

small area, so that it is distinctly felt in a way that the Rájá's general claim over a large area cannot be. When, in course of a generation or two, this chief's descendants form a considerable body, these *jointly* claim the entire area as a body of 'landlords'; or, dividing it up into ancestral shares according to their descent, constitute what the books call 'pattídárí' communities.

We have now to see how the Kolarian village system was modified by being taken into the Dravidian system.

The Kól tribes had no central government. The tribal groups, distinguished by a flag[1], were called 'parhá,' and over which was a chief called 'Mánkí' or 'Mánjhí.' These were independent; they might meet for counsel and combine for defence, but often they were at war with each other. The parhá territory was divided into villages, each under its 'mundá' or headman, who was hereditary. There was a 'páhan,' or priest; but he was tribal, not local.

The Dravidians did not alter this organization, but their chiefs and Rájás took the rule over the *mánkís*, who, having no special estates, dropped into a secondary or inferior official position. What distinguished the Dravidian plan, was that in every village the Rájá or the chief took a *certain area of land*, the whole produce of which went to his State granary. It was easy to carry out this plan, because the whole village was divided into lots, according to certain principles. The lots were called (originally) 'khúnt'—a term said to mean stock (Latin *stirps*), and imply the allotment for a family group of the same order. The term 'khúnt-káti,' or the clearer of the holding, is still a term used to mark the right which, in the public estimation, attaches to the clearer of the primeval jungle. The 'khúnts' consisted of plots of different qualities of land, and in some places were periodically re-distributed, so as to give the person who enjoyed each a certain equality of advantage[2].

[1] These are still displayed at ceremonial or festive gatherings.

[2] In the Chutiyá Nágpur villages we find an institution which is common in Southern and Western India: where the level land was cultivated with rice, some uplands, called 'tanr,' to supply grass and stuff to burn for manure, were allotted with each holding.

When the Dravidians conquered, and desired to find a 'lot' in the village for the Rájá (or chief in an estate not held by the Rájá himself), it was easy to do so by a slight re-adjustment of the 'khúnt' system.

§ 4. *Official Allotments.—Royal Lands.*

Originally it seems that a lot was reserved for the old tribal mánjhí—and this became the Rájá's royal farm, and was called majh-has. The 'bhúíñhár,' or original families (founders [1]) of the village, had their allotments. One of these was for the headman, mundá, whose family was of course 'bhúíñhár.' Another was for the priest (láyá), which was subdivided into a lot for the *village* god (grám deotá bhút-khetá), and the district god (desaulí bhút-khetá); the Dravidians added a third, the earth-god, or deity of the whole nation (whose secret symbol was the snake)—this was called 'dálikátarí [2].' It is hardly necessary to add that petty allotments were made for the support of the village menials—watchmen, &c., and the artisans, not forgetting the 'ojhá,' or witch-finder.

§ 5. *Changes effected by the Rájás.*

In the course of time, but very early in the history, the Rájás became dissatisfied with merely the produce of the 'majh-has,' and began to levy a grain-share from the land generally, but always excepting the official and religious allotments. In this stage all the land that paid the share was called 'Ráj-has' land. Possibly this was in imitation of the Kols. This people paid no regular revenue, but used to give informal offerings of grain to their tribal chiefs, which may have suggested to the Dravidian Rájá to make a regular or formal levy of grain. Then it was that the Rájá grafted on to the old village staff, a steward or

[1] Called also Khúnt-kátí (clearers of the lot).

[2] These were again subdivided, as e.g. into 'páni-bhará' for support of the priests' assistants who carried water: 'murghí-pakowá' for those who cooked fowls on festival and ceremonial occasions.

headman, in the royal interest, and called 'Mahto.' This official was provided with an *ex officio* land-holding (called 'mahtoáí), like the earlier village authorities. In order better to provide for the tillage of the majh-has lands, the king also established allotments (called beṭ-kheta) for labourers who cultivated the royal farm; these allotments were held revenue-free.

When these changes were accomplished, the lands in each village became distinguished as (1) majh-has, (2) the bhúíṅhárí and other privileged lands, (3) the other lands paying a royal share and called ráj-has accordingly.

§ 6. *Later condition of the Village Lands.*

When the Rájá's dominion passed away, the 'majh-has' land became the special holding of the person, whoever he might be, that retained or acquired the superior or quasi-landlord right over the village. Meanwhile the idea of *lots* for cultivation was carried further than is above indicated; for, after these original allotments were provided for, there remained all the rest of the available waste and other land. At the present day we find it held by a variety of what we may call tenants, as distinct from the 'búíṅhárs.'

In some villages, a lot of the land is called sájwat or khundwat, meaning that it was held by tenants who had cleared the jungle: these were not the original village founders, but people called in at a later period to extend the cultivation and, as 'first clearers,' were to some extent privileged. Then there would be a large area of 'jíban,' held by people who got the right to cultivate a certain area (defined by local measures, with reference to amount of seed required), and here the holdings were not fixed, but were distributed from year to year by exchange. Then another part of the available area would be held by ordinary tenant-labourers, called 'útkár.' This distribution of area varied according to locality and circumstances. In some places, settlers of other tribes admitted, were called 'khorkár,' holding rent-free for three years, and then paying half rates. I find also tenancies called 'báibalá,' 'áriát,' and many others. One called 'jalsázan,' or water-providing, meant a permanent tenure, where the holder got the angle of a ravine, dammed it up, and so formed a small tank; then he carefully terraced some rice-fields below, which he watered from the tank.

§ 7. *Later history of the Rájás.*

The Muhammadan conquest brought no real change to the local chiefships; the holders were accepted as Zamíndárs, and some of them got *sunads* on submitting to pay a 'peshkash' or tribute.

But among themselves, the usual course of events overtook both chiefs and Rájás: quarrels, feuds, and the usurpations of the more energetic members of families who threw off their allegiance, occurred. Some families rose, others fell. At first the seat of the chief authority was at Patkúm (Mánbhúm district); but, in time, 'the chiefs, who had previously governed outlying provinces under the control of the descendants of their first leader, proceeded, like the Maráthá chiefs who separated themselves from the authority of the Government at Satára, to set up independent kingdoms for themselves; while the Patkúm chiefs sank from being lords paramount to being merely subordinate barons.' These changes appear to have come about gradually, and without such violent disturbance as would have left traces in the traditions of the country[1].

The next change was one that also happened in Assam. Brahmans and others began to penetrate the country, and in time the chiefs were 'Hinduized.' As usual, they became 'Nágbáńsi' Rájputs, and adopted caste. The result was that the outsiders began to get lands and influence, and to override the rights of the original inhabitants, causing much discontent.

[1] *Asiatic Quarterly Review*, vol. iii. p. 410.

When British rule began, some of the surviving Rájás chiefs, and grantees, were recognized as 'Zamíndárs,' with a Permanent Settlement; and then, as landlords, they began to grant 'taluqs' and 'ijáras[1],' or farms of their villages, to eject tenants and enhance rents, on the (ráj-has or) revenue-paying lands. A few peculiar land-tenures are the result of the chiefs becoming Zamíndárs. They made grants for their brothers, called 'Hákimáli,' 'Kuṅwarkár,' &c. (according to locality), for relations called 'Khor-o-posh.' A number of these obtained recognition separately, and became Permanently-Settled estates. When the old Rájás (or their successors) became 'Zamíndár' landlords, the *majh-has* lands became their home-farm or special property, unless rights had arisen in them, owing to grants, family divisions, &c. as might be the case. The 'ráj-has' became the ordinary 'tenant-lands.' The landlords did their best to reduce to a minimum the rights of the 'bhúíṅhárs,' in their free allotments; and this led to so much discontent as to cause rebellion in 1831–32, and again in 1858. The districts were then (by Regulation XIII of 1833) separated from the Regulation Districts and placed under the 'South-West Frontier Agency,' the political control being guided by simple administrative rules. At the present time the districts are 'Scheduled Districts' under Act XIV of 1874. The Revenue-sale law has never been enforced.

§ 8. *Modern attempts to adjust rights.*

In 1869 it was determined to put an end to the uncertainty and discontent which arose from the encroachments of the landlords, who had ignored the old tenures, and infringed the bhúíṅhári rights. Bengal Act II of 1869 provided for the appointment of a Special Commissioner, whose duty was to define and record all classes of rights.

[1] Thus, for instance, in Mánbhúm, the Zamíndár of the Barábhúm estate had granted the entire pargana on an ijára or managing lease for 21 years to an English firm of indigo planters.

It is stated (but on this matter I am not competent to form an opinion) that the Act does not correctly represent the real state of affairs. I understand that it does not apply to the 'ráj-has' or ordinary proprietary lands, in which the tenants of all classes have their holdings. Tenants there have the protection already afforded them by the Rent law, presently to be mentioned. The Act certainly makes no mention of the 'ráj-has' lands and their tenants, but directs that a record of rights shall be made, giving an accurate list of the lands that belong to the majh-has class[1], and those which were 'bhúíñhári'—i.e. set apart for the hereditary headman, mahto, priest, and privileged families. It was to be ascertained what were the services required from, and the rights enjoyed by, the holders.

Anciently the theory was that no 'bhúíṇhár (of an original founders' family) could ever lose his lands; so that after years of absence he might return and claim it from the present holder. This was so far recognized by the Act, that a bhúíñhár who had been dispossessed, could claim to be restored if his loss occurred within the twenty years preceding 1869. No tenure originating within twenty years was to be recognized as really bhúíñhári, unless it was a proved case, not of originating, but of regaining, a former bhúíñhárí *status*[2]. The bhúíñhárs had been so long made to pay *some* rent to the 'Zamíndár,' that this could not now be reversed; but the holder could claim to commute any service he had to render, for a money payment.

[1] Including the beṭ-kheta holdings of the special tenants who work the majh-has land.

[2] I have mentioned that rice-land holdings were accompanied by a certain appendage of hilly upland, which supplied grass, wood, and stuff to yield ash-manure, &c., for the rice. No doubt originally the allotment of such areas among the villages and tribes was well understood; but in time the Rájás and others encroached, and so the bhúíñhárs, though always allowed certain rights of user in the waste near the village, were not given an actual right over the waste (tanr) unless they could prove a definite occupation and possession.

§ 9. *The Chutiyá-Nágpur Tenancy Act.*

The value of the record made under this Act is to a great extent secured by the existence of another special Act—(B.) I of 1879—which regulates the relations of landlord and tenant in Chutiyá Nágpur.

This Act makes no attempt to draw any theoretical distinction between tenants and tenure-holders, but speaks of taluq-holders and persons having a permanent and transferable interest in land, as well as of raiyats. A twelve years' holding gives a right of occupancy to a raiyat in all lands *except* in the majh-has lands, or in waste reclaimed by the landlord (the khámár of the Permanent Settlement), or in his 'nij-jot' or home-farm, or in lands called 'mán' lands (held in virtue of office[1]), or as 'saiká,' i.e. lands held by contract from year to year, or under a contract containing express stipulations.

The usual rule was made about holdings which have paid the same rent since the Permanent Settlement; they are unenhanceable. Moreover, no tenant who is a 'bhúíñhár' or a 'khúnt-káti' (the reader will now understand this term) can be enhanced, except on proof of custom or a written agreement; and a number of tenancies specified in Section 20 are similarly exempt. All occupancy tenants, as such, are liable to enhancement *only* on certain terms stated in Sections 22, 23, 24.

§ 10. *Ghátwálí Tenures of Mánbhúm.*

A special notice of these tenures, which exist not only in Chutiyá Nágpur, but in Monghyr (Munger), the Santál Pergunnahs, Bánkura, and other districts, will throw some

[1] The reader will note how the landlord claim had grown. The old Rájá was content with his majh-has and his grain-share; but the Zamíndár took, besides waste which he reclaimed, private lands of his purchase or original possession; and had land (mán) held—no doubt free of revenue—in virtue of his office, a privilege one would have supposed to be already provided for in the *majh-has*. The exemption of the special holdings of the landlord from the growth of tenant-right is on the usual principle observed in modern Indian Tenant Acts.

light on the Permanent Settlement and its effects, as well as on the influence of revenue-free grants, in originating tenures. (See Book I. Chap. IV. Sec. iii. § 9.)

The outlying districts of a conquered country were, as I have before stated, usually occupied by chiefs who were bound to maintain a force to keep the passes. In the end it often happened that these very forces proved a source of trouble; instead of defending, they attacked; and the 'Poly-gar wars' of Southern India originated in this manner.

When the Permanent Settlement arrangements were made, there were a number of local chiefs all round the frontiers of Chutiyá Nágpur, in Rámgarh (Hazáribágh), Singhbhúm, Mánbhúm, &c. Their territories adjoined the more settled districts, and formed what were called 'the jungle mahláls' in early days. Our administrators accepted these chiefs as 'Zamíndárs,' imposed a small and fixed revenue, and left them very much to themselves. In Mánbhúm this was the case. In the days before 1793, and even at the Permanent Settlement, we hear nothing about ghátwáls, under that name at least. In 1793, indeed, there is some mention of 'paikán' lands; but they were virtually looked upon as lands for the support of rural police or páiks, which did not demand any special notice.

But the existence of ghátwálí lands was a matter of real importance, for it is to be remembered that in these tenures not only is the chief (*the* Ghátwál *par excellence*) entitled to his privileges, but every head of a troop in his own grade and rank, and every militia man, had his lesser share in the privilege—a certain area of land revenue-free, which he either worked himself, or, if his caste and rank demanded it, let out to his own tenants. When, therefore, the chief of the locality became 'Zamíndár,' and the collections from the raiyats became his rents, it followed that every acre or bíghá that could be claimed as held by a subordinate in ghátwálí tenure, was so much cut out of his profits: he got nothing but (at most) a small quit-rent from it. The sort of militia men who held the land, were taken over, so to speak, by Government, who tried to organize them into rural police and make them render service; and there were, from time to time, Regulations passed with this object. Such subordinate tenures represented a very large area of land, and they were held by a series of holders in a graded order.

In 1877–78 the inefficiency of the local police called attention to the system, with the result that, under the Bengal Survey Act V of 1875, it was determined to have a survey and record of all the ghátwálí lands, and of the rights of the Zamíndár and minor ghátwáls respectively, so that disputes might be at an end and proper service demanded in return for the holdings allowed. Mr. Risley, C.S., was in charge of the ghátwál survey of Mánbhúm, and submitted to Government an elaborate report. The report is somewhat difficult for the uninitiated to understand, but it is full of curious information.

It appears that ghátwálí lands were found in 25 out of the 38 parganas of the Mánbhúm district; there were 591 holdings, covering an area of 785,192 standard bíghás, or 408 square miles[1]. These were distributed among 1974 persons, who formed the organized body,—organized, that is, according to their own custom.

The chief grantee has become the 'Zamíndár,' and under him the various grades are as follows:—

At the head of a group of villages, now called a taraf, is the 'sardár-ghátwál,' or leader, of whom there are twelve in all, and they, of course, have the largest holdings. There is also a body of 'digwárs,' and náib- (or deputy-digwárs, whose functions formerly were to 'show the way,' i.e. guide or protect travellers and caravans in transit. They are now subordinate heads of small companies of 'tába'-dárs.' In the ghátwál villages there were headmen called 'village sardárs,' and persons called 'sadiál,' about whose origin there was some doubt. It was first supposed that they were 'sarbarákár,' or managing collectors of rents[2]; but their true position seems to be

[1] *Report* (No. 6, dated 20th Dec., 1883) *to Board of Revenue*, § 7. These tenures represent the shares of various grades,—sardár-ghátwál, digwár, náib-digwár, sadiál, village-sardár, and tába'dar, as will appear presently.

[2] In the special note on the

that of chiefs of the 'parhá' (the old Kolarian union or group of villages); being thus a relic of earlier times they were respected, but in subordination to the 'taraf-sardár.' The rank and file are the 'tába'dár,' who have their petty holdings. The local name for ghátwál is 'chhuár[1].'

It must be remembered that this is the country of the Bhúmij Kols. There seems reason to believe that the militia-organization was created *over* and amalgamated with, the *village* organization on the Kol system. The village lands being divided into lots or 'khúnts' held by the office-bearers and original settlers, the tába'dárs represent the body of ordinary village landholders: the village sardár represents the mundá, and the sardár-ghátwal and sadiál take the place of the 'mánkí,' or chief of the 'parhá' or union of villages.

It did not follow, of course, that the whole of the chief's (now become Zamíndár's) lands were held by his subordinates on ghátwálí tenure: some were so held, others as ordinary tenancies: and, as there was no real knowledge of land-measures in old days, it became a burning question at the survey what lands should be demarcated as ghátwálí, i.e. held on that favourable tenure, and what as 'mál,' i.e. land liable to pay full or tenant-rent to the 'Zamíndár.'

The ghátwálí lands were described in various ways, e.g. as 'land sowed with one maund of seed' (which may be taken as about eight bíghás), or as so many 'rekhs'—a rekh meaning a sixteenth of the total cultivated area, whatever that might be. The consequence was, as might be expected, that the minor ghátwáls got to claim, and hold, a good deal more than they were really entitled to; and that any attempt to define would, under the large licence of

Barábhúm pargana, Mr. Risley discusses the 'sadiál' at length, and thinks he was a real part of the system—a senior chief.

[1] The ghátwáls are not good cultivators, and the lands are poorly managed. Notwithstanding their poverty, 'the sardár-ghátwáls keep up the pretence of being Zamíndárs. They have seals, execute 'sanads,' and grant muqarrari rights in complete disregard of the nature of their own title. They even keep so-called 'diwáns,' disreputable Hindus, who do whatever writing is necessary and absorb whatever profits are to be made out of the lands. Even the sadiáls and village-sardárs copy this system on a small scale.' (*Report*, § 43.)

dispute given by the Survey Act, result in the ghátwáls claiming more on one side, and the Zamíndár striving to reduce the allotments on the other. In one case it happened that the original estate-holder—the old Bhúmij chief, who had first been transformed into a Hindu 'Rájá,' and then into a Permanent-Settlement Zamíndár—had granted an ijára or managing lease of the whole pargana to an English firm. These gentlemen were, of course, anxious to watch every demarcation; it was the Zamíndár's interest to see that no more was allowed as 'ghátwálí' land than could be helped. In Mánbhúm there was fortunately a kind of list of the ghátwáls, with their rights stated in *rekhs*, &c., drawn up in 1833, and spoken of as the 'Ismnavísi' (or 'nominal roll' of ghátwáls). Mr. Risley gives reasons at length for relying on this; and in the pargana we are speaking of, it was made the basis of a compromise by which certain lands were demarcated as 'ghátwálí,' the rest becoming 'mál' or liable to rent to the Zamíndár. In consideration, however, of the fact that many of the rent-payers were probably the original clearers of the land, even though not entitled to it on ghátwálí terms, they were to be allowed a rent-Settlement at fixed rates, something in this way: the holders were to pay fixed rates per bíghá; the Zamíndár took 50 per cent. from the headmen of tarafs (sardár-ghátwáls and sadiáls); the 50 per cent. that remained was then shared according to fixed percentages between the grades of ghátwál; 25 per cent. to the village sardár, and so on.

The ghátwálí tenure does not carry with it any *title* to a share in the village upland waste or 'tanr,' but certain rights of user are allowed.

The ghátwálí land is not held entirely free. It pays the landlord a 'panchak' or quit-rent[1]. But extra land pays rent and the 'mángan' or cesses.

[1] The use of this term throws light on the 'panchaki' and 'upanchaki' tenures: (p. 573). Calculating on the old fashion of sharing the grain, 'one-fifth' would be a light share, as a full rent was often the half or very commonly the 'panch-do' or two-fifths.

§ 11. *Similar Jágír Tenures.*

Somewhat analogous to the frontier police tenures were the jágír grants found in Palámau and Lohárdaggá, and called báráik, cheru, and bhogtá. They were grants of land held on condition of the holder being ready to turn out armed at any moment to defend his Rájá's lands and make reprisals [1].

§ 12. *Law relating to Ghátwáls.*

I shall not go further into detail regarding the law of ghátwálí tenures, as this can be found at p. 256 of Finucane and Rampini's *Tenant Act* (2nd ed.) There are ghátwál grants created under the Mughal rule (as in Bírbhúm, and now in the Santál Pergunnahs) which have become proprietary tenures, alienable and governed by Regulation XXIX of 1814, and Bengal Act V of 1859. Others (as those of Kharakpur in Munger) are on a different footing; they are not alienable (without consent of the superior), and the ghátwál may be dismissed by the Government, or the Zamíndár, as the case may be, for misconduct.

Police ghátwáls, like those of Mánbhúm, are on a different footing; if the ghátwál is dismissed for misconduct, he forfeits the holding [2].

[1] For further details, see *Statistical Account*, vol. xvi. p. 371, &c.

[2] See *Indian Law Reports*, vol. v, Calcutta Series, p. 740.

SECTION X.—THE TENURES OF THE SANTÁL PERGUNNAHS[1].

§ 1. *General Account.*

The district was made up (1) by the withdrawal from Murshídábád of some of the Zamíndárí tracts; (2) from Bírbhúm of certain parganas belonging to the Nagu Rájá's estate; (3) from the Bhágalpur district, of certain Zamíndárí tracts, as well as the hilly territory known as the Rájmahál Hills, and formerly called 'Jungle Terry' (jangal tarái). The chief feature of the district, indeed, is this hilly tract, forming a broad strip beginning at the Ganges and extending downwards to the south-east corner, which is indicated on the map by a separate colour showing it to be a 'Government estate.' It is locally known as the Dáman-i-Koh, and here no formal recognition of any proprietary right has been made, though, of course, the occupants have all their interests practically respected and recorded.

The Santáls colonized this district about the middle of the last century. In consequence, the population is a mixed one, although it is evident that the Kol village system was generally prevalent.

§ 2. *The Permanently-settled portion.*

I. In that part of the district taken from the older collectorates on the east, west, and north-west, all the earlier settled tracts are under the Permanent Settlement, and their tenures exhibit no peculiarity, except that they have all been surveyed and rights recorded under Regulation III of 1872. Here (as elsewhere under the Regulation) the

[1] For this section I am mainly indebted to a *Report on the Settlement*, by Mr. C. W. Bolton, and to a *Note on the Tenures*, by Mr. W. Oldham, kindly prepared expressly for my work.

village headman is employed to collect the rents from his villagers, unless there is any special reason for allowing the Zamíndár directly to interfere in the management. The village headman will be a 'mánjhi' in a Santál village, a 'pradhán' in other tribal villages, and a 'mustájir' or a 'mandal' in the Bengálí villages. The office and its appurtenances cannot be transferred by sale. For every raiyat actually cultivating at the time of Settlement, and whose name was entered in the Settlement proceedings, after due inquiry, as the occupant, it has been recorded that he cannot be ejected without an order of Court. This refers to tenants who have not already a right of occupancy, so that *all tenants have virtually rights of occupancy.* A further effect has been that the tenures so recorded, no matter of how short standing, are bought and sold and sub-let: whether such transfers will hold good against the Zamíndár (or his rent-farmers—patnídárs, muqarrarídárs, &c.) has yet to be decided. But a portion of this Zamíndárí and Permanently-Settled tract may be distinguished by the fact that the great mass of the cultivators are Santál immigrants. This consists of the portion nearer the hills, and where there is much forest to clear. Here especially, the rules about the headmen as managers, and the occupancy rights above stated, are applicable.

§ 3. *The Dáman-i-Koh.*

II. The Dáman-i-Koh itself is entirely distinct. It was originally occupied by Pahária or 'hill' tribes under local chiefs who got spoken of (though that, of course, is only a Persian office nomenclature) as 'sardárs' and 'naíbs.' As early as 1780 this tract was placed on a special footing; no revenue was demanded from the Pahárias, who roamed the tops and sides of the hills, living by shifting cultivation in the forest (júm[1]). Government made a cash allowance monthly to support the 'sardárs' and 'naíbs'; and then left the land and all its products to the

[1] Locally called 'Kurowabárí.'

people, contenting itself with declaring, but never otherwise practically asserting, its own title. The valleys lay uncultivated till the Santáls immigrated and established villages under their mánjhís or headmen: these have now been settled and their rights recorded under the Regulation. They are thus tenants on a Government estate. The mánjhí pays direct to Government, receiving 8 per cent. on the collections as his commission.

This immigration has confined the Pahárias to the hillsides. 'In the hills,' says Mr. Oldham, 'left to themselves, tenures innumerable have grown up among them. Every hill is claimed as private property and the hills are bought and sold.' . . . 'None of their claims have been acknowledged by Government, and are all at variance with its declaration that the Dáman-i-Koh is its own and the inhabitants its direct raiyats.'

§ 4. *Law of the District.*

The whole district called the 'Sonthal (Santál) Pergunnahs' was removed formally from the Regulation law within the limits stated in Act XXVII of 1855 (amended by Act X of 1857). But the managers of the several Zamíndárí estates, and especially some of the contract-farmers, had been in the habit of oppressing the people, by raising their rents, and that even in the case of those who had cleared the jungle and therefore ought to have been respected. In 1871 the ill-feeling culminated in a very general agitation. In Mr. Bolton's report will be found in detail the various complaints which the local inquiry elicited[1].

It is to the credit of one of the Zamíndárs, the Mahárája Gopál Singh of Maheshpur, that some of the main sugges-

[1] As a specimen it may be noted that a European contractor from a Rájá had (in 1267, Bengal era) taken a seven years' contract for R. 30,052, the jamabandi or rent-roll being R. 41,566. At the close of the lease he had run the rents up to R. 81,637. He then got a lease for another seven years at R. 50,000 (thus making a profit of over R. 31,000). Four years later the rental was run up to R. 1,12,296. Granted that some of this was due to extended cultivation or legitimate increase, a rental rise of 270 per cent. in twelve years, could not have been effected without grievous oppression.

tions on which the Regulations of 1872 are based, came from him. They were, that the whole body of the 'Regulation' laws should not be enforced[1]; that the cultivator of a first clearing should not be ousted, but that the rent should be adjusted by a public officer; and that no cesses beyond the rent so fixed should be levied.

Regulation III of 1872 declares what laws are in force, and limits the interest that may be levied on debts to 24 per cent. as a maximum, any agreement to the contrary being disallowed, and compound interest in no case being permitted. The interest is also never to exceed the principal debt, and if the interest is for not more than a year, it is not to exceed one-fourth of the principal.

The rest of the Regulation is taken up with the Settlement and record of rights. The decisions of the Settlement Courts are to have the force of decrees. Mr. Bolton thus describes the chief provisions of the special Regulation:—

'The Settlement Officers were to inquire into, decide and record the rights of Zamíndárs and other proprietors, the rights of tenants or ryots, the rights of manjhees and other headmen as against both proprietors and tenants, and also any other landed rights to which, by the law or custom of the country or of any tribe, any person may have legal or equitable claims. The claimants must, however, have had possession personally, or through others, since the 1st January, 1859, a limitation of twelve years being thus fixed. (Section 12.)

'The record of rights must show the nature and incidents of the rights and interests of each class of occupiers or owners, or, if need be, of individuals. Notice must be given to the people on the Settlement Officer proceeding to a village to record the rights. (Sections 13 and 14.)

'The boundaries of each village must be demarcated, areas of waste or forest beyond the reasonable requirements of the village being excluded, unless one-third of the total area of the village is already cultivated or is fallow in due course of agricultural rotation, and such waste or forest has been hitherto enjoyed by the village. (Section 15.)

[1] It would seem that, in spite of Act XXVII of 1855, and partly owing to an erroneous legal opinion, later Acts, and notably Act X of 1859, which worked great mischief, were practically put in force.

'The Settlement Officers were empowered to review and modify any previous decision of the ordinary officers of the district, regarding the rights of manjhees and other village headmen, which was found erroneous. (Section 16.)

'With regard to the manjhees and other headmen, it was laid down that any manjhee or headman who had lost his village since the 31st December, 1858, was entitled to restoration if he had a fair and equitable claim; and that he should not be excluded because he had been described as a mustájir or farmer. The Settlement Officers might abate the existing rents of manjhees or headmen if they were inequitable, or enhance them if they were low, the rates being determined according to the prevailing rates of the neighbourhood, the number of ploughs in the village, and other relevant matters. If necessary the lands might be measured. (Section 17.)

'The following principles were to apply in the case of ryots:—

'(*a*) Twelve years' possession conferred occupancy rights.

'(*b*) Ryots who had acquired occupancy rights before the 31st December, 1858, to be restored to possession, if justly entitled.

'(*c*) Ryots to be held to have acquired rights of occupancy in fields taken in exchange for other fields in the same village in the same manner as if no exchange had taken place.

'(*d*) Any custom regulating the mode of paying rents to the manjhee or headman to be recorded.

'(*e*) The Settlement Officer to record the rents of the ryots, if they are fair and equitable. If they are not, he should inquire into and re-settle the rents according to the number of ploughs owned by each ryot, or the area of cultivated land held by him, or in any other manner which might be customary and equitable. (Section 18.)

'After adjustment and record, the rents of both headmen and ryots shall remain unchanged for seven years, and thereafter until a fresh Settlement or agreement is made. (Section 19.)

'In adjusting rents, the Settlement Officer might take into consideration the agricultural skill and habits of life of the rent-payers, or the fact that the headmen or ryots, or those through whom they claim, had reclaimed the land from forest or waste. (Sections 20 and 21.)

'The instalments of rent and dates of payment by ryots and manjhees or headmen respectively[1] were to be fixed by the Settlement Officer, who was empowered to alter existing instalments and dates if they pressed hardly on the people of any village. The amount and dates of the instalments are to remain unaltered until otherwise ordered by the Lieutenant-Governor. (Section 22.)

'A record of local customs on the following matters was to be drawn up for every village :—

'(*a*) The existence of the office of manjhee or other village headship, and the duties and emoluments of each headman, and the customs of succession to the headship by inheritance, election, or otherwise.

'(*b*) The removal or suspension of a headman for misconduct, and the appointment or election to a vacant headship.

'(*c*) The devolution of the lands held by proprietors or under-proprietors or headmen, or cultivated by ryots, any custom contrary to the ordinary Hindu or Mahomedan law being noted.

'(*d*) The tenure of houses in the village, and the payment of ground-rents and dues by non-cultivating residents.

'(*e*) The duties and dues of village watchmen and other village servants, and their succession to, and removal from office.

'(*f*) The management and usufruct of the waste land, and other matters relating to the internal arrangement of villages.

'The record of rights must be published by being posted conspicuously in the village or otherwise, and persons interested may bring forward objections in the original or appellate Settlement Courts. (Section 24.)

'After one year from the date of publication the record of rights becomes conclusive proof of the rights and customs therein recorded, except in regard to those still under objec-

[1] It will be remembered that the headmen are constituted the sole rent-collectors of their villages, thus saving the raiyats from having to deal with the landlord's officials.

tion before the Settlement Court. Such record having become final, shall not be reopened or modified without the sanction of the Lieutenant-Governor, save as provided by the customs of the village; but the Lieutenant-Governor may order the revision of any material error.' (Section 25.)

§ 5. *Special Land Tenures.*

The special tenures that deserve notice are the results of the Kol organization. As before stated, in the permanently-settled portions of the district, we have Zamíndárs with patnídárs and other tenure-holders leasing their estates in the usual way. These need no remark.

A considerable area of land is held by ghátwáls who employ farmers, 'mustájirs,' to collect their rents. The ghátwáls (as far as they differ from those described in Mánbhúm) will be described presently.

Throughout the Zamíndárí and ghátwálí villages, there are the usual rent-free taluqs for religious or personal service; lands allotted to members of the family (bábúána), and in the Deogarh ghátwálís 'khor-o-posh' grants for the same object; and there are the village-service lands, especially those of the 'Gorait,' or village watchman.

Where the Santál villages are the predominant element, we find that the village has its headman or 'mánjhi' (the heads of other villages are called pradhán or mustájir). A group of villages, now called a 'chakla' (borrowing the Persian term), has a 'pramánik' over it (also called 'chakladár'). A still higher chief, called a 'des-mánjhi,' used to preside over the pramániks; these have now no functions, but are still remembered. The head of an entire 'pargana' was called 'parganáit.' In the 'Dáman-i-Koh' his position was regularly recognized; he gets a commission of 2 per cent. on all rents punctually paid, and an allowance from each village. Elsewhere he is not so generally recognized, and sometimes does not exist. These officials have all more or less retained lands held in virtue of office, rent-free or lightly assessed. The holding is called 'mán'; thus, 'mánjhimán' is the headman's holding[1].

In the Dáman-i-Koh, I may notice, only levelled and prepared rice-land is called 'zamín' (or in the dialectic form 'jamí'). This is one of the many indications how little the *soil*, as such, is regarded as the subject of property; it is the cleared, prepared, utilizable surface, or, in other words, the use and productivity of land, that is regarded as the object of ownership. The Pahária, wandering about and getting a crop from the ashes of the burnt forest, is not regarded as owning any 'land.'

§ 6. *Ghátwálí.*

I have already described the tenures of this class in Mánbhúm: but the ghátwáls of Deogarh and other parts are, in some respects, peculiar, so that I may reproduce *in extenso* the account kindly sent me by Mr. Oldham:—

'It was the practice throughout the district, and in the portions transferred from Bírbhúm, Bhágalpur, or Múrshidábád, for the great Zamíndárs to assign grants of land, generally at the edges of their estates, in selected passes (gháts) or other spots suited for forts, to check the incursions of the forest tribes, as the remuneration of the person or family entrusted with the guardianship of the pass, and of the specified number of armed retainers whom he was bound to maintain.

'This was the general character of the ghátwálí tenure. The grants were rent-free. The grantees held while they performed the conditions of their grant. The establishments of retainers varied much in size, according to the purpose for which they were wanted; and the extent of the lands assigned varied in proportion. Some of the holders were wardens of extensive marches, and their successors at this day occupy the position of considerable Zamíndárs. Other grants were merely for the purpose of checking the ravages of wild beasts; one in particular was given for the destruction of elephants.

[1] Note that here we have the same idea as involved in the *watan* of Central India.

'In the Bhágalpur district the grants were considered "police lands," and when the need for the grantee's services passed away, they were resumed by Government and held for some time as Government estates. One proprietor, however, appealed against this mode of dealing with them, and the Privy Council decreed that he, and not the Government, had the right of resumption; and most of those resumed have been restored and absorbed in the Zamíndárís, of which they formed a part.

'In the part of the district which once belonged to Bírbhúm, no resumption or restoration has taken place. The grants, with an exception to be noticed, are of small extent, and are still held as rent-free lands, and a nominal service rendered for them. Many of them have changed hands by sale and by encroachment, though such alienations are not recognized or permitted when known by Government.

'An exception to the ghátwálí, as thus generally described, is the subdivision of Deogarh, which consists entirely of ghátwálí tenures of a distinct kind. This country, which consisted of a forest tract, amid which rise precipitous, isolated hills, was held by a number of Bhúiya chieftains of an aboriginal or semi-aboriginal race, and was conquered by the Muhammadan sovereign of Bírbhúm about A.D. 1600. The conquerors, however, were never able to bring the tract into complete subjection, and at last effected a compromise with the Bhúiya chiefs, under which the latter were to hold half of their respective tenures rent-free, on condition of their maintaining retainers and performing the services of warden of the marches as above described. Engagements on both sides were never properly fulfilled, and in A.D. 1813 the Government finally intervened and concluded an arrangement with the ghátwáls by which their quota of rent was paid directly to itself, and they were still bound to render what the Government of the day styled their police duties.

'Their system of sub-tenures coincides with that existing in the precisely similar tenures in the Chutiyá Nágpur division, on which Deogarh abuts. They held watch and ward, and maintained militia and police, and farmed out each village to a person called mustájir, on whom fell fiscal responsibilities only. These farmerships became hereditary, and consequently at Settlement, the holders were unwilling to accept the lower status and more onerous duties, as well as the restrictions as to sale and transfer, fixed for the village headman. They made an application to the Government, which conceded in return the right of sale to mustájirs of certain specified villages.[1] '

[1] The British Government made certain Ghátwálí grants to pensioned or invalided soldiers on the banks of the Ganges; these are known as 'Inglís (English) Grants.' In parts of the district the (Persian) term mustájir has been naturalized and turned into mustágir (with the hard *g* instead of *j*).

CHAPTER IV.

THE RELATION OF LANDLORD AND TENANT.

SECTION I.—THE LOCAL VARIETIES OF TENANTS' HOLDINGS.

THE preceding chapter has dealt with landlord estates or those involving proprietary right, and also with 'tenures,' technically so called, which form a sort of secondary class, intermediate between the first grade of interest and the lowest which is that of the *raiyat*. Properly speaking, no fresh start is necessary before proceeding to describe *raiyatí* rights; an account of the varieties of these, as they are found in different districts, is as much a part of our study of Bengal land-tenures, as is the description of the Zamíndár or the hawáladár. It is only the magnitude of the subject and the necessity for subdivision into sections, that makes me begin a new 'chapter' for tenants and their rights. In reality, a large number of the persons who have become legally tenants, but are still called by the old name of *raiyat*, were the original soil-owners of, at any rate, their individual holdings. Their present position is due partly to their own decay, partly to the gradual overlaying of their rights by the growth of the 'Zamíndárs'; it is therefore necessary to bear in mind that in Bengal, as in other parts of India, we must not be surprised to find 'tenants' many of whom owe their position to no kind of *contract* with any landlord whatsoever. That is a main point to be borne in mind. We may now proceed to notice some of the local forms of *raiyatí* tenure, and then proceed to the history of the relations of landlord and tenant, and to the provisions of law actually in force. And first of certain very common terms describing tenants generally.

§ 1. *Main Classes of Tenants.*

In the ordinary revenue language, but hardly in the common speech of the people, tenants in the Permanently Settled districts were spoken of in two classes—'*khudkásht*' and '*pahi-kásht.*' *Khudkásht* properly means a man who cultivates his *own* land; and, in reality, it points back to a time before the Zamíndárs' time, when the village cultivator was either a member of a body which had cleared the waste and established the village, or had become, by conquest or grant at some remote date, the virtual owner of it. Where such persons were of a cultivating caste and worked their own holdings personally or with the aid of their servants, they were said to be 'khudkásht,' or cultivating their own. But there were always others in the village who, though not on the same footing, were nevertheless *resident* and privileged cultivators, just as we see in Panjáb villages at the present day. When the proprietary right of the village cultivators became lost or obscured by the turmoils of the times and the influence of overlords, both the original village owners and their resident helpmates became practically undistinguished, and were called *raiyats* under the Zamíndár; but as both were by custom privileged, and were not liable to eviction, both came to be equally called 'khudkásht'—with a slight change of meaning, for the word now implied tenants 'cultivating in their own village.' The 'tháni' (or stháni) cultivator is only a Hindí name for exactly the same thing; and 'chapparband,' the man who has his 'roof' or house 'fixed' in the village, is also the same. Pahi- or pái-kásht meant a man who came from abroad and took up land to cultivate without belonging to the village permanently. He retained the appellation of origin, even though he in fact continued to till the land year after year.

As the modern tenant-law has given privileges, after a lapse of years, to the 'pahi' cultivators as well as to the khudkásht, the distinction found in the Regulations and in the older reports has ceased to be of practical import, and has given place to the legal distinction of 'occupancy' and 'non-occupancy' raiyat.

§ 2. *Local Names for Tenants.*

The common local names for tenants are various. 'Jot' is a term commonly used for any tenancy [1], especially in the Bihár districts, where it has not the special meaning explained (in Chap. III. Sec. VI. § C, p. 546). 'Prajá' is a common word for tenant, and also 'karshá' (*Sansk.* krishán).

As regards the term 'jot,' Mr. Cotton remarks that it is used with the most elastic application. It has already been stated that in Jessore it means a class of persons who are in fact substantial *tenure-holders* with an acknowledged right to hold at fixed rates; and so it is explained in the district of Rangpur. In general the raiyat who holds direct from the landlord is called 'jotdár,' and his holding is a 'jot,' whatever its size, and which may, and does, vary from one paying a rent of one rupee to one of which the rent is half a lakh [2]. It will then be remembered that 'jot' may be either a 'tenure' or a raiyatí (tenant) holding according to locality.

§ 3. *Hál-hásila.*

In the Bhágalpur division a form of tenancy is spoken of as 'hál-hásila' (which means 'what has been realized for

[1] *R. and F. Ten. Act*, p. 33.

[2] The term 'jot-jama' merely implies that a lump rent is fixed on the whole holding, say, of five to ten bíghás, including the site of house and garden and paddy-fields. The rent is 'be-miyádi,' without a fixed term, or 'miyádi,' for a term, or 'sarásar,' fixed from time to time, and so on.

the time being, or actually'). This almost explains that the tenant is *only bound to pay according to the crop which actually comes to maturity.* The tenant cultivates such lands in the holding as he judges best, so that the fields occupied and the rent, vary from year to year; but it is understood that the tenure is a continuing one. Certain *rates* for each crop, called 'bera,' are known; and at the close of the year, the account is made out by taking the area of crops of different kinds matured, and working out the rent by aid of the 'bera' or rates[1].

So much of the holding as is left fallow is either not paid for at all or according to a 'fallow' rate, as may be agreed on; but it will be observed that, whether fallow or not, the *entire area* is at the disposal of the tenant. The landlord has no power to hand over to some other person such fields as the tenant has not elected to plough up. It is said that these tenures are held by the higher castes, and that, in some cases, they are regarded as transferable, having been sold in executing decrees.

A modern form of this, only on a *yearly* agreement, is found on the banks of the Ganges and Kúsi rivers, by non-resident cultivators, locally called 'dotwár[2].'

§ 4. *Otbandi or Útbandi*[3].

This is a new form of temporary contract tenancy, and only resembles 'the hál-hásila,' which is a permanent tenancy, in this one particular, that the rent depends on the *area* cultivated, and on the actual crop raised; nothing is paid for the fallow, if, as in some cases, the útbandi

[1] There is a more extended account in the *Statistical Account* (Purneah), vol. xv. p. 324, and Malda (vol. vii. p. 81). The questions there raised about an occupancy-right accruing, are all set at rest by Act VIII of 1885, under which it is not needed that the very same plots should have been continuously held.

[2] Unless the name is (as I suspect) a misprint for aotwár or ôtwár (as in the following note).

[3] Commonly written 'utbandi.' Wilson gives it as a Maráthí word Áút, a plough, from Sanscrit áyúdh, a weapon. But Platt, with much more probability, spells it 'oṭ,' which means a 'scotch' (to fix a thing down); and hence a fixed rate for the use of a plough and pair of bullocks.

raiyat holds for two or three years; for it is a local feature that the land (owing to its infertility) must be given rest. This form of tenancy is commonest in Nadiya, but is found in Jessore, Murshidábád, and in Pabna under the name of 'Uthitpatít' or 'charcha jot.' It is said that 'jama'i' raiyats—i.e. tenants paying a lump rental for their holding—pay at rates about half as high as those which are paid by útbandi raiyats on their actual cultivation.

§ 5. *Grain-tenants.*

Before closing the notice of varieties of tenant, I must mention the 'bháoli' or grain-paying system of Bihár. The process of division is much the same as it is in the Panjáb, or any other place where it survives, or had survived till of late years. As usual, the grain division is effected either by weighing out the grain at the threshing-floor (agor-bátái), or by appraising the standing crop (dáná-bandi), in which case the tenant makes over as many maunds of the grain as it was estimated would be the share in the field as it stood. It is surprising how accurate an appraisement of this sort can be when made by persons accustomed to the work.

In Gáyá, it is said, four-fifths of the land is held on grain-paying tenures. I have found a report on these tenures written by Babu Bhúb-Sen Singh, of Gáyá, which graphically describes them [1]:—

'It is the distinctive feature of the grain-rents that the payment consists not in any fixed quantity but in a fixed proportion of the actual out-turn of the crops grown. The rent paid or payable accordingly varies from year to year. The land is tilled and the seed sown is supplied by the raiyat or at

[1] *Report on the Rent Bill in* 1884. The account is also curious as it is written from a strongly landlord point of view. When it is recollected that a large proportion of the bháoli tenants are what was once, in byegone days, the village proprietary body, and that the 'gorait' whom the 'Zamíndár maintains,' is one of the regular servants of the village community, and that the Zamíndár was always bound to keep the embankments, the author certainly does not underrate the landlord's equitable interest in the cultivation.

his cost—the cost of hoeing and transplanting, of weeding and clearing, being also borne by him. But the water is supplied by the landlord at his own cost. The cost of gilandázi (throwing up of earth), division of lands into plots, by *al* and *ail* (ridges) according to their levels, for the storage of the necessary quantity of water, and of erecting embankments on the banks of rivers for the protection of the villages from being over-flooded, are exclusively paid by him. In dry years, when water cannot be supplied from rivers and village reservoirs and artificial water-courses, he pays the raiyat the cost of sinking wells. It is not only that the landlord supplies water for irrigation, but as the rise or fall in his income depends upon the increase or decrease in the produce of the lands, he naturally shows as much anxiety and takes as much care in the proper and timely ploughing thereof, as he would have done had he been a cultivator himself; and his servants are always found to be busy in superintending the tilling of the soil, the sowing of the seed, the transplanting of the rice, and so forth, according as the case may be.

'If the raiyat's bullock happens to die in the ploughing season, and the raiyat is unable to procure one in its stead, the Zamíndár would come forward and help him with one, even at the risk of running into debt, if he is poor. Seed is also supplied by him in the same way. For similar reasons, the landlord is interested in seeing that the best crops are grown upon the land it is capable of producing. No raiyat has the right to sow any crop inferior to what the land is capable of producing, nor can he be allowed, without the express consent of his landlord, to grow crops for which, by the custom of the country, a cash rent is paid, or which are incapable of being appraised or stored in the threshing-floor or barn for division. From the time the crops are sown to the time they are appraised and stored, the landlord watches the crops with keen interest and protects them from being wasted or otherwise injured by men or cattle. For this purpose he has to maintain an establishment of Barahils and Goraits, the former of whom receive their salary from the Zamíndár, ... while the latter are remunerated by the Zamíndár with rent-free land' [and some grain-payment which is exacted from the tenants]. 'This kind of tenure, it may be remarked *en passant*, is a peculiar one and has not its like anywhere else either in

Asia or Europe: and it would be a mistake to compare it with the European metayer system and to condemn it as *having all the evils of that system without any of its advantages*[1]. . . .

'The "bháoli" crops are by custom and the circumstances under which they are grown, regarded by the parties concerned as their joint property.' [!] . . . 'The whole of the straw and the chaff, which are not without value, goes to the raiyats. It is only out of the grain-produce that the Zamíndár gets a share which, though everywhere more than half, is different in different parganas, and almost in different villages, and which again varies with the different classes of raiyats, whether Ra'iyán or Shurfá[2], the former delivering a higher and the latter a lower share: and we shall be very near the true figure when we state that the Zamíndár's share, with the customary abwábs or cesses, is $\frac{9}{16}$ of the grain-produce. But, if the value of the straw and the chaff, which are, in these days, as much valuable commodities as grain, be taken into consideration, the highest share which the Zamíndár gets in lieu of rent, would be much less than even half of the total gross produce. The value of the straw and chaff may fairly be assumed to be one-third of the grain-produce.'

. . . .

'As soon as the crops are ripe for harvesting, the Zamíndár deputes an *amín* (assessor) and a *sális* (arbitrator) to make an estimate of the grain-produce. In the presence of these officers, the raiyats, the village *gomásta*, the patwárí, and the *jeth* (headman of raiyats), who generally knows how to read and write, representing and watching the interests of the raiyats; the village chainman, called *kathádár* (holder of the rod or bamboo), measures the field with the village bamboo, which in this district is nowhere less than 8 feet 3 inches or more than 9 feet in length. The *sális* then goes round the field, and from his experience guesses out the probable quantity of the grain in the fields, holds a consultation with the *amín* and the village officers, and when the quantity is unanimously agreed upon, it is made known to the raiyat. If he accepts the estimate so arrived at, the quantity is entered by the patwárí

[1] I should have thought that the author's own description fully justified the condemnation in italics, which, if I recollect rightly, is Dr. Field's!

[2] Ra'iyán are ordinary 'subjects.' Shurfá are the higher castes (from sharíf = noble), very often ex-proprietors.

in the *khasra* or field-book. If he objects, other raiyats are called in to act as mediators, and if they fail to convince either party, a *partál* or test takes place. On behalf of the landlord, a portion of the best part of the crops is reaped, and an equal portion of the worst part is reaped on behalf of the raiyat. The two portions so reaped are threshed and the grain weighed. On the quantity thus ascertained, the whole produce of the field is calculated and entered in the *khasra*. From the time the estimate is made, the Zamíndár withdraws his supervision from the crops, which are then left in the exclusive charge and possession of the tenant.' . . . 'After the appraisement of the field, the raiyat is allowed the full liberty of reaping the crops and taking them home at any time that may suit his convenience. Out of the estimated quantity, a deduction at the rate of two *seers* per *maund* is allowed to the raiyat, which is called *chhuthi* (let off). I have not been able to ascertain the exact reason for which this allowance is made. But, as in the *agorbatái*, the reapers who also thresh out the grain are paid from the joint crop, I presume this is allowed to the raiyat to meet the cost of reaping, gathering, and threshing. The landlord's share is then calculated on the quantity left after the *chhuthi* has been deducted.'

The writer, however, goes on to describe how the landlord exacts several cesses (here called 'ḥubúb'), which include the dah-haq, which is an extra 'tenth' (4 seers in the maund), besides pau-sera ($\frac{1}{4}$ seer), 'nocha,' and others. With these he says 'the Zamíndár's total share would come to, in some cases, a little less, and in others a little more, than $\frac{9}{16}$.

§ 6. *Sub-tenants.*

When the tenant's holding is of considerable size and importance, it is not surprising that sub-letting should be usual. The commonest name for a tenant's tenant, or under-raiyat, is, perhaps, 'kúrpha' (often written 'koorfa,' &c.)[1]. A sub-tenant paying grain is called bargáit or

[1] As the term is supposed to be of Hindi or Bengali origin, of course the letter 'f,' which does not occur in these languages, must be wrong; but I believe it is not settled what the real derivation of the term is.

ádhiyadár. The term 'shikmí' is used for under-tenants, but not in Gáyá, where it means a kind of money-paying tenant who is permanent, and probably refers to the class of tenant who was not on equal terms with the descendants of original village settlers, though privileged as long resident and settled.

§ 7. *Local terms for Tenants.*

Where there are special terms for 'tenures,' or for raiyatí holdings, there are also special terms for tenants or sub-tenants; as, for instance, the chukánidár under the jotdár in Rangpur and other districts, and the kol-karshádár in Bákirganj. For a variety of terms which I do not think it would be interesting to reproduce, as merely indicating kinds of contract, it will be sufficient to refer to the note at p. 35 of Finucane and Rampini's *Tenancy Act.*

§ 8. *Tenancies in Waste-land clearings.*

Chittagong presents to us certain peculiarities in the system of tenancy which deserve to be noticed, because they throw light on the difficulties of a tenant law, and how provisions which may be effective in one place, and under one set of circumstances, fail to apply in another. The account that has been given both of land-tenures and of the method of land-revenue Settlement adopted in this district, will have made the subject so far familiar that what follows will be intelligible. We have, in fact, a country where land is extremely abundant in proportion to tenants, and where there is indeed never likely to be much pressure, because the neighbouring district of Arakan is still a virgin wilderness to a great extent, and, like so much of Burma generally, only awaits the overflow of population to turn it into a source of wealth to the agriculturist. Not only is land abundant, but it is held in small patches which are still distinguished by the names of origin. The taluq is the individual holding, whether old-settled revenue-free, assessed (i. e. resumed) revenue-free, or nauábád. The result is (1) that every one ekes out his subsistence by taking, as a tenant, some patch of land belonging to another; (2) that every one desires to have some land of which he is owner, or at least permanent tenure-holder (qáimi), because that gives him the *power of letting it out.* A mere occupancy-right is not valued; for it does not enable a man to get land on any better terms than circumstances always secure for him as a casual tenant; while of itself it is not a right which enables him to let the plot and get money by it.

A considerable portion of the cultivation is in the hands of tenants-at-will, called (as usual) 'jotdár' or 'chásá,' or sometimes 'karshai-raiyat' (karsha=plough). And of course a man may be a 'chásá' tenant on one plot, while he is owner (or taluqdár) of another.

'Settlements with the cultivators' (writes Mr. Lowis, the Commissioner[1]) 'are made in March or April, when each jotdár settles what rent is to be paid for the land he proposes to cultivate, the rate being governed by the state of the rice market and the demand for the land. . . . Sometimes written engagements are taken, but as often as not the arrangement is verbal. It is not absolutely necessary that a fresh engagement should be entered into every year. When a chásá has held the same land for several years, he is allowed to hold on at the old rate without attending at the cutcherry to settle afresh. . . . It is always assumed, however, by both parties that, on the occasion of a marked rise or fall in the price of rice, there shall be a corresponding change in the rent, after mutual discussion.'

A trusted chásá—

'will be allowed to hold on for some years without a fresh agreement, while a new man will be required to attend at the beginning of each season to settle his rent.'

In many cases rents are settled only for one year, and at the end of it either party is at liberty to dissolve the con-

[1] Commissioner of Chittagong to Board of Revenue, No. 72 C.T., dated 8th December, 1882.

nection. Such a system, Mr. Lowis remarks, would, on a large estate, result in rack-renting; but it does not here, as the tenant is independent, owing to the small size of the holdings; and if he cannot get one bit on terms that suits him, it is no question of breaking up his home and going to a distant village—he is sure to find another, or half a dozen other plots, within a stone's throw, the owners of which are only too anxious to secure him. A man is not absolutely bound to get land or starve; he is pretty sure to have some of his own, by which he can live; and if he does not get extra land on a tenancy as it pleases him, he can afford to let it alone.

The taluqdárs have thus the complete control of the land, but subject to conditions which compel moderation; the tenants prefer to be free also. 'The taluqdárs,' says the Collector regarding the Kutabdiya estates,—

'argued that no terms whatever could pay them if the control of the land were taken out of their hands and the cultivators under them were recorded with fixed rights. The reason of this is, that the cultivators under them cannot be relied on for a fixed rent year by year. They prefer to pay heavily on a good crop and lightly in a year when they have reaped less or got lower prices, or have left a larger area uncultivated. Moreover, each taluq has its own small embankments, and the taluqdárs must be entitled to demand the labour of the cultivators to ensure these being kept up. In short, the cultivators do not want fixity of tenure, and it would be ruinous to the taluqdárs if it were given to them.'

§ 9. *Alluvial Tenancies in Noakhálí district.*

Noakhálí is another district where land is abundant, owing to the constant formation of more or less rich silt islands or 'chars' out of the river-branches that intersect the district.

These 'chars,' of course, vary in their durability: some last but a short time; some remain for many years, or permanently. Most of the recent chars, and even much land on the older ones, is cultivated by 'jotdárs' on a purely annual tenancy. Tenants of this class will come at the proper time to the office of the *hawáladár* or other tenure-holder, and offer to take a certain plot, at a rate which varies, and depends on the quality of the land and its advantages. The agreement being completed, the tenant passes a plough-furrow across the land, as the sign of his taking possession.

The Commissioner writes as follows[1]:—

'For the first ten or even twenty years of its existence, a char is thus cultivated by jotdárs pure and simple,—non-resident, nomadic, and unsettled. Gradually, however, some of them settle near their cultivation, and come to be looked on as settled-raiyats, who hold at some sort of fixed rate of rent. There is a rate for settled-raiyats, and this is not usually altered; but even a settled-raiyat often sits loose to his holding, and so a custom has become recognized that he should be allowed some remission in a bad season, and should not be expected to pay for land not cultivated.

'This rule is not invariable, but I am led to believe that in a bad season, after some haggling, a settled-raiyat does generally get some remission, while in a good season he has to pay something extra in one shape or another; in either case the rate is not altered, but the arrangements made are the result of mutual compromise.

'There is very little actual difference between a settled-raiyat and a jotdár. They neither of them hold under leases; the usual rate for both is about the same: only the jotdárí rent is admittedly variable; that of the settled-raiyat is not variable, but—which comes to much the same thing—he can generally get some remission when things are bad.

'There has always been more land to be cultivated on the islands than cultivators; and land once cultivated so soon gets covered with rank vegetation—all the ranker for the earth having once been opened up—that cultivators are in demand, and have always been able pretty well to dictate their own terms; while the facilities for obtaining fresh land rent-free, or at low rates, have induced unsettled and nomadic habits, so

[1] To Board of Revenue, No. 116 C.T., dated 11th February, 1882. A similar state of things is described in Tipperah (Típra).

that even where cultivators have been for a considerable period apparently settled, the hawáladár knows that they sit very loose to the holding, and, if discontented, are apt to abandon them in order to acquire land elsewhere.'

§ 10. *Comparison of this class of Tenancy with the state of Tenancies generally at the Permanent Settlement.*

Mr. J. S. Cotton compares the present state of things in the alluvial districts to the condition of the 'páhi-kásht,' or casual or non-resident tenants generally, at the time of the Permanent Settlement; and the existence of such conditions no doubt largely contributed to the old belief that the relations of landlord and tenant (generally) would *settle themselves*—a belief which resulted in the silence of the Regulations as to any definite terms of protection.

'The country was then three parts waste, still slowly recovering from the effects of famine. The demand was on all sides for *raiyats* to bring the land under cultivation; the rates of rent were uniformly low, since, as soon as the demand was raised above what the raiyat chose to pay, he would migrate to the lands of a neighbouring landlord[1].'

But as time passed, this state of things gradually ceased, and in the end Government was obliged to devise protective measures, which it did in 1859, and again in 1885.

'But in Chittagong, and throughout the new alluvial formations of Noakhálí and Tipperah, population is still sparse, land still plentiful, and the demand is still for raiyats to bring land under cultivation.' . . .

'There is no rack-renting in Chittagong, for there is always the probability that if the rent is fixed too high the land may not be taken up; and if not engaged for, the loss would, of course, fall on the taluqdár or hawáladár, as the case may be.

'The Chittagong raiyats are, in short, entirely independent

[1] And this to the 'páhi-kásht' was not what a removal would be to an old resident of a village. There was no breaking up of an ancestral home—even though a humble one—and severing lifelong ties and associations; the casual tenant soon packed up his *lotá* (drinking-pot) and his bedding and few moveables; and as to his hut, a frame of mud and bamboos and a thatch roof is easily renewed in one place as well as another.

of the influence and interference of their landlords, and cultivate as they please on a yearly tenure. It is not surprising that under such circumstances they do not attach much importance to the right of occupancy as our law defines it. They are naturally indisposed to bind themselves definitely to a particular plot of land for which they will have to pay rent whether they cultivate it or not. Their real ambition is to get a permanent lease ['tenure'] and then to let this to other raiyats for cultivation; but, if they cannot get this, they prefer to make their own terms with their landlord for such lands as they may themselves cultivate.

'A similar state of things exists in the Dwárs [1] of Jalpáigúrí, where so much land is available that an under-tenant who feels himself aggrieved will at once desert his holding and take up other land.

'It is the same in the estates belonging to the Jaipur Government [2] in the district of Bogra (Bagurá). Owing to the abundance of fallow and waste land in this part of the country, the raiyats seldom occupy the same holding for any lengthened period, and rights of occupancy are almost entirely unknown. The Zamíndárs compete for raiyats, and "the latter are almost masters of the situation." The figures given by Mr. Macpherson in paragraph 8 of his report show that nearly 10 per cent. of the holdings on these estates had been vacated during the three years, 1879-80 to 1881-82, and no less than 1,320 bíghás, which were cultivated three years before, had gone out of cultivation. The amount of new land taken under cultivation had prevented the rental of the estates from being reduced by more than R. 48; but the results vary considerably in different villages, and from year to year.'

[1] Commissioner to Board, No. 868, dated 2nd March, 1878, paragraph 11; and Board to Government, No. 211 A., dated 25th March, 1878, paragraph 12.

[2] Mr. Macpherson's report to the Board, No. 61, dated 22 Jan. 1883, paragraph 4, published on p. 201 of the *Selections from the correspondence on the preparation of Tables of Rent Rate.*

SECTION II.—A SKETCH OF THE HISTORICAL CHANGES IN THE RELATION OF LANDLORD AND TENANT.

§ 1. *Introductory Remarks.*

I must now endeavour to give a sketch of the relation of Landlord and Tenant in Bengal. Among the legacies which the Permanent Settlement has left us, the controversies excited by the question of the Zamíndár's right to the estate, and of the permanence of the assessment, sink into insignificance beside the burning question of the rights of tenants and their liability to ejectment and to enhancement of rent. On this subject, the difficulty, once more, is to deal with the mass of official literature that the question has evoked, and to place before the student just as much as is really important and really authoritative.

The main points I have to bring out are—*first*, that from 1769 onwards the Government was perfectly alive to the fact that the raiyats of all classes—from the permanent tenure-holder to the humblest resident cultivator—needed protection and were entitled to it; *second*, that they only contemplated certain means for this protection, which were, perhaps, in any case, theoretically inadequate, and which certainly, in the course of actual events, proved absolutely futile. *Thirdly*, I shall have to illustrate and explain the difficult subject of *rents and their liability to enhancement*, which our ablest administrators of 1789 certainly had very confused ideas about. On this subject I shall have to point out that a great portion of the controversy has arisen from a failure to draw the distinction which a careful consideration of the original condition of the raiyats will be found to warrant, and to an utterly mistaken view of what the early Regulations really laid down. It has been sedulously maintained—notably (for instance) in an elaborate volume of authorities, entitled the *Zamíndárí Settlement of Bengal* [1]

[1] An anonymous work in two volumes. Calcutta: Brown & Co., 1879; already alluded to.

—not only that the 'raiyats' were the original owners of the soil, which is true only to a limited extent (if we take into account not merely historical facts of a remote past, but also the actual conditions which ages of change brought about), but also that the 'raiyats' had a general right [1] to an absolutely unchangeable rate of payment, which it was intended to make permanent and unalterable, just as much as it was to fix the revenue of the Zamíndár. I do not understand that even the author of this work goes so far as to assert that tenants really owing their position to contract—i. e. located on the *waste* lands—were or could be entitled to have a fixed rent, never to be enhanced; and that alone would seriously affect the question, for at least one-third of the whole presidency was uncultivated at Settlement: in many districts two-thirds would be nearer the mark.

But, as regards the raiyats on cultivated land, it cannot be contended that they were all on the same footing. Even as regards those that had once been the real proprietors of the holdings (before there were any Zamíndárs, or under the rule of Rájás who were overlords, but never proprietors), it is quite impossible to assert that their revenue contributions were not liable to increase [2]. It is true that, by a mere tradition, the Settlement of Rájá Toḍar Mal was remembered and looked back to as a sort of fundamental assessment or starting-point; but it was nowhere actually in force, or had been within recent memory. It is a matter of the plainest fact that the Mughal Government from time to time re-assessed the lands and raised the rates, just as our own Government does (only in a more methodical way) in temporarily-settled provinces [3]. It is a mere question of form that sometimes the assessment was raised by actual re-measurement and re-valuation, and sometimes, in later days, by the expedient of adding 'cesses'

[1] I. e. not limited to particular cases where general and prescriptive usage could be proved, in which case no one ever doubted that the possession and the payment were fixed.

[2] See *ante*, p. 277, and *Fifth Report*, vol. i. 104 (Shore's Minute, §§ 13-39, 63, 279).

[3] This fact is expressly asserted in Reg. I of 1793, Sec. 7 (Article VI of the Proclamation).

but nowhere expressed, circumstances would soon have rendered its maintenance impossible. Remembering what a large part of Bengal was waste, and how rapidly new land was brought under the plough, it was to be expected that new rates of rent would arise; and as population increased and competition for land arose, those new rates would be higher than the old ones. Again, when an estate was sold for arrears (as was frequently the case), the existing leases were all voided, except certain specified ones, and therefore the purchasers would make new terms with the tenants, and rents would be raised to the level of the higher rates 'prevailing' from the cause first mentioned [1].

'Now,' says Dr. Field, 'if one-half of Bengal was waste in 1793, and could therefore be let by the Zamíndárs upon their own terms, and if half of the landed property in Bengal changed hands between 1793 and 1815, under a law which authorized the purchasers to avoid previous engagements, it was easy to see that the majority of the *raiyats* were, in the matter of rents, subjected to the uncontrolled will of their landlords, and the 'prevailing rate of rent being thus raised, there was little difficulty in enhancing the rents of the remaining *raiyats* up to the same level [2].'

§ 6. *Summary of the Argument.*

It has sometimes been asserted that it was the declared intention of the Regulations that no raiyat should be made to pay more than 'pargana rates of 1793.'

There is no doubt a great deal of uncertainty in the State papers preceding the Regulations; it is possible to pick out phrases from which some writers could be argued to suppose that every raiyat was to be protected for ever in paying a rate ascertained and fixed in a *patta* at the time of Settlement; but it is equally easy to show that what was really meant was, that the rates fixed by lawful authority,

[1] Compare Maine, *Early History of Institutions*, p. 184, and Hunter's *Orissa*, i. 57-8. In twenty-two years succeeding the Permanent Settlement one-half the estates were sold.

[2] Field, p. 559.

and not according to arbitrary exaction, should be paid (how or by what rule fixed was never determined), and that these rates could only be departed from by a consent which altered the mode of cultivation, and also by the increase of land under cultivation.

I may briefly also summarize the reasons why it could not have been intended by any one (as it certainly was never declared by any Regulation) that all raiyats' rents were to be absolutely invariable :—

(1) that no class of raiyats (except of course those who had special grants) was ever exempt from having the revenue periodically raised by State authority from time to time, even when there was no question that the raiyat was the practical owner of his holding; and when Government limited its demand on the middleman it did not follow that the revision of the raiyat's rent was also foregone, unless it was specifically so provided, which it never was[1];

(2) that no such thing as a pargana rate, fixed for all time, existed, but only a rate from time to time fixed by authority;

(3) that the change in the value of money and of produce, the gradual change of circumstances whereby, as population increased (under a peaceful rule), tenants would become more abundant and begin to *compete* for land,—all tend to produce a state of things in which an unchangeable rent for all classes is a practical impossibility;

(4) that the very fact that some raiyats held 'muqarrarí' or fixed rate leases, showed that a fixed rent was the exception, not the rule;

[1] Indeed, exactly the contrary. The preamble to Regulation XLV of 1793 expressly states that the raiyats were bound to pay a proportion of the annual produce of every bighá of land (in money or kind according to custom), and that the Government fixed a demand on the proprietor of every estate, and left him to 'appropriate to his own use the difference between the said proportion' and the fixed demand. The whole preamble would have no point if it were not that the 'proportion' payable by the raiyat had not been (in the absence of express grant) liable to be fixed from time to time on periodical revisions.

(5) that even if some of the old village cultivators were specially entitled to consideration, all raiyats were not, by custom, on the same footing;

(6) that considering the enormous areas of waste that in time would be brought under cultivation, the tenants who undertook it, could not be on any other footing than that which depended on contract, and these would, in time, become a very large class;

(7) rents in kind are still common, especially in Bihár, and in the nature of things, these would *really*, if not nominally, increase, and could not escape being converted into money rents in time. In short, when the value of produce increased, and the money commutation took place, and when the cultivation of new land called for a reassessment, the 'nirkh-bandí' or often appealed to list of 'pargana rates' would necessarily rise (see Field, page 546).

§ 7. *Actual Provisions in Regulation VIII of* 1793 *regarding Rent.*

The features of the Permanent Settlement law, as stereotyped in Regulation VIII of 1793, have already been stated, and at p. 433, I expressly reserved the provisions *relating to tenants*. Let us now consider them briefly.

The Regulation notices that there are persons called taluqdárs or 'muqarrarídárs' (on grant of fixed rent), &c. Some of these, as I have explained, were recognized as proprietors and were settled with independently. With such we are not now concerned. The others then remained 'dependent' or holding 'tenures' *under* the proprietors; but if Section 49.
they had held at a fixed rent for more than twelve years, or if their grant or title-deed showed a fixed rent, then these tenures were 'not liable to be assessed with any increase' (unless the Zamíndárí was held by Government or let in farm). And in any case these 'dependent' tenures were not Section 50.
to be enhanced, except upon proof that it was the custom of the district or the special condition under which the tenure

Section 51. was created. A certain provision was also made for one other class—the old resident (or khudkásht) raiyats. Their existing terms of holding could not be interfered with (except on proof of fraud in the title), and the right to raise these rents was limited to cases—

(1) where the rent paid within the previous three years had fallen below the nirkh or rate of the pargana, according to the kánúngo's lists[1];

(2) upon a general measurement of the pargana for the purpose of equalizing and correcting the assessment. (This did not apply to Bihár, where rents in kind are taken[2].)

Then comes a provision about the 'remaining lands,'—i.e. all that are not of the classes just named. These lands are to be *let*, under the prescribed restrictions, in
Section 52. whatever manner the Zamíndár may think fit. The 'prescribed restrictions,' as stated in the Regulation, are, that persons appointed to collect rents are to get authority by a written ''amlnáma[3]'; that all cesses (abwáb, máthaut,

[1] These, as I remarked, were often incorrect, since the irregularities of many years would either have resulted in arbitrary and various rates, or else in some old rates being continued, which could not be expected to last for ever without revision. It was the *want of any rule* for getting equitable and correct rent-rates that led to all the trouble. Mr. Shore observes: 'In every district in Bengal, where the licence of exaction has not superseded all rule, the rents of land are regulated by known rates called "nirkh" (and the list of these pargana rates is the "nirkh-bandí"). These rates are formed with respect to the produce of the land, at so much per bighá. Some soil produces two crops in the year of different species; some three. The more profitable articles, such as the mulberry plant, betel-leaf, tobacco, sugarcane, and others, render the value of the land proportionately great. These rates must have been fixed upon a measurement of the land.' And he might have added, must have varied from period to period according as the money value rose, and according to other circumstances.

[2] In 1789, Mr. Harington gave a full statement of the arguments *pro* and *con* as to enacting that the 'permanent raiyats' should be entitled to hold for ever at fixed rents (Harington, iii. pp. 461–463). He recommended, as the result, that for the decennial settlement, the proprietors should be obliged to fix, during the first three years, a rent which was to hold good for the remaining seven. When the decennial settlement was made permanent the protection given to the permanent tenants was that stated in the text, which is perhaps not very definite or satisfactory, for there is nothing to show how often the 'general measurement' might have come round. But an absolute fixity of rent and tenure is nowhere conceded, unless proved to have been acquired by grant or by prescription.

[3] So that the raiyat may know

mángan, &c.) are to be consolidated with the substantive rent (*'asl*) in one sum; that no *new* cesses are to be imposed. Where it was the custom to vary the terms of holding for lands according to the 'articles produced thereon,' this was allowed to be done, the law, however, '*expecting* that the parties (specifying both landlord and tenant) *would find it for their mutual advantage*' to enter into agreements for a specified sum, for a certain quantity of land. All rents were to be specifically stated in *pattas* or written leases (and details are given as to how this was to be done); forms of *patta* were to be prepared and get the Collector's approval, and be given out to the *raiyats*; leases existing at time of assessment, unexpired, and not contrary to anything in the Regulation, nor collusive nor fraudulent, were to hold good till expiry. Accounts were to be kept by patwárís, &c.; receipts for rent were to be given; rents of persons who absconded were not to be demanded from those that remained (called *nájái* payments). *Instalments* of rent were to be fixed with due regard to seasons of reaping and selling the produce.

These were the only 'restrictions' on the Zamíndár 'letting' his 'remaining lands' in any way he pleased. But there was a restriction imposed on the other side. For fear that Zamíndárs should be too liberal, or rather too eager to get rid of trouble, by granting away their estates on long leases, and so disabling themselves from meeting the Government demand, another Regulation, passed at the same time (XLIV of 1793), prohibited *pattas* being issued for more than *ten* years. It is obvious that such a provision contemplated a periodic increase of rents, which might be foregone for ten years, but not for more, or it has no meaning[1].

who he was paying to, and not be tricked into handing over his rents to some one who could not discharge him legally.

[1] Mr. Field has given a number of authorities (p. 523 *et seq.*) showing that this was the meaning of the Regulations.

§ 8. *Eviction.*

It also follows from these provisions that the question of *eviction* of tenants was undetermined. The tenure-holders (taluqdárs and others similar) were of course not liable to be dispossessed. And the resident raiyats were protected to a limited extent. But nothing is said about other tenants; if they would not agree to the terms offered, and were not holding under an unexpired lease, there was nothing to prevent their being removed. Probably in 1793 the demand for tenants was so great (see p. 610 *ante*), that it was not thought likely that the Zamíndár would evict many; he would be only too glad to keep them. However this may be, there is no provision in the early law on the subject, except as above indicated. When once the idea of the Zamíndár being landlord, in the English sense, became familiar, it was not surprising that people should begin to talk of the 'inherent privilege of giving him (the tenant) due warning to quit [1].'

§ 9. *General Conclusion.*

I cannot here forbear extracting Dr. Field's just and lucid summing up of the discussions and orders which preceded the Settlement, giving the result of Mr. Shore's and Lord Cornwallis' minutes and the orders of the Home Government. He says [2]:—

'It will be clear to any unprejudiced person that the Directors, and those who, under their authority, conducted the Government of Bengal, were well aware of the indefinite relations which subsisted between *Zamíndárs* and *raiyats*, were well apprized of the uncertain nature of the rights of the cultivators of the soil [3]; that practically nothing effectual had been

[1] See, for instance, the correspondence quoted by Dr. Field (p. 531), and *Land Tenure, by a Civilian*, p. 104—'In point of law and fact, the raiyats can claim [that is, *ordinary* tenants can claim], under the provisions of Lord Cornwallis' Code, no rights at all.'

[2] Page 503, § 267.

[3] Uncertain, in the first place (I may repeat), because all village cultivators were not originally on an

done between 1765 and 1790 to define or adjust the rights and the payments to be made by the raiyats . . . that Mr. Hastings and Mr. Shore were of opinion that these rights and payments should be defined and adjusted before the Government limited its own demands upon the Zamíndárs and settled for ever the amount of revenue payable by them ; that it was admitted on all hands that up to 1790 there were not sufficient materials for this definition and adjustment ; that Lord Cornwallis was sanguine that the combined effects of the limitation and permanent Settlement of the State demand, and of the *patta* regulations, would have the ultimate effect of adjusting the relations between the *Zamíndárs* and the raiyats . . . ; that the Court of Directors adopted Lord Cornwallis' views, and instead of directing the rights of the cultivators of the soil to be ascertained, adjusted, and defined once for all[1], contented themselves with reserving a general right to interfere *afterwards*, if these expectations and those of Lord Cornwallis should be disappointed, and such interference should be found necessary for the protection and welfare of the *raiyats*. Any unbiassed individual who will read the whole of the papers must be satisfied that both Lord Cornwallis and the Court of Directors acted to the best of their judgment and entertained a very honest belief that (*a*) the elimination of the element of uncertainty by the permanent fixing of the Government demand, (*b*) the mutual interests of the parties, and (*c*) the enforcement of the rules as to *pattas*, would together operate to assure and improve the condition of the raiyats.'

equal footing. Some were certainly originally proprietors, others only privileged helpmates (I will not call them tenants) of these proprietors ; others equally clearly only casual cultivators, but who, from lapse of time or other circumstances, had even then great claims to consideration. 'Uncertain,' in the next place, because rights get irretrievably abandoned, changed, and lost, in the lapse of years, and the confusion caused by two centuries of doubtful government ; and at best it is 'uncertain,' whether the original right, whatever it was, had not been, in a great many cases, thoroughly and really lost.

[1] A task which indispensably necessitated a *survey* and a *Settlement* staff to discover and *record* rights. How impossible such a work seemed in 1789 I have already remarked. The power of doing it was not discovered till 1822, when a new epoch of land administration commenced.

§ 10. *Result of the Regulation Law.*

It will now be amply clear that there was neither law nor custom by which even the old resident cultivators of a village, and still less other tenants, could expect to go on from decade to decade without any increase in their revenue (now become rent) payment. It was also in the nature of things that tenants on waste land and tenants offering themselves and willing to compete for available holdings, should hold at variable rates of rent fixed by contract and mutual understanding; and, finally, the Regulations prescribed nothing as to any principle of rent enhancement, because the information on which different classes of tenants and their privileges could be distinguished and formulated, was wholly wanting.

'The necessary and natural result,' says Dr. Field,—

> 'was that for all things for which the legislature did not make provision, the new course of things under British rule created a practice and an usage which adjusted and regulated those relations with which Government did not concern itself to interfere; and a common law (i. e. unwritten usage and practice) came into existence which was largely compounded of the ideas of the ruling race, to which practical operation was given by a strong executive and by means of the Courts of Justice.'

SECTION III.—PROGRESS OF THE TENANT-LAW FROM 1793 TO 1859.

§ 1. *The 'Patta' Rules.*

The first disappointment experienced was the failure of the attempt to enforce the issue of written leases for all tenancies, to which I have alluded[1]. Some tenants, who regarded themselves as really or originally proprietors of their holdings, refused (and very naturally) to take a lease for fear of its being an admission of a *lower status* on their part, implying that their right and title was derived from

[1] See p. 629 *ante*.

the grantor of the *patta*, that it was terminable (the *patta* could not be granted for more than ten years), and that the rent-rate was liable to alteration. Many of the tenants also, feared the *pattas* as means of extortion, and refused to take them [1]. The earlier Regulations supposed that if *pattas* were required, the *parties would agree as to the rates*, and yet nothing was said as to what was to happen when *pattas* existing (or those first granted) expired. Regulation IV of 1794 attempted further legislation. Disputes as to rates were to be settled in the Civil Court, with reference to 'rates established in the *pargana* for lands of the same description and quality.' This applied both to existing tenancies and to new ones; the 'pargana rate' was not to be exceeded [2]. The facts about the pargana rates have already been stated (see §§ 4, 5, p. 620). It was provided also that, if people did not take *pattas*, the landlord might post up at his office a list of rates, and offer *pattas* at those rates, and that then he might recover by suit or distraint at such rates. 'Thus,' says Dr. Field, 'the Zamíndárs were enabled to claim any rates they pleased, and to distrain for rent at those rates, and to put on the raiyats the *onus* of proving that the rates so claimed were not the "established" rates [3].'

These suits, moreover, became numerous, and so swamped the Courts, that the Zamíndárs in turn suffered, as they could not get decrees for rent really due.

§ 2. '*Haftam.*'

The next step taken, therefore, was to facilitate the recovery of rents by *improving the law of distraint*. Re-

[1] They feared that they would be bound to pay for the whole land specified, even if crops failed, or cattle died.

[2] Field, p. 563. The rate might easily be raised by getting tenants to take some private land of the Zamíndár's at high rates, which were then appealed to as examples by which to raise the average rates of the whole neighbourhood (*Land Tenure by a Civilian*).

[3] In 1811 the Collector of Ráj-sháhí reported that the Regulations had then been in force eighteen years, and that as to *pattas* and their counterparts (*qabúliyats*) 'these are as few now as ever.' He attributed this to the fact that the rights of raiyats had never been defined, and that those who claimed a certain *status* refused pattas for fear of compromising their claim. The letter is given in detail by Field, pp. 565–66.

gulation VII of 1799, popularly known as 'Qánún haftam' (seventh Regulation)[1] recites that the revenue collections had suffered because the landlords could not readily get in their rents, particularly when the land was sub-rented and the crop not in the immediate possession of the *raiyat*[2]. The law empowered landholders and farmers to delegate the power of distraint to their collecting agents; distraint might be exercised without sending notice to any Court or public officer, and included crops and cattle and personal effects; tools of tradesmen were, indeed, exempt, but ploughs and seed-grain and plough cattle were only exempt if other property could be found; and as the distrainer was the judge of this, the exemption was a dead letter. No written demand was required before distraint, except in the case where the tenant had no written specification of the exact time when his instalment fell due. After the distraint was made, notice was to be given of sale; if the arrear was not at once paid, and if the tenant absconded or was *otherwise absent*, then a list of the property was sent to the nearest official who had power to hold a sale, and the law only required five clear days between notice and sale. The tenant must either pay or find security to institute a suit to test the rent and to pay whatever the Court decreed with interest.

It was stated that tenants sometimes delayed proceedings by making unfounded (criminal) complaints of misfeasance and abuses in attachment. Magistrates were to repress

[1] The 'haftam' was followed, in 1812, by 'panjam,' or Regulation fifth (of which presently): the peasantry of to-day attribute all their misfortunes to 'panjam' and 'haftam'.

[2] See *Fifth Report*, i. pp. 76, 77. In Feb. 1802 the Collector of Midnapore reported that 'complaints were very general among the Zamíndárs . . . they had not the same powers over their tenants which Government exercised over them. It was notorious that many of them had large arrears of rent due to them which they were utterly unable to recover; while Government was selling their lands for arrears of assessment . . . Farmers and intermediate tenants were till lately able to withhold their rents with impunity, and to set the authority of their landlords at defiance. Landholders had no direct control over them: they could not proceed against them, except through the Courts of Justice, and the ends of substantial justice were defeated by delays and costs of suit.'

these and fine the complainant if his case appeared vexatious; and other provisions were added. Practically this meant that no one, unfamiliar with new Courts and new procedure, would venture to bring a complaint, for fear of his powerful adversary making out that it was a vexatious one.

There were other provisions regarding the arrest of persons intending to abscond, and authorizing the seizure of tenures and farms in arrears, the landlord managing them direct, and ultimately putting up the title to sale if the management failed to realize the arrear. When default occurred in the case of a lease-holder or tenant 'having a right of occupancy, only so long as a certain rent . . . was paid without any right of property or transferable possession' the landlord was to have the right of evicting the defaulter. No application to a Court was needed, but farmers, proprietors, &c., were responsible for any act exceeding their powers. The Regulation stated that it was not intended to limit or define rights of any class, but to point out in what manner defaulting tenants might be made to pay, leaving them to recover their rights, if infringed, with full costs and damages, in the established Courts of Justice.

It was stated that 'in all other instances the Courts of Justice will determine the rights of every description of landholder and tenant . . . whether ascertainable from written engagements, defined by law, or dependent on custom.' Nothing in the Regulation took away the power of landlords to 'summon, and if necessary compel, the attendance of tenants for the adjustment of their rents, or any other just purpose.'

No doubt this law was passed in the *bonâ fide* belief that tenants were in fault, that the hands of the landlord needed strengthening, and that his power would be exercised fairly, and that the Courts would give relief if needed. But when it is recollected how impossible it was for the poor and ignorant to apply to distant Courts under a new and strange procedure, which took an immense time—always a serious difficulty to people who want to be in their fields;—when it was further recollected that such a law could not fail to be abused, it is difficult to read its monstrous provisions without indignation.

That this law produced the most evil results goes almost without saying[1].

§ 3. *Proposals for Relief.*

In 1811, the evils produced were remarked on by the Board of Commissioners at home, and in India the Government issued a circular of inquiry, which still shows a spirit of belief that complaints were exaggerated, and that if rents were not collected regularly, there would be a heavy accumulation of arrears of Government revenue. Among the opinions elicited, Mr. H. Colebrooke's was among the most valuable. Other officers followed suit. Having clearly pointed out that the remedy of appeal to the Courts was, in the case of poor people, quite inefficient—'many of the rules designed for the protection of the *raiyats* having been perverted into engines for their destruction,—it was urged that definition of rights should be undertaken, and that if people had no rights they should be told so.

The abolition of the local native offices of kánúngo and patwárí during the first years, was appealed to as facilitating the destruction of rights; but this may be doubted. The village accountant is of no use if the whole system of village organization has perished. And the district accountant can be of no use under a system where there is no public control of the details of revenue collection, but where the landlords pay their lump sums into the Collector's treasury direct. Both officers naturally became mere servants of the Zamíndár, and therefore they had been abolished. This step was taken because it was found that the formal records which they still prepared were useless; in some cases these were altogether neglected; in

[1] Those desirous of some details may read the quotation from Official Reports in Field, p. 584, *et seq.*

others they were falsely framed to suit the purposes of the Zamíndárs.

Among the points discussed by Mr. Colebrooke were the restriction of *pattas* to ten years, prescribing the form, and invalidating all that, though definite, were not in due form; the invalidating *en bloc* all existing leases and tenures on a sale of an estate for arrears; above all, he exposed the fallacy which lay at the root of the reference so often made to 'established pargana rates' (see p. 621).

Mr. Colebrooke proposed that where 'pargana rates' were not available, definite protection should be given to the resident (khudkásht) raiyats: 'This will silently substitute a new and definite rule in place of ancient but uncertain usages.' He proposed that in individual cases of renewed *pattas* or new *pattas* in place of an old one voided by a sale, the rate should be that which was actually paid for similar land in the vicinity; and that where there had been a wholesale cancelling of the *pattas* of a village or estate consequent on a sale, new rates should not exceed the highest rate actually paid in the three preceding years. And in the case of *taluqdárs*, after calculating the raiyats' *jama'* on these principles, the tenure-holder was to be definitely allowed 10 per cent. on the total, plus a reasonable allowance for cost of collection.

I only state the proposals generally and in outline, for the purpose of indicating the historical *birth of the modern tenant law*, which substitutes defined rules practically securing certain advantages, for pretended references to ancient standards impossible of access.

§ 4. '*Panjam.*'

The main proposals of Mr. Colebrooke were adopted in 'Qánún Panjam,' or Regulation V of 1812.

The ten-years' restriction as to leases was removed, and *any form* of lease was allowed as long as it was definite, but this was not to be construed to sanction 'cesses' and exactions in any guise. It limits the avoidance of existing leases on sale of the estate for arrears ; it declares the uncertainty of 'pargana rates,' and substitutes rules similar to those above stated for adjusting rents on renewal of pattas. Enhancement was to be preceded by a formal notice, without which no enhanced rent would be recoverable. The law of distraint was softened, and implements of husbandry, plough cattle, &c., were absolutely exempted.

The Regulation still made no provision for defining rights by record, and thus only dealt with a part of the evil ; it would, however, have been a relief were it not for the fact that it was unfortunately neutralized by other Regulations [1].

§ 5. *Farming Estates.*

It was during this period that the creation of farming tenures, which I have fully explained under the name of 'Patní,' came to notice, and it was found desirable to recognize them. (See p. 543 *ante.*) Their advantages I have already pointed out. On the other hand, they may tend to oppression. The manager or leaseholder often re-transferred portions of the estate to sub-lessees, and such a person had no other interest but to amass the largest profit to himself, regardless whether, on going out, he left behind him an estate sucked dry and tenants verging on misery. In 1843, the system was described as 'striking its roots all over the country, and grinding down the poorer classes to a bare subsistence.'

It should, however, be remembered that it is in the Central and North-West Bengal that those 'patnís' were most common. In East Bengal generally, the tenants have rather the upper hand of the Zamíndárs than the reverse.

[1] It is not necessary to go into this in detail. At p. 654 of Dr. Field's book will be found a footnote which will explain how it came about.

§ 6. *Alteration of Sale Laws as affecting Tenants.*

The next series of enactments that affected tenants were the modifications in the sale laws, and especially what was provided about the *clear title* which the purchaser would get, that is, a title free of encumbrances created by the defaulter or his predecessors being representatives of the original engager. It was, of course, impossible equitably to avoid *all* encumbrances, and Regulation XI of 1822 made certain exemptions; among them it protected 'khud-kásht-qadími raiyats or resident and hereditary cultivators having a prescriptive right-of-occupancy [1],' and the purchaser was not to demand a higher rate of rent from such a tenant than was receivable by the predecessor, unless in specified cases where a rent lower than was justly demandable had been fixed by him. 'This gave rise,' says Dr. Field, 'to a doctrine that *khudkásht* raiyats who had their origin subsequent to the Settlement (1789) *were* liable to eviction, though, if not evicted, they could only be called on to pay rents determined according to the law and usage of the country; and also that the possession of all *raiyats* whose title commenced subsequent to the Settlement, was simply a permissive one, that is, retained with consent of the landlord. The establishment of this principle left the Zamíndárs free to enhance the rents of all but a small class of *raiyats* up to any point that competition could run them; because, though the provisions of the Sale Regulations applied only to estates which had been sold for arrears, yet the principle being established, it was soon extended by the power of the Zamíndárs, to other estates also. Quite apart from this power, the raising of rents in one place tended to create a higher 'prevailing rate' which could by law be imposed on the tenants of any estate independently of there being a revenue sale. Moreover, those tenants well knew that if they resisted, the *Zamíndár* would accomplish his

[1] Construed to mean resident raiyats who had been in possession for more than twelve years before the decennial Settlement. (*Bengal Law Reports*, Supplementary Vol., p. 215.)

purpose by allowing the estate to fall into arrears and be sold, purchasing it himself (free of the old leases) in the name of a relation or dependent[1].

This law remained in force till 1841, when Act XII provided that a sale should void all tenancies and tenures created since the Settlement, and leave all tenants to be *enhanced at discretion* after notice given, except certain specified cases, which were certainly made more definite than before. Some changes, not affecting the rent question, were made by Act I of 1845; and this law remained in force till 1859, when the Tenant Act X of 1859 was passed, and the Sale Law (XI of 1859) also (five days after Act X)[2]. The great feature of the modern sale law, as it affects tenures, is, that it, for the first time, hit upon a proper device for protecting them, by registration. Entry in a General Register protects them against auction-purchasers, and entry in a Special Register protects even against the Government.

We shall recur to the Sale Laws in the following chapter on Revenue Business.

[1] These 'banámi' transactions as they are called, are a favourite device all over India for concealing the property really belonging to one person by making it appear to belong to another.

The term is '*ba*-nám,' *in* the name of (another),' not, as incorrectly written, *be*-nám, which would mean (*be*) *without* a name.

[2] The connection of the sale law with the tenant's rights was important when sales were frequent. The whole body of the tenants was alarmed, because there was no means of making the defaulter hand over his papers to the purchaser. The latter came in as a stranger, not knowing one tenant from another, nor the protected classes from the unprotected.

'Affrays and litigations cannot but ensue. There must always, in every case, be years of enmity between the new landlord and his tenantry. There being no record of the *protected*, he assumes that none are protected, while the tenants set up groundless claims to protection, often-times supported by the late Zamíndár . . . I can imagine no condition more pitiable than that of the inhabitants of a *Zamíndári* transferred by sale for arrears.

. . . We can talk and write with indifference of it (*re-adjustment of rent*), but to the tenants on an estate, a sale was as the spring of a wild beast into a fold, or the bursting of a shell in a square.' (*Sir H. Ricketts*, 1850.)

SECTION IV.—MODERN TENANT LAW.

§ 1. *Act X of* 1859.

This Act came at a time when the evils of the existing state of things were so patent, that, in giving his assent to the Act as passed by the Legislative Council on 29th April, 1859, Lord Canning was able to say, 'no objection is suggested to the nature of the Settlement which tho Bill contemplates.' In fact, almost the only serious discussion which arose was on the provision which *made over rent cases to revenue officers sitting as Courts* (with only a reference, by way of appeal, to the Civil Court in certain cases).

I will borrow Dr. Field's excellent analysis[1] of the Act under nine heads, and make a few remarks on each. These will not be out of place, because there are still a few districts where the Act is in force (as I will presently explain), and in any case the student will hardly understand the effect of the law of 1885 without some idea of what the reforms effected by the first 'modern' tenant law, if I may so call it, actually were.

The Act exhibited these main features :—

I. The abolition of the landlord's power to compel attendance of *raiyats* at their offices.

II. The definition of a few classes of 'tenants' whose rent was *fixed* (not then classifying or attempting any distinction between heritable and transferable *tenures* and *tenancies*).

III. A right of occupancy for tenants (with exception of those on the landlord's home farm—sír, nij-jot, and khámár land—who held on lease from year to year; and excepting also sub-tenants). This right was acquired *by continuous holding* (personally, or by the predecessor from whom the holding

[1] The whole chapter on Act X in Dr. Field's book may well be read by students desiring to go a little more into detail (p. 743 *et seq.*).

descended) *of the same land for twelve years.* It was conditional, of course, on duly paying the rent (which was enhanceable, but only on the conditions prescribed in the Act).

IV. Making provision for settling rent-disputes and questions of abatement and enhancement.

V. A renewed attempt to bring about an interchange of pattas (leases) and qabúliyats (counterparts).

VI. An attempt to compel *receipts* for rent and to prevent exaction of excess rent.

VII. *Distraint* was modified but not abolished.

VIII. Transfer of original jurisdiction in suits between landlord and tenant from the Civil to the Revenue Courts (limited *appeal* to the principal Civil Court of the district).

XI. Registration of transfers of permanent transferable interests intermediate between the cultivator and the landlord.

§ 2. *Remarks on these Heads.—Special classes of Tenants.*

I. The first head calls for no remark; its natural result was that duress and coercion were prevented, to an extent dependent on the raiyats' knowledge of the law, and the perfection of the *subdivisional* system, whereby local courts and the protective action of the 'Sub-Deputy Collector and Magistrate' were brought nearer to the people's doors.

II. The tenures called '*muqarrarí*' and '*istimrárí*,' which were always permanent, and, in the former case had the benefit of a fixed rent, had been acknowledged, as we have seen, from the days of the Regulation VIII of 1793; a rather uncertain protection had also been given by Regulations V of 1812, and XI of 1822, to the old resident cultivators called qadímí-khudkásht. The Act of 1859 extended this by allowing *every dependent taluqdár or other person possessing a permanent, transferable,* interest in land[1] who held at a fixed rent, which had not been changed since the Permanent Settlement, to be exempt from enhancement. Even raiyats (who had not a permanent, transferable interest) whose rents had not been changed since 1793 were also exempt, being entitled *to pattas at those rates.*

And as it was often difficult to carry evidence so far back, the privileged classes were aided by a *presumption of law* that if the rent had not been changed for twenty years before suit, it had been unchanged since the Settlement. The landlord might rebut by showing that a change *had* taken place, or that the tenure or raiyat's holding had been created, and therefore the rent fixed, at some time subsequent to the Settlement.

Dr. Field remarks that the only class who would have had any difficulty in producing the rebutting proof (if any existed), supposing they had kept proper accounts, would be the auction-purchasers, a class not entitled to much sympathy.

Head III. The occupancy-right after twelve years, was a sort of cutting the Gordian knot of a complicated question. It was quite certain that all the old village cultivators at the time of Settlement were—if in the lapse of ages they had lost actual proprietary rights—certainly entitled to be considered 'ex-proprietors' in some sense. Yet it was not *all* of these that could get the protection mentioned under Head II; and even if they could, there were many tenants of less pretensions who were still, in the belief and feeling of the people, entitled to occupancy-rights. In the sixty years that had elapsed since Settlement, a number of such rights had grown up, and tenancies had been held from father to son; so that a general rule of the kind was more likely to be just in the long run than any attempt to distinguish or classify[2]. I have stated the exceptions

[1] Dr. Field thinks this left it uncertain whether the 'jót,' 'hawála,' 'gánthí,' and similar tenures I have described were protected; in *popular estimation* they were certainly permanent, heritable, and transferable, but perhaps this could not be legally proved (p. 755).

[2] The draft *Bill* limited the rule to *resident* raiyats, but this was not adopted in the Act as passed. If *some* tenants got, under this clause,

which were intended to protect the landlord's home-farm, and give him the full benefit of that.

It was further enacted that a decree of Court must, in all cases, be the means of ejectment; and that decree could only be passed on the ground of non-payment of *rent*. It is obvious, however, that a protection from *ejectment* is not sufficient of itself; for if *enhancement* is not also regulated, the landlord might demand such a rent that the tenant could not pay it, and so be evicted on that ground. It was, therefore, necessary to add two more provisions: (1) that the landlord *could not enhance without order of the Revenue Court*, and (2) that the Court should only enhance on certain principles.

§ 3. *Enhancement; and other Rent-rules.*

Head IV.—The principles of enhancement were:—

(*a*) The Court started with the presumption that the existing rent was fair and equitable till the landlord showed the contrary.

(*b*) The 'contrary' was shown when it appeared that the rent paid was below the prevailing rate payable by the same class of raiyat for land of a similar description and with similar advantages in the places adjacent;

(*c*) that the value of the produce or the productive powers of the land had been increased otherwise than by the agency (or at the expense) of the raiyat;

(*d*) that the quantity of land held by the *raiyat* proved on measurement to be greater than that for which rent had been previously paid.

I may dismiss (*d*) without remark, as it is not *really an enhancement* at all.

(*b*) is also a question of enhancement only as regards the

rather more than an absolutely accurate criterion of right would have allowed, it was no more than a compensation for years of suffering. The landlords had had *their* innings for sixty years, and if the tenantry now got a little more than was due, it would be hard to complain of it.

individual; it makes one man pay as much as his fellows: it does not *raise the rent* payable by the class generally.

(*c*) This is the important ground: but it proved very difficult of application. The Great Rent Case of 1865 [1], in which all the fifteen Judges of the High Court gave judgments reviewing the whole history of rent since the Permanent Settlement, was an endeavour to settle it; but while the decision of the majority gave a rule, it was one which it was difficult, if not impossible, to apply in practice.

The enhanced rent was to be calculated so as to bear to the old rent the same proportion that the proved increase of value in produce did to the old value. Or in a *formula* thus:—

$$\left\{\begin{array}{l}\text{Former gross}\\ \text{value of pro-}\\ \text{duce (average}\\ \text{of 3–5 normal}\\ \text{years).}\end{array}\right\} : \left\{\begin{array}{l}\text{Present gross}\\ \text{value of pro-}\\ \text{duce (average}\\ \text{of 3–5 normal}\\ \text{years).}\end{array}\right\} :: \left\{\begin{array}{c}\text{Former}\\ \text{rate}\end{array}\right\} : \left\{\begin{array}{c}\text{Enhanced}\\ \text{rate.}\end{array}\right\}$$

The first three terms had to be proved, but the difficulty of proving *when* the rent was previously fixed, so as to give the *date* at which the 'former' value was to be taken for comparison with 'present' value, was very great. 'The most experienced officers,' says Dr. Field, 'have pronounced the rule to be unworkable, and the Zamíndárs have confirmed the verdict by giving up all attempt to work it in their own interest.'

We must also notice that Act X gives some general rules for *all* tenants. No tenant can be made to pay a higher rent than the rent payable for the previous year, unless a written notice has been served on him before the close of the agricultural year, specifying the higher rent claimed and the reason of the enhancement; and the tenant can contest this, either by suit or in answer to a suit for arrears. This applies to tenants not holding under any agreement, or under an agreement indefinite as to period,

[1] Thakuráni Dási *vs.* Bisheshur Mukharjí—*Bengal Law Rep.*, Supp. Vol. (Full Bench) 202. See also another case—Hills *vs.* Ishar Ghos. *Weekly Rep.* (special volume).

or under one which has expired or become void by sale of the estate for arrears of revenue.

§ 4. *Pattas and Receipts.*

Heads V and VI require no remark. It is now recognized that, what with decrees of Court and improved means of record, it is immaterial whether *pattas* are given or not.

§ 5. *Law of Distraint.*

Head VII.—Distraint is to be made only against *cultivators* (i. e. not against farmers, patnídárs, &c.), and only for the rent of one year; no distraint is allowed for any sum in excess of the rent payable for the same land in the preceding year, unless a written engagement for the payment of such excess had been executed by the cultivator.

Before distraint, a written notice specifying the demand, and the grounds on which it was made, is required. After distraint, application must be made to the proper officer for *sale* within five days. If the distraint was made while the crop was standing, the cultivator may reap and gather it.

It is stated that these provisions, good as they seem on paper, were not useful in practice.

§ 6. *Revenue Courts.*

Head VIII.—The transfer of jurisdiction in 1859 was cancelled ten years later; but that Act (B. C. VIII. of 1869) did not apply to all districts[1]; so that where it or the subsequent Act of 1885 does not apply, Act X of 1859 still retains the Revenue Courts. The reason for giving revenue officers power in these matters, is that the experience of Civil Courts is not always such as enables them to understand revenue practice, and that the settlement of rents depends on facts and circumstances not 'easily reducible to

[1] See § 9, *post*.

the usual forms of evidence.' Officers daily dealing with land-management, and knowing the local details in many cases, acquire a sense of fitness and a practical power of adjusting rents which are invaluable, but cannot always be adequately explained in a formal judgment.

§ 7. *Transfer of Tenures.*

Head IX.—The provisions for registering transfers of farms, taluqs, and tenures intermediate between the cultivator or the landlord, were thought necessary, and have been retained on a somewhat different basis even in the later law of 1885 (as we shall presently see). But they are said not to work, owing to a fear (which is legally groundless) that registry of a transfer would imply the landlord's admission of its validity. On the other hand, the rules were supposed to check secret transfers and transactions whereby one man held in the name of the other, and thus created difficulties in cases where the real owner of the tenure was required to be known; and it was believed that they prevented litigation.

§ 8. *Some objections to the Act.*

Act X of 1859 was not a complete Code of Tenant law, and yet contained no provision that it was not intended to touch any customary right not inconsistent with, or expressly or impliedly disallowed or modified by it. It also failed to recognize, as distinct from raiyats' holdings, tenures which, if not easily definable, were, nevertheless, in the popular estimation, permanent, heritable, and transferable.

The landlords also objected to the working of the enhancement clauses, which failed where they considered they had a good claim [1].

[1] 'The principal faults of Act X of 1859 have been said to be that it placed the right of occupancy which it recognized in the tenant, and the right of enhancement, which it recognized in the landlord, on a precarious footing. It gave, or professed to give, the *raiyat* a right which he could not prove, and the landlord one which he could not enforce.' (*Introduction to R. and F. Tenant Act.*) Minor amendments have been made in Act X, and appear incorporated in the Legislative Department edition in the 'Lower Provinces Code.'

§ 9. *Bengal Act VIII of* 1869.

This Act of the Bengal Council was merely a new edition of Act X of 1859, with certain amendments of detail (not of principle as regards tenants' rights). The details need not occupy our attention here; they relate to matters of limitation of suits, to powers of measurement of estates, and so forth. The important change was the re-transfer of landlord and tenant cases to the Civil Courts.

The Act only applied to districts to which it was expressly extended, and these were the permanently-settled, and what I may call 'regular' districts, in the Bhagulpore, Patna, Rájsháhí, Bardwán, Presidency, Dacca, and Chittagong Civil Divisions; and the law did not apply to Jalpáígúrí, Darjíling, the Orissa districts, the Chutiyá Nágpur districts, and the Santál Pergunnahs. It is therefore a local question whether Act X of 1859 (and its amending Acts) still remains in force: it does if declared in force, and if neither Bengal Act VIII of 1869 nor Act VIII of 1885 has superseded it. Act VIII of 1885 is in force in all the Bengal and Bihár districts, not being Scheduled Districts, and is not in force in Orissa.

§ 10. *Local operation of the several Acts.*

Full details on this subject will be found in the notes to Section 1 (3) of Act VIII of 1885. The following table is generally correct:—

Regulation Districts in the Divisions of—		
	Bhagulpur	Act VIII of 1885.
	Patna	
	Rájsháhí	
	Bardwán	
	Presidency	
	(Dacca) Dákha	
	Chittagong	
Orissa	Katák [1]	Act X of 1859 and amending Acts.
	Bálásor	
	Purí	

[1] Bánki, formerly a scheduled tract, has now (Act XXV of 1881) become part of Katák. Angul in Orissa is a scheduled tract, and Act X has not been applied to it.

Chutiyá Nágpur	Hazaribágh ...... Lohardaggá......... Singhbhúm.........	Bengal Act II of 1869 and also I of 1879.
Mánbhúm		Act X of 1859 and Bengal Act II of 1869.
Santál Pergunnahs		Regulation III of 1872 and Rent Rgulation II of 1886.
Chittagong Hill Tracts		See Act XXII of 1860.
Jalpáigúrí	(a) South of district, once part of the old Rámgarh District.	Act X of 1859, &c.
	(b) Western Dwárs.	See Act XVI of 1869.
Darjíling		Act X of 1859, &c.

The Act of 1885 may be extended to any of the Scheduled Districts (by Section 3, Act XIV of 1874), and may be extended to Orissa (by the Act itself, Section 1 (3)).

§ 11. *The origin of Act VIII of* 1885.

As no one is likely to enter on a detailed study of the present law applicable to the larger and most important part of Bengal and Bihár, without Rampini and Finucane's edition in their hand, it will be my part only to call attention to the salient points.

In 1876 a bill for a serious alteration as regards definition of rights was commenced with, but only led to the appointment of a *Rent Law Commission* (in 1879) to inquire into the whole subject, aided by a Committee of experienced officials, indigo-planters, and landlords, to consider the special difficulties of Bihár. A complete draft law was prepared by their means in 1880; but the Government could not accept the draft in its entirety. Several other drafts were then made under various authority, and the present law was introduced into the Legislative Council of India in 1883, and received assent on 14th March, 1885. It was declared to come into force on 1st November, 1885 [1], except certain portions, the operation of which was by law (Act XX of 1885) deferred to 1st February, 1886.

[1] Notification, *Calcutta Gazette*, 4th September, 1885.

§ 12. *Analysis of the Law of* 1885.

In this Act (as amended by Act VIII of 1886) the following classes are recognized :—

(1) Tenure-holders and under-tenure-holders (e.g. the patnídár and darpatnídár) ;

(2) Raiyats { Raiyats at fixed rates ; Occupancy-raiyats ; Settled-raiyats ; Non-occupancy-raiyats.

(3) Under-raiyats (or sub-tenants).

This, it will be observed, obviates the objection to the old Act, as regards reducing holders of *tenures* to being merely a kind of *tenant*.

Any non-proprietary holding exceeding 100 bíghás, is presumed to be a 'tenure' till the contrary is shown.

The tenure-holder, who has paid a fixed rent from 1793,
Sec. 6. is, as before, protected from enhancement, except on proof that local custom, or the terms of the tenure, warrant an increase, or that the tenure-holder, by receiving reduction of his rent (not being on account of loss of area) has subjected himself to the payment of the increase demanded, and that the lands are capable of affording it[1]. And in this (rare) case of enhancement, the limit is (subject to any contract between the parties) such customary rate as other tenure-holders in the vicinity are paying; if such a rate does not exist, then the limit is what the Court thinks fair and equitable. And in drawing conclusions the Court will never leave the tenure-holder with a less profit than 10 per cent. on the gross collections of rent, and will have regard to the conditions under which the tenure arose, whether it paid a fine to begin with, or was for reclamation, and what
Sec. 7. improvements have been made. The rent once enhanced cannot again be raised for fifteen years.

[1] This resulted from an old standing custom that if a taluqdár accepted remission or reduction at one time, he must accept increase at another. It is explained in § 384 of Shore's Minute, printed in the *Fifth Report*, vol. i. p. 162.

The tenure-holder cannot be ejected, except on breach of some express condition, not inconsistent with the Act. A tenure is heritable and may be bequeathed, and is transferable by registered instrument, or by course of law.

Sections 12 to 15 are the ones altered by Act VIII of 1886 and represent the amended form of the 'Registry' rules for securing that it be known who was the actual tenure-holder, repressing 'banámi' holdings (see note, p. 640), and preventing litigation—noted under Head IX of Act X of 1859.

§ 13. *Raiyats.*

The first class of *raiyat* may hold either at a fixed rent or a fixed *rate* of rent; the distinction is obvious. He is subject to the same provisions as to succession and transfer as a tenure-holder, and he cannot be ejected except on breach of a condition (consistent with the Act), whereby he Sec. 18.
becomes, by contract, liable to ejectment. The second class (occupancy-raiyats) includes, generally, all who, immediately before November 1885, had the right of occupancy, by the operation of any law, by custom, or otherwise; so that all existing rights are saved.

Not only so, but any tenant (before or after the Act) who has held for twelve years continuously *any* land in the village, whether under a lease or not, becomes a 'settled-raiyat.' It need not be the same plot of land (as under Act X), so that a landlord cannot evade occupancy by shifting the site of the cultivation within the same village.

The holding may have been by means of the person whose heir the present holder is.

A person is a 'settled-raiyat' as long as he holds any land as a raiyat in the village, and for one year thereafter: and even if the tenant *abandon*, but return in time, under section 87 he does not lose his right. The raiyat starts with the presumption in his favour that he has hold for twelve years; it is, of course, much easier for the landlord to show Sec. 20 (7).
how long he really has been there, if he is not a twelve-years' tenant.

Section 21 should be read with Section 178, and the notes; these will explain the object, which is generally, to prevent an ignorant tenant *contracting himself out of the benefit of occupancy*; and especially doing so between March 1883 and the passing of the Act, when the whole matter was in Council, and sharp landlords might have brought pressure to bear on tenants to make such contracts.

Section 22 makes provision in cases of *merger* of rights by transfer, succession, &c.

The occupancy-tenant has to pay rent 'at fair and equitable rates.' He cannot be ejected except by Court decree, on the ground that he has used his land in a manner which renders it unfit for the purpose of the tenancy, or has broken a condition (consistent with the Act) on breach of which he is by contract liable to ejectment [1].

An occupancy-right (subject to any custom to the contrary) descends by inheritance; but in default of heirs it dies out (i.e. does not lapse to the Crown).

It will be observed that the law is *intentionally* silent as to whether occupancy-rights are *transferable* by bequest, sale, gift, mortgage, &c., or not. The matter is regulated by *custom*, which is saved by Section 183. (See illustration 1 to the section [2].)

The 'private lands' of proprietors are (as before) protected from the growth of occupancy-rights, only that the subject is specially dealt with in chapter xi of the Act, which provides clearly for determining what *are* private lands.

Thus, it will be seen that comparing Heads II and III of the abstract Act of 1859 (p. 642) a very considerable advance has been made in the law.

[1] And even then section 155 must be read, as it affords a remedy against absolute ejectment.

[2] The law on the whole subject of transferability is given at pages 70–2, F. and R. *Tenancy Act*.

§ 14. *Enhancement.*

It will here also be interesting to look back to p. 644, Head IV (Enhancement). Here we found the law of 1859 was somewhat impracticable. It was one of the main objects of the law of 1885 to effect an improvement. As far as the *landlords* are concerned, the new rules for deciding an enhancement suit are certainly made easier and more practical; while the *tenant* has been protected by not being allowed, in his ignorance, to bind himself to submit to an unreasonable enhancement, so that 'a raiyat cannot now contract himself out of almost any of the rights conferred upon him by the Act[1].'

The initial presumption (as under the former Act) is, that the existing rent of an occupancy-tenant is 'fair and equitable'; the landlord must prove that it ought to be enhanced.

A money rent *cannot be enhanced except as provided by the Act.*

A produce rent cannot be enhanced at all, and very naturally so, for it is a question of sharing the produce, and this really enhances itself by the rise in value of the share which naturally occurs.

Section 40, however, gives either the landlord or occupancy-tenant power to apply for a commutation of a grain-rent into a cash-rent.

The specific provisions of the Act stand thus:—

I. Enhancement by Contract.

The conditions are that—

(*a*) Contract is to be written *and registered*; Sec. 29.

(*b*) The rise agreed on must not exceed 2 *annas in the rupee*;

(*c*) The rent fixed is not to be liable to further enhancement for fifteen years.

[1] F. and R. *Tenancy Act*, Introduction, p. xiii.

There are, however, provisoes added, which should be referred to; for instance, (*b*) will not apply where a higher rate is contracted for on the express ground that the landlord has made, or will make, an improvement to which the raiyat is not otherwise entitled. The provisoes explain themselves, except, perhaps, the first, which refers to the case where a tenant, though entitled to ignore the contract, because not in writing or not registered, has actually paid a certain rate of rent for three consecutive years (which he might have refused if he had chosen).

II. Enhancement by Suit in Court.

The grounds on which a decree can be made are:—

Sec. 30. (*a*) That the rate is below what other occupancy-tenants pay, in the absence of special circumstances;

(*b*) Rise in *average local price of staple food-crops* during currency of present rent;

(*c*) Increase in productive powers of the land—

(1) By landlord's improvement;

(2) Fluvial action (which includes a change in the course of the river rendering irrigation possible).

These three grounds are nearly but not quite, the same as the older law, and are such as are usually entered in modern Tenancy Acts[1].

In order that these principles of enhancement may be applied properly, the Act goes on to explain their use.

Secs. 31, 32, 33, and 34. As to (*a*) the rates generally paid during the previous three or more years are to be looked to; and enhancement will not be decreed unless there is a substantial difference between the rate so discovered, and that which the *raiyat* is paying. A 'local inquiry' may be ordered with a view of discovering the prevailing rate.

The caste of the cultivator will only be taken into consideration when it is proved that the local custom requires it.

[1] The student will find it instructive to turn to the similar sections in Act XII of 1881 (N.-W. Provinces), section 13, Act XXII of 1886 (Oudh), section 33, and compare them with section 17, Act X of 1859, and this section 30.

As to (*b*), the average prices for the ten years immediately preceding the suit are compared with the average prices 'during such other decennial period as it may appear equitable and practicable to take for comparison.' Then the rule of enhancement, stated in the form of a proportion sum, so that the student may compare it with the old rule (cf. p. 645, *ante*) will be—

Value of produce in selected 10-years period.	:	Value in 10-years period immediately before suit.	::	Former rent.	:	Enhanced rent.

Provided that the excess of the second term over the first term is to be reduced by *one-third* in order to give the enhanced rate; and if a ten-year period is not practicable a shorter period may be used.

As to (*c*). The landlord's improvements must have been *registered*. The registration (in a book kept for the purpose) will obviate any dispute as to whether an improvement has been made or not. And, naturally, as 'improvements' vary, the increase of rent will depend on the amount of increase in the productive power of the soil which is likely to result; the cheapness and costliness of the improvement; the question whether the improvement will require a costly style of cultivation to benefit from it; and lastly, it is important to consider whether the rent is not already so high that the land, even as improved, cannot well bear a higher rate.

As all these matters are, to some extent, matters of expectation and probability, any decree made is liable to reconsideration, 'in the event of the improvement not producing, or ceasing to produce, the estimated effect.' For the case of 'fluvial action,' Section 34 may be referred to.

Sections 35 and 36 contain the important general provisoes that in no case is an enhancement to be decreed 'which is, under the circumstances of the case, unfair or inequitable'; and that if a sudden enhancement would press hardly, the increase may be gradual, i.e. by rises extending over not more than five years till the full rate is reached.

Section 37 is also by way of general proviso, since an enhancement on the ground of 'prevailing rate' or of 'rise in prices' (*a*, *b*) will not be allowed, if, *within the fifteen years* next before the suit, there has been—

(1) A contract for enhancement dated after March 2nd, 1883;

(2) A decree for commutation of grain-rent to cash (Section 40);

(3) A decree for enhancement (or a decree of dismissal of suit on the merits) on the same grounds, 'or grounds corresponding thereto.'

It should be added that to facilitate, in future, these
Sec. 39. inquiries about the value of produce, the law prescribes the maintenance of *price lists* by the Collector.

§ 15. *Reduction of Rent.—Commutation.*

As rent can be enhanced, so there are occasions when a reduction may be called for and justly enforced by law if
Sec. 38. refused voluntarily. And it has already been mentioned that grain-rents (still so common in Bihár, p. 602, *ante*) *can*
Sec. 40. *be commuted* to cash, on demand of either landlord or tenant.

Grain-rents are both natural and useful in certain cases and in the early stages of society. If, for instance, in outlying and precarious tracts crops are liable to loss by flood or drought, or locusts or wild beasts, the tenant who has to give only a fraction of the grain—*actually produced and garnered*, receives a practical reduction in bad years; the calamity of season and uncertainty fall on both parties equally. But in other places, where this ground does not exist, other objections come to light—fraud and concealment on one side, over-estimate and extortion on the other, and the loss to the tenant of a rise in value. As the country becomes more settled, and cultivation reaches its limits, the tendency is always to give up grain-rents.

§ 16. *Non-occupancy Tenants.*

The ordinary *raiyat* is not, and ought not to be, in any country in India, left entirely to 'competition.' All tenant laws admit the principle that *some* protection he requires.

If a tenant accepts land for the first time, he must naturally accept the terms offered[1]; if he does not like them, let him give up his attempt to get the land, in favour of some one who does; and if the landlord finds that no one will accept his terms, naturally he will come down.

But once the tenant has accepted, he cannot be subject to extortion. Further enhancement must be by *registered* agreement[2] or by means of what the Act calls an agreement under Section 46, of which presently.

Ejectment has, also, to be regulated. It is obvious that it is of no use regulating *enhancement* without regulating ejectment, and *vice versâ*.

Section 89 has here to be read, because it applies to *all* tenants. There is no ejectment, except by *decree* of Court; Section 44 gives plainly the grounds on which an ordinary raiyat can be decreed against[3].

Section 46 requires some remark. Supposing the tenant refuses to accept a landlord's demand for enhancement and so becomes liable to a suit for ejectment; the landlord must, as a preliminary measure, put into Court a proposed agreement which will be served on the tenant in a specified way. If the tenant fails to accept this, a suit for ejectment will be lodged. When such a suit is lodged, the Court will declare what is a fair and equitable rent and give the tenant the option of paying that,—which will *not be subject to any further enhancement for five years*.

[1] See, however, Section 47. A man must be *bonâ fide* a new-comer, not a man really already on the land, whom the Zamíndár proposes to treat as a new-comer.

[2] Unless, as in a previous section, the tenant has *de facto* waived this, by paying for three years the enhanced rate which he might have refused.

[3] The ordinary *raiyat* is ejected for arrears. The tenure-holder and occupancy-raiyat of both classes is not; his tenure is put up to sale (Section 65).

If the tenant will not have this, of course a decree for ejectment will issue. Under-raiyats are protected by Sections 48 and 49, which need no comment.

§ 17. *General Provisions as to Rents.*

It will be observed that the whole question of *pattas* has been allowed to drop. Receipts for rent are retained, and various provisions are made.

The general principles of rent need only be read (Chapter VIII) to be understood.

The old principle about rents not changed since Settlement is retained, and with it the twenty years' prescription already explained.

An alteration in *area* of a tenancy may always involve an alteration of rent without infringement of the privileges already noticed.

Rent is always payable, subject to agreement or established usage, in four (quarterly) instalments.

Sections 56–60 go into details about receipts for rent, and counterparts, which will, perhaps, not prove very effective, or be easily enforced.

§ 18. *Arrears of Rent.*

Sections 65 to 68 should be read on the subject of arrears; interest is allowed by law, and damages in some cases of wilful non-payment; but not both. Any decree for ejectment on the ground of arrears (amount to be specified) can be avoided, if the tenant, within fifteen days, pays the amount with costs.

The landlord cannot harass a tenant by successive suits for arrears; having got his decree, he cannot sue again for
Sec. 147. three months. The restrictions on execution of decrees for rent have been removed to a great extent by reason of the application of the Civil Procedure Code subject to certain modifications. A decree for arrears of rent must be executed by the landlord himself or a transferee of the

landlord's interest in the land, not by any chance assignee of the decree; on the other hand, there is no restriction as to the order in which certain property must be proceeded against, &c., other than what the Civil Procedure Code prescribes.

The tenant's holding is treated as hypothecated for the rent due, and no transfer is valid while any arrears of rent which have accrued are unpaid[1].

§ 19. *Produce Rents.*

The Sections 69 to 71 provide for various matters likely to be in dispute, e.g. appointing an officer to make an appraisement of the standing crops, and to make a division (see p. 602 *ante*), and defining the right of possession of the crop and the grain at the threshing-floor.

§ 20. *Improvements.*

Chapter IX deals with a number of additional matters between landlord and tenant, which will give relief. The whole question of improvements is dealt with, defining what an *improvement* is, settling that occupancy and fixed-rate raiyats can always make improvements of all kinds, but that non-occupancy tenants can only make improvements of certain kinds, and giving a convenient power of reference to the Collector, whose decision is final. There is special provision for registering improvements and recording evidence as to their being made, intended to save future disputes.

There are, of course, provisions for *compensation* for improvements on ejectment. Also, when ejectment takes place, there is a protection in respect of growing crops and Sec. 156.
land prepared for sowing. As the number of tenants fixed in their holdings is now great, a reasonable facility is given

[1] In these remarks, I have gone out of the order of the Act in order to complete the subject; the procedure sections about execution of decrees, &c., come later on in the Act.

to landlords to apply to the Civil Courts for an order to retake a plot of ground wanted for religious, charitable, or educational buildings, on fair terms.

§ 21. *Miscellaneous Provisions.*

Section 85 regulates the raiyat's power of sub-letting, and Section 90 the landlord's power of measurement. Section 93, *et seq.*, call for some remark, as these provisions will probably smooth over many cases of dispute, where there are co-sharers on an estate, and they are at feud as to the management; this harasses tenants greatly, and a 'common manager' can now be appointed.

§ 22. *Distraint.*

Passing over some intermediate chapters, it will be observed that Chapter XII regulates the power of distraint. It can now only be done through the Civil Court; and notwithstanding the attachment, the tenant can reap, gather, or store the produce, and do everything necessary to its preservation.

§ 23. *Record-of-Rights.*

I left out of its place Chapter X, which is really the most important feature of the Act, and if I may venture a prophecy, will be gradually acted on, till the only complete satisfaction for all classes of rights is gained, viz. a cadastral survey and record-of-rights for every estate, large and small, in the province.

Under circumstances stated in Section 101, a survey and a record-of-rights can be ordered for a local area *in any case* with the sanction of the Governor-General in Council, and in certain specified cases without such sanction.

And among such cases I may mention that the procedure applies to all estates under the Court of Wards and all khás maháls or estates which are or have become the property of Government.

Where this Act is in force, Act VIII of 1879 is repealed; and as Government, in its own estates, as landlord, is subject to the same liabilities to tenant-occupancy and other rights as other landlords, it desires to have those rights defined and protected and its own management facilitated, provision is made for a record-of-rights and a *settlement of rents*. (See page 459).

In any area in which this survey and record-of-rights is ordered, the ordinary Courts are precluded from entertaining any suit for alteration of rent or the determination of the *status* of any tenant.

§ 24. *Jurisdiction.*

The law of 1885 retains the jurisdiction of Civil Courts over suits between landlord and tenant, except in the case of a survey and record above mentioned. The High Court is empowered to make rules, declaring that any portions of the Civil Procedure Code do not apply, or apply with modifications: and, as already stated, the Act itself, in Chapter XIII, makes certain special provisions as regards procedure.

§ 25. *Sale of Tenures for Arrears.*

The sale law has (as we have seen), from time to time, dealt with the 'clear-title' to be given when an estate is put up to sale for arrears of the Government revenue; and as tenures, and certain raiyatí holdings, can be sold for arrears of rent, in executing a decree, there are similar questions as to voiding the subordinate contracts or rights. These are dealt with in Chapter XIV. Briefly, all such subordinate rights are classed into (1) 'protected interests' and (2) 'incumbrances'; the former are not voidable, the latter are, but only in certain cases.

CHAPTER V.

THE REVENUE OFFICERS OF BENGAL.

§ 1. *Introductory.*

THE system of public administration by means of District Officers throughout the Provinces, may be said to have been derived from Bengal. There the system originated; there it was modified from time to time by way of experiment, and ultimately issued from the crucible of a very severe testing, in its modern form. It is natural to expect that the system, ultimately perfected in BENGAL, has, to a large extent, been the model on which district government has been developed in all the other provinces.

It will be desirable therefore to examine the administrative machinery of Bengal and to follow the steps by which it has attained its present form, somewhat more in detail than we shall need to do in the case of other provinces.

§ 2. *General Outlines of Provincial Administration.*

I have stated (p. 389), as a general fact, that the main outlines of the administrative system are everywhere the same. Immediately under the Local Government or Administration, with its Revenue Secretaries, i.e. Secretaries who take charge of the correspondence relating to revenue matters, we shall generally find, first, a central controlling revenue authority over the whole province[1], whether under the name of a 'Board of Revenue' or of one or more 'Financial Commissioners.'

[1] Bombay is an exception, as presently noted.

The whole of the province is divided out into a number of DISTRICTS, and these are generally, but not always, formed into groups of three to five as DIVISIONS under Commissioners, who form a supervising and controlling agency, intermediate between the chief authority and the District Officer [1].

The DISTRICT is presided over by a COLLECTOR, who is also the District Magistrate. His general official title is 'Magistrate and Collector,' while in provinces or parts of provinces where formerly what was called the Non-Regulation system prevailed, the District head is styled 'Deputy Commissioner [2].'

The local sub-division of districts, though always carried out, is not so uniform, and will be spoken of later.

The Department of 'Land Records and Agriculture' has now become an integral and important factor in the revenue administration (Bk. I, Chap. V, p. 349); the 'Director,' who may or may not have the charge of Settlements, as 'Commissioner of Settlements,' assists the district officers by systematizing, directing, and constantly inspecting, the preparation of local maps and land records and statistics. These not only concern the Settlement work of districts where that is subject to periodical revision, but intimately concern the revenue administration, as the means of keeping the Collector informed of the progress and state of all estates, with reference to their management, to advances for agricultural improvements, and to the remission or suspension of land-revenue which calamities of season may call for.

Now we must return to the special system of Bengal.

[1] In Madras no 'Division' intervenes between the District and the Board of Revenue. But the districts are large and are subdivided. *To some extent*, therefore, the officer of a sub-division may be regarded as the real district officer, and the Collector rather as a sort of Commissioner over him. Again, the Board now consists of an aggregate of 'Commissioners,' in charge of different branches of work; and the reader may, if he pleases, look on the Board as in fact a body of Commissioners, only aggregated in one central office.

[2] The title is still maintained. Formerly, the Deputy-Commissioner had Civil Court powers: moreover, the latter was always a covenanted civilian (by statute); the former might be, and still often is, an Uncovenanted or a Military officer.

§ 3. *The Board of Revenue.*

It has already been indicated more than once, that on first assuming the government of 'Bengal, Bihár and Orissa,' no attempt was made to interfere with the native method of revenue management. In 1769, as we shall see, an attempt at supervision, excellent in theory but impossible in practice, was made. In 1770, two 'Revenue Councils,' sitting at Patna and Murshidábád, were established, and soon after, 'District Collectors' were tried. A Board of Revenue was appointed at Calcutta, to supervise the revenue generally; it consisted of the Governor and Members of Council, with an Accountant-General. After the Regulating Act of 1773, a new experiment was made; the Collectors were withdrawn from districts and aggregated into six 'Provincial Councils[1].'

These were supervised by the Calcutta Board remodelled as a 'Committee of Revenue.'

In 1781, it was found, as might be expected, that district control was indispensable, so the six Councils were dissolved, and Collectors remanded to the districts. The Controlling Committee at Calcutta, up to this time, consisted only of members of the Government. But this was found inconvenient, as the members, in their other capacities, had more than enough to occupy their time. The Committee gradually became a separate body of Civil Servants, but in 1786 the President was still a member of the Government[2].

Reg. II of 1793. The Regulations of 1793 recognized this 'Board of Revenue' and conferred powers—

[1] Sitting at Calcutta, Bardwán, Murshidábád, Dacca, Dinájpur, and Patná.

[2] 'It is therefore full time,' wrote the Court of Directors, 'to adopt a settled plan, and for that purpose we direct that there be a "Board of Revenue" to reside in Calcutta, to consist of one of the junior Members of Council, and four others of the most intelligent of the senior servants of the Company.'

For the information regarding the official staff, I am indebted to a very good historical sketch prefixed to the *Report of the Salaries Commission* (Calcutta, 1886), to the *Report of the Salaries Commission* (Ministerial Officers), 1868, and to *Papers relating to Village and Indigenous Agency Employed in the Census of* 1872 (Calcutta, 1873).

(1) To summon any officer to the Presidency to explain and justify his conduct, to impose a fine not exceeding a month's salary, and to suspend him from office [1].

No further alteration was made till 1807, and then only to provide supervision for other acquisitions of territory. By Regulation X of 1807 a 'Board of Commissioners' was appointed for the 'Upper Provinces,' and in 1817 a Board for Benares and Bihár, including two districts of Bengal. (This was rescinded by Regulation I of 1819.)

By Regulation III of 1822 (still in force) provision was made for the better division of labour; three Boards of Revenue were constituted—one for the 'Lower Provinces,' one for 'Central Bengal,' and one for the 'Western Provinces.'

In 1829 a final change was made. The previous history of the Boards marks the difficulty which was increasingly felt as the revenue system developed, cultivation extended, and work increased. The Boards were directly responsible for too much detail and too much judicial work. The idea therefore soon gained acceptance, that it would be better to arrange for the direct supervision of manageable groups of districts by Revenue Commissioners, and restrict the scope of the Board's duties to a general and ultimate control at head-quarters.

The Board of Revenue at Calcutta (at first called the Sudder (Sadr) Revenue Board) remained for Bengal, and the Board for the Upper Provinces became the Board which now sits under the Lieutenant-Governor of the North-West Provinces; the third Board (Central Bengal) was abolished. Bengal was then apportioned into eleven Divisions [2].

The functions of the Central Board at Calcutta being thus restricted to the superior control, it was possible to unite with it what had been, since 1819, a separate Board for Trade, Customs, Opium, &c. This was effected by Act XLIV of 1850, and the title 'Sudder Board' was dropped.

[1] These provisions were never rescinded till Act XII of 1873 declared them repealed as obsolete.

[2] And the North-Western Provinces into nine.

The 'Board of Revenue for the Lower Provinces' is henceforth the official designation. Regulation III of 1822 (still in force) enables the Government to empower any Member of the Board to exercise all or any of the powers of the whole Board[1]; this Regulation also states the general powers of control possessed by the Board, though, of course, other Regulations and Acts have to be referred to in order to trace the entire scope of legal provisions giving powers.

The Board of Revenue now consists of two members with two Secretaries[2]. It exercises general powers of control and sanction, and regulates, by the issue of Standing Orders and Circulars, the procedure and conduct of official business in all revenue departments whenever these matters are not directly provided for by Acts of the Legislature, or rules having the force of law made pursuant to such Acts. Some idea of the extent and variety of the duties and powers of the Board of Revenue, in supervising officials, reviewing decisions and orders, sanctioning Settlements, controlling sales for arrears of revenue, controlling the Land Registers, Irrigation, Embankments, Customs, Salt, Opium, Excise, the Court of Wards, Stamps, and many other matters, may be gained by a glance at the columns under the head of the 'Board of Revenue, Bengal,' in the 'General Index to Enactments relating to India,' or to the volumes of Standing Orders.

§ 4. *Commissioners.*

As already indicated, the appointment of Commissioners of Divisions, with general powers of supervision and control, but subject to the Board of Revenue, dates from 1829 (Regulation I of that year). The territorial extent of the Commissioner's charge was then wisely determined to be such, that the presiding officer might 'be easy of access to the people' and be able 'frequently to visit the different

[1] An order has recently been issued (1889) empowering each Member to exercise the whole power of the Board, one in matters of Revenue, the other for Miscellaneous Revenue, Opium, Stamps, Excise, &c.

[2] By the 24 & 25 Vict., cap. 54, the members and Secretaries are to be Civil Servants.

parts of their respective jurisdictions.' At first the Commissioners had Civil Court powers and were Criminal Judges of Circuit. They were, however, relieved of Civil Court duties by Act III of 1835[1]; and afterwards were relieved of criminal duties by the appointment of separate Sessions Judges under the Code of Criminal Procedure.

In other provinces, it may be mentioned, the union of civil and criminal powers in the Commissioner's office lasted much longer, and has not yet altogether ceased in some provinces. In the Panjáb it lasted till the Courts Act of 1st November, 1884. In the Central Provinces it still exists, and so in some other places.

Even in provinces where the ordinary civil and criminal (appellate and original) jurisdiction of Commissioners has ceased, the Commissioners have some judicial or *quasi*-judicial duties, inasmuch as under the Tenancy and Revenue Laws, a number of matters are excluded from the cognizance of Civil Courts, and are disposed of by Revenue Officers, and by such officers sitting as Revenue Courts, and the appeal lies to the Commissioners.

In Bengal, rent cases and appeals are heard by the Civil Courts[2], but there are still important revenue matters in which an appeal of a *quasi*-judicial nature lies from the Collector's order to the Commissioner.

Commissioners also retain a general control in police matters. The minor changes in the law between 1837 and 1861, which have occurred, do not directly concern us here.

The wide scope of the duty of a Commissioner of Division in Bengal is well summed up in the *Salaries Commission Report* (1885–86), and as this gives an excellent general idea of what the Commissioner's duty is everywhere, it may be quoted *in extenso*:—

[3] 'Nearly every one of the numerous duties of the District Officer is exercised by him subject to the supervision of the Commissioner of Revenue and Circuit, and even in those

[1] *Salary Commission Report*, chapter II. § 9.
[2] Except in Orissa, Chutiyá Nagpúr, and the Santál Parganas.
[3] § 18 of the *Report*, 1886.

branches of public business which do not, ordinarily, come under his immediate observation, he is at any time liable to be called on by Government to interfere or to give an opinion. His work, like that of the Magistrate-Collector, may be divided into administrative and judicial—the former is far more onerous than the latter. A Commissioner's administrative work is very difficult to define, and there is hardly anything, except perhaps taking command of a fleet, or performing a surgical operation, that he may not be called upon, at one time or another, to undertake. He has to inspect the offices of all the Collectors under him once a year, and the Sub-divisional Officers, as far as he can, and to see not only that work is properly performed, but that the people in all parts of the division are treated with due consideration, and all that affects their interest is carefully watched and reported by District and Sub-divisional Officers as well as by the Police. He has to collect information from his District Officers concerning a vast variety of matters, and present it in a suitable shape to Government. He receives constant applications from the Collectors for sanction to the disbursement of money, and the performance of official acts, and to these he replies in some cases by giving sanction himself; in others by referring the question to higher authority. He is also referred to for instructions on all sorts of questions by his subordinates, and these references, if he is an active man, not afraid of responsibility, he answers himself; if he is not such a man, he merely sends them on to Government, or to the Board for orders. He has to write carefully considered opinions on legislative measures while passing through the Council, and a large number of annual reports and occasional reports on a number of subjects. . . . His *judicial* work consists in hearing appeals in Settlement, partition, certificate sale, wards' and Government estates, and under several other revenue laws: as well as appeals from ministerial and police officers regarding dismissal or other punishment. Lately, also, the Local Self-Government Act has added considerably to his work; and some Commissioners have also a large amount of political and civil work. Thus, the Commissioner of Orissa is also Superintendent of the Tributary States, a duty which entails on him a large amount of civil and criminal work, besides that of supervision, advice, and guidance to the Rájás of the several estates.

'The Commissioner of Chutiyá Nágpur has similar work, but

on a smaller scale. The Commissioner of Bhágalpur has civil and criminal jurisdiction in the Santál Parganas, and the Commissioner of Chittagong in the Hill Tracts of his Division.'

There are now in Bengal nine Divisions over groups of districts:—

1. Bardwán,	over 6	districts.
2. Presidency,	,, 6	,,
3. Rájsháhí,	,, 7	,,
4. Dacca (Dháká),	,, 4	,,
5. Chittagong,	,, 4	,,
6. Patna,	,, 5	,,
7. Bhágalpur,	,, 3	,,
8. Orissa,	,, 3	districts (besides political charge of the Tributary States).
9. Chutiyá Nágpur,	,, 4	districts.

§ 5. *Collectors.*

In speaking of the Board of Revenue, mention was made that, as early as 1769, 'supervisors' were appointed, with a view to collecting information of all kinds, and to keeping a check on the work of the Muhammadan district officers [1].

They did not continue long: in May, 1772, they were styled Collectors; and in 1773 they were withdrawn, as already stated, and the districts left to native officers—'Díwán' and ''Ámil.'

After the various attempts at revenue administration by means of local and central committees, District Collectors were again appointed in 1786. The main changes in the office since that time have been with reference to the union of Magisterial and Civil Court powers with Revenue duties. At first (in 1787) it was considered desirable that the 'people accustomed to despotic authority should look to one master.' But in the course of time, and after several changes enacted by law, the Civil Court powers were

[1] See p. 392. The letter describing their duties is given in Field, p. 463. The best account of Supervisors I have seen is in Hunter's *Annals of Rural Bengal*, pp. 262 65.

withdrawn and Criminal powers alone remained in union with the Revenue powers. It was in 1831 that the Regulations gave rise to the modern office of 'Magistrate and Collector.' But in 1837 the double function was for a time divided, owing to the pressure of Revenue work. The separation was gradually carried out, and up to 1845, Collector after Collector was relieved of Magisterial duty. It was only in 1859 [1] that the Magisterial and Revenue functions were again, finally, united.

Though the possession of Magisterial authority in the district is deemed essential for the Collector's position, it is not to be supposed that time would suffice for the chief officers to take a large share in the disposal of the daily work of the Criminal Courts. Various expedients were resorted to, such as the creation of 'Joint-Magistrates' (Act XV of 1843), with which a Revenue Manual is not concerned.

The division of Criminal and Revenue labour has been much facilitated by the modern system of sub-dividing districts and giving local officers charge.

At the present time all grades of Magistrates, whether District Magistrates, or Assistants, or Joint-Magistrates, or Uncovenanted Deputy Magistrates, derive their Magisterial powers from the Code of Criminal Procedure. And under that Code there may be Honorary and other Magistrates who have no official position as Revenue Officers.

The Revenue duties of the Collector, with which alone we are here concerned, were originally enumerated in Regulation II of 1793. His duties have increased in many directions. The land-revenue, which in the days of the decennial Settlement is quoted as 285 lakhs, had risen in 1888–89 to over 380 lakhs [2]. The Collector has to look after the collection of this LAND-REVENUE, involving the sale for arrears in the case of the 'Zamíndárí' estates, and the certificate procedure, as it is called, under the 'Public

[1] Despatch of Secretary of State, No. 15, dated 14th April, 1859.

[2] The list of districts and the number of permanently-settled and other estates can be seen in the table at pp. 470–1. See also p. 442.

Demands Recovery Act' (B. Act VII of 1880) in others. He has also the collection of the local or provincial rates, which consist of the Public Works cess (B. Act IX of 1880 [1]), a cess levied for roads and provincial public works; and the Postal cess (B. Act VIII of 1862) which provides for local official postage. Besides this, there is the whole subject of the EXCISE revenue under his care (this revenue in 1884–85 exceeded 10 lakhs). To this must be added the supervision of the LICENSE-Tax and INCOME-Tax, and the STAMP Revenue. Besides the collection of these revenues, there are all the connected duties which the land-revenue system entails, viz. the registration of titles to land; issue and recovery of loans for agricultural improvements; embankments (on the maintenance of which agriculture in many parts depends); irrigation (in some districts); the opening of separate accounts, for sharers and others in estates paying one sum of revenue; management of patwárís in Bihár; various applications under the Tenancy Law (Act VIII of 1885); the management of estates of minors under the Court of Wards, and of attached estates (for recovery of debts due by the owners).

Besides all these matters, there are various miscellaneous duties connected with supply of provisions for troops on the march; the occasional acquisition of land for public purposes; Municipalities and Local Boards; Ferries; Pounds; Emigration; Primary Education, and others; to say nothing of his responsibility as Magistrate for the Police and Criminal administration of the district. The District Officer is designed to be the central authority, the 'Hákim,' *par excellence*, of his district. Sir George Campbell wrote in 1871–72 (*Administration Report*, Part I, p. 66):—

'It is the Lieutenant-Governor's wish to render the heads of districts (the Magistrate-Collectors) no longer the drudges of many departments and masters of none, but in fact the general controlling authority over all departments in each district. . . . Departments are excellent servants, but, as he considers, very

[1] With amending Acts, e. g. II of 1881, and VII of 1881.

bad masters. He has, therefore, striven to make the Magistrate-Collector of a great Bengal district, generally comprising one-and-a-half to two-and-a-half millions of inhabitants, the real executive chief and Administrator of the tract of country committed to him, and supreme over everyone and everything, except the proceedings of the Courts of Justice.'

§ 6. *Collector's Office.*

The Collector has under him both an 'English Office,' i. e. clerks and accountants for the correspondence and accounts kept up in English for communication with other offices and departments, and a 'Vernacular Office,' of which, however, the members mostly know English, and make use of it to some extent.

In *Bengal*, the Vernacular Office has long been divided into departments, the sarishtadár, the treasurer (khazánchí), the record-keeper, and the 'taujíh-navís'; these are all assisted by native readers and clerks (*Munshí* and *Muharir*).

The 'Sarishtadár' (as his name imports) keeps the 'files' that are pending, and is, in fact, responsible for the supervision of the whole vernacular office and for the care of different records, petitions, and papers, that are undergoing inquiry and are awaiting orders.

The Native treasurer is under the Deputy or Assistant Collector who is in charge of the district treasury, and his duties require no notice here.

The Record-keeper takes care of the records. There is, always, one department for English correspondence, and another for files of vernacular 'cases.' He arranges and classifies the records, keeps the general registers prescribed by the Land Registration Act in Bengal, and makes reports regarding mutations of proprietors, and other matters which the registers show, and he supervises the issue of authenticated copies of papers.

The taujíh-navís maintains the revenue-roll and prepares the returns showing the state of the collections, what payments of land-revenue fall due, what are in arrears, and so forth.

There is also the district Názir or 'Sheriff' and his Náib or Deputy. This person acts as the guardian of property attached, and sees to the issue of processes and notices. Besides which he is the general sort of 'housekeeper' to the District Officer, looking after the furniture, 'pankhas,' the district tents, and so forth.

Some such distribution of business as this—varying of course in details, and in the local titles of the officials—will be found in every Collector's head-quarters office in India.

§ 7. *The Collector's Assistants.*

From an early date there were, besides the Collectors, officers called Assistant-Collectors, but they had no legal powers. By Regulation IV of 1821, the Collectors were first formally empowered to delegate to their (Covenanted) Assistants any part of their duties to which they could not themselves give due attention. By Regulation IX of 1833 the appointment of Uncovenanted Officers with the title of 'Deputy Collectors' was legalized.

These provisions resulted (in connection with different laws giving magisterial powers) in the official titles of 'the Magistrate and Collector,' 'Joint Magistrate and Deputy Collector,' 'Assistant Magistrate and Collector,' 'Deputy Collector and Deputy Magistrate (Uncovenanted).'

In 1872, Executive Revenue Officers called 'Sub-Deputy Collectors' were appointed for the purpose of giving local or special aid for particular places or departments of duty. The Sub-Deputy Collector is appointed by executive authority, and can be invested with such powers of a Deputy Collector under various Acts and Regulations as may be necessary. Even Kánúngos (of whom hereafter) are now reckoned on the staff of the revenue-agency, as, where they are employed, they can be utilized in various ways, supervising partitions of estates, making assessments in connection with the levy of cesses or rates, and so forth.

In order to facilitate the district management and turn to best account the powers of the various grades of officers, the plan of sub-dividing the district and giving the charge of the sub-division to one of the district officers in subordination to the District Officer, was long ago thought of. In 1845 thirty-four sub-divisions were made, but as the system developed, the number rose to its present figure of ninety.

Attention should be directed to this feature of the Bengal district, because it marks an important difference between that province and the other provinces, where the Native Government had not introduced the system of revenue collection by Zamíndárs. In all other provinces, speaking generally, the districts are divided up into small local revenue divisions, known variously as the 'tahsíl,' the pargana, or the taluka; and when this is the case, there is a native or other officer in charge (called by various titles—tahsíldár, mámlatdár, &c.), with his writers and revenue-accountants and treasurers. There are often, under this officer, other subordinates, to aid in the general work of the tahsíl, or taluka, and help in the supervision of the village officials; and finally for each village or group of villages [1], a system of headmen and village-accountants. Thus there is a complete revenue hierarchy, from the District Collector at the top to the village officer at the bottom. In provinces where this system exists, in more or less completeness, there may be primary sub-divisions of districts in case the district is large, and there is some important town with its connected territory, at which it is desirable to relieve the Collector by posting an Assistant or Deputy.

In Bengal, the revenue history has already shown us how the Zamíndárí system gradually swept away [2] all but the memory of local limits of parganas, destroying the agency of 'Ámils or Tahsíldárs, with their Kánúngos and the village Patwárís or accountants. Deprived then, of

[1] Village *patwárís* generally look after groups of villages or 'circles.'

[2] I am, of course, speaking generally. Patwárís in villages (for instance) survived in the Bihár districts, and other features of old revenue days in other places.

what I may call the natural sub-division of revenue-work which facilitates administration in other parts, and there being no field-registers and maps of each village, revenue-management would be now impossible, were it not for the Sub-divisions in charge of Sub-Deputy Collectors subordinate to the Collectors. It may be asked why the need of sub-division of labour has arisen and why such an increase of official work has taken place? The Salaries Commission remarks in answer :—

'This increase in the superior executive staff, is accounted for by the gradual development and perfecting of our Administrative system, the chief feature of which has been a cautious and gradual advance. New laws have been and are being constantly enacted to provide for the growing requirements of the people, to remedy abuses, and to regulate procedure. New measures, undreamt of a hundred years ago, have been introduced as experience showed the necessity for them, and matters once considered of so little importance as to be left to be disposed of by Collectors according to their own ideas, have been made the subject of intricate legal provisions and fenced about with safeguards and restrictions of all kinds. Large as the present executive body may seem when contrasted with that of the early years of the present century, there is little doubt that it is even now barely strong enough for all the work it has to do.'

At this point, then, our account of the Revenue Officers of Bengal ceases to be a guide to what exists in other provinces, and we must therefore devote a brief special study to the local pargana and village agency as it exists in Bengal.

§ 8. *Village Officers in Bengal.*

After looking through all the evidence collected in 1872. I see no reason to think that the villages of Bengal were different from those which were found wherever the Aryan conquests extended, or where kingdoms, which, if not Hindu had adopted the Hindu constitution, existed. I do not include in this remark the districts of Chutiyá Nágpur or the Santál Pergunnahs, the villages of which I have elsewhere described.

In Chittagong and other places, where the colonization of the waste has been of comparatively recent or modern origin, there are also special features. It is impossible to carry on cultivation in jungle country in India without co-operation; and that implies a grouping of cultivators, a headman—or headmen of the different castes or sections associated, and some artisans and helpers. I am aware of no form of Indian cultivating settlement of which this is not true.

In Chittagong, for instance, with its local institutions—the 'tarf' and the associated 'taluqdárs,' we find that there are headmen of local groups known as 'Mátabar' (corruption of the Arabic mu'tabir = respectable or trusted man), though they are not officially recognized.

In the ordinary districts in Bihár as well as Bengal, the old constitution is so far traceable, that the 'headman' survives with the almost universal name of 'Mandal.' He is still hereditary as a rule; but the elective element is not wanting; and the villages would reject an incompetent heir, and elect a more promising one. In some cases the term 'pradhán' is used, but in more than one district I find it doubted whether this does not really indicate a *parvenu* headman, not of the old organization, but one who has gained the position by official interference, and by his own wealth and influence. In villages where, from the earliest days, we can find no trace of any idea of proprietorship except in the lot occupied by the family for clearing and cultivation, we are probably in presence of the 'raiyatwárí type' of village, which was discussed in Book I, Chap. IV. And this is a form of land-holding which lends itself to change; for there is a tendency for persons of various kinds to assume the landlord position, the old holders of land becoming his 'raiyats,' or under-proprietors, or something analogous. And thus it is we so often have traces of the effects of a Rájá's grant, and other forms of over-lordship, which, at a remote date, or perhaps at a comparatively modern one, introduced a change. A proprietary body, being the multiplication of a grantee's or of a chief's family, claims the village and divides it into sections, called 'pattí,' or 'muhalla,' and when we find that there are several 'mandals,' one at the head of each section, we may reasonably conclude that something of the kind has occurred. In fact, every member of the proprietary families calls himself, and is called, 'mandal' in Bengal, 'pátel' in Central India; though only one man is the official head, or two or more if there are sub-divisions of the village. These have a certain precedence on occasions—appear first on the *punyá* or first day of rent payment, and receive small offerings, and such like marks of superiority.

Directly the *village* system falls into abeyance, and the State officers no longer deal with the village-heads, for rent collection, but look to larger estate-holders as Zamíndárs, taluqdárs, and the like, the headman drops out of consideration;—but not altogether, for he is still useful, and in some places the estate-holder will assume to appoint him, or rather confirm or recognize his appointment. But the *village accountant* either disappears or becomes the mere servant of the landlord, keeping his accounts with his tenants, without any sense of *public* duty or responsibility, or dignity. The village watchman (gorait, budhwár, &c.) remains, and so the 'chaukidár' or guardian of roads, and other similar functionaries: and the artisans remain of course, still receiving certain grain-dues, or perhaps rewarded by a bit of 'chákarán' or rent-free service land, which the landlord does not, out of policy, resume.

That is, I believe, in brief, the true state of the case as regards the village headmen, and the village accountants in Bengal. In Bihár, the old institutions survived more perfectly, because there the villages seem to have been held by minor chiefs or even petty officers of the Rájá's army;—at any rate, the circumstances were such, that the landlords were small holders: the greater chiefs did not often develop into Zamíndárs; and therefore, even though the village gained a 'proprietor,' or several joint proprietors, the form of its constitution survived: moreover as villages paying grain-rents require the services of village officers more than those paying cash rents, the patwárís more generally remained.

§ 9. *The Kánúngo and the Patwárí.*

As the *village* system disappeared under the later plan of farming or contracting for the revenues, so the *pargana* system, of which the *kánúngo* was the representative, disappeared also. 'Qánún-go' means[1], the 'teller,' of the 'rule,' but it rather refers to the rule or standard of what was proper in assessment, and measurement, than to any general legal knowledge possessed by the pargana officer. In 1793 it was thought that the retention of the kánúngo would be a good check on the Zamíndár; and the latter was required to maintain *patwárís* in the villages, and they were, in turn, to render accounts to the kánúngo. But they did no such thing; the one idea of the Zamíndár had originally been—in the days of Mughal decline—to pay as little to the treasury as possible, and therefore to conceal what he really got out of the villages. Under British law, it is true, his payment was positively fixed, but still he felt that, perhaps, something would happen if it was known accidentally what was the real rent-total he got; hence he took care that any accounts he sent in were framed so as to suit his interests. Naturally enough, both kánúngos and patwárís were soon abolished, the latter being employed by Zamíndárs as their clerks.

But the growing evils which I have described in the last chapter gradually attracted attention; and in 1815 the Court of Directors conceived that the patwárís might be made Government servants; the scheme fell through, and

[1] The word ought always to be written with '*q*' to represent the true vernacular word, but Kánúngo with a '*k*' has become such a common revenue term, that I have generally retained the usual but incorrect spelling.

the patwárís, where they existed, remained as servants of the landlords. Then it was thought the *kánúngos* might be revived, so as to supervise the patwárís. Regulations were accordingly passed in 1817, 1818, and 1819. Regulation I of 1819 directed the re-establishment of kánúngos and defined the duties of patwárís. But these offices are part of certain machinery; they are calculated to work with the machinery as a whole; they cannot be detached and introduced into a totally different system. In 1827 it was found that the kánúngos had done nothing, and that the land-owners had been determined in their opposition. In Orissa alone (where the Settlements are temporary village Settlements) kánúngos and patwárís have survived.

'Efforts have, of late, been made,' says the author of the Report of 1883 on the Land-Revenue system,—

'to revivify patwárís. Throughout the province provision was made for their appointment, or for the performance of their duties in all Settlements, under instructions issued in 1872[1]. As a rule, in every estate of which the revenue was above R. 300, remuneration for a *patwári* formed a set-off against the assessment: and in a smaller estate, the Settlement-holder engaged himself to perform the duties required of a *patwári*. Except in Orissa and Bihár, however, no successful results sprang from the attempt. . . . The system was generally condemned by officers in *Bengal proper* as being vexatious and irritating to the landlords, useless for all practical purposes, wasteful of Government money, and opposed to the present customs and traditions of the land-owning classes. The Government, therefore, at the suggestion of the Board, directed that no further attempts should be made to revive the institution, and that allowances granted in the estates should be resumed.

[1] By Sir G. Campbell, whose official life had mostly been passed where village Settlements were in force, and where the patwári, being a natural feature of the system, was indispensable. The use of patwárís in Orissa and in Bihár illustrates this: in these districts there is more of 'village' management in the system; and just in proportion as that is the case, the utility of the village accountant becomes more manifest:—it may be but little, for even the Orissa patwárís' accounts are said to be quite untrustworthy.

'In Bihár (and in the Mungér district) steps were taken to give the system a more effective existence. The re-organization has been completed in Mungér, and has reached an advanced state in the Bihár Districts.'

The report from which this is quoted is dated 1883, and it is there stated that fresh legislation would be required: but I have not seen any proposal on the subject during the six years that have since elapsed[1].

The *Settlement Manual*, 1888, at p. 18, gives the rules for entertaining patwárís in Government estates, or estates held direct, or under farm. In temporarily-settled estates where Government is not proprietor, the Settlement naturally makes provision for the patwárís who will maintain the records. A patwárí is separately found for each estate, or group of estates, having a rental of R. 2000.

§ 10. *Chittagong Local Establishments.*

The Chittagong District has always been an exception; there being no Zamíndárs of large estates, but only small holdings in groups of very independent taluqdárs, almost like a raiyatwárí country, the kánúngo has always been useful, and the country is now divided into 'tahsíls,' with tahsíldárs under whom the kánúngos work very much as in Northern India.

[1] It was still undetermined in 1887 (see Board's *Annual Report*, Section 137). Regulations XII of 1817 and I of 1819 are still in force (nominally).

If I may venture an opinion, further legislation may give a certain legal status to the officers, but it will not infuse life into them. Patwárís require kánúngos, under orders of the Land Record Department, to inspect them: but the patwárí can do nothing unless he has accounts, maps, field-indexes, and records determined by authority to start with. That he has not in Bengal; herein lies the futility of all schemes for utilizing them.

CHAPTER VI.

LAND-REVENUE BUSINESS AND PROCEDURE.

SECTION I.—INTRODUCTORY.

I DO not propose to go into any *detail* on these subjects; the object of this chapter is merely to indicate how certain main heads of administration are provided for. For the Permanent Settlement, with its total absence of survey and record-of-rights, has left a necessity for a variety of special laws.

For example, there is the Registration of landed property. I do not here speak of the ordinary Registration law under which bonds, mortgages, and other documents, are either compulsorily or voluntarily registered, but to the maintenance of registers or lists of the various landed interests, which shall have public credit or authority. The preparation of such registers has also been brought about indirectly in various ways. There is the direct law, beginning with the old regulation for making five-yearly registers of Proprietary estates in the Collector's office. Then another record grew out of the necessity for imposing on all estates a cess for maintaining roads, and local public works, as will presently appear. A still further registration was brought about by the sale-law. We have already seen how early it was perceived to be necessary to give full value to the prior lien of the State on all land for its revenue-dues. This could not be effective if the land were so encumbered by the defaulting holder that at sale it would fetch nothing. So that in some form, or to some extent, it became a matter of necessity to record such encumbrances, and distinguish those subordinate interests, which, in common fairness, ought not to be avoided; such (for instance) as might not have been created by the landlord in full knowledge that his acts would be held subject to the prior claims of the State. After many changes which have been incidentally sketched in the preceding pages, the device was hit on of opening certain registers, and allowing that interests registered in the one or the other should have a certain protection in the event of the estate going to auction for arrears of revenue.

Another outcome of the special system is the 'Certificate Procedure' of Bengal. When an estate cannot, or will not, pay its revenue, it has always been the legal remedy to put it up for sale. But in Bengal, besides the Zamíndárí estates which are so dealt with, the Government has a number of estates, held by itself, or under its management, and has rents and other dues to get in where there is no *estate* to sell, and where some other less formal and (to the State) less troublesome method than a law-suit and the execution of a decree, had to be devised.

The special *Survey law* was another outcome of the state of things which has grown up out of the Permanent Settlement.

Again, the local circumstances of Bengal, and the action of rivers in some districts, have also necessitated a special law regarding *drainage*, by which important works can be carried out by local Commissioners under the supervision of Government. A similar law also deals with watercourses and *embankments*, or works both for retaining water in tanks or reservoirs, as well as keeping out water where, but for the embankment, it would flood the land and convert it into a marsh. Formerly, it would seem the native Governments entrusted the duty of maintaining public watercourses and embankments to the Zamíndárs as public officers, and allowed them to deduct from the revenue certain charges under the name of 'púl-bandí' and the like. At Settlement our Government determined to assess the revenue in one sum, on which no deductions were to be allowed. But the Zamíndárs still bound themselves to some extent, and in general terms, to maintain embankments[1]. All this was, however, very indefinite, and from time to time Regulations were passed to deal with the subject. The existing law is in Bengal Act II of 1882.

Besides these more special branches of Bengal Collectorate law, there are the usual subjects (relating to land) of partition of estates, acquisition of land for public purposes, management of estates by the Court of Wards (Act (B) IX of 1879 and amending Acts)[2].

I now proceed to notice specially, a few of the more important branches of business, confining myself to those directly connected with land-revenue.

SECTION II.—REGISTRATION OF LANDED PROPERTY.

§ 1. *Object and Practice of Land-Registration.*

It was the intention of the legislature from the first, that there should be at least one Register kept up, showing the extent and particulars of each estate separately assessed with revenue payable to Government. The object was to enable the Collectors to apportion the revenue in cases of partition, and to enable the Civil Courts to know when an estate changed hands, or happened to be transferred from one district to another. The registers were first directed to deal with the land as grouped by estates only[3], but after-

[1] But *construction* was to be undertaken by the State. One of the clauses of the Zamíndár's engagement used to be: 'the construction of "berí" (small embankments), the excavation of silt from "khál" (water-courses), the construction of "gangura" (larger embankments) in connection with the salt and sweet lands of the pargana, shall be made by the Government of the Hon'ble Company.' The whole history of the Regulations relating to embankments is given in a High Court judgment (I. L. R., 7, Calcutta, 505) quoted at length in H. A. D. Phillips' *Revenue and Collectorate Law*, p. 165.

[2] The New Guardian and Wards Act, VIII of 1890, which has simplified and consolidated the general law of minors, &c. (and repeals the old Act XL of 1858) does not touch the Bengal Act quoted in the text. (See Sec. 3 of the new Act.)

[3] And any estate might have lands belonging to it scattered over half the district or extending into other districts. Reg. XLVIII of

wards 'pargana registers,' dealing with the lands as they lay, and accounting for every plot in each pargana and its subdivisions, were ordered. The law on this subject was never very well carried out, and the Regulation was both cumbrous and incomplete. It is, however, unnecessary in this place to dwell on the history of the past; it is enough to turn to the present law (Bengal Act VII of 1876)[1].

The object of the registration is simply to know who is the person answerable, as in possession, for every plot of land in the district, whether revenue-paying or revenue-free. Every person in possession, whether as owner or manager of the land, or of any share in it, is bound, under heavy penalty, to register. Registration is optional in the case of mortgagees who have a lien but not possession of the soil.

The Act does not apply to certain special localities, e.g. the Western Dwárs, the Kolhán estate, and the political estates in the Singbhúm district. The possibility of overcoming the difficulties of the old system is largely owing to the land-survey, of which mention will presently be made. In the course of the survey, descriptive lists of the land were prepared (and the survey followed the local areas or villages, or was, in revenue language, *mauzawár*). Registers showing the *estates* as made up of lands in different villages, or of groups of villages locally compact (i. e. mahálwár registers), are easily prepared from those first mentioned, by simply abstracting them. In September, 1888, the Board noticed in a circular, that proposals for legislation to enforce the record of all changes subsequent to the initial registration, had been abandoned for the pre-

1793 was the first law: that directed an (English) alphabetical register, with a supplementary register of changes by sale, inheritance, &c., and every fifth year the registers were to be written out anew. The Regulation was amended by No. VIII of 1800; but up till 1876, practically, the registers were not properly kept, nor were any penalties enforced. Such registers as there were did not explain who the owners were, and furnished no information at all about under-tenures and raiyats.

[1] As amended by Act V of 1878. See also Chapter V of the *First Volume of the Rules of the Revenue Department* (edition of 1878), with additions prescribed in September, 1888, by Board's *Circular*.

sent. But 'various disqualifications are now imposed by law on those who neglect to register. Under Section 78 of Act VII (B.C.) of 1876, no one is bound to pay rent to an unregistered proprietor. A revenue officer making a Settlement of rents under the Tenancy Act (1885) may refuse to entertain an application for enhancement or settlement of fair rents from a proprietor who is not registered. It is only registered proprietors who are entitled to partition (batwára), or to open separate accounts with the Collector whether for revenue or cesses, to bring a *patní* to sale, to object to common or special registry (of this hereafter), and to claim surplus sale-proceeds on the estates of which they are proprietors being sold for arrears of revenue.' In order to facilitate registration, the Board supply, free of cost, *forms of application* which are to be had from stamp-vendors and others.

§ 2. *Form of Registration.*

The registers at present required by law are :—

(A), a register showing the revenue-paying lands in the district. This is divided into two parts, to show the lands which belong to estates the revenue of which is payable in the district, and lands within the district, which form portions of estates whose assessment is payable in other districts.

(B), a register of revenue-free lands. This is divided into three parts showing (1) perpetual revenue-free grants; (2) lands held by Government or companies for public purposes free of revenue; and (3) unassessed waste land and other lands not included in part 1 or 2.

(C) is a register of lands paying revenue and those held revenue-free, arranged 'mauzawár,' i.e. the register is a list of the villages in each local sub-division (adopted for the purpose by order of the Board) and accounting for all the lands in each village, showing to what estate each belong, which are revenue-free, and so on.

(D) is an 'intermediate' register for all kinds of land,

showing the changes in proprietary rights resulting from sale, succession, lapse, or other transfer, and changes caused by the alteration of district and other boundaries.

The registers are only re-written when the changes have become so numerous as to affect the original register very considerably and make it no longer of any use for reference. The Act makes it obligatory on persons interested to give information with a view to the preparation of the registers. It should be borne in mind that registration only describes the person in possession. It decides no question of right. Section 89 of the Act expressly states that any one may sue for possession or for a declaration of right, the Act notwithstanding.

§ 3. '*Dákhil-khárij*.'—*Subsequent Changes.*

The proceedings for reporting and registering changes in proprietorship are spoken of as 'dákhil-khárij,' and closely resemble the same procedure in other provinces. The 'dákhil-khárij' proceedings are solely concerned with the fact of, or right to, possession. If the applicant's possession of, succession to, or acquisition by transfer of the property is disputed, the Collector will summarily determine the right to possession, and will then see that the party is put in possession, and will make the entry in the register accordingly[1].

The details of procedure for obtaining mutation of names will be found in the Act.

The work of registration is now practically complete, or will shortly be so. In 1887 it was reported complete in thirty-seven out of the forty-three districts to which the law applies, and was practically complete in the remaining districts. In the Orissa districts and in Chittagong there was a source of unusual labour in the number of petty revenue-free holdings, and the work was brought to a close by rejecting from registration very small free-holdings.

[1] Bengal Act VII of 1876, section 55, as amended by Act V of 1878. Dákhil means 'entering': khárij is 'putting out.'

§ 4. *Registration of subordinate Interests in Land.*

It will be observed that these registers do not profess to *deal with any subordinate rights or interests*; there is nothing in Bengal which answers to the 'Record-of-Rights' of the North-West Provinces[1]. It so happens, however, that the Road and Public Works Cess, Bengal Act IX of 1880[2], has resulted in a record of subordinate rights also. The results are, however, vitiated by the system of summary valuation (for purposes of the Cess calculation) which the Act necessarily provides. This summary valuation 'withdraws from sight all details of tenures, under-tenures, and *raiyatí* holdings contained in such estates or tenures as are summarily valued.' 'In the instructions issued to officers[3] under the Act IX of 1880 (B.C.) an attempt has been made to remedy this defect in the returns, by declaring that the least possible recourse should be had to the process of summary valuation.' The Road Cess is a tax levied on all classes of proprietors, including every grade of tenure-holders, down to a limit of cultivators paying R. 100 in the year as rent; and hence a register has to be made of them. There is no legal validity, as evidence of right, attached to these returns.

There is another method, however, of registering under-tenures. We have seen that it has been always the law that when an estate is sold for arrears of revenue, all leases and under-tenures (with certain exceptions[4]) are liable to be voided, and the purchaser gets a clear and complete 'Parliamentary' title. This is so under the Sale Law (Act XI of 1859) and its Amending Acts[5]. To protect such

[1] Except of course in Government estates or in temporary Settlements under Regulation VII of 1822, or in cases where, under the Tenancy Act, Chapter X, or other special (local law), records-of-rights are made.

[2] Acts X of 1871 and II of 1877 have been repealed and superseded by the Act quoted in the text.

[3] The Board has issued a collection of Rules called the *Cess Manual*, 1888.

[4] Now contained in section 37 of Act XI of 1859.

[5] Act (B. C.) III of 1862, Act (B. C.) VII of 1868. Act (B. C.) II of 1871, and Act VII (B. C.) of 1880.

Act XI of 1859, sec. 38 to 50. tenures, the Act provides[1] that they may be registered either in a 'common' or a 'special' register[2]. Registration in the former protects them from being voided on sale of the estate for arrears, *by any party other than Government*; and special registration protects them *absolutely*. The Act also provides that the rights of *sharers* may be protected (and this is important, because otherwise the default of one sharer might cause the whole estate to be sold). 'Separate
Sec. 10. *accounts*' are opened with sharers on application. Separate
Sec. 11. accounts can also be opened for sharers, who not only have a specified fractional interest in an estate (and therefore are liable for a known fraction of the revenue), but whose shares consist of 'a specific portion of the land of the estate': Section 70, Act VII of 1876, also contemplates separate accounts of 'complex shares' as therein described. And Part V of Act VII of 1877 (Land Registration) should be read as to 'separate accounts' generally.

For the procedure necessary to the registering, the Act itself must be consulted.

SECTION III.—COLLECTION OF THE LAND-REVENUE.

§ 1. *The Taujih Department.*

For the purposes of revenue collection, besides the lists of estates just described, there must be kept up lists showing the revenue payable by each estate or separately assessed portion of an estate. There is a general district revenue-roll, divided into two parts—one showing the revenue fixed permanently or for a time, and payable by

[1] See Board's Rules, vol. i. ch. xiv.

[2] Up to the end of 1887, the 'common register' contained 2502 holdings with an area of 28,037,819 acres, and a revenue of R. 1,21,94,842. The 'special register' contained 256 holdings, of 8,861,964 acres, with a revenue of R. 30,85,888. The *tenures* registered were 'common' 4440 (rental R. 24,35,234), and 'special' 389 (rental R. 46,099). Separate accounts (under section 10) were 40,524, with a revenue demand of over 60¾ *lakhs*. Accounts for specific shares (section 11) were 3680, with a revenue demand of over 4¾ *lakhs*. Accounts under section 70 (Act VII of 1876 B.C.) were 7,061, with a revenue demand of something over 5 *lakhs*.

proprietors, farmers, or other engagees for the whole; the other showing the rent or revenue in estates in which the raiyats pay direct to Government. It is not necessary to go into further detail on the subject[1].

§ 2. *Sale Laws.*

The effects of the Law of Sale for arrears have been noticed in previous chapters.

The present law on the subject is to be found in Act XI of 1859, as amended and amplified by Bengal Acts III of 1862 and VII of 1868, and still more recently by Bengal Act VII of 1880 for the recovery of 'Public Demands.'

An 'arrear' accrues, if the 'kist' (properly *qist*) or instalment of revenue due for any month remains unpaid on the first of the following month. In some cases notice for fifteen days before sale is required, and the later Act enables Government to empower Collectors to issue warning notices in all cases. Act XI of 1859, secs. 2 and 5. B. Act VII of 1868, sec. 6.

Sharers of joint estates can protect themselves from their shares being sold for arrears along with the rest of the estate, by applying for and obtaining an order for a 'separate revenue account' of their share, as I mentioned at page 688. But if on a sale being notified (subject to the exception of the separate shares), it is found that the estate, subject to such exception, will not fetch a price equal to the amount in arrear, then notice is given that, unless the recorded sharers make up the arrears and so save the estate, the whole estate will be sold. I pass over the rules for re-sale in case the auction-purchaser fails to pay the purchase-money in due time, and here only notice that there is an appeal (final) to the Commissioner against a sale in certain cases. The Commissioner may also suspend a sale in cases of hardship, and report to the Board, on B. Act VII of 1868, sec. 2. Act XI of 1859, sec. 26.

[1] The detail may be found in chap. vi. *Rules of the Revenue Department*, vol. i. (1878). The revenue roll is written up by the Taujih-navis: the establishment which keeps the rent-roll and the accounts of each estate, with the amounts, collections, and balances, is spoken of as the Taujih Department.

whose recommendation the sale may be annulled (after it
Act XI of 1859, sec. 33. has taken place) by the local Government. The jurisdiction of the Civil Courts to annul a sale, on a regular suit being brought for the purpose, is also defined.

As already noticed, a sale for arrears hands the estate over to the purchaser with a clear title: the purchaser may void and annul all leases and subordinate tenures, except those specified in Section 37 of the Act XI, and those which are protected by registration. 'Tenures,' and interests like fisheries, and other interests arising out of lands not being
Act VII of 1868, sec. 11. 'estates' (land or shares in revenue-paying land) may be sold like estates for arrears of revenue.

The sale law, which at first worked very hardly, is now little felt. The average annual number of defaulting estates and *shares* during the last ten years, has been 9126, of which only 1624 or 17·8 *per cent.* have actually been sold.

For the details of Sale Law Procedure the student will naturally refer to Mr. Grimley's *Manual of Sale Law* published by the Bengal Government. But I must warn him that the Sale Law is being consolidated and redrafted by the Board of Revenue, but the Bill will not be completed nor come before Council in time for me to give any information about it in this chapter.

§ 3. *Certificate Procedure.—Public Demands Act.*

There is a *Certificate Procedure Manual*, 1885, which gives the detailed rules on this subject[1]. As sale of the estate is the only remedy for revenue default, it follows that some further procedure is needed for the collection of rents in Government estates and other public demands to which the sale law is inapplicable. Bengal Act VII of 1868 was intended to provide for the recovery of such demands, and Act VII of 1880 amended the law. It is only necessary to allude to the subject; the practice being quite simple. Briefly, the Collector records a 'certificate of arrears'

[1] To be had in the Bengal Secretariat Press.

which acts like a decree of Court, and can be executed continuously till all is paid, subject, of course, to the law of limitation.

SECTION IV.—SURVEY.

I have already given a description of the survey work in Bengal (see p. 456 *ante*). Here it is only necessary to allude to the laws applicable.

Previous to 1875, as far as permanently-settled estates were concerned, the process of revenue-survey was carried on without any authority given by law. Regulation VII of 1822 could not be quoted, since it applied to non-permanently settled estates, and could not warrant any action with reference to estates in which there could be no question of re-settlement. In 1847, indeed, a law had been passed regarding the survey of lands liable to river action [1], and the principles of this law are still maintained under the Survey Acts. The whole business of survey is now regulated by Bengal Act V of 1875 [2]. It is not my intention to go into any detail as to the procedure, but a general outline may be given so as to furnish a clue or guide to the study of the Act itself when necessary.

The Act allows a survey to be made extending not only to districts and to estates, but, if ordered, to defining fields and the limits of tenures [3].

[1] Act IX of 1847 (amended by Act IV (B.C.) of 1868). In the case of the alluvial lands the survey is treated as a special matter; it is required only along the banks of the great rivers. At present the special branch which deals with this work—the 'Diyára (Dearah) Survey' as it is called—is confined to the Dacca Division. It is worked by non-professional agency under the Deputy-collectors. The object is to 'identify and relay on the ground the boundaries of villages which have been subject to fluvial action and of which the boundaries cannot in consequence be identified; also to ascertain and assess lands which have been added to the estates by accretion.' (*Board's Revenue Administration Report*, 1879-80, § 92.)

[2] As amended by Act VII (B.C.) of 1880, with regard to the recovery of demands under the Act (sec. 5).

[3] But, of course, has nothing to do with defining or recording rights; that has to be done under chap. x. of the Tenant Act, 1885, or the Settlement Act of 1879, as the case may be, in the cases where it is lawful to order it.

After provisions relating to establishments, the Act requires a proclamation to be issued, and persons to attend and point out boundaries, clear lines, and so forth, so that the survey may begin.

When the demarcation is complete, the persons who pointed out the boundaries are required to inspect the papers and plans representing such boundaries, and to satisfy themselves as to whether the boundary-marks have been fixed according to their information. The plans and papers are to be signed by these parties, in token that the marks *are* shown in the maps or papers in the places where they declared they should be.

The Collector can always set up temporary marks, and may also set up permanent marks; after notifying their number and cost and giving opportunity for objections to be heard, he may direct the cost to be apportioned among
Secs. 19, 20. the land-owners or tenure-holders concerned. Provision is made for the permanent maintenance of these marks.

Passing over the detailed provisions for determining who shall bear the cost of the boundary-marks, and how it is to
Act, Part V, sec. 40, &c. be apportioned, I proceed to the subject of boundary-disputes. Here the Collector is to decide on the basis of actual possession, and his order holds good till it is upset by competent authority. If possession cannot be ascertained, the Collector may attach the land till one party or the other obtains a legal decision; or the Collector may, by consent of the parties, refer the matter to arbitration. There are also excellent provisions for relaying any boundary which has once been decided, but which has become doubtful or disputed.

Full provisions also will be found for protecting boundary-marks from injury and restoring them when damaged.

The Act, it will be observed, does not say anything about the records and registers which the Survey Department prepare.

These particulars, and rules about the scale, and so forth, must be sought for in the Board's Revenue Rules.

SECTION V.—PARTITION OF ESTATES.

This generally finds a place among the topics of revenue procedure. Owing to the fact that by the native laws the sons or other heirs succeed together, it follows from our modern ideas, that any one of a joint body may require that his interest and share should be separated off and assigned to him. This process is called 'batwára' or partition. But, then, such a separation may affect the Government revenue: since, if an estate assessed with, and liable as a whole for, one-sum of revenue, is afterwards divided into, say, four properties, the Government interest would be considerably affected, unless the whole group remained, as before, liable for the entire revenue.

This fact has led in Northern India to a distinction between 'imperfect' and 'perfect' partition. When the partition is imperfect, the different shareholders get their private rights separated and declared, but the whole estate still remains liable to Government for the whole revenue. In 'perfect' partition the responsibility to Government is also divided, and the shares henceforth become separate estates, entirely independent one of the other. It has always been therefore a moot question how far partition should be allowed. The question, indeed, has most interest in those provinces where the village Settlement-system is in force. That system, as the student will have sufficiently gathered from the Introductory Chapters in Book I, is based on the joint responsibility of the community, for the lump sum assessed on the village area.

In Bengal the land unit is different; but still the breaking up of a compact estate liable to sale as a whole, for the revenue assessed on it, into a number of petty holdings, each separately liable for its fractional assessment, and possessing a very reduced market value in consequence of its small size, has been felt to be a real difficulty. On the other hand, there are interests which benefit by partition.

The tenants on a joint estate are often seriously harassed by having to pay their total rent in a number of fractions to different shareholders, each insisting on collecting his own separate payment. A separation of the interests tends to alleviate this[1]. The question, therefore, of regulating partition long remained under discussion. It had been dealt with by Regulations in 1793, 1801, and 1803. In 1807 a limit had been put to the division, and no share assessed with less than R.500 revenue was allowed to be separated. This Regulation, however, was thought to go too far, and was afterwards repealed[2]. The subject has been more recently set at rest by the passing of Bengal Act VIII of 1876.

This Act contemplates only one kind of partition, i.e. the complete separation of the estates, not only as regards the private rights, but as regards the responsibility for the revenue. But no partition made after the date of the Act coming in force (4th October, 1876) other than under its provisions, though it may bind the parties, can affect the responsibility for Government revenue. There is a limit, but only a very low one, to partition: if the separate share would bear a revenue not exceeding one rupee, the separation cannot be made, unless the proprietor consents to redeem the land-revenue, under the rules for this purpose. Partition can be refused when the result of it would be to break up a compact estate into several estates consisting of scattered parcels of land, and which would, in the opinion of the Collector, endanger the land-revenue.

B. Act VIII of 1876, secs. 11–13

For the procedure of a partition case, how disputes are settled, how the final order is recorded, the Act must be referred to. The proceedings are held 'on the Revenue side' before the Collector.

[1] This difficulty of fractional payments will be found discussed in Macneile's *Memorandum*, chap. xvii.

[2] By Regulation V of 1810.

Section VI.—Estate Management.

§ 1. *Government Estates.*

While speaking of the Collector's general revenue duty, it is impossible to avoid mentioning one branch which is not represented by any particular Act. I refer to what is called 'khás,' or direct management, of estates belonging to Government, where no one is entitled to a Settlement, or of estates where a person entitled declines the terms of Settlement and is therefore excluded for a term (with a 'málikána' allowance). 'It was formerly the custom to let estates of this kind in farm, but in 1873 the practice was condemned as injurious to the interests of the property, and the tenantry. . . . There are 1061 estates with an annual revenue of R. 26,27,360 under the direct management of the revenue officers throughout the Lower Provinces[1].' Estates are either managed by the revenue officers as part of their ordinary duty, or, in case of larger estates, by special managers with suitable collecting establishments. The management charges are met by setting apart 10 per cent. of the total collections as a fund (credited to Land-Revenue Receipts in the public accounts) for meeting the costs; 7½ per cent. is placed at the disposal of the Board of Revenue for expenses of management, Settlement, measurement, and improvements and 2½ per cent. is devoted (not under the Board) to education and roads.

§ 2. *The Court of Wards.*

A most important branch of management duty is the care of Wards' estates, regulated by Act IX (B. C.) of 1879 (amended by Act III of 1881). There is also an excellent manual of rules issued under the authority of the Board of Revenue.

I cannot forbear making another extract from the *Report* (*on Land-tenures*) of 1883, on the results attained

[1] This is exclusive of such estates as are still, for special reasons, farmed. (*Report* 1883, p. 29.)

by the management (under the Court of Wards) of the great estate of Darbhangá (1860–1879). The extract not only speaks of the benefits conferred, but incidentally affords a vivid sketch of the varied subjects which come under the Manager's notice. I will only add that effort is made, when an estate comes under the Court of Wards, to get a survey and record-of-rights, but it is not always that the resources and circumstances of the estate make such a course possible.

'The Darbhangá Ráj is the largest property which has, for many years past, been under the charge of the Court of Wards. When the Court took charge, in 1860, its condition seemed almost hopelessly bad. The gross annual rental was nominally R. 16,39,357, and the Government revenue only R. 4,07,484. But the management had for years been left entirely in the hands of underlings. All the villages were leased to farmers, most of them relatives of the Ráj servants, who had got their leases on favourable terms. Others were outsiders, men of straw, who had nominally undertaken to pay rents far above the value of the lands, and who made what they could by rack-renting the ryots and levying illegal cesses, without attempting to satisfy the Ráj demand. Security for payment was never taken from the farmers. *Pattas* and kabúliyats were seldom interchanged. The correct rental of the villages was nowhere recorded. Patwárís' papers were seldom forthcoming. The outstanding arrears of rent, at first unknown, proved to amount to R. 56,44,972. There were other debts due to the estate, aggregating R. 3,37,775. The debts alleged to be due by the Mahárájá to creditors amounted to a crore of rupees, of which the Court of Wards was compelled to admit R. 71,88,427. The estates were destitute of roads and bridges. The palace was neglected and in ruins; its courtyards quagmires; its environs a hopeless waste of jungle, pools, and filth. Notoriously all the epidemics of the town took their rise in the Rájbárí. There were no refuges for the sick; no resting-places for travellers; not a school in the whole estate. No productive works of any kind had anywhere been attempted.

'On the surrender of the estate to the Mahárájá, in 1879, all this had been changed. The rent-roll had been re-adjusted; and although reductions of rental had been made, amounting to R. 5,92,323, the gross rental (including that of a few small properties purchased) was R. 21,61,885. The outstanding arrears of rent due to the estate were R. 18,51,397 (less than a year's demand), of which R. 14,51,664 were good and in process of realization. All debts had been paid off long before. There was a cash balance in hand of R. 2,75,733, besides Government securities of the value of R. 38,54,500. Over 150 miles of road had been constructed and bridged (in many places with screw-pile viaducts). Upwards of 20,000 trees had been planted along their sides. Feeder and village roads had been made and improved. In Kharakpur, extensive irrigation works, securing that property against famine, had been made and opened. A large bazaar had been built at Darbhangá, including a handsome public serai[1]. The old palace was considerably improved and was made the centre of a pretty garden some fifty acres in extent. In lieu of the ruinous system of farming leases, the whole estate had been brought under direct management. Collections were made without friction or difficulty. The outlying zirát lands[2] had been equitably settled with indigo-planters, while those in the vicinity of villages had been reserved for the ryots, thus putting an end to the constant disputes between the factories and the cultivators. Hundreds of small embankments, water-channels, tanks, and wells had been constructed from advances made without interest to the tenants. Complete surveys had been made of the greater part of the property, and a considerable area had been resettled to the advantage both of the estate and of the cultivators. Twenty vernacular schools had been established by the Ráj, educating 1000 children; aid being at the same time given to other educational institutions not belonging to the estate. Three admirable hospitals were kept up for the use of the tenantry, while assistance was also afforded to six charitable dispensaries in various places near. Above all, both the Mahárájá and his brother had received a thorough English education, were proficient in manly exercises, and free from the vices which are too often the ruin of native magnates. The Mahárájá had been trained to manage his own affairs, and to take a lively interest in the welfare of his people, while his brother had been deemed

[1] Saráŭ or Saráí (P.) is a public inn or resting-place.

[2] Zirát (zirá'at A.) means 'cultivation,' and is one of the several terms used to indicate the private or home farm of the landlord: it is practically equivalent to nij or nij-jot, or kámat or khámár land.

fit for appointment to the civil service of the province, in which he is now an Assistant Magistrate.

'During the incumbency of the Court of Wards, the aggregate demand of rent due to the estate amounted to R. 4,26,79,578. Of this, R. 3,54,66,458, or 83 per cent., were collected, and R. 55,39,610 remitted. The total receipts from all sources during the management were R. 4,84,50,669, and the total disbursements R. 4,80,86,228, of which R. 32,90,934, or only 6 per cent. of the receipts represents the cost of management. R. 80,41,113 were expended in payment of Government revenue, and R. 31,98,000, or 6 per cent. of the receipts in the allowances of the family, including social and religious ceremonies. The collection of rent was on several occasions during the management seriously affected by drought and scarcity. These calamities serve to explain the heavy remissions of rent shown in the accounts. The total expenditure on public works from first to last was R. 54,92,245.'

Section VII.—Other Branches of Revenue-Duty.

There are other branches of a revenue officer's duty which occupy a considerable space in the Revenue manuals. It is not within the scope of this work to deal with these branches; they are all fully provided for by special Acts and by Revenue Rules.

As an example I may instance the question of agricultural loans (Act XII of 1884), the rules for 'Taqáví,' or advances made for land improvements (Act XIX of 1883).

The road cess assessment and collection under Bengal Act IX of 1880, to which incidental allusion has already been made, forms, in Bengal, another special branch of a revenue officer's duty. In other provinces, as a rule, a cess for the same purposes is assessed along with the land-revenue, and is collected at the same time and by the same process. In Bengal, the arrangements of the Permanent Settlement did not include this, and therefore an Act was required, which makes not only estates, but every kind of tenure and cultivating holding, liable to pay a small contribution to the maintenance of a fund for roads and communications. (There is a Cess Manual, 1888, issued by the Board which gives all the rules.)

The acquisition of lands for public purposes under Act X of 1870 is practically a branch of revenue duty, as it is the Collector who makes the first award of compensation; moreover, when the land is expropriated the revenue on it has to be remitted, so that the 'taujih' department is also concerned.

Full instructions regarding the form of submitting a proposal to expropriate lands, and other details of procedure, are to be found in the Board's Rules; a reference to these and to the Act X of 1870 will make the whole matter clear. Further detail here is not required.

The Waste Land Rules have also a great importance in Bengal, as there are still lands available, about Darjíling, and in the Sundarbans. I have already given some account of the working of these Rules, as far as the tenures resulting from them are concerned[1]. I have here only to add that some revised rules were issued in 1888; and that the whole subject is now to be studied in the *Waste Land Manual*, 1888.

[1] See p. 479, *ante*.

END OF VOL. I.

Published by

Facsimile Publisher
Ashok Vihar, Delhi-110052 (India)
Website: www.facsimilepublishers.com

Distributed by

Gyan Books Pvt. Ltd.
5, Ansari Road, Daryaganj, New Delhi-110002 (India)
E-mail: books@gyanbooks.com, Website: www.gyanbooks.com

9 789333 311779